JURISPRUDENCE: REALISM IN THEORY AND PRACTICE

KARL N. LLEWELLYN, 1893-1962

JURISPRUDENCE

REALISM IN THEORY AND PRACTICE

THE UNIVERSITY OF CHICAGO PRESS

Library of Congress Catalog Card Number: 62–12634
The University of Chicago Press, Chicago & London
The University of Toronto Press, Toronto 5, Canada
© *1962 by The University of Chicago. All rights reserved*
Published 1962.
Printed in the United States of America

PREFACE

This book is not a general collection or "representative" selection of papers. It is, instead, an organization of a number of papers (which appeared from 1928 to 1960) around a single theme: the bearings on Jurisprudence of the approach I have been seeing and urging for some thirty-five years as Realism—an approach which seems to me as fresh and needed today as it was in the twenties and thirties, and as it had been in the hands of Aristotle, Machiavelli, Montaigne, or Montesquieu.

Hence the start is with those of the fundamental papers of the modern revival which happened to come from my pen. There follow various more concrete applications. Due attention is given to the positive results which have developed in one of the original centers of attention, the area of appellate judging. In that, as throughout, I have sought to keep even concrete application uncluttered by such elaborated technical material as was necessary to my *Common Law Tradition* or to my studies on Warranty or Divorce; for which reason my work in Commercial Law, in general, has also been almost entirely omitted. It has proved possible, however, especially by drawing on scattered little-known papers, to offer some introduction to such things as the problem (and not merely in the criminal field) of spotting the significant type-situation, or the importance to Jurisprudence of intensive study of the crafts and of craftsmanship, or of the concept of period-style or of analysis in terms of the nature of an institution and of an institution's basic jobs or functions—indeed, in "Law and the Social Sciences" there is even a first suggestion of the value of substituting Law-Government for Law as the most significant organizing focus of the institution which Jurisprudence should take as its subject matter. There is an effort, also, to open up for serious study the fascination of legal (and governmental) esthetics, and to restake the old and rightful claim of legal study to status among the humanities as well as among those arts known as liberal.

Two lacks I regret. There is no paper here which picks up for sustained development the theory of Justice as being not an attainable or even describable substance, but a quest—as being an idea conditioned in the first instance by each quester's view of the Universe, and conditioned secondly (as Law-Government must always be) by the fact of scarcity. Whether within an organized group with firm legal-governmental traditions or within an emerging, half-chaotic world, the *justified* desires and demands have always exceeded the wherewithal to fulfill them, and they always will. I should have liked to wrestle also with the peculiar bearing of what may be called the "Justice-explosion" in the world today.

The other lack I regret is that of a paper which would give some detailed attention to the need in the "criminal" field for a real double standard: for the individual, as regards himself, a standard of complete personal responsibility; for the legislator or administrator, as regards the actual or prospective offender, a standard largely dominated by the concept of genetic and social conditioning. I feel like urging the inclusion of a pocket on the back cover, to accommodate these two still unborn members of the clan.

ADDITIONS TO THE TEXT

In the main, the text is presented as it originally appeared. In half a hundred places I have simply sharpened or tightened or clarified a phrase; but never so as to change the original meaning. Where meaning is affected, due notice is given: 1) either the new language is inserted *in square brackets,* or 2) there is a *footnote* which signals its supplementary character by being *not numbered, but lettered.*

KARL N. LLEWELLYN

University of Chicago Law School
February 5, 1962.

Mr. Llewellyn died eight days after the preface was written and before he had a chance to see page proof or prepare the index. I acknowledge with gratitude the proofreading and index preparation which was taken over by Thomas B. Rutter with the assistance of his wife, Fred K. Grant, and Dori Dressander. Without the loyal devotion of these students and friends, this book would never have been readied for publication on May 22, 1962, the date of what would have been Mr. Llewellyn's sixty-ninth birthday.

SOIA M. LLEWELLYN

March 26, 1962

CONTENTS

vii

REALISM

A REALISTIC JURISPRUDENCE—
THE NEXT STEP [a] [*]

THE PROBLEM OF DEFINING LAW; FOCUS VERSUS CONFINES

The difficulty in framing any concept of "law" is that there are so many things to be included, and the things to be included are so unbelievably different from each other. Perhaps it is possible to get them all under one verbal roof. But I do not see what you have accomplished if you do. For a concept, as I understand it, is built for a purpose. It is a thinking tool. It is to make your data more manageable in doing something, in getting somewhere with them. And I have not yet met the job, or heard of it, to which all the data that associate themselves with this loosest of suggestive symbols, "law," are relevant at once. We do and have too many disparate things and thinkings to which we like to attach that name. For instance, legislators pass "a law," by which we mean that they officially put a new form of words on the statute books. That calls up associations with regard to attorneys and judges, and to suits being brought "under the statute." But it also calls up associations with regard to those sets of practices and expectations and people which we call political parties and machines and lobbies. The former we should want, in some way, to include under the head "law," I suspect. If we did not, we ought to stop defining and think a little further. The latter—the parties and lobbies—we

[a] From 30 COLUM. L. REV. 431 (1930).
[*] The substance of this paper was presented at the Round Table on Current Trends in Political and Legal Thought of the American Association of Political Science, December, 1929, under the title *Modern Concepts of Law*.

might have more doubt about, even if we did stop and think. Again, it seems fairly clear that there has been something we could not well dissociate from our symbol "law" in places and times when there was no legislature and even no state—indeed when there was no organization we can call "political" that was distinct from any other organization. You cannot study the simpler forms of society nor "the law" of such forms without looking into the mechanisms of organized control at such times and places; but today you will be likely to distinguish such types of control as *non-legal*. Of course, you would not disregard them, if you wanted to know anything about "law" that was worth knowing. But you would regard them as background, or foreground, or underground, to your center of interest. They would be something that you would compare and contrast with "law," I suspect, in the present order of society. And yet I also suspect you would have your hands full if you set about to draw the line between "the two." Or again, there are gentlemen who spend a good deal of time discussing "the ends of law," or "what law ought to be." Are they talking about "law"? Certainly their postulates and conclusions, in gross and in detail, have no need to look like anything any judge ever did; and at times some of those gentlemen seem to avail themselves of that freedom; but it would be a case-hardened person who denied that what they are dealing with is closely connected with this same loose suggestive symbol. What interests me is that when a judge is working in a "well-settled field" he is likely to pay no attention to what such gentlemen say, and to call it irrelevant speculation; whereas when he is working in an "unsettled field" he seems to pay a lot of attention to their ideas, or to ideas of much the same order. This I take to mean that *for some purposes* they are talking something very close to "law," under any definition; and for *other* purposes, they are talking something whose connection with "law" as just used is fairly remote. And this problem of the word calling up wide-scattered and disparate references, *according to the circumstance,* seems to me vital.

So that I am not going to attempt a definition of law. Not anybody's definition; much less my own. A definition both excludes and includes. It marks out a field. It makes some matters fall inside the field; it makes some fall outside. And the exclusion is almost always rather arbitrary. I have no desire to exclude anything from matters legal. In one aspect law is as broad as life, and for some purposes one will have to follow life pretty far to get the bearings of the legal matters one is examining. I say again, therefore, that I shall not attempt a definition. I shall not describe a periphery, a stopping place, a barrier. I shall instead devote my attention to the *focus* of matters legal. I shall try to discuss a *point of reference;* a point of reference to which I believe all matters legal can most usefully be referred, if they are to be seen with intelligence and with appreciation of their bearings. A focus, a core, a center—with the bearings and boundaries outward unlimited. Pardon my saying it so often; but I find it very hard to make people understand that I am not talking about putting or pushing anything *out of* the field or concept of law. People are so much used to definitions—although definitions have not always been of so much use to people. I am, therefore, going to talk about substituting a somewhat unfamiliar, but more exciting and more useful focus for the focus that most thinking about law in the past has had.

Two references to the course that thought has taken will help to set the perspective: one, to the tenets of the nineteenth-century schools of jurisprudence; one, to the development of the concepts of rights and of interests.

For the nineteenth-century schools I am content to accept one of Pound's summaries.[1] It fits with what reading in the field I have done; it is based upon vastly more reading in the field than I shall ever do. With regard to the analytical jurists, Pound stresses their interest in a body of established precepts whereby a definite legal result is supposed to be fitted to a definite set of facts; he stresses the centering of their definition upon the "aggregate of authoritative legal precepts applied by tribunals as such in a given time and place," and their presupposition of a state which makes those precepts and tribunals authoritative. The historical jurists, on the other hand, he finds making little distinction between law and other forms of social control; with them customary precepts, irrespective of whether they originate in the organs of politically organized societies, come in for heavy attention; central in their picture of law are the traditional techniques of decision and the traditional or customary notions of rightness. (All this, it may be added, without any too close analysis as to what is meant by "custom.") For the philosophical jurists, finally, Pound finds that "philosophical, political and ethical ideas as to the end of law and as to what legal precepts should be in view thereof" occupy the center of the stage.

I have no wish to put the tenets of these schools to the test, nor

[1] LAW AND MORALS, 25 *et seq.* (1924).

to pursue them further. Their value here is limited, but great within its limits: taken together, they hammer home the complexity of law. Each school was reaching for a single definition of all that was significant about law. Each school wound up with a definition which stressed some phases and either overlooked or greatly understressed others. Each had a definition with which, for its purposes, and especially in the hands of its creative thinkers, it made striking headway. But too close attention to any one of the definitions—in its *ex*clusion aspects—for too long, would have meant ultimate barrenness. And I gather that one lesson Pound has drawn from his study of these and other schools has been to insist rather on what goes into the idea of law than on what is to be kept out of it.

PRECEPTS AS THE HEART AND CORE OF MOST THINKING ABOUT LAW

Moreover, you will have noted running through his summary of their views the word "precepts." This is traditional. When men talk or think about law, they talk and think about *rules*. "Precepts" as used by Pound, for instance, I take to be roughly synonymous with rules and principles, the principles being wider in scope and proportionately vaguer in connotation, with a tendency toward idealization of some portion of the *status quo* at any given time. And I think you will find as you read Pound that the precepts are *central* to his thinking about law. Along with rules and principles—along with precepts proper, may I say?—he stresses for instance "standards" as a part of the subject matter of law. These standards seem to be those vague but useful pictures with which one approaches a wide and varied field of conduct to measure the rights of a particular situation: a conception of what a reasonable man would do in the circumstances, or of what good faith requires, and similar pictures. They differ from rules, though not from principles, partly in their vagueness; they differ from both in being not propositions in themselves, but normative approaches to working out the application of some one *term* in a major proposition. The principle, let us say, would read: a man must answer for what good faith requires. But a standard (like a concept; like any class-term, loose or sharp) functions chiefly or exclusively as *part* of a precept. Consequently, it belongs in much the same world. It, too, *centers* on precepts. But Pound mentions more as law than precepts and standards. Along with the standards he stresses also ideals as to "the end" of law. These I take to be in substance standards on a peculiarly vague and majestic scale; standards, perhaps, to be applied to rules rather than to individual transactions.[2] Finally, he stresses—and we meet here a very different order of phenomena—"the traditional techniques of developing and applying" precepts. Only a man gifted with insight would have added to the verbal formulae and verbalized (though vague) conceptual pictures thus far catalogued, such an element *of practices,* of habits and techniques of action, of *behavior.* But only a man partially caught in the traditional precept-thinking of an age that is passing would have focussed that behavior on, have given it a major reference to, have belittled its importance by dealing with it as a phase of, those merely verbal formulae: precepts.[a] I have no wish to argue the point. It will appeal, or it will not, and argument will be of little service. But not only this particular bit of phrasing (which might be accidental), but the use made in Pound's writings of the idea, brings out vigorously the limitations of rules, of precepts, of *words,* when made the focus, the *center of reference,* in thinking about law.[3]

[2] Not only ideals, but standards, not only standards, but concepts, not only concepts, but rules, involve of course generalized mental pictures which play a part in shaping both rules and the actions of courts. But as traditionally dealt with this ideal element, even where observed, is promptly related in the first instance to rules.

[a] Here, as so often, "merely" (like "and-not") is a trap for the jurisprude. I cannot today think of any but exceptional rules, in exceptional circumstances, as "merely" verbal.

[3] Pound's work in this aspect is as striking in its values as in its limitations. It is full to bursting with magnificent insight. It is to Pound we owe the suggestion of "the limits of effective legal action" (worked out in terms of *court* decisions). It is to Pound we owe the contrast of law-in-books and law-in-action (the latter limited again, in his working out of it, to what *courts* do; though in other places he insists upon *administrative* organs as the present center of legal growth). It is to Pound we owe the formulation "individualization of treatment of an offender," and the reference to the proceedings of the Conference on Charities and Corrections to see what the criminal law is really doing. And so it goes. I am not concerned here with whether prior writers may have contributed to, or anticipated, some or all of these ideas. Pound saw them, he formulated them, he drove them home. But these brilliant buddings have in the main not come to fruition. No one thinks them through in their relation either to each other or to the bulk of received jurisprudence. "Balancing of interests" remains with no indication of how to tell an interest when you see one, much less with any study of how they are or should be balanced. "Sociological jurisprudence" remains bare of most that is significant in sociology. "Law-in-action" is left as a suggestion, while further discussion of "the law" centers on "precept." "The limits of effective legal action"—a formulation that fairly shrieks for study of the habit and control set-up of society (that *complex,* industrialized, partially urban, indirect-cooperation society he has given us words for)—is left without study of the society to which law is supposed to have relation. The more one learns, the more one studies, the more light and stimulus

Remedies, Rights and Interests: A Developing Insight

Indeed, those limitations appear throughout the current analysis of law in terms of interests, rights, and remedies. The growth of that analysis requires a short digression, but one that I believe worth making. It has to do with the *subject matter* of the rules and precepts of which men regarded the legal system as made up. Both with us and in the Roman system that subject matter has in the course of time undergone striking changes.

In the earlier stages the rules were thought of almost exclusively as rules of remedies.[4] Remedies were few and specific. There were

---

Pound's writings give. But always peculiarly on a fringe of insight which fails to penetrate at all to the more systematic set-up of the material. One is tempted to see in the thinking of the one man and of the American school of sociological juris-prudence a parallel to the development of case law as a whole: accepting in the main what has been handed down; systematizing compartment-wise; innovating where need shows, powerfully and surely—but *ad hoc* only, with little drive toward or interest in incorporating the innovation into or aligning it with the mass of the material as received.

Critical reading of Pound's work, it may be noted in passing, and especially the phrasing of any concrete criticism, are embarrassed by the constant indeterminacy of the level of his discourse. At times the work purports clearly to travel on the level of considered and buttressed scholarly discussion; at times on the level of bed-time stories for the tired bar; at times on an intermediate level, that of the thoughtful but unproved essay. Most often, it is impossible to tell the intended level of any chapter or passage, and the writing seems to pass without notice from one to another. Now it is obvious that three successive, mutually inconsistent generaliza-tions, though no one of them sustainable as the deliberate propositions of a scholar, may all be illuminating and indeed all true at once—on the level of the after-dinner speech, or even of the thought-provoking essay. All of which gags the critic at the same time that it perhaps stimulates his critical faculties. There is value in this. There is value, even in the legal bed-time story. But there is greater value to be had. What would one not give for the actual appearance of the long-awaited *Sociological Jurisprudence,* if its author would integrate it in terms of those pioneer-ing thoughts of his which thus far have been waiting to be called together in a Constituent Assembly?

[The *Sociological Jurisprudence* never appeared. The five-volume *Jurisprudence* which did appear made some headway on the matter of "interests," but little on either the administrative phase of legal life or law's relations to society. It is further discussed below at p. 495.]

[4] I am presupposing the presence of "rules of law," *i.e.,* at least assuming law as a semi-specialized activity of control distinguished from other mechanisms of control; and also presupposing generalization to have set in. Just how far this first assumption reaches I am sure I do not know; I should be inclined to regard any special assembly held for the purpose of adjusting disputes, by say village elders otherwise without official position or authority (*cf.* Gutman, Das Recht der Dschagga, ch. *Der Spruchrasen*), as one instance of its presence. The second assump-tion presupposes that prior decision has begun to be dealt with as precedent; that *Themis* is not merely an oracle, but marks a norm. But I am insisting that it be a norm *of law.* Vinogradoff cogently points out that Maine's *Themis* is not a pure creation of the judgment maker; before the *Themis* was a societal life in

a few certain ways to lug a man into court and a few certain things that you or the court could do with him when you got him there. We are concerned here not with why that was (why "can" a court of law give no injunctive relief today?) but only with *that* it was. The question for the man of that day took this shape: on what facts could one man make use of any specific one of the specific ways of making the court bother another man? And the rules of law were rules about that. They clustered around each remedy. In those terms people thought.[5] They thought about what they could see and do. Their crude minds dealt only with what they could observe. What they observed, they described.

To later writers this seemed primitive. The later thinkers find a different kind of order in the field of law. Remedies seem to

---

which norms were both explicit and implicit. I hesitate, however, to call the *im-plicit* norms either "rules" or "legal," and see nothing but confusion to be had from so doing. I see only *practices*, more or less definite, more or less conscious, plus a generalized attitude that whatever is practice is right, and whatever varies widely enough is wrong. Certainly the process of making the implicit norm express calls for difficult creative work (two pieces of gold as the reward, on the shield of Achilles!) though any man can *recognize* the result once arrived at *as* right, if it is right (the crowd will award the gold!). Certainly also the "explicit-making" permits a twisting. Finally, once the judgment is made, it is both clearer to see, firmer in outline, more rigid, and perhaps more authoritative than it was before. If authoritative at all *because of who made it,* or because of the circumstances of its making, moreover, it has certainly begun the differentiation out of the general social matrix into the specific character of legality. (Malinowski's analysis in CRIME AND CUSTOM IN SAVAGE SOCIETY (1926) is somewhat similar; but it moves in terms of dominant authoritativeness of the norm, not of the functionary. If, *when appealed to,* a norm will prevail over an inconsistent norm of common practice, he thinks of it as legal. An illuminating discrimination.) [These matters are further developed in my *The Normative, the Legal,* etc., 49 YALE L. J. 1355 (1940), and LLEWELLYN AND HOEBEL, THE CHEYENNE WAY (1941) esp. ch. III.]

[5] Here and in the following I am talking about the thinking of what my friend T. R. Powell calls the "postmortemizers," those who hash over events that are past, and write books about them, or build taught law. Such persons typically show a wider range of thought than the practical man of similar ability, but a greater naiveté. The practical man seems to think in two water-tight compartments. One half of his mind grinds out the ideology of the day, as gospel, over pippins and cheese or from the rostrum; that half belongs to the postmortemizers. The other half deals cannily with existing institutions, of whatever holiness, to shape (at times it verges on twisting) them to the needs of the practical man or of his client. This side of the practical man's mind must have been at work in every legal system from the days of the most formal rigidity. (Compare the whole preparation and sequence of the lawsuit in Dasent's *Njals-Saga.*) And some persons—conscious creators—must have taken thought of the relation of interest and remedy since there has been law. (Compare the protection of the Church in the old English laws.) But the tone and ideas of the postmortemizers have changed from age to age, and while not altering the basic attitudes of the practical man, have changed his words and his stock of ideas, his tools, seemingly with powerful effects on his results.

them to have a *purpose,* to be protections of something else. They
could imagine these somethings and give them a name: *rights,*
substantive rights. Thus the important, the substantial rules of
law become rules defining rights. Remedies are relegated to the
periphery of attention. They are "adjective law" merely—devices
more or less imperfect for giving effect to the important things,
the substantive rights which make up the substance of the law.
The relation of rights to rules is fairly clear: the two are aspects
of the same thing. When a rule runs in favor of a person, he has
a right, as measured by the rule. Or, if he has a right, that can be
phrased by setting out a rule ascribing to him and persons in like
situation with him the benefits connoted by the rights. Rights are
thus precise counterparts of rules, when the rights are ascribed
generally to all persons in a class in given circumstances; and this
is the typical postmortemizer's line of discourse. Or rights, when
ascribed to particular individuals in specific circumstances, are
deductions which presuppose the rule; the major premise is the
general rule on rights; the minor is the proposition hooking up
this individual and these circumstances with that general rule.
Rights and rules are therefore for present purposes pretty much
interchangeable; the right is a shorthand symbol for the rule.[6]

Substantive rights and rules are spoken of as prevailing between
people, laymen: one has, *e.g.,* a right to the performance of a
contract. It is a heresy when Coke or Holmes speaks of a man
having liberty under the law to perform his contract or to pay
damages, at his option. It would likewise be a heresy to argue that
the vital real evidence of this supposed "right" lies in an action for
damages, and that the right could rather more accurately be
phrased somewhat as follows: if the other party does not perform
as agreed, you can sue, and *if* you have a fair lawyer, and nothing
goes wrong with your witnesses or the jury, *and* you give up four
or five days of time and some ten to thirty percent of the proceeds, and wait two to twenty months, you will *probably* get a
judgment for a sum considerably less than what the performance
would have been worth—which, if the other party is solvent and
has not secreted his assets, you can in further due course collect
with six percent interest for delay. To argue thus would be to
confuse the remedy (which you can see) with the substantive right

[6] For present purposes the dubious distinction taken by the German thinkers:
"objective *Recht*" (rather "law" than "right") and "subjective *Recht*" (close to our
pre-Hohfeldian 'right') can be disregarded. It fits the discussion in that the subjective
Recht is viewed first of all as a deduction from the rule of law, and then as an
independent something.

(which you cannot see, but which you know is there—somewhere; people tell you so). The substantive right in this body of thought has a shape and scope independent of the accidents of remedies. And herein lies the scientific advance involved in the concept. You are freed of any necessity of observing what courts do, and of limiting your discussion to that. You get back into the ultimate realities behind their doing. Obviously you can think more clearly among those ultimate realities. They are not so much obscured by inconsistency and divergence of detail. They are not answerable to fact.

Most lay thinking, it may be noted in passing, is on this level today. Typical is the current acceptance of a paper rule or statute as meaning something simply because it has paper authority—indeed, as meaning all it says, or all it is supposed to have been intended to say, simply because it has paper authority.

Far be it from me to dispute that the concepts of substantive rights and of rules of substantive law have had great value.[7] They moved definitely and sharply toward fixing the attention of thinkers on the idea that procedure, remedies, existed not merely because they existed, nor because they had value in themselves, but because they had a purpose. From which follows immediate inquiry into what the purpose is, and criticism, if the means to its accomplishment be poor. They moved, moreover, to some extent, toward sizing up the law by significant life-situations, instead of under the categories of historically conditioned, often archaic remedy-law: a new base for a new synthesis; a base for law reform.

THE AMBIGUITIES IN THE CONCEPTS OF RULES AND RIGHTS

But that should not obscure the price that was paid for the advance. A price first, as already described, of moving discussion away from the checkup of fact. To a legal reformer in his campaigning, in his getting of new views across, this may have value, if "the fact" in question be existing positive law. He may move more comfortably if he can keep people from observing that his moves mean change. To a scientist, observing, or to a reformer engaged not in selling his reform, in propaganding, in putting ideas over, but in inquiring what is before him, where he wants

---

[7] Neither would I be understood to deny practical consequences to this mode of thinking, in our case results, in constitutional law, limitation of actions, etc., or to urge that describing the immediate remedy describes the whole situation, today. It *does* describe the most important, and a much neglected, aspect of the situation.

to get, and how to get there, this obfuscation of the facts is another matter.

Secondly, a price was paid, of ambiguity—indeed of multiguity. "Rules" is a term sufficiently ambiguous. A rule may be prescriptive: "this is what *ought* to be; what the judges *ought* to do in such cases." Or it may be descriptive: "this is what *is*; what the judges *actually* do in such cases." Or it may be both at once: "this is *both* what they do *and* what they ought to do." [7a] And when theorists discuss, they will move from one of these meanings into another without notice, and with all and any gradations of connotations. In the particular case of rules "of law" a further ambiguity affects the word "rule": whether descriptive or prescriptive, there is little effort to make out *whose* action and *what* action is prescribed or described. The statement "this is the rule" typically means: "I find this formula of words in authoritative books." [8] Does this connote: *"Courts are actually proceeding* according to this formula"; or *"Courts* always *rehearse* this formula in this connection"? Does it connote: *"People* are conducting themselves in the light of this formula"; or even "People are conducting themselves as this formula suggests that they ought to." The theorist will rarely trouble to tell you how many (if any) of these connotations are implicit in his statement: "this is the rule." But he will reason, on the next page, from some one of such implications. Which means: confusion, profuse and inevitable.[9]

[7a] Put another way, prescriptive rules are rules *for* doing something; descriptive rules are so-called rules *of* doing something—statements of observed regularity. But "rules *of*" in common speech includes both aspects at once, and "rules *for*" as often as not connotes the presence of a corresponding practice. I shall limit my term "rules" to "rules for," and shall not *imply* any such connotation.

[8] I omit from discussion here one other troublesome confusion: whenever rules are discussed in their prescriptive aspect, it is frequently difficult to tell whether a writer is giving *his own* view of what ought to be, or, on the other hand, a view sanctioned by authority—the prevailingly accepted prescriptive rules. In this last case the *prevalence* of a given prescriptive rule is a fact capable of description (or misdescription); but it always remains to be noted whether that prevailing prescriptive rule has any counterpart in *practice,* or remains in the paper or lip-service stage.

[9] Refinement of terms goes some distance to avoid this confusion. "Rule" is well confined to the *pre*scriptive sphere. "Paper rule" is a fair name for a rule to which no counterpart in practice is ascribed. "Working rule" indicates a rule with counterpart in practice, or else a practice *consciously* normatized. *Cf. supra* note 4. "Practice" indicates an observable course of action, with no necessary ascription of conscious normatizing about it. In an earlier paper (*The Effect of Legal Institutions on Economics,* 15 AM. EC. REV. 671—1925) I failed to make this last distinction; it seems obvious, however, that it refines one's descriptive and reasoning technique in an important detail. Consider, *e.g.,* the double value Ehrlich's work would have had, if his stock of terms had served to keep such distinctions clear, and to let his magnificent thinking work itself out free of confusion.

The confusion is stirred blacker with the concept "right" poured in. "Right" adds nothing to descriptive power. But it gives a specious appearance of substance to prescriptive rules. They seem to be *about* some *thing*. So that to clothe one's statement about what rules of law are in terms of rights, is to double the tendency to disregard the limitations actually put on rules or rights by practice and by remedies. At the vital core of thought about law, at the very place where one thought impinges on another, or where one part of law impinges on another, one sees the impingement in terms of idealized somethings which may not, which mostly *do* not, accurately reflect men's actions. In terms of words, and not in terms of conduct; in terms of what *apparently* is understandable *without* checking up in life. So that one makes the assumption—without the urge to inquiry—that one is dealing with reality when he talks of rights, and proceeds to use these unchecked words for further building.

There is another confusion, found in dealing with rules, and strengthened by the associated idea of rights, within the field of doctrine itself. Having come to regard words as sound bases for further thinking, the tendency is well nigh inevitable to simplify the formulations more and more: to rub out of the formulations even the discrepancies in paper doctrine which any growing system of law contains in heaping measure; doubly so because the word "rights" introduces *sub rosa* at this point the additional notion of "rightness" (in the sense of what ought to be)—before which unwanted discrepancies must fall. I am speaking here of the effects of the idea of rightness on the rejection of some of the existent purely doctrinal materials in favor of other equally doctrinal materials, the case of conflicts in and within legal doctrine—a matter of vast concern to a lawyer, though commonly enough of no great moment to a political scientist.

But the same tendency carries over quite as well into the confusion of legal with non-legal materials, where it concerns political scientist and lawyer in common; and here the idea of "rights" seems to be the heavy tool of confusion, with no help at all from the idea of "rules." "Right" eternally suggests its connotation of inherent "rightness"—social, political, economic, and especially moral. It takes more careful self-analysis than most have been interested in giving to keep the *non-legal* "right" (which was a reason for claiming or striving toward or awarding a legal right) distinguished from the "legal right" which was conceived, I take it, as something not quite a mere description of an available remedy, but at least an official recognition that some kind of remedy could be had. The threat of ambiguous middle is obvious.[9a] The natural rights theorists did little to make it less.

INTERESTS

This third confusion (but, be it noted, neither the second nor the first) was cleared up by the controversy that centered about Ihering. Since that controversy we take some care to limit our term "rights" to legal rights ("substantive," if nothing more be said), and are thereby aided in keeping the legal separate from the social factors at work in a situation. The term *interests,* on the other hand, comes in to focus attention on the presence of social factors, and to urge that substantive rights themselves, like remedies, exist only for a purpose. Their purpose is now perceived to be the protection of the interests. To be sure, we do not know what interests are. Hence, behind substantive rights (which we need not check against anything courts *do*) we now have interests (which we need not check against anything at all, and about whose presence, extent, nature, and importance, whether the interests be taken absolutely or taken relatively one to another, no two of us seem to be able to agree). The scientific advance should again be obvious. Complete subjectivity has been achieved.[b]

At this stage of the development, then, one arrives at a double chain of purposes. One starts with the interest. That is a social fact or factor of some kind, existing independent of the law.[10] And it has value independent of the law. Indeed, its protection is the purpose of substantive legal rights, of legal rules, of precepts of substantive law. "Security of transactions" is such an interest. The rules and rights of contract law exist to protect and effectuate it. The rules and rights are not ends, but means. But they are means which in another aspect (like most means) themselves become ends: remedies exist as means to effectuate the substantive rights, to realize the substantive rules. Obviously the means may be inadequate, badly chosen, wasteful, even self-defeating, at either

[9a] Wherever the plaintiff has a [legal] right to recover, he can recover at law. This plaintiff has a [social, moral, economic] right to recover. Therefore this plaintiff can recover in this action at law.—This may improve the law. It has. It is not, for that, any the better thinking for a *scientist* to use.

[b] This caricature was directed not at Ihering, but at some of the looser stuff Pound had been publishing in the '20's. But Pound wrote me an extraordinary congratulation on the paper: *"Veni post me, me fortior."*

[10] This is an overstatement. Past law may have contributed much to the present existence of an interest, and to its shape and extent.

stage. They may be so, cumulatively, at both stages. The rule that consideration is necessary to make an offer irrevocable for three days, even when the offer is fully intended, business like, signed, in writing, and expressed to be irrevocable for three days, may be thought not adapted to further security of transactions. The rule that certain oral and essential terms of an agreement are without force, if the balance of the agreement has been committed to writing, and looks on its face to be complete, raises considerable doubts as to its furtherance of security of transactions—sufficiently so as to have made our rules on the subject rather intricate and uncertain, and our judicial practices at times highly erratic. The rules standardizing the remedies in contracts for the sale of goods, limiting the remedy to a suit before a jury, and for damages, and measuring the damages in the great body of cases by arbitrary standards which presuppose a frictionless market, may be thought to give inadequate remedy, even if the basis of supposed substantive rules and rights be thought wholly adequate to *its* purposes. The means, I say, may be inadequate; but the analysis invites discovery of the inadequacy. Hence, whatever one thinks of the sufficiency in the large of the analysis in the threefold terms of interests, substantive rights and rules, and remedies, one can but pay homage to the sureness with which it forces law on the attention as something man-made, something capable of criticism, of change, of reform—and capable of criticism, change, and reform not only according to standards found inside law itself (inner harmony, logical consistence of rules, parts and tendencies, *elegantia juris*) but also according to standards vastly more vital found *outside* law itself, in the society law purports both to govern *and to serve.*

On the other hand, the set-up in these terms has carried over its full measure of confusion, as I have tried to indicate above. And the confusion thus carried over is not—like the virtues of the analysis—familiar, well understood, and regularly taken account of. Which brings me again to the suggestion made above, that the use of precepts, or rules, or of rights which are logical counterparts of rules—of *words,* in a word—as the *center* of reference in thinking about law, is a block to clear thinking about matters legal. I want again to make sure that I am not misunderstood. (1) I am not arguing that "rules of substantive law" are without importance. (2) I am not arguing that it is not humanly *possible* to use the interests-rights and rules-remedies analysis and still think clearly and usefully about law. (3) Least of all am I attempting to urge the exclusion of substantive rights and rules from the field of

"law." Instead of these things, I am arguing (1) that rules of substantive law are of far less importance than most legal theorizers
have assumed in most of their thinking and writing, and that they
are *not* the most useful center of reference for discussion of law;
(2) that the presence of the term "rights and rules" in the interest
set-up (a) has a persistent tendency to misfocus attention onto that
term; (b) that the avoidance of that tendency is a great gain in
clarity; and (c) that to both attempt such avoidance and retain
the term is to cumber all discussion with embarrassing and quite
unnecessary baggage; (3) that substantive rights and rules should
be removed from their present position at the *focal point* of legal
discussion, in favor of the *area of contact* between judicial (or
official) *behavior* and the *behavior* of laymen; that the substantive
rights and rules should be studied not as self-existent, nor as a
major point of reference, but themselves with constant reference
to that area of behavior-contacts. Let me take up the second and
third of these positions together, and turn then to the first.

The Interests-Rights-Remedies Analysis: Words v. Practice

I see no value to be gained from the interests-rights and rules-
remedies set up except to bring out, to underscore, that law is not
all, nor yet the major part, of society; and to force attention to the
relations and interactions of law and the rest of society; and as a
matter of method, to provide words which keep legal and non-legal
aspects of the situation and of the interactions distinct. And it
would seem to go without demonstration that *the most significant*
(I do *not* say the *only* significant) aspects of the relations of law
and society lie in the field of behavior, and that words take on
importance either because and insofar as they are behavior, or
because and insofar as they demonstrably reflect or influence other
behavior. This statement seems not worth making. Its truth is
absurdly apparent. For all that, it reverses, it upsets, the whole
traditional approach to law. It turns accepted theory on its head.
The traditional approach is in terms of words; it centers on words;
it has the utmost difficulty in getting beyond words. If nothing be
said about behavior, the *tacit* assumption is that the words do
reflect behavior, and if they be the words of rules of law, do influence behavior, even influence behavior effectively and precisely
to conform completely to those words. Here lies the key to the
muddle. The "rules" are laid down; in the type-case they are
"ought" rules, prescriptive rules: the writer's prescriptions, the

writer's oughts, individually proclaimed oughts—the true rule is that judges should give judgment for the plaintiff on these facts. From this we jump without necessary notice into equivalent oughts as *accepted* in the legal system under discussion: prevailing oughts—the authorities agree that judges should give judgment for the plaintiff on these facts. Here, again without notice and without inquiry, we *assume* that *practice* of the judges conforms to the accepted oughts on the books; that the verbal formulations of oughts *describe* precisely the is-es of practice; that they *do* give such judgment on such facts. A toothed bird of a situation, in law or any other walk of life. Where is men's ideology about their doing, about what is good practice—where is that ideology or has it ever been an adequate description of their *working* practice?

This is the first tacit imputation of factuality to the rules of ought. A second such imputation follows forthwith—again without explicitness, again without inquiry, again (save in odd instances) without challenge or suggestion or doubt. The paper rule of ought which has now been *assumed* to *describe* the judges' *working* rule of ought (*i.e.,* to correspond with the judges' practice of decision) is now further assumed to *control* the practice of the interested laymen, to *govern* people's conduct. Pray for the storm-tossed mariner on a night like this! What hope is there for clarity of reasoning with such a waste of billowing to build on?

Do I suggest that (to cut in at one crucial point) the "accepted rules," the rules the judges say that they apply, are without influence upon their actual behavior? I do not. I do not even say that, *sometimes,* these "accepted rules" may not be a very accurate description of the judges' actual behavior. What I say is that such accuracy of description is rare. The question is how, and how much, and in what direction, do the accepted rule and the practice of decision diverge? More: how, and how much, *in each case?* You cannot generalize on this, *without investigation.* Your guesses may be worth something, in the large. *They are worth nothing at all, in the particular.* The one thing we know now for certain is, that different rules have totally different relations to the behavior of judges, of other officials, and of the particular persons "governed" (optimistic word!) by those different rules. The approach here argued for admits, then, out of hand, *some* relation between *any* accepted rule and judicial behavior; and then proceeds to deny that that admission involves anything but a problem for investigation in the case in hand; and to argue that the significance of the particular rule will appear only *after* the investigation of the vital, focal, phenomenon: the behavior. And if an empirical *science* of law is to have any realistic basis, any responsibility to the facts, I see no escape from moving to this position. Thus, and only thus, is the real gain sought by the interests-rights and rules-remedies analysis to be made tangible.

I do not deny, be it noted, that those who have cast their thinking in that set-up are from time to time aware of the importance of what is here urged. "Law-in-books and law-in-action." Indeed, whenever challenged on the point, any one of them will proceed to remodel his emphasis *ad hoc;* he will, for a moment, fix his stress on the remedy, even on the effects of the remedy, as used, in life. *But* it is an *ad hoc* remodelling. It is forgotten when the immediate issue is passed. It is no part of the standard equipment of investigation, discussion, synthesis; it is a part only of the equipment of defense. When used apart from combat, as a result of a worker's own curiosity or of some sudden fact-stimulus from outside, it flares like a shooting star, and disappears. Always the night of words will close again in beauty over the wild, streaked disturbance.

INTERESTS: WHAT ARE THEY?

This emphasis on behavior, on the observable, on *attempts* at objective cross-check on the data under discussion, on *attempts* to find words which describe and do not misdescribe those data, ought to bear fruit in the discussion of interests, as well. The attribution of "interest" quality to anything of necessity involves a value-judgment over and above those value-judgments inherent in any scientific inquiry.[11] At that point the behavior approach ceases to promise objective agreement, except in this—that isolation of the value-judgment, in presentation, from the observed phenomena on which it in part rests, would clarify much discussion. Above all, such an approach to interests would move in terms of *demonstrating the existence of groupings* of behavior claimed to be significant, as the part of scientific decency when any "interest" is set up for discussion. The current approach tends instead to set up the broadest of formulae about interests, and to attribute them

---

[11] As, *e.g.,* that it is worth while finding out; that it is worth while checking conclusions constantly by facts; and striving to state conclusions which stay within the observed facts; probably also that it is worth while to publish such conclusions for discussion irrespective of what prejudices they may affront, or what accepted values they may disturb.

to situations in magisterial unconcern for the specific facts. I have paid my disrespects briefly above to some aspects of "security of transactions." I would not be understood thereby to deny that those three words are highly useful, or that they refer to very significant aspects of our life. But I am very eager to be understood as questioning how much is accomplished, for any given specific problem, by resting merely on the magic of those words. I think my friend Patterson has wisely described the interest-concept, in its present stage of development, as merely a red flag to *challenge investigation* in certain general directions—as leaving in any concrete situation most of the fact gathering and most of the fact weighing still to be done. "Security of transactions," in the contract cases I have put above would, to him, mean the most useful raising of a query: what kind of transactions is involved? Better, what *kinds* of transactions are involved? How many? What results, at present? What disappointments? What effects would any proposed change have? What possible undesired effects, in the hands of interested parties? And so on. "Security of transactions" would settle nothing. It would, as facts become clear, suggest one line of policy which has come in many phases of the law to be regarded as important; but it would leave the importance of that line of policy in any case to be illumined by the facts relevant to the situation in that instant case. No elimination of the subjective value-judgment, then; but an illumination by objective data of the basis and bearings of a subjective value-judgment. Insofar, a comparison of *facts* with *facts,* and not of *words* with *words.* Not a comparison of a mere formula of words about an interest with a formula of words said to be a "rule of law," a precept with no man knows what unexamined meaning in life. Nay, rather the objective data, the *specific* data, *claimed* to represent an interest, compared with the *actual doings* of the judges and the *actual effects* of the doings *on the data claimed to represent an interest.* If the judges' *sayings* have *demonstrable* effects, add those to the comparison. What else is relevant? Better: is anything else anything like *so* relevant?

I have said above that this can be done under the more cumbersome three-fold analytical set-up.[12] I have said that it semiocca-

[12] Throughout this paper I am speaking primarily from the viewpoint of the postmortemizer, the observer, the orderer, the scientist. But in passing let me pay my respects to four other lines of legal thinking in which the utility of the suggested approach seems equally striking.

(a) That of the practicing lawyer. In his moments of action, in his actual handling of a case or situation, the measure of his success is the measure in which he actually

sionally has been done. I have said that it is rarely done, and that
the definite tendency of that set-up is to block off the doing of it.
I venture to predict that without the shift of emphasis, of focus,
to behavior, that tendency will continue cheerfully in evidence.

uses this approach. (The question of how far he uses it consciously, how far
intuitively, is immaterial to that fact.) His job is either to guide a specific client
through the difficulties of action in a concrete situation, or to bring the personnel
of a specific tribunal to a specific result. The desired results, and not formulae, are
his focus, and he uses formulae as he uses his knowledge of both judicial tradition
and individual peculiarity: as tools to reach his desired result. He can be more
effective, as any other practical man or artist can, if his technique be consciously
studied. This is not to say that all that goes to make up his technique can be laid
down or be consciously imparted. Still less is it to urge that he is himself a trustworthy reporter of his own technique.

(b) That of the legislator. Here is a man who wants results. How can one doubt
the added utility to be derived from his wrestling with the observable facts of
official action and lay action as those facts exist? Indeed, the successful practitioner
and the successful politician are precisely the men whose grasp of the realities of
law puts the word-beclouded theorist to shame.

(c) That of the philosopher of law—on the side of the "ends of law" and social
values. He takes his data for philosophizing from somewhere. The worthwhileness
of his philosophy is to a considerable degree conditioned by those data. If they
be data of life, his problems become more real, his check-up easier, his basis of
thinking more actual. This would mean at least, when he comes to apply his
chosen values to the criticism of "positive law," that he would bridge to the law-
in-action of his day, not merely to the books. If he be a pure mystic, this may be
immaterial; otherwise the gain seems inevitable.

For the devotee of formal logic in the law the picture is somewhat different. He
will be concerned with words, with propositions. Probably almost wholly with propositions which move within the realm of ought—of doctrine—presumably the
accepted doctrine of the system. Once he has his propositions, he runs free of the
approach here discussed. He meets that approach in two places: the first, when
he puts concrete content into his symbols, to start with. He will be no more accurate a logician, but a more useful one, if he reaches into observed fact, not
merely into paper words, for that life content. And again, when the logical process
is over, and he wishes to compare his results with something, to see whether he
would not prefer another line of systematizing, he can use the behavior-area effectively for his comparison.

But what I have said of the logician suggests the making express of a matter
implicit throughout the paper. To say that the area of behavior contact is the most
useful point of reference for all matters legal is *not* to say that a specialist may
not do the most useful of work, conceivably, without even reaching to that point
of reference. A careful study of the formal logic of judicial opinions would be a
useful study. But I would urge that even its usefulness would be hugely increased
by an equally careful study of the instrumentalism, the pragmatic and socio-psy-
chological decision elements in the same cases. And that an equally geometric increase
in illumination would follow a further careful study of the effects on the society
concerned of the same cases. Under the present "words" and "rules" approach, all
the tendency would be to stop with, or slightly modify, the first of these hypothetical
studies. Under the behavior-contact approach each would be welcome, but the
insistent drive would be toward completing the last before the significance of the
others would be thought even measurably understood.

(d) That of the judge. His approach as one member of a bench to his colleagues

Meaning of Rules and Rights Under the Behavior Analysis

What now, is the place of rules and rights, under such an approach? To attempt their excision from the field of law would be to fly in the face of fact. I should like to begin by distinguishing real "rules" and rights from paper rules and rights. The former are conceived in terms of behavior; they are but other names, convenient shorthand symbols, for the remedies, the actions of the courts. They are descriptive, not prescriptive, except in so far as there may commonly be implied that courts *ought* to continue in their practices.[13] "Real rules," then, if I had my way with words, would *by legal scientists* be called the practices of the courts, and not "rules" at all. And for such scientists statements of "rights" would be statements of likelihood that in a given situation a certain type of court action loomed in the offing. Factual terms. No more. This use of "rights," at least, has already considerable stand-

does not seem to me to differ significantly for the present purpose from that of the practicing lawyer. His approach *for himself* involves (as does the approach of the philosopher) his forming a value-judgment on the case in hand, in addition to observation and prediction. How his value-judgment can fail of higher utility if he sees his problem not as the mere making of an abstract paper formula, but as the devising of a *way of working* in court *which will in due course affect people* is hard for me to see. The latter approach will certainly force him toward using all facilities he has available to *visualize* in advance the effects of the decision. Such visualization has been thought—and, I conceive, rightly—to be the essence of case-law wisdom-in-action. The approach described should make this wisdom-in-action a reality in a higher percentage of cases. I have developed elsewhere that whereas the net effect is undoubtedly an expansion of the traditional field of discretion and judicial law-making, yet this should give even a conservative no cause for alarm: first, because even when expanded, that field remains amazingly narrow, taken in relation to law as a whole, or to the movement of law—only cumulative changes over decades being in the main of much note[c]; second, because it involves the introduction of no technique of change not already hallowed by conservative tradition, but only a reorganization, for conscious utilization, of techniques accepted for centuries as good; third (this an article of faith, not a matter capable as yet of proof) because the type of change produced under these circumstances is change which moves official action more into keeping with current needs; and another type of change, now constantly occurring, though hidden, tends to be eliminated: change by way of over-simplification of verbal formulae and over-"application" of such formulae to cases they never had before been applied to, and do not fit. Präjudi-zienrecht und Rechtsprechung in Amerika (1933).

[c] A corrected view, showing the process and importance of the daily change, is developed in my The Common Law Tradition—Deciding Appeals (1960).

[13] Eliminating such an implication would to my mind be pure gain. The question of desirability of continuing a given practice, when it comes up for discussion at all, is better made express. [This seems to me today to be a confused passage which fails to spot the true goal and existing fact of reasonable regularity in judicial behavior, and also fails to distinguish trial from appellate courts.]

ing among the followers of Hohfeld. This concept of "real rule" has been gaining favor since it was first put into clarity by Holmes. "Paper rules" are what have been treated, traditionally, as rules of law: the accepted *doctrine* of the time and place—what the books there say "the law" is. The "real rules" and rights—"what the courts will do in a given case, and nothing more pretentious" —are then predictions. They are, I repeat, on the level of isness and not of oughtness; they seek earnestly to go no whit, in their suggestions, beyond the remedy actually available. Like all short-hand symbols, they are dangerous in connotation, when applied to situations which are not all quite alike. But their intent and effort is to describe. And one can adapt for them Max Weber's magnificent formulation in terms of probability: a right (or practice, or "real rule") exists *to the extent that* a likelihood exists that A can induce a court to squeeze, out of B, A's damages; more: *to the extent that* the likely collections will cover A's damage. In this aspect *substantive* rights and "rules," as distinct from adjective, simply disappear—on the descriptive level. The measure of a "rule," the measure of a right, becomes what can be done about the situation. *Accurate* statement of a "real rule" or of a right includes all procedural limitations on what can be done about the situation. What is left, in the realm of *description,* are at the one end the facts, the groupings of conduct (and demonstrable expecta-tions [and/or needs]) which may be claimed to constitute an interest; and on the other the practices of courts in their effects upon the conduct and expectations of the laymen in question. Facts, in the world of isness, to be compared directly with other facts, also in the world of isness.

A reversion, do you say, to the crude and out-moded thinking of rules in terms of remedies only, to confining legal thinking to the vagaries of tradition-bound procedure? Not quite. It is a re-version to the realism of that primitive point of view. But a sophisticated reversion to a sophisticated realism. Gone is the ancient assumption that law is because law is; there has come since, and remains, the inquiry into the purpose of what courts are do-ing, the criticism in terms of searching out purposes and criticiz-ing means. Here value-judgments reenter the picture, and should. Observing particular, concrete facts of conduct and of expectation which suggest the presence of "an interest," one arrives at his value conclusion that something in those facts calls for protection at the hands of state officials. What protection is called for, and called for in terms of what *action* of the state officials? Again a matter of judgment—but a matter of judgment which at least foots on reality and comes to results in terms of action. With that hypothetical action, the actual conduct of those officials can be directly compared. Room for error, in plenty, in diagnosing interests, and in imagining the forms of official conduct suited to their protection. But realism in discussion; realism at each end of the comparison; a narrowing as far as the present state of knowledge will permit, of the field for obstructing eyes with words that masquerade as things without a check-up.

THE PLACE AND TREATMENT OF PAPER RULES

Are "rules of law" in the accepted sense eliminated in such a course of thought? Somewhat obviously not. Whether they be pure paper rules, or are the accepted patter of the law officials, they remain present, and their presence remains an actuality— an actuality of importance—but an actuality whose *precise* importance, whose bearing and influence become clear. First of all they appear as what they are: rules of authoritative ought, addressed *to* officials, telling *officials* what the *officials* ought to do.[14] To which telling the officials either pay no heed at all (the pure paper rule; the dead-letter statute; the obsolete case) or listen partly (the rule "construed" out of recognition; the rule to which lip-service chiefly is paid, while practice runs another course) or listen with all care (the rule with which the official practice pretty accurately coincides). I think that every such official precept-on-the-books (statute, doctrine laid down in the decision of a court, administrative regulation) tacitly contains an element of pseudo-description along with its statement of what officials ought to do; a tacit statement that officials do act according to the tenor of the rule; a tacit prediction that officials will act according to its tenor. Neither statement nor prediction is often true *in toto*. And the first point of the approach here made is skepticism as to the truth of

---

[14] This I think holds true of *all* official ought-rules, irrespective of their form. I speak of their effects, not of their purposes. And the rights of laymen result through the screen of the official's practice, by a kind of social reflex. Ehrlich described the phenomenon cogently, so far as concerned the rules governing the set-up of the state government machine. A legal philosopher or a normatizer, with his mind fixed on the purpose of rules to ultimately affect the conduct of the "governed," will quarrel with this. A sociologist is content to see and describe what happens—and *compare* that with what is purposed.

How joyously sharp, under this addressing of the rule to the judge, becomes the distinction between a rule telling him what to *do,* himself, and one telling him how to instruct a jury!

either in any case in hand. Yet it is an accepted convention to act and talk as if this statement and prediction were most solemn truth: a tradition marked peculiarly among the legal profession when engaged officially. It is indeed of first importance to remember that such a tradition contains a tendency to verify itself.[15] But no more so than to remember that such a tendency is no more powerful than its opposite: that other tendency to move quietly into falsifying the prediction in fact, while laying on an ointment of conventional words to soothe such as wish to believe the prediction has worked out.

Thus the problem of official formulations of rules and rights becomes complex. First, as to formulations already present, already existent: the accepted doctrine. There, I repeat, one lifts an eye canny and skeptical as to whether judicial behavior is in fact what the paper rule purports (implicitly) to state. One seeks the real practice on the subject, by study of how the cases do in fact eventuate. One seeks to determine how far the paper rule is real, how far *merely* paper.[16] One seeks an understanding of *actual* judicial behavior, in that comparison of paper rule with practice; one follows also the use made of the paper rule in argument by judges and by counsel, and the apparent influence of its official presence on decisions. One seeks to determine when it is stated, but ignored; when it is stated and followed; when and why it is *expressly* narrowed or extended or modified, so that a new paper rule is created. One observes the level of *silent* application or modification or escape, in the "interpretation" of the facts of a case, in contrast to that other and quite distinct level of express wrestling with the language of the paper rule. One observes how strongly ingrained is the tradition of requiring a good paper justification, in terms of officially accepted paper rules, before any decision, however appealing on the facts, can be regarded as likely of acceptance. And by the same token, one observes the importance of the official formulae as tools of argument and persuasion; one observes both the stimuli to be derived from, and the

[15] Ehrlich, again, brings this out beautifully.

[16] And on moving into the further fields of contact between judicial or official behavior and lay behavior, one gets into much deeper water: how does the paper rule work out (*i.e.,* have a reflection or a counterpart in behavior) in lower court cases, unappealed? How often does it have any influence? What influence on administrative officials? On transactions between laymen which never reach any officials? All signs point to this being vastly more important than the set-up of doctrine, or even than the actual practices of higher courts. What is documented takes on a specious appearance of value—even of typicality—as against the unexplored.

limitations set by, their language. Very rapidly, too, one perceives that neither are all official formulae alike in these regards, nor are all courts, nor are all times and circumstances for the same formula in the same court. The *handling* of the official formulae to influence court behavior then comes to appear as an art, capable only to a limited extent of routinization or (to date) of accurate and satisfying description. And the discrepancy, great or small, between the official formula and what actually results, obtains the limelight attention it deserves.

PAPER RULES AND NEW CONTROL

I am tempted, however, to regard the *new* formulation of official rules as even more vitally affected by the approach here suggested than is the dealing with existing formulations. For such new formulation is always with a purpose.[17] The effectuation of this purpose (one recalls "the protection of an interest," *supra*) *must be sought by means of verbal formulation.* In part the need is based on our legal tradition: our officials move to a great extent on the stimulus of and in the light of verbally formulated rules.[18] In part, moreover, verbal formulations, and especially those in regard to *new, planned* change in action, are an inherently essential tool of communication in a complex society; they are pecul-

[17] This hopelessly over-simplifies. There may be as many divergent purposes as there are participants. And almost regularly the formulator's purpose and the purpose he publicly assigns are in part disparate.

[18] This factor has by no means the exclusive importance the devotees of paper rules tend to attribute to it. The keener observers constantly stress this: what other meaning has the emphasis on the traditional techniques "for developing and applying precepts"; the *practice* of the office, or of the Constitution, which shift emphases, and often create or abrogate whole institutions; the "interpreting away" of a rule; the importance of experience in the office, of the "trained" incumbent? And so forth.

On the other hand the factor of verbally formulated rules has enough importance to explain why they have so long been considered the core of even the substance of law. They are not the sole machinery for *producing* regularity. Habit, practice, unverbalized experience and tradition, *are* vital to regularity. But they are *a* factor in *producing* it—to the extent that officials react to words, and read words, alike. They are, moreover, the main device for *checking* on regularity, for letting outsiders get an idea whether officials stay within the due limits of discretion. And they are, as indicated, a most vital element in introducing change in regularity. Where official behavior occurs *without* regularity, the older views tend to deny it the character of law (the assumed irregularity or caprice of cadijustice, and the like). On this I differ. I should of course stress as the more perfect illustration of the concept *regular* official behavior; but I regard the behavior as more vital than the regularity, and the mere paper expression of desired regularity—save so far as it expresses an ideal—well, as paper.

iarly important in a society which depends in good part upon
written records to maintain continuity of practice between successive incumbents of an office, and between successive generations.
But since the ultimate effectuation of a purpose is in terms of
action, of behavior, the verbal formulation, if it is to be an efficient
tool, must be such as will produce the behavior[19] desired. *This
turns on the relevant prevailing practices and attitudes of the
relevant persons.* In one familiar doctrinal illustration, language
used in a statute "will be read" in the light both of the existing
common law, and of prior judicial construction of that language.
But that is a matter of the top, the most superficial, level. Below
that are the more vital practices prevalent as to *handling* official
rules, described roughly above; practices, *i.e.,* of courts and of
lawyers.

But in regard to the new (and especially the statutory) formulation, the behavior problem goes much deeper than such practices
of the legal elect. The ways of appellate courts in handling existing official rules presuppose the cracking of the toughest nut the
statutory draftsman has to crack: the case is already in court;
someone is already making an appeal to the official formula.
Whereas one of the statutory draftsman's major problems is to
look into existent behavior beforehand, to make sure that his
formula, when it becomes an official rule, will not merely bask
in the sun upon the books. He must so shape it as to *induce its
application* (with all the discrepancies that may entail) or else (for
any purpose save that of pacifying clamorous constituents content
with words) his blow is spent in air.[20]

Only as a second job does he have to wrestle with making his
formula so impinge upon judicial tradition that the results in
action will be those desired *if* a case gets into court. Again there is
little to be gained by laboring the point. It seems patent that only
a gain in realism and effectiveness of thinking can come from
consistently (not occasionally) regarding the official formulation
as a tool, not as a thing of value in itself; as a means without

---

[19] I have not attempted in this paper to define conduct, action, behavior. I have
no desire to exclude such things as the arousing and disappointment of expectations,
the creation of hopes and fears, etc. The approach advocated would, however, go
vigorously to inquiring into the grounds for claiming the arousing or disappointment of expectations in any given case—as also to inquiring into what expectations,
and whose. So, too, for example, with the thought processes of judges, the influence
of ideology on judges and laymen, etc. *Cf.* 15 AM. EC. REV. 670, n. 17; 675, n. 32.

[20] Other aspects are developed in my paper *Law Observance and Law Enforcement,*
PROCEEDINGS OF CONFERENCE OF SOCIAL WORK (1928), at 129 *et seq.,* infra, p. 399.

meaning save in terms of its workings, and of meaning in its workings only when these last are compared with the results desired. In the terms used above: as *prima facie* pure paper until the contrary is demonstrated; and as at best a new piece of an established but moving environment, one single element in a complex of practices, ideas and institutions without whose study the one element means nothing. Hence what the proposed approach means is not the elimination of rules, but such setting of words and paper in perspective as can hugely step up their power and effect.[d]

THE PLACE AND TREATMENT OF CONCEPTS

Like rules, concepts are not to be eliminated; it cannot be done. Behavior is too heterogeneous to be dealt with except after some artificial ordering. The sense impressions which make up what we call observation are useless unless gathered into some arrangement. Nor can thought go on without categories.

A realistic approach would, however, put forward two suggestions on the making of such categories. The first suggestion rests primarily upon the knowledge that to classify is to disturb. It is to build emphases, to create stresses, which obscure some of the data under observation and give fictitious value to others—a process which can be excused only insofar as it is necessary to the accomplishing of a purpose. The data to be singled out in reference to that purpose are obviously those which appear most relevant. But true relevancy can be determined only as the inquiry advances. For this reason a realistic approach to any new problem would begin by scepticism as to the adequacy of the *received* categories for ordering the phenomena effectively toward a solution of the new problem. It is quite possible that the received categories as they already stand are perfect for the purpose. It is, however, altogether unlikely. The suggestion then comes to this: that with the new purpose in mind one approach the data afresh, taking them in as raw a condition as possible, and discovering how far and how well the available traditional categories really cover the most relevant of the raw data. And that before proceeding one undertake such modifications in the categories as may be necessary or look promising. In view of the tendency toward overgeneralization in the past this is likely to mean the making of

[d] For a quick and easy illustration compare Uniform Commercial Code, Art. 2, with the older Uniform Sales Act.

smaller categories—which may either be sub-groupings inside the received categories, or may cut across them.

The other suggestion of a realistic approach rests on the observation that categories and concepts, once formulated and once they have entered into thought processes, tend to take on an appearance of solidity, reality and inherent value which has no foundation in experience. More than this: although originally formulated on the model of at least some observed data, they tend, once they have entered into the organization of thinking, both to suggest the presence of corresponding data even when these data are not in fact present, and to twist any fresh observation of data into conformity with the lines and shape of the categories. This has been discussed above in its application to rules; it holds true, however, of any concept. It is peculiarly troublesome in regard to legal concepts, because of the tendency of the crystallized legal concept to persist after the fact model from which the concept was once derived has disappeared or changed out of recognizability. A simple but striking instance is the resistance opposed by the "master-servant" concept to each readjustment along the lines of a new industrial labor situation. The counsel of the realistic approach here, then, would be the constant back-checking of the category against the data, to see whether the data are still present *in the form suggested by the category-name*. This slows up thinking. But it makes for results which means something when one gets them.

Background of the Behavior Approach

All this is nothing new in social science. It is of a piece with the work of the modern ethnographer. He substitutes painstaking objective description of practice for local *report* of what the practice is, or for (what is worse) a report either of local practice or of local ideology pleasantly distorted by the observer's own home-grown conventions. It is of a piece with the development of objective method in psychology. It fits into the pragmatic and instrumental developments in logic.[21] It seeks to capitalize the methodological worries that have been working through in these latter years to new approaches in sociology, economics, political science. The only novel feature is the application to that most conventionalized and fiction-ridden of disciplines, the law. In

[21] Mortimer Adler suggests to me that the operational approach to modern physics is a classic analogue and precursor.

essence the historical school of jurists from the one side, and Bentham and later Ihering from the other, were approaching the lines of theorizing here put forth. Holmes' mind had travelled most of the road two generations back. What has been done in the last decades that has some touch of novelty is for theorizers to go beyond theorizing, to move, along such lines as these, into the gathering and interpretation of facts about legal behavior: Ehrlich, Nussbaum, Hedemann, Brandeis, Frankfurter, Moore, Clark, Douglas, Moley, Yntema, Klaus, Handler, Lambert [22]—I name only enough to show that neither a single country nor a single school is involved, and to make clear that the point of view has moved beyond the stage of chatter and has proved itself in operation. That out of the way, I should like to glance at a few further implications of the approach.

ADMINISTRATIVE ACTION AS LAW

Three of them appear together. First, to focus on the area of contact between judicial behavior and the behavior of the "governed" is to stress *interactions*. Second, central as are the judges' actions in disputed cases, there is a vast body of other

[22] The work of the different men moves in somewhat different fields, and is uneven in value. The same holds often of different work of the same man. And an exhaustive bibliography of all that has been done along the lines discussed would be long. Probably most titles would fall in the useful but less advanced field of discovering the appellate courts' real practice as distinct from the paper pattern of courts or writers. The names listed were chosen with reference to work at the next stage beyond: facts as to lower court operations, and the beginnings of inquiry into the contact-area between official and layman's conduct. EHRLICH (Czernowitz), GRUNDLEGUNG EINER SOZIOLOGIE DES RECHTS, and see PAGE, PRO. ASSN. AM. L. S. 46, (1914). Unfortunately most of the findings of his investigations into "living law" are inaccessible. NUSSBAUM (Berlin), in his RECHTSTATSACHEN-FORSCHUNG; HEDEMANN (Jena), REICHSGERICHT UND WIRTSCHAFTSRECHT; Brandeis, the brief in *Muller v. Oregon,* and his opinions, repeatedly; FRANKFURTER AND LANDIS (Harvard), THE BUSINESS OF THE SUPREME COURT (1928); FRANKFURTER AND GREEN, THE LABOR INJUNCTION (1930); Underhill Moore (Yale), mimeographed and MS. materials on banking in relation to the law of banking; Moore and Shamos, *Interest on the Balances of Checking Accounts,* 27 COLUM. LAW REV. 633 (1927); C. E. Clark (Yale), MS. materials on the actual practice of litigation in Connecticut and New York; partial results appear in the CONN. BAR J. for July, 1928, April and July, 1929, and the W. VA. L. J. for Dec., 1929; Wm. Douglas (Yale), study in bankruptcy and insolvency practice, still under way; Moley (Columbia), the crime surveys, generally; Yntema and Theo. Hope (Johns Hopkins), pending investigations into the use of federal jurisdiction and into the actual course of litigation in state courts; Klaus (Columbia), *Sale, Agency and Price Maintenance,* 28 COLUM. LAW REV. 312, 441 (1928); Handler (Columbia), *False and Misleading Advertising* (1929) 39 YALE L. J. 22; ISHIZAKI, LE DROIT CORPORATIF INTERNATIONAL DE LA VENTE DE SOIES (1928); and Klaus' excellent review, 28 COLUM. LAW REV. 991 (1928).

officials whose actions are of no less importance; quantitatively their actions are of vastly greater importance, though it may well be that the judge's position gives him a leverage of peculiar power. In what has preceded I have somewhat lightly argued as if judge and court were the be-all and end-all of the legal focus. It is time to reformulate, to grow at once more accurate and more inclusive.[23] The actions of these other officials touch the interested layman more often than do those of the judge; increasingly so, and apparently increasing at a rising rate of increase as the administrative machine gains in function and in force. More often than not, administrative action is, *to the layman affected,* the last expression of the law on the case. In such a situation, I think it highly useful to regard it, for him, as being the law of the case. I see no gain whatever, and much loss, from setting up a fictitious unity in the law, when some officials do one thing, some another, and the courts now and again a third. Realistically, the law is then not one, but at least three, and by no means three-in-one. If what the courts do ultimately prevails *and is translated into* administrative practice, that is that. If such an event is predictable in advance, I find it vastly more useful to think of that event as the emerging unity of the law, which until it happens may be an ought, and is already an opportunity (at a price) for him with gumption and money to reach for it, but is not *yet* the probable law for the ordinary case. What—more than one law, on a single jurisdiction, according to the whim or practice of an official, or according to the funds or temperament or political complexion of the layman affected? Just that. What else expresses the facts? Why blink and squint because the paper tradition is annoyed? As long as there are words to describe the court rule which will ultimately prevail (in a case where it will!), and to describe the situation differently before and after the victory, what is gained *in a science of observation* by using the same words to describe both conditions—except a sure confusion? [24]

[23] The reformulation would complicate the preceding argument, but would not essentially change it. Except insofar as the argument would thereby gain cogency.

[24] On the *normative* side of law no confusion or doubt would exist in this case. The "right rule" would be the same all along. But that is no reason for obscuring the divergence in the results, on the level of description and prediction. We need, precisely for such purposes, to sever the normative from the descriptive aspects of law. Moreover, results affect norms, quite as much as norms affect results. If the outcome were going to be the overthrow of the judicial by the administrative practice, in the case put, the norm would pending outcome be in considerable doubt. And one of the (quite incidental) advantages of the approach contended for is to make explicit, understandable, *and non-shocking* the fact and realm of occurrence of such doubts as to norm.

Hence I argue that the focus, the center of law, is not merely what the judge does, in the impact of that doing on the interested layman, but what *any* state official does, officially.[25] Lawyers are curious. As to a *court* of first instance, though it be the court of a lay J.P., they would have no difficulty seeing this.[e] They could even see that a wrong decision below, appealed from and reversed, would be part of the troubles of a litigant, would reduce his effective rights—how often do they jockey the case to bring about a settlement, by trading on just such friction-factors! But to say that the decision of the eighteen hundred dollar clerk in Bureau *B* that certain expenses are not deductible from my income tax return *is* the law in my case, gives a lawyer's ideology the same shock that it gives to a political scientist to urge that for purposes of that decision, that official *is* the State. One needs again to wash the matter down with Holmes' "cynical acid" and see what is left. In the same manner, if the official's decision is adverse and erroneous, I should include as a subtraction from my effective rights, if I proceeded to get a reversal, the ill-will and subsequent trouble I might incur at the hands of that official; as a part of the law, if I won; and its predictability as a determining part of the law, if in view thereof I decided not to fight.

Laymen's Behavior as a Part of Law

Interactions between official behavior and laymen's behavior, first; and second, the recognition of official behavior of all officials as part of the core of law. Third, and an immediate part of both, the recognition of what Nicholas Spykman so strongly and properly stresses: that the word "official" tacitly presupposes, connotes, reaches out to include, all those patterns of action (ordering, initiative) and obedience (including passivity) on the part both of the official and of all laymen affected which *make up* the official's position and authority as such. Something of this sort is the idea

[25] If we were dealing with a society which lacked political organization, this obviously would be a bad terminology. But another of the futilities of overgeneralization in the law has been the attempt to find *one* set of terms to cover the institutions of disparate societies. Before political organization we find control, and often specialized or semispecialized control institutions. But in describing a politically organized society it is exceedingly convenient to limit the term to the official Big Stick. A convenient term for the closely similar "law" of the subgroup in such a society is "by-law." Sociologically the two are often more similar than dissimilar. *Cf.* Max Weber, Wirtschaft u. Gesellschaft, 16, 17, 27 etc.; and 15 Am. Ec. Rev. 672 *et seq.*

[e] This difference in approach has been beautifully developed by Arnold, especially in Symbols of Government (1937) and Bottlenecks of Business (1940).

underlying "consent of the governed," "ultimate dependence upon public opinion," and the like; but these older phrasings have no neatness of outline; they do not even suggest the need of sharp-edged drawing, which I take to be the reason why they act as a soporific, while the Spykman formulation acts as a stimulant to the curiosity and imagination. In a passing it is well to note that here, too, Max Weber's method of formulation becomes classic: the official exists as such precisely *insofar as* such patterns of action and obedience prevail.[26] I agree whole-heartedly that these patterns are an essential part of any phenomena we call law. The more whole-heartedly because Spykman's formulation brings out with fresh emphasis the difference between paper rules and resultant behavior, and the extent to which the behavior which results (if any) from the official formulation of a rule depends on the patterns of thought and action of the persons whose behavior is in question.

The Need for Narrower, More Concrete Study

How far these patterns can be presupposed, how far they require specific examination, depends on the individual case. Here as throughout we run into the need for reexamining the majestic categories of the romantic period of jurisprudence. The old categories are imposing in their purple, but they are all too big to handle. They hold to many heterogeneous items to be reliable in use. What is true of some law simply will not hold of other law. What is true of some persons as to some law will not hold of other persons, even as to the same or similar law.[27] I care not how reclassification be made, so long as it is in terms of observation and of organizing the data usably, *and* with back-check to the facts. But reclassification is called for. From another angle, what we need is patience to look and see what is there; and to do that we must become less ambitious as to how much we are going to look at all at once.

An illustration may make the point clearer. Some "rules" are aimed at controlling and affecting the behavior of persons whose

[26] In the same way (borrowing Spykman again) *to the extent* that the official's behavior plays into these interlocking patterns of action it becomes "official" rather than personal behavior, and so of direct interest here. "Purely" personal behavior of an official approaches inconceivability; but substantially personal behavior may take up a great bulk of a given official's time.

[27] Cf. *Law Observance and Law Enforcement,* Pro. Conf. Social Work, 129, 131, *et seq.* (1928), *infra,* p. 399.

whole set and interest is opposed to making the adjustment desired; others are aimed at affecting behavior of persons who are not only willing to adjust, but have an existing effective machinery for accomplishing the adjustment. A type of the first is almost any phase of professional crime; a type of the second, perhaps, would be some change in the law affecting city real estate transactions which happens to be desired by the dealers. Most cases are compounded of both elements. If city real estate alone is involved, much might be said at first blush for law reform being peculiarly easy and quick, because the practice is firmly entrenched of never entering a real estate deal without consulting a lawyer. But other practices are also entrenched, such as relying upon first mortgage finance from a particular type of concern which in turn insists upon a title policy which in turn is under control of companies whose interest runs counter to certain types of law reform. The troubles of Torrens titles in New York City are an instance. They are substantially unmarketable; no mortgage company will loan on them because no title company will insure them.[28] That is, however, an instance of attempted "helpful-device" legal innovation. It is a different problem from the "ordering-and-forbidding" legal innovation. Barring questions of constitutionality, and barring the political question of how far legislation running counter to the desire of a well organized and powerful group can be achieved at all, it is obvious that enforcement of a new prescribed style of doing business upon New York City title companies would be *prima facie* a promising problem of legal engineering, precisely because their business is localized, well organized, and run by relatively few business units. Unlike the professional criminal, they could not dive underground and survive. The problem of detection would therefore be one of detecting not persons, but infractions by known units; and their deals could almost certainly be forced into the open. The major policing problem would therefore in all likelihood become one of anticipating and barring out in advance "evasions" undertaken by changing the methods of business under advice of counsel: *i.e.,* a problem of initially or subsequently so framing the official formulae of ordering and forbidding that transactions could not be accomplished (at a profit, after deducting fines, etc.) except along lines of the general purposes of the legislation. True, unless the engineering were so

[28] Thus one Torrens title to one lot in a block makes the block unavailable for large-scale improvement. R. R. B. Powell tells me that Torrens titles have even on occasion been de-registered, in order to gain access to mortgage money.

successful that a somewhat comparably profitable new turn to
the business developed, the legislator would have to reckon not
only with initial, but with persistent and highly skilled resistance
—which might even take the line it once did with the railroads,
of seeking to capture the governmental machine. And it is of
course this type of resistance which would in fact (contrary to our
hypothesis) keep the constitutional issue in the forefront of the
fight. The parallels and the divergencies from regulation or prohibition of liquor traffic would be instructive. As one moves to
bank robberies or jewelry thefts the parallels begin to fade out and
the divergencies to sharpen. I have purposely chosen an illustration from a field in which I am blankly ignorant, in order to bring
out the lines of thought and inquiry which open, under the approach, *even before the gathering of data is begun.* It is obvious
that the set or attitude of those affected or sought to be affected
by any piece of "law" is at the heart of the problem of control;
it should be equally obvious that the style of organization of
those persons, their group ways of action—whether among themselves or with regard to society at large—is equally vital. Behavior
effects depend in important part upon present behavior conditions.

The Narrow Applicability of Most Rules—
and Its Implications

This leads directly into the next point: most pieces of law affect
only a *relatively* small number of persons ever or at all, with any
directness—or are intended to. Where that is the case, the *organization, attitude, present and probable behavior of the persons
sought to be affected* is what needs major consideration, from the
angle of getting results (or of understanding results). Indeed, the
very *identification* of those persons may be a precondition calling
for much study. Which is a somewhat absurdly roundabout way
of saying that unless those matters are studied, the rules drawn,
and the administrative behavior adapted to the persons in question, results will be largely accident. *"To the persons in question,"*
and, indeed, "to those persons *under the conditions in question."*
It cannot be too strongly insisted that our attitude toward "rules"
of law, treating them as universal in *application,* involves a persistent twisting of observation. "Rules" in the realm of action
mean what rules *do;* "rules" in the realm of action *are* what they
do. The *possible* application and applicability are not without

importance, but the *actual* application and applicability are of controlling importance. To think of rules as universals—especially, to think of them as being applicable to "all persons who bring themselves within their terms"—is to muffle one's eyes in a constitutional fiction before beginning a survey of the scene. To be sure, constitutions purport to require rules of law to be "equal and general." [29] But most rules, however general as to the few they cover, are highly special, when viewed from the angle of how many citizens there are. And most rules "applying" to "all who come within their terms" (all those who set up barber shops, or are tempted to commit murder, or to bribe officials, or to embezzle from banks or certify checks without the drawer having funds, or to adopt a child, or to run a manufacturing establishment employing five or more persons) do not and will not, realistically considered, ever be "applicable" in any meaningful sense of the term, to *most* people in the community. Such rules are indeed open. Persons do move in and out of the sphere of their applicability. But that sphere is much more clearly seen when viewed (as compared with the community) as narrow, as special, as peculiar. Obviously even more special is the sphere of *real* application: of official *behavior* with reference to application. (And is it not clear that this most special sphere is commonly the one of greatest consequence to the persons on whose behavior any results depend: the objects of the "regulation"?)[30]

I know of no consequence of the approach here contended for —the approach in terms of organized behavior interacting with

[29] In practice this comes to: "*equable* in the choice of the very limited class to be affected." *Equality* of rule is impossible in a specialized society. It is true that some few of the lines of discrimination which are under our system excluded from consideration, are suggested by the word "equality." But it is not particularly significant, save historically.

[30] I have stressed elsewhere that the vital problem in such cases is that of creating in the conduct of the relevant persons new *practices* (folkways) which conform to the purposes sought *via* the new legal rules. *Law Observance and Law Enforcement, infra*, at p. 399. And that the effectiveness of legal rules, old or new, is not to be measured simply by how often officials act in accordance with them. *Ibid.*, and 15 AM. EC. REV. 682. Indeed the ideal effectiveness is not achieved until officials do not have to act at all. But if the rules are of the kind which coincide roughly with ancient, established lay practice (*mores*) it becomes a serious problem how far we have in such cases effectiveness of the *legal rule*, or of the occasional official behavior with reference to the rule. Contrast the extreme opposite case: an entire organized line of activity all units of which are prepared to move or not to move along lines newly prescribed, according to the outcome in court of a deliberately chosen test case. It is not behavior of officials *alone*, but behavior of officials in its *interaction* with that of the relevant laymen, which is most important.

organized behavior—no consequence more illuminating than this immediate opening up for study of the subgroup and institutional structure both of "governors" and of "governed." Its opening up for study as a first essential to any understanding at all, as making the study of law a study in first instance of particularized situations and what happens in or can be done about them.[31]

REALISM AS TO "SOCIETY"

"What can be done," and by whom? I have spoken of law as a means: *whose* means, to *whose* end? Discussion of law, like discussions of "social control," tend a little lightly to assume "*a society*" and to assume the antecedent discovery of "social" objectives. Either is hard to find in any sense which corresponds with the facts of control. Where is the unity, the single coherent group? Where is the demonstrable objective which is "social," and not opposed by groups well nigh as important as those which support it? And law in particular presents, over most if not all of its bulk, the phenomenon of clashing interests, of antagonistic persons or groups, with officials stepping in to favor some as against some others. Either to line up the dissenter in the interests of his own group; that is one broad phase. Or to regulate the relations between two groups, or to alter the terms of the struggle (competitive or other) between them. Hence the eternal fight for the control of the machinery of law, and of law making, whereby the highly interested *A*s can hope partially to force their will upon the equally but adversely interested *B*s, and to put behind that control the passive approval and support of the great body of *C*s—who happen to be disinterested, or, what is equally to the point, uninterested. To the truth of this observation it makes little difference whether the ends of the *A*s are material or idealistic, whether wholly selfish or dedicated most altruistically to some concept of the welfare of the whole. And while this welter with regard to change in law may, if you will, be thought of as political, the presence of the welter raises problems in defining "interests." One must also recur to the fact that it is on the same welter that official behavior is expected to be brought to bear when the new

[31] What is wanted in the way of generalization must come from a resynthesis of such particularized studies, once we have them. Meantime, we have our common sense and tradition-given understanding of *some* of the regularities of official behavior, and sufficient traditional skills in predicting, influencing, managing official or other behavior to get on after a fashion, in practice, while we learn more.

"rule" has been proclaimed.[32] Thus raising all the problems raised above, with this addition: the possibility, not there mentioned, of a group of laymen pushing to help the official program along.

One matter does need mention here, however: the eternal dilemma of the law, indeed of society; and of the law because the law purports peculiarly among our institutions to "represent" the whole. There is, amid the welter of self-serving groups, clamoring and struggling over this machine that will give power over others, the recurrent emergence of some wholeness, some sense of responsibility which outruns enlightened self-interest, and results in action apparently headed (often purposefully) for the common good. To affirm this is to confess no Hegelian mysticism of the State. It leaves quite open any question of the existence of some "life principle" in a society. It merely notes that, lacking such a self-sanation in terms of the whole, the whole would not indefinitely continue as a whole. And to deny that would be folly. It would be to carry emancipation from the idle ideology of "representation of the whole" into blindness to the half-truth around which that once-precious ideology was built. But to deny the emancipation, to worship the half truth without dire and specific concern for the details of the welter, would be a folly quite as great.[33]

---

[32] Not quite the same. The fight and victory may have somewhat changed the picture. And the enactment of a new formula has some consequences in itself: among others, that the formula chosen imposes temporary (though sometimes wide) limits upon what the officials can do, whereas the prior struggle is typically in terms of policies more than of measures.

[33] It is along the same line that I feel strongly the unwisdom, when turning the spotlight on behavior, of throwing overboard emphasis on rules, concepts, ideology, and ideological stereotypes or patterns. These last, as we have them, are, by themselves, confusing, misleading, inadequate to describe or explain. But a jurisprudence which was practically workable could not have been built in terms of them, if they had not contained a goodly core of truth and sense. To be sure, it was not the precept-ideology of jurisprudence, but the practice that jurisprudence only partly mirrored, which actually worked. But one thing sociological study ought to do for the advance of science is to school the advocates of new insight no longer to junk wholesale the old insight against which they are rebelling. The rebelling indicates inadequacy in the old. It does not indicate that the old did not have much solid basis. The bare fact that the old exists, could come into existence and persist, evidences that it had. If we can examine it for what it has, and carry that with us into a new alignment, we shall do much to reduce the well-known pendulum swing from exaggeration to exaggeration. This is of less moment in the earliest stages of a new movement. The innovator carries over willy-nilly the virtues of the same training against which he is in intellectual revolt. But those newly trained in the new school will be half-trained unsound exaggerators, if the original innovators fail to incorporate *in their doctrine as in their practice* the life-power of the older school, even while attacking the latter's false emphases and implications.

What Law Is Thought to Be: Folk-Law

In all the emphasis placed upon behavior I may have created the impression that a "realistic" approach would make itself un-realistic by disregarding what people *think* law is. Not so. But a realistic approach would cut at once into analysis and subdivision of the terms "people," "think," and "law" in such a phrase. For the great mass of persons not particularly concerned, I suspect that "law" in this aspect, *so far as* it concerns themselves, means "what I ought to do" and is not much distinguished from those selective slight idealizations of current practice we think of as morals. At times the issue certainly gets closer: "I want this contract to stick"—and doubtless I will then think of putting it in writing, and will meditate on reciting a formula I saw somewhere (in a deed, was it?): "for one dollar and other good and valuable considerations"; I may get a witness to the signing, too. In the field of private law we know singularly little of this folk-law-in-action. In that of the older criminal law we can suspect a very rough coincidence of folk-law-in-action with folk-morality-in-action,[34] except that here and there the thought of cop and jail will work deterrently when plain external and internal non-official social sanctions might not wholly click; we can suspect further that over considerable fields criminal law is too new and too specialized to have much background or counterpart in folk-morality; and, finally, that some fairly wide bodies of non-moral (or not yet moral) criminal law aspects will have percolated into folk-law: I think of traffic law (as known to the traffickers) as distinctly in advance in most places of traffic morality, and of similar discrepancies in regard to liquor, gambling, and sex matters, as to some portions of a population with variant morals. Now clearly what people think law to be, as regards themselves, has some effect at times upon their action. My guess is, however, that the effect on the side of forbidding is much slighter than the lawyer is likely to imagine, whenever any important pressure of self-interest is present, except for a relatively small minority, or over relatively small areas of action for any particular person. On the other hand, my guess is that in the field in which law provides "helpful devices" —the attempt to use which presupposes concurrent self-interest—

[34] May I insist again at this point that "folk morality" really means often at least as many important varieties in specific details as there are subgroups within the main group?

folk-law has very considerable influence in shaping conduct. The problem calls for exploration, from the realist's angle, by cautious study of detail. Even more important, I suspect, is the problem of what law is supposed to be with regard to others than the supposer. But important in accounting less for action than for inaction. For it seems likely that in this aspect law is mainly conceived simply as being all right, without concern for detail; and that this aspect of folk-law is close to the heart of that grand-scale passive cooperation of the uninterested which makes control of the political machinery a prize.

Ideals as to What Law Ought to Be

No less important than what people think law is, is what people conceive that law should be. Any change in law is in good part a reflection of someone's desire to produce a difference. And just as attitudes and expectations must be taken into account along with overt behavior, so must purposes and the ideal pictures toward which purposes drive. Thus far, even from the angle of a purely descriptive science.

Into another aspect of ideals as to what law ought to be this present paper does not attempt to go. I make no effort *here* to indicate either the proper rule or the proper action of any legal subject. I do, however, argue, and with some vigor, that as soon as one turns from the *formulation* of ideals to their *realization*, the approach here indicated is vital to his making headway. It is only in terms of a sound descriptive science of law (or of what is roughly equivalent, a soundly built working art, which takes equal account of conditions) that ideals move beyond the stage of dreams. Moreover, as has so often been pointed out, both the feasibility of accomplishing a policy and the cost of its accomplishment are in a world of limited possibilities vital elements in arriving at a judgment of the worthwhileness of the policy itself.

Conclusion

In conclusion, then, may I repeat that I have been concerned not at all with marking a periphery of law, with defining "it," with *excluding* anything at all from its field. I have argued that the trend of the most fruitful thinking about law has run steadily toward regarding law as an engine (a heterogeneous multitude of engines) having purposes, not values in itself; and that the clearer visualization of the problems involved moves toward ever-decreasing emphasis on words, and ever-increasing emphasis on observable behavior (in which any demonstrably probable attitudes and thought-patterns should be included). Indeed that the focus of study, the point of reference for all things legal has been shifting, and should now be consciously shifted to the area of contact, of interaction, between official regulatory behavior and the behavior of those affecting or affected by official regulatory behavior; and that the rules and precepts and principles which have hitherto tended to keep the limelight should be displaced, and treated with severe reference to their bearing upon that area of contact —in order that paper rules may be revealed for what they are, and rules with real behavior correspondences come into due importance. That the complex phenomena which are lumped under the term "law" have been too broadly treated in the past, and that a realistic understanding, possible only in terms of observable behavior, is again possible only in terms of study of the way in which persons and institutions are organized in our society, and of the cross-bearings of any particular *part* of law and of any particular *part* of the social in the social organization.

Included in the field of law under such an approach is everything currently included, and a vast deal more. At the very heart, I suspect, is the behavior of judges, peculiarly, that part of their behavior which marks them as judges—those practices which establish the continuity of their office with their predecessors and successors, and which make official their contacts with other persons; but that suspicion on my part may be a relic of the case law tradition in which we American lawyers have been raised. Close around it on the one hand lies the behavior of other government officials. On the other, the sets of accepted formulae which judges recite, seek light from, try to follow. Distinguishing here the formulae with close behavior-correspondences from others; those of frequent application from those of infrequent. Close around these again, lie various persons' ideas of what the law is; and especially their views of what it or some part of it ought to accomplish. At first hand contact with officials' behavior, from another angle, lies the social set-up where the official's acts impinge directly on it; and behind that the social set-up which resists or furthers or reflects the impingement of his acts. Farther from the center lies legal and social philosophy—approaching that center more directly in proportion as the materials with which it deals are taken directly from the center. Part of law, in many aspects, is all of society, and all of man in society. But that is a question of periphery and not of center, of the reach of a specific problem in hands, not of a general discussion. As to the overlapping of the field as thus sketched with that of other social sciences, I should be sorry if no overlapping were observable. The social sciences are not staked out like real estate. Even in law the sanctions for harmless trespass are not heavy.

{ 2 }

SOME REALISM ABOUT REALISM [a] [*]

Ferment is abroad in the law. The sphere of interest widens; men become interested again in the life that swirls around things legal. Before rules, were facts; in the beginning was not a Word, but a Doing. Behind decisions stand judges; judges are men; as men they have human backgrounds. Beyond rules, again, lie effects: beyond decisions stand people whom rules and decisions directly or indirectly touch. The field of Law reaches both forward and back from the Substantive Law of school and doctrine. The sphere of interest is widening; so, too, is the scope of doubt. *Beyond rules lie effects*—but do they? Are some rules mere paper? And if effects, what effects? Hearsay, unbuttressed guess, assumption or assertion unchecked by test—can such be trusted on this matter of what law is *doing?*

The ferment is proper to the time. The law of the schools threatened at the close of the century to turn into words—placid, clear-seeming, lifeless, like some old canal. Practice rolled on, muddy, turbulent, vigorous. It is now spilling, flooding, into the canal of stagnant words. It brings ferment and trouble. So other fields of thought have spilled their waters in: the stress on be-

[a] From 44 HARV. L. REV. 1222 (1931). The paper was prepared as a reply to Pound, *The Call for a Realist Jurisprudence*, 44 *id.* 697 (1931).

[*] Jerome Frank refused me permission to sign his name as joint author to this paper, on the ground that it was my fist which pushed the pen. But his generosity does not alter the fact that the paper could not have been written without his help. I therefore write the first sections, in partial recognition, as "We," meaning thereby Frank and myself. In the description of the realists, I turn to the first person singular, partly because any alignment of such diverse work is individually colored; partly because any phrasing which would seem to suggest a non-existent school would be unfortunate.

havior in the social sciences; their drive toward integration; the physicists' re-examination of final-seeming premises; the challenge of war and revolution. These stir. They stir the law. Interests of practice claim attention. Methods of work unfamiliar to lawyers make their way in, beside traditional techniques. Traditional techniques themselves are re-examined, checked against fact, stripped somewhat of confusion. And always there is this restless questing: what *difference* does statute, or rule, or court-decision, make?

Whether this ferment is one thing or twenty is a question; if one thing, it is twenty things in one. But it is with us. It spreads. It is no mere talk. It shows results, results enough through the past decade to demonstrate its value.

And those involved are folk of modest ideals. They want law to deal, they themselves want to deal, with things, with people, with tangibles, with *definite* tangibles, and *observable* relations between definite tangibles—not with words alone; when law deals with words, they want the words to represent tangibles which can be got at beneath the words, and to represent observable relations between those tangibles. They want to check ideas, and rules, and formulas by facts, to keep them close to facts. They view rules, they view law, as means to ends; as only means to ends; as having meaning only insofar as they are means to ends. They suspect, with law moving slowly and the life around them moving fast, that some law may have gotten out of joint with life. This is a question in first instance of fact: what does law *do*, to people, or for people? In the second instance, it is a question of ends: what *ought* law to do to people, or for them? But there is no reaching a judgment as to whether any specific part of present law does what it ought, until you can first answer what it is doing now. To see this, and to be ignorant of the answer, is to start fermenting, is to start trying to find out.

All this is, we say, a simple-hearted point of view, and often philosophically naïve—though it has in it elements enough of intellectual sophistication. It denies very little, except the completeness of the teachings handed down. It knows too little to care about denying much. It affirms ignorance, pitched within and without. It affirms the need to know. Its call is for intelligent effort to dispel the ignorance. Intelligent effort to cut beneath old rules, old words, to get sight of current things. It is not a new point of view; it is as old as man. But its rediscovery in any age, by any man, in any discipline, is joyous.

Speak, if you will, of a "realistic jurisprudence." And since the individual workers who are the cells of ferment cry their wares, find their results good, see the need for more workers, more results, speak, if you will (as Dean Pound has) of a *Call for a Realist Jurisprudence*.[1] If advance is insistent on advancing further, such a call there is. But it is a call which rests on work done as well as on work to do, on experience as well as on hope, on some portion of past experiment proved useful as well as on perceived need for further experiment.

Dean Pound has discussed the call and the ferment. One portion of his discussion calls in turn for our attention. He welcomed the ferment. He described it. The general terms in which he described the fermenters we seemed to recognize: "the oncoming generation of American law teachers";[2] "our younger teachers of law" who are insistent on a realistic jurisprudence;[3] "the new juristic realists";[4] "the new school . . . current juristic realism." [5] These general designations we say, we seemed to recognize (except the "school"). There were more specific attributes which also struck responsive chords: "By realism they mean fidelity to nature, accurate recording of things as they are, as contrasted with things as they are imagined to be, or wished to be." [6] "Insistent . . . on beginning with an objectively scientific gathering of facts." [7] "Psychological exposure of the rôle of reason in human behavior, of the extent to which so-called reasons come after action as explanations instead of before action as determining factors, has made a profound impression upon the rising generation of jurists." [8] "Looking at precepts and doctrines and institutions with reference to how they work or fail to work, and why." [9] "There is a distinct advance in their frank recognition of the alogical or non-rational element in judicial action which the legal science [philosophy?] of the nineteenth century sought to ignore." [10] If these were the attributes of the "new realists," we knew who they were. We rejoiced that a scholar of Dean Pound's standing and perspective

[1] 44 HARV. L. REV. 697 (1931).
[2] *Id.* at 697.
[3] *Ibid.*
[4] *Ibid.*, and *passim*.
[5] *Id.* at 701.
[6] *Id.* at 697.
[7] *Id.* at 700.
[8] *Id.* at 705.
[9] *Id.* at 706.
[10] *Ibid.* This square-bracket insertion was in the original. Of course I still indorse it.

found much in their fermenting to appreciate. We agreed with him that it was important for the older thinking and the newer to make contact.

But the Dean's description did not stop with the points mentioned. It continued. On bones we knew was built a flesh we knew not of. An ugly flesh. The new realists, or "most of them," had, as the Dean read them, been guilty of a goodly number of things that careful thinkers would in the main not be proud to be caught doing. These intellectual offenses Dean Pound criticized. He criticized them tellingly. The question is one of fact: whether the offenses have been committed. For if they have, the Dean's rebukes are needed. Spare the rod and spoil the realist.

The question is one of fact. By fact it must be tried. And tried it must be. When Dean Pound speaks on jurisprudence, men listen. The profession has too long relied on him to discover, read, digest, classify and report on jurists foreign and ancient not to rely again when he speaks of would-be jurists modern and at home. We regret, therefore, peculiarly that he departed in this paper from a practice he has often followed,[11] of indicating, in each instance when he presented a view, precisely whose view it was, and precisely where that person had set it forth. Freed of the check of the concrete, the most learned err. And error in perceiving or describing the attributes of these new fermenters would be unfortunate. For "here is an important movement in the science of law, and it behooves us to understand it and be thinking about it."[12]

Into a series of further points in his description—these are supposed points which he does not approve of—we have inquired, and present the results.[13] We speak, be it noted, for ourselves alone, and for the facts alone, not for the men whose work we have canvassed. Interpretations, judgments, and responsibility are ours. We are no spokesmen for a school.

The method of the inquiry is set forth in a note. The detailed results are printed in part in an appendix. We indicate the results here in summary, to clear up some things that realists are not.

[11] *The End of Law as Developed in Juristic Thought*, 27 HARV. L. REV. 605 (1914); 30 *id.* 201 (1917); *The Progress of the Law—Analytical Jurisprudence, 1914-1927*, 41 *id.* 174 (1927); LAW AND MORALS (1924); INTERPRETATIONS OF LEGAL HISTORY (1923). AN INTRODUCTION TO THE PHILOSOPHY OF LAW (1924) contains only a general bibliography.

[12] Pound, *supra* note 1, at 697.

[13] One matter we reserve for treatment in a later portion of the paper: the repeated suggestion of the Dean as to "a school" of realists.

There will then be set forth an interpretation of the new ferment
and its bearings, by way of contrast, along lines of organization
independent of the points made by the Dean.

One further preliminary needs mention. Dean Pound was careful to recognize that "one may point out work to be done in the
progress of a school without implying that those engaged in the
task are ignorant thereof, or that they do not intend to direct their
energies thereto in due time." [14] And to recognize that "it is
unfair to take any one item, or even set of items, from one or more
of its adherents and assume that it may be fastened upon the
formative school as characteristic dogma." [15]

Nonetheless, he states: "five items are to be found so generally
in the writings of the new school, *that one may be justified in
pronouncing them, or most of them, the ideas of current juristic
realism.*" [16] The points of description here involved are taken
with three exceptions from these five items or from their detailed
development in his paper.

I

The trial of Dean Pound's indictment is not easy. It is a blanket
indictment. It is blanket as to time and place and person of each
offense. It specifies no one offender by his name.

We have the general indications above-mentioned: "new realists" and the like. We have the more specific indications also mentioned. Taken together, they narrow the class that may come in
question.[17] We can, therefore, check the particular items against a
reasonable sampling of the men whom the rest of the description
fits.[18] We have chosen twenty men and ninety-odd titles; repre-

---

[14] Pound, *supra* note 1, at 709.

[15] *Id.* at 700.

[16] *Id.* at 701 (our italics).

[17] We had hoped to be more precise. We wrote Dean Pound to ask whom he
had had in mind when he wrote his article. The cumulation of his work at Washington and his regular work was the reason of his not going into detail. He did
mention three names specifically. Bingham and Lorenzen he had had in mind.
C. E. Clark he definitely had not.

[18] *The sampling of men.* We set up the following criteria: (a) those chosen must
fit the general and the more specific items set forth above; (b) they must include
the leading figures in the new ferment; (c) in order that we may turn up most
passages supporting the items we challenge, the men chosen must include all who
may be reputed to have taken extreme positions; (d) a wide range of views and positions must be included.

(1) Bingham and Lorenzen are included as of course [because Pound named them
—Lorenzen presumably because of his adoption of Hohfeld's forum-centered approach to conflicts.] (2) We add those who we believe are recognized as figures of central stimulus in the new ferment; C. E. Clark, Cook, Corbin, Moore, T. R. Powell,

sentative men and pertinent titles. These we have canvassed in order to ascertain the extent to which the evidence supports the Dean's allegations. The results of our investigation are presented in summary under each point.

Oliphant. (3) We add further men peculiarly vocal in advocating new or rebellious points of view: Frank, Green, Radin. (4) We stir in all others whom we have heard criticized as extremists on one or another point mentioned by the Dean: Hutcheson, Klaus, Sturges. (5) We fill out with as many more as time permits: Douglas, Francis, Patterson, Tulin, Yntema—chosen partly because their writing has explicitly touched points of theory, partly because their writing was either familiar to us or not too bulky. (6) We throw in Llewellyn, as both vociferous and extreme, but peculiarly because he and he alone has issued a "Call for a Realist Jurisprudence" under that peculiar label. *A Realistic Jurisprudence—The Next Step*, 30 COLUM. L. REV. 431 (1930), supra, p. 3. This gives us twenty names. There are doubtless twenty more. But half is a fair sample. We check back and find that our men range from right to the four or five prevailing lefts. They are either characteristic or extreme. They are in print more fully than most on these matters. If they do not bear out Dean Pound's challenged points of description, we feel safe in saying that those points can not stand.— (Dean Pound to the contrary notwithstanding, we must include Clark. His thirst for facts and influence in procedural research force his inclusion. Corbin, *The Law and the Judges*, 3 YALE REV. 234 (1914), is, we think, the first rounded presentation of the realistic attitude, except for Holmes and Bingham. Frankfurter we do not include; he has been currently considered a "sociological jurist," not a "realist." It profits little to show that one not thought a realist does not fit an alleged description of "realists.")

The sampling of writings. We selected such writings as seemed to speak most directly to points of legal theory, or most likely to contain evidence on any of the Dean's allegations. We wrote to the men, requesting from each his suggestion as to where he had expressed himself, and were thereby led to a number of papers we might otherwise have missed. Bingham, Clark, Corbin, Douglas, Green, Klaus, Patterson, Powell, Radin, and Sturges were generous enough of their time to supply such references, often to specific pertinent passages. They are in no way responsible for what we say, or for our plan of organization. In every case, moreover, we are solely responsible for including or excluding the passages they referred us to, or any others from their works, and for the classification thereof, and especially for the general judgments expressed. But their references greatly lightened our labor. A complete list of the authors and titles is given in Appendix I, *infra*. [Appendixes I and II are omitted in this reprint.]

Procedure of testing. Each paper listed, whether quoted from or not, has been read or reread entire for the present purpose, to make sure that countervailing evidence was not present, and to make sure that any passage cited was in key with the whole. If nothing to the contrary is said, passages quoted or cited *against the Dean* are offered as in substantial harmony not only with the whole of the paper in which they appeared, but also with the author's work in general. Passages cited in the Dean's favor are often unfair to the men cited, for which we tender our apologies. Judgments as to general tone or afterglow of a writing (a matter sometimes very different from its specific phrasing) are ours.

We had prepared for use in Appendix II, in Dean Pound's language, the statement of the positions here challenged, which in his view the realists, or many of them, or some of them, hold. Under each such point the evidence was arranged. (a) *All* passages we have found which support the Dean's description. (b) Such passages as might colorably be adduced in support, and our judgment as to writings whose general flavor or afterglow might be colorably adduced in support. In each such case further passages from the same author which clarify

The Results of the Test

These statements of the Dean's points here set out are *in our language, not his.* We have done our best to reach and state his meaning. But we may misinterpret. We purport therefore to give *not what Dean Pound meant but what a reasonable reader may be expected to understand from his language.*[19]

Point 1. Much of the realists' discussion of judges' thinking sets forth what such thinkings "must" be, under some current psychological dogma, *without investigation of what recorded judicial experience reveals.*[20]

his position were adduced, if found. (c) Some of the passages which display inappropriateness in the Dean's description. These were so many that they often required to be merely cited or even disregarded. Of the passages truly supporting the Dean's description we do not believe we have missed many. They stand out, to readers of our leanings. But the "colorable, but rebutted" passages here given are probably only a fraction of those present in the materials we have canvassed. Colorable passages take color from the mind of the reader. They camouflage themselves to one who (however he tries to find them) colors them with the meaning of the whole paper in which they are found.

As indicated in Appendix II, space forbade the printing of all of this material. Its form was mainly that of Point II, there set forth, which must serve as a sample.

Each point was closed with a nose-count summary of results, under the rubrics: (a) Supporting; (b) Colorable: (i) unrebutted, (ii) rebutted; (c) Negating; (d) No evidence noted. The category "No evidence noted" is almost as significant as any other: the Dean's description is expressly rested *on the writings* of the "new realists."

Passages published after Feb. 1, 1931, were canvassed. They are significant of the newer thinkers' views, which we wish to present. Such passages can not, however, be regarded as accessible to the Dean when he wrote. They bear only on the accuracy of his diagnosis of trends of thought.

Frank is responsible for errors and omissions as to Bingham, Green, Frank, and Radin; Llewellyn as to the others.

Finally, we write, as the men whose work we are discussing wrote, for readers patient and careful enough to *read* what stands on the page. Gratuitous implications are air-castles. There is no arguing with persons who insist on building them. Realists write for the literate. We take a writer's words in first instance for what, under reasonable and careful reading, they appear to say. We attempt to take separate account of general tone and after-impression.

[19] For Dean Pound's language in points 1, 10 and 11 together with a detailed account of the results of our investigation concerning those points, see Appendix II, infra. To avoid misinterpretation by us, we asked Dean Pound for permission to submit our manuscript to him and have misinterpretations corrected. His time, unfortunately, did not permit. So that misinterpretation is undoubtedly present, for we have as much trouble at times in getting the Dean's meaning as he at times has in getting the meaning of realists. Which is inevitable. Words are read against the reader's background, and distorted accordingly.

[20] See 44 Harv. L. Rev. 1260. Since this paper was prepared Yntema has given some warrant for being shifted into the Negating column. Yntema and Jaffin, *Preliminary Analysis of Concurrent Jurisdiction,* 79 U. of Pa. L. Rev. 869 (1931), esp. 881–86. And the internal evidence is abundant in the same direction, as to all three men named.

(a) Supporting: perhaps Bingham, Francis, Yntema: 3;
(b) Colorable: None;
(c) Negating: 16;
(d) No evidence noted: 1.

Point 2. One of the most common items found in the writings of the new school is *faith in masses of figures as having significance in and of themselves.*[21]

(a) Supporting: None;
(b) Colorable: (i) Unrebutted: None; (ii) Rebutted: 1;
(c) Negating: 9;
(d) No evidence noted: 10.

Point 3. Much insisted on is the *exclusive* significance of an approach to law by way of exact terminology. Some realists believe problems are solved by terminology.[22]

(a) Supporting: None;
(b) Colorable: (i) perhaps Unrebutted: Cook, Moore:[23] (ii) Rebutted: 1;
(c) Negating: 14;
(d) No evidence noted: 3.

Point 4. A strong group of realists expect rigidly exact and workable formulas about law to be developed in ways analogous to mathematical physics; and these formulas are expected to be workable without more as rules of what to do.[24]

(a) Supporting: None;
(b) Colorable: (i) Unrebutted: Cook: 1; (ii) Rebutted: 1;

---

[21] See Pound, *supra* note 1, at 701, lines 1–5; 703, lines 13–15.

[22] See *id.* at 702, first full paragraph.

[23] The colorable passages (all cited in Appendix I) are Cook, *Scientific Method and the Law* 233; *The Alienability of Choses in Action,* II 452, 461, 481 (but *cf. ibid.* 484); *The Logical and Legal Bases of the Conflict of Laws* 473, 484, n.75 (but *cf. ibid.* 475, 479, n.60). Colorable from Moore is only the afterglow of such writings as *An Institutional Approach to the Law of Commercial Banking.*

[24] See Pound, *supra* note 1, at 702, lines 4–5, 25–26, last full par.; 703, lines 13–15. Cook, *The Jurisdiction of Sovereign States and the Conflict of Laws* 380: "The postulates in question contain inherently contradictory assertions, *and so can never furnish a satisfactory basis for sound doctrine* in the field of the conflict of laws." (Our italics.) Somewhat allied in implication, *Privileges of Labor Unions in the Struggle for Life* 785; and on the *descriptive* side only, *The Utility of Jurisprudence in the Solution of Legal Problems* 337; *Scientific Method and the Law* 233; *The Jurisdiction of Sovereign States and the Conflict of Laws* 371, n.12; *The Logical and Legal Bases of the Conflict of Laws* 457–58. On the *normative* side, *cf. The Utility of Jurisprudence in the Solution of Legal Problems* 365; *Scientific Method and the Law* 230–31; *The Logical and Legal Bases of the Conflict of Laws* 485–86. But compare *ibid.* at 470, defining what he means by "sound theory." And in the context even the main passage means only that Story's postulates fail *when tested by their own premises.* (Complete citations in Appendix I, *infra.*)

(c) Negating: (i) As to expecting any results *via* techniques closely analogous to mathematical physics: 5; (ii) As to awareness of great limitations on what may be expected from quantitative methods: 4 (one duplication).

(d) No evidence noted: 10.

Point 5. Many of the realists insist *that the rational element in law is an illusion.*[25]

(a) Supporting: Conceivably Frank: 1;

(b) Colorable: (i) Unrebutted: Green: 1; (ii) Rebutted: 4;

(c) Negating: 13;

(d) No evidence noted: 1.

Point 6. Realists usually have a presupposition that some one of the competing psychologies is the *unum necessarium* for jurisprudence.[26] (The theory of rationalization is, we believe, employed by all our subjects. It is employed by none of them as an exclusively valid attack.) We read "competing psychologies" as referring to general bodies of doctrine: *e.g.,* behaviorism or psychoanalysis in some brand. As to this:

(a) Supporting: None;

(b) Colorable: (i) Unrebutted: None; (ii) Rebutted: 2;

(c) Negating: 4;

(d) No evidence noted: 14.

Point 7. Many of the realists seek to ignore the traditional common-law technique "of application." [27]

Examination develops that no triable issue of fact, as distinct from opinion, is joined here, since the Dean apparently conceives the traditional techniques primarily as techniques *of applying rules,* whereas the realist would include *all* the traditional techniques of deciding cases, or of the lawyer's art.

The canvass shows only that our subjects are much interested in study of the traditional techniques, so far as they can get at them, and that they weight the rule-applying aspect less heavily than does Dean Pound.

Point 8. Realists are blind to how far the administration of justice *attains certainty through rule and form.*[28]

[25] See Pound, *supra* note 1, at 698, lines, from bottom, 7–3; 705, lines 4–6; last 5 lines; 707, last par., first three lines. Supporting: FRANK, LAW AND THE MODERN MIND, the afterglow (but *cf. id.* at 37, 121, 138, 152, 169, 288, 343, 362, and esp. 155–59; Frank informally repudiates any such opinion, and denies that his writings warrant this classification). Colorable: GREEN, JUDGE AND JURY, e.g., at 145, 146, 148, 151, and the afterglow.

[26] See Pound, *supra* note 1, at 705, first full par., first sentence; 706, same.

[27] See *id.* at 706, last par. to its end.

[28] See *id.* at 707, lines 4–9.

Again no triable issue of fact, as opposed to opinion, is joined. The canvass shows that our subjects are much concerned with how far justice obtains certainty, and with how far it is attained —or hindered—through rule and form. But that they tend to differ with the Dean on the "how far" in both cases.

Point 9.[b] A characteristic of the realist is conceiving of the administration of justice rather as a mere aggregate of single determinations than as an approximation to a uniform course of behavior.[29]

Our evidence is directed to the proposition that our subjects do not conceive of judicial (and other legal) behavior as involving uniformities.

(a) Supporting: Frank: 1;
(b) Colorable: (i) Unrebutted: Green: 1; (ii) Rebutted: 4;
(c) Negating: 14;
(d) No evidence noted: None.

Point 10. Many of the realists have an exclusive interest in the business aspects of the law, and this exclusively from the standpoint of the purposes of business, rather than of society as a whole.[30]

This could, of course, apply only to the ten commercial lawyers among our subjects:

(a) Perhaps supporting: Sturges: 1;
(b) Perhaps colorable: (i) Unrebutted (in print): Moore: 1;
    (ii) Rebutted: None;
(c) Negating: 7;
(d) Inadequate evidence noted (in print): 1.

Point 11. By clear implication: the work of the realists is not concerned with questions of what ought to be done by way of law.[31]

(a) Supporting: None;
(b) Colorable: (i) Unrebutted: None; (ii) Rebutted: 3;

---

[b] I have never been able to understand how either Pound or those who accepted his criticisms of the realists could rime this alleged characteristic #9 with alleged characteristic #4.

[29] See *id.* at 707, first full par., first sentence; 708, lines 1–8. The supporting material: FRANK, *op. cit. supra* note 25. But see *ibid.* at 104, 130–32, 166–67, 251–52. GREEN, *op. cit. supra* note 25. Green insists on predictability of procedure and formula, as distinct from outcome. Both Frank and Green are focussing on the trial court, [whereas Pound's emphasis was on the appellate level. *"The* judicial process" cannot wisely be discussed as if there were significant unity as between *e.g.* trial by jury, trial by court, appeal of the entire case, and appeal on points of law.]

[30] See 44 HARV. L. REV. 1261 (1931).

[31] See 44 HARV. L. REV. 1262 (1931).

(c) Negating: 17;

(d) No evidence noted: None.

Point 12. By clear implication: the realists, *in their attempts at description,* disregard the effects of the judges' own ideal pictures of what they ought to do.[32]

(a) Supporting: None;

(b) Colorable: (i) Unrebutted: Moore: 1; (ii) Rebutted: None;

(c) Negating Passages adduced from 11; but they are not particularly significant.

What counts here is the whole tone of a man's work. We should have thought the realists' concern as to the effects of the court's ideal picture of delusive certainty would be enough to negate.— Significant in this canvass is chiefly the absence of positive support.

Point 13. By clear implication: the realists are unmindful of the relativity of significance, of the way in which preconceptions necessarily condition observation, and are not on their guard against their own preconceptions, while investigating.[33]

(a) Supporting: None;

(b) Colorable: None;

(c) Negating: 12;

(d) No evidence noted: 8.

SUMMARY: Of eleven points on which evidence in support could be diagnosed and counted, we find such evidence as to seven— but how much? We can adduce some support for *one* point from *three of our twenty men,* for each of four further points from two of our twenty, for each of two further points from one of our twenty. *One of our twenty men* offers some support for *three of the eleven points,* three offer some support each for two of the eleven points, four offer some support each for one point. *In no instance is the support offered strong, unambiguous, or unqualified,* even on the printed record.

Let it be conceded that we have missed men or evidence which would support these points of description on which so much of the Dean's criticism of realists is based. Let it be conceded that (though aided by his lines of criticism) we have in part misinterpreted what it was that he was criticizing. We submit, nonetheless, that *any* description of what "realists" think, or what "most of them believe" or what "many of them write"—and especially

---

[32] See Pound, *supra* note 1, at 700 from line 3 through the par. Colorable: Moore, *Legal and Institutional Methods Applied to the Debiting of Direct Discounts,* 40 YALE L. J. 555, 563 (1931). See Pound, *supra* note 1, at 698, lines 3–7; 699, lines 1–16; 700, second par.

[33] See *id.* at 698–700.

any description made the basis of criticism—will in the light of our canvass need evidence by man and chapter and verse before it can be relied on as meaning more than: *the writer has an impression that there is someone, perhaps two someones, whose writings bear this out.* We accept the implications of this statement for ourselves. What we here further say of realists is, where no evidence is cited, to be read as giving a vague and very fallible impression.

II

REAL REALISTS[34]

What, then, *are* the characteristics of these new fermenters? One thing is clear. There is no school of realists. There is no likelihood that there will be such a school. There is no group with an official or accepted, or even with an emerging creed. There is no abnegation of independent striking out. We hope that there may never be. New recruits acquire tools and stimulus, not masters, nor over-mastering ideas. Old recruits diverge in interests from each other. They are related, says Frank, only in their negations, and in their skepticisms, and in their curiosity.[35]

[34] Both Adler (*Law and the Modern Mind—Legal Certainty*, 31 COL. L. REV. 91 (1931)) and Morris Cohen (*Justice Holmes and the Nature of Law*, 31 *id*. 352 (1931)) discuss "realism" adversely, Cohen addressing himself especially to Frank, Moore (uncited specifically), Bingham, and Oliphant; Adler to the same (except Moore), especially Frank, and to Cook, Yntema, and Green (all uncited) as well. Dickinson, *Legal Rules: Their Function in the Process of Decision*, 79 U. OF PA. L. REV. 833 (1931), bases his criticisms (especially of Cook, Frank, Llewellyn) largely on specific citations. Radin and Yntema publish admirable papers on the matter with which I concur almost *in toto*. Radin, *Legal Realism*, 31 COLUM. L. REV. 824 (1931); Yntema, *The Rational Basis of Legal Science*, 31 *id*. 925 (1931). Citations of realists are lacking in their papers also: they speak not of or for a school, but for themselves. So far as the present paper purports to be descriptive, it sins in non-citation. (As did my controversial paper, *supra* note 18, in non-specificity as to where the views criticized might be found. *Mea maxima culpa!* and may whoever feels that he was caricatured forgive me. Preparing the present discussion has shown me that error of my ways.) I had hoped in this part to build a fair bibliography of the literature but time has not served. Felix Cohen has been kind enough to aid me in this and I include his references, marked "(C)."

[35] Names for them vary. I call them realists (so do Frank, Radin, and often, Yntema; Bingham also recognizes the term. And I find it used in the same sense in the work of Cook, Douglas, Frankfurter)—stressing the interest in the actuality of what happens, and the distrust of formula. Cook prefers to speak of scientific approach to law, Oliphant of objective method—stressing much the same features. Clark speaks of fact-research, Corbin of what courts do. "Functional approach" stresses the interest in, and valuation by, effects. Dickinson speaks of the skeptical movement.

There is, however, a *movement* in thought and work about law. The movement, the method of attack, is wider than the number of its adherents. It includes some or much work of many men who would scorn ascription to its banner. Individual men, then. Men more or less interstimulated—but no more than all of them have been stimulated by the orthodox tradition, or by that ferment at the opening of the century in which Dean Pound took a leading part. Individual men, working and thinking over law and its place in society. Their differences in point of view, in interest, in emphasis, in field of work, are huge. They differ among themselves well-nigh as much as any of them differs from, say, Langdell. Their number grows. Their work finds acceptance.

What one does find as he observes them is twofold. First (and to be expected) certain points of departure are common to them all. Second (and this, when one can find neither school nor striking likenesses among individuals, is startling) a cross-relevance, a complementing, an interlocking of their varied results "as if they were guided by an invisible hand." A third thing may be mentioned in passing: a fighting faith in their methods of attack on legal problems; but in these last years the battle with the facts has proved so much more exciting than any battle with traditionalism that the fighting faith had come (until the spring offensive of 1931 against the realists) to manifest itself chiefly in enthusiastic labor to get on.

But as with a description of an economic order, tone and color of description must vary with the point of view of the reporter. No other one of the men would set the picture up as I shall. Such a report must thus be individual. Each man, of necessity, orients the whole to his own main interest of the moment—as I shall orient the whole to mine: the workings of case-law in appellate courts. Maps of the United States prepared respectively by a political geographer and a student of climate would show some resemblance; each would show a coherent picture; but neither's map would give much satisfaction to the other. So here. I speak for myself of that movement which in its sum is realism; I do not speak of "the realists"; still less do I speak *for* the participants or any of them. And I shall endeavor to keep in mind as I go that the justification for grouping these men together lies not in that they are *alike* in belief or work, but in that from certain common points of departure they have branched into lines of work which seem to be building themselves into a whole, a whole planned by none, foreseen by none, and (it may well be) not yet adequately grasped by any.

The common points of departure are several.[36]

(1) The conception of law in flux, of moving law, and of judicial creation of law.

(2) The conception of law as a means to social ends and not as an end in itself; so that any part needs constantly to be examined for its purpose, and for its effect, and to be judged in the light of both and of their relation to each other.

(3) The conception of society in flux, and in flux typically faster than the law, so that the probability is always given that any portion of law needs reëxamination to determine how far it fits the society it purports to serve.

(4) The *temporary* divorce of Is and Ought for purposes of study. By this I mean that whereas value judgments must always be appealed to in order to set objectives for inquiry, yet during the inquiry itself into what Is, the observation, the description, and the establishment of relations between the things described are to remain *as largely as possible* uncontaminated by the desires of the observer or by what he wishes might be or thinks ought

[36] As to each of the following points I have attempted to check over not only the general tone of work but several specific writings of the twenty men named and a number of others—*e.g.,* Kidd, Maggs, Breckenridge, Morse, Durfee, Bohlen, Bryant Smith and Goble—and to make sure that each point was applicable to each. Errors may have crept in. Note how closely the description fits Holmes' work as early as 1871-72: "It commands the future, a valid but imperfectly realized ideal."

On the common points of departure, see especially Corbin, *The Law and the Judges;* LLEWELLYN, CASES AND MATERIALS ON THE LAW OF SALES, Introd.; Oliphant, *A Return to Stare Decisis;* Patterson, *Can Law Be Scientific?,* all cited in Appendix I. See also Arnold, *Criminal Attempts—The Rise and Fall of an Abstraction,* 40 YALE L. J. 53 (1930); Arnold, *The Restatement of the Law of Trusts* (1931) 31 COL. L. REV. 800; Clark, Douglas and Thomas, *The Business Failures Project—A Problem in Methodology,* 39 YALE L. J. 1013 (1930); Douglas and Thomas, *The Business Failures Project—II. An Analysis of Methods of Investigation,* 40 *id.* 1034 (1931); Burch, *The Paradoxes of Legal Science: A Review,* 27 MICH. L. REV. 637 (1929); Radin, *The Permanent Problems of the Law,* 15 CORN. L. Q. 1 (1929); Yntema and Jaffin, *supra* note 20; Yntema, *supra* note 34. And see (C) Isaacs, *How Lawyers Think,* 23 COL. L. REV. 555 (1923); Laski, *Judicial Review of Social Policy in England,* 39 HARV. L. REV. 832 (1926).

On checking rules descriptive against the facts of the decisions, see especially Corbin, Douglas, Klaus, Tulin, *infra,* Appendix I; (C) Finkelstein, *Judicial Self-Limitation,* 37 HARV. L. REV. 338 (1924); Finkelstein, *Further Notes on Self-Limitation,* 39 *id.* 221 (1925); Isaacs' more recent work in general, but especially *The Promoter: A Legislative Problem,* 38 *id.* 887 (1925); Brown, *Due Process of Law, Police Power, and the Supreme Court,* 40 *id.* 943 (1927); Hamilton, *Affectation with a Public Interest,* 39 YALE L. J. 1089 (1930).

(ethically) to be. More particularly, this involves during the study of what courts are doing the effort to disregard the question what they ought to do. Such divorce of Is and Ought is, of course, not conceived as permanent. To men who begin with a suspicion that change is needed, a permanent divorce would be impossible. The argument is simply that no judgment of what Ought to be done in the future with respect to any part of law can be intelligently made without knowing objectively, as far as possible, what that part of law is now doing. And realists believe that experience shows the intrusion of Ought-spectacles *during the investigation of the facts* to make it very difficult to see what is being done. On the Ought side this means an insistence on informed evaluations instead of armchair speculations. Its full implications on the side of Is-investigation can be appreciated only when one follows the contributions to objective description in business law and practice made by realists whose social philosophy rejects many of the accepted foundations of the existing economic order. (*E.g.*, Handler *re* trade-marks and advertising; Klaus *re* marketing and banking; Llewellyn *re* sales; Moore *re* banking; Patterson *re* risk-bearing.)

(5) Distrust of traditional legal rules and concepts insofar as they purport to *describe* what either courts or people are actually doing. Hence the constant emphasis on rules as "generalized predictions of what courts will do." This is much more widespread as yet than its counterpart: the careful severance of rules *for* doing (precepts) from rules *of* doing (practices).

(6) Hand in hand with this distrust of traditional rules (on the descriptive side) goes a distrust of the theory that traditional prescriptive rule-formulations are *the* heavily operative factor in producing court decisions. This involves the tentative adoption [better: exploration] of the theory of rationalization for [what light it can give in] the study of opinions. It will be noted that "distrust" in this and the preceding point is not at all equivalent to "negation in any given instance."

(7) The belief in the worthwhileness of grouping cases and legal situations into narrower categories than has been the practice in the past.[e] This is connected with the distrust of verbally simple rules—which so often cover dissimilar and non-simple fact

---

[e] The quest for narrower, more significant, categories is always a sound *first* approach to wide categories which are not giving satisfaction-in-use. But of course, once satisfactory narrower categories have been found and tested, the eternal quest recurs, for wider synthesis—but one which will really stand up in use.

situations (dissimilarity being tested partly by the way cases come out, and partly by the observer's judgment as to how they ought to come out; but a realist tries to indicate explicitly which criterion he is applying in any particular instance).

(8) An insistence on evaluation of any part of law in terms of its effects, and an insistence on the worthwhileness of trying to find these effects.

(9) Insistence on *sustained and programmatic attack* on the problems of law along any of these lines. *None of the ideas set forth in this list is new.* Each can be matched from somewhere; each can be matched from recent orthodox work in law. New twists and combinations do appear here and there. What is as novel as it is vital is for a goodly number of men to pick up ideas which have been expressed and dropped, used for an hour and dropped, played with from time to time and dropped—to pick up such ideas and set about *consistently, persistently, insistently to carry them through.* Grant that the idea or point of view is familiar— the results of steady, sustained, systematic work with it are not familiar. Not hit-or-miss stuff, not the insight which flashes and is forgotten, but sustained effort to force an old insight into its full bearing, to exploit it to the point where it laps over upon an apparently inconsistent insight, to explore their bearing on each other by the test of fact. This urge, in law, is quite new enough over the last decades to excuse a touch of frenzy among the locust-eaters.[37]

The first, second, third and fifth of the above items, while common to the workers of the newer movement, are not peculiar to them. But the other items (4, 6, 7, 8, and 9) are to me the characteristic marks of the movement. Men or work fitting those specifications are to me "realistic" whatever label they may wear. Such, and none other, are the perfect fauna of this new land. Not all the work cited below fits my peculiar definition in all points. All such work fits most of the points.

Bound, as all "innovators" are, by prior thinking, these innovating "realists" brought their batteries to bear in first instance on the work of appellate courts. Still wholly within the tradition of our law, they strove to improve on that tradition.

[37] Since everyone who reads the manuscript in this sad age finds this allusion blind, but I still like it, I insert the passage: ". . . Preaching in the wilderness of Judea, And saying, Repent ye. . . . And the same John had his raiment of camel's hair, and a leathern girdle about his loins; *and his meat was locusts* and wild honey." Matthew III, 1, 2, 4.

(a) An early and fruitful line of attack borrowed from psychology the concept of *rationalization* already mentioned. To recanvass the opinions, viewing them no longer as mirroring the process of deciding cases, but rather as trained lawyers' arguments made by the judges (after the decision has been reached), intended to make the decision seem plausible, legally decent, legally right, to make it seem, indeed, legally inevitable—this was to open up new vision. It was assumed that the deductive logic of opinions need by no means be either a *description* of the process of decision, or an *explanation* of how the decision had been reached.[38] Indeed over-enthusiasm has at times assumed that the logic of the opinion *could* be neither; and similar over-enthusiasm, perceiving case after case in which the opinion is clearly almost valueless as an indication of how that case came to decision, has worked at times almost as if the opinion were equally valueless in predicting what a later court will do.[38a]

But the line of inquiry via rationalization has come close to demonstrating that in any case doubtful enough to make litigation respectable the available authoritative premises—*i.e.*, premises legitimate and impeccable under the traditional legal techniques —are at least two, and that the two are mutually contradictory as applied to the case in hand.[39] Which opens the question of what made the court select the one available premise rather than the other. And which raises the greatest of doubts as to *how far* any supposed certainty in decision which may derive merely [or even chiefly] from the presence of accepted rules really goes.

(b) A second line of attack has been to discriminate among rules with reference to their relative significance. Too much is written and thought about "law" and "rules," lump-wise. Which part of law? Which rule? Iron rules of policy, and rules "in the absence of agreement"; rules which keep a case from the jury,

[38] *E.g.*, Tulin, *The Role of Penalties in Criminal Law*, 37 YALE L. J. 1048 (1928); Douglas, *Vicarious Liability and Administration of Risk*, 38 *id.* 584, 720 (1929); Corbin, *Contracts for the Benefit of Third Persons*, 46 L. Q. REV. 12 (1930).

[38a] Moore and Oliphant certainly, and I think Sturges, would differ from me, to a greater or less extent, as to how far this is "over-enthusiasm." Moore's three years' quest reached for some more objective technique of prediction. Moore and Sussman, *Legal and Institutional Methods Applied to the Debiting of Direct Discounts*, 40 YALE L. J. 381, 555, 752, 928 (1931). And Oliphant, *A Return to Stare Decisis*, 14 A. B. A. J. 71, 159, n.5 (1928).

[39] For a series of examples, see Cook, *The Utility of Jurisprudence in the Solution of Legal Problems* in 5 LECTURES ON LEGAL TOPICS, ASSOCIATION OF THE BAR OF THE CITY OF NEW YORK 335 (1923–24); T. R. Powell, *Current Conflicts Between the Commerce Clause and State Police Power, 1922–1927*, 12 MINN. L. REV. 470, 491, 607, 631 (1928).

and rules as to the etiquette of instructions necessary to make a verdict stick—if one can get it; rules "of pure decision" for hospital cases, and rules which counsellors rely on in their counselling; rules which affect many (and which many, and how?) and rules which affect few.[40] Such discriminations affect the traditional law curriculum, the traditional organization of law books and, above all, the orientation of study: to drive into *the most important* fields of ignorance.

(c) A further line of attack on the apparent conflict and uncertainty among the decisions in appellate courts has been to seek more understandable statement of them by grouping the facts in new—and typically but not always narrower—categories. The search is for correlations of fact-situation and outcome which (aided by common sense) may reveal *when* courts seize on one rather than another of the available competing premises. One may even stumble on the trail of *why* they do. Perhaps, *e.g.*, third party beneficiary difficulties simply fail to get applied to promises to make provision for dependents;[41] perhaps the pre-existing duty rule goes by the board when the agreement is one for a marriage-settlement.[42] Perhaps, indeed, contracts in what we may broadly call family relations do not work out in general as they do in business.[43] If so, the rules—viewed as statements of the course of judicial behavior—as *predictions* of what will happen—need to be restated. Sometimes it is a question of carving out hitherto unnoticed exceptions. But sometimes the results force the worker to reclassify an area altogether.[44] Typically, as stated, the classes of situations which result are narrower, much narrower than the traditional classes. The process is in essence the orthodox technique of making distinctions, and reformulating—but undertaken systematically; exploited consciously, instead of being reserved until facts which refuse to be twisted by "interpretation"

[40] Compare the work of Bohlen and Green on torts or of Llewellyn on contracts, for attempts to carry this type of old insight through more consistently.

[41] Note 31 COLUM. L. REV. 117 (1931).

[42] An unpublished study by Moore. Another example is Handler and Pickett, *Trade Marks and Trade Names—An Analysis and Synthesis*, 30 COLUM. L. REV. 168, 759 (1930).

[43] Perhaps they should not—but that is an Ought question. One will be forced to raise it, if he finds courts in their results persistently evading the consequences of what accepted doctrine declares to be the general rule. Compare Moore and Sussman, *supra* note 38ᵃ, at 555, 557; Oliphant, *supra* note 38ᵃ, at 159, 160.

[44] Sometimes the effort fails. Durfee and Duffy, *Foreclosure of Land Contracts in Michigan: Equitable Suit and Summary Proceeding*, 7 MICH. ST. B. J. 166, 221, 236 (1928). It is a grateful sign of a growing scientific spirit when *negative* results of investigation come into print.

force action.[45] The departure from orthodox procedure lies chiefly in distrust of, instead of search for, the widest sweep of generalization words permit.[46] Not that such sweeping generalizations are not desired—*if they can be made so as to state what judges do* [or ought to do.]

All of these three earliest lines of attack converge to a single conclusion: *there is less possibility of accurate prediction of what courts will do than the traditional rules would lead us to suppose*[47]

[45] It may sometimes be not *convenient* to draw rules *for* courts to use in terms of these narrower categories. Williston argues that the set of official formulas must not be too complex; they are to be "applied" by ordinary men, not by intellectual giants. WILLISTON, SOME MODERN TENDENCIES IN THE LAW 127 (1929). That does not touch the present point. Even with broad formulas prevailing, as at present, one still gets better results in *describing* where courts get to if he thinks in terms of narrower classifications of the facts. But a fair portion of present unpredictability is certainly attributable to the fact that the courts are using official formulas which fit, only part of the time, what the facts seem to call for. Sometimes the facts win, sometimes the formula. See note 46, *infra*.

[46] When this procedure results in a formulation along lines strikingly unorthodox (*cf.* my own approach to title—CASES AND MATERIALS ON THE LAW OF SALES (1930) [and *Through Title to Contract, etc.* 3 (N. Y. U.) LAW—A CENTURY OF PROGRESS, 80 (1937)]), but one which the worker finds helpful in prediction or in generalizing results, Dean Pound's query as to *how far* courts achieve certainty by traditional rule and form becomes pressing. At times Moore (chiefly in conversation), Oliphant (*supra* note 38, conversation, and theory of contracts), and Sturges (*Legal Theory and Real Property Mortgages*, 37 YALE L. J. 691 (1928)), seem to me to verge upon a position which escapes my understanding: that the judges' reactions to the facts in such cases are only negligibly influenced by the orthodox rules. My experience is that when measures (here "the rule") do not fit purposes (here the line of discrimination discovered by the fact-issue-judgment approach) the result is *always* some inadequacy in accomplishing purposes. And my experience is that when purposes do not become conscious, there is commonly inadequacy at times in locating a measure for their adequate accomplishment. (Compare Corbin's results on the English cases: Corbin, *Contracts for the Benefit of Third Persons* 46 L. Q. REV. 12 (1930)). What one has gained by the new formulation, if it proves significant, seems to me to be a tool for clarifying the situation and the purposes; a means of bringing a hidden factor, perhaps *the* hidden factor in past uncertainty, into view; perhaps also a new insight into wise objectives, and so a key for reform. Compare Llewellyn, *What Price Contract?—An Essay in Perspective*, 40 YALE L. J. 704, 732, n.62 (1931).

[47] Partly, as I have tried to develop elsewhere (Llewellyn, *Legal Illusion*, 31 COLUM. L. REV. 82, 87 (1931); PRÄJUDIZIENRECHT U. RECHTSPRECHUNG IN AMERIKA § 52 *et seq.* (1933)), because the "certainty" sought is conceived verbally, and in terms of lawyers, not factually and in terms of laymen. Neither can commonly be had save at the cost of the other. We get enough of each to upset the other. One effect of the realist approach is to center on certainty for laymen and improve the machinery for attaining it. The present dilemma is quickly stated: if there is *no* certainty in law (rules and concepts *plus* intuition *plus* lawmen's practices) why is not any layman qualified to practice or to judge? But if the certainty is what the rule-believers claim, how can two good lawyers disagree about an appealed case? *Cf. also* (C) Isaacs, *supra* note 36, at 890 *et seq.*; Isaacs, *infra* note 61, at 211–12.

(and what possibility there is must be found in good measure out-side these same traditional rules). The particular kind of certainty that men have thus far thought to find in law is in good measure an illusion. Realistic workers have sometimes insisted on this truth so hard that they have been thought pleased with it. (The danger lies close, for one thinking indiscriminately of Is and Ought, to suspect announcements of fact to reflect preferences, ethically normative judgments, on the part of those who do the announcing.)

But announcements of fact are not appraisals of worth. The contrary holds. The immediate results of the preliminary work thus far described has been a further, varied series of endeavors; *the focussing of conscious attack on discovering the factors thus far unpredictable, in good part with a view to their control.*[d] Not wholly with a view to such elimination; part of the conscious attack is directed to finding where and when and how far *un-certainty* has value. Much of what has been taken as insistence on the exclusive significance of the particular (with supposed implicit denial of the existence of valid or apposite generaliza-tions) represents in fact a clearing of the ground for such attack. Close study of particular unpredictables may lessen unpredicta-bility. It may increase the value of what remains. It certainly makes clearer what the present situation is. "Link by link is chain-mail made."

(i) There is the question of the personality of the judge. (Little has as yet been attempted in study of the jury; Frank, *Law and the Modern Mind,* makes a beginning.) Within this field, again, attempts diverge. Some have attempted study of the particular judge[48]—a line that will certainly lead to inquiry into his social

---

[d] It is interesting, thirty years later, to meet this formulation out of the days when anything other than rules, principles, etc., was suspect as being, if not illegitimate, at least subject to unforeseeable arbitrary abuse. Yet the problems of regularization and control remain. See my COMMON LAW TRADITION (1960), and esp. 323–332.

[48] *E.g.,* Powell's insistence on the particular judges in successions of decisions. *Supra* note 39; *Commerce, Congress, and the Supreme Court, 1922–1925,* 26 COLUM. L. REV. 396, 521 (1926); (C) *The Judiciality of Minimum Wage Legislation,* 37 HARV. L. REV. 545 (1924); *The Nature of a Patent Right,* 17 COLUM. L. REV. 663 (1917); Haines, *General Observations on the Effects of Personal, Political, and Economic Influences in the Decisions of Judges,* 17 ILL. L. REV. 96 (1922); Brown, *Police Power —Legislation for Health and Personal Safety,* 42 HARV. L. REV. 866 (1929); Cush-man, *The Social and Economic Interpretation of the Fourteenth Amendment,* 20 MICH. L. REV. 737 (1922); FRANKFURTER AND LANDIS, THE BUSINESS OF THE SUPREME COURT (1928), and the supplementary series of articles in 42 HARV. L. REV. 1 (1928); 43 *id.* 1 (1929); 44 *id.* 1 (1930).

To be added, especially, is the growing volume of judicial self-revelation:

conditioning.[49] Some have attempted to bring various psychological hypotheses to bear.[50] All that has become clear is that our government is not a government of laws, but one of law through men.

(ii) There has been some attempt to work out the varieties of interaction between the traditional concepts (the judge's "legal" equipment for thinking, seeing, judging) and the fact-pressures of the cases.[51] This is a question not—as above—of getting at results on particular facts, but of studying the effect, *e.g.*, of a series of cases in which the facts either press successively in the one direction, or alternate in their pressures and counteract each other. Closely related in substance, but wholly diverse in both method and aim, is study of the machinery by which fact-pressures can under our procedure be brought to bear upon the court.[52]

(iii) First efforts have been made to capitalize the wealth of our reported cases to make large-scale quantitative studies of facts and outcome; the hope has been that these might develop lines of prediction more sure, or at least capable of adding further certainty to the predictions based as hitherto on intensive study of smaller bodies of cases. This represents a more ambitious development of the procedure described above, under (c); I know of no published results. [Here the recent University of Chicago studies need attention.]

Cardozo's work: Hutcheson, *infra* Appendix I; Judge Amidon's beautiful opinion in Great Northern Ry. v. Brousseau, 286 Fed. 414 (D. N. D. 1923); and parts of such earlier work as Young, *The Law as an Expression of Community Ideals and the Law Making Functions of Courts*, 27 YALE L. J. 1 (1917).

[49] Nelles, Book Review, 40 YALE L. J. 998 (1931).

[50] Freudian: beginnings in FRANK, LAW AND THE MODERN MIND (1930). Behaviorist: an attempt in Patterson, *Equitable Relief for Unilateral Mistake*, 28 COLUM. L. REV. 859 (1928). Semi-behaviorist, via cultural anthropology: Moore and Sussman, *supra* note 38.

[51] Llewellyn in 3 ENCYCLOPAEDIA OF THE SOCIAL SCIENCES 249 (1930); LLEWELLYN, CASES AND MATERIALS ON THE LAW OF SALES (1930); PRÄJUDIZIENRECHT U. RECHTSPRECHUNG IN AMERIKA (1931). With which last compare Pound, *A Theory of Judicial Decision*, 36 HARV. L. REV. 641, 802, esp. 940 (1923); HENDERSON, THE POSITION OF FOREIGN CORPORATIONS IN AMERICAN CONSTITUTIONAL LAW (1918); CARDOZO, THE NATURE OF THE JUDICIAL PROCESS (1921); Corbin, *supra* note 37; Haines, *supra* note 48; Berle, *Investors and the Revised Delaware Corporation Act*, 29 COLUM. L. REV. 563 (1929); Finkelstein, *supra* note 36; Hamilton, *Judicial Tolerance of Farmers' Cooperatives*, 38 YALE L. J. 936 (1929); Patterson, *infra* Appendix I.

[52] The famous Brandeis brief and its successors mark the beginning. In commercial cases both Germany and England have evolved effective machinery. [The importance of type-fact-situation pressures is more fully discussed in my COMMON LAW TRADITION—DECIDING APPEALS (1960).]

(iv) Repeated effort has been made to work with the cases of single states, to see how far additional predictability might thus be gained.[53]

(v) Study has been attempted of "substantive rules" in the particular light of the available remedial procedure; the hope being to discover in the court's unmentioned knowledge of the immediate consequences of this rule or that, in the case at hand, a motivation for decision which cuts deeper than any shown by the opinion.[54] Related, but distinct, is the reassertion of the fundamental quality of remedy, and the general approach to re-stating "what the law is" (on the side of prediction) in terms not of rights, but of what can be done: Not only "no remedy, no right," but "precisely as much right as remedy." [55]

(vi) The set-up of men's ways and practices and ideas on the subject matter of the controversy has been studied, in the hope that this might yield a further or even final [56] basis for prediction. The work here ranges from more or less indefinite reference to

[53] Here, as throughout, one notes the contact of the realist movement with a tradition of practice (single state law, interest in procedure, "automobile juris-prudence" and the like, damage and procedure points treated in conjunction with the relevant substantive law, interest in the facts and atmosphere) which the older academic tradition was prone to scorn. But this progress backwards takes with it, and fertilizes the practical tradition with, the interest in theory, generality of outlook, and long-range thinking of the older academic tradition. Fortunate media for this type of work are the local law reviews. Such work, long continued, will force a radical revision of thought about "the common law" and, one may hope, educate the "national" reviews. See also (C) Kales, *An Unsolicited Report on Legal Education*, 18 COLUM. L. REV. 21 (1918).

[54] *E.g.*, Tulin, *supra* note 38; Pound, *supra* note 51, at 649 *et seq.* on the art of administering justice through damages. And *cf.* the remedy canvass in Patterson, *Equitable Relief for Unilateral Mistake*, 28 COLUM. L. REV. 859 (1928); Durfee and Duffy, *supra* note 44.

[55] *E.g.*, Klaus, *Identification of the Holder and Tender of Receipt on the Counter Presentation of Checks*, 13 MINN. L. REV. 281 (1929); Handler, *False and Misleading Advertising*, 39 YALE L. J. 22 (1929); Handler and Pickett, *supra* note 42; *cf.* Tulin, *infra* Appendix I; LLEWELLYN, CASES AND MATERIALS ON THE LAW OF SALES c. III.

[56] Moore, *An Institutional Approach to the Law of Commercial Banking*, 38 YALE L. J. 703 (1929); Moore and Sussman, *supra* note 38, might be so read; or rather, so misread. His study of behavior is not based on a belief that it will by itself lead to final results; it is rather (as is the intelligent behaviorist program in psychology) a "Let us see how far we can get with this" approach. And it is hard to justify a quarrel with that. See Moore and Sussman, *supra* note 38, at 556–64, esp. 561. And though prediction should be achieved, there still remains the question of Ought—if in no other guise, then as a legislative matter. Compare also L. K. Frank, *An Institutional Analysis of the Law*, 24 COLUM. L. REV. 480 (1924) (a mag-nificent example of what the outsider can contribute); Moore, *Rational Basis of Legal Institutions*, *infra* Appendix I; (C) Ketcham, *Law as a Body of Subjective Rules*, 23 ILL. L. REV. 360 (1929).

custom (the historical school), or mores (Corbin),[57] through
rough or more careful canvasses[58] of business[59] practice and
ideology (*e.g.*, Berle, Sturges, Isaacs, Handler, Bogert, Durfee and
Duffy, Breckenridge, Turner, Douglas, Shanks, Oliphant and indeed Holmes) to painstaking and detailed studies in which practice is much more considered than is any prevailing set of ideas
about what the practices are (Klaus) or—even—to studies in which
the concept of "practice" is itself broken up into behavior-
sequences presented with careful note of the degree of their frequency and recurrence, and in which all reference to actor's
own ideas is deprecated or excluded (Moore and Sussman). While
grouped here together, under one formula, these workers show
differences in degree and manner of interest in the background-
ways which range from one pole to the other. Corbin's main
interest is the appellate case; most of the second group mentioned
rely on semi-special information and readily available material
from economics, sociology, etc., with occasional careful studies of
their own, and carry a strong interest into drafting or counselling
work; Klaus insists on full canvass of all relevant literature, buttressed by and viewed in the light of intensive personal investigation; Moore's canvass and study is so original and thorough in
technique as to offer as vital and important a contribution to
ethnology and sociology as to banking practice. This is not one
"school"; here alone are the germs of many "schools."

(vii) Another line of attack, hardly begun, is that on the effect
of the lawyer on the outcome of cases, as an element in prediction.
The lawyer *in litigation* has been the subject thus far only of
desultory comment.[60] Groping approach has been made to the
counsellor as field general, in the business field: in drafting, and
in counselling (and so in the building of practices and professional
understandings which influence court action later), and in the

[57] Recently becoming much more specific—see *Third Parties as Beneficiaries of
Contractors' Surety Bonds*, 38 YALE L. J. 1 (1928).

[58] Ideals here largely outstrip scholarly achievement. But most realist scholars
are in their work materially ahead of what they have printed. It should be noted
that Douglas' business failures study, *supra* note 36, proceeds to a level comparable
to Klaus or Moore.

[59] Or practice in criminal law administration, as in the crime surveys; or on
family matters: JACOBS AND ANGELL, A RESEARCH IN FAMILY LAW (1930); Powell and
LOOKER, *Decedents' Estates—Illumination from Probate and Tax Records*, 30
COLUM. L. REV. 919 (1930).

[60] One exception is Sturges, *Law's Delays, Lawyers' Delays, and Forwarded Cases*,
12 MINN. L. REV. 351 (1928); *cf.* Wickser, *Bar Associations*, 15 CORN. L. Q. 390
(1930). Yet no more vital field exists. Consider merely the effect of skillful or
dumb-skulled presentation on the growth of case-law.

strategy of presenting cases in favorable series, settling the un-favorable cases, etc.[61]

All of the above has focussed on how to tell what appellate courts will do, however far afield any new scent may have led the individual hunter. But the interest in *effects* on laymen of what the courts will do leads rapidly from this still respectably tradi-tional sphere of legal discussion into a series of further inquiries whose legal decorum is more dubious. They soon extend far be-yond what has in recent years been conceived (in regard to the developed state) as law at all. I can not stop to consider these inquiries in detail. Space presses. Each of the following phases could be, and should be, elaborated at least into such a rough sketch as the foregoing. Through each would continue to run interest in what actually eventuates; interest in accurate descrip-tion of what evenuates; interest in attempting, where prediction becomes uncertain, some conscious attack on hidden factors whose study might lessen the uncertainty; and interest in effects—on laymen. Finally, insistence that Ought-judgment should be bot-tomed on knowledge. And that action should be bottomed on all the knowledge that can be got in time to act.

I. *There is first the question of what lower courts and especially trial courts are doing, and what relation their doing has to the sayings and doings of upper courts and legislatures.*

Here the question has been to begin to find out, to find some way, some ways, of getting the hitherto unavailable facts, to find some significant way or ways of classifying what business is done, how long it takes, how various parts of the procedural machinery work. (*E.g.*, Warner, Sunderland, Millar, Clark, Yntema, Marshall, Oliphant, Douglas, Arnold, Morgan, Frankfurter, Greene, and Swazie.) Another attack begins by inquiry not into records, but into the processes of trial and their effects on the outcome of cases. (Frank, Green.) This, on the civil side, where we have (save for memoirs) been wholly in the dark. On the criminal side, beginnings lie further back. (Pound, Frankfurter, Moley and the Crime Surveys; where lawyers have drawn on the crimi-

---

[61] Something of this in Elizabeth Sanford's forthcoming THE UNIT RULE; something in LLEWELLYN, BRAMBLE BUSH (1930) c. X; and Frederick, *The Trust Receipt as Security*, 22 COLUM. L. REV. 395, 546 (1922), is not only itself a step in such a sequence, but esp. at 409 *et seq.* presents, in the Farmers and Mechanics Bank cases, thence to importing, and thence to the automobile line, both materials and suggestion for such a study. And see Isaacs, *Business Security and Legal Security*, 37 HARV. L. REV. 201 (1923); (C) Isaacs, *How Lawyers Think*, 23 COLUM. L. REV. 555 (1923).

nologists.) All that is really clear to date is that until we know more here our "rules" give us no remote suggestion of *what law means* to persons in the lower income brackets,[62] and give us misleading suggestions as to the whole body of cases unappealed. Meantime, the techniques of the social sciences are being drawn upon and modified to make the work possible.[63]

II. *There is the question of administrative bodies*—not merely on the side of administrative law (itself a novel concept recently enough)—but including all the action which state officials take "under the law" so far as it proves to affect people.[64] And with this we begin departing from the orthodox. To be sure, the practicing lawyer today knows his commission as he knows his court. But the trail thus broken leads into the wilds of government, and politics, and queer events in both.

III. *There is the question of legislative regulation*—in terms of what it *means in action, and to whom,* not merely in terms of what it says. And with that, the question of what goes into producing legislative change—or blocking it [65]—especially so far as the profession participates therein; legislative history on the official record; but as well the background of fact and interest and need. And, no less vital, there is the fact-inquiry into areas of life where maladjustment capable of legal remedy exists.[66]

IV. Finally, and cutting now completely beyond the tradition-bounded area of law, there is the matter not of describing or predicting the action of officials—be they appellate courts, trial courts, legislators, administrators—but of describing and predict-

[62] Little has been done in print to follow up REGINALD SMITH's path-breaking JUSTICE AND THE POOR (1924); but allied is the growing literature on poor man's financing, and Bradway's work.

[63] Especially useful Wm. Clark, Douglas and Thomas, *supra* note 36; C. E. Clark, *Fact Research in Law Administration, infra* Appendix I.

[64] One may cite generally Freund, Frankfurter, Henderson, Dickinson, Landis, Magill. Also PATTERSON, THE INSURANCE COMMISSIONER (1927); *cf.* Stason, *Judicial Review of Tax Errors—Effect of Failure to Resort to Administrative Remedies,* 28 MICH. L. REV. 637 (1930). And much of the Crime Survey and criminological work fits here. So, *e.g.,* Sheldon Glueck, Fosdick.

[65] See (C) Berle, *supra* note 51; CHILDS, LABOR AND CAPITAL IN NATIONAL POLITICS (1930).

[66] In general *cf.* Berle and Weiner in the corporate field; FRANKFURTER AND GREENE, THE LABOR INJUNCTION (1930); Clark, *infra* Appendix I; Sunderland. In brief, who not, realist or non-realist, who has ever touched facts and found no solution in case-law? What the realist offers is only thirst for *more* facts, better gathered, more clearly interpreted. And *not* merely selected (though accurate) to point an argument. For which reason not all the work just mentioned, despite its value, can count as fully "realistic."

ing *the effects of their action on the laymen of the community.*[67] "Law" without effect approaches zero in its meaning. To be ignorant of its effect is to be ignorant of its meaning. To know its effect without study of the persons whom it affects is impossible. Here the antecedents of court action touch its results. To know law, then, to know *anything* of what is necessary to judge or evaluate law, we must proceed into these areas which have traditionally been conceived (save by the historical school) as not-law. Not only what courts do instead of what courts say, but also what difference it makes to anybody that they do it. And no sooner does one begin such a study than it becomes clear that there can be no broad talk of "law" nor of "the community"; but that it is

[67] I quote Felix Cohen: "In the economic analysis of judicial rules and theories much valuable work has been done by Hale, Bonbright, Richberg, Henderson, Julius Cohen, Goddard and Weiner, particularly in the field of public utility valuation. Otherwise there is simply the call for facts, *e.g.*, Weiner, *Payment of Dissenting Stockholders* (1927) 27 COL. L. REV. 547." Except that the "otherwise" comes several lines too soon, I concur *in toto*. As to the point of difference, before I even open the books to search I think, e.g., of Breckenridge, J. M. Clark, J. R. Commons, Douglas, Fredericks, Herman Finkelstein, Handler, Kidd, Klaus, Patterson, Radin, Ripley, Roscoe Steffen, Vold, Wilbert Ward, all (save Clark and Commons) as to work inside the field of private commercial law.

Such analysis seems to be on the increase. Comparing, *e.g.*, the Cornell Law Quarterly, vols. 14–16 with vols. 4–6, and the Michigan Law Review, vols. 27–29 with vols. 17–19, one finds reference to facts and analysis of effects of rules of private law increasing—not so much in frequency as in scope and care and objectivity, and integration into the essential framework of the papers. (On public law the older material often rivals the recent; there the fact-impetus developed earlier.) Striking in the earlier materials is Rogers, *An Account of Some Psychological Experiments on the Subject of Trade-Mark Infringement,* 18 MICH. L. REV. 75 (1919); but perhaps even more striking is that in the later, Billig, *What Price Bankruptcy: A Plea for "Friendly Adjustment,"* 14 CORN. L. Q. 413 (1929) (and compare Billig, *Extra-Judicial Administration of Insolvent Estates: A Study of Recent Cases,* 78 U. OF PA. L. REV. 293 (1930)) using figures and more systematic approach of facts and effects, does not stand alone, but stirs up prompt and competent discussion of his *data,* not merely of his conclusions: Gamer, *On Comparing "Friendly Adjustment" and Bankruptcy,* 16 CORN. L. Q. 35 (1930). Competent discussion is to the single study what the incorporation of a new tool of approach into a thinker's standard working kit is to the insight which once came and then was forgotten. Compare my own use of risk-allocation as early as 1920, *Implied Warranties of Wholesomeness Again,* 29 YALE L. J. 782 (1920), only to wholly overlook it in 1922 in a problem that shrieked for its use (*Certified Altered Checks Under the Negotiable Instruments Law,* 31 id. 522 (1922)) and to almost disregard it in two papers in 1923, both in fields where it yields results. *Supervening Impossibility of Performing Conditions Precedent in the Law of Negotiable Paper,* 23 COLUM. L. REV. 142 (1923); *C. I. F. Contracts in American Law,* 32 YALE L. J. 711 (1923). In short I did not *have* the idea in 1920; I *had had* it then—once. Contrast its consistent employment, wherever it promised help, since 1925. It is the growing *normality* of appeal to facts and of their critical use which marks the intrusion of this aspect of realism into the literature.

a question of reaching the particular part of the community relevant to some particular part of law. There are persons sought to
be affected, and persons not sought to be affected. Of the former,
some are not in fact materially affected (the gangster-feud); of
the latter, some are (depositors in a failing bank which the bank
laws have *not* controlled).[68] There is the range of questions as to
those legal "helpful devices" (corporation,[69] contract, lease) designed to make it easier for men to get where they want and what
they want. There is all the information social scientists have
gathered to be explored, in its bearings on the law. There is all
the information they have not been interested in gathering, likewise to be explored—but, first, to be gathered.

Here are the matters one or another of the new fermenters is
ploughing into. Even the sketchy citations here are enough to
make clear that their lines of work organize curiously into a whole.

But again rises the query: are the matters *new?* What realist
knows so little of law or the ways of human thought as to make
such a claim? Which of the inquiries has not been made, or started,
or adumbrated, in the past? Which of the techniques does not
rest on our prior culture? New, I repeat, is one thing only: the
systematic effort to carry one problem through, to carry a succession
of problems through, to *consistently,* not occasionally, choose the
best available technique, to *consistently* keep description on the
descriptive level, to *consistently* distinguish the fact basis which
will feed evaluation from the evaluation which it will later feed,
to *consistently* seek *all* the relevant data one can find to *add* to
the haphazard single-life experience, to *add* to general common
sense [—so as, in possible due course, to produce that *un*common
sense we know as horse-sense.]

Is it not obvious that—if this be realism—realism is a mass
of trends in legal work and thinking? (1) They have their common core, present to some extent wherever realistic work is done:
recognition of law as means; recognition of change in society that
may call for change in law; interest in what happens; interest in
effects; recognition of the need for effort toward keeping percep-

---

[68] Further developed in Llewellyn, *Law Observance and Law Enforcement, infra*
Appendix I.

[69] The literature here is vast. Peculiarly striking: Weiner, *Conflicting Functions
of the Upset Price in a Corporate Reorganization,* 27 COLUM. L. REV. 132 (1927);
Douglas and Shanks, *Insulation from Liability Through Subsidiary Corporations,*
39 YALE L. J. 193 (1930); Posner, *Liability of the Trustee Under the Corporate
Indenture,* 42 HARV. L. REV. 198 (1928); Berle, *Corporate Powers as Powers in Trust,*
44 HARV. L. REV. 1049 (1931).

tion of the facts uncolored by one's views on Ought; a distrust of the received set of rules and concepts as adequate indications of what is happening in the courts; a drive toward narrowing the categories of description. (2) They have grown out of the study of the action of appellate courts, and that study still remains their potent stimulus. Uncertainty in the action of such courts is one main problem: to find the why of it; to find means to reduce it, where it needs reduction; to find where it needs reduction, where expansion.[e] (3) But into the work of lower courts, of administrative bodies, of legislatures, of the life which lies before and behind "law," the ferment of investigation spreads.

Some one or other of these realistic trends takes up the whole time of many; a hundred more participate in them to various degrees who yet would scorn the appellation "realist." The trends are centered in no man, in no coherent group. There is no leader. Spokesmen are self-appointed. They speak not for the whole but for the work each is himself concerned with—at times with little or no thought of the whole, at times with the exaggeration of controversy or innovation. Yet who should know better than lawyers the exaggeration of controversy; who should have more skill than they to limit argument and dictum to the particular issue, to read it in the light thereof. One will find, reading thus, little said by realistic spokesmen that does not warrant careful pondering. Indeed, on *careful* pondering, one will find little of exaggeration in their writing. Meantime, the proof of the pudding: are there results?

There are. They are results, primarily, on the side of the descriptive sociology of law discussed thus far. They are big with meaning for attack on the field of Ought—either on what courts ought to do with existing rules, or on what changes in rules are called for.

Already we have a series, lengthening impressively, of *more accurate* reformulations of what appellate courts are doing and may be expected to do. We are making headway in *seeing* (not just "knowing" without inquiry) what effects their doing has on some of the persons interested. We are accumulating some *knowledge* (*i.e.,* more than guesses) on phases of our life as to which our law seems out of joint.

We have, moreover, a first attack upon the realm of the unpre-

---

[e] On the value and vitality of the concept of "reasonable regularity" in contrast to that of certainty—a major contribution of John R. Commons—see my COMMON LAW TRADITION, esp. at 215 ff.

dictable in the actions of [appellate] courts. That attack suggests strongly that one large element in the now incalculable consists in the traditional pretense or belief (sometimes the one, sometimes the other) that there is no such area of uncertainty, or that it is much smaller than it is. To *recognize* that there are limits to the certainty sought by words and deduction, to seek to define those limits, is to open the door to that other and far more useful judicial procedure: *conscious* seeking, *within the limits laid down by precedent and statute,* for the wise decision. Decisions thus reached, *within those limits,* may fairly be hoped to be more certainly predictable than decisions are now—for today no man can tell when the court will, and when it will not, thus seek the wise decision, but hide the seeking under words. And not only more certain, but what is no whit less important: more just and wise (or more frequently just and wise).

Indeed, the most fascinating result of the realistic effort appears as one returns from trial court or the ways of laymen to the tradition-hallowed problem of appellate case-law. Criticized by those who refuse to disentangle Is and Ought because of their supposed deliberate neglect of the normative aspect of law, the realists prove the value, for the normative, of temporarily putting the normative aside. They return from their excursion into the purest description they can manage with a demonstration that the field of free play for Ought in appellate courts is vastly wider than traditional Ought-bound thinking ever had made clear. This, *within* the confines of precedent as we have it, *within* the limits and on the basis of our present order. Let me summarize the points of the brief:

(a) If deduction does not solve cases, but only shows the effect of a given premise; and if there is available a competing but equally authoritative premise that leads to a different conclusion —then there is a choice in the case; a choice to be justified; a choice which *can* be justified only as a question of policy—for the authoritative tradition speaks with a forked tongue.[70]

(b) If (i) the possible inductions from one case or a series of

---

[70] *Cf.* Radin, *The Theory of Judicial Decision: or How Judges Think*; Cook, *The Utility of Jurisprudence in the Solution of Legal Problems;* LLEWELLYN, THE BRAMBLE BUSH chs. IV, V; FRANK, LAW AND THE MODERN MIND; GREEN, JUDGE AND JURY; Corbin, *Contracts for the Benefit of Third Persons;* Powell, *The Logic and Rhetoric of Constitutional Law,* all *infra* Appendix I. See also Radin, *supra* note 36; (C) Dickinson, *The Law Behind Law,* 29 COLUM. L. REV. 113, 285, 296–99 (1929); Brown, *supra* note 36; Waite, *Caveat Emptor and the Judicial Process,* 25 COLUM. L. REV. 129 (1925).

cases—even if those cases really had each a single fixed meaning —are nonetheless not single, but many; and if (ii) the standard authoritative techniques[71] of dealing with precedent range for limiting the case to its narrowest issue on facts and procedure, and even searching the record for a hidden distinguishing fact, all the way to giving it the widest meaning the rule expressed will allow, or even thrusting under it a principle which was not announced in the opinion at all—then the available leeway in *interpretation of precedent* is (relatively to what the older tradition has *consciously* conceived) nothing less than huge. And only policy considerations and the facing of policy considerations can justify "interpreting" (making, shaping, drawing conclusions from) the relevant body of precedent in one way or in another. And —the essence of all—*stare decisis* has in the past been, now is, and must continue to be, a norm of change, and a means of change, as well as a norm of staying put, and a means of staying put.[72] *The growth of the past has been achieved by "standing on" the decided cases;* rarely by overturning them. Let this be recognized, and precedent is clearly seen to be a way of change as well as a way of refusing to change. Let that, in turn, be recognized, and that peculiar one of the ways of working with precedent which consists in blinding the eyes to policy loses the fictitious sanctity with which it is now enveloped *some of the time:* to wit, whenever judges for any reason do not wish to look at policy.

(c) If the classification of raw facts is largely an arbitrary [better: *creative*] process, raw facts having in most doubtful cases the possibility of ready classification along various lines, then "certainty," even under pure deductive thinking, has not the meaning that people who have wanted certainty in law are looking for. The quest of this unreal certainty, this certainty unattained in result, is the major reason for one self-denying ordinance of judges: their refusal to look beyond words to things. Let them once see that the "certainty" thus achieved is *un*certainty for the non-law-tutored layman in his living and dealing, and the way is open to

[71] I mean not those approved by the schoolmen, but those *used* by authoritative courts in dealing with "authority." On this as on other matters, the rules of the schoolmen are to be subjected to the check of fact—here, of what courts do, and do both openly and with clean conscience. See LLEWELLYN, BRAMBLE BUSH (1930) c. IV. Contrast Goodhart, *Determining the Ratio Decidendi of a Case,* 40 YALE L. J. 161 (1930). [And see the demonstration in my COMMON LAW TRADITION—DECIDING APPEALS (1960).]

[72] See especially Corbin, *The Law and the Judges; Contracts for the Benefit of Third Persons;* Llewellyn, *Legal Tradition and Social Science Method;* Tulin; all *infra* Appendix I, also LLEWELLYN, BRAMBLE BUSH chs. III, IV.

reach for *layman's* certainty-through-law, by seeking for the fair or wise outcome, so far as precedent and statute make such outcome *possible*. To see the problem thus is also to open the way to conscious discrimination, *e.g.*, between current commercial dealings on the one hand and real estate conveyancing or corporate indenture drafting on the other. In the latter the *lawyer's* peculiar reliance on formulae may be assumed as of course; whereas in the former cause needs to be shown for making such an assumption.

Thus, as various of the self-designated realistic spokesmen have been shouting: the temporary divorce of Is and Ought brings to the reunion a sharper eye, a fuller equipment, a sounder judgment—even a wider opportunity as to that case-law which tradition has painted as peculiarly ridden by the past. That on the fact side, as to the particular questions studied, the temporary divorce yields no less gratifying results is demonstrated by the literature.

When the matter of *program in the normative aspect* is raised, the answer is: *there is none.* A likeness of method in approaching Ought-questions is apparent. If there be, beyond that, general lines of fairly wide agreement, they are hardly specific enough to mean anything on any given issue. Partly, this derives from differences in temperament and outlook. Partly, it derives from the total lack of organization or desire to schoolify among the men concerned. But partly, it is due to the range of work involved. Business lawyers have some pet Oughts, each in the material he has become familiar with; torts lawyers have the like in torts; public lawyers in public law. And so it goes. Partly also, the lack of programmatic agreement derives from the time and effort consumed in getting at facts, either the facts strictly legal or the "foreign" facts bearing on the law. Specialized interest must alone spell absence of group-program. Yet some general points of view may be hazarded.

(1) There is fairly general agreement on the importance of personnel, and of court organization, as essential to making laws have meaning. This both as to triers of fact and as to triers of law. There is some tendency, too, to urge specialization of tribunals.

(2) There is very general agreement on the need for courts to face squarely the policy questions in their cases, and use the full freedom precedent affords in working toward conclusions that seem indicated. There is fairly general agreement that effects of rules, so far as known, should be taken account of in making or remaking the rules. There is fairly general agreement that we need

improved machinery for making the facts about such effects—or about needs and conditions to be affected by a decision—available to courts.

(3) There is a strong tendency to think it wiser [for purposes of initial inquiry] to narrow rather than to widen the categories in which concepts and rules *either about judging or for judging* are made.

(4) There is a strong tendency to approach most legal problems as problems in allocation of risks,[73] and so far as possible, as problems of their reduction, and so to insist on the effects of rules on parties who not only are not in court, but are not fairly represented by the parties who are in court. To approach not only tort but business matters, in a word, as matters of *general* policy.

And so I close as I began. What is there novel here? [74] In the ideas, nothing. In the sustained attempt to make one or another of them fruitful, much. In the narrowness of fact-category together with the wide range of fact-inquiry, much. In the techniques availed of, much—for lawyers. But let this be noted—for the summary above runs so largely to the purely descriptive side: When writers of realistic inclination are writing in general, they are bound to stress the need of more accurate description, of Is and not of Ought. There lies the *common* ground of their thinking; there lies the area of new and puzzling development. There lies the point of discrimination which they must drive home. To get perspective on their stand about ethically normative matters one must pick up the work of each man in his special field of work. There one will find no lack of interest or effort toward improvement in the law. As to whether change is called for, on any *given* point of law, and if so, how much change,

[73] *E.g.*, Patterson, *The Apportionment of Business Risks Through Legal Devices;* Douglas, *Vicarious Liability and Administration of Risk,* both *infra* Appendix I. See also Isaacs, *supra* note 61. Contrast Breckenridge and Llewellyn, 31 YALE L. J. 522 (1922) with Breckenridge, *The Negotiability of Postdated Checks,* 38 YALE L. J. 1063 (1929), and LLEWELLYN, CASES AND MATERIALS ON THE LAW OF SALES (1930). Or Corbin's earlier work with his article *supra* note 57. Compare the work of Green, Y. B. Smith, Turner, Weiner; BRANNAN, NEGOTIABLE INSTRUMENTS LAW 572 (Chafee's ed. 1926); Clark's conception of procedural handicapping, CODE PLEADING (1928). Holmes, as usual, set the mark: THE COMMON LAW (1881) chs. VIII, IX.

[74] Reports Felix Cohen: "Pound can be cited for all the planks for the realistic platform—and against many of them." My unchecked memory would endorse this (save for the rigorous temporary severance of Is and Ought?). But it is also probably true (perhaps in lesser degree because they have written less) of most realists who did not happen to be laid and hatched by other realists. Our good fortune is that the world we live in is neither static, nor, as to those who people it, too consistent.

and in what direction, there is no agreement. Why should there be? A *group* philosophy or program, a *group* credo of social welfare, these realists have not. They are not a group.[f]

Bibliography: The Literature Canvassed for the Test

Bingham, W.: *What is the Law?*, 11 Mich. L. Rev. 1 (1912); *Science and the Law*, 25 Green Bag 162 (1913); *Legal Philosophy and the Law*, 9 Ill. L. Rev. 98 (1914); *The Nature and Importance of Legal Possession*, 13 Mich. L. Rev. 535 (1915).

Clark, C. E.: *Relations, Legal and Others*, 5 Ill. L. J. 26 (1922); *The Code Cause of Action*, 33 Yale L. J. 817 (1924); *Fact Research in Law Administration*, 2 Conn. Bar J. 211 (1928); *New Types of Legal Research* (June 30, 1929) Buffalo Daily L. J.; *Some of the Facts of Law Administration in Connecticut*, 3 Conn. Bar J. 161 (1929); *Methods of Legal Reform*, 36 W. Va. L. Q. 106 (1929); *Legal Education and Research at Yale*, Yale Alum. Weekly (March 7, 1930); *Present Status of Judicial Statistics*, 14 J. Am. Jud. Soc. 84 (Oct. 1930).

Cook, W. W.: *The Alienability of Choses in Action*, 29 Harv. L. Rev. 816 (1916); *The Alienability of Choses in Action: A Reply to Professor Williston*, 30 *id.* 449 (1917); *Privileges of Labor Unions in the Struggle for Life* (1918) 27 Yale L. J. 779 (1918); *Hohfeld's Contributions to the Science of Law*, 28 *id.* 721 (1919); *The Utility of Jurisprudence in the Solution of Legal Problems* in 5 Lectures on Legal Topics, Association of the Bar of the City of New York (1923–24) 335; *The Logical and Legal Bases of the Conflict of Laws*, 33 Yale L. J. 457 (1924); *Scientific Method and the Law*, 15 Johns Hop. Alum. Mag. 213 (1927); *The Jurisdiction of Sovereign States and the Conflict of Laws*, 31 Colum. L. Rev. 368 (1931); Book Review, 31 *id.* 725 (1931).

Corbin, Arthur Linton: *The Law and the Judges*, 3 Yale Rev. 234 (New Ser. 1914); *Legal Analysis and Terminology*, 29 Yale L. J. 163 (1919); *Jural Relations and Their Classification*, 30 Yale L. J. 226 (1921); *Democracy and Education for the Bar*, 19 Proc. Am. L. S. Ass'n 143 (1921); Book Review, 38 Yale L. J. 270 (1928); *Third Parties as Beneficiaries of Contractors' Surety Bonds*, 38 *id.* 1 (1928); *The Restatement of the Common Law by the American Law Institute*, 15 Iowa L. Rev. 19 (1929); *Contracts for the Benefit of Third Persons*, 46 L. Q. Rev. 12 (1930).

Douglas, W. O.: *Vicarious Liability and Administration of Risk*, 38 Yale L. J. 584, 720 (1929); (with C. M. Shanks) *Insulation from Liability Through Subsidiary Corporations*, 39 Yale L. J. 193 (1929); (with Wm. Clark and D. S. Thomas) *The Business Failures Project—A Problem in Methodology*, 39 Yale L. J. 1013 (1930).

Francis, J.: *Domicil of a Corporation*, 38 Yale L. J. 335 (1929).

Frank, J.: Law and the Modern Mind (1930); Book Review, 40 Yale L. J. 1120 (1931).

Green, L.: Book Review, 38 Yale L. J. 402 (1929); Judge and Jury (1930).

[f] For specific test results on Points 1, 10, and 11, see Appendix II in the original, 44 Harv. L. Rev. at 1260 ff., here omitted.

Hutcheson, Jr., J. C.: *The Judgment Intuitive:—The Function of the "Hunch" in Judicial Decision*, 14 CORN. L. Q. 274 (1929).

Klaus, S.: *Sale, Agency and Price Maintenance*, 28 COLUM. L. REV. 312, 441 (1928); Book Review, 28 *id.* 991 (1928); *Identification of the Holder and Tender of Receipt on the Counter Presentation of Checks*, 13 MINN. L. REV. 281 (1929); *Introduction to* EX PARTE MILLIGAN (1929); *Introduction to* PEOPLE V. MOLINEUX (1929); Book Review, 30 COLUM. L. REV. 1220 (1930).

Llewellyn, K. N.: *Free Speech in Time of Peace*, 29 YALE L. J. 337 (1920); *Implied Warranties of Wholesomeness Again*, 29 *id.* 782 (1920); *C. I. F. Contracts in American Law*, 32 *id.* 711 (1923); *The Effect of Legal Institutions on Economics*, 15 AM. ECON. REV. 665 (1925); Book Review, 40 HARV. L. REV. 142 (1926); *Law Observance and Law Enforcement*, PROCEEDINGS NATIONAL CONFERENCE SOCIAL WORK 127 (1928); *A Realistic Jurisprudence—The Next Step*, 30 COLUM. L. REV. 431 (1930); *The Conditions for and the Aims and Methods of Legal Research*, AM. L. S. REV. (1930); CASES AND MATERIALS ON THE LAW OF SALES (1930); THE BRAMBLE BUSH (1930); *Law and the Modern Mind: A Symposium: Legal Illusion*, 31 COLUM. L. REV. 82 (1931); *What Price Contract?—An Essay in Perspective*, 40 YALE L. J. 704 (1931); *Legal Tradition and Social Science Method* (Brookings) ESSAYS ON RESEARCH IN THE SOCIAL SCIENCES, 89 (1931).

Lorenzen, E. G.: *The Renvoi Doctrine in the Conflict of Laws—Meaning of "the Law of a Country,"* 27 YALE L. J. 509 (1918); *Causa and Consideration in the Law of Contracts*, 28 *id.* 621 (1919); *The Theory of Qualifications and the Conflict of Laws*, 20 COLUM. L. REV. 247 (1920); *The Statute of Frauds and the Conflict of Laws*, 32 YALE L. J. 311 (1923); *Territoriality, Public Policy and the Conflict of Laws*, 33 *id.* 736 (1924).

Moore, U.: *Rational Basis of Legal Institutions*, 23 COLUM. L. REV. 609 (1923); (with Hope) *An Institutional Approach to the Law of Commercial Banking*, 38 YALE L. J. 703 (1929); (with Sussman) *Legal and Institutional Methods Applied to the Debiting of Direct Discounts*, 40 *id.* 381, 555, 752, 928 (1931).

Oliphant, H.: *Mutuality of Obligation in Bilateral Contracts at Law*, 25 COLUM. L. REV. 705 (1925); 28 *id.* 997 (1928); *Trade Associations and the Law*, 26 *id.* 381 (1926); *A Return to Stare Decisis*, 14 A.B.A.J. 71, 159 (1928); (with Hewitt) *Introduction to* RUEFF, FROM THE PHYSICAL TO THE SOCIAL SCIENCES (1929).

Patterson, E. W.: *The Apportionment of Business Risks Through Legal Devices*, 24 COLUM. L. REV. 335 (1924); *Equitable Relief for Unilateral Mistake*, 28 *id.* 859 (1928); *The Transfer of Insured Property in German and in American Law*, 29 *id.* 691 (1929); *Can Law be Scientific?*, 25 ILL. L. REV. 121 (1930); (with McIntyre) *Unsecured Creditors' Insurance*, 31 COLUM. L. REV. 212 (1931); *Hedging and Wagering on Produce Exchanges*, 40 YALE L. J. 843 (1931).

Powell, T. R.: *The Study of Moral Judgments by the Case Method*, 10 J. PHIL. PSYCH. 484 (1913); *Law as a University Study*, 19 COLUM. U. Q. 106 (1917); *Law as a Cultural Study*, 4 AM. L. S. REV. 330 (1917); *The Nature of a Patent Right*, 17 COLUM. L. REV. 663 (1917); *The Logic and Rhetoric of Constitutional Law*, 15 J. PHIL. PSYCH. 645 (1918); *The Changing Law of Foreign Corporations*, 33 POL. SCI. Q. 549 (1918); *How Philosophers May be Useful to Society*, 31 INT. J. ETHICS 289 (1921); *The Business Situs of Credits*,

28 W. VA. L. Q. 89 (1922); *An Imaginary Judicial Opinion,* 44 HARV. L. REV. 889 (1931).

Radin, M.: *The Disseisin of Chattels: The Title of a Thief,* 11 CALIF. L. REV. 259 (1923); *The Theory of Judicial Decision: Or How Judges Think,* 11 A.B.A.J. 357 (1925); *Scientific Method and the Law,* 19 CALIF. L. REV. 164 (1931); *Legal Realism,* 31 COLUM. L. REV. 824 (1931).

Sturges, W. A.: *Unincorporated Associations as Parties to Actions,* 33 YALE L. J. 383 (1924); *Commercial Arbitration or Court Application of Common Law Rules of Marketing,* 34 *id.* 480 (1925); Book Review, 35 *id.* 776 (1926); Book Review, 40 HARV. L. REV. 510 (1927); (with S. O. Clark) *Legal Theory and Real Property Mortgages,* 37 YALE L. J. 691 (1928).

Tulin, L. A.: *The Role of Penalties in Criminal Law,* 37 YALE L. J. 1048 (1928).

Yntema, H. E.: *The Hornbook Method and the Conflict of Laws,* 37 Yale L. J. 468 (1928); Book Review, 39 *id.* 140 (1929); *The Purview of Research in the Administration of Justice,* 16 IOWA L. REV. 337 (1931); *Mr. Justice Holmes' View of Legal Science,* 40 YALE L. J. 696 (1931); *The Rational Basis of Legal Science,* 31 COLUM. L. REV. 925 (1931).

LEGAL TRADITION AND SOCIAL SCIENCE
METHOD—A REALIST'S CRITIQUE [a]

I

In one way it seems absurd for any devotee of the most back-ward of social disciplines to attempt to discuss problems of method in social science. In another way a strong *prima facie* case can be made for letting a lawyer speak. Out of contrast comes clarity. The very backwardness[1] of law makes its material stand to observa-tion more readily than is the case in those more sophisticated sciences in which men have learned how error of method along one line can be artfully concealed under the mantle of advance along another. I shall ask your leave, moreover, to indulge in what may seem at first sight unconscionable repetitiousness in recurring again and again to the same phenomena. For if my guess is right, here too may lie a suggestion for general method. It sometimes pays to walk seven times around the walls. In different contexts the same facts take on new meaning.

But before I can well start talking about "law," especially in

---

[a] From BROOKINGS INSTITUTION, ESSAYS ON RESEARCH IN THE SOCIAL SCIENCES 89 ff. (1931)—a paper for a general seminar.

[1] Backwardness as a *science of observation,* not backwardness as an art of life. As an art law is backward, too, but unevenly; more here, less there, and sometimes not at all. For whereas one may readily admit Ogburn's "social lag" as applied to law in general, law shares with other aspects of culture a concentration of growth processes on particular areas at particular times, a shifting around of growth-buds, almost as striking as that seen in the embryo. And an area in which growth is coming to conclusion commonly has achieved rather effective shape.

this day of new conflict between schools,[2] I must give you some idea of what the term means to me, of what I shall be talking about when I use it.[3] You need not look upon me distrustfully as I do this. I have no intention of framing a *definition* of law, of laying a foundation for argument, of inveigling you into acceptance of something for me to pull conclusions out of later on. It is merely a matter of sketching out the subject matter which is under primary consideration in the rest of this discussion. I shall sketch that subject matter from the standpoint of a legal realist, concerned *in this particular discussion* primarily with law as a science of observation, and secondarily with law as an art of life, and concerned—*in this particular discussion*—almost not at all with law as a philosophy, or with value judgments as to social objectives. Obviously, "law" extends into all of these spheres, and covers as well a body of authoritative doctrine: those official, prevailing legal "rules" which are often said to "be the law."

But one concerned with law as a social *science,* a science of *observation,* must center his thought on behavior, on the interactions between the behavior of law-officials and behavior of laymen. The behavior which comes chiefly in question has two aspects: (*a*) the settling by somewhat regularized official action of disputes that do not otherwise get settled; and (*b*) the use of somewhat regularized official pressures to get people to do (or not to do) particular things, or to do (or not to do) what they do in particular ways—more briefly, the directing and channeling of the conduct of people.

There are a number of points in these over-abstract formulae which call for a bit of elaboration, if the formulae are to be more than words. And they must be made to take on meaning if the ground is to be cleared for any comparison of work in law with work in other social fields. For comparison we need, here as always, first a common ground, and then a point of difference. The

[2] Basic is Holmes, O. W., e. g., *Collected Legal Papers*, p. 167. See also Moore, Underhill, *The Rational Basis of Institutions*, 23 COLUM. LAW REV. 609 ff. (1923); Oliphant, *A Return to Stare Decisis*, 14 A.B.A.J. 71, 159; 6 AM. L. S. REV. 215; LLEWELLYN, THE BRAMBLE BUSH (1930); FRANK, LAW AND THE MODERN MIND (1930); Llewellyn, Adler, and Cook, Symposium, 31 COLUM. L. REV. 82 ff. (1931); Cohen, *Justice Holmes and the Nature of Law*, 31 *id.* 352 ff. (1931); Pound, *The Call for a Realist Jurisprudence*, 44 HARV. L. REV. 697 ff. (1931); and the reply to this last by Llewellyn, *ibid.*, June, 1931, above, p. 42.

[3] These matters are developed more fully in *A Realistic Jurisprudence—the Next Step*, 30 COLUM. L. REV. 431 ff. (1930), *supra*, p. 3. And various of the present suggestions on method, as applied to legal research, appear in *The Conditions for, and the Aims and Methods of Legal Research*, March 1930, AMER. L. S. REV. 672 ff.

common ground I hope to find in the interest common to all social scientists in what men do, and how they do it. The points of difference have to do with the peculiar attention thus far paid in law to rules.

As to the first phase of behavior here in question (the settling by somewhat regularized official action of disputes which do not otherwise get settled), a further word is called for on "disputes," and on "not otherwise settled," and on "official action," and on "somewhat regularized."

"Disputes." Disputes are the eternal heart and core of law. They do not mark its circumference, but they will always mark its center. It is when two people are in a dispute, it is especially when they are in a dispute not otherwise settled, that law shows its first societal value: the cleaning up of the matter in such a fashion that we can leave it behind, forget it, and get on.

"Not otherwise settled" because so many disputes are settled in one way or another by argument or by wrangling or simply by self-assertion on the one side and submission on the other, or by bargaining or compromise or mediation. The primary business of law is not with these. Law on its dispute side is the machinery of last resort, when these others have failed.

Of last resort, by *"official action."* It is the intervention of the official in the dispute which insures that the action in this last resort will stick. Since I am dealing here with a developed system of law and not with the law of a primitive society, it is unnecessary to discriminate between action by officials and action by the parties themselves which has, because of its form or circumstance, official character. But there is another aspect of official action which does need attention. Do I mean the officials *of the state* and only these? For purposes of this discussion I can answer, yes. All that it is necessary to point out in passing is that when disputes require settlement inside of any smaller group within the state (or, for that matter, inside of any group, large or small, that cuts across states) there may be a body of *group* officials devoted to the maintenance of group order, whose functioning for purposes of that group will be official, and so will constitute *group* "law." When this is contrasted with the work of state officials it is convenient to speak of it as *by-law.*

No less important is the element of *regularization.* When we think of law (or by-law) we think, in the main, not of emergency action, not of one-time action, but of repetitive action, of more or less predictable action; not of the outcome of a given ballot, but

of the institution of balloting; not of executive decisions in time
of famine, flood, or war, but of a semi-permanent change by
legislation. And in the decision of a given case, while we may, if
we have to, recognize a wholly arbitrary decision of the single
dispute as law (or near-law), we think of it as a very imperfect kind
of law unless we have some assurance that later like disputes will
have like outcome.

As to the second aspect of law, the directing and channeling
of conduct by regularized official pressures, we must draw similar
lines.

It is *official, not non-official pressures,* that we are concerned
with; the pressures exerted not by private individuals, but by
state officials. True, behind the action of private persons and
groups, and affording one major fulcrum from which they gain
leverage, is the general legal system. That system guarantees the
peace; it furnishes some and buttresses more of the phases of
private property. In a broader view we should have to take into
account these, law's indirect effects.[4] For the moment they can
be disregarded.

Regularization again plays in. It is with legislation and administrative fiats of regular application that we are concerned; and
especially with administrative *practice.* It is not primarily, if at all,
a question of policy determination by executives nor of their
solutions in isolated cases, but of their dealings with repetitive
cases. In a word, not [as much] leadership, [as] administration.
And it will be observed in passing that from this angle I am including vastly more than the lawyers commonly understand
under the heading of "administrative law," since I would take in
all regularized administrative operations.

Whereas, as indicated above, we can disregard tonight such
very indirect effects of law as are reflected in unequal distribution
of property rights, we cannot well throw out what I may class as
the *semi-direct effects of law,* as when a whole line of practices in
income tax collection is changed because of a single test case in
court, or when the rule laid down in a private case at law leads to
change in the practices of bankers or of merchandizers.

Above all, however, what looms large in this connection is the
difference between the *words* and the *practices* of officials. It is not

[4] See R. L. Hale, *Coercion and Distribution in a Supposedly Non-Coercive State,*
38 Pol. Sci. Q. 470 ff. (1923); K. N. Llewellyn, *What Price Contract?* 40 Yale L. J.
704 ff. (1931).

what stands on the books, but what happens, which is the center of attention. It is not the *purpose* of any legal rule, or the *purpose* of official action, but the kind and quality of *the action itself* which is of primary concern. Long ago Holmes pointed out that law in the pinch was significant for what it meant to a bad man who cared only what could or would be done to him. This is not to deny the importance of the purposes of rules or acts, nor to deny the importance of the rules themselves. The very phrase "law observance," points to their vitality. You have law "observance" when you have action by non-officials which squares roughly with the purpose at which official action and official pronouncements aim.[5] None the less, and however important either purposes or rules, we remain concerned *primarily* with what officials *do* and the *effects* of their doing. (Including of course their saying in their doing, *if, as, and when* their saying makes a difference.) One point to be clinched as we get into this is that the effects are differential. They are not the same for all persons. We live in a specialized, a differentiated society. We live in groups, in constellations, unlike, far from, hardly aware of most of those others who are the rest of us. The effects of official action *must* then be different for different persons or groups, according to the interests, habits, complexes, occupations; according to the type of organization, if any, of different persons in the community, [and, indeed, according to the area of the official action.]

II

All of this is miles apart from the traditional approach to law. Wherefore it affords an excellent vantage point from which to view that same traditional approach. And the first observation that one makes from the vantage point is that the traditional approach to law has not been primarily concerned with a science of observation at all. Its center has been either an art (how to *get* disputes settled, how to *get* conduct channeled) or else a philosophy (what *ought* to be done with disputes, what *ought* to be done about channeling conduct)—or else an indiscriminate stew of both together. In this, law calls up memories of the beginnings of economics, political science, sociology. But with a difference. None of those disciplines found it easy to get far enough away from the check-up of hard facts to set abroad the idea that they were *made*

[5] See *Law Observance and Law Enforcement*, PROCEEDINGS OF THE CONFERENCE ON SOCIAL WORK 128 (1928), *infra*, p. 399.

up exclusively of rules. The analogue of law in this is the applied religious dogma of the casuists.

For in the traditional approach law *is* a question of *rules.* Sometimes they are said to be rules of "external conduct"; sometimes they are said to be rules "laid down by a superior to an inferior." Always the question, in one form or another, is of rules. [Almost] Always it is of rules either laid down or enforced by the state, and always a question of rules with an *Ought* content. In a word, under the traditional approach the bulk of the subject matter of law is exhausted when the writer has expressed in words what ought to be done, or, if he is a legal "positivist," when he has expressed in words what those rules are which in the state he is discussing are *officially accepted* as laying down what ought to be done ("positive law"). What actually *occurs,* what actually *is done,* on the part either of courts and other state officials, or on the part of people who are not officials, is either ignored, or is hinted at vaguely and obscurely. It hides from sight and interest beneath this veil of words.

From this fact there flow immediately a number of warnings as to social science method.

In the first place, there is the *threat of the available.* This is the lesson from the almost inevitable tendency in any thinking, or in any study, first to turn to the most available material and to study that—to study it exclusively—at the outset; second, having once begun the study of the available, to lose all perspective and come shortly to mistake the merely available, the easily seen, for all there is to see. The simple available thing in law consists in the rules laid down on the statute books by the legislature, or laid down authoritatively by the supreme court of any given jurisdiction. The statute book is in print. The reports of the supreme court are in print. Both are collected and arranged in libraries. And the easiest thing to extract from either or both is the set of rules which they purport to contain. What wonder, then, that these have been the subject matter of our study? What wonder, either, that once the study is begun we come to think of them as occupying the whole field? At the same time, what an absurdity. Useful and influential as these rules may be (and I do not deny either their influence or their necessity or—when they are soundly handled—their high utility) surely it is clear that they offer the most dubious of pictures of any social behavior outside themselves. How many cases come into the city and municipal courts in comparison with those in the supreme court of a state we know little of. But we may suspect that the former number is close to a full thousand times the latter. Neither do we know how far either statute books or rules laid down in the supreme court are reflected in the action of these lower courts—or whether they are reflected at all. Still less, if that be possible, do we know the relation between what governing officials do outside of court and the "supreme" official rules. Least of all do we know what influence either rules or even acts of courts or other officials have on the conduct of "the governed."

We suspect that these things differ from rule to rule, from court to court, from group to group among the governed. We suspect. In the suspicion buds our hope.

The amazing thing, the thing to be stressed, the thing of significance for every study in any social discipline, is that over decades, over centuries, lawyers have regarded these *unavailable* behavior aspects either as immaterial, lacking in interest, not worth pursuing, or else as quite adequately, quite accurately sampled and reflected in the particular *available* material that they did (as of course) take as their subject matter. That danger, I say, is present in every discipline, and in every study. The evil of the actuality happens to glare peculiarly in ours.

Another suggestion for general method lies in the *threat from apparent simplicity*. The urge to find things simple, to establish their simplicity, has panic power. The assumption that things *must* be simple seems well-nigh compulsive. Whence that persistent posing of false issues against which we are never warned enough: "Is it this *or* is it that?" Whereas in sober study it will some day prove to be neither, or both, or both plus several others. Of a piece with the "which-of-the-two" issue is the "and-not" answer, and the war of schools—with the suggestion to the recurrent rising generation that while their elders are undoubtedly wrong, they are rarely *all* wrong; and that to junk *all* of the accepted approach by "and-not" thinking is commonly to fall into error as great or greater than that from which one has escaped.

Finally, the threat from simplicity reveals itself in that curious drive to create a seeming simplicity, when nothing else will do it, by *verbal* unification, by manipulation of verbal or other symbols which correspond to nothing in the facts. The sign-post of this in the law is the naive anouncement so often met: "The principle is clear, but there is difficulty, there is uncertainty, in its application." This means that cases unlike in facts and outcome have been successfully verbalized into one jumbled pile. But the statisticians are as bad when they "smooth" their data into curves which have no warrant in the data smoothed, and then proceed to manipulate the curves as if the curves had been precise description. Further exhibits are offered by those simpler souls among statisticians who lack the mathematics to see the presuppositions of particular statistical formulae, and so "apply" the formulae light-heartedly, whether they are adapted to the data in hand or not. Finally—the crassest cases—the system-builders in social science pour examples of this would-be simplifying from their horn of plenty.[aa]

The third suggestion for general method lies in the *fusion or confusion of the realms of Is and Ought*. This confusion is rooted with dire firmness in our thinking. We glimmer at times toward escape. Ethnographers have discovered that the ethical preconceptions of the missionary darkened his observation of simpler cultures. Economists move to the discovery that a theory of prices is without [decisive] bearing on the field of economic welfare, a field of value-judgments. But all the disciplines which deal with contemporary society and yet leave room for ideals remain afflicted. Not only do the workers insist (as they well may) on combining in the same person the observer, the scientist, and the idealist or reformer, but (which is sure confusion) too many of them insist on talking about both observation and reform at once, in hodgepodge, with magnificent disinterest in which is which. Commonly this means badly designed reforms; always it means the skewing of observation.

Both the word *rule* and the word *principle* invite confusion. "Rule" masks two meanings. A rule may be a rule *for* doing something, a precept, an instruction, an ideal. Or else a rule may be a rule *of* doing something, a practice, a pattern of behavior, an observed regularity of recurrence. Out of such regularities there may and do grow concepts of what ought to be done; but almost never will such a concept coincide wholly with the practice which gave it birth. The presence of a "rule for," *per contra,* may indicate the presence also of a somewhat similar practice, but it need not do so; and almost never, even when it does, will the practice wholly coincide with the "rule for." But one who thinks in terms of rules—without analysis—will have his mind either on the precept or on the practice, without telling us or himself which; at

[aa] Until rather recently I had thought I was shock-proof against even such intellectual fads as exclusive quantitavism in the social disciplines. But it has recently been suggested to me that there may be "built into" the "tables" a 5 per cent margin for error even in regard to *recording* of the alleged *facts*. This would shock me at my most unshockable.

times he will have his mind on both at once and presuppose their identity; in any event he will pass, both in his thinking and in his discussion, from one to the other *without giving notice*—or taking it.

What is thus true of "rules" is *a fortiori* true of "principles"— which, being conceived as broader, invite even more to looseness of thinking. Which of you has not seen books "on social *science*" in which the "principles" laid down were now descriptive of prevailing practices, now of prevailing aims or values, now the author's notion of what people ought to do to get where *they* wanted to go, and now *his* notion of where people ought to want to get to—with the reasoning proceeding as if all these were mudpies of a single mud? What is needed is not, of course, to throw the world of Ought out of the window and concentrate exclusively upon the description of what Is. A descriptive science in the social field is not enough. Yet without a descriptive science which *describes,* we make no advance; and without keeping description uncontaminated by our desires and ideals[6] we acquire no clean-limbed descriptive science. The facts which we must investigate begin in isolated observations as to occurrences, behavior; where we can find such, they take in recurrences, regularities, patterns found in the behavior. In the second instance, and on a slightly different level, but again as given facts and as nothing else, we observe the actually prevailing concepts of what ought to happen —not our own notions of what ought to happen, but the notions which prevail among the persons being observed. One of our jobs is to note how far these prevailing notions correspond with the prevailing practices; how far, too, they influence the practices which make up our first line of observation. But obviously this observation material is not enough to *live* by, nor yet to *do* by, except for the occasional freak who only wants to know. We have to add value judgments as to where people Ought to want to go; we have to criticize both their practices and their ethics with that in view. But what we must not lose sight of (and what we are

[6] I mean just this. I do not deny that ideals are valuable, and that some arbitrary value judgments are indispensable, *to set a problem for inquiry,* nor do I deny that in good part the setting of the problem determines the observation. I do say that, *once the problem is set,* every effort must be bent on keeping observation uncontaminated by other value judgments than the desirability of finding out, of being objective and accurate, and of so recording as to invite the cross-checking of other observers. *After* the purely scientific problem has thus been solved, as far as it can be solved, *the hour of ideals and value judgments recurs.* And "as far as it can be solved" may, when need for action presses, mean before inquiry is well begun. That does not affect method.

forever losing sight of despite all "must"), is that as we move
into these value judgments we desert entirely the solid sphere of
objective observation, of possible agreement among all normal
trained observers, and enter the airy sphere of individual ideals
and subjectivity. One would have thought that as clear a stat-
ment as Merriam's of the difference between political *science* and
political *prudence* would have made further discussion of this
point unnecessary.[7] But I cannot find that it has, either in the
political disciplines, or in the economic, or in law.[aaa]

Every social science begins with an art of life, a craft, a doing
by laymen. That art, that doing, does not stop because a science
begins. The hope of the science is to inform the art from which it
has branched off and which goes on beside it. The curious thing is
that it can achieve this ideal, or indeed contribute to any others,
only by divorcing itself *temporarily* from all ideals. And what
the older approach to law writes on the sky is just this truth.

Meantime, the fusion and confusion of Is and Ought is so unnecessary. All that the social scientist need do is, in his writing,
as in his thinking, to mark off for the reader's observation and for
his own the place where his *science* ends and his *prudence* begins.
We all recognize the difference between a statement of established
facts based on a thorough investigation and a statement of the
probable or suggested facts based on a fragmentary canvass. In
the realm of fact we attempt with care to distinguish the two, and
to distinguish both from mere guesses. But when it comes to
the realm of objectives, of values, too many of us find neither
patience for nor interest in running up the red flag to mark the
place where our personal judgment, our personal preferences, our
personal hunches, our profound convictions, our intuitions of
absolute rightness, begin and where by the same token any *scientific* agreement (as distinct from the agreement of some group
upon particular ethical values) leaves off. Let me repeat. I do not
wish to suggest that a social scientist has no function to perform in
announcing his preferences and hunches and in urging, planning,
campaigning for their adoption. On the contrary, what one may
call the informed hunch of the informed man as to objectives is a

[7] MERRIAM, NEW ASPECTS OF POLITICS (1925).

[aaa] There is, for me, a disheartening flavor, among some of my own home-town
thinkers in the economic field, which seems to see price-economics (with amazing
judges in regard to the price-data) as somehow giving indication of how an economy
Ought to be run. Whereas price-economics (without judging) is merely a *descriptive*
system. Any value-judgment is intrusive. Even the description is not, today, too
hot: consider the Defense-Budget.

pearl of price. Rarely is it to be bartered for a thousand hunches of the uninformed. Despite that, I do urge that nothing could more endanger either one's own thinking or the reputation of a discipline than the putting forward of such hunches *as if they were statements of scientific truth*. Science does not teach us where to go. It never will. To fuse Is and Ought is to confuse the gradually accumulating semi-permanent data on which any *science* must rest with the flux of changing opinion as to social objectives —that welter of objectives *any* of which a science can be made to serve.

Nor will it do to shrug off this confusion of the world of Ought and the world of Is as being exclusively a problem of what one may speak of as the normative disciplines, such as law or ethics, or, for that matter, business administration, or government, or farming, or social case work. If anything, the danger may be less in the normative disciplines than elsewhere. For in the normative discipline *one* important subject of study does and must consist of the prevailing or, as the case may be, the officially accepted norms (I use norm in the ethical and not in the statistical sense). In the art of law, as in the art of procuring legislation, one major line of success lies in convincing oneself and then convincing others that the norm which he desires is in fact the right norm. With luck he can then at least secure its adoption as the official norm. Furthermore, in law at least, both in the hearings before legislative committees and in the debates in the legislature, and more particularly in the hearings before a court, an established corrective technique has been developed which in part counteracts the dangers of mistaking Ought for Is: the technique of dispute, *immediate* dispute. The opponent is there. He will fight, at once. The opponent may to a considerable extent be trusted to detect whatever error *in description* has been made through the confusion, and to give the arbiter the wherewithal to set it right.

Much less does this corrective operate in the field of scientific literature. There the dispute is not joined at once and head on; there the one claim may gain considerable acceptance before the other side is heard; there, consequently, progress with decent speed depends as much on the self-discipline of each contributor as on correction by an opponent. The aim of scientific literature is not debate, but co-operative thinking. Co-operative thinking presupposes disciplined, enlightened, deconfused co-operators [—indeed, co-operators who are not concerned in major aspect in their own careers.]

Let me recur now to the beginning: to the fact that it is the *official,* the authoritative *rules* (rules for and/or of) which have taken in the past as the subject matter for legal study. Let me develop some of the implications in new context. The relation to the fusion of Ought and Is is obvious. I need only mention again the still prevailing practice among most lawyers of looking more sharply at the rule a court purports to lay down than at the outcome of the case upon the facts. But what I wish to speak of now lies in two other aspects. First, in continuing concentration upon a single supposed key position, and second, in the matter of pseudo-deduction.

Concentration upon the one "key position" means in law concentration upon the supreme court or the legislature, upon the ultimate seat of authority. It has already been mentioned in regard to the fascination of the available and of the apparently simple. But the key-position approach is in the law peculiarly interesting in comparison with some other disciplines. It corresponds somewhat to the dynastic aproach to history. It corresponds somewhat to the economics of the enterpriser. Even more, it corresponds to a political science based exclusively upon officials and their official pronouncements. In all four cases a supposedly key position is selected as being a guide, a safe guide to the understanding of the whole. A good beginning, perhaps the best beginning. The danger lies in stopping with it. Thus we are getting away from the dynastic approach to history; increasingly doubt is being raised as to the adequacy of economics based exclusively upon the enterpriser. How much more so does the key position prove a pit, in law. In history it can at least not be denied that the leading political and military figures are in times of crisis of transcendent importance. It is recognized that we must go beyond them, but disregard them we cannot. Again and again they are the crux and source of vital change. And this is even truer, if that may be, of the enterpriser in economics. He remains still the great lever of readjustment, or re-establishment of some balance in our system at large. Both in history and in economics, moreover, a major portion of emphasis must lie upon the processes of *change.* In law, on the other hand, the focus of study is not change, but regulation; not flux, but constancy. This lies in the very nature of law's stuff. However important the rôle of legal readjustment (in regard to which both supreme courts and legislatures play their important part) the fact remains that in this discipline as contrasted with the others, readjustment is the lesser [better: the less pressing practical] problem [, so that concentration upon the "key-position" can and does take attention almost wholly off of it.] Hence, here again, the example of the older legal thinking serves as peculiarly striking and peculiarly horrible; this time, to illumine the defects of the *exclusive* "key-position" approach—in any discipline. As a cut-in, no man can quarrel with it. But half done, even in the proverb, is as far as "well begun" will take you.

Turning now to the matter of *pseudo-deduction,* we are presented in law, as in every other discipline, with the fierce distinction between a science and an art. In the work of an art, in practical creation, in the manipulation of men or institutions for any purpose, fiction enters of necessity. It must. The job cannot be done unless the new can be made most of the time to pass as being old. Inertia and its emotional consequences, the rebellion of human reason at the displacement of beloved symbols, human difficulty in grappling with ideas clothed in new symbols—these require such manipulation. If the art be not only an art, but also a dogmatic art (law, most phases of religion and ethics, much of education and business administration) fiction must not only enter, but enter unnoticed. The authoritative premises are given. The language of the constitution may not be changed at will. None the less, needs must be served. Consequent adaptation of slogans or shibboleths or formulae under the guise of "interpretation" is therefore with us. It must always be.

But in scientific writing resort to such devices means pure confusion, slows up understanding, and slows up advance. There is no excuse for it. And the only way to avoid encroachment upon science by the fiction device and the slippery thinking so necessary in the practical arts is by keeping the mind alive to the difference between the two spheres of activity. What was said above in regard to the sphere of Is and the sphere of Ought applies again, but this time as between the sphere of observation and the sphere of action, between the realm of science and the realm of the craft.

You will gather from this that my quarrel with the faulty logic indulged in by courts in their opinions is as slight as my quarrel with the faulty logic indulged in by the pseudo-systematizers of social science is great. So far as I can gather, the "systematizers" of social science have been like the legal philosophers. They have lacked the courage to be good logicians. So, too, have they lacked the patience to forego until time ripened an attempt to systematize the whole. I say they have not the courage to be good logicians.

To be a good logician requires first of all, as any mathematician knows, utterly rigorous definition of concepts, utter rigor in staying within the confines of the definitions made, a painstaking canvass for the postulates involved, a flawless concatenation of the propositions set up. Since no social thinker has yet been able to find concepts which adequately gather and box all his relevant facts, he is faced with the necessity either of arriving at deductions which are absurd on their face when applied to life, or else of playing plug-hat and wizard with his concepts, via omission or looseness of definition, via verbal manipulation of his slippery terms. This latter, for the scientist, is inexcusable. The former we have seen too little of in social science to know much of its utility.[b]

The judge, on the other hand, has as his prime duty to keep within measurable distance of filling social needs as they arise, and as his second duty to stay within the bounds of legal decency —which as the system we impose upon him stands, means keeping measurably within the tradition-hallowed formulae. He must do both at once. If his concepts come to him outmoded, he must either fall down on his job or juggle concepts. They do come to him outmoded. Let him then juggle. Like Our Lady's Tumbler in the sweet medieval tale: let him tumble and juggle reverently; let him turn upon his juggling all that is best in him and all his skill.[8] The quarrel which one has with the judges is rather that

[b] Kelsen, in law, offers the closest approach to truly courageous logical system; with, in my view a consequent almost complete sterility—save in his by-product remarks.

[8] This, with one qualification rooted in hope. The text *presupposes* the existing ideological tradition, as imposed on judges by society, and as accepted by judges and developed and reimposed by them on their successors. The elements of the tradition here concerned are (1) the notion that law is, in the main, fixed; *and fixed in words;* (2) the notion that deductive reasoning from a fixed formula is the perfection of law, always to be striven for at all costs; (3) the notion that what actually happens in the courts is reasonably consistent with the supposed fact of (1) and the supposed ideal of (2). But I am rather firmly of opinion that this tradition is capable of change. Society caused it, but I doubt that modern society will prevent its alteration. Supreme courts operate at a sufficient remove from life and in an atmosphere sufficiently protected by respect so that a change in judicial technique, though consciously undertaken by the judges, would effectively remake the tradition of what constitutes legal decency. Within wide limits we look today to the judges to tell us what legal decency is, rather than imposing our ideas on them.

And a change in the tradition is called for, if the ideology of courts is to be geared to their work. Holmes has again and again insisted on the inevitable legislative power of judges and the need for its intelligent use. Brandeis has spoken by action, piling up facts to justify or persuade to decision. Cardozo (especially in THE NATURE OF THE JUDICIAL PROCESS, 1921) has been peculiarly effective in giving cur-

they do not play sleight-of-hand enough or, better, that their sleight-of-hand is too often uninspired routine; is not always lit by passionate, conscious battle with the problem of ends and purposes which presents itself before honest juggling can begin.

---

rency to the idea that interstitial legislative work by the judges is legitimate. In constitutional matters the truth is easiest to see, because the official formula remains verbally fixed over decades or centuries. In private law, on the other hand, as soon as sufficient change has occurred to strike attention, a re-formulation of "the" rule on the new base is common—which obscures further legislation by making discrepancies less obvious. Yet constitutional law insists in our system on taking much of the flavor of its technique from private law. A change in the private law tradition would therefore react at once and in double measure on the constitutional side, just as the continuance of the outworn private law tradition of thought now cripples constitutional judgment.

Meantime the innovators themselves (innovators be it noted, merely in theory; innovators merely in stating the existing practice to be what it is) have happened to fall upon phrasing which puts an unfortunate obstacle in the way of their own views (as, indeed, it has hampered somewhat their own perception of their own position) by treating judicial legislation in the main *as if it involved abandonment of precedent*. (Especially Cardozo, *ibid.*, ch. IV.) Occasionally it does. Much more often and more importantly, it does not. The trouble is that this same traditional ideology (as a fourth element) moves still along the lines that each case holds or stands for *one single rule*, its *"ratio decidendi."* (This concept is nowhere better presented than in A. L. Goodhart, *Determining the* Ratio Decidendi *of a Case*, 40 YALE L. J. 161 ff. (1930); nor has any body of material been brought together which better shows the utter hopelessness of such a notion of "the" *ratio decidendi* to describe or cope with precedent-in-practice.) *Ratio decidendi* in this sense means "what a case stands for *after* its decision, and with respect to future cases." In fact the case stands not for one thing, but for a wide choice of things. In fact the established and honorable judicial theory and practice of precedent covers, includes, techniques for narrowing or evading, techniques for extending, techniques for shifting direction, as well as techniques for staying put. Yet the particular symbol "precedent" or *"stare decisis"* calls up (even to Cardozo) chiefly connotations of standing pat upon the past, of refusing to open up the policy questions in the new case (cf. the three elements of traditional ideology, *supra*). *Change*, on the other hand, calls up connotations of upsetting traditional technique, upsetting expectations, endangering stability. This is as regrettable as it is misleading. It confines the NAME *stare decisis* to a single one among the many phases that doctrine takes in action. In fact our case law is, and has always been, in constant process of change. *And in fact the change has been brought about, let me repeat, by the process known as "standing" on precedent, stare decisis.* You must know where you want to go in the case in hand before you *can* utilize the precedents effectively. They can limit you, before you decide, but they cannot deprive you of choice. A decision on policy remains inescapable, because the precedents are multiform, ambiguous, *never* fixed; and because the tradition-hallowed techniques for dealing with them (*wholly within the "principle" of stare decisis*) permit you to squeeze out of the same set of precedents any one of a dozen *different* conclusions or rules. The only thing gained by pretending that to abide by precedent is to cut out questions of policy is, on occasion, the saving of effort and the evasion of responsibility as you make a blind decision on policy instead of an intelligent one. But the effect is effort which should not be saved, and the responsibility is responsibility which it is the judge's job to face. Wise choice of policy is his function.

The only other quarrel would be that, juggling too often *un-awares,* they may be dupes of their own magic of yesterday, dupes of the game instead of its masters, and sometimes fail in their job because the wizard's hat they play before the multitude seems even to themselves to bring forth rabbits, white or pied, by some spontaneous generation.

III

Flaws in the older legal thinking go hand in hand with virtues. Not only its weaknesses but its strengths offer suggestions for social science. Here, too, the hints from the law may be found elsewhere. Here, too, one wonders whether they are set anywhere in bolder type.

The emphasis on rules and, in our own case law, the particular emphasis on the derivation of rules from case-to-case decision, forces particular attention to the *problem of induction.* The common drama in the doubtful case presents two lawyers dealing with precisely the same body of data, two lawyers arguing vigorously, each for a rule which will contradict the other's rule in its application to the case in hand. Yet each urges that the rule he contends for is necessarily contained in, necessarily derivable from, indeed the one necessary conclusion from that single set of opinions and decisions under discussion by both. This situation reaches its extreme when there is only a single case in point, and when that case is not quite on all fours with the case in dispute. There then unfolds impressively the trickiness of generalizing from the single instance. Be it as to the direction in which the

---

I do not of course mean that judges are free. I mean that the leeway which strict "adherence to precedent" has always allowed is infinitely greater than the current conscious ideology (in contra-distinction to the standard going judicial practices) gives any inkling of. The result is that we profit by the leeway only some of the time, not all; we profit therefore by the judges' wisdom on whether to change or not and if so, in what direction, only some of the time, not all. But once the leeway is seen, once demonstrated from the *work* of respected courts with precedents to be *constantly* present, it may be hoped, sooner or later, to make the conscious facing of the policy questions difficult to escape. It may be hoped, even, to lessen word-juggling in the opinions by lessening the pretense that the precedents are firm and sure. Word-juggling becomes unnecessary when judges *know* what they have been *doing.*—The demonstration is not hard, and I hope shortly to attempt it. The line of argument is sketched in THE BRAMBLE BUSH, chs. IV, V; in the Symposium (at pp. 87 ff.) cited in footnote 2, p. 90; and in Adler's insistence (*ibid.,* p. 105), on the pluralistic character of any system of positive law—but peculiarly of a case law system. Especially illuminating is A. L. Corbin, *Contracts for the Benefit of Third Persons,* 40 L. Q. REV. 12 (1930). [THE COMMON LAW TRADITION—DECIDING APPEALS has finally provided the demonstration above referred to.]

generalization is to run, be it with reference to its extent, the needle swings to the will.[9] But the problem is not ousted, it is merely reduced in scope, when one has half a dozen or more cases to base his induction. I have been tempted to formulate the experience somewhat as follows: Every social phenomenon is multiguous when viewed in itself. It shifts color, shape, light, meaning, as you turn it. But before it can be made a datum for use in an inductive process it must first be frozen into one fixed shape. You can attempt induction only from *fixed* data, data fixed at least for the purpose in hand. To fix the data you must be arbitrary: as given in nature, they are not fixed, they cannot be. And the manner of your thus freezing the data will condition your resulting induction. In the manner of the freezing the conclusion lies concealed. More, commonly you must not only freeze but weight your data, before you can proceed. The weighing, too, conditions your result. This is as true of the data of observed behavior as it is of the records of judicial decision. And it is trite. But I know few trite things more often overlooked. And few more tricky.

Hand in hand with induction goes *deduction*. And here a social scientist can learn as well from the lawyer's art as he can from the physical scientist. Every dispute on a point of law involves in the first instance hypothetical thinking in purely deductive terms. "*If* this is the rule of law, *then* it dictates the outcome in this case which favors me." The case should be and commonly is lost if there is any flaw in this portion of the reasoning. And to that extent it is fair to describe this set-up as the legal hypothesis of the argument. The beauty of the legal situation, almost unique among social phenomena, is that it brings out so clearly the *hypothetical* character of applying the deductive process. There is *always* an opponent setting up a similar hypothesis which leads to a flatly contradictory result. The hypothetical character of the reasoning must stand clear to any man with eyes. The crux of the matter becomes inducing the court to accept the major premise set up. But the legal argument is in this like any piece of social research: that unless it *begins* with an adequate hypothesis for *orientation* it can lead somewhere only by accident. The hypothesis, the *preliminary deductive* thinking, is an utter essential to intelligent advance.

Hand in hand with this (and forced on the attention of the legal thinker peculiarly by the necessity to which I have already

[9] See Oliphant, *supra* note 2, at 71, 159.

referred, of using fictions and sloppy logic in the practical application of any dogmatic art) goes recognition of the dangers of loose definitions of concepts. Here, I suppose, social science has sinned more vigorously than any other modern field of thought. Some of the reasons I have discussed above. The phenomena to be integrated, if integration be tried on any large scale, escape any conceptual system which has yet been set up. But that does not deny the utility of *orientation via conceptual systems* built on a less ambitious scale. Until one wrestles with the problem of putting the entirety of the available information together, the bearings of one segment of information on another must elude the grasp. The superciliousness now manifest among social scientists toward logical development of concepts is based not at all upon any disutility of systems, but upon their hopeless misuse by armchair book-builders to whom the card-castling of a System was a last word, an end in itself, a truth free of all need to check up the hypothetical conclusion. But the framing of concepts and the integration of a conceptual system for the purpose of finding out where we are at, as a preliminary to seeing whither we are to go next—that will remain eternally necessary to scientific advance. And at this point the process of argument in court, or the judicial process, affords in the rival claims of the opposing lawyers a clarity of appreciation forced upon few other men as to the weasel ways of verbal symbols, as to the need for rigorous definition, the need for hunting postulates to their foul holes and yanking them out into brutal, healthy sun, the need for step-by-step reasoning which stays at every step within the premises as defined, whenever one sets about any such integration. Let me, at whatever risk, say this again: without rigid definition of concepts no hypothesis which means anything is possible, and without a hypothesis which *unambiguously* means *one* thing, attempted observation or research into new data or old is somewhere between 90 and 95 per cent waste motion. Granted—as is granted above—that the hypothesis conditions observation, and so is dangerous. Granted—as is granted above—that the shaping and fixing (partly by the hypothesis) of the multicolored data in turn conditions the conclusion, and so is dangerous again. The fact remains. Without the unambiguous hypothesis, no advance. Between perils, the path. From which derives that fundamental of science: only the gift of posing meaningful hypothesis leads anywhere. Poet first, then workman; artist, then patient artisan. The one, alone, is like to be a liar, though he lie in beauty, though he lie our dreams. The other, lone, is blind grub. He who is both may hope to be a scientist.

Another point which the legal conceptual structure brings out with force is an essential pluralism in the nature of any system of ideas which is socially given, that is, of any systematization either of the existing prevailing ideas or of the existing prevailing practices in a complex society. Neither practices nor ideas nor society can be harmonious. They are a welter of divergent tendencies with divergent implications; unity in the whole spells out not harmony, but balance. Pluralism is thus inevitable in descriptive presentation of things social. Much of the reason for the lasting ambiguity of such terms as capital, instinct, culture area, is based upon this *given* pluralism in the organization of the stuff which men desire to cram into a single term.

Yet if I were to pick out the biggest single message which the orthodox approach to law voices to social science, it would be *the importance of concepts.*

First, the importance of concepts to observation, the foundation of science: the concrete demonstration in heaped-up recorded experience of the truth announced by the metaphysicians that you see in terms of your own eyes, observe in terms of your own prior thinking; approach a fresh set of phenomena to see not what is there, in point either of existence or of arrangement or of working interrelation, but to see *almost* exclusively that which you are looking for, and to see *almost* exclusively in terms of the categories with which you start to look. One thing that drives this home in law[10] is the comparison of the state of information actually before a court with the "statement of facts" in that "opinion" of the judge which crowns the controversy on appeal. Writing with a result in mind, the judge picks, leaves, emphasizes, slights, even twists, the facts as an actor builds a character out of the raw material of his face. Writing (and thinking, seeing, judging) with a set of legal rules and categories as the tradition-given scaffolding of his expression, the judge finds certain facts legally "material"; he is alert for them. He finds certain other facts legally "immaterial," and dulls his eye. Hence (often in the measure of his skill) your

[10] Another is the way that cases leap into line to "sustain" the position of one's client, and the relative trouble which a lawyer then has in even *seeing* other possible interpretation. Still another is the amazing diversity in analysis of the same problem or material when two able young graduates of say Columbia or Yale (modernistic, heterodox, realist) and of Harvard (more orthodox) are working together in the same office [Differences of importance among recent graduates of different schools remain, still, striking, in their lines of analysis.]

judge presents you with a *selected distortion* of the facts which were before him, *as if they were the whole.* He looks, and sees. But what he sees is not what is before his eyes. Much that is there he does not see at all. What he does see he sees not in terms of life, or love, or holes-in-one; not in terms of wage-earning or investment; of stimulus-response, Gestalt-configuration, claustrophobia; but in terms of tradition-molded *legal categories* whose existence, shape, and meaning are a part of him as he observes. This is or is not "a contract" or a "trust." The facts take meaning only as they bear on that culture-conditioned intellectual artifact: the legal concept. To which is to be added the judge as artist, and the artist's triumphant disregard of detail he finds non-significant. Thus the judge's selection among facts (as indeed the lawyer's, in the initial preparation of "the case") illumines the selective process for any thinker, but illumines it with a documented profusion you will find it hard to match. Nowhere is this so clear as when more than one opinion is delivered in the same case. Everywhere it is present. Please note that I do not criticize it. It is inevitable. Here again the test for when it is good, when bad, escapes objective statement. The distortion must be significant, *so significant that its effect is true.*[11] This calls in scientist or in judge for the poet, for the seer. In the posing of problems, subjectivity remains. On the other hand, something the investigator can do, to counter-act the inevitable. He can be aware of it. He can *try* to be awake for data which make initial categories look silly, make his hypothesis look non-significant, make his observations to date call for the junk-pile. For concepts do not *wholly* condition observation—else we could never add to what we know. And he who knows their power holds a key which may bring him escape.

The rôle of concepts extends much further than merely to the influencing of a scientist's observation. Law affords illustration, too, e.g., of the necessary rôle of concepts in any type of conscious social pressure. In this law is to be distinguished from the simpler learning processes, or from those indirect pressures which function, for example, by way of suggesting imitation of a prevailing way or set of ways of doing. Most teaching (as opposed to learning), on the other hand, and any social pressure which is consciously directed at a delinquent or at one who varies from the accepted ways, presupposes recognition by the persons exerting the pressure of some discrepancy in the behavior from the conceptual picture

[11] CARDOZO, LAW AND LITERATURE, par 7 (1930).

that they hold as to what in the circumstances is proper and right. So with the law. And *a fortiori* concepts play into and condition any type of mobilization or direction of pressure by a number of persons; if it requires communication, it requires concepts.

The mutually contradictory character of those concepts which are socially given—the matter spoken of above as pluralism—and the almost inevitable looseness of definition of such concepts appear also with peculiar force in law. And as with pseudo-deduction, one must distinguish sharply the utility of such mutual contradictions and of such loose definition to an *art* on the one hand and to a *science* on the other. Loose, inaccurate, and partial summations of much experience are valuable in an art even though no one of them is complete, even though their totality is never self-consistent. They call up to the craftsman a body of material for which he needs a convenient symbol and summary. The presence of an opposing and inconsistent symbol and summary of another, different body of experience, so far from being in the way, is in most aspects an advantage. Still water grows stagnant. A rolling stone gathers no moss. Two such summations, for all their inconsistency, are an advance. *They narrow the range of possibilities* to be considered. What is needed in addition to the two summations is, for a science, the search for quantitative comparison of the possibilities, together with the search for some discriminating factors over at least a part of the material. Pending that, what is needed is the intangible something we know as hunching-power, or skill, or judgment, in determining when to call on which summation. More often than not the *craftsman* himself at the moment of use wholly overlooks the presence of the nonapplicable slogan. His doing is better than his rationalization. But no lesson of the law is more vital to social science than recognition that work, useful work, skilful work *in the art* by means of such a self-inconsistent system of concepts and propositions is no sign of the existence of a *science* which will satisfy the observer. Thus the eternally self-inconsistent set of precepts— concepts and propositions: rules—in law does *not* describe the behavior of courts, nor yet of people. And the self-inconsistent set of concepts and propositions of the psychoanalysts describes the behavior neither of the psychoanalysts nor of their subjects. Proverbs, again, for all the wisdom that they contain, cannot be put into a consistent arrangement which describes human action. The same holds throughout the realm of social life. It holds more particularly (and this is of particular interest to the social scientist) as to *any* ordinary active man's description of what he does, when contrasted with what the same man does in truth. So of the business man, so of the politician, so of the statesman, so of the ethnological subject, when interviewed. *Their accounts do not describe their actions.* Their ideology does not accurately reflect their current doing. Their accounts are partial, they are selective, they are cast in terms of their current ideology, which is at best the ideology of an art, not a scientist's ideology; and which is commonly enough molded on practices of a generation back. Such accounts by the doer are not, for this reason, to be neglected. But they are, for this reason, not to be believed without examination.

From which follows directly, *inter alia,* the untrustworthiness of the most careful of questionnaires, no matter how skilfully built, no matter how honestly filled out. *If the filling out is left to the unsupervised work of the questionee.* I do not reason from this that questionnaires may not be useful, if they are non-suggestive in their question set-up, if they are skilfully planned, especially if they ask for concrete items, for cases of experience. I do reason that a questionnaire filled out by the inquirer, and by an inquirer trained to ask for such concrete incidents, not merely for opinions, tendencies, or values (a questionnaire, i.e., which serves as a guide to inquiry and observation and serves as well for the assuring of complete and comparable records) is likely to be worth nine times as much as any questionnaire filled out merely by the subjects of the questioning.

Closely connected with the foregoing is a suggestion for which the opinions of judges again afford more cogent support than almost any other coherent body of material. That is, the process of rationalization and the relative merits of rationalization and action. Any social scientist can profit by the conclusions to be derived therefrom: namely, first, that reasons given for action are rarely an adequate explanation of the action; second (so often overlooked by those who perceive the first), that reasons given for action today will become a factor in influencing action tomorrow; and third, that action is with considerable regularity wiser than the reasons given therefor, just as in the main institutions are vastly wiser than the reasoning of their apologists.

IV

It would not be proper to close what might be construed as an attack on the orthodox legal technique without giving voice to a firm conviction, one closely related to what has just been said as to the relative wisdom of rationalizations and of action. By and large, for all the slipperiness of logic, for all the hide-bound verbalism occasionally found among the judges, the fact remains that on the private law side the work of appellate judges has been amazingly adequate to the needs of the community. (Of the lower courts I cannot speak: we do not know. We doubt.) Social science students have their attention so largely and so vigorously fixed upon the peculiarities of our own constitutional system that their reactions on isolated constitutional decisions tend to set their picture of the work of the appellate bench entire. Nothing could be less true to fact. Nothing could be more of a distortion. Even on the constitutional side it may fairly be argued that the attention of social science students turns almost exclusively upon the sore thumbs in the law.[c]

But law is more than sore thumbs; it is a going whole. Yet see. If a desirable statute is upheld, that fact passes as a matter of course. Whatever wisdom the court exercises is taken for granted, sinks out of sight, is honored by burial, by oblivion. But to the court's mistakes [whether real or imagined] the trumpets blare. And blare again. I do not quarrel with this. The court has need of it. Yet if a scientist is interested in his perspective he must [, even when a mistake may be real and deep,] look to the rest of the court's work as well. Excavations among the legal records as on ancient sites will yield their buried treasure, and without stint. The somewhat astounding achievement of making a document a century and a half old meet the needs of a community which insists upon retaining the document in substantially its ancient verbal form, despite a tenfold expansion of territory, despite a twentyfold expansion of population, despite the shattering onset of an industrial order, seems by non-legal critics to be taken almost without comment. A word for Marshall, who died before industrialism had begun. A word for Marshall—and then silence. And this although it may fairly be said that such a minor change in our judicial machinery as making declaration of unconstitutionality require a vote of seven judges would eliminate three-quarters of the current criticism, so few are the instances on which that criticism rests. Let me be clear. I share the criticism. I sputter scorn and dismay into the trumpet, as do

---

[c] Today—always with the usual emphasis on the Supreme Court—it is other people who are finding their thumbs sore. But the point of the text remains.

you.[d] But I would have you, as reasonable accountants, tot up the credit column before you judge the net worth of the judges' work.

Meantime, what does this examination of the legal tradition come to—this survey of the time-honored ideology which has both helped and hindered the judges at their labors? I have spoken of a new approach to law as a social science, as a matter of behavior to be seen, recorded, and studied as we see and record the work of men in industry. I have contrasted with this the traditional approach to law in terms of rules, official rules, the rules laid down by the supreme authorities within the state. From the contrast I have sought to draw suggestion: the threat of the available; the threat from apparent simplicity; the dangers of confusing Is and Ought, and the way in which, when unconfused, they can be made to serve each other; the fallacy of concentrating forever upon the one supposedly key position; the utility of pseudo-deduction in an art, but its danger to a science; the caution to be observed when one (as he must) freezes data arbitrarily, for his induction from them; the need of concept-building and of systematization of concepts, to orient thinking and to frame hypothesis for further study; the barrenness of investigation not oriented by an hypothesis and by one which has a single meaning; and finally, the effects of prior concepts—be they consciously built up or not—and of the hypothesis itself, in conditioning (at times in crippling) observation.

As a last word, this: again a suggestion of method. The matters above discussed turn neither upon an analysis of the orthodox approach to law alone, nor yet upon an analysis, alone, of the now growing realistic approach. They turn upon a view of the one from the standpoint of the other; upon climbing outside of one aspect of thought for purposes of looking back into it, without at the same time kicking the mind free of what that aspect has to offer. In intellectual life as in civilization, and within each discipline as between disciplines, the contact of cultures is the blow of flint on steel.

[d] This speaks as of 1931. I have no such scorn, dismay or criticism with reference to the results of the Supreme Court decisions of the '40's and the '50's, though I do think the judicial method of these later years can be improved. See THE COMMON LAW TRADITION, esp. 384 ff. (The text there contains by accident a reflection on Mr. Justice Douglas which has no basis, which I withdraw, and for which I apologize.)

{ 4 }

FRANK'S LAW AND THE MODERN MIND [a]

This book excites. It is keen, cogent, well-integrated. Its range is wide. Its grasp is sure. It is well-nigh unique in attempting exploration of emotional drives and genetic psychology for their contribution to our understanding of the ways of law. Rarely[aa] in legal literature has prior writing been handled with such critical insight. Frank makes a striking contribution to that neglected and important field: general jurisprudence. The contribution comes from a practicing lawyer, a practical lawyer. It is realistic in the best sense of the word. That has high value for jurisprudence. It reminds anyone who cares to be reminded that law may still be made a study of man and society. And that may have a certain value for the Bar. In its eager attack on the illusion of complete certainty it under-emphasizes what certainty there is; in its perception of the importance of particulars it well-nigh denies the importance of generals. But what of that? Are pathfinders to have no prerogative of exaggeration?

The argument: That law can and should be simple and certain and invariable (the author seems to use "certain" and "invariable" as almost interchangeable), is lay belief and settled legal dogma. It is a bad myth for the lawyer: the layman will curse him for injustices if he fails to change the law, and curse him for breach of duty if he does. He is damned by one litigant, in any event, and out of his own mouth. Meanwhile, the idea itself is false. It is the basic myth of law. Myth, but basic. It colors all legal operations. Yet change in law, more or less sharp, is constant. Else, with

[a] From 31 COLUM. L. REV. 82 (1931).
[aa] And never again, in J. Frank's writings.

changing conditions, law would be intolerable. Lawyers, in a word, are inveterate prey to common-sense-in-action, followed by rationalization which outrages common sense. All this is honest, for most lawyers, most of the time. It is not lie, but myth: *self-deception.* The change in law, to repeat, is needed. But the myth of immutability must be perceived neither to produce immutability, nor to be serviceable; it but obscures, embarrasses, encumbers the process of adjustment. It obscures and embarrasses in the interest of making rules *seem* to continue, verbally. "Certainty" is supposed by the myth makers thereby to be attained. But law is in fact what law does. What law does is decision of cases. And it helps lawyers and laymen little *in their predicting,* that rules are preserved in verbal fixity, if results wobble and shift. "Certainty" with meaning is predictability in fact. The legal fundamentalism ("Bealism") of principle supposed to exist above and beyond decision has little connection with life. It assumes that "law must be" something that decisions are in fact not. It is related intimately to Platonic abstractions. Its "certainty" is a certainty in a non-factual world. So, too, the syllogistic reasoning which derives from it obscures change by hidden manipulation of major or minor premise, by manipulation of verbal symbols. Uncertainty of decision in the world of fact is not wiped out thereby. (All this, one may be certain, the author would argue with equal vigor as to the supposedly "fixed" rules of codes, if they should come in question.) Now this illusion of certainty—clung to with the clutch of the drowning by professionals and laymen alike, clung to in the face of the evidence—is present in law peculiarly, and *far more than elsewhere.*

All this holds for the work of the judge. He judges backward: Conclusion first. Rationalization to follow. Nor is this talk that the great bulk of the action of courts presents "mere routine application of accepted rules" to be allowed to deceive. We cannot tell from the reports what has been routine, and what has not. The judge's selection, stress and arrangement of "the facts" can make the most peculiar case look like routine. We know from life that most cases are, before this fact-manipulation begins, peculiar. Manipulation—nay, perception—of "the facts" is all-important; judges, like witnesses, *observe* differently according to temperament and circumstances. Judges read the evidence they get with an eye to their views of justice; "the facts" take shape in court in the light of the result to be achieved. Not rules, then, but likeness among the reactions of the judges, is the source and hope of any uniformity of "law," *i.e.,* any uniformity in *decision.* The road to partial consistency is to be found not in further word-be-clouded illusion as to the importance of "rule" and "principle," but—as with the natural scientist—in study of and wrestling with the problem of eliminating, to the degree possible, individual subjective factors. Yet the whole approach of the lawmen has been and is, instead, to scout and shrink from the very possibility that it is the judge and not the rule that does the deciding of cases, to hide from seeing that "law" and "discretion" are inseparable. Even Gray saw in law only rules. Not so Holmes: "what the courts will *do,* in fact." Holmes is the true prophet. *The law of any case is what the judge decides*—decisions, not rules. (Through here the author builds also on Bingham,[1] Walter Wheeler Cook, Leon Green, Keyser.) Hence the concern of judges with the illusory task of laying down new rules to guide future cases does little but trouble present litigants. Meantime the jury presents, in the general verdict, the crowning example of the futility of the certainty-illusion; what is certain there is only the mouthing of a ritual and the total impossibility that the ritual will seriously influence the result. Only an emotional *need,* a desperately strong emotional need, to continue in illusion can explain our practice in the matter. Thus the argument.

Thus far, too, the author's exposition is clear, his buttressing material impressive, his argument essentially sound. Not less so his attack on Pound's attempt to divide "property" and "commercial law" from "human conduct" and the "conduct of enterprises" as fields in which fixed rules and discretion are supposedly, respectively in order. (Though this does not touch Pound's underlying insight into the presence, and need, of divergent degrees of

[1] Frank chides me gently for not having cited Bingham in my article *Realistic Jurisprudence,* 30 Colum. L. Rev. 431 (1930) (which, however, appeared too late to come under his fire in detail). I had thought of that article as rather obviously purporting only to give a more rounded picture of the bearings of a point of view well-known as the common working equipment of a goodly number of thinkers. It did not occur to me that any misconstruction of the purpose of the paper was possible. To remedy the difficulty as far as may be, let me here acknowledge specifically that my paper was built on the published work and private discussion (in addition to Holmes, from whom we all derive, and Sumner and Max Weber to whom I am peculiarly indebted) of Corbin, Cook, U. Moore, Oliphant, L. Frank, John Dewey, J. R. Commons, and the Boas school; and that Sturges, Max Radin, Yntema, and Leon Green had preceded and Jerome Frank paralleled me in many points in print. Even on my own assumptions, however, Frank is wholly right as to Bingham. Bingham had pioneered and had worked through to ripe conclusions at a time when the other legal writers named—Holmes and Weber excepted—were still in the earlier stages of struggling free of rules, and I can only regret having failed to acclaim that in my article.

fluidity in various divergent types of cases which may some day be adequately defined.) Not less so, either, is his critique of Jhering, Cardozo, Cook, Dickinson, Green, and Bingham.

But this is for the author not enough. He wishes to do more than establish the existence of a basic legal myth and its family of myth-children, and more than show the results of their prevalence. He wishes to explain the why of the disease, and to indicate the manner of its cure. So that he would regard my presentation of the argument, above, as an emasculation. Yet there is reason for the emasculation. It will not do for this book by any accident to fail of its accomplishment merely because the intrusions of psychoanalytic borrowing may fail to persuade. *Cut them out, and the book still stands.*[aaa]

Is there then any need to cut them out? This part of the author's argument runs somewhat as follows: The illusion of certainty is so strongly and peculiarly present in the law that it must answer to some vital need. No *practical* need appears which is strong enough to explain the phenomenon. Practicality, indeed, requires change as well as stability. Indeed, the very stability and security which we need in a changing society is (Demogue) *dynamic* security quite as well as static. But we find neither myth nor current ideology nor even current recognition, of change. One major cause of this lopsidedness of illusion—all toward certainty—may be found in the nature and growth-process of children. Here is a *recurrent* factor, recurrent in every lawyer, every layman, every generation. No way has yet been discovered to produce adults from the egg. The child yearns for his pre-natal serenity. He finds something approaching it in the family. His father becomes the embodiment of power and stability, on which he relies, which he "worships." Discovery of his father's limitations destroys the reliance; it does not destroy the need. In his rôle of the object from which satisfaction of the stability-need was expected, the father replaces the womb, God and the law replace the father. The need being emotional, deep-seated, often unconscious, *intellectual* maturity does not displace it. The human mind, granted such a need, is adept at putting bridges of rationalization between the illusion which makes the need seem satisfied and any unpleasant countervailing facts or experiences. Other facts, such as the nature of

---

[aaa] Frank wrote me, on the basis of a MS. of this review, that I had showed a curious empathy; and we collaborated on the reply to Pound. But the very choice by him of the folk we would each study—p. 48, above—indicates the then unnoticed lines of divergence.

language (Ogden and Richards) enter to help and ease the process of rationalization. Plato's reification of abstractions represented a flight from the intolerable uncertainty of his predecessors. So with "fixity" in the law: uncertainty is conjured out of consciousness by way of words. And this is again strengthened by other trends in the child: his phantasy and wishful thinking; his assumption of a coherent, orderly, satisfying universe; his employment of the former to produce the latter—inside his own head (Piaget). But neither word-consciousness nor an understanding of the logic and method of science are enough to effect a cure. What is needed is *emotional* adulthood, a zest in uncertainty and adventure, a pleasure in instead of a flight from the "pain of suspension"; to which word consciousness and scientific method can then be added as tools, to usher in the era of realism in the law. This is not mere cry for a change of heart, since even in the child the dynamic tendency is present as well as the static. It is capable of conscious development, in child and adult-in-years alike.

One's first reaction to this is amazement. How is it possible for the canny student who discriminates so skilfully the proved from the dubious when reading a legal writer to swallow at a gulp a yearning for pre-natal serenity which is not only unproved but unprovable? How can the same mind which cuts through rule and *legal* concept to bare decision accept as dogmatic Must-Be's such stereotyped psychoanalytic concepts as womb-yearning, father-omnipotence, father-substitution, law as the father-substitute—accept them as applying not to *some* persons, but to almost all. The basic fallacy of whole-hog psychoanalytic theory is the assumption that what may well be possibly or even probably *often* true is always or almost always true. May be; but, pending proof, the man who has learned the unreliability of generalizations in the law can best remain skeptical. I recognize the unwisdom and unfairness of talking in the loose about "the psychoanalysts" or "psychoanalytic theorizing." I recognize that a strong case can be made for psychoanalytic hypotheses and concepts as very useful "as if" concepts which help the user in dealing with concrete situations, and so as somewhat related to the theories and concepts, say, of modern physics. Yet I stand to my position, as to their utility for the outsider. They are to be handled with gloves and circumspection. Few indeed even of the psychoanalytic writers or thinkers recognize these concepts and theories *habitually* as fictions. Few indeed recognize their essential difference from the fictional concepts of physics. The concepts of physics are very carefully defined, and are used with a sustained effort at consistency with *all* relevant observation. The psychoanalytic concepts are *not* carefully defined, and are regularly inconsistent with a great body of relevant observation, and are available *in mutual inconsistency* for "application" to concrete situations or for "explanation" of such situations. They are, in this, subject to all the ambiguity and uncertainty which Frank himself castigates in "rules of law" and which all careful legal thinkers have pointed out in legal maxims. Only art, experience, "judgment," give the wherewithal to determine when to turn to which. (Which is why psychoanalytic therapeutics and legal practice so far outrun their respective dogmatics.) This means that they are rich sources of suggestion, condensations of *much* experience. As such those noted above have value in this present book. It means simultaneously that they are untrustworthy *bases* of building—condensations of only *some* experience which is *not* typical of all. And untrustworthy they prove themselves in this book by distorting at times even the author's *observation* of legal phenomena.

For all this, there is solidity in much of the author's argument. It *is* demonstrated that withdrawal of support from the newborn leads to squalling. It *is* demonstrated that *one* tendency of children is early and heavy setting of habits, objection to their interruption, and a strong demand for certainty. It *is* strongly suggested that the conditions of language-learning favor the fresh growth in every generation of word-magic. It *is* certain that the personality models immediately at hand, and especially the father, are commonly looked to as authority-sources, as endowed with powers and wisdom beyond the lot of man, and that there commonly develops in the child a dependence and reliance on these persons for security, which is slow to pass, and which can often be observed to transfer. It *is* demonstrated that wishful thinking and thought-systematization apart from reality are also characteristic of the child-mind. It would be strange if these factors were without important effect on adults who began as children, and on the law which the adults shape.

It would be unjust to Frank, moreover, to take the setup of his argument and emphasis as proclaiming father-substitution to be *the* important spring of the illusion of certainty. I risk suspecting that underneath he has a half-belief that it is. But he is very careful in several places expressly to negate claiming for it either exclusive causation, or constant or even dominant causation at all times. (One wishes that he had been equally careful to point out the fictional character of the concept itself.) However, there is little question that the gain he achieves by deliberate over-emphasis of this factor, to drive it home to his reader, is bought at a price in the occasional skewing of his own observation.

Skewing is present in a number of points. Law, in the sense of decision, is in fact much more predictable, and hence more certain, than his treatment would indicate. In his very proper enthusiasm for illusion-smashing he paints the illusion as somewhat more illusive than it is. For while we may properly proclaim that general propositions do not decide concrete cases, we none the less must recognize that *ways* of deciding, *ways* of thinking, *ways* of sizing up facts "in terms of their legal relevance" are distinctly enough marked in our courts so that we can know a lawman, by his judg-ing-reactions, from a layman. It is not merely decisions, but de-cisions *in this setting* of their semirregularity, which make up the core of law. Somewhat similarly as to certainty to the layman. *Real* certainly is not *real* stability. Nor is it true that what law a layman does not know is immaterial to his planning. To the extent that *when the court is called upon* its judgment will jump with the layman's prior non-legal expectation, that layman can plan safely, counting on the law, although without knowing it. In a régime of change, *certainty* in law is attained whenever change in the judges' ways moves in step and pace with changes in the ways— and so in the expectations—of the relevant laymen. Certainty fails for most laymen, whatever the fixity of the formula, when the judge's reaction fails to jump with the change in laymen's ways, and only then. For the professional lawyer, so far as he is relying on a verbalistic ideology, the case is almost the reverse. Certainty for the one is uncertainty for the other. "Stability," for either, exists despite any change, if the change goes unperceived. And of the outcome of future decisions at their best Carter's saying as to custom holds: "more and better than known—felt." This—like the unconscious expanding power of words in a legal formula, at the impact of the *slightly* novel fact set-up—is of importance to Frank's problem, for it goes far to explain why the law often *seems* fixed even in its flux, not by fiction, nor yet by myth, but by the pragmatic test of fulfilled expectations. The new which suits appears as if it *had* always been. The point, finally, strengthens Frank's position that open-eyed judicial change means greater *real* certainty—at least for laymen. And for lawyers as soon as they learn a reasonably open-eyed technique of prediction.

Certain further remarks to Frank's main theme: "Why the illusion?" It seems to me rather clear that one important factor in producing the illusion is the notion that law is *right,* coupled with the equally vigorous notions that right is very permanent, and that there *can* be in a given situation only one right answer. But these notions inhere pretty largely in the nature of men-in-groups (apparently by virtue chiefly of those tendencies which lead to habit and to the limitations of any in-group outlook). This factor would seem to have roots separate from, and quite as vital as, psychoanalytic motivations. Moreover, when the question arises why law *in particular* should be the victim of an overdose of certainty-illusion, I should be tempted to argue that law is a phase of the control machinery of society, and in the main a stabilizing phase. That is its office, society being what it is. What moves less often, less fast, and wobbles in its moving less than things about it, must tend to seem at rest with reference to them. I do not suggest that traditionalism was consciously introduced into law for any such practical purposes; but I would argue that traditionalism has persisted in law more strongly than elsewhere partly (and this is bad) because the law is not *directly* in contact with the checkup of hard fact, but works at one remove from business, which itself works at one remove from things. But partly (and this has virtue) because one great value of law lies precisely in opposing and braking change; in choosing late among experiments, after they have competed long enough to afford a better guess at which of them is best; in crystallizing the experiments chosen as the new and solid basis for new experiments, which then can work from a common foundation. Law's precise office is not change, but to prevent change; or when that will not do, then to adjust with the least possible rearrangement to the new conditions. Obviously this job of conservation is overdone, much overdone, as things stand. The machinery for gradual readjustment should be consciously improved. But the question is: Why the illusion of certainty? And I should answer, because (at least in part) even adventurous spirits want some footing to adventure from. That need is practical. I am not persuaded that it depends on a transfer of father-dependence.

Similarly with the minor question: Why no ideology of *constant* change? Laymen do not want *constant* change. They want such particular change as they want, and they want the particular new basis then to continue without further change: to have a pleasant foundation to build on, a pleasant help in downing their opponents. The *gradual* readjustment via decision is for the lawyer to work out, and at its best is for the layman never to notice. *He will notice only its absence.* He wants law "stable"—*i.e.,* largely unnoticed—as he wants the ground stable. So that to me the problem of "Why the illusion of certainty?" narrows down to the lawyers themselves as the proper insects to put under the lens. Much of the layman's illusion, indeed, is traceable to what he has been taught by lawyers. But the lawyers do the changing, and should see it. Theirs, then, the illusion. Whence does it come? Certainly "professional tradition" plays a great part. That leaves us with the further question Frank might ask: Why the professional tradition? How of father-authority there?

But for "the modern mind" the problem has now been simplified. We no longer have to explain why or how the tradition *arose,* but only why it *persists.* And we have three-quarters of it solved by the answer *that it exists.* A tradition coupled with an ideology and a machine for breaking new men into it persists almost of itself. One of its elements, the argument by deductive logic, is a powerful constant suggestion to reinforce it. Frank is right that the lawyer's constant job is change. But he does not emphasize nearly enough that that job is *for the lawyer himself* built in terms of fixity. The whole of the law, *except that bearing on the case in hand,* the lawyer can most conveniently regard as indeed fixed. He has no more occasion to notice change in the great whole than he has to notice the shifting of the stars throughout the year. But even as to the case in hand, the law is for the lawyer *in flux* only during that tiny fraction of his effort in which he *builds his theory* [for his particular impending case. For that one case.] This may be two minutes, two hours, two weeks. But, that theory once built (and during the building all authorities *were* fluid), the argument freezes into deductive form, is cast into form *as if* premise and conclusion had always been, is fought for on that basis. This must inevitably tend for most men, most of the time, to wipe away the memory of the short fluid period—as to the same case, the same facts, the same change—and to leave behind a memory rather in terms of one's own skill in perceiving the hidden something that was always there. Thus, the experiencing of change is by legal tradition itself kept from becoming *cumulative* and from having the effects which cumulative experience ought to have. Judges might be expected to break through more quickly than lawyers. But their sense of duty to follow authority must make their observation somewhat selective; and the opinion works on the writer as does deductive argument on a lawyer. Neither should one overlook that *enough* of the ways of judges are regular to offer a firm foothold to selective observation.

My own conclusion comes down then to something like this: The problem Frank puts is there to solve. But vastly less for laymen than for lawyers. And for lawyers considerably less than he suggests; there is much certainty which in any pragmatic sense is real and no illusion. What is left is in good part explained by the mere going tradition plus the extent to which the traditional ideology really does work out. Finally, one chief basis for his argument that a deep-seated emotional drive is necessary to any explanation (namely, that law is so peculiarly subject to the illusion) is in good part removed from cogency by the nature and office of law; and what is left may demonstrate an emotional need for an illusion of certainty in law, but does not demonstrate that father-worship is the genesis, or even a step in the genesis thereof. Maybe, of course, it is. Probably, I should guess, it plays some part. For surely my arguments, even if accepted, do not *negate* that. They aim only to show that factors which seem a step or so closer to tangibility offer some hope of nearly adequate explanation.

One protest as to vocabulary is in order, namely, against Frank's denial that precedents (or indeed, I think he would argue, accepted rules of any kind) are "authoritative." What he means by the word I do not get in any clarity; apparently, however, some *absolutely* binding force. If so the wording says nothing that any sane man will dispute, and tends rather to mislead. We know that precedents have no such force. But force they have. We know the doctrine of precedent, and the effect of rules, as studiously ambiguous. Yet ambiguous within margins which in the main are reasonably defined. Rules guide, although they do not control, decision. The rule of the case or the code does lay its hand upon the future, though one finger or several may slip or shift position.

Despite my differences with the author, I repeat: The book excites; it illuminates; it breaks new ground; it is an important contribution.

ONE "REALIST'S" VIEW OF NATURAL
LAW FOR JUDGES [a]

Even if sometimes bewildered by technical detail, plagued by woodenness of administration, or outraged by cynical lawyer's trading on the fact that a given matter turns "not on justice, but on law," no man can wrestle long with the things of law without becoming aware that under the very things which sometimes bewilder, plague or outrage him there pulses an urge for right, or decency, or justice: a drive toward an ideal attribute which men may well conceive as a proper and indeed the proper ultimate objective of all law and of all legal institutions. The concept of Natural Law seems to me an expression of this urge: an expression informed by the urge, and directed to its greater realization; yet an expression only partially effective, because baffled in part as it moves toward realization, baffled by the very legal technique which its objective is to criticize and remedy.

In saying this I am conscious of departing from one solid tradition in regard to the use of the term. "Natural Law" has been used as the designation of a body of principle for the right ordering of any human society; principle which for that reason is so broad as to require perplexing labor to give it any application concrete enough to be of service in practical legal work. To me principle as broad as that appears to be not a *lawyer's* Natural Law, nor Natural Law in a *lawyer's* sense. A lawyer, or indeed a jurist, has as one major function the dealing with detailed principle and rule applicable to a given going society, in terms accurate

[a] From 15 Notre Dame Lawyer 3 (1939).

enough and sharp enough to let any relevant particular persons or groups know where they stand. A *lawyer's* Natural Law is an effort to bring the philosopher's Natural Law to bear in lawyerlike actual regulation of the multiple specific problems of human conflict. There is even another tradition in regard to the use of the term, Natural Law: a tradition of which some of Grotius' writings and some of Mansfield's decisions may remind; a tradition in which Natural Law is conceived as a body of *applicable* rules. I have no desire to choose between the two traditions, which are indeed wholly consonant with each other. I do suggest, however that Natural Law in the philosopher's sense bears on the work of the normal legal scholar who is concerned with Natural Law as a keystone and as a touchstone for his own labors, while it leaves those actual labors still to be done. The labors themselves must be concerned in good part with the formulation, detail by detail, of apposite rules, of apposite rules for the particular legal scholar's own society—rules which are consistent with, and perhaps crowned by, the philosopher's Natural Law. But few of those rules will be *dictated* by the philosopher's Natural Law. Their purposes may often be, but rarely if ever their form. Whereas matters of legal form are for the lawyer matters of his very substance.

I shall speak of such a legal scholar, in this aspect of his distinctively legal work, as a Natural Lawyer; and it is *his rules for his society* which this paper is dealing with under the designation Natural Law.

In one important aspect it is convenient to conceive Law as made up of rules and normative concepts; broad rules (commonly spoken of as "principles") and more precise ones (commonly spoken of as "rules"); ideal terms of dynamic normative character, both relatively precise ("concepts"—if this is what Pound, say, means by "concepts") and relatively vague ("standards"). Insofar, Law is conceived as something which can and does envisage its own occasional disregard by layman or by lawman, and which can and does nonetheless hold, and hold valid. The breach of duty produces the enforcement, the error produces the reversal. The formulated rules, and those semi-formulated rules which are *felt* rather than stated, remain as guides to conduct initially, and as guides for the correction or rebuke of aberrant conduct which occurs. They remain also as material to be subjected to critique in the light of the objectives of all law, and, one hopes, to be slowly themselves corrected and readjusted in the direction of more adequately reflecting justice.

It is at this point, as I see it, that the lawyer's Natural Law enters the picture. His Natural Law bears a relation to positive law (positive law viewed as a body of actually prevailing rules and concepts) which is curiously similar to the relation of such positive law to actually prevailing human behavior. Discrepancies in positive law do not affect the validity or virtue of the Natural Law; it continues, despite all such discrepancy; it affords a concrete guide to the making of proper positive law, and a concrete guide for the correction of positive law which has gotten itself badly and aberrantly made.

This does not exhaust the similarity. There is another phase, and one which is crucial both to the effectiveness and to the limits of utility of the lawyer's Natural Law conception. That phase is that Natural Law meets positive law (as positive law meets particular behavior) within the case-law *judge's* realm of thinking and discourse. The lawyer's or jurist's Natural Law is properly formulated in rules, in normative propositions attaching prescribed legal consequences to described types of possible fact. They claim, these rules of Natural Law, to be right rules, true rules, *the* right and true rules, the *only* right and true rules, the only right and true rules *of law*. At every step in the judging process they sit at the judge's side, and counsel steadily that all leeway properly entrusted to case-law judges be utilized to correct any incorrect positive rule-formulation so that it may more closely fit *the* correct rule-formulation. It is the aim and function of such Natural Law to be thus drawn upon continually as a source of positive law; and this ought to hold no less as to the reading ("interpretation," "construction," "application") or development of statute law than it does in regard to the continuing reformulation of case-law and principle.

This same characteristic accounts for what seems to me an inherent limitation upon such Natural Law. Conceived as Law, it must undertake the ordering of a society. Conceived as a guide to positive law, it must deal with the ordering of a society not too greatly dissimilar from the society whose positive law it is to guide. Such a society, as given by history, is always a society which has had to compromise with much which is plain injustice, if justice be viewed as at all determined by the good, as distinct from the necessary. Views will differ about where such injustice is found; but views can hardly differ about the presence of injustice, and of injustice compromised with. And Natural Lawyers have, it seems to me, whenever they dealt with a given social structure, found themselves with some regularity doing similar compromise. They have allowed themselves indeed materially greater leeway in working toward their view of justice, than have purely "positive" lawyers; but from compromising they have not escaped.

As indicated, this seems to me altogether proper. Guidance for a particular society must plant its feet in that society. And guidance for a positive legal scheme must either rub elbows with that scheme or grow chimerical.

The above views on Natural Law seem to lead to a number of conclusions which will doubtless be subject to even sharper challenge than the views themselves. The first is that most of a jurist's or lawyer's Natural Law will in a diversified world fail of its very function if its content be sought in formulations so broad as to apply to too many legal times, systems, and societies at once. Its very virtue lies in concretization so great as to invite its infiltration into a particular given body of positive law—its infiltration in terms not only of large guidance, but of detailed rule. That other type of "natural law" study to which Wigmore's The Pledge Idea is a monument—the search for inherent coincidence at all times of certain conditions with certain types of legal institution, or of inherent sequences all over the world in the development of certain types of legal institution—that is a study looking for "natural law" in the sense of sociological sequence of effect upon cause. It sheds lights on the right only insofar as it sheds light upon the necessary, and again only insofar as the necessary conditions the right. Natural Law in the more proper sense has Natural character in that different sense in which Natural means "conforming to ideal essence."

The second conclusion is that Natural Law has a peculiarly fertile field wherever the precepts and concepts of positive law are malleable, are not caught into unchangeable authoritative words, and are subjected by the going tradition itself to constant re-examination and reformulation. It is thus peculiarly at home, it is indeed peculiarly needed, in a case-law system; for a case-law system places responsibility for day to day *reformulation* of rule and principle upon the bench. In a case-law system the verbal garb of rules is not fixed, and rephrasing to constantly and more closely approach a *righter* phrasing is not only proper, but is a bounden duty of scholar and of judge.

In such a system the Natural Law of a lawyer is, again, peculiarly at home, and is peculiarly needed, at a period when stress of change and circumstance in the surrounding society is forcing upon the particular body of case-law not only a fuller utilization, but a fuller *conscious* utilization, of that flexibility which is inherent in any case-law system. Reformulation *for* the future, but *upon* the past, has been the pride of our case-law through the centuries; and the extra touch of emphasis upon the future which was the life of American case-law a century ago has for two decades been with us again. No wonder, then, that we find Natural Law in vigorous revival here today.

The third conclusion is that it should occasion mild wonderment to find any Natural Law man and any so-called realist engaged in pegging brickbats at each other. Each sees the positive rules and concepts of here and now as present and potent. Each regards them as requiring re-examination in terms of their effective going value. Each sees one major guide to their evaluation in the service which they prove on examination either to render or not to render to the society which brought them forth. Each labors for the utilization of the greater leeways afforded by legislation, and the lesser leeways afforded by that case-law system which is built out of the rulings of a nation, to produce a finer and more effective set of guides for conduct and for judging. And it is difficult for me to conceive of the ultimate legal ideals of any of the writers who have been called realists in terms which do not resemble amazingly the type and even the content of the principles of a philosopher's Natural Law.

Finally, it is my belief that the *working methods* propounded, and followed in actual work, by writers who profess various jurisprudential faiths which have come into labels, and labels which seem to have become rather more combative than descriptive— it is my belief that the working methods of these differently labelled writers form an interesting and highly useful complement to one another. At any rate, this "realist" welcomes the modern Natural Law movement—including those parts of it which he doubtless does not yet understand. Nor does he feel at all backward in urging upon workers in that movement that the so-called realists have been getting the rust off quite a number of ancient and rather admirable legal tools, which any worker in law would do well to look over and even install over his own workbench. Such a distinction as that between Philosopher's and Lawyer's Natural Law, for example: it is so old, so obvious, so useful— and in these latter days so rusted in neglect.

{ 6 }

IMPRESSIONS OF THE CONFERENCE
ON PRECEDENT [a] *

If one puts together the proceedings at your Conference on Judicial Precedent—on which may I congratulate your Association?—two things stand out like radio towers:

First, lawyers and judges and professors all agreed that we have a system of precedent, and that under it we have very considerable guidance. But above all, it was clear that the speakers, each and all, *felt an overpowering need for guidance-from-the-law;* and it was clear that, each and all, they felt our *system* of judicial precedent to give them *almost* enough guidance; they knew how to find their way about with it pretty well. But they were still hungry for more and better guidance. And,

Second, when it came to *stating* what our system of judicial precedent was, the speakers could find no agreement, and knew in advance that they would be unable to.

I say that there was agreement that our system of precedent gave us pretty fair guidance, and enough to get on with, at need. It is true that here and there along the line there was suggestion or complaint—chiefly from practicing lawyers—that the doctrine of precedent, or the stability which that doctrine-in-its-application has been affording us, had seemed recently to suffer serious recent undermining; and the Supreme Court of the United States came in for some particular attention in that respect.

[a] From 14 U. CINC. L. REV. 343 (1940).
* After Professor Llewellyn returned to New York, he wrote this letter in which he states his impressions of the Cincinnati Conference.

The lines of the complaint and the lines of its discussion both seem to me extremely interesting. Apart from *Erie R. R. Co. v. Tompkins*,[1] the complaint ran along two primary lines: first, and especially in tax cases, the Supreme Court has recently shifted ground, with a noticeable trend toward widening the available lines of taxation. Second, the Supreme Court has openly expressed the idea that where older decisions have been mistaken, they can do with re-examination. From such observations the somewhat amazing conclusion was drawn that the Supreme Court, and constitutional cases in particular, are suffering from a serious shaking or undermining of the doctrine of precedent.

Fortunately your Conference itself provided the necessary correction and perspective. On the matter of open discussion of any change of rule which might be needed, there is, for instance, Chief Justice Weygandt's clear position that that is exactly what the proper way is to handle any rule which may need re-examination. And the emergence into judicial respectability was noted, of the procedure of safeguarding those who had relied on prior clear rules, even while the Court made clear a new rule for the future—a procedure which has been under discussion for twenty years, whose constitutionality was the subject of one of Justice Cardozo's finest opinions, and which had been advocated by him while he was still holding office in New York. Indeed, the quotation from *Taney* came into the picture to make clear that re-examination of mistaken doctrine was nothing new on the part of the Supreme Court itself. And, finally and most particularly, no one even suggested that the Supreme Court or any other court, in re-examining any portion of precedent, was proposing to depart from the foundation of that doctrine, which is to always keep in mind the reason for the rule, to extend the rule as far as the reason extends, limit the rule where the reason stops, and alter the rule when the reason is discovered to have ceased or been mistaken, and then to stay with the results of any re-examination and correction of any reason. This aspect of precedent has been with us always; Judge Traynor emphasized its importance as a vital part of the law as law has been for a century; Pound and Cardozo and Wright were brought in to buttress his view. The "ideals" Dean Pound rightly speaks of as part of the law itself include the search for proper reason and objective, the "techniques" which he rightly sees as equally a part of the law itself, consist in first instance of the ways in which the courts handle their prece-

[1] 304 U. S. 64, 58 Sup. Ct. 816 (1938).

dent material. And it is almost amusing to recall that Jerome
Frank's demonstration, ten years ago, of the presence of important
leeway for decision *within the law,* was directed not to the Supreme
Court, nor to constitutional cases, nor to the events of the depression, but to the every day, in the common law courts at large.

So that when particular current series of cases come up for
particular attention, one's mind runs back for instance to a
series of older cases from 1901, 1914, 1925, associated with the
names Lochner, Muller, and Adkins. And when older tax law, as
understood by the profession, seems in process of remaking, one
recalls the remaking of the older law of sealed contracts, and
Wright's remarks (in which I can join) on the progressive remodeling of the law of Sales. Indeed, as to the tax cases in particular, it
has seemed to me that one who has followed the current of opinion, judicial and other, over the past ten years, and has observed
the pressure all over the country to open sources of revenue, must
have been aware that *some* important shifts of ground have been
impending. One never knows in such a situation exactly what
the shifts will be, nor exactly where they will stop; as in the seal
cases instanced by Traynor and Cardozo, the order in which
cases arise has something to do with the net result. But that is
nothing new in a precedent system; and the uncertainty attending it is due to the older precedents which are coming under
pressure not having been so based on good and explicit reason
that they could become modified gradually and almost imper-
ceptibly, instead of by sudden jerks.

The truth is that what has been happening recently in the
Supreme Court is thrown out of all perspective by a number of
accidental factors. Of these the first is that the Court stands to
observation for all of us, whether we come from Ohio or from
Texas or from Indiana or from Massachusetts; so that each of us
comments on the Supreme Court, and the very repetition of the
comment makes things which happen there seem to happen much
oftener than they do. The second accidental factor is that whereas
when our home courts upset or modify the expectations which
members of the profession happen (with or without sound justification) to have built on the prior cases, it is rather rare that
more than forty lawyers at a time find the single decision affecting their immediate work; so that instead of feeling upset about
the past, we proceed to feel instructed about the future. The
Supreme Court, however, especially in regard to tax cases, is
listened in on by thousands of lawyers, on each decision. When

it then proceeds to deal with its precedents exactly as all the other courts have been dealing with theirs, *it* gets *noticed.* And because the *other* courts have not been *noticed,* the Supreme Court seems to be doing something *different.*

As a matter of cold fact, the Supreme Court, in its ways of handling precedent, is only just catching up with what the courts of the country at large have been doing for twenty years. For a few decades after about 1880 the courts of the country tended to be somewhat literal-minded and word-minded about their precedents, and where they did creation, to create along the lines Judge Traynor quoted from Choate. By and after 1920, the whole tone of the decisions can be seen to have shifted; the way of work with precedent—while still staying cleanly within the doctrinal possibilities, except on rare occasions—the way of work with precedent has become noticeably different. But lawyers did not notice this, or if they did, they did not write about it, nor did they change their general views to fit the change in the courts' way of work. They did begin, without thinking too much about it, to put more stress in argument on the flavor of the case. In *argument,* they came more and more to remember, in Wright's words, the Court's "prime duty to do right according to law in a particular case." "Do right" means "get the right result, the result that satisfies." "According to law" means two things, and they must not be confused. The one is: "stay within the accepted and correct authorities, if that is at all possible"—and that does *not* mean: within any particular lawyer's interpretation of the authorities. And the other thing that "according to law" means is: "according to a rule and reason which will be a good rule and reason for the future"—and that does not mean to freeze decision upon any *particular* interpretation of the past.

Now the interesting thing is that the older "lawyer's" doctrine of precedent, which always pretended that there was only one answer to a legal question, and that the precedents, all by themselves, gave you the answer—the interesting thing is that that doctrine began, long ago, to give difficulties, all over the country, to judges. Justice Cardozo found it didn't do his work, and wrote about that fact, and tried to get into more communicable form the something else that was in the picture. Judge Hutcheson found it didn't do his work, and tried to do the same. Moschisker of Pennsylvania, and Pound of New York, and Burch and Mason of Kansas, and Beach and Gager in Connecticut, Hough and the Hands and Bingham on the federal bench—such men were reaching into their experience and conscience as judges, and trying to get clear for themselves and their brethren and the bar what these *ways of using* precedent were which, they had come to realize, were as important as the precedents themselves. What I hope your Conference may do is to awaken lawyers to the fact that the Supreme Court, on this point, is only catching up with what the courts of the country have been doing these twenty years and more; and that we need to dig into the job of shaping up doctrine that reaches the ways of handling precedent as well as the rules.

Thus it is true that there was common ground among the judges, the lawyers, and the professors. The only seeming dissent was about the Supreme Court, but what the Supreme Court was shown to be doing was exactly what the other courts were doing. And about the other courts they did not complain too loudly. They did want more certainty, though, there, too.

Nonetheless, when it came to *stating* what our system of judicial precedent was, the speakers found no agreement, and they knew in advance that they would be unable to.

Judge Hutcheson, for instance, talked about "my" doctrine of precedent—"if you agree with it;" and the doctrine was one of what would *control* him even against his own better judgment. It was not one of guidance, but one of what he was bounded by. Within the leeway thus allowed, he used his own best judgment. That makes for admirable judging; but it means, inescapably, that if lawyers want to find out *just from the Rules, as the Rules Stand,* what is law to Judge Hutcheson, then in two cases out of four they will have to litigate, and they will know the answer only if, as and when Judge Hutcheson hands down his decision, and thereby adds to the Rules.

Now it is vital to note at this point that there was no unsureness at all about Judge Hutcheson's demeanor, nor about his talk, nor about the lines of his judgment. And as one who has studied Judge Hutcheson's opinions long and hard, I can testify that those opinions run with a gratifying and even uplifting consistency, and with as much predictability as the judgments of any living judge whose work I have followed. My point is going to be shortly, that the certainty which is in them, and which judges need, and lawyers need, is found by adding *something else* to the Rules as They Stand; and that the System of Precedent as we have it and practice it includes a *something else* which is not in the System of Precedent as we commonly describe it.

Chief Justice Weygandt was inclined to feel that "these troubles" were materially less with a "syllabus court." The reaction was again: first, that things were moving with rather adequate certainty and guidance in his actual work; and yet, there were difficulties; second, the System which he happened to have—this time, the syllabus system—was what was doing the work. Judge Weygandt's position goaded me into renewed examination of the Ohio cases; because it was hard for me to believe that any syllabus system could be enough to escape the eternal judge's job of working out the *best* one of the various answers which the Rules as They Stand happen to allow.

Here are a few results. In *State v. Taylor,*[2] decided December 20th last, the syllabus court splits twice. There is a special concurrence on the merits, which means some less than perfect clarity of the precedents on those merits. There is a dissent on whether the case is before the court, which means the same on procedure. The concurring judge voices as to a statute a view which must have its psychological weight also in sizing up a past syllabus: "It is not well, however, to attach too much importance to one passage or to allow the letter of the law to obscure its purpose. After all, the spirit of the law is the touchstone of interpretation."

The next case, decided the same day, *State ex rel. Rae v. Industrial Commission,*[3] carries another dissent, but by a different judge. The majority reasoning, in this syllabus-state in which the entire opinion is "not" available for use as authority, but only the syllabus, relied as to two of the three judicial authorities it cites on language from the opinions which is *not found in the relevant syllabi;* and, amusingly, quotes from the *body* of the opinion of a third case that case's quotation of one of the syllabi of the second.

The next case, decided the same day, *Patton v. Pennsylvania R. R. Co.,*[4] involved a rule so clear as a guide that the court of appeals had split, the majority giving a judgment which it felt to be in conflict with that of another court of appeals. One judge again found it desirable to limit his concurrence, in this case. And the nub of the case is not concluded by any of the authorities relied on; had the court chosen to stress the time period which a train abiding by the ordinance would have taken to reach the crossing, and the distance probably travelled by

[2] 136 Ohio St. 174, 24 N. E. (2d) 591 (1939).
[3] 136 Ohio St. 168, 24 N. E. (2d) 594 (1939).
[4] 136 Ohio St. 159, 24 N. E. (2d) 597 (1939).

decedent's truck before the actual sixty mile speed of the train could register through his eye, a different conclusion would, under precisely the same authorities, have been *possible. But it would not have been probable*—due to the "something else" which is not written in the Rules.

That is the end of the December 20th opinions.

In *Losito v. Kruse*,[5] decided on the next opinion-day, January 3rd, the court deliberately extends a quotation from a prior case to cover a situation known to be distinguishable; the extension is because of announced identity of the underlying reason. The reader knows what was done, why it was done, and has a good clear indication of what will be done tomorrow. The companion case, *Herron v. City of Youngstown*,[6] proceeds not into extension, but into heavy distinguishing of prior cases, and further fixes for future use the clearly announced solving rule and its clearly announced solving reason. This work is on a par with the very best in the New York work at the July 11th session[b]; what is to be stressed, however, is that in achieving it two utterly variant and mutually inconsistent precedent-techniques are employed upon the prior holdings.

Now in the light of such results, recorded from the successive cases reported from two successive opinion-days only two weeks apart, it does not seem to me possible to conclude that Judge Weygandt and his court stand, in their ways of dealing with their high judicial function, on materially different footing from Judge Hutcheson and his court, from the New York Court of Appeals, and from the Supreme Court of the United States, as these were discussed in so much of the proceedings as I was well enough to hear.

(1) Common to all are lines of compulsion in the precedents, which to a great extent limit, and which to some extent control their action. And which, to some extent, control them even when their judgment is that the case would better be decided the other way.

(2) But when the urges of justice and policy are clear enough, they *can* find a distinction to avoid or whittle almost any precedent or line of precedent.

(3) Within limits wide enough to spell success or disaster for a

[5] 136 Ohio St. 183, 24 N. E. (2d) 705 (1940).
[6] 136 Ohio St. 190, 24 N. E. (2d) 708 (1940).
[b] The reference is to the 300-page opinion day July 11, 1939 in the N. Y. Court of Appeals, discussed at the Conference, and discussed fully, THE COMMON LAW TRADITION 96, 102, 135.

lawyer's case, the precedents are capable of being shaped as they are followed or applied, so as to bring judgment out on one side or the other.

(4) But such shaping is *not* arbitrary. And

(5) Such shaping or its non-occurrence is indeed largely predictable. And

(6) The judges who do the shaping, as they are doing it, *feel*, to a large degree, *controlled.* They [commonly] *feel* that the *Rules* as They Stand should allow and do allow only one proper answer.

And the trouble for lawyers, and indeed for judges, comes, I submit, from the confusion which now follows:

(7) *Feeling* controlled, as they apply and shape precedent to the tough and troubling case in hand, the judges *attribute* the manner and nature of the control *to the Rules as they Stand,* as if it were those Rules which contained but a single possible and legitimate answer.

(8) Whereas in fact the control is a control over the way in which the judges may properly *use* those Rules; the actual final control lies not in any rules of law or rules of precedent, but lies instead in a combination of judicial conscience, judicial judgment, and what I can best describe as the net lines of force of the particular field of law, which press judgment in a given direction, and resist any expansion or turning in another direction. A judge, like a lawyer, sizes up the situation in terms of the way The Law sizes it up; there is no rule and no precedent to lay down how to do that—we just do it. We classify the case in terms of the feel of the law. And the feel of the law then proceeds to push judgment in one direction, and proceeds to block judgment off from moving in another technically possible direction. When the feel of The Law and the feel of good sense are at odds, courts may be expected to divide, because their office is, somehow, to combine the two.

The evil comes from the general pretense that there is in each case only a single legitimate meaning to the precedent itself, or to the line of precedents. Because courts write opinions as if this were so, they feel no sustained need, when they follow, or when they slightly reshape a precedent or line of precedents, to say *why* they find the precedents good to follow *in just that form.* Sometimes, as in the *Losito and Herron* cases, they tell us, with clarity and precision. That, as things stand, is our fortune, not our right. They feel no sustained need to tell their successors and us just what the *reason* is for *not* distinguishing, nor yet for *not* following some interesting language; they feel also no sustained need to tell their successors and us just why a case which they do distinguish needs to be distinguished; they write often as if it were enough that "that could not have been decided, because it was not before the court."

Yet the best judicial practice has always been to make explicit the reason and spirit of the law, which "is the touchstone of interpretation" for precedent as well as for statute. Where there is both a precedent *and* a satisfying reason under it, the precedent comes close in most cases to both applying and distinguishing itself. Such a precedent *does* give certainty to lawyers.

Where, on the other hand, all you have is precedents, or rules phrasing decision, with the reasons obscure, then one lawyer can build a letter-perfect case on the language, or some language, announced in the process of actual decision; the opposing lawyer can show the language to be distinguishable stuff, and can bring other language. If lawyers are good, two technically letter-perfect cases are the rule, on just the Rules as They Stand. This is not certainty, *for lawyers*. It may bring business, but it is not certainty. It may be good enough for judges, because judges always can add, they always do add, they cannot help but always add, their feel for the law, and their feel for good sense in the case. That produces an effective choosing, and the winning brief *can* then produce an opinion. But if the opinion does not tell the judge's successors and us *why* the technically solid argument of the loser had no business to be listened to, then uncertainty remains, *for lawyers*, as to whether this new precedent will be followed (or which part of it will be followed—even in Ohio), or extended, or turned, and if turned, then turned in which direction; or distinguished down, and if distinguished, *how* and how far it will be distinguished.

The picture is the picture of a bough on an apple-tree, in winter, before the pruner comes. There is no question that that bough stretches northeast, and that it runs rather flat. There is no question that no apples will grow from the empty air around it, nor will that air support a climber's foot. The bough is the solid, the utterly solid, the solidly limited, line of law. Yet even the solid bough puts forth vertical shoots of doctrinal possibility. In our feel for orcharding, we can disregard such shoots; they are like, say, the attack on the constitutionality of the late Eighteenth Amendment. Under the formal rules of precedent, they are conceivable; but the feel of the situation is that the pruner's shears will snip them inevitably, as soon as his attention is called to them. There is also a side-shoot working over under another bough; it also is foredoomed to pruning, foredoomed by the general setup of the law. But had it been working over toward an unoccupied space free to the sun, one might think it likely to be encouraged rather than pruned. Out at the end of the branching (where lawyer's litigation is likely to occur, and twigs, not boughs, decide the question) there is a three-way start, all fresh, strong, sap-filled stuff, fed with life from the bough. To choose between such doctrinal possibilities, or to leave them all, that is the typical problem of the emergent case. The line of precedent and bough and language says: Northeast only—clip the side shoots! The emergent case may argue: Northeast it has been, but the time has come to spread to right, or to left, or to both; there is new space here for growing needed apples. The system of precedent lays it down that you must follow the bough; that you can have no twigs or apples from the air; that no twigs[e] can come into being, save solidly on and from a prior branching; that any twig thus growing can be spared, regardless of its new, distinguishable direction; that you can properly clip even the middle end-shoot, and start the bough off in a new direction; that a dying or wrongheaded bough, even, can at utter need be taken off at the tree-trunk. An orcharder would think you silly if you told him that those rules led to one single answer as to what to do with a given problematical shoot. He just looks and clips, like a judge, when an outlandish vertical shoot is presented to him. Or he looks and puzzles, sizing up the situation, and figuring which way is best, in view of the whole setup. The orcharder *takes for granted* every last thing that is in our rules about how to handle precedent. His whole mind is on the *reasons for using those rules one way, or another way*—on the wise choice of which of them to use in the particular instance.

But judges have as their business to be more than orcharders. The shoots from precedent they prune or leave are shoots by whose probable future our counsellors and laymen and advocates must guide future action. We need to know the *reasons* not only for pruning a shoot, but for leaving it. We need to have explicit principles of pruning, if there are any. We need to know the reasons for using one of the legitimate techniques with any prec-

---

[e] This is of course an exaggeration. Fresh creation does occur—but even there the effort is, and rightly, to stay within the "feel" of the Law. THE COMMON LAW TRADITION, esp. 88–91, 217–223.

edent or line of precedents rather than some other of the equally
legitimate techniques. Without this, our "certainty" is our skilful
or unskilful insight and guesswork about particular judges', or
particular benches', *ways* of orcharding among the limited but
very plentiful supply of shoots from the boughs of precedent.

We do moderately workable guessing now; but most of us get
fooled too often, and even the best of us get fooled sometimes.
And, believing that the Rules as They Stand afford a single
unambiguous answer, we often fool ourselves, because we need
an answer to run one way, and we find a good *technical* basis to
sustain that answer. The precedents and the lines of precedent
which do *not* fool us, but guide us clearly, and which guide the
judges too, are the precedents which do two things together:
first, they state a clean *reason* along with a rule which really sorts
out different states of fact for easy sizing up; and second, they
state a reason which satisfies as making sense. Such rules, our
best rules, control and guide and satisfy, and open clear lines for
their own limitation or development. Such rules, and such rules
only, afford *dynamic* certainty. They are hard to make, but the
case-law process is continuous. No formula for action can produce
clean rules out of muddy minds; nor can any formula make
judges do their more inspired work day by day and every day.
What a formula can do it to ease the road a little by making the
goal more clear; to raise the average performance a little, and to
help inspiration to come oftener. That is much.

Certainly the making of the finer type of rule is slowed up by
the pretense that a precedent has only one single legitimate and
authoritative line of possible meaning; so that there is no need
to show why the meaning chosen is the proper one to choose.
Certainly the making of the finer rules is furthered and speeded
by conscious accounting by our judges of *why* they find a given
precedent or line of precedent vital to shape as they shape it,
or to distinguish, or to "merely" follow. Lawyers need guidance
on the reasons for the judges' manner of orcharding. And judges
aiming at a more rational system of law will judge better for
rendering more explicit account, to themselves, of *why* they know
so clearly and so often that some technically flawless line of argument from the precedents simply will not do. Because, sometimes,
when counsel on the other side have missed their own available
technically good road, a technically flawless line of argument has
led judges into nonsense, as if by sheer authority.

In a word, the road to that greater certainty and wiser guidance which we need from case-law is to open our eyes to what makes up the amount of certainty and guidance which we have. And to see that there are *two* main lines of factor in it, one, the precedents and rules; the second, the ways of using them, *as employed* by the judges in the conscientious practice of the judge's art and duty. And then to take steps to move the second of these lines of factor onto a basis of clarity and reasonedness, so far as we are able, not occasionally, but regularly; so that certainty may move further out of the area of incommunicable guesswork, and wisdom may move further out of the area of uncommunicated intuition.

Again, my congratulations on the Conference. I thought it an achievement, in plan, and in result.

{ 7 }

ON READING AND USING
THE NEWER JURISPRUDENCE [a] *

When discussion of leading writers on Jurisprudence is found referring equally to their books or articles and to their opinions laying down doctrine for the Supreme Court of the United States,[1] there is reason for feeling that the long-standing exile of Jurisprudence into the duskier and dustier portions of the libraries may have come to an end. When two of the most discussed modern writers occupy strategic policy-shaping positions in Washington,[2] and an American Bar Association report on that vital question, Administrative Law, is made up and rested in major part upon jurisprudential material,[3] and decisions such as the *Sunburst Oil* case,[4] or *Erie R. R. v. Tompkins*[5] turn flatly on answers to such

[a] From 40 COLUM. L. REV. 581 (1940).

* To the thoughtful criticism and illuminating stimulus of my colleague, Elliott Cheatham, this paper owes more than I find it easy to express. (This article is appearing simultaneously in the April and May, 1940, issues of the AMERICAN BAR ASSOCIATION JOURNAL. 26 *ibid.* 300, 418. ED.)

[1] As holds not only of Holmes and Cardozo, but also of Brandeis, Hughes, Stone, Frankfurter, Douglas; and as was earlier the case with, *e.g.*, Kent and Story.

[2] Jerome Frank and Thurman Arnold, discussed *infra;* one can remind of Landis and Douglas. The phenomenon, though on the increase, is not purely recent: Wigmore, *e.g.*, was important in the Judge Advocate General's office in the last war; Pound was an influential member of the Wickersham Commission; in both cases, views on jurisprudential matters demonstrably influenced their work.

[3] PROC. A. B. A. (A Pound job). 155, 331 (1938).

[4] Great Northern Ry. v. Sunburst Oil & Refining Co., 287 U.S. 358 (1932). This opinion of Cardozo's is fraught with destiny. Yet how glacially slow the movement of ideas can be is evidenced by a wait of six years before the first State court starts on the new path; see 23 J. AM. JUD. SOC. 32 (1939).

[5] Erie Railroad Co. v. Tompkins, 304 U. S. 64 (1938).

jurisprudential questions as the essential nature of our common law or of our judicial lawmaking, then there is reason to feel that Jurisprudence is again becoming part of the practicing lawyer's necessary practical equipment. When skilful practitioners report that critical study of modern jurisprudential writing (as distinct from either the plain swallowing of it, or its plain neglect) gives them useful and effective leads on building briefs,[6] and a bar association finds it useful to have put in a three-session meeting on working the theory of precedent into more communicable shape,[7] then it appears probable that modern thought in the field is beginning to pass beyond the stage of groping into that of grasping.

At least, that some of it is. For it would be a hardy jurisprude who would recommend, indiscriminately, all writings that may have been appearing in the field or under the label of jurisprudence; or indeed who would recommend everything in anything which has appeared (except perhaps the products of his personal pen). The truth is that jurisprudential writing contains, as most writing does—including texts on straight law—its proper human proportion of twaddle, misconception and exaggeration. Indeed, I fear the truth is that the jurisprudential writing of the last ten years may contain a bit more than its proper human proportion of these, for it has been a literature of groping, of half-discovery, and of controversy, and of all of these together; which means that it contains blind leads, exaggerations, waste motion. Yet it contains also sap, health, light. It is a lively literature and a zestful one; it rings with a small boy's enthusiasms, with his "See what I found!", with his shouts of "You're another!", with his swift and sometimes aimless fisticuffs. It has, in a word, more life than form. But it has been growing up fast, its formlessness is assuming shape and usability, its over-enthusiasms are weeding out, it is settling to its job, it is a youngster who has ceased to be merely obstreperous or merely promising, it has become a young fellow who is taking hold and whose work needs to be followed.

This paper is an effort to set out the scheme of growth which underlies what has seemed like a welter, but has been in fact a development; to focus the vital and practical issues not in terms of the unwise things which have been written, but of the con-

[6] On this I suspect that any active writer's correspondence will show the same picture as my own: rather frequent responses ranging over the past decade from dominantly indignant protest to dominantly active participation in inquiry.

[7] Conference organized by Cincinnati Bar Association under the auspices of the Ohio State Bar Association, February 17, 1940, at Cincinnati, reported 14 U. CINC. L. REV. 203–355 (1940).

stantly building core of vision and accomplishment. It is an effort
to see recent jurisprudential writing as one would see a body of
"confused" case-law, disregarding the untenable extremes, the
wilder misformulations; hunting, instead, for solid central stuff,
distinguishing dictum and obiter, repudiating any announced
ratio decidendi which proves to have been ill-advised and to have
won no following; searching for the true issues and the true guiding principles which can help to advance the ball, and around
which the bulk of the work has somehow grouped itself by native
common law juristic intuition.

The older Jurisprudence which is current among lawyers is one
which the profession did not have occasion to study particularly;
a lawyer just absorbed it, largely through the fingers and the pores,
as he went along. It was, and is, in essence, the homely and effective
philosophy of active men about their work. And it has the solid
virtues which are commonly a part of any going, working institution. The going, working institution which the philosophy seeks
to reflect is not merely our rules of law, but the whole scheme of
our law, our courts, our lawyers, and their work; it includes our
ways of work, and the goals toward which our rules of law drive, as
well as rules of law themselves. At the heart and core of that institution lies the fact that judges, and administrative officials who
do not happen to be judges, are not free to do what they choose
or to decide as they choose; that their action in matters which
concern the rest of us is circumscribed and limited, and is guided
by something independent of the individual preferences or vagaries of the judges and officials. That is a fact, it is an observable
fact, it is a vital fact. In addition to that there is laid down in our
legal system a judgment of policy, powerfully express and even
more powerfully implicit. This judgment is that it is good and
right that our judges and other officials should not be free to act
and decide as they happen to please. The policy is one which is
very dear to us; and it is a policy which needs constant vigilance
lest officials, or indeed judges, overlook it. The older Jurisprudence proceeded, in consequence, to give us a rationale or doctrine
which was intended to express both the fact and the policy, and
which was intended to make future facts conform to the policy. In
its less sophisticated form the doctrine runs that "this is a government of laws *and not* of men," and that "the rules of law determine
the right decision."

As will appear in a moment, this particular phrasing of rationale or doctrine, while useful, is yet exceedingly inadequate. It wraps its words around half of the truth, and that is good; but it is also so phrased as to obscure the other half of the truth, which is not good at all. Regardless of their exactness or adequacy of phrasing, however, these particular formulations of the older Jurisprudence have a value in men's minds and more particularly in the minds of lawyers. They have a fighting value. They are prized, they will be fought for, they will be defended from any challenge at all, because they have (without our quite knowing how) come to symbolize and indeed to embody the great and essential truth that judges are not free, nor are administrative officials. Indeed, these particular formulations have come to appear to most of us (without our thinking particularly about how this has happened) as the *sole* established and available means to keep our officials and our judges reminded of our vital need that neither judges nor officials shall be free to decide and do as they just happen to please.

We cannot leave our judges or officials wholly free, or let them utterly loose, without chaos; that is clear. We cannot hold them down and direct them, without proper institutional machinery for holding them down and directing them; and that is clear. So much is common ground among all responsible jurisprudes, new or old. What the newer jurisprudes are worrying over is how to find a better, a more effective, a more reliable machinery for directing judges and other officials than the older rationale and doctrine have managed to give us.

For the older doctrine has not only the sturdy virtues which commonly inhere in the active man's philosophy of a going scheme of things; it has also the defects which commonly inhere in any unstudied and haphazard wisdom about a very complex human institution. Unstudied and haphazard wisdom on the lips of active men is commonly partial, it is commonly self-inconsistent, it commonly needs to have its various and variant partial expressions put down side by side, and thought through all together. The folk saws about marriage, for instance, are almost all of them rooted in deep truth—such as that man was not meant to live alone, and that marriage is a battle, and that a good woman is a pearl above price, and that it takes two to make a marriage, and that two are not enough. The trouble is that no single one of such going expressions gets its words around the whole, or even an adequate part, of the truth. Similarly, the older Jurisprudence has wrestled from time to time with certain inadequacies of the two major doctrinal formulations which have been mentioned—

inadequacies which affected not only full description of the actual working of our legal system but also the full expression of our legal system's judgment on what is right, needed, and established policy. Thus akin to the saws of marriage there run saws of law: "Hard cases make bad law" means that in our going scheme judges pay attention to the justice of the individual case, but that they probably shouldn't quite as much as they do. "Bad law makes hard cases" means that rules have a function beyond certainty, and that we do not like it and judges probably ought to do something about it, when the rules are merely certain and are not also just. "The law looks not to the form, but to the substance" means that courts do and should have one sharp eye out for what they see as effective justice in the case in hand, despite all building and reliance which may have rested on the rules of law. All of these expressions mean that in our system as we have it, the judge or other official does, to some (unspecified) extent, and should, to some (equally unspecified) extent, operate in ways not clearly laid down in the explicit rules of law. So that even lawyers who were troubled when Holmes stated that "General propositions do not decide concrete cases" watch judicial appointments or elections with concern because, apart from the question of character or bias, they know that the question of skill and temperament in the individual judge makes a difference both to decision and to law.

All of this plainly calls for some qualification on "a government" of laws "*and not* of men." Cardozo found the interaction of "stability and change" in judge-made law to be a "paradox"; he saw the presence of change, and he valued it; indeed, he felt a judicial duty to further it, within the proper limits. Exactly what the proper limits are he did not describe; he *felt* them, and then used them. What they are, you gather not from his books; those books tell you chiefly that there is some freedom for a judge, and that it is severely restricted.[8] To find out what the freedom is, as Cardozo saw it and used it, and on what the restrictions are, you have to go to Cardozo's opinions and piece the matter together for yourself.[9] Pound, again, poses as a major problem for Jurispru-

---

[8] That freedom is present, but severely limited, is the major theme of THE NATURE OF THE JUDICIAL PROCESS (1921), repeated in the superb and neglected address before the New York State Bar Association, *Jurisprudence*, 55 N.Y.S.B.A. 263 (1932), HALL, SELECTED WRITINGS OF BENJAMIN NATHAN CARDOZO, 20 (1947). The paradox is stated, not resolved, in PARADOXES OF LEGAL SCIENCE (1928).

[9] The opinions reveal a judge in whom the following five characteristics are developed in almost exactly equal intensity, and in whom any one or any combination of them may in a given instance gain the ascendancy and dominate the shaping of the result—though never without all the others being perceptibly at work. (1)

dence—in its immediately practical bearings—the problems of marking out and guiding the interaction of "rule and discretion"; and in Pound's descriptions of that "Law" *under* which courts and other officials do move and must be made to move, we find a very considerable array of factors other than "rules." [10] These factors turn out, moveover, if one examines them, to be factors that do three things at once: (1) They help control and guide the judge or other official in ways and places in which the rules of law, as such, fail to control and guide. (2) They are factors which are given and present in the legal system as we have it, so that they can be known, felt, even seen by a lawyer, and they therefore *can* guide him both in predicting and in working out an argument to a court. (3) They are factors which afford, however, some very real degree of flexibility of adjustment both of the outcome of a particular case and of the rule laid down in a case to changing times and needs and case-situations. Such factors include the "principles" of our law, which Pound wisely sees as broader than rules, and as capable of reshaping narrower rules that fall within their scope; and the "concepts" of our law—such as "Contract," which is different in connotation from "Property" or "Tort"; such "concepts" classify a situation and thereby give it a frame of reference and tendency, and so help decide a case even if there is no

---

Sensitivity to immediate felt justice of the immediate outcome in the particular litigation. (2) Sensitivity to long-range felt policy in the line of cases and situations typified by the case in hand. (3) Sense of duty to the rules theretofore laid down by court and legislature, but rather to their substance and felt purpose than to their form. (4) Profound sense of duty of the court to shape in words some explicit guidance for the future. (5) Love of lawyer-like dialectic to a degree which, when you like it, you feel as utterly superb, and when you do not like it, you feel as spiderweb sophistry, but which in any event had the capacity to honestly mislead the dialectician himself, when the safeguarding characteristics, for any reason, failed to afford it full balance. I know of no judge in whom these five attributes have been so equally balanced, in high development. Another judge, following policy, may be impatient of authority; Mansfield is the type. Or, following the justice of the case, he may be muddy of analysis, or slipshod of formulation; a typical American procedure. Or, following certainty and the rule, he may disregard the need of the case or the situation; as did Parke, or our elder Sanborn in commercial cases. Cardozo never does any of these things; but repeatedly he does grow oversubtle in their reconciliation.

[10] For earlier passages, see *The Theory of Judicial Decision*, 36 HARV. L. REV. 641, 802, 940 (1923); LAW AND MORALS 25 (1924). For more recent passages, which have come to stress ever increasingly the institutional and ideal phases of our tools of legal guidance, see *The Ideal Element in American Judicial Decision*, 45 HARV. L. REV. 136 (1931); THE FORMATIVE ERA IN AMERICAN LAW (1938), especially ch. III; "What is the Common Law," in *Future of the Common Law*, HARVARD TERCENTENARY PUBLICATIONS (1937), also in 4 U. OF CHI. L. REV. 176 (1937). On the relation of rule as discretion, see my COMMON LAW TRADITION (1960), esp. 217–219.

rule to tell whether that case *is* one of "Contract." [11] "The law of conveyances," says a court in one of the last advance sheets on my desk, "is not the law of contracts"; and the decision in the case turns, as decisions should in good part turn, on the classification which the court then makes of the situation. Such classifying is only sometimes dictated by existing rules.

What has been said can perhaps be summed up thus: the fact that judges and officials are not wholly free and must not be wholly free, divides on analysis and closer examination into two facts. The one fact is concerned with the control, the restraint, the holding down, of judges and officials; the other fact is concerned with the allowing to them of a limited degree and a limited kind of leeway, and the putting on them of a duty to exercise their uttermost skill and judgment within that leeway. Both of these facts must be seen, and both must be reckoned with, by any Jurisprudence which aims to cover the plain facts and the settled policies of our legal system. For there are two kinds of judicial or other official freedom which come in question, and the two kinds are very different. It is a fact in our legal system that judges are by no means free to be *arbitrary,* and our vital need that they shall not be free to be *arbitrary* has been caught into these rationales or doctrines about "laws and not men," and about "rules determining cases." But it is also a fact that our legal system does adjust to the individual case *and* to changes in our conditions and

---

[11] A current illustration is found in the division of the Circuit Courts of Appeal over whether it is a refusal to "bargain collectively" to refuse to commit the results to writing. If the matter be sized up as one of Contract, a "bargain" has been achieved and completed by oral agreement, and the court has no business to presuppose bad faith. If the matter be sized up as one of effective adjustment of labor relations by collective agreement, the men bargained for are seen as needing protection against their own leaders' possible misrepresentation of results: the writing amounts to credentials of the returning emissary, and the printed copies of it to the individual's record of whatever security it gives him about the terms of his employment. Thus seen, the signed writing is a voucher for the auditors. Classification, once made, dictates flavor; and flavor makes the case require decision its way.

Of late years, Pound's own writing has tended to soft-pedal "concepts" and put more stress on that "relational thinking of the common law," which was developed in THE SPIRIT OF THE COMMON LAW (1921). What this means is that the sharper study of the concept "concepts" by such writers as Cook drove Pound into discomfort in the use of that term; but he had never used "concepts" to mean ideas with clear edges; he had been reaching (and very wisely) for expression of the shaping and dynamic character of the *given classifications,* and for the common law *ways* of making classifications around dynamic situations.

The shaping effect of context on decision, produced by classifying, is beautifully brought out in Arnold's books, if one can forget the political purpose of his illustrations. See esp. SYMBOLS OF GOVERNMENT, 47 f. (1935).

institutions; and that fact means that judges and other officials are free to some real degree to be *just* and *wise,* and that we have a vital need that judges and other officials shall continue to be to some real degree free to be *wise and just.* That fact happens, however, *not* to have been caught into an equally familiar, equally sharp, or equally precious rationale or doctrine. Yet it needs to be; it is no less a vital part of our legal system and of our judges' duty. There is the law, which we know as impersonal, and think of as clear; there is the right outcome, which we feel as also impersonal, and think of as hard to find, but capable of being found, and the office of the judge is to fulfill the demands of *both,* together.

Here one sees as under a microscope the essence of method and accomplishment of the newer Jurisprudence. The method is to take accepted doctrine, and check its words against its results, in the particular as in the large. The method is to attempt to take a fresh look, and a sustained, careful look, at what goes on. The method is then to try to keep all the relevant results in mind at once, to see whether Tuesday's results check with Monday's, and Wednesday's with either; and to be content with no formulation which does not account for *all* of the results. That is the first part of the method. The second part of the method, if the accepted doctrine does not seem to square wholly with all of the results, is to attempt another fresh look from some other angles: If a doctrine does not do all that it purports to do, then why do people cling to it so hard? If a doctrine does not, in and by itself, do all that it purports to do, then *what else* is at work helping the doctrine out? For there is something else at work, helping all doctrines out. There is the tradition of the judge's craft, stabilizing the work of our judges, and guiding it; and there are the ideals of that craft, which also stabilize and guide. Is this *something else* a something wholly ineffable or spiritual or personal, so much so as to yield nothing at all to careful study, so much so as to lay no foundation for more effective doctrine which can get closer to really doing what the doctrine we have is supposed to be doing? The idea underlying modern Jurisprudence is that harder and more intensive study of what goes on, and harder and above all more sustained study of the wisdoms and part-wisdoms in the books, checking them again and again against what goes on, can lay the foundation for more solid doctrine. On the particular matter of judging, the newer Jurisprudence is persuaded that the older, by putting on the doctrines of law more weight than those

doctrines do bear or can bear alone, have put too little weight on
the *art and craft of the judge's office*. One studies that art and
craft by studying particular officers at work in their office, and
seeking for the similarities in their attitudes and behavior. This
has been misconceived as being a delving into the vagaries of individuals; what it is, instead, is a search for predictabilities and
proper lines of work in the judge's office which transcend individuality. These can be dug out only by case study.

What has been discussed seems to me an illustration of this. For
it is a real gain to discover how much, in a regime of "law," we
have been leaving first, to the untutored, unguided conscience of
our judges, and second, to the training which they are left just to
pick up. "Better a poor judge with experience than a good one
who isn't broken in," runs a lawyers' saying; and that saying is not
directed to the judge's conscience. But what *is* directed to the
judge's conscience is the notion of not being influenced in decision
by unjudicial considerations. And unjudicial considerations are
not just "considerations outside the record"—though charges
have been framed and sustained in those terms. They are *some
kinds* of consideration outside the record, of which we can effectively name one or two, such as "bribery," but which at present
we mostly know only by feeling. For there are *other kinds* of consideration outside the record whose skilful use marks a judge as
great: "true" insight into justice and policy, for instance, whence-
soever derived. And it is a good man who at present writing can
lay down the difference between "yielding to public clamor or
political power" on the one hand, and "feeling and serving the
demands of the times for justice" on the other. About all that is
yet clear on that point is that the discrimination does not turn
wholly on motive, but turns also on insight, for we are not content
with the steadfast blind; nor wholly on insight, regardless of
motive, for neither are we content with even prophetic judgment,
if it rests on favor or on fear.

What I am trying to say can be almost summed up in this: that
when we take a fresh look at what really goes on, then we see
before us, along with our doctrines of law, and giving to those
doctrines much of their meaning, the crafts of law, and the ideals
and traditions of those crafts; of which judging at trial is one, and
judging on appeal is another, and different one. And that to leave
unstudied and almost wholly implicit the ideals and traditions of
the crafts is to leave unspoken and undiscussed half of the guidance and control and soundness which lies in our actual going legal

scheme of things. So that if the newer Jurisprudence, following
its basic approaches of a realistic *fresh* look at what goes on, and
a *sustained* effort to account for *all* of it, can open up these crafts
for communicable study, it will be offering real help.

Pound has attempted to combine the two phases in his slogan
"Justice under Law"; but the heart is taken out of that slogan by
an unfortunate accident of phrasing in Pound's writings; the
accident that he regularly and indistinguishably uses the word
"Justice" to mean *either* what most men mean by Justice *or,* as
the case may be, to mean the mere process of adjudication, whatever the result; so that in little, if any, of his writing does *"Justice*
under Law" have any inescapable flavor of *"Attaining* the *goal* of
Justice, though working under Law." [12]

But much more troublesome to understanding than any accident of any individual's phrasing, are the facts of the work and
thought of lawyers at large. Lawyers think law, lawyers argue law
in court. And the job of a lawyer is to show how the goal of
"justice" in his case can be attained within the framework of the
law. And—a point to which we shall recur in a moment, a vital
point—the fact is that in a huge number of cases *there is enough
leeway and give within the framework of our law* to allow of what
is felt as justice being attained in the case without departing from
that framework. This fact means that when a lawyer openly
argues "Justice" as a major argument, instead of arguing law first
and justice as showing what the "true" rule or principle or application of the law must be seen to be, then that lawyer is practically
advising the court either that he has not thought the law of his
case out and made clear its bearings on his case, and so ought not
to be seriously listened to; or else he is advising the court that
his case really falls outside what it is proper for a court to remedy.
But this means, in turn, that when a lawyer is thinking about the
use and work of "law," in general and in the large, it is law-in-
rules which comes to his mind, and the slogans about "decision
dictated by the rule of law," and "laws and not men" loom ten
times as large in his mind as even the best slogan about needed

---

[12] For recent discussion, see Pound's two last items in note 10. The ambiguity, or
better, multiguity of the word "justice" runs throughout Pound's writings: now it
means "justification," now "administration," now "the socially just," now "the just
as between these litigants," and again any combination of these elements. The context commonly indicates the dominant meaning; except of course on this crucial
question, where exactness is necessary to getting to the juice, and only the two
last-given concepts—which frequently need themselves to be distinguished—are
important.

change in rules, or justice for individual cases, could hope to loom. For the very changes that he urges in actual argument are urged nine times out of ten as *already* clearly "law." It is only in the particular, when the lawyer is thinking about how to shape up some one case actually in hand, that the felt justice of his cause, the need for making the court see and feel that his client is *right,* looms large in his mind; and even then, it looms as a problem in fact, not as a problem in law.

I wish I had the skill to make this clear. For it is simple fact that when men think consciously about a problem in its general aspects—such as the problem of what rules of law do, what effect they have on courts, what effect they ought to have, or indeed, under our legal system which works on "right rules" and "true rules," what effect they must have—it is simple fact that when men start to wrestle with such a problem, they think especially about the *parts* of that problem which are intellectually hard and intellectually articulate, about the parts which call for research and careful planning, and most especially about the parts to deal with which they must resort to books and to the definite, printed word. The rest of what goes into the problem they mostly forget or else assume; in any event they do not talk or write about it. So that the very lawyer who is most careful about the "atmosphere" of his every case, and who most deftly works each time to make the court feel justice on his side of it, to make the court want to accept his good and solid line of legal argument and reject his adversary's line of legal argument (which really, just as *legal* argument, is about as good and solid as his own)—that same lawyer will be telling you next day that it was the rules which decided that case; he "simply" got the court to "see" "the true" rule and its bearing. But if he is right in this, then a less skilful lawyer entrusted with the case might have lost it; and then the "true" rule would have turned out to be a different rule, at least for that case, perhaps for the whole line of cases: "settled in this State" thereafter. Indeed, it is a rare lawyer who has lost a case who does not feel that the court in deciding against him "departed" from the "clear" rule; but he does not so often feel that the courts make a practice of so departing—except in the cases he loses.[b]

[b] As indicated in THE COMMON LAW TRADITION, my own experience over the past twenty years has forced me to the conviction that such feeling, resentment and worry have been growing steadily and alarmingly among the bar. I note that those reviewers who differ most sharply do not seem to me to have had very full firsthand conversation-experience with either non-metropolitan lawyers or the less successful members of the metropolitan bar.

With this we come to the newer lines of Jurisprudence. From this foundation we can see what they are about, how far they have gotten (and how far they have *not* gotten), the queerly and immediately practical bearings of their theory, the reasons for these lines of Jurisprudence being so widely misunderstood, and where some of their next lines of fruitful inquiry must lie.

For the basic problems to which they are addressed are these. Taking as given the two facts, first, that judges and officials are not free to be "arbitrary," and must be held down and directed; and second, that they are and must be to some extent free to be just; then, first, is the rationale and doctrine about "laws *and not* men" and about "rules deciding cases"—is that the best description we can give of how in our legal system judges and officials are in fact held down and directed? Indeed, does not our legal system itself contain some other and better machinery, some more effective, more reckonable machinery, for holding them down when they need to be held down, for leaving them free where they need to be left free, and for directing them, inside this latter area? You can put this another way. There *is* in our legal system a vital and needed measure of stability and reckonability and control. There *is* also in our legal system a vital and needed measure of give and adjustment, of development and change, and of individualization, of which the study of rules of law alone, and as they stand at any given moment, gives no adequate indication. As a practical matter it is vital for lawyers to have the best intellectual wherewithal they can get, to judge when the court is going to be governed by the one and when it is going to be governed by the other. And as a practical matter lawyers need help in making that judgment about individual and particular counselling situations, individual and particular matters of litigation. The large and the long run, the sweep of the decades, will not do the lawyer's work here. He needs in this to get down to cases. It is not enough that "the course of decision has been characteristically steady and uniform." The lawyer needs light on the particular case which will be up tomorrow. The older Jurisprudence never did get down to particular cases, on this problem.

Hence, and naturally, the newer Jurisprudence began just here, began as a lawyer's Jurisprudence, built on worry over lawyers' needs in dealing with lawyers' problems about lawyers' *individual* cases: "The prophecies of what the courts will do in fact" is language addressed to the counsellor. But the newer Jurisprudence, wherever it begins, cannot fulfill its mission if it stops with the counsellor—though I should hate to see it leave off its interest in his work. There follows at once an interest in law from the angle of the advocate and his work—an angle revealing, among other things, the extraordinary leeway which our legal system allows in the particular case for reaching *either* result contended for, and for reaching either of those results *"under law."* There follows then, and no less, and indeed inescapably, an interest in the judge and his work.

In that portion of the newer Jurisprudence directed mainly at the *counsellor's* work, judges figure chiefly as officials whose prospective actions must be foreseen if possible; the figuring is in terms of probabilities; account has to be taken of the chance that a case may come up in an unfavorable setting, that it may be handled and argued abominably on one side and magnificently on the other; account has to be taken of intervening factors, possibly personal to judges and utterly irrelevant to any rule of law, which a client's proper protection simply does not allow a counsellor to ignore because that counsellor (or a jurisprude) may view their presence or possible presence with concern, or with alarm, or even with disgust. It is no infatuation with the ugly or the nasty or the wrong which leads the newer Jurisprudence, when studying the counsellor's work, to deal with the possible presence of official irregularity as affecting a client's realization of his rights. It is the practical need for studying how law's gears sometimes slip, in order that the slipping of law's gears may be effectively reduced. Thus even that "state of the judge's digestion" which has been the subject of considerable deprecatory comment on jurisprudes or by them[13] is still a matter which no cautious counsellor can leave out of his reckoning; instead, he tries to stay on legal and factual ground and record so solid as to guard against any state of any judge's digestion, any death of any witness, any prejudice of any jury.

In that quite different portion of the newer Jurisprudence which is directed at the work of the *advocate,* the study of judicial personality becomes not indeed the central, but certainly one central focus; for in the advocate's work not courts in general, but

[13] The difficulty in scientific use of any hypothesis resting on personal idiosyncrasy is to find adequate *evidence* to justify attributing any particular decision to any such factor. Guesses are of little use. But sometimes, as with Mansfield in *Stuart v. Wilkins* [see 52 HARV. L. REV. 725, 742 *et seq.* (1939)], a decision is so utterly out of known character as to call for some unusual factor to explain it. [Emery Anderson, in an unpublished thesis, has since persuaded me that I misread *Stuart v. Wilkins,* and that on its exact issue and exact language it is sound.]

one particular court, or in the event of appeal, then one particular series of courts, and at one particular time, and on one particular case, is concerned. Study of particular personalities becomes essential to the advocate; hence important for Jurisprudence if Jurisprudence is not to ignore the facts of life. In the case of a particular judge subject to dyspepsia, the unfortunate effects of a particular ill-advised breakfast do alter the advocate's practical problem. I confess to total inability to understand why, when the subject of study is the effect of advocacy and the bearing of the advocate's work on the result of cases and the growth of law, such matters should be regarded as either unilluminating or indecent to discuss. They are not, in acute forms, too frequent of occurrence; they are not always disturbing when they do occur; they do not alter the basic importance of law and law's rules and principles. But I have yet to meet an effective advocate who did not worry over them, who did not when they crossed his path work with or against them, who did not regard as bearing on his case, its presentation, and its outcome, even such matters as that "the judge is certainly feeling good this morning." And so long as law exists not for itself and *in vacuo,* but to serve the people, and so long as advocates and counsellors continue to be those through whom law's results are mediated to the people, and through whom the facts are strained and shaped for the court's use in reformulation of the law for the people, just so long will it be one fair part of Jurisprudence, to my mind, to study more in detail exactly how this great task of mediation is now being accomplished, in order that we may learn how to accomplish it more effectively, with less waste, and with fewer slip-ups.

Let me make plain that I have never discussed the judge's breakfast or headache before; I do not regard either as a peculiarly fruitful line of study. I mention them here simply to put into perspective the whole problem of the idiosyncrasies of particular officials. The perspective is that elimination of things we do not like, or coping with them, is best accomplished by trying to see what they are, where, how frequent, how they operate. Then we can get at them.[e]

But obviously the branch of Jurisprudence which is concerned with the *judge* and the *judge's work* must see the judge in a

[e] And surely we should note that *every* kind of idiosyncratic factor—including stomach-ulcers in general and any particular attack of acute dyspepsia—raises jurisprudential problems peculiarly for a bench where the one judge sits alone, without either the conditioning which accompanies being broken in to a bench or the immediate impact of the person, persuasion and vote of brethren in the case,

wholly different light. A counsellor has to worry over what a judge
will do, whether that doing is right or whether it is not right;
right or wrong, it decides a case; right or wrong, decent or indecent, it may make or remake a rule. For a counsellor at work
on counselling, what the courts *do* is thus the most important part
of law; whether, I repeat, the doing is right or not. But *judges*
(trial judges or appellate) cannot see law that way, nor can jurisprudes when they are working over either of the judges' functions
see law that way, nor can citizens, as citizens, see law that way
(though, as interested parties, they will do well to see law in fair
part that way). This is not to say that the "Prediction-of-official-
action" way of seeing law is a bad way or a wrong way to see
law; it is to say that the prediction way is an *incomplete* way to
see law. Indeed, and on the other hand, it would be an incomplete
way for even a judge to see law, if he should ignore this matter of
what courts will do, and sometimes do wrongly; for their doing—
even wrongly—is likely to make positive law which later courts
have to attend to; and what an upper court will do is what determines prospective affirmance or reversal of the court below. For
all this, the branch of Jurisprudence which deals with the judge
and his function must center no less upon the "just" solution
than upon the solution which other courts will reach, or even that
which the rules of law may seem to indicate. It must center no
less upon that idea and duty of the judge's office which requires
that somehow he is to arrive at a just outcome in the case before
him than upon that ideal which requires that he stay within and
follow the scheme of our prevailing law.

And by revealing this double job—imposed upon him by our
legal system *as* a double job—by revealing this as peculiarly the job
of the judge (or indeed of any responsible administrative official)
the newer Jurisprudence seems to me to get the matter a full
step further toward clarity and toward guidance. When we stop
talking just about "Law" in the large and what "Law"—in the
vague indefiniteness of "All Law at once"—is and does, then
certainty of prediction for a counsellor can stop getting all confused with good guidance for the judge, and then the judge's
peculiar problems, at trial or on appeal, come into much clearer
focus. The Jurisprudence of advocacy makes clear that the rules
of law as we have them do not alone provide certainty of prediction, or opposing counsel just could not make worthwhile arguments on two sides of the same case. The Jurisprudence of advocacy thus centers attention upon the need for the judge to get some

guidance and help in *choosing between two tenable lines of legal argument from the authorities. Over and above the guidance and partial control given by the rules of law which we have, there is further guidance needed.* Rules giving that further guidance— rules akin to, but deeper than, our rules on use of precedent— need articulation, and are in process of getting that articulation, and of providing the further guidance which we need. And that is a problem that does not come out of hiding for sustained and articulate and rational study until we observe that the mere rules of law, in their combination, and indeed in their language, speak to the particular case so very often with a forked tongue. Any advance the newer Jurisprudence can make along this line will rather obviously advance certainty in the results of law and further the articulate rational guidance of decision—a certainty and articulate guidance of which we now have less than we need, because of our overemphasis on the rules of law alone as being *the* great factor, the *only* observable and recordable factor, and hence the *only rationally manipulable* factor, which controls judges—and other officials.

Pound has done good pioneering here, in regard to the part played by "ideal elements" in law; and by his more recent emphasis on the stabilizing force of "taught traditions"; but what these mean in detail, when one gets down to cases, lies still unexplored. Almost wholly unworked out is the reduction of these ideas and their bearings to concrete normative form for use in practice by judges and by other law-officials faced with decision under law of some particular doubtful case in hand. Indeed our rules of precedent themselves need going over, as do those for statutory construction. For any lawyer is aware that whereas we have clear and established practice, and even rules, to tell, for instance, *how* to distinguish a precedent, and *how* to give even bold dictum full weight by quotation and citation of what "this court has declared," as "a true expression of the principle," we yet have no unambiguous rules at all to tell *when* to do the one or the other or anything between or different. And the same holds as to, say, "remedial" and "strict" construction of statutes. Pound's line of initial approach to the matter is thoroughly sound: the necessary basis for better doctrine does lie in the laying out of new and more effective lines of descriptive study of the actual work of the courts with our rules of law, and within the frame of action, which those rules mark out. For it is by careful and accurate description of what the courts are doing that we can see when and wherein existing doctrine fails to *guide* them effectively in being wise, and fails to hold down their freedom to be "arbitrary." Yet any attempted description will for the next decade need repeated testing in *detail* on particular series of cases in particular courts, so as to check up on just how good and accurate a description it may be; and above all, so as to bring out for study what else and more there may be which also needs description and comparison. Only so can the basis be laid for clearer and more unambiguous doctrine on how judges are to go about the judge's job. To date, we have left much more of this to mere untutored and unguided experience than a system of Law has any business to.[14]

The philosophy of this can be stated briefly: Legal doctrine cannot wisely attempt to achieve what is impossible of achievement. To make courts either stand still or ignore the justice of the case in hand is impossible. (It is also undesirable.) Doctrine which purports to cut down all freedom of the judge or other official is therefore unserviceable doctrine. In practice, it leads to the production and use of *de facto* leeways which *de jure* are left unmentioned; and *de facto* but unmentioned leeways are both confusing and not subject to easy control. But to merely see this and then insist that judges—and other officials—are in fact as free to move as the *rules of law now leave* them whenever they really *want* to move; or to insist that they *ought* to use all the freedom which the rules of law now leave them—either of these things is to make doctrine fit only for the super-judges, the Mansfields and Marshalls, and not for the McWhirtles and McWhortles who, though good and solid men, do yet need guidance and may sometimes need control. To see just what we have, in the way of either control or guidance, is a job for realistic observation, observation of fact, of detailed fact, observation which cuts beneath formula, sustained observation. To see just what is needed, in control of freedom to be arbitrary, while leaving the necessary freedom to be just, is a job for such observation plus legal statesmanship. To formulate for practical use rules and principles which can help materially in accomplishing the desired gain in both certainty and justice, is a

[14] For an extremely interesting sequence on this point, see Radin, *The Theory of Judicial Decision: or, How Judges Think*, 11 A.B.A.J. 357 (1925); Dewey's papers cited by Patterson; MORRIS, HOW LAWYERS THINK (1937) and my review thereof, 51 HARV. L. REV. 757 (1938); Levi, *Natural Law, Precedent and Thurman Arnold*, 24 VA. L. REV. 587 (1938); Patterson in the forthcoming THE PHILOSOPHER OF THE COMMON MAN (Ratner ed. 1940); and the forthcoming papers at the Cincinnati Bar Association Conference on Judicial Precedent (1940); with all of which compare Hamilton, *The Jurist's Art, infra* note 15, and Moore and Sussman, *The Lawyer's Law*, 41 YALE L. J. 566 (1932).

job for legal engineering. The task is not chimerical, because we know that there can be training for the art of advocacy; the Greeks accomplished that, and so did the Scholastics. We know, too, that there can be training for counselling; the offices "break men in," year by year. *Some* of the art of advocacy, *some* of the art of counselling, can be reduced to helpful rules and principles. Judging, too, is a craft and art of law. Well, then?

The "Well, then?" is a challenge, not a performance. The newer Jurisprudence is yet far from having worked out with clarity the relation, in the judge's actual work, of the ideal and ideological elements in our legal system to the words of the rules of law, or the relation of either of these to the going institutional practices of courts and judges. That is a plain next problem for study. The newer Jurisprudence can claim to have gotten it into the clear, to be seen as a problem. That is not too much. But what there is of it, is good.

Another problem, on which a beginning has been made, is the examination of the three major aspects of the judge, and of their relations to one another in his work. He is a *human being,* and in our system he is an American. He is a *lawyer,* and in our system he is a common-lawyer. He is a *judge,* and in our system a common-law judge of the modern American type—which is very different not only from being a Continental or English judge, but also from being merely an American, or merely a lawyer, or merely an American lawyer. Some of the older Jurisprudence is written as if a judge were practically nothing but a mechanical lawyer on a bench; some of the newer reads almost as if he were nothing but a human American in a black robe. Neither of these points of view is to be simply scorned, because there are facts under each; but no such point of view, *alone,* has value as more than a reminder that certain very real factors in the picture are never to be forgotten.

With the above serving as a rough indicator of what the newer Jurisprudence started from, and of the problems it is opening for study—as well as of how far it is as yet from fulfillment of its mission—let us glance over a few of the more striking writers and see what they may thus far have contributed, and why what seems so sane a line of inquiry should have elicited so much opposition. I shall for convenience deal with a few men who have written books, though much of the best material is in articles; and I shall choose books on Jurisprudence, though much of the most telling material is in monographic papers on specific legal topics.

Let me premise one word of caution. American jurisprudes are case-trained lawyers. Case-trained lawyers are trained to think with the middle of an idea, with its core; they have the case-law habit of using words very loosely around the edges of an idea. Their arguments are built to the issue in hand, and their dicta, if only the dicta help argue the issue in hand, can be grandly obiter, giving no indication at all of what they have any intention of standing to, when some *different* case or issue may be in hand. Our judges write law thus, and thus our jurisprudes have written jurisprudence. It makes for lively reading; it also makes for inexactitude, and it makes for very easy misconception. However, it is the way of our law, and it has been the way of most of our Jurisprudence. Holmes did it, Pound does it, practically all the newer writers do it more or less. But two things will be noted which indicate that the ball is really moving forward. One is that those writers whose practice, while phrasing their jurisprudential *rationes decidendi,* is to look the wording over with most thought to issues other than the one immediately in hand, are those who have been least attacked: the writings—and they are worth reading[15]—of Radin, Hamilton, Fuller, and Morris Cohen have not,

[15] The more prolific writers, such as Radin, Hamilton, and Pound, are extremely uneven. Each, at his best, is very fine. In addition to material cited elsewhere herein, the following are characteristic, and illuminating:

Radin: *The Permanent Problems of the Law,* 15 CORNELL L. Q. 1 (1929); *The Chancellor's Foot,* 49 HARV. L. REV. 44 (1935); *Solving Problems by Statute,* 14 ORE. L. REV. 90 (1934); and presumably the forthcoming Storrs lectures at Yale: THE LAW AS LOGIC AND AS EXPERIENCE. [These last were in my opinion not up to Radin's standard before and since.]

Hamilton: *Institution,* in 8 ENCYC. SOC. SCIENCES 84 (1932); *The Jurist's Art,* 31 COLUM. L. REV. 1073 (1931) (on Brandeis); *Cardozo, The Craftsman,* 6 U. OF CHI. L. REV. 1 (1938); *Preview of a Justice,* 48 YALE L. J. 819 (1939) (on Frankfurter); 39 COLUM. L. REV. 724 (1939) (on Blackstone); (with Adair) THE POWER TO GOVERN (1937); PRICE AND PRICE POLICIES (Hamilton ed. 1938).

Fuller: *American Legal Realism,* 82 U. OF PA. L. REV. 429 (1934); *On Williston's "Contracts",* 18 N. C. L. REV. 1 (1939). The forthcoming lectures at Northwestern on THE LAW IN QUEST OF ITSELF should be of equal value. [I did not find them so, but there has been much fine later work.]

M. Cohen: LAW AND THE SOCIAL ORDER (1933).

Carter: LAW, ITS ORIGIN, GROWTH, AND FUNCTION (1907) is the best known work; much more satisfactory is the little-known pamphlet, THE IDEAL AND THE ACTUAL IN LAW (1890). GRAY'S NATURE AND SOURCES OF THE LAW (1909, 2d ed. 1921) is a more rounded, and wiser, book.

Pound: *The Scope and Purpose of Sociological Jurisprudence,* 24 HARV. L. REV. 591, 25 *id.* at 140 (1911–12); INTERPRETATIONS OF LEGAL HISTORY (1930). In general, and with exceptions, the articles published before 1921 assay high, and those after 1930 lower, *e.g.,* that cited in note 16, *infra,* which re-slaughters a dead horse. In the particular field of Torts, under discussion in that paper, one cannot, for instance, dispose of the good modern work as one does and should of Brooks Adams' naivetés. Compare Douglas, *Vicarious Liability and Administration of Risk,* 38 YALE L. J. 584, 720 (1929); Steffen, *Independent Contractor and The Good Life,* 2 U. OF CHI.

for example, come in for the drubbings administered to those of Carter, Pound, Frank, Hutcheson, and Arnold. The second thing is that the drubbings undertaken in the Donnybrook of Jurisprudence have almost never been undertaken upon any writer's central and basic thought, upon the good *core* of what he was either saying or trying to say, but have instead whaled the daylights out of some loose-hanging piece of the thought's verbal clothing. This happens with treble ease in Jurisprudence because there is in that field no accepted machinery of pleading to produce an issue before battle. Which again makes for a lively spectacle, as two armored and embattled knights charge clashing past each other.

Let me now try to sketch briefly one of the major lines of recent writing. To my mind, the central one is the inquiry into "certainty of law"; in any event, it has produced bound books and the merriest bonfires. Ten years ago Jerome Frank, then a practitioner, came out with *Law and the Modern Mind,* and followed the book with a series of articles. The essence of the book was to take the doctrine that rules of law decide cases in certain and predictable fashion and to demonstrate and document that, taken as description of what happened in court, it wasn't so. What Frank was worried about was why lawyers thought it was so when it wasn't so,

---

L. REV. 501 (1935); Hamilton, *The Living Law,* 26 SURVEY GRAPHIC 632 (1937); Evatt on Pound on spring-guns, below, note 16.

Indeed, and in general, modern use of economic factors for study of the drives influencing law brings out results rather comparable to Pound's own results with "security of transactions" and "security of acquisitions," but more tentative than these latter, because more detailed. Compare Steffen and Danziger, *The Rebirth of the Commercial Factor,* 36 COLUM. L. REV. 745 (1936); Lerner, *John Marshall and The Campaign of History,* 39 COLUM. L. REV. 396 (1939); Llewellyn, *On Warranty of Quality,* 36 COLUM. L. REV. 699; 37 *id.* at 341 (1936–37); *Horse-Trade and Merchant's Market in Sales,* 52 HARV. L. REV. 725, 873 (1939). For admirable very recent work by Pound, see *A Hundred Years of American Law,* 1 LAW—A CENTURY OF PROGRESS 8 (N. Y. U. 1937). *What is the Common Law?* cited *supra* note 10. Pound's strength lies in tremendous reading coupled with a peculiar flair for flashing suggestion that lights up significant currents. His weakness lies in impatience about fitting his multitude of good ideas together, where they overlap or conflict; with a consequent tendency to use any one of his own suggestions at any given time as a solid, safe major premise, out beyond where, unqualified, it is neither safe nor solid. His keen juristic instinct then signals trouble. At this point he either goes into new and closer examination of the data, and works out an enlightening relation between the overlapping ideas; or else he allows the rhetorician in him to curtain the felt uncertainty with waving words.

Hutcheson: JUDGMENT INTUITIVE (1938), especially the title essay; *The Glorious Uncertainty of our Lady of the Law,* 23 J. AM. JUD. SOC. 73 (1939); and the forthcoming addresses at Cincinnati last February. LAW AS LIBERATOR (1937) came too early to reflect Hutcheson's recent advance in analysis.

and he proceeded to explore at some length a psychoanalytical hypothesis which, from then to now, does not appear to have appealed much to anyone except Frank.

In this three things are significant. First, Frank cleared the ground. He cleared the ground because he met the older doctrine, in its less sophisticated form, head on, and in its own terms, and showed it to be unsound description: Do rules do a one hundred percent job of deciding cases with predictable certainty? They do not. Frank advanced the ball on this issue that far, and no further: after his documentation it is no longer possible for an intelligent jurisprude to argue seriously the contrary position; and once the first shock was over, no one has seriously argued the contrary position. But what that does is only to show that one particular half-true formulation never should have had currency as being a whole truth. It does not show "uncertainty" in the law, in any sense of coin-flipping chanciness. What it shows is lack of 100 per cent certainty, and that is all it shows. Whereas 100 per cent certainty is not a thing anybody ever had any business to think that we had. What law needs is a manageable degree of certainty and pre-dictability—enough to get on with; more here and maybe less there. Have we that sort of *Certainty-Enough?* Frank gives no answer. He does open the way for posing the problem intelligently and for doing inquiry where inquiry can count.

The second significant thing is the way both Frank and his adversaries argued. Having posed the issue: "Is there (100 per cent) Certainty?" Frank first cut to results, as being the essence of Law, *for his issue:* for the litigant, certainty is as certainty does. He cut then to the results of litigation, because there unpredictable results were to be found; and he went into the trial court by preference, because he found evidence his way fastest there. Frank's adversaries, on the other hand, talked normative rules as being the essence of Law, because occasional or even frequent improper results do not upset a *rule* (though it is plain enough that they do upset certainty for the interested parties); and then the Anti-Franks talked situations in which counsel had shaped the transaction in advance, and which never came up for litigation; and in regard to litigated cases, they talked appellate courts, where at least the records are settled, and benches sit instead of individuals. Such argumentation leads to no issue; and at the moment of controversy it leads to little light. Each side can celebrate a pseudo-victory; each does; each did. With bonfires. But after the smoke blows off, even such controversy proves to have gotten us a further step along. In this instance, we can now begin to see such things as these: (1) that where counsellors are consulted, there is a body of very solid and predictable law (rules *and* practices) which makes possible the shaping of such transactions as are at all reasonable and decent, with a high degree of certainty—though even these are not utterly proof against skilled perjury; and though when counsellors attempt to accomplish things too outrageous the courts are likely to break over the seeming rules, and to upset what was really injudicious counselling. (2) Whereas there is a great body of less certain law in which rival theories (say, as to just how far a precedent extends) are available, and much will depend on the case which happens to come up, and on the relative skill of the rival advocates, and even on the personnel of the court, as well as on the rules, principles, and classification-concepts of the law. And (3) that the individual litigation, especially where it does not rest on a carefully and skilfully prearranged transaction, offers material elements of uncertainty which no student of our law can afford to hide under any general theory that Law is Certain, but the reduction of which to a greater reckonability is one major task of the profession. This begins to mark out workable subdivisions of "the" problem "of Certainty in Law"—subdivisions whose marking out is a gain for clarity of understanding, a furtherer of intelligent inquiry. To take a single practical application, it is astonishing to discover how clear and sure a rule one can build out of the usury cases when one sets as his inquiry not a question in the second area just described (what is the full distance you can go, and yet avoid the usury prohibition?—a most uncertain matter, as Corpus Juris shows), but a question in the first area (how far can you go in proper ways and still be almost certain to avoid the usury prohibition?). To answer this second question, one discards the chancy cases, one builds on the clear cases, and works out in consequence a solid investment apparatus instead of a speculation. Such differentiation is old stuff *to the best lawyers*. It is not old stuff to the run of the profession. The newer Jurisprudence has as one major function to make this kind of working wisdom more explicit, and so more communicable, and so more teachable, and so more common.

Indeed it is a fair generalization that almost nothing the newer Jurisprudence has yet found, and little that it seems likely to find within the next few decades, will prove in any manner *new*, to the *best* lawyers. It will be, as it has been, a putting together of different pieces of what the *best* lawyers know—different pieces which

even the best lawyers do not commonly put together and *compare*
—so as to make the resulting Whole give other lawyers, and
especially new lawyers, a clearer and more usable picture of how
the various crafts of the lawyer are best carried on: counselling,
advocacy, judging in either aspect, and administration.

The third significant thing about the work of Frank is, on the
one hand, that by dragging into his book a dubious psychoanalytical hypothesis, he opened the solid part of his work to the dialectic
reproach that it rested on Freudian psychology. Which it did not.
The solid part rested on sound observation, tested and recorded.
The Freudian part of the work, on the other hand, is Frank's individual excursion; it is useful to have had somebody do it so
that others may see how far he did not get. On the other hand,
the Anti-Franks not only have sought to make hay out of his
Freudian sowing, but with equal dialectical acumen have read
into his work a desire which is there neither in letter nor in
thought—a desire to exalt brute power and official arbitrariness
at the expense of the right, the orderly, the lawful, and the just.
This is a typical example of the cross-purposing of words in the
Non-Joinder of Issues in Jurisprudence. As we have seen, Frank's
concern is with certainty, for lawyers, in lawyers' daily work. Certainty finds its essence for lawyers and their clients in certainty of
outcome, and the tribunal determines the outcome. Hence what
the official does is the particular kind of "law," the "certainty" of
which Frank is testing. But the Anti-Frank is seeing as "Law"
only a right and approved rule or norm *for* action by judges or
officials. When he sees anything given the name of "Law"—for
any purpose at all—that means to him that the thing so named is
being called "right," and is being approved as a guide "for" action
by officials. When read in this perhaps understandable but sadly
twisted way, Frank's words can be made to take on shocking character. And the misreading is doubly easy if the misreader himself,
sure that we need to keep judges and officials from acting according to their "arbitrary" will and desire, happens also to believe
that the sole way to serve that need is by maintaining the beloved
doctrine and rationale "Laws and not Men" or "It is the rules
which (alone) decide the cases." For those are formulations of
doctrine which Frank does certainly attack: first, as being untrue
descriptions; second, as being inadequate doctrine. Rules and
principles are part of what produces decision, says Frank. There
is more, much more. What more? How much more? How can we
bring the "more" under more rational control? Frank did not

know, for sure. Neither do you. But we need to know. And as for further study of the matter, the way to resume is to resume.

Into this certainty controversy Pound, in the post-Frank whirl, injected at least four ideas which have real fertility, and whose implications need following up as much as does that subdivision of the field of study which is the first conclusion to be derived from Frank's work. The Pound ideas with their appropriate caveats are these: first, no study of law which is to cover the whole of the ground can take its eye off the ideal elements which the facts only partially reflect. This holds even for purely descriptive study; ideals—notably those two ideals, so often inconsistent in their seeming bearings on a particular matter, the ideal of certainty and the ideal of justice—ideals do show observable effects on the behavior of judges, and of other people. The caveat is that the effects they show which we thus far know about are mass effects, and that lawyers, and judges, need a Jurisprudence which can get closer to guidance as to tomorrow's *individual* cases. Pound's second useful idea was to challenge any assumption that because such a doctrine as "rules of law decide cases" is inadequate as a full description of what happens, it is therefore inadequate as doctrine. Bad description may, as he points out, be admirable doctrine; for one function of doctrine is to get facts and results shaped out of what they are into what they ought to be. The caveat is that this *particular* piece of doctrine needs supplement not because it is bad description, but because it too often fails to give clear guidance in the particular case; if left unsupplemented, it leaves to the hunching process the determination of such matters as when a precedent will be distinguished, when on the other hand it will be followed flat, or even have its "principle" extended. Pound's third contribution has been mentioned: the re-emphasis on the "concepts" of our law, our "relational thinking," our "legal techniques," as being clusters of elements in our law which, over and above the rules and principles of law, help guide decision and control it; and his introduction of the formula "taught tradition" into the picture, as a further cluster of guidance. The caveat is that all of these are multiguous both in the large and in the particular; again the lawyer's vital question goes unanswered—to wit, which technique is the correct technique to use on this statute or precedent in this case. But the ideas mentioned remain magnificent focussing glasses for further deailed study. And Morris Cohen, for example, in his insistence on a phenomenon in law akin to "fields" of force and strain-in-a-given-direction in physics, advanced the ball here; as does Levi with his inquiry into what leads us to find "similarities" for the application or extension of rules. Such work needs to be built together, tested out concretely on series of cases, refined, further developed. A further caveat on this matter of the "taught" tradition runs to the fact that a goodly portion of our effective tradition is not taught at all, but remains hidden in the unspoken; it is only learned, it is absorbed through the pores or through haphazard imitation, or it is reinvented, man by man, in the process of doing the job. This untaught portion of the tradition, especially of the tradition of judging, is acquired unevenly, and we have as yet no convenient or communicable way of checking up on how or how far it has been absorbed, or indeed on what it is. But efforts at reduction of its content and use to more rational description and control are of the essence of increasing certainty and wisdom in judging. Pound rightly warns us in a current essay that we must not expect too much from reason in the law;[16] one can go with the warning, and yet feel it essential to use, in consistent, sustained, self-corrective effort, such reason as we have, in an effort to reduce to somewhat greater manageability those silent aspects of the law which lie in the judges' *ways of work*.

The fourth contribution of Pound to the advancement of the ball is difficult to describe, but was the most serviceable of all. Again and again, in language often difficult to make clear meaning out of, and often enough at intellectual odds with itself inside the same essay, he recurs to one vital point: if these modern jurisprudes are forgetting that the goal of law is justice, and forgetting also that judges and other officials must not be free to be arbitrary, then they need correction at once and, if need be, with a club. For to Pound the heart and core of Jurisprudence is what the heart and core of Jurisprudence ought to be to any scholar: to wit, right guidance to the judge—or to the legislator—or to the administrator. And I for one am ready to do open penance for any part I may have played [17] in giving occasion for the feeling that

---

[16] *The Economic Interpretation and the Law of Torts,* 53 HARV. L. REV. 365, 368 *et seq.* (1940). [The general thesis of this paper of Pound's needs the corrections suggested above in note 15, p. 146, and the re-examination of some of the basic data provided by Evatt, *Judges and Teachers of Public Law,* 53 HARV. L. REV. 1145, 1148–1152 (1940)].

[17] Especially, so far as I can make out, by one remark on page three of my BRAMBLE BUSH, although half that book is devoted to rules and their meaning, and my own doubts had been as to whether it did not contain more preaching of ethics than students would stand for. In any event, BRAMBLE BUSH, *page three,* is cited almost wherever this matter is under adverse critical discussion, and the rest of BRAMBLE BUSH is not. So, *e.g.,* by Auburtin, Kantorowicz, Dickinson, Goodhart,

modern jurisprudes or any of them had ever lost sight of this. I do not think any of them ever has. They seem to me to be singularly affected, one and all, with zeal for justice, and with zeal for improving the *legal* techniques for doing the law's business. But it is certainly in large part the result of Pound's indefatigable reaffirmance of the basic truth about the heart of Jurisprudence that the other moderns are taking pains these days to make sure that they get and keep these interests of theirs from being overlooked or misconceived.

This problem of finding guidance for the judge is the core of Cardozo's jurisprudential thinking; upon it all his descriptive study centers. It is the core of Hutcheson's writing as well. Neither doubts the presence and importance of precedent and rule of law, of principle and concept; nor does either show impatience with these things. But each, facing at once the rules of law and the judicial task, found that the rules provide not *the* answer, but only part of the answer, for the task. Each, therefore, set about to see what could be said about what *also* there was to the task, and what *other* guidance there might be available for the doing of it. Each, thoughtfully but gropingly, in careful searching of his experience and his conscience, came out with some light, which is not as yet enough light. Hutcheson's contributions must be considered as hardly more than begun. The "judicial hunch" and the "little, small dice" expressed deep conviction on three points: first, that there was more to it than the rules of law, and that the "more" was frequently the most vital part. Second, that it thus became a question of individual judicial responsibility to the case and to the country. Third, that the judge himself was often puzzled as to how he got the answer, even when he had become certain that he had it. But first in the address on "glorious uncertainty," and again and more clearly at Cincinnati last February[b] Hutcheson's analysis moved a definite step forward: he marked out what the field of the judge's *limitation* was; he marked out where the judge came very close to being *controlled* by precedent. To get that down and get it clear is to subdivide the original problems for study; with *control* largely clarified, the search for ar-

Pound, Kocourek. One high authority makes that ill-starred single page lead off a long list of citations whose every other member is a book or a full article. I hereby repudiate BRAMBLE BUSH, page three, save when taken in conjunction with chapter V of that book; even then, I regard its emphasis as out of balance; let me set with it also 1100 pages of study of the law of Sales, which appeared in the same year. [On this, see the later editions of BRAMBLE BUSH, the *Foreword*.]

[b] 14 U. CINC. L. REV. 259 (1940), and my comment, *ibid.*, at 283.

ticulating the lines of *guidance* in the area left open becomes much more sure. Hutcheson's next writings will prove exciting.

Indeed when one takes as the central theme this problem of guidance to the judge—or to the legislator—or to the administrator—one finds every line of work in modern Jurisprudence falling into an organization as clear as that of spokes around a common hub, building themselves together into a common wheel. Any one of these lines may be pursued in a single paper or by a single writer, in utter independence of the others, in complete "narrow" specialization of effort, in seeming variety of direction among the different jobs; yet each in its own way works to and from the common center, each contributes toward the total central task which calls for use of all of them together. Let me illustrate by a number of lines of modern work which would seem to be at war, if any of them should be misestimated as being what it is not, namely as being an effort to stake out an exclusively valid approach to the *whole* field of Jurisprudence. None of these lines is to be soundly conceived as denying the worthwhileness, utility, necessity, of other, complementary lines of work. What each does is to insist that its own line has sufficient value, actual or potential, to warrant careful and sustained labor on its exploration. The older writers—such men as Bentham, Savigny, Ihering—seem sometimes to have written as if work in Jurisprudence had no point unless it could at the moment of its doing be brought into its right relation with a whole and rounded view of all of law and all law's work. The current writers, even along with the impatience they sometimes display with one another or with a tough-minded and sometimes tough-hided profession, do show a gratifying intellectual patience in this: that they are willing to work hard over one small piece of the picture, just as being one needed piece, in an effort to get *that piece* into better shape for synthesis tomorrow, and perhaps by someone else who may happen to take synthesis as his line of labor.[18]

[18] Much of the controversy turns on cross-purposing of this sort: X alleges that the psychology of judges needs study, and tries some study along behavioristic lines. Y reads that X is trying to *substitute* behavioristic psychology for rules and principles, to deny free will to judges, and to urge as right law whatever judges take it into their heads to do. *I.e.*, much cross-purposing turns on reading an X's insistence that something or other goes into or is part of Jurisprudence—is a spoke—as being an allegation that the something is the exclusive *all* of Jurisprudence: wheel and hub. This is an inevitable accompaniment of exploratory writing. The explorer commonly overstresses, in language and in flavor, the value or significance of the particular thing he is after. Even if he does not, it is the novel which stands out to the reader, and by filling his *attention* and being the

There is for instance the logical work of Michael and Adler on the problem and law of proof.[19] They work out a formal logical analysis in much greater detail and with much greater rigor than is the practice of our law. Accepting thus what is already one of the recognized working tools of the law, logic, they explore the light and guidance to be had from using that tool with a precision and incisive impact which practice has edged away from because the practice of our law has been to treat *sustained* and accurate formal logic as impractical. Yet the results of the Michael-Adler effort are extremely illuminating, and a similar effort would, to my mind, illuminate any field of law in which some single fairly well-accepted postulate is alleged to control. To put an instance, the conception that contracts are made by the parties as they will to make them could no longer maintain itself if its consequences were once worked out cleanly and fearlessly, and put down to be looked at in their utter inconsistency with that half or more of contract law which real acceptance of that postulate would require our courts to junk: constructive conditions, for one typical example, or the law of penalties, or the infant's privilege, or the requirements of consideration and of the statute of frauds.[20]

Such work in formal logical analysis, while it is going on, requires temporary utter contentment with the premises on which it rests; else the logical development will not be clean. It requires temporary utter indifference to the consequences derived from the premises, else the unpleasant or distasteful consequences contained in the premises will not be deduced and expressed; the logical operation will instead be fudged. But this does not mean that the men of formal logic are at odds with such other men as Felix Cohen when these latter are insisting on the utter need for digging out the ethical premises underlying rules of statute or decision, for making those premises explicit, and for testing out whether they are good premises.[21] There is another line of work

---

Whole for the moment, to him, it almost by necessity appears to reek with implicit denial of everything else.

[19] THE NATURE OF JUDICIAL PROOF (1931); *The Trial of an Issue of Fact*, 34 COLUM. L. REV. 1224, 1462 (1934).

[20] A first indication of the degree to which the postulate does not hold up, in either established law or accepted doctrine, is found in Cook, *Review of Williston on Contracts*, 33 ILL. L. REV. 497 (1939). And see the lovely illumination of the criminal law in Michael and Wechsler's forthcoming book, by following the particular variant premises of our criminal law through rigorously, and displaying the bearings of the various conclusions on one another. Compare their *Rationale of the Law of Homicide*, 37 COLUM. L. REV. 701, 1326 (1937).

[21] FELIX COHEN, ETHICAL SYSTEMS AND LEGAL IDEALS (1933).

which fits into the picture. One finds much written by the newer jurisprudes about the importance of the effects of law, the importance of seeing what actually happens in or out of court, the importance of the actual behavior of judges or other officials, the importance of what the laymen concerned are actually doing, doing under the law, or with it, or in spite of it. What this means, in the perspective, is that the total picture of law and law's work extends beyond either the rules alone or the ideals alone, and indeed beyond the immediate legal institutions such as courts; and that it pays, on any given matter, to go exploring. To a lawyer actively engaged on a case this seems somewhat obvious, as to that case. It has sounded a little strange when the context has been that of Jurisprudence, because Jurisprudence has been conceived as a Philosophy of *Law*, and Law has commonly been distinguished from Fact. But Jurisprudence as a Philosophy of Law is too narrowly conceived to reach its full development; the modern writers are conceiving it as a philosophy *not only* of Law, *but also* of Law's Function, *and* of Law's Operation, *and* of Legal Institutions: *i.e.*, of Law *and* Law's Work,[22] *and* Law's Personnel.[23] Such widening

[22] The evidence of this pervades the law reviews. The last five to ten volumes of CHICAGO, COLUMBIA, HARVARD, YALE, LAW AND CONTEMPORARY PROBLEMS can be cited almost in bloc, with special emphasis on the student notes. Neither is the discussion and investigation of fact-situation and of law's effects limited to the more important and even theatrical issues in the forefront of public attention ranging from, say, labor and corporate finance (with 77B) on into the alphabetical administrators and the problems of taxation—the bulk of which material in the reviews mentioned alone is enough to cause wonder at Nussbaum's judgment that "the amount of fact research is slight." 40 COLUM. L. REV. 189, 200 (1940). Of course, all perspective is distorted if reading concentrates upon the polemical or programmatic writings, as most critics have, or even upon the signed writings. The test of vitality in the movement lies in the bulking student work, in the spread of research beneath the doctrinal surface into the odd corners where public interest is *not* focused, and in the cumulation of such work. Some scattered sampling is cited from the earlier work in my *Some Realism About Realism*, 44 HARV. L. REV. 1222 (1931), in the footnotes and the appendix. The type of thing I mean is the symposium on small debtors, 42 YALE L. J. 473–642 (1933), followed up by such papers as Elson, *Collection of Unpaid Wages and Financial Responsibility of Employers*, 5 U. OF CHI. L. REV. 609 (1938); Garrison, *Wisconsin's New Personal Receivership Law*, (1938) WIS. L. REV. 201; Stone and Thomas, *California's Legislature Faces the Small Loan Problem*, 27 CALIF. L. REV. 286 (1939). Or the delvings into odd corners of contract law cited *infra* note 27. Or Britt, *Blood Grouping Tests and the Law*, 21 MINN. L. REV. 671 (1937); Galton, *Blood-Grouping Tests and Their Relationship to the Law*, 17 ORE. L. REV. 177 (1938). Or Goble, *The Moral Hazard Clauses of the Standard Fire Insurance Policy*, 37 COLUM. L. REV. 410 (1937). Or the extraordinary mass of material which has accumulated, some of it informative and penetrating, on the subject of the consumer's action for defects causing serious damage. Or the material sampled in French, THE AUTOMOBILE COMPENSATION PLAN (1933); Symposium, *Financial Protection for the Motor Accident Victim*, 3 LAW AND CONTEMP. PROB. 465 *et seq.* (1936).

of scope involves not elimination, but illumination, of rules and principles of Law. In much the same fashion the emphasis placed on descriptive study is to be understood. To deal with conditions, you have to know what they are. To see what they are, you have to do your best, while you are trying to observe and record, to keep your vision from being tinted with what you either desire or abhor; neither viewing with alarm nor pointing with pride is a good road into balanced observation. If descriptive studies, or would-be descriptive studies, are viewed as spokes of the great wheel, they fit, and they help. If they are misviewed, as being efforts to cover the whole ground of Jurisprudence with reference to their subject-matter, they shock, because they are then given the sad semblance of attempting to eliminate the proper function of Law, which is to control and direct; or what is almost worse, such misviewing gives them the semblance of attempting to make Law merely follow and conform to what may be evil practices found to exist among laymen or officials.

The newer Jurisprudence has in all of this shown one rather gratifying quality. It is plain enough from what has been said that different men have been working in different areas, along different lines, and that any of the lines, if mistaken as seeking to be an effort to stake out the Whole of Jurisprudence, can be made to look pretty awful. In addition, the temptation to lump all the newer writing into one "School" lies very close; for all of it contains at least the common element of a strong feeling that the older Jurisprudence is not alone sufficient unto our needs. But a "School" whose characterizing attributes are supposedly found at the extremes of the several spokes is bound to be a terrifying thing for a man to be accused of belonging to; and it gratifies, that most of the newer writers have gone their ways attending as best they could to the jobs that they were on, and trying to go on learning, without too much regard for the labels which were pasted on them.

Such case-books as Durfee and Dawson's on REMEDIES, Steffen's on AGENCY and on COMMERCIAL PAPER, Powell's on TRUSTS AND ESTATES, Michael and Wechsler's on CRIMINAL LAW, my own on SALES, and, despite the practical absence of notes, Thayer's on the LAW MERCHANT, are effective studies on how the law works and what lines of law work best, and why, and on how to use the law, as well as teaching tools for instruction in the law.

[23] Symposium, *The "Unauthorized Practice of Law" Controversy*, 5 LAW AND CONTEMP. PROB. 1–174 (1938); A. B. A. COMM. ON PROFESSIONAL ECONOMICS, THE ECONOMICS OF THE LEGAL PROFESSION (1938); Stone, *Certain European Legal Aid Offices*, 25 CALIF. L. REV. 52 (1936); Garrison, *Low Cost Legal Service in Sweden*, 26 A. B. A. J. 215, 293 (1940).

Let us go on to observe another spoke or two of the wheel. Here are men like Brendan Brown, trying to work out in clear detail the implications for our common case-law and for our detailed legislation of the Natural Law as developed, say, by Aquinas.[24] They are going to be using, in making their determinations of what health of our society calls for under Natural Law premises, the fact-grubbing of realistic writers who are at the moment of grubbing no closer to philosophy than the study of such things as what language the certification-stamps of Chicago, St. Louis, and Pittsburgh banks contain.[25] Or, here is a "behaviorist" at work on trying to add to the techniques for guiding judicial decision.[26] For the moment he is disregarding judicial language, and may seem to superficial observation to be "warring on rule and principle." He may gather twenty or two hundred cases on some situation, and try to play facts and issue straight against result. But if he succeeds, what he will bring out will be a *new and better rule or principle of case-law:* "The factor which the judges have been feeling for, and responding to, in this situation, has not yet been clearly articulated in the rules in vogue. Here it is. It focuses the real issue; it lines up the cases; stating it this way helps you predict more accurately what will happen; it helps a judge see more clearly what to do, and why. It is 'the true rule' of the situation." [27]

Run through the branches—or the budding twigs—of the newer Jurisprudence, then, and you will see each one growing and hardening to become a good spoke of the wheel: the branch of logical analysis, that of philosophical postulates, that of ethical values, that of the psychology and experimental logic of judicial decision, that of recanvass of the concepts and principles of any

[24] *Natural Law and the Law-Making Function in American Jurisprudence,* 15 NOTRE DAME LAWYER 9 (1939).

[25] *Cf.* Steffen and Starr, *A Blue Print for the Certified Check,* 13 N. C. L. REV. 450 (1935); Bogert and Fink, *Business Practice Regarding Warranties in the Sale of Goods,* 25 ILL. L. REV. 400 (1930).

[26] *E.g.,* Oliphant, *A Return to Stare Decisis,* 14 A. B. A. J. 71, 107, 159 (1928); 6 AM. L. S. REV. 215 (1928). For a court at work along similar lines, *see* Cochran, J., in Cincinnati Traction Co. v. Cole, 258 Fed. 169 (C. C. A. 6th, 1919). It is *one* of the standard case-law traditions.

[27] Compare for efforts along such lines: Havighurst, *Services in the Home—A Study of Contract Concepts in Domestic Relations,* 41 YALE L. J. 386 (1932); Shattuck, *Gratuitous Promises; a New Writ,* 35 MICH. L. REV. 908 (1937); Eno, *Price Movements, etc.,* 44 YALE L. J. 782 (1935); Campbell, *The Protection of Laborers and Materialmen under Construction Bonds,* 3 U. OF CHI. L. REV. 1, 201 (1936–7); and compare the notes and papers cited in my paper in 37 COLUM. L. REV. 341 (1937), from 374 on.

field of case-law, that of inquiry into the facts about the life under law and of law's effects on that life, that of the nature and work of legal institutions, that of the working principles of each one of the legal crafts, that of the general philosophy of law, that of battle upon extravagant dictum—each seeks to supplement the others in dealing with law's jobs of here and now. And no particular writing comes into perspective until one notes which, and how many, of such spokes it is addressed to. Compatible with all such lines of work is the type of detailed and vigorous critique to which Kennedy has been exposing some of the results.[28] The fresh look at what actually goes on, the sustained insistence that all that is observed must be accounted for—exploration, testing, correction: this is the line of advance. And obviously compatible is such work as has been going on in the companion statutory field (*e.g.*, Radin, Landis).

*   *   *   *   *

The next writer who needs discussion as we recur to the particular problem of certainty, hit into the puzzle from a novel angle. Moore and Oliphant, in an effort to get a more reliable basis for work than the accepted rules, had made two divergent efforts. Moore had attempted study of the background of people's practices as a guide to decision of cases; the essential result on our question of certainty is that the technique attempted proves unworkable for the run of cases. Oliphant had attempted to correlate facts, issue, and results of cases independently of the reasoning of the opinions; the essential result from his work is that— as case-law history shows—this is frequently, but not always, an excellent road out of confusion, but that its effect is to give us new and clearer doctrine, to be dealt with still along the familiar case-law lines. And that on the grand scale of statistics, the method is impracticable.

But Arnold, instead of reaching for ways of decreasing the uncertainty of law, conceived of examining uncertainty for the utility which it might have; which was akin to adding Carlyle's *Sartor Resartus* to the work of Bentham. Where rules speak with a forked tongue, said he, the way is open for judges to do justice in the case in hand: the rules leave them free to deal with their

---

[28] *E.g.*, especially on Felix Cohen: *Functional Nonsense and the Transcendental Approach*, 5 FORDHAM L. REV. 272 (1936); Cohen's letter *id.* at 548; *More Functional Nonsense*, 6 FORDHAM L. REV. 75 (1937); on Arnold: *Realism, What Next*, 7 FORDHAM L. REV. 203 (1938); on Eno: 8 FORDHAM L. REV. 45 (1939). *Cf.* also Kennedy's forthcoming paper, *Psychologism in the Law.*

main job. And especially as to the criminal trial, he put his finger
on a matter too often overlooked: an impressive ceremonial has
a value in making people *feel* that something is being done; this
holds, whether the result is right or wrong; and there is some value
in an institution which makes men content with fate, whatever
that fate may be. The Certainty Boys, argued Arnold, are impossible idealists; they want what no living system of law can
give them, so they fool themselves into thinking they have it. The
Uncertainty Boys, he argued further, are just as bad; they really
want the same thing, which is why they are making a terrible noise
over discovering that there is no Santa Klaus. But the wisdom of
that great institution, our Law, lies in providing everybody with
a satisfying ceremonial and in providing the judges—or other
officials—with a wherewithal to do their best from case to case.

This much of Arnold's work is an exceedingly useful contribution and, though overstated, contains a huge core of truth. But it
is not on our major issue, which is: How, by taking thought and
giving study, can we achieve more of manageable certainty than
life has been willing to just drop into our laps? And how can we
keep the freedom of judges—and other officials—to do their best,
and be just, from being freedom to do their worst and be arbitrary?
So that Arnold's books,[29] though illuminating and stimulating, do
more to clear ground than to advance this particular ball. He
makes one suggestion which is the procedure of our case-law put
into generalized advice: work it out case by case, and recanvass
your generalizations, case by case. But that, being what our
judges have been doing for some centuries, is only reaffirmance of
tradition.

There is another suggestion which results from Arnold's work.
If he is right, then men of the law who venerate even those parts
of legal ceremonial which can be shown to give no guidance or
actually to further confusion in decision—such men are yet on
the trail of a real value which it is also the office of the law to
serve. If Arnold is right, any reframing of particular legal doctrines, any addition to or clarification of the techniques of
decision, must not only better serve control of arbitrariness and
guidance to justice, but must also satisfy men's craving for reason-

---

[29] FOLKLORE OF CAPITALISM (1937) had the greater circulation; but the ore of
SYMBOLS OF GOVERNMENT (1935) is richer. [But see BOTTLENECKS OF BUSINESS (1940),
in which after he had assumed office as head of the Anti-Trust Division, Arnold laid
out one fair portion of his application of his realism.]

able certainty of *form* as well as substance, and for dignity of process as well as dignity of result. This is a necessary conclusion from Arnold's work, if he is right on the point; and I think he is. One must not "unsettle doctrine," even to get better results, or lawyers will refuse to come along, and so will judges. This has interesting implications. It means that new and better doctrine must be produced along old and familiar lines of doctrine-production, in order that it may be a "discovery," and not an "unsettling." And that is a very neat addition to the objectives and methods of a newer Jurisprudence which had tended to think too exclusively in terms merely of increased certainty and increased justice and wisdom of results.

Why, then, does Arnold's discussion set off so much commotion—in terms, *e.g.*, of its supposedly vicious "tendencies"? I should like to try to answer that with two figures. The first is from football, in the days when play could pile at the side-lines. Arnold attempts an end-run. It gains quite a few yards, on our certainty problem, but its major service is to get the ball into the middle of the field. Is such an end-play to be judged for its seeming "tendency" into the far grandstand? It seems to me wholly characteristic of the essential nature of the *game* (as distinguished from the particular play of the moment), as the game was seen in essence by both Arnold and Frank when they wrote, that Frank, the "uncertainty" man, the alleged atomizer of all rules and their denier, was at the time engaged in writing successful briefs, giving effective counsel, with rules of law and from them; and that he is now making and applying effective regulations of legal character; and that Arnold, the alleged describer of unprincipled guidelessness, the alleged mocker of law as empty ceremonial, is working out the most consistent, reckonable, guidesome, and wholesome administration of anti-trust laws which we have seen since we have had such laws.

The second figure has to do with the irreverence of Arnold, along with other modern jurisprudes. For their manner of writing has involved its portion of verbal thumbing of the nose. The figure is that of a roof, a shingle roof. The modern jurisprudes have, so far as I can make out, an appreciation of the roof our legal system puts over us all which is a deal more live than that of most. They think it serves a noble function, as well as a useful one—so much so that they get impatient of any leaks at all. But they view that roof as made of many little pieces put down by many different hands at different times, some of which pieces are wearing out, or threatening to, or have worn out already. Any particular piece they happen to be looking at is suspect. *It* is entitled to no reverence, while the looking goes on. It is to be tested as if *it* might be the leaky one. As a piece under examination, not one tiny presumption holds in its favor. To indulge presumptions while inspecting is to endanger the roof. And if the shingle is found faulty, it must be replaced, and at once, and with a solid shingle. Such is the line of work which catches and cures leaks before they happen and keeps a whole roof whole and worthy of devotion. Even if, when a gob of dirty drip hits such a shingle-worker in the eye, he utters colorful remarks about "that . . . roof," the part of wisdom—as well as mercy—in reading his Jurisprudence is to assume that such remarks are obiter.

Indeed, one can lay down by this time a principle for reading modern Jurisprudence. If the writing is colorful rather than merely graceful, then the chances are strong that it has not been thought through, and is to be read for its suggestion rather than for its conclusion. There is indeed a little graceful Jurisprudence abroad in print which is shoddy, or is shallow; but there is no heated Jurisprudence abroad which has worked out into wholeness. One can even proceed to lay down two further principles for reading this modern Jurisprudence: if readability, absence of heat, and some grace of expression are one first indication of probable ripeness of the product, the two others are, first, that one should have to stop at least once on a page, to call up, in his mind, out of his own experience, illustrations or further illustrations of the point which the author is making; and, second, that if appropriate illustrations do not come, either the page is unripe or the reader is unripe for it. If they do come, the page is already paying for the time its reading has consumed.

Before leaving the point of form, and so, this time, the subject, let me call attention to one fascinating facet of modern Jurisprudence: the reintroduction into that field of satirical and ironical writing. I refer not merely to the sprightly style and pungent exaggerations of, say, Frank and especially Arnold, matched, from a more conventional jurisprudential approach, by Kennedy, Jacobs, and Leach. I refer to whole straight pieces cast in a tone reminiscent of the ironists. T. R. Powell's *An Imaginary Judicial*

Opinion[30] is the first that comes to my mind. Rodell in his *Farewell to Law Reviews*[31] presents a beautiful example. The art lay there in such delicate, cumulative, dispassionate scarifying of undeniable weaknesses as to present a seeming case not for reform but for Abolition outright. Teufelsdröckh's *Jurisprudence, The Crown of Civilization*,[32] though heavier and not so neatly architectured, attempted the Swift tradition of solemnly glorifying all that was worst in the trade practice of the jurisprudes. Jervey's *Foam* (or, *The Jurisprudence of Ice-Cubes*)[33] moved from pseudo-jurisprudential principles gathered from a galaxy of parodied theories into triumphant demonstration of absurdity, flinging garlands on the way. The point for the present purpose is that this type of fun-making is a symptom not only of exuberance, but of strength; not only of irreverence but of self-critique. And that it may presage for modern Jurisprudence some reintegration of the fine arts into the study and critique of law along lines familiar enough two centuries ago, or even one, lines healthy for law and lawyers. It must be confessed, though, that Rodell's last venture along this line is less successful. *Woe Unto You, Lawyers* follows the basic pattern of *Farewell to Law Reviews; i.e.,* it sets up weakness after weakness calling for reform, and builds them into a seeming case for Outright Abolition—this time, Abolition of The Technical Law as lawyers perpetrate and mangle it, Abolition of The Technical Courts, Abolition of The Lawyers themselves. This is a lovely project. It is big at once with belly-laughs and with reform. And Rodell's chapter on *Senior v. Braden* is, for example, superb. The difficulty is that such a project calls for an almost superhuman craftsmanship, on the extended scale of an integrated volume. A. P. Herbert's *Uncommon Law* carries only because it is broken into pieces. Even Swift, after his sustained satirization of humanity in Lilliput, broke down as to the giants of Brobdingnag, because he could not simultaneously put over greatness of soul and gross-

---

[30] 44 HARV. L. REV. 889 (1931). The full bearing of the Imaginary Opinion, in wisdom and beauty balanced and restrained, is presented in *Some Aspects of American Constitutional Law*, 53 HARV. L. REV. 529 (1940). The Imaginary Opinion is a distinct advance in technique over that of Sidney Smith, in *Man Traps and Spring Guns* (WORKS, ed. Phillips, Sampson, 1856, p. 227); which might have been a mere law review article.

[31] 23 VA. L. REV. 38 (1936).

[32] 5 U. OF CHI. L. REV. 171 (1938).

[33] KENT'S COMMENTARIES (Columbia Law School, 1938). And there is admirable material in the little circulated HARVARD LAW REVUE, and the YALE LAW JUMBLE, as they spasmodically appear.

ness of body. Rodell's *Woe* book attempts a similarly incompatible combination. His satire rests at once on uncertainty and chicanery. Now one can make a biting burlesque along either line; but to develop "chicanery" with artistic clarity requires that the rules with which the chicanery is practiced be shown not as themselves uncertain, but as *clear,* in both purpose and phrase. And that cannot help but undermine all "showing up" of "inherent uncertainty." In result the book leaves the reader emotionally and esthetically confused; and the Great Proposals at the end, instead of being at once funny and stimulating, become merely silly and boresome. Good satire, moreover, cannot afford to call the name; the line of the burlesqued nose and squinting eye must show the rascal. Rodell's purpose was thus defeated when he first introduced the word "racket" into a satire, whether of the Law and Lawyers, or of any other thing. Get out your Gulliver and contrast Swift's clean-lined job when Gulliver is describing to the Houyhnhnms the work of our tribe in Merry England. It is a pity, too, because Rodell has the rhetorical advantage none of the rest of us can claim, of being able to open a Hogarthian sketch with the grave announcement that *he,* at least, is no member of the bar.

In sum, not all of the newer Jurisprudence, viewed as square feet of print, has wholly paid its way. But a series of important areas, of import both theoretical and immediately practical, it has opened. The central problem is the working out of rational techniques for marking off the area where freedom to be just is necessary, from that in which freedom to be arbitrary is to be excluded; and for working out more rational techniques for guidance of judges and other officials, within the former area. Call it sustained and realistic examination of the best practice and art of the best judges in their judging. Call it the effort to develop out of that best practice, and into communicable, serviceable form, rules and principles for the right and rational and more unambiguous use and development in day to day detailed work, of the rules and principles and concepts of our law. In addition, a goodly number of other problems emerge, as to making the practices and the art of the best *lawyers* more communicable, and as to the law itself, and how it is working. Further laboratory and other work is under way, by many hands. The results will, most of them, have to be read as suggestive rather than as conclusive, as has always been the way of Jurisprudence. But a fresh, needed, vital current is flowing—flowing with more vigor, more volume, more effect as every year goes by. The newer Jurisprudence is just beginning. Writers who are "discovering" that this newer Jurisprudence is coming to "shift its ground" have, I fear, never understood the ground on which it started work. But that makes little difference. The work goes on. And sometimes its material makes good reading, just as such.

OBITER STILL

Judgment goes panoplied in awe,
 whether his brow be grim or mild.
Judgment is son to hallowed Law—
 but Obiter still is Fancy's child.

  I find the wayside berries sweet,
  and wind across the wayside grass,
  rock-slopes where fern and cedar meet.—
  Words may be fragrant as they pass.

By robe and office more than dust,
 lit with strange fire that kindles clay,
Lawmen put forth the doom they must—
 to bind tomorrow by today.

  Sweetly the rills of wayside water
  babble and gurgle through the grass.
  Obiter still is Fancy's daughter,
  and words are fragrant as they pass.

Who hews too close must miss the mark;
 truth too much true is dying truth.
Obiter glows in gathering dark,
 colors the clouds of doom with youth.

{8}

ON THE GOOD, THE TRUE, THE BEAUTIFUL, IN LAW [a] [*]

PROLOGUE

In the first two lectures of this series, I tried to show the succession of overemphasis on one, another, and ever another vital phase of the institution of law, in presenting what the thinker, his public, or both, took to be a rounded view of the whole; and

[a] From 9 U. OF CHI. L. REV. 224 (1942).

[*] The text represents the last two of four lectures read at the University of Chicago in the spring of 1941. Changes made since are minor. The substance of the first lecture, "Ancient Issues and a Forgotten Institution," is somewhat indicated in my paper in MY PHILOSOPHY OF LAW 181 (1941). The second lecture, "On the Problem of the True, in Law," dealt with differences between objectively verifiable truth, and truth of other kinds, and with the need for keeping them distinct; it dealt also with the problem of finding and stating true law in those areas of flux which are so troubling, and attempted a reconciliation between Fuller's position and my own. It also introduced a certain non-existent legal philosopher who has been of much service to my thinking; he will be met here in the Prologue.

It is plain that the subject-matter is hardly scratched in these lectures. The material for one needed companion piece, which might be called "On the True, about Law," has appeared in *The Theory of Legal "Science,"* 20 N. C. L. REV. 1 (1941). A second companion piece, which might be called "On the Problem of Official Truth," has not been written and would deal with the perennial problem when action, or settlement, is imperative, and data, or the needed "forms," are inadequate or absent. Again, the present lecture requires to be companioned by one on "The Esthetics of Legal Craftsmanship," with discussion at the very least of advocacy and counseling. It is plain, for example, that the esthetics of advocacy are closely related to the performing arts—music, drama, dance—and also to composition for such arts, especially for self-direction and self-performance, and again especially to those ages and branches in which much was left to improvisation.

I suggested that the needs of a man within himself, and of his times around him, made the swing from exaggeration to exaggeration all but inevitable.

That, I take it, is why no flesh-and-blood philosopher about law, or of law, can really be trusted to maintain balance in his any effort to present a picture of the whole. Let him touch law, and he touches, of necessity, and then of necessity responds to, a deflecting need of his own here and now. Hence I crave your indulgence to introduce a philosopher who is not flesh and blood, and never has been. He is a Euclidean result of a set of non-Euclidean axioms about what an ideal philosopher of law should rightly be. He came into his own type of existence as a test and checkup, in an effort to keep personal vagaries and the needs of my own here and now from too greatly distorting my efforts at a picture of the whole. And, having lived with him for a couple of years, I find him assuming an uncontrollable way of his own, with results by turns shocking, dazzling, and trite, as various unforeseen consequences of the axioms of his being proceed to discover themselves.

To philosophize about law for our use, such a philosopher had to be rooted soundly in the human, and had both to know our own system intimately and to be apart from it. Plainly, also, he had to be intimate, in firsthand experience, with a homely, well-worked simple system of law adjusted to a largely pre-industrial economy such as gave all Western law its basic concepts. No less plainly, he had to be familiar also, and thoroughly familiar, with the code-trend, with the intellectualization and systematic thoroughness of Continental legal work. He had to know British thinking from its

---

There should also be a lecture on "The Esthetics of Substance," which lap over interestingly upon technical efficiency, on the one hand, and upon the Good, on the other. Indeed, if I were arranging a more complete set of lectures, I should be inclined to place the one on "The Esthetics of Substance" at the end, because it not only must draw so vigorously upon the True and the Good, but also, on pain of utter failure, must work the three phases into harmony. And I am rather clear that in a fuller presentation, there would have to be included under "The Good," a study of "Justice, Efficiency, and Warmth," developing not only the problem of finding the first, and of weaving the three together, but also that of finding a symbol for law of very different character from that of a large, cold, figure, distant, blind, and carrying a sword—a symbol earth-rooted and friendly as an oak.

While the lectures here presented purport to offer nothing but a point of view, they do purport to offer a point of view carefully considered and carefully phrased. And they both evidence and hope to persuade of my conviction that any sound socio-jurisprudence turns on analysis of what the institution of law is for, and how it goes round, with one's fighting convictions on the former never allowed to interfere with accurate *observation* of the latter.

formal side, which nowhere found finer expression than in Queen Anne's time, with Swift, and he had to understand it, again, from the side of its humanitarian and democratic rebellion and form-bursting, of which Carlyle serves almost as an incarnation. He had to pierce all sham, yet he had to have a rich understanding for form, ritual, for the significance peculiarly to law of the garb of *means* which requires to be laid upon reason, goal, or meaning. He had to know us and our law, as I have said, yet to have no silly, easy urge to lump us indiscriminately with the British, as "*the* Anglo-American."

So far I had gotten when it dawned upon me that there had already appeared in the literature a somewhat fantastic figure, one Diogenes Jonathan Swift Teufelsdröckh, whose name and whose style were a curious mélange of echoes of Carlyle and Swift; whose works were given as including a treatise on *The Roots and Powers of the Doctorate,* who himself held five-powered J.U.D.'s—surely a guaranty of proper Continental schooling—but who had lived and taught his life out in Nempenusquam, of which no man has ever heard, and which could only be some Liechtenstein or Andorra on the untouched fringes of the modern scene. If such a person proved to be the grandson of his namesake, the great Philosopher of Clothes,† and if he had devoted his life to applying the Science of Things in General more particularly to law, we should begin to have the outlines of the very man we were seeking.

There were, however, about this fantastic Teufelsdröckh certain things which would not fit at all. There was no coherence of style in the major paper in question. But the perfect philosopher of law had to be a sound artist; he had indeed to be an eager artist, though never so eager as to forego balance. The paper showed humor, without which balance in law would be superhuman; but it showed little sympathy, it did not show an understanding patient with all men's vagaries, such as must belong to the perfect philosopher of law. Thus the Teufelsdröckh of a pair of vagrant papers§

---

† It will be remembered that Diogenes Teufelsdröckh wrote SARTOR RESARTUS. The common attribution to Carlyle is not unlike the Baconian theory concerning Shakespeare.

§ *Jurisprudence, the Crown of Civilization—Being Also the Principles of Writing Jurisprudence Made Clear to Neophytes,* 5 UNIV. CHI. L. REV. 171 (1938); *The Universal Solvent of Jurisprudence; or The Riddles Contradicted and the Contradictions Unriddled,* 8 HARV. L. REVUE 1 (1940).

If I were forced to, I could make a rather cogent case that the *Crown* rests on an actual MS of Teufelsdröckh, manhandled here and there by some American editor

began to change form, began to gather other attributes, as a necessary consequence of rather inevitable axioms. It is clear, for instance, that the required sympathy and human breadth, merged with the required drive toward the Ideal, would, if left to themselves, yield us a saint, not a philosopher. Our man, to become the ideal philosopher, had need of a weakness: a touch of intellectual snobbery would let him see men, and understand them, and feel for them, without losing the urge to think it all through, without exhausting his energy on immediate personal healing of abuse. Again, the qualities thus far named will give us no philosopher of *law* at all, but a general philosopher, or a prophet, or if he turns to dealing with the world direct, a leader into action. Hence our man had to have a bit more (in W. I. Thomas' terms) of the "wish for security" than of either the "wish for new experience" or the "wish for recognition"; and he had to have at the same time something of a farmer's earthiness; else his mind would never settle adequately to those practical engineering problems on whose continuing solution good law turns, or to their long-range study, rather than their dangerous practice.

Such are the axioms about attributes which set themselves to work, and lesser human qualities grew up about them, merged with them. I may have thought out the axioms. I suppose I did. But I did not think out Teufelsdröckh. He happened. He is still happening. He sheds light for me on problems I have never thought to look into. He produces perspectives I should never think of looking for, myself. I have come to admire him intensely. I learn from him. I cannot always agree with him; I lack the qualities which make up the perfect philosopher of law, and that leads to differences in judgment even when I can see why he must view some matter as he does. I am, too, both materially more of an experimenter and much more of a believer in the common man than any such passionate devotee of technicians' "safe" craftsman-like leadership and control could ever be. But in the main, I find that Teufelsdröckh persuades me; and when he puts a matter better than I can, I have felt free to quote him. As I quote him,

---

in the manner at once of those who tack bawdy-"comic" stanzas onto *Frankie and Johnnie,* and of Garrick's rewriting of Shakespeare. The fine core is still clear. The paper, for the initiate, is half-satire, yet contains a true description of the "veil" dealt with in the Solvent, which hangs between the High or Inner Jurisprudence and the vulgar, and performs its own function—one which Arnold has described, though incompletely, in his SYMBOLS OF GOVERNMENT (1935). The brief *Solvent,* on the other hand, is, save for a printer's error or three, unmistakable Teufelsdröckh, as anyone can see who compares it with the passages quoted hereinafter.

I understand what novelists and dramatists have told us, of figures who go their own way, refusing to fit into any scheme or plot laid out for them—"writing themselves," at times to the serious inconvenience of their "author." And I understand with an intensity new to me the wonders of geometry.

I. ON THE BEAUTIFUL: FORM AND STYLE

Beauty in things of law has been slighted as if by law; and where not slighted, has been seen off-center and in spiraled distortion. Law, men have thought, is a thing of words, and literature is the appropriate art to measure by; and how shabby does the resulting measurement appear, when "art" in things of law is seen or sought in an image or a turn of phrase stuck on or stuck in. Such is a common run of thinking among those who have meditated upon law as being thus a matter of words: an ill-advantaged distant cousin of belles lettres, too doltish, for the most part, to be hungry for improvement. The horrible mark of this, even after Holmes had shown modern Americans what style could be in legal writing, was the persistent misconception of Holmes' aphorisms as mots: removable singlenesses which, if anything, gained by dislodgment from a context of mere "law." It is my belief that Holmes himself, in later life, half-held this feeling; the true artist in him fought it, always, in his actual work; his vision laid out wholes, not bits, his mind and pen made vivid the whole vision. But his climate of appreciation of the 'teens and 'twenties was for mots— "plums"; Holmes had appreciation for that climate.

I shall recur to Holmes, whose major lesson to the beautiful in things of law I find in another aspect of the "five-word jewels." Here I want to move on to the tale told of Stendhal, the shaping of personal style in a writer of lay material by ceaseless study of the packed simplicity of Napoleon's Code. That code contains no ornament or imagery. The beauty of language which it holds is functional beauty, the beauty of "dam-race" and turbine.

The same code introduces, however, another partially sound but mistwisted view of esthetics in things of law, one much more widely held by lawmen—who have too rarely given more than casual thought to beauty in words. This other view of legal esthetics sees law not as a matter of language in general, but as a matter of rules cast into language. The rules of law, you remember, have become to most, today, the thing of law; language, then, but clothes and serves them. The rules, and the concepts which build into and are built out of them (for the process runs, willy-nilly, both ways), are to stand together; they are to merge into majestic harmony; they are to be a structure. Structured beauty becomes thus the esthetic goal—an intellectual architecture, clean, rigorous; above all, carried through in sharp chiseling to body out the predetermined plan in every vault, in each line, into each angle. The great monument to this esthetic ideal is the German Civil Code, read not as it stands on the page, merely, but read also against the rigorous, almost rigid German theories of construction and dogmatics which were in vogue for a decade after its adoption. It is a type of legal esthetics little practiced among us. The Langdell school's amazing theory of consideration and unilateral contract is not only the most familiar American example, but the one most clean of line, most bald of eye-deflecting cover: the consideration needed to support a promise must be bargained for; it must be the precise something bargained for; the something bargained for must be precise. Acceptance and the provision of consideration coincide like equal triangles, superposed, and, superposed, exclude all variant dimensions of "conditions." If "an act" is called for by an offer, that very "act," complete, and nothing else or less, though by a hair, is what is needed. Only the other party to the bargain can accept; only "he" can give consideration; only "he" acquire rights. Nothing could be more simply stated, more rigorously thought, more tightly integrated, more fascinatingly absurd to teach, more easy to "apply."

Another example is the law of the c.i.f. contract, which Lord Wright has recently held up to admiration as perhaps the most "elegant" of our legal institutions.[1] It is in my mind—though I may be unjust to Wright's shrewd juristic insight—that what stirs his praise is the logical clarity, the singleness, the sharpness of line, in the law governing this once standard contract for overseas commerce. The patterned succession of the seller's proper actions, as he arranges, as he ships, as he sends forward promptly the batch of documents; the neatly matched mortising of the due steps by the buyer, honoring the draft when the documents are presented, then paying the freight in cash before outturn of the merchandise, proceeding then, and again promptly, to inspection of the merchandise itself, until which all the built-up seeming rights stand subject to possible defeat; the courtly grace with which the steps and rights of one intervening banker, or two, or three, are laid out as in a minuet—this, I say, is what I suspect Wright to have primarily

[1] Introduction to THAYER, CASES ON THE LAW MERCHANT (1939).

in mind when he speaks of "elegance" in the law of this institution. What concerns me is that the aspects of that elegance are two; that but one of the two is basic to legal beauty; that that one is utterly basic, while the other is either an efflux or a tool, and, lacking the one, would be a simulacrum. It is not the structure, however sweet of logic and of line, that is the essence. Langdell's construct points that moral: magnificent in conception, impeccable in workmanship, it yet would not *function;* men do not, and courts will not, work according to that pattern. And that, in things of law, bars beauty. The history of the Langdell conception is one of a delighted welcome by law-teachers, which continues still, while piece after piece of the integrated whole continues to be junked; the holes consume the structure. The c.i.f. construct, on the other hand, has proved in test after test as surely, as cleanly, as smoothly gauged to the work it had to do as any legal engine man has yet designed. As a result, or as a means, a logical clarity is present, too. But the prime test of its legal beauty remains the functional test. Structural harmony, structural grandeur, are good to have, they add, they enrich; but they are subsidiary. So is ornament. Legal esthetics are in first essence functional esthetics.

If, with this in mind, one turns back to Holmes, the "five-word jewels" take on another significance. One ceases to be content to see them arranged on the walls of a museum. One begins to smoulder when any man quotes one of them, and does not give the source; when, in this wonder-world of words, in which a part can be taken and the whole yet left intact, a man hides from us the location of the whole monument which he has plundered. For Holmes' opinions are not mere jewel-cases; nor are they merely structured prose. They drive to a point; [especially on the Supreme Court,] they drive to a policy; they drive to technical accuracy, to justice in the case in hand, to right guidance for the future. Love them, or leave them, it is rare that you can miss in any of them any of these attributes. Their beauty is functional; the prose is clean by the nature of the man, but it is thrice clean because hewn powerful to purpose. Carven pillar and keystone sing, but the song is the song of the arch they hold and bind. Else —as occasionally—there is a mot; no more.

So it comes about that right craftsmen of the law can discover that they have "been talking prose all their lives"—which means, in this instance, that they have been *doing* legal poetry. They have been artists, they are artists, art is of the essence of their daily work. The search after ornament alone, apart from function, is for the single worker in the law a search after false gods; footless, but relatively harmless, because it commonly hurts few except the searcher. The larger-scale search, that after structured harmony of rules, alone, is also a search after false gods. This time, however, it is a tragic search. "For," wrote Teufelsdröckh,[2] "a Structure of Rules, however majestic in Simplicity or Grandeur, in logical Design and Harmony—such a Structure, if it be once accepted into a legal System, must house People and the Work of People. If its Beauty be a Beauty for the Eye only, or of the Mind only, if it be not in first instance a *working* Beauty in and for the People and the People's Needs, then it is false. It is falser than mere false Architecture. False Architecture, save when it crashes, is but Waste, Inconvenience, or Hypocrisy. But a Structure of legal Rules, howsoever fair of Face, must function well or be an active Evil to the Men and Work it houses."

This "housing" figure is not to be taken lightly. The esthetic phase of a legal system is cognate to architecture as it is not, for instance, to painting, and as it rather rarely is to music. Architecture and engineering strike most closely home—perhaps because both look so directly and so inescapably to use. Indeed, in regard to the rule-structure of a developed legal system,[b] it is fascinating to follow the semi-analogue of one of those medieval cathedrals whose building reached across the centuries. In the law—at least in our own—there has never been an original entire plan by any master architect; but that I think highly probable also in regard to some of those cathedrals which rested content over generations with a choir. In any event, for structured rules and structured stone alike, one finds unit after unit, set up aforetime, in a "style" whose reason has lost meaning to the later user, but whose form will bind him still. I do not, of course, mean here by "style" an individual's manner of handling words or work, as when one speaks of the style of Swift, or of Renoir's early style. I mean the pervading unmistakable manner of a period, the period-style of a craft—and I shall argue that style in that sense is not only applicable, but important, to work in law.

And as with a medieval cathedral, work done in an older period-style persists beyond its own day. One finds shift of plan, sudden, irreverent, even rebellious—old wall, old stone, old ornament,

[2] Quotations are not herein referred to particular works. That would serve no purpose until the fuller story of Teufelsdröckh's life and works becomes available.

[b] By "legal system" in this context I meant and mean the body of doctrinal material—not the going-whole of Law-government.

being pressed into "modern" service, in a new design. Too, change small enough in scope can sometimes alter an entire aspect, as when the fourteenth-century chapel-rows were built between the buttresses, and window and wall pushed outward to make great, smooth space—the buttresses, as the phrasing goes, "drawn in"; or when Gothic vaulting was made to upheave a nave designed for the balanced measure of the Romanesque; or ornate plaster masked upon ancient stone or brick or varicolor, and the horizontal whirl of baroque, in every image, thrown in to force upon eye-lifting Gothic an almost jazz-like rhythm.

Such things one meets a-plenty in a case-law system to which no master architect has ever set a hand: the cases of a few years can make a Constitution seem made over. One meets, in law, too, the impatient, relentless clamor for modernity—whether need or fad. One meets, in law, too, the intrenched insistence upon the unchanged immediate past—whether dead or living. One meets also in law the romantic trend, the urge to cure the immediate past by recourse to the "good" past, more remote. Consider—if I may now with decorum avoid certain more burning contemporary issues whose smoke obscures a larger scene—consider a certain body of rules of law on contract. One ancient form, the signed promise with a seal, persisted long. Being ancient in style and architecture, its rules of law were at once revered and scorned, respected as of peculiar dignity, turned to irreverent everyday uses, decried as intolerable trickeries. State after state demolished the structure as outmoded, as in the way of progress; they did this, for the most part, hastily, scrappily, putting nothing in its stead. Other states maintained the structure with some piety, though with disquiet. Now the most modern reformers are putting forth designs for rebuilding the signed promise with a seal in all of its ancient solemnity, but freed of its ancient, hidden, tortuous passages[3]—somewhat as highly utilitarian yet traditionalized dormitories *can* rise in a sufficiently sophisticated "college Gothic."

All of this is a phantasy; it will be unwarranted digression if it does not serve to drive home at once the conglomerate, the dis-

---

[3] Compare Symposium on Consideration, 41 COLUM. L. REV. 777 *et seq.* (1941). Contrast the Uniform Written Obligations Act with the New York statutes dealt with by Hays, *Formal Contracts and Consideration: A Legislative Program,* 41 COLUM. L. REV. 849 (1941), and Revised Sales Act, Second Draft, Section 3(2) and Alternative Section 3-C. [These became UNIFORM COMMERCIAL CODE § 2–205, on firm offers.] Also see Havighurst, Consideration, Ethics and Administration, 42 COLUM. L. REV. 1 (1942). [See Fink, *Obviating the Necessity for Consideration in Amendatory Agreements,* 9 U. CHI. L. REV. 293 (1942).—Ed.]

unified, the eternally groping, nature of our own structure of
legal rules, and one other thing: the fact that the shaping of
rules of law, like that of buildings, changes what can only be called
pervading style, from era to era.

"Style," in art, is a term abused; it is badly defined, badly
described; it is treated lightly as explanation for what it does not
explain; it is vaguely "explained" by factors which do not explain
it. Nonetheless, the term says something, and it says something for
the aspect of the law. That aspect changes. It changes, as I see it,
in first instance in regard to the *ways of thinking and working in
the legal crafts*. Style-change, in any art, stands in some intimate,
as yet not surely fathomed, relation to the ways of at least some
important section of the people—the relevant "public". Such a
change, in matters of law, will of necessity show in the attitudes
and shifting ways of thought and work of the craftsmen before it
shows in the resultant structured rules. Again, by looking to the
going institution of law, to petty process in the men's work within
the institution, one gains light on its recorded word.

This holds, indeed, throughout art: pervading style, and style-
change, will be understood, if at all, by way of the craftsman and
especially of the craftsmen. But for the legal field it holds peculiarly; save for an Eike von Repgow, and his *Sachsenspiegel*, where
one man's sole creation came to print itself for centuries on half
a nation, save for a Mansfield, the individual craftsman's work is
slow to leave a mark. And since in case-law the structured rules,
once built, can persist almost as do built parts of a cathedral, the
craftsmen's attitudes and ways of work may change, and change
again, yet leave great portions of the prior builded structure
almost untouched. What will best show the style of an era, are of
course the parts fresh-built in that era. But what must not be
forgotten, is that even while those parts are building, the other
parts are largely being used in the style of that building.[4] I beg
leave to insist again that the craftsmen's ways of using their materials mean as much or more to the result as do the materials them-

---

[4] Compare the warranty-picture in New York after 1870, Llewellyn, *Courts, Quality
of Goods, and a Credit Economy*, reprinted from 36 COLUM. L. REV. 699 (1936), 37
COLUM. L. REV. 341, 365, 371 *et seq.* (1937); and compare especially the bill of
lading cases of the 1880's when forward contract-thinking had drowned the "feel"
of courts for the factorage market. Llewellyn, *Horse Trade and Merchants' Market
in Sales*, reprinted from 52 HARV. L. REV. 725, 873, at 894 *et seq.*, esp. 901 *et seq.*
(1939). Or observe the horse-sense view of rewards first undercut by the conception
that recovery without intentional acceptance is "anomaly," and then struggling, in
the newer drive back toward horse-sense, to develop new lines of recovery.

selves. I beg leave to repeat also that in style, as in service, it is the craftsmen who mediate between the people and the structured rules and forms of law. For a broad contrast, consider the general German temper, in all fields, of building a broad premise (often enough half-mystical) and following it then with rigor into the most untoward conclusion; consider then the American temper of empiricism, of case-to-case thinking, of loose ad hoc wording, of sudden revision of premise whenever a consequence comes to be perceived as unwanted. Is the broad, controlling manner of German law, pervading lesser style-change from Savigny's pounds of pages on *Possession* through to 1931, in its contrast to our own broad, pervading, manner of case-law and spasmodic statute, to be considered in any fairness as a phenomenon of law alone?

I shall want to recur to style in the American legal institution, but this reference to the German should not be allowed to slip away without a reminder of one other exciting parallel between rule-structure and physical building: the fact that the art of either is conditioned by, or, as the case may be, encouraged by, the available technology. What materials are there, to work with? What skills in using those materials have been devised, have entered into *general* use in the crafts? What is available need not of course make its way into general use, over indefinite periods (as, steel, glass, pre-fabrication); for all that, its presence seems to urge somewhat toward its utilization. But whatever depends for use on devices still technically unavailable, that simply cannot get built— or, if sought to be erected, will not stand.

In things of law, the worded rule is one such technical device. Writing, and again printing, are others.[5] But a fourth lies in man-stuff which is reckonably at hand, and so in the organization and tradition of that man-stuff: most particularly, therefore, in the available quantity and kind of official personnel. If one turns, for example, to the tidy pre-Hitler working out, in the German rules, of how to handle tender, one finds the problem which lies at the root of our own confusion solved by way of a technical device which the American simply does not have at hand to call on; it lies outside the field of rules of law proper; it consists in a trustworthy, skilled, cheap, relatively nonpolitical bureaucratic machine, there on call. You set up an appropriate office, and there

[5] Someone at the Contracts Round Table at the Association of American Law Schools in 1941 likened the invention of transferability of contract-rights, notably credits, to the invention of the wheel, in regard to its importance and effects on our institutions.

the refused tender can be deposited. All risk can then pass in comfort from the debtor; "payment" *by* him can happen in complete clean severance from payment *to* the creditor. That severance once achieved, a tidy mind can proceed to work out all the other problems—and is invited to begin. But without that severance of payment *by* from payment *to,* I submit that even a tidy mind will find itself faced with alternatives none of which are tidy. As the development of rib and buttress, and the development again of skilled masonry, conditioned the emergence of Gothic vaulting, as the substitution of chisel and chisel-skill for adze let both relief and shadow vivify stone sculpture, so the development of unified legislative control, or of effective administrative techniques and personnel and institutions, condition the vaulting of puzzled spaces in the law.[c] Teufelsdröckh's image is more homely: A suction-pump, or one law-official lifting by himself, can raise water or the work of law but a scant single atmosphere; nor can the flow be ever enough to serve a people. A water system, or a legal system, demands the force-pump, demands channeling pipe that can take the stronger pressures: personnel toughened and hardened in a schooled tradition; advanced techniques that rest on prior patient study and experiment.

In our own history of the last hundred years or so, one can distinguish with some clarity three marked style-periods. Pound has noted them, with that singular flair of his for feeling, and commonly enough for charting, significant currents where another would find nothing but a waste of waves. And I should like to do honor here to his insistence, over the years, on the presence of *periods* in our law—an insistence which, wherever it has chanced to carry into the teaching of doctrine in the day-by-day undergraduate classroom, adds to case-study a new dimension of richness, of time-perspective, and of process.[6] Pound has distinguished a

[c] Consider the building of the Corpus Juris in some seven years under Tribonian, that of the Code Civil in some five years, with the guidance of Portalis. Each called for well-worked preliminary materials, powerful technical leadership with vision, available skilled staff and craft-public, and, most of all, centralized power in Justinian and Napoleon to put the results into effect without need for debate or compromise. Thus also, in contrast to medieval cathedrals, Hagia Sophia, as huge and detailed as any, and more original, came into being within six years. In contrast, the American Uniform Commercial Code, a relatively small-scale enterprise, has already been mutilated by conditions and by the ignorant of the bar, and will take a quarter-century to come in to dominant force.

[6] For which reason alone I should have thought that Jurisprudence would have been seen these many years as essential to right undergraduate work in law study[,

"formative era," roughly the first half of the last century,[7] a period of "maturity of law," centering from perhaps 1880 to 1900,[8] and a modern "sociological" period, involving new movement,[9] but threatened these latter days (as Pound has come to see it) by absolutism and associated evils.[10] The sequence "movement-consolidation-movement" holds, without question. Beyond that, I find myself differing from Pound's analysis almost in the measure in which I have learned from it. But his setting of thought has been "stages" of legal history, or else sequences of so-called "schools" of jurisprudence. Mine, here, is period-style.

The first style to be discussed, which I shall center on the later 1830's and earlier 1840's, is in every sense an "early" style; Pound's "formative" suggests this well enough, though the term is chosen with reference more to the now *body of doctrine* than to the then *method,* and if Pound does not talk of style, he nonetheless inescapably communicates about this period both the presence of one and its flavor.[11] It was, however, a style in its own way quite as "mature" as that of the following period, if mature is to mean ripe in effectiveness, vigorous in coping with new tasks, wise against tough problems; indeed, such lines of maturity in workmanship are attributes of any "early" style, when it is carried by the powerful craftsmen of a powerful people, once that style has passed beyond groping and has begun truly to shape.[d] "Formative," I repeat, goes thus to *content* of American legal doctrine, in the first half of the last century, not to the *method* of the law crafts at that time. [The "Style of Reason," or the "Grand Style," would offer much more significant designation.]

One can follow that craft-method in the opinions, often also in the reports of argument; one can conclude much about craft-

---

and for which reason the course in Constitutional Law—a long time-sweep with a single court—offers peculiar educational values *apart from its subject-matter.*]

[7] Not nearly so well handled, to my mind, in the book of that name as, say, in the exaggerated but powerful paper in 1 ACTA ACAD. UNIV. JURIS. COMP. 183 (1928).

[8] Discussed, *e.g.,* Pound, *Fifty Years of Jurisprudence,* 50 HARV. L. REV. 557 (1937), 51 HARV. L. REV. 444, 477 (1937).

[9] Compare Pound, *The Scope and Purpose of Sociological Jurisprudence,* 24 HARV. L. REV. 591 (1911); 25 HARV. L. REV. 140 (1912), and repeated shorter references since.

[10] These fears are voiced in perhaps the most sustained manner in Pound, *Contemporary Juristic Theory* chs. 1, 2 (1940). On which see my review in 26 A.B.A.J. 876 (1940).

[11] So also FULLER, THE LAW IN QUEST OF ITSELF (1940).

[d] Consider early Gothic in Normandy, or the sudden blossoming of painting under Iknaton, or Hagia Sophia, or the early Romantics in literature.

method from the relatively clean-running statutory texts.[12] Systematized law they do not present; craftsmanship they do. Directness, fluidity, vigor, and a surpassing average rightness are the
marks. *Reason* is tool, method, goal.

To make clear what I mean, let me now differ most explicitly
with my brother Radin in his recent unwise equating of "reason"
and of "logic" in legal work—an equating curiously at odds with
the wise insistence in the same book on the prime importance of
rules being laid down for the "future." [13] In a developed system,
well provided with authorities, reason and logic, as they appear in
action, are more likely than not to be at odds. "Reason" in law-
work always implies more than reasoning; it implies also the use
of Reason in *choosing premises* which have a reason, and it implies in addition the use of Reason in judging the reasonableness
of any outcome or any goal. "Reason" is thus the main guide and
measure by which "experience" works its way into legal results,
whereas "logic," in legal work, tends powerfully to take authoritative premises as given and to reason simply thence. So that I speak
here not of true logic—of which there was plenty—but of "Reason" as the dominant tool, method, and goal of the 'thirties and
'forties, because it was the constant recourse to "Reason" *to determine the premises for logic* which gave fluidity, power, directness,
and direction to the style. It was craftsmanship in the on-going use
of both true logic and the rightest Reason the craftsman could
manage, coupled with the relative access of even a single individual, in those days, to some fair understanding of the whole
going society, which gave the style simplicity. I note one other
thing which has been altogether too little stressed: the progres-
sives of the legal system[e] of the 'thirties and 'forties were, the bulk

[12] Contrast the sweet-running craftsmanship of the American Factors Acts of the
1830's with the strictly comparable "negotiability" clauses of those anti-wildcat-
warehousing statutes of the 1870's which came up for construction in Shaw v.
Railroad Co., 101 U.S. 557 (1879).

[13] RADIN, LAW AS LOGIC AND AS EXPERIENCE (1940). I agree with most that Radin
has to say about law "as experience"; save that his insistence on the second-hand
and *therefore* non-reliable character of any "experience" law can make contact with
is, to my mind, the chasing of paradox materially too far. The matter is significantly
similar for any contact of man with "experience"; it is the problem of reaching
the *Ding an sich*, coupled with the problem of meanings, *and law is not peculiarly
worse off than other disciplines.* An initially good point can be pressed to where
it loses virtue. [Frank in his later work falls into similar error re "facts" in court.]

[e] "Legal system" here refers obviously to the *going whole*, but only of the
appellate judicial phase of the *Law*-side of Law-government. Jurisprudes need
schooling in care with terms. Legislatures were not conservative in the reforming
'40's.

of them, strong conservatives in general politics. The schooled men, the skilled men, the "safe" men—these had at this period a beaver's building job to do for the legal system.† The "best" men, the most "solid" men, of bar and bench were in their daily work, in good part, in creative alignment with the surely felt unambiguous needs of the country. Such a conjunction has not occurred again (though something comparable seems to be happening in Government, today[14]). In any event, I mistake both my sociology and my esthetics if that conjunction a century ago does not go some distance to account for the unity of the legal style of the period, for its superb sureness of line, and for its passionate, though restrained, simplicity. For let me remind that period-styles as such need not reflect "the people." Nor did the style of our law-work in the 'thirties in any vital measure reflect that tidal wave that had swept Jackson into power. A style needs a sufficient public; no more. Does any person have the illusion that Louis Quinze furniture reflects the "France" of Louis Quinze? But a style in work of law must reflect not only an unremitting but also a sensitively accurate concern for *general* welfare, or else go wooden on decay. No craftsman can long escape the essential

† I should view "legal system" here as meaning "the whole Law-side."

[14] Conversation about this with Evan Haines and Jack Dawson elicited some extremely interesting suggestions. Haines noted that leadership of the men of law, responsible and conscious leadership, persisted in their attitudes even while it was waning in their powers; that, when the Jacksonian wave was followed by the election of judges, and then by the dominance of industrial and financial leaders, both external and internal foundation for courageous sustained creativeness tended to slip away; and he noted, again, that in a real sense the legislative and administrative attitude of today had again become one of conscious and responsible leadership to get done needed things which, seemingly, only law and government could get done, for the whole-of-us.

Dawson reached for currents common to the Western World, and noted especially the misinterpretation of the situation in France, if one drew his views on French judicial practice, say at mid-century, from the formalistic doctrinal writings. And both men raised the question whether at the present juncture, in regard to the appellate bench, we were not reaping important benefit from the combination of solid horse sense and drive for justice with a sufficient relative ignorance of the full range of our tangled law to keep horse sense from being frustrated by a feeling of the mere mass of the Augean mess. It seemed to all of us that one thing which stamped Cardozo's private-law work with the mark of greatness was the intellectual power and the relentless industry displayed, when he had found a light-giving answer in a particular area, in straightening out and clarifying the entire body of precedent which had lain, confused, behind. So that in the current work of the appellate courts, in general, one felt much less the conscious leadership of the whole which typified the '30's and '40's of the last century, than a recapture of that *way* of Reason which was submerged in the formal period. But I see courts re-emerging as *one* focal point of leadership. Compare my THE COMMON LAW TRADITION [esp. 333 ff.]

nature of his medium, and the material of law loses life fast, in selfish interest. It may retain power; life, no.

Two caveats I should now like to lodge. A "style," though strongly marked, is not a uniformity; it is, as it meets the learner in the craft, a set of pressures channeling technique and imagination, a set of pressures which have come (rarely by design) to interlock into a sensible whole. But some resist, some escape; even those who are craft-schooled may vary widely. Thus you will find in the same volume opinions with the clean, clear lift of Laon Cathedral—and with Laon's imaginative daring—from the New York Supreme Court, and, from the senatorial Court of Errors and Appeals, opinions with the polysyllabled fanfare of the public oration of the day. It is the former which mark the age, for me. If you will not go with me in that, then let me state the claim more modestly, to meet your prejudice: the lasting law-work of that era, the best work, the distinctive work, has the style I have described; and the craftsmen had it when they wrought that work.

The other caveat is this: borrowing from England there was, in substance and in technique; and in that aspect the concept of "reception" of the English common law, i.e. of its substance—in rule, and somewhat in spirit—has real meaning. But the *style* of the then English law was borrowed not at all, and no talk about "reception" must be allowed to obscure that fact.[15] The American work was not that satirized by Dickens, nor that in which Parke satirized himself. In commercial law, which is the only nineteenth-century English Law I have followed carefully along its time-dimension, the period in question has in England, dominantly, rather the aspect of the American period next to be described; whereas between say 1860 and 1880 the English style moves for a time into Blackburn's relative flexibility. Their style is hardly, however, even then, a simple or "early" one: there is more of rationality, less of direct "Reason," in the work; there is craftsmanship, sound craftsmanship, functional craftsmanship, and more "elegant" craftsmanship than in our early style, but there is little passion: Amiens (the "classic model" of Gothic), not Laon or

---

[15] Pound misleads on this; and he misleads severely, in regard to the effect of civil law writers. What was doing the work was informed horse sense, in the highly skilful manipulation of available, many-tendencied, precedent material. Almost regularly, save perhaps for Story's work in Conflicts, the references to the civilians are grace-notes of rhetoric, not sources of light. The real test of this last is the essentially non-civilian character of that basic legislation of the period which Pound and I both admire. There, despite a free hand, the work is a wholly common law type of work.

Chartres (where you hear Our Lady breathe). I do not, indeed, understand why the disciples of idealism in our law leave unremarked the passionate quality of our period of the Style of Reason: restrained, but burning. One's admiration for Blackburn is intense, but Cowen must be loved—as, later, Scrutton must. "Law's true Peaks," Teufelsdröckh observed, "bring both far Vision and a throbbing Heart. That is their Glory. But a schooled, a sure, a steady Hand is needed. And," he continued, "lone Climbers fall."

The next style in our own legal system which becomes pervasive enough, distinct enough, to be clearly seen as such, seems to me that which characterizes Pound's period of "maturity of law"— which he sees as a period of "consolidation and development of the received materials." The characteristics are well enough known to all of us: authoritarian, formal, logical. If the 'thirties and early 'forties have the flavor of Gothic-in-growth,[16] this period centering on the last decades of the nineteenth century can be likened best to English Perpendicular. And Pound seems to me off perspective with the "development" part of the above phrasing; the characteristic of the period is indeed consolidation, but it is a consolidation by cutting down, rather than by development. *Lawrence v. Fox*,[17] for instance, had got off to a very good start on third-party beneficiary; the office of *Vrooman v. Turner*[18] was then to limit the implications so far as authority would in any way allow. That was in 1877. Charitable subscriptions, again, had done fairly well in the earlier period; *Presbyterian Church v. Cooper*,[19] in cold alleged regret, then labored to squeeze all life out of each earlier case. That was in 1889. The very growth in the documentary sales cases was a growth in terms appropriate, and almost calculated, to rigidify an all-pervasive rule of exact performance for the future. It did. That process ran through the 'eighties. Authority was authority; logic was logic; certainty was certainty; heart had no place in legal work; esthetics drove in the direction of cold clarity. Now cold clarity is not achieved by

---

[16] A less familiar, but much closer, analogy, is that of German brick Gothic in the fourteenth and especially the fifteenth centuries: a vibrant, independent, provincial-national offshoot, bourgeois and half-secular in flavor and with strong democratizing tendencies, striking out along new lines conditioned both by new material (brick) and new conditions, at a time when the French "center of diffusion" had gone into formalism. BECHTEL, WIRTSCHAFTSSTIL (1930), makes, on the whole, an impressive case in terms of tangible process, about this "Sondergotik."

[17] 20 N.Y. 268 (1859).

[18] 69 N.Y. 280 (1877).

[19] 112 N.Y. 517, 20 N.E. 352 (1889).

that type of work which extends, which *develops,* prior implications when they need it; esthetically clean poles with esthetically clean lines (if that is what you want) are made by neatly smoothing the growth-branches off.[20] I do not want to go psychoanalytical in a discussion of a period-style in American law; nor have I any intention of putting forward here a theory of why, in general, periods of formalism recur in law and flourish. But I do think it odd enough to call for speculation, that with the American economic world in almost frenzied expansion, and with systematization dominant in no other branch of our intellectual life of which I know, the craftsmen of our law should have been swept by this particular esthetic urge: the Formal Style.

In general, one expects intellectual tides, and tides of action, to show somewhat similar effects in the various aspects of life and thought. Eddies challenge to study. Here speculation cannot rest with the prevalence of a severely positivistic legal philosophy, because a philosophy does not just prevail of itself; it displaces a prior philosophy; it has to get itself accepted. Once accepted, indeed, it enters as an independent factor; but *why* was it accepted? Nor can I accept any semi-conspiracy theory, which would find the formal way of work best fitted to rapacity, though I do feel strongly that, once the way of work got under way, the lawyer for the exploiter and developer took to it like the skunk to little chickens. I cannot avoid the feeling that, with religious fundaments under known fire from biblical criticism on the one side, from the Darwinian controversy and, later, Spencer on the other, those older lawyers who sat upon the bench found comfort in a next most solid foundation; that they preferred authority to expansion, preferred a way of law which brought clarity and approached system, though at the price of lopping off the growing branches. And I am far from clear, in addition, that such a way of law did not provide a comfortingly solid foundation in what was beginning for the first time to become an economic world which a single busy man had to see that he could no longer compass with his mind. I find it difficult to forget Henry Adams' disgusted withdrawal from dirty politics into history—into the period of his fathers, then into the unified thirteenth century. I find it difficult to forget Holmes' labors over Kent, and over legal history, and over system, giving himself a known and tested (and

[20] There is a passage from Holmes to Pollock explaining Holmes' delight at finally having found a chance to prune off an anomalous (highly sensible) excrescence. But the point made rests on feel and result of the mass of the cases.

rather tight, growth-proof) foundation, before he emerged at forty to match himself against events—and at least one passage argues that such preliminary labor had been a conscious need. I note that Holmes himself in non-constitutional doctrine was of the clarifiers from within the legal system, one of the very slow to move;[21] and that in constitutional doctrine his stand was in essence one against the innovating expansion of "due process" law. I remember his suggestion that that particular expansion might well reflect a fear of socialism, and I remember then my own puzzlement when I began to discover common law cases somehow similar in tone and flavor, which long antedate the constitutional cases. What was going on was a consolidation and withdrawal into a formal shell of fixed authority; and, I repeat, it was a cutting down, *not* a "development," of prior doctrine.

I am quite unwilling to "explain" this in that "private" law field which (despite the much talk of the constitutional lawyers) set the dominant tone of the period—I am quite unwilling to "explain" this by the mere philosophy of laissez faire. I am ready to hook it up with such a philosophy, if I can find the way; the fact of relation is, I think, perceptible. But to see that the two fit well together is not to solve the problem of *process*, the problem of how it happened. The formal style, I repeat, had a better and different style to displace, before it could itself become dominant. Here I face my ignorance. May I speculate? May I guess at a touch of breakdown in the transmission of the older craft-style, in the 'sixties, or even as a delayed result of Jacksonianism? May I guess at a "best" bar beginning then to specialize in clients (industrial clients who needed steadiness of law) and so coming to lose somewhat the earlier constant appeal to Reason and to select, among the earlier techniques, chiefly those which rested flatly on authority? This does not satisfy me. The manner and detail of the process are among the most puzzling unexplored and vital problems of our law.[g] This we can say: laissez faire does

[21] The opinion in Vegelahn v. Guntner, 167 Mass. 92, 44 N.E. 1077 (1896), is an expression of unwillingness to create. The two main creative phases of Holmes' work on the Massachusetts court seem to me to be his work in constructive conditions and in criminal law, in both of which fields his thinking in The Common Law had arrived at a systematic base which made the *non*-sense in the law seem the anomalous. Contrast the story in bailments, or in conflicts, or in the consideration phase of contract.

[g] One can surely add, as further factors, the growing pressure of business, the growing body of *local* precedent, and the absence until West's first National Digest of any easy access to authorities which offered different conclusions and reasons. I remain unsatisfied.

discourage legal inquiry into policy and does discourage deliberate urge to reshape in terms of policy. It does encourage a feeling for minimum interference, and for clarifying predictability. Out of urges thus initiated, the creative impulses could turn toward tidy structure—what is there left for them to work on? But some of the results remain distinctly queer, in such a view. Prima facie, for instance, laissez faire does not too directly encourage a way of dealing with commercial materials judge-made and largely already on the books which is not only formal, but almost anti-commercial, in effect.[22] Laissez faire moved onto the stage in clarity rather with "liberty of contract" and the due process clause. As against prior case-law, these represented not contraction, nor yet continuance, but inventive expansion of the range of doctrine. Laissez faire, or "business-industrial" thinking, and fear of disturbance of an order seen as good, produced also an enormous creative expansion of prior doctrine in the injunction field—be it anti-labor, or anti-government. In a word, where either economic philosophy entered more unmistakably, or the ideal of a society rightly and happily centered on "business" opportunity, or (as commonly) the two as brothers, they entered to induce expansion of doctrine in a manner at odds with the general style of the period. Powerfully felt policy could do what heart could not, and break the bonds of form. The elaboration of the defenses against the injured workman is doubtless in part also apt, to point that moral; but again the matter is not a simple or a clear one: there is a touch of perverse logic in the development of the common law defenses which fits with style, pure.

Now here belongs an observation of some moment, because the marks of what one may call the Authoritarian or Formal Style are with us still. Under the early style, with right Reason plainly dominant, the outcome of a particular case at law can be moderately certain in the bulk of instances, and can and will at the same time give guidance in words, for the future, which is moderately clear. It is the felt reason of the situation which is stated; the rule and its application shift, at need (as they should),

---

[22] Soia Mentschikoff suggests here that Commerce is a mediating and central line of work, encouraging a broad view and a responsible control; but that Industry is met in specialization and leads readily to failure either to see or to feel for the whole; that this period is the era of Industry; and that judges learn, like other lawyers, in terms of the problems of their prior practice and of the thinking of their times. The cases I have in mind have as their archetype, Shaw v. Railroad Co., 101 U.S. 557 (1879), note 12 *supra*. For an effort at explanation, see Llewellyn, *Horse Trade and Merchants' Market in Sales*, note 4 *supra*.

with any shift in reason; shift can then be moderately well fore-felt, if not foreseen. Again, and under the Formal Style, certainty both in outcome and in verbal guidance can be had; the court states its position, and then refuses to budge, for whatever cause, save to whittle away "anomaly."

But what produces confusion, persistent and inevitable, is to *act* in terms of the felt reason of the situation—i.e., in the early style—but to *talk* in terms of the *Formal Style*. That confusion was introduced, as a practice, in the creative phases of the time-span here under consideration: the due process and injunction lines of expansion. And so long as any part of that confusion of style in law continues in the courts, so long will litigants have unnecessary uncertainty, lawyers have both uncertainty and wholly impolitic leeway, and courts have more work, and more baffling work, than there is call for. Courts will, also in consequence, go wrong, under pressure of work, more often than they need to—and they will harvest less solid satisfaction from their labor. For esthetically satisfying work is a vital return to the craftsman. Either of the styles described, pure, can yield that return to its disciples. The mixture does not, nor can it.[23]

The work of the craftsmen of the law, other than judges, in this formal period, I do not know in detail. What I gather of it fits what has been said. Since law in an era of terrific change would not stand still—whether as institution or as doctrine—both practical work and theoretical thought under the Formal Perpendicular had of necessity to be somewhat confused. Carter's book[24] is a belated monument to that. Yet the precision of concept and rigor of logic which marked the work of a Holmes and a Gray and a Langdell are not, it seems to me, to be wisely attributed either to a single teaching institution or to scholar's seclusion. I believe them to have been rather of the time. Field's drive to codify seems to me to have been a thoroughly appropriate stylistic ex-pression; what stood in the way—apart from J. C. Carter—was that men had neither the training nor the time to check up on an attempted "systematization" on so vast a scale. The historical scholarship of the period, on the other hand, I take to be neither causative of the style, nor too important a factor in it, nor even a

[23] This is developed in LLEWELLYN, THE COMMON LAW TRADITION.

[24] CARTER, LAW, ITS ORIGIN, GROWTH and FUNCTION (1907). Consider his difficulty with "custom," when specialized practice is under discussion, and the consequent confusion in dealing with the interaction of the specialized practice of the courts and that of some relevant body of laymen. This, though his initial attack ought, as against formalism, to have furthered clarity.

true expression of it; it seems to me rather a derivative and a parallel. It is not like Coke's "historical" work; it is a work of the schools, not of the bar or the bench or the political arena. Nor were scholars enjoying any large place in the legal sun. Still, if anomalies and asymmetrical forms are to be ironed out, history may help get rid of them; if it does not, it at least puts some explanation under them; meantime, it does stay put, whereas the disturbing economy does not. One may delve for love, but he is likely to delve also in relation with the dominant intellectual currents of *the field* at the time, and with the interests of his brethren.

In contrast with the two styles described, a third not only is emerging, but has emerged, today. [What I refer to is a style not of appellate judging (where today's style, despite unmistakable moves toward recapture of the Style of Reason, is still hampered by remainders of the Formal Style); it is a style rather of our whole institution of Law—Government—in action.] Its groping period seems to me largely over. Its causes I take to be, first, the unwieldy complexity of modern life; second, the perception that the *rules* of law built in the formal period out of the pruned-down materials which had then been at hand cannot cope with the problems heaped up by two succeeding generations, a half-perception also that the *techniques* of law built in the formal period are no adequate techniques for that transition or reform which for three decades and more has been in process. The third cause is a slow awakening to the fact that the relative balance of the 1830's and 1840's has slipped increasingly so far away—both as to the fact of balance and as to its foundation—that there are great gaps which need vaulting, great backward areas which need development, large-scale work to be done. And a fourth, if I am to list things, would be the perception that specialized, skilled, powerful units professionally on the job can be dealt with only by other powerful, skilled, specialized units *also* professionally on the job.

The basic element in the new style is thus conscious and overt concern *about* policy. The preposition has been carefully chosen. For concern, and conscious concern, *with* policy has been a part of work in law from the beginning—even when that concern extended only to the duty of "standing on" the precedents or producing, by vigorous surgery on the precedents, a doctrinal symmetry. But policy today opens neither to uninformed right Reason nor to mere tradition; policy has become a thing to worry over. Such worry, once, was for the queer case. No longer is that so. If, now, you should find such conscious and overt concern *about* policy non-typical of today's run-of-the-mine advance sheet, or of today's run-of-the-mine work of the law office, you might be right enough. Half of the law-work of the country may, indeed, still be going on in a style corresponding to the two-story-and-basement brownstone front, in rows, or to the well-gim-cracked small-town frame house of my birth. But if you should undertake such a mental canvass as a test of whether we are living a new style in law, then you would be missing not only that it is the characteristic, with forward thrust, that marks a strong young style; you would be missing also that one focal point of style in law has shifted from judges and from lawyers in practice to legislators and to lawyers in government. The other focal point is still the appellate bench, as I have tried to show elsewhere; but the appellate bench has not yet voiced its new style clearly, and the bar is not as yet responding to it. Rather is it out of that growing center of legislation and administration, with taxation as the dominant single channel of contagion, that changes in style of law are spreading through the crafts of legal practice. Conscious concern about corporate policy from within had been building, as a style-factor, independently; but conscious concern about relation to the governmental policies of all-of-us has to add itself, when taxes bite.

The next feature of the modern style which strikes one could be called factuality; it could be called realism; it could be called technological contact. Its essence is the supplementation of legal authority on the one hand, and of ordinary common sense on the other, with such technical data of fact and expert opinion as are available, or can in the time at hand be made available, to inform a judgment. In legislation, in advocates' work, and in work of courts; in counseling, above all in administration; everywhere this comes to the fore. It is a vital style-factor; it changes the whole relation of a legal craftsman to his work and to his society: instead of being *the* expert, by mere command of his own craft in command of all crafts, he becomes *one* expert, in immediate command only of his own craft—otherwise a co-worker. It pays to think over courts' emotional resistance to the earlier administrative tribunals in terms of this.

Meantime, a paradox appears. Precisely in the circumstance of losing both dominance and competence to command by mere virtue of his craft, the man of law embarks upon larger-scale, more powerful legal creation than ever in our history. The statute in the new style is no minor change, no mere detailed corrective. It vaults areas on a scale heretofore undreamed of; it does not codify and mildly reform on the basis of past legal experience; it brings forth at one stroke a policy, a measure, a whole new field of operation, an appropriate administrative machine, and blanket provisions for what (the nicer distinctions of constitutional law to the contrary notwithstanding) is in effect continuing large-scale delegated sublegislation. And here I should like to recur to a point made earlier, in regard to the conditioning of legal building, as of architecture, by the available technological wherewithal. A legal vaulting that presupposes an adequate administrative machine, with adequate administrative personnel—trained, restrained, skilful, diligent, forceful, tactful—such a vaulting does presuppose just that kind of personnel. You cannot span with stone what you can span with steel. You cannot span with flawed steel what you can with right steel. You cannot disregard outthrust; you cannot forget internal stress. Beauvais rose overproudly—and it crashed. And American legal building in the modern manner strikes me, thus far, as paying altogether inadequate attention to that engineering discipline on which a permanent magnificence of legal architecture must depend: the creation of adequate traditions and machinery for training and holding and continuously breaking in an adequate supply of right personnel. The feature of scale remains, however, characteristic. Nor is the reference alone to federal legislation of the last years; consider, for example, the style of work, in private counsel's hands, which used to go into arranging, capturing, and controlling a railroad receivership, or which still goes into legal planning for a national market. Or consider, in these days when the "dwindling of states' rights" is so much talked of, the *expansion* of state government, and the problem of building personnel —which means, of building craft-traditions—to handle that expansion.

There is a further matter to be noted before we leave the point of scale; it goes again to the heart of style in legal work. In the early style, the work of law is in command of the community; it is so felt; the doing shows it. In the Authoritarian Perpendicular, whether or not the courts are to be viewed as retreating into formalism to escape coping with events beyond their compass, the counselor is certainly to be viewed as sliding steadily into the position of a hired hand. The position of a corporation lawyer in 1910 was not a noble one. Scale alters that position; it reverses that trend. In legal creation, and in specialized administration, the man of law does indeed need to draw on co-workers, independent experts, and becomes and remains insofar himself a dependent worker. The men being equal of ability, however, there is no question, once the work gets well under way on the great scale, as to who moves into command. Initial dependence of the man of law yields then, even in the most technical field, to dominance of the one craft that speaks for the Whole and to the Whole. That craft no longer stands alone and sufficient, but it holds command. By force of scale of legal work, then, the modern man of law regains his soul. And one thing for which the private lawyer of tomorrow will be grateful to the government lawyer of today, when spitting bitterness has come, a bit, to mellow, is that increasingly, in the modern battle with the government, counsel are ceasing to take orders from their clients. They give the orders. At the worst, they consult as equals.

Conscious concern over policy, technological contact, scale—these seem to me more than likely of continuance through the next generation. A fourth characteristic, not yet so clear to see, seems to me no less so: a craftsmanship conscious and articulate in a new way, a craftsmanship along lines explicitly communicable, whether in advocacy, or in counseling, or in legislation, or in administration—or, yes, in either branch of judging. Though, as I see it, an outgrowth primarily of pressing maladjustment and of large-scale needs, this articulate craftsmanship can, and in my view will, carry over into daily, even petty, work. At least with regard to advocacy and counseling, such a conscious tradition was not undeveloped under the early style: apprenticeship and circuit riding favored it, though I find little evidence that it was ever systematized. In any event, it died, as training moved into the schools and as these latter came to center thought on rules of law alone [better: on legal doctrine.] But men who these days shudder at the recrudescence of the careful study of craft-work,[25] as being the begetter or the spawn of cynicism, should take heart as they remember that such a tradition of conscious craftsmanship was what sustained bar and bench in our high "early" period.

If an alleged style be indeed a style, its dominant characters

[25] The perception is slowly growing more general, as the smoke of the fireworks blows away, that the so-called "realistic" line of work is in essence a new and sound drive into more effective legal engineering techniques; not in any way a philosophy of law, but useful in the more adequate service of any philosophy of law. This has been clear from the start. Llewellyn, *Some Realism about Realism*,

should show some unified relation. These do. There is the faith, courage, drive, and conscious quest for balance in the whole, which they have in common with the early style. There is a daring of scope, and a range of exploration of "outside" as well as "inside" material for light on why, whither, how, which are new— save for Mansfield and, later, Brandeis. The unifying feature seems to me to be the clear-eyed wrestling with the possibilities and problems of great-bodies, as units—be they private groups, or governmental, or great scattered unorganized rucks of like-circumstanced persons—this, in a system whose whole conceptual tradition is still that of our friends A and B and C. From this feature all else flows. The feature itself flows—a touch belatedly— out of the time. And infusing the whole is a further feature that had been missing within the law-crafts, save for individuals, under formalism, a healthy feature, a feature proper to all law that lives and serves. As in the great days of the style of Reason, passion informs the modern style again: faith and vigor in a "calling."

I had not intended to spend so much space on this matter of period-style. Yet the concept has a striking-power, a range, and an ignoredness, which warrant the space. What would not be warranted would be failure to follow through a bit further the functional evaluation of esthetics in the institution of law, and also to indicate some places at which it ceases to be an adequate line of evaluation.

In the first place, as I attempted to bring out in the second lecture,[26] a functional evaluation moves as does no other line to knit together problems and results in regard to the True, the Beautiful, the Good. This would be a purely intellectual value, a reconciliation for mental peace alone, if the problems posed by the True, the Beautiful, and the Good were merely problems of an intellectual tradition—if they were that type of received issue which men have disputed over for centuries because truth lies on both sides, the question itself never having cut to essence. I find no such situation here. Taking, so far as I am able, a child's fresh view of matters legal, starting over, as best I can, from bedrock up, with all legal questions re-forming in consequence, I seem to find these three lines of philosophical inquiry still standing firm as vital aspects of man's quest. On the side of philosophy I am of course entirely unlearned. I have tried there to come as a dilettante

---

[26] On the True, in Law (unpublished).

should, conscious of technical ignorance and eager to be shown;[27] conscious also, however, that technicians can go haywire, and so, insistent on being shown. It seems to me that I have been shown. Hence the knitting together, in law, of the three great lines of inquiry seems to me a high virtue of the functional evaluation.

The knitting is obvious. There can be no test by effect, no working test, no test for functional Beauty, without inquiry into situation, process, and result in fact. Determination of the True becomes thus an inherent part of search for the Beautiful. But again, neither can there be test by effect, without inquiry into purpose against which to measure that effect, nor can there be such inquiry without search for the Good. It is a fortunate field to work in, this of law, in which the three great ultimates so clearly merge.

One thus gets here, as one does not in most fields of esthetics, some help in evaluating one style as against another. With working adequacy to go by, it becomes clear that a formal style will grade high in beauty only where conditions are stable enough, and the concepts and rules of law are, in addition, surely enough hewn to the conditions, to make results fit ongoing need. In our own law the best example I think of lies in many of the provisions of the Negotiable Instruments Law in regard to charging secondary parties; yet even here, the courts had to reach into purpose to do justice when checks were put into new standard banking channels of collection; and the rules on protest stand out rigid and obstructionist in supervening metropolitan conditions. A formal style, in a word, is foredoomed, sooner or later, to *become* a bad style, and lawyers will have to groan under fiction, spurious interpretation, and their progeny at once of confusion and of a discretion which escapes accountability. "Vouloir guignoler la noblesse de la robe" was Teufelsdröckh's expression of his scorn, "c'est finir par se guignoler soi-même." Which I suppose one can render: A theory or a people which seeks to put law's high ministers on puppet-strings ends up itself a puppet in their hands. What grows very clear is that in the high flux of our latter nineteenth century the Formal Style was an esthetic aberration. Law out of harmony with

---

[27] I got particular stimulus from PEPPEREL MONTAGUE, THE WAYS OF THINGS (1940), reading which set off this series of lectures. There is an old debt to Dewey, and another to Morris R. Cohen, and, for me, a more recent one to Aquinas. On application of natural law postulates, compare Llewellyn, *One "Realist's" View of Natural Law for Judges*, 15 NOTRE DAME LAWYER 3 (1939), *supra*, p. 111; Brown, *Natural Law and the Law-Making Function in American Jurisprudence*, 15 NOTRE DAME LAWYER 9 (1939).

life, ways of law which grind gears with law's society, these cannot have right beauty. Not the rules, but the living institution,
not mere certainty for lawyers, but certainty plus justice for the
folk law is to serve, define the need.

When one turns to the modern, the case is not so simple. Too
much depends, there, on variant conceptions of the Good. Too
much depends, also, on whether a great-scale measure be taken
first in terms of grandeur of conception and soundness of intent
and largely of design, or first in terms of such disturbing lines as
mar its rhythm, or of worry over whether the man-material will
bear up under the outthrust and the strain. For myself, I hold
this modern style to be one of unfolding loveliness, its lines of
self-restraint perceptible, challenging, and, rightly handled, ready
of development from its own sound premises.[28]

With the idea of functional evaluation I have no desire to take
over into legal esthetics the exaggerations, and to my mind
absurdities, of those extreme "functionalists" in architecture and
related arts who hold no form, no piece, no ornament to be
esthetically legitimate which is not, with maximum economy and
efficiency, a working portion of the thing designed. I hold another,
and I hope a saner, view. I hold, first, that even under such a
bare "efficiency" conception of functional esthetics, purpose is yet
an inherent part of any functioning structure; and so, that whatever expresses purpose expresses also an inherent part of function. Thus, to recur to the Gothic Cathedral, sculpture and glass-
painting did not require to help hold up the edifice in order to
be a right esthetic part of it. I hold, moreover, that man's love of
play, and—yes—of loveliness, is as rightly satisfied as is his desire
for work well done, or for economy, or for clean form. And objects
of use are those which grow closest to the heart. Thus the only
esthetic rule which I recognize about adornment in relation to
function is that adornment is best when it can be made to serve
function, and is bad when it interferes with function; beyond that,
the quest for richness of beauty and meaning seems to me a right
quest. You may call these prejudices; to me, they are considered
values. But whether you like them or not, in general, you will
have difficulty in dodging their applicability to things of law.

Consider the single legal rule. Its esthetics are functional, in

<hr>

[28] See LLEWELLYN, THE COMMON LAW TRADITION chs. 4, 5. [These projected chapters—delivered as Storrs Lectures—dealt with administration and with some aspects
of planning legislation, and do not appear in TRADITION as published.]

the strictest sense. It has room for not one jot of ornament; and the measure of its beauty is the measure of its sweetness of effect. Spencer's approach to style in terms purely of economy and efficiency seems to me to have application to one sole type of literature: to wit, stripped technical discourse. That is the rule of law. In it, a waste word is not waste only; it is peril.

But Spencer's approach does not exhaust the esthetics of the individual rule of law. Besides economy and efficiency, the rule of law requires rightness. The situation must be rightly grasped, the criterion rightly seen, the effect neatly devised to purpose, else neither clarity nor economy of language can serve true beauty.[h]

Whether Spencer's concept of economy extends to cover a certain other aspect of the esthetics of the single rule of law, I shall not try to determine. I refer to what was mentioned earlier: elegantia. Tersely, elegantia is simple grace in larger structure, each detail serving. It suits economy. But I feel another something in it, for I can conceive a thoroughly economical legal filing system which lacks grace and proportion. But here the dominant interest is again a caveat. Let me put it thus: a graceful structure of doctrine can intoxicate—as Langdell's has. But if it does not serve sense, it remains bad legal esthetics. Per contra, to seek merely to serve sense, case by case, will yield a welter. A welter also is plainly unesthetic.

The larger whole of rules must thus serve not only the immediate, but the larger need: sense, finder-value, balance—as well as relative precision. That is, to be esthetically satisfying. Here, there is a range of creative effort which no individual rule can offer.

And still, in regard to the rule of law itself, there remains an esthetic aspect undiscussed. It will be urged in the next lecture that right law must be intelligible, intellectually accessible, to the people whom that law is to serve, whose law it is, the law-consumers[29] and the citizen "makers" of the law. "Function," conceived purely in terms of the staff of legal technicians, could indeed be achieved by language which would carry no meaning or wrong meaning to such laymen. But as I have tried to develop elsewhere, even the high temporary effectiveness which can be had by skilful

[h] I should today certainly include, as well, the esthetic handling of the minimum of right words. It can be said effectively and briefly, and yet either bump or sing. And there is the job of letting purpose shine through a rule.

[29] A phrasing which it was a delight to find David Riesman using, too. Proceedings, A.A.L.S. (Dec. 30, 1941).

black-art language is unsound because it cannot be relied on to
continue effective. Only the rule which shows its reason on its
face has ground to claim maximum chance of *continuing* effectiveness;[30] *so that to satisfy, in this, the lay need of relative accessibility, of friendliness and meaningfulness of the reason, is at the
same time to do a functionally more effective job on the side of
pure technique.* There is thus no need, in widening one's view of
what the function of rules of law is, to risk confusion on the marks
of beauty. Quite the contrary. For to see the wider function is to
find the road back to that rightest and most beautiful type of legal
rule, the singing rule with purpose and with reason clear, whose
nature, whose very possibility, the Formal Perpendicular has led
our legal thinkers to forget—almost to deny.

  I have said nothing of ceremonial and symbol, of ritual beauty,
of emotive symbols. I have said nothing of the esthetics of certain
legal arts I deeply love: counseling, advocacy, teaching of prospective lawyers. I have said almost nothing of the esthetics of judging,
and nothing on the writing of opinions. Instead, I have dealt
chiefly with rules of law, and with structures of such rules. Is this
because, though of the realist persuasion, I find myself driven back
to the Rules as in truth the essence and the center? I trow not.
When I get opportunity, I hope to show how infinitely richer
in esthetics are the crafts of law than doctrine and rules can ever
be.
  No, I have stayed here with the rules of law neither because I
see them as "the law," nor because I like their esthetics better
than I do the esthetics of any other phase [of Law-Government],
but because they make peculiarly the vital point which a cut-in
at any other place would [might] leave obscure: that the foundation of any legal esthetics is service to function.

  Perhaps there is another point almost as vital: one comes to
the soberest, the allegedly dullest portion of the whole institution
of the law, and finds both Beauty and a theory of it. Is it not fair
to conclude, then, there can be no part of our institution of law
which may not yield fresh light, if one knocks at it asking, there
also, after Beauty?

  [30] See Llewellyn in MY PHILOSOPHY OF LAW 181 (1941); Llewellyn, THE COMMON
LAW TRADITION, esp. 183 f,

II. ON THE GOOD, IN LAW||

The threshold question as one knocks at the door of the Good *in* the institution of law, or *for* that institution, is that of the ethical or moral neutrality of the inevitable and of the impossible. *In* law, the inevitable and the impossible are doubtless to be taken as ethically neutral, as setting given conditions and given limits of action. Work *in* law is work within and under a given system of severely limited leeways; the Good, as the judge sees it and must do it, for example, is a Good whose most striking single element is the need to stay within the limits laid down for him as an official, and as that particular kind of official known as judge. The Good, again, for our legislators, is limited, this side of revolution, by their duty to our Constitution. The Good, even for the revolutionary, remains dream, not law-work, so long as it remains beyond his powers. "The Good in Law," says Teufelsdröckh, "roots in the good Earth of the Possible." [1]

Yet the inevitable and the impossible are not ethically neutral *for* law or even *in* law. Teufelsdröckh continues: "The Possible for Law, however, must include much that is not at the Moment possible wholly, or at all. Law's Purposes and Law's Ideals stand, and should stand, as Kelsen sees, in constant Tension with Law's Acceptance—but also with Law's Accomplishment. The Art is to keep that Tension at its Maximum, this side of Snapping. The Cable of the System, moreover, can carry Tensions which would snap single Strands; Strands which remain long almost purely hortatory thus can have their Uses."

This comes to the proposition that the purposes of a particular legal measure can often wisely far outrun either the measure or its execution, but that in each case both execution and measure need rigorous attention, and that high judgment is called for before any gap gives warrant for being left too large.[31]

|| This lecture is shorter than the preceding one not because I conceive the problem of the Good to be a simpler problem, but because the Good, in law, is at least a familiar problem, with a familiar vocabulary, whereas discussion of the Beautiful, in law, must, these days, build from the ground up.—[Today I should discuss Law-Government.]

[1] "It calls also," the passage continues, "for sun and rain. But it calls most for a farmer who has both a back and a brain."

[31] Those portions of the Bill of Rights which gather around the concept of toleration and the ideal of active tolerance offer well-nigh a perfect illustration. The ideal remains almost wholly unachieved; even the measure, "toleration," is hardly approached in practice. Yet enough is accomplished to keep the ideal in effective

There is, however, another reason for being loath to allow the inevitable or the impossible to count as ethically neutral. That reason goes back to our test for Truth.[32] "Inevitable" and "impossible" are terms whose use *in dealing with practical life,* as contrasted with their use in dialectic, requires application in a world only partially explored. Our only test of what in fact falls under either category is either experience, which is inadequate, or intuition, which is unchecked upon. Take the problem of the reshaping of human nature. In the sixteenth century Ignatius Loyola devised means for utterly remaking an adult personality, given that the individual was not unwilling to cooperate. In the early nineteenth century the Zulu Chaka devised and put into execution the remaking of a governmental, military, and social system, and of the people within it, without regard to any man's unwillingness to cooperate. This was so "impossible" that William Graham Sumner himself forgot to wrestle with its implications. In the twentieth century, that ancient monopoly known as Chinese literacy was cracked wide open, in a fashion which all informed men had known to be impossible, by a series of moves as skilful and as undreamed of as anything in the history of natural science.[33] Within a decade and a half Hitler has invented and put into execution measures for the mass-remaking of the culture and the whole youth of a modern nation—a thing, again, well known to be impossible. Chaka and Hitler both centered up their work by way of what men know as the institution of law. Loyola and Hü Shih used other means. Now what such remodeling of human nature can *cost* is not my problem here. I am dealing only with that shift of the impossible into the possible which keeps the "impossible" of today within the field of ethical significance.

The lesson I draw is that objectives may be attainable tomorrow

---

tension with both the society and its legal system. Not only does the ideal remain live, a heritage of our more sober moments to influence our wilder ones, but the ideal lures us toward its own greater actualization in our lives, and in our spirit. This despite the patent fact that to make the ideal a truly working part even of our legal system is flatly impossible into the indefinite future. [A newer experiment, large-scale and with thus far unexplored range of consequence, has been presented by the de-segregation cases.]

[32] On the True, in Law (unpublished).

[33] The team-combination of a scholar like Hü Shih to pick the Thousand Characters and front the movement, a popularizing orator like Jimmy Yen, and the selfless labor of a whole generation of the intellectuals of New China, to spread the Thousand Characters through isolated country villages, is a saga as epic as it is unbelievable. [It is on this great first demonstration that Communist China is building, in producing literacy.]

which seem impossible today, and, by the same token, that the inevitable of today may not be inexorably inevitable tomorrow. It would, for instance, when I began law study, have been regarded as inevitable that the best brains among outgoing graduates should all be drawn into the service of private clients, while government made out, save for occasion, with staffs overladen with political hacks. That inevitability has, seemingly, vanished—and without giving notice.

Hence the problem of the Good *for* the law has no limits which I can see. And yet it is the more vital to keep that problem separate from the problem of the Good *in* law, for this latter must be wrestled with in direct lawyer's terms: i.e., in terms which include always the problem of the feasible working measure whose tension with the existing remains this side of snapping, or of reaction.

By the same token, the initial and more pressing inquiry about the Good *in* law falls within the field of the foreseeably feasible.

In another place,[34] I have attempted to group the major jobs of law in any group or in any society around five, or perhaps better six, significant themes. There is first of all the cleaning up of those grievances and disputes which societies secrete as surely as babies produce a diaper-problem. Intimately related, but distinct, is the problem of channeling conduct in situations fraught with potential tension and conflict, so that, negatively, grievances and disputes are avoided, and, positively, men's work is geared into team-play.[35] In any mobile society, the needed *re*channeling along new lines is hardly less important. The fourth great job centers around allocation of that *say* which in case of doubt or trouble is to go, and around the procedures for making that say an official

[34] Llewellyn, *The Normative, the Legal, and the Law-Jobs*, 49 YALE L. J. 1355 (1940); see also Llewellyn and Hoebel, *The Cheyenne Way* chs. 10, 11, 12 (1941), reviewed by Redfield, 9 U. CHI. L. REV. 366 (1942).

[35] Let me insist again that any approach either to the sociology of law or to the philosophy of law which goes to bat purely in terms of the restrictive or repressive phases must miss some of the most significant aspects. Again, the conception of *institution* is the key. Rule by rule, case by case, one sees one thing, and it is chiefly repression or restriction. But complex, geared *wholes* of such rules, concepts, practices, lead and drive in *directions*, to positive accomplishment. They *build* teams of indirect or direct cooperation. Take "Contract," or Taxation plus Budget. A fortiori does this hold of the whole going legal system. I think it touching that realistic workers, who see these greater structures, should have been mistaken by critics for decisionistic atomizers, merely because they cannot regard a rule as effectively *prevailing* in our courts unless it effectively and continually reflects and guides decisions.

and binding say. The fifth, altogether too little studied as a job of law, has to do with producing a net organization and direction of the work of the whole group or society, and in a fashion which unleashes incentive.[36] And, as the last, I have suggested the job of juristic method, that of building and using techniques and skills for keeping the men and machinery of all the law-jobs on their jobs and up to the jobs.[j]

Now each of these things I take to be a good, if the existence of groups or societies is a good. And in each of them I sought to distinguish, first, a bare-bones aspect which was the minimum condition of the group's continuance as a group. What concerns me here is that these basic bare-bones needs must be met before we can get on at all into any other aspect of the Good, *for* law. To start with high goals is to risk forgetting this; it is no good thing to forget. The matter bites, these days, when the high goals themselves seem threatened.

Yet the reason for careful thought is obvious: when basic needs which have been forgotten raise their heads suddenly, men who have forgotten those needs are likely in turn to lose their heads, and panic lightly sacrifices high goals to the moment. But if men steadily keep in mind the bare-bones needs, even amid security, then threat to security brings with it no cause for panic, because it brings up no forgotten problem; it calls then only for shrewder planning and for resolution and for the *due* measure of temporary decrease in individualistic elbow-room.

In addition, as to each of these lines of the job of law in a society, I sought to distinguish two aspects, beyond the bare-bones problems, of questing for the Good. The one I may call here the technician's quest: it looks to effectiveness of legal machinery—including in machinery the rules of law; it looks to efficiency, and to reduction of cost, waste, and undesired by-product; it looks, at its peak, to smoothness up to the point of grace, to order up to the point of beauty. And I did not say before, and should like to say here, that the eternal ideal of this technician's quest, rightly understood, heads up in a simplicity which transcends complexity, and which can make once more accessible to the people at large

[36] Consider the problem of taxation, that of mobile status, and that of pressure to team up in corporation, union, or political group, in their bearings on this matter of unleashing incentive. Or consider the utility, now that a reserve of trained drafted men is available, of a regime taking *all* future officer-candidates from the ranks of those who have gone in at the bottom.

[j] Today I should see not Law, but Law-government, as the more useful area for analysis, and should in consequence count in a few other basic jobs: e.g. Defense.

a contact with, an understanding of, warmth for that institution of law which is theirs, and of which they are a part.[37] This is a good in law which in general is afar off, still. It is one, too, that has been sought through centuries by many, and mainly sought thus far in vain. It has been sought, I think we are beginning to see now, by the wrong road. One of the most amazing results, indeed, which seems to be emerging from two decades of realistic work over our law, is the glimmering of a road toward the kind of essential technical simplicity which may yet bring law home to law's people. I shall recur to this. For it will not do to let right technique in law appear to be a minor or collateral good.

The other phase of questing for the Good, in the doing of the eternal law-jobs, has to do with what I suppose most people think of first. I have not put it first, because it is too important that these other phases be not overlooked. But it is time now to come to the use of the institution of law to work toward what one conceives as the Good for a Society, and as the Good for its constituent people.

Now in this aspect, and with regard to law, there is an inveterate tendency to identify the Good with Justice. Justice, to many, suggests only so much of the Good as it is wise and right to seek by way of law. And indeed, *with direct bearing on law,* Justice may well be conceived as bounded by what *can* be achieved by way of law; which is one main reason why, for law, Justice must always be sought under the dire influence of the principle of scarcity: rarely, rarely indeed, is there enough of good and warranted Justice to go round.

Yet it is unwise, even in dealing with law and legal possibilities, to limit words too sharply or to constrict the view wholly within the range of lawyers' thinking or of lawyers' work.[38] There is an-

[37] This is touched on at the close of the preceding lecture; it represents, for instance, a full half of the problem of the Revised Uniform Sales Act, Second Draft (1941). [Which has become UNIFORM COMMERCIAL CODE, Art. 2, without too material change of form or feeling.]

[38] Most illuminating, on this, is Pound's introduction to GURVITCH, SOCIOLOGY OF LAW (1942), in which it becomes clear that most of Pound's writing on "Jurisprudence," and some of his less fortunate criticism of others, have rested on his intention of dealing with Jurisprudence *from a lawyer's angle,* solely. Which, as he points out, has great value, but also has limited value. The sociologist of the legal is concerned with much that comes to interest the lawyer only indirectly, though hard-eyed sociological study of lawyers' and judges' work is at the moment a main key to desperately needed juristic reform. But the doing of such study is, despite that, not a lawyer's job, nor is it done from a lawyer's angle. It is *utilization* of the *results* of such study which presents a lawyer's job proper, to be done from a

other use of the word Justice which obscures the whole picture unless it be dealt with first—and it is a use with its own legitimacy.

The first meaning of Justice which makes sense to me is what I shall call net Justice in the social scheme. It has to do with the organization of the whole society, of which the whole institution of Law [-Government] is for most purposes but an efflux and a voice—though the institution of law is of course also capable of being made one major tool for *re*organizing society.

This net Justice, as I conceive it, however, does not in first instance voice an appeal to Law, not even to change in Law. It voices in first instance a yearning that the less pleasant attributes of men-in-groups and indeed of men-as-individuals might disappear, and that something other and better might be substituted for them. It then expresses clearly that aspect of the Good, as the thinker sees it, which has to do with men's equal access to desired things—positions, powers, enjoyments, opportunities—things of which there are too few to meet all desires. Let me say further that as I read and try to think, I have been able to find no ultimate postulate for a thorough demand for such net Justice which does not involve at the same time a revolt against the native inequality of men, and that a through-driving demand for net Justice as Equality or Deservedness seems to me capable of philosophical harmony with no view of the world which fails to provide, outside the life we know, either for just causation or for just subsequent balancing of these inequalities with which men continue to be born. Let me say also and promptly, however, that this philosophical difficulty in no way impairs my own drive toward, and faith in the virtue of, a wider net Justice here on earth. For one of the things which goes with my own notion of the Good, as with my notion of the True, is that when you get done with all the use of Reason you can manage, you will find yourself still taking the heart of it all on a faith of whose validity you can persuade only another man who shares it. It seems, for instance, to my limited reason that if Aristotle is right that it calls for a just man to know Justice, then forthwith all effort to make a so-called rational "science" about Justice be also an objective science becomes futile, since every man of conscience must hold his own perceptions of Justice to be the basic ones.

What makes the concept of net Justice quite at home, however,

---

lawyer's peculiar angle. In much the same way, here, I wish to deal with Justice from the angle of a social philosopher, to *clear the ground* for a more effective treatment of the idea within the area of the "lawyer's" approach.

in my own concept of Justice, is the presence of four attributes. First, it is an aspect of the Good. Second, it has to do with conflict between people and with removing or avoiding or regulating that conflict. Third, it is heavily affected by the idea of fairness, and again by that phase of fairness which we speak of as even-handedness. Fourth, it operates under the sad fact of scarcity: in result, there will not be enough of it to go round,[39] and "solution" will be driven into preferring some to others, or into compromise. This is to me an essential attribute of Justice as man knows it: that there is not enough of it to go round, save when singular skill is joined to singular good fortune.

It is thus clear that I get little help out of Aristotle's famous discussion of Justice. It helps me little either in philosophy or in practical work.[k] Indeed, I have no hope of meeting any formula regarding the substance of Justice which accomplishes much more than the focusing of issues and then some suggestion about desirable direction, of the nature of "somewhere between East and Northeast." In regard to net Justice, for instance, it is clear to me that such an ideal as "to each according to his need" requires modification by the ideal of opportunity, training, and power, to some, according not to *their* needs, but to *ours:* our need for eliciting sound leadership. Under the fact of scarcity, this throws out even-handedness, in distribution. I think it not only must, but ought to. And to me the flattening of the idea into "equality of opportunity" seems to be a cover-up that, even when not consciously indulged, verges on intellectual cowardice. Per contra, "fairness," to me, includes a right portion of favor, of unearned aid or indulgence to those who need it, provided the favor be so handled as not to turn its beneficiaries into laggards, spongers,

---

[39] How it comes about that conflicting claims can yet from any angle of human feeling and direct social justification both or all be just, is developed in the material cited in note 4 *supra*. The issue is sufficiently pointed in any new marriage, in which an extension by Mr. Hubb into the "legal" order of the new marriage-whole, of the family ways of the house of his birth, plus the men's ways of his bachelorhood, with "due" adjustment, is commonly just; but so is the extension by Mrs. Hubb into the same new "legal" order of divergent norms and solutions derived from the family ways of the house of her birth, and from the of-coursenesses among women. It simply obscures the picture to see "Justice" only in the "correct" solution. The eternal problem is the finding of the *best* solution, when each of the conflicting claims is sociologically, even ethically, *justified*. If one of them is not justified, or neither is, the problem is or would be vastly simpler.

[k] This is not at all so in regard to the little passage using sense of Injustice to help define Justice, from which Cahn has also profited. I suggest that this most difficult bull's-eye may be better approached by near-misses than defined.

sluggards.[40] And on this point, I think talk of even-handedness to be mere cover-up of the character just described. I have, in this paragraph, no particular persons in mind. I am attacking points of view in which I was raised, and which, on testing, I find to be unsolid.

Perhaps I can get the matter into focus thus: to pick the state or the nation as the dominant repository of the Good to be sought is to ignore the fact that either consists of human beings. Whereas to pick "The Individual" as the dominant repository is to ignore two other facts: first, that individuals differ vastly, and that there is no "The Individual," save in a way of thinking too hopelessly over-simplified for practical meaning; second, that individuals exist only in the context of a society which is itself a context of groups and needs. The problem of social Justice—net Justice— begins, as I see it, with getting something to be just *with;* and that is a group-job. It takes precedence. That group-job calls for organization, discipline, leadership, and leaders. The ensuing problem of net Justice looks then peculiarly to the development of the disadvantaged. It looks to that development from two angles: the first angle is that of fairness and of the dignity of human beings; the second angle is that of wisdom, because refreshment out of the undeveloped is the way of hope for all. In this there is nothing concrete, and you could fit the formula, if you want to call it that, about as well to Hitler's state as to ours, or to some really ideal or actual democracy. With due hesitation, as I ponder on deep thinkers who have found otherwise, I conclude, thus far, that that is about as far as the available ultimate goals give guidance for concrete applications. I do not find them *dictating* even such major ways and means as form of government. The democratic way, or so much of it as we either have (which is not too much) or want (which is not for most of us too much more), rests to my mind on preference and on faith. I am content to let it rest on faith. Faith is a good foundation.

What I do find with what I take to be my reason is that even net or "social" Justice does not begin to exhaust the problem of the Good in law. No phase of life which is directed primarily to handling the scarce can exhaust the problem of the Good. And if I am right, that one of the major law-jobs has to do with the net

[40] On this, nothing officially in "legal" philosophy can remotely compare with HENRY ADAMS, MONT SAINT MICHEL AND CHARTRES ch. 13 (1904). Bryce's famous chapter on Tammany is the nearest. And which of the "legal" philosophers has made its implications into one of his foundation-piers? [Bienenfeld, for all his silliness, has here come closest. THE REDISCOVERY OF JUSTICE (1947).]

positive driving and directing aspect of the whole institution of law [better: Law-Government], then over and above any "distributive" net Justice there remains for law that phase of the Good which goes to enrichment of life, for more of us, or for all of us. Wherein such enrichment consists, I see with clarity only in minor part. For no man does it mean going flabby. That is clear. Clear, too, is that for men of law this Good includes right pride of craft and joy in craftsmanship.

This last leads into those other and more pedestrian phases of Justice which, though pedestrian, are quite enough to occupy most of the time and strength of legal craftsmen. They are: legislative Justice and Justice in particular cases, Justice, as the phrase goes, "under the law." I am of course not using the word "Justice" here in the bastard and confusing sense of the processes of adjudication or of litigation or of law-administration—say, to sum up that misuse of the word: justiciation.[41] I speak instead of a kind of *result,* a kind of *goal* to be achieved. I speak of what is with decency, and without confusion, called "Justice": an *ideal.*

And in regard to legislative search for Justice I wish I might be brief, instead of exhausting most of my remaining time upon it. I much prefer discussing a field more familiar to me: that of search for Justice "under the law." [42]

Legislative Justice is Justice sought by way of particular and deliberate change of law. I see it in four aspects, three of which, and often the fourth, present—along with the intimately related device of executive discretion—the only machinery whereby practically all-of-us support specialized delegates in efforts to revamp this or that portion of the institution of Law—[government] in ways supposed to make it work more effectively toward net Justice.

The first aspect of legislative Justice seems to me to move under the ideal of restoration of a Balance, assumed to have been, but assumed somehow to have gotten lost. The men of law say that legislation is prospective; and, with regard to legal effect, this is commonly true. But in the aspect I am mentioning, legislation

[41] Pound has sinned for decades, and impenitently, on this point, and he ought to stop sinning. Nothing but confusion to reader and to writer can come out of Jurisprudence or Philosophy written with a single word to describe justiciation, a human process for handling trouble by limited institutional means with human officers, and Justice, which is a goal eternal, as intangible as the other is tangible, as free in its nature of human or traditional foibles as justiciation is bound to them.

[42] Dealt with [most inadequately] in Llewellyn, *On Reading and Using the Newer Jurisprudence,* 40 COLUM. L. REV. 581 (1940) [supra, p. 128.] and in LLEWELLYN, THE COMMON LAW TRADITION.

is *pro*spective, looking *backward*. If ever there was illustration of Holmes' aphorism, it is here: "Continuity with the past is not a duty; it is merely a necessity."

Now I have no objection to efforts at recapture of lost balance, per se; for I think balance one of the most important ideals of law. Yet looking merely backward can cripple legislative imagination, and has, and does. To Holmes' aphorism let me add the gloss of Teufelsodröckh: "By Contrast, Vision is a Duty; though also a Necessity, it is that Necessity which Law too often sacrifices to its Twin: to Continuity with the Past."

Yet there are found pieces of legislation which drive not backward by repression, as was the objective of the original Sherman Act, nor into a desired recapture of balance by new devices, as with current schemes to help out agriculture, nor Back into Balance by setting up a governmental counterweight to concentrated economic power, as with the utilities commissions and the SEC. There are pieces of legislation also which drive plainly forward. In our earlier history, one thinks of internal improvements and of the school systems; later, of emancipation, and of the general incorporation acts; today, one thinks of highways, of social security, and of defense, and of the still halting program for gearing youth into the ways of work and opportunity. It seems to me vital, in any consideration of the Good in law, to keep distinct the urge Back into Balance—which is likely enough to be good— from the urge Forward into Better—in which lies the hope for a rounded people.

The third line of legislative Justice, which interests me as a man of law peculiarly, and on which each other line depends for its results, is that of improving the machinery for making rights real. If this be not a Good, in Law, I know not what a Good may be: to make provision and purpose of statute or of case-law come to life, become effective actuality—to take rules of law and goals of law and ideals of law out of the realm of *mere* doctrine, *mere* paper, *mere* words, *mere* dreams, and body them forth among law's people in vibrant realization. It is at this point, in talking of the Good in law, that I am proud to look back over the work of those many scattered and disunited stump-pulling and cabin-raising pioneers of modern law maligned as "realists." For it is hard-eyed realistic technical work that serves to make rights *real*.

Such technical work has been, and still is, badly needed. Slowly, and without noticing, we have drifted in three aspects curiously far from what is healthy for any institution of law, and farther from what is healthy for our own. The first aspect is the slow but horribly effective growth of a barrier of ignorance between men and their rights—between men and their law. The second is the slow and almost equally effective growth of a barrier of delay, un-certainty, and expense, in our legal procedures, that tends to make reality of rights at law a privilege. The last lies in the development, amid most attempts to cure the first two, of an attitude of having it done *for* you which as little becomes a healthy citizenry as does a hired army.

I have spoken of the complexity of our rules of law and of our procedures of law. I have not spoken of such causes of that com-plexity as are remediable. I have of course no illusion that the relations of a technologically uncompassable age can be all reduced to words of regulation which open their meaning to a high school junior. Nor have I any illusion that the peculiar legal system we have inherited, of forty-eight largely independent bodies of tech-nically divergent rules of law within a single nation which con-stitutes a single economy, each of the forty-eight paired differently with the complicating federal forty-ninth—I have no illusion that that inherited legal system is going to boil down readily or soon into a something intelligible to a citizen—or, indeed, to a man of law. But I do not think it needs to. The major fault lies today in our tradition-ridden errors of technique in stating rules of law and in work with them. We work still, we legal technicians, an unpredictable half of the time, and we talk still an unpredictable three-quarters of the time, as if fixed rules of law were all of law, as if all rules were of a single kidney, as if, finally, the *reason,* explicitly and accountably stated for guidance and for explana-tion, were not the heart of all sound work in things of law. Now in law, as in all other disciplines, there are to be discovered major lines of guidance which can be stated, which focus the problems of policy for seeing, and which indicate the lines along which their solution is to run. Such "general propositions" of guidance do not indeed "decide concrete cases" by any deductive process, be-cause their edges are unclear, because, also, two or more of them can commonly overlap a situation in conflicting ways. What such lines, when well stated, do, instead, is to make the nature of the controversy clear, and to point up the place and nature of the doubt or trouble, and to suggest *lines* of wise *direction* of solution, for consideration. Rules wisely built, clearly phrased, with goal and reason clear, such rules do these things for an advocate; they do

these things for a counselor; they do these things for a judge; and
they do them in much the same way for all three. No other type
of rule does talk the same way to all three. What is in some ways
even more important, rules of this right and largely unused type
do these things also for the interested layman, for the law-consumer, for the law-supporter, for the man whose law our law is.
Once that man can see clearly "what is up," and "where the
trouble lies," and why, he can take decision against him, and
realize that he has had a fair deal, though he has lost. He can
take decision for him without thinking that his lawyer was just
good enough to put one over. He can respect and honor the law
which his ingrained—I am almost ready to say "innate"—but
baffled yearning is to respect and honor.

But we technicians have become so habituated to the trees of
mere authority and rule that we have forgotten how a well-run
woodland, intended for a public, needs sign-posts, roads, and maps.
Ours is the fault, and on us the burden of the cure. Law is complex
and vast, but there are not many fields of law of which any particular citizen needs to know the guiding lines. However, where
he knows his stuff, he does need and he feels need to see that the
main lines of his law make sense, raise sensible problems, come to
decision in terms that talk and make sense in life.

This can be done for him. I have been utterly amazed, this past
year, after wrestling through the squashy mud of sales law for two
decades, at discovering how much sense, for a non-sales lawyer or
for a businessman, could come out of rather minor reformulations,
once one or another underlying idea got itself out into the clear
to be looked at. I find the same thing, wherever I have worked,
or have watched the relevant work of others.[43] Technicalities we
cannot get rid of. What we can do, is to make the technicalities
take shape and meaning *around* communicable lines of sense.

Today, this is best bodied forth in legislation, when well drawn,
with lines of policy that any interested man can understand made
clear, with technical detail left then to be handled flexibly by
administrative regulation. I sing no paean. Much of the ensuing
administrative regulation makes my hackles rise at its sheer un-
intelligibility in the worst manner of legal garbage. But we are on
our way, and have been, for some time.

The new Sales Act can serve to point the argument.[1] I suggest

---

[43] Consider the Beckwith A.B.A. Committee's work in getting the draft regulations
reformulated into relative accessibility of meaning.
[1] UNIFORM COMMERCIAL CODE, Art. II.

it not merely because I happen to be more familiar with it, but peculiarly because I want to avoid any misconstruction to the effect that in the foregoing I am becoming mushy, mystical, or vague, or that I am overlooking a lawyer's job of phrasing clearly, to give clean guidance to a fellow-craftsman. Quite the contrary. I stand on the proposition that the new Sales Act has as its job not only to make its sense and purposes far clearer to the non-specialist and to the interested layman than does the older phrasing of the legal rules, but that it must also give to counsel and to court a sharper and a more predictable guidance. I am not arguing that Pollock was wholly right when he opined that almost any rule of law could be translated into English which an ordinary man could understand. I am arguing that he was to my knowledge partly right, and that so far as he was right—and that needs testing, case by case—so far as he was right, it is a sad thing for the law of any people to leave the translation unattempted. It is a dire thing for the law of a democracy.

It will be observed that I have been concerned in this matter only indirectly with Justice. Justice plays in, and importantly; for it is well for a man to have some direct inkling of his rights, and knowledge goes far in many cases to shape expectation. It is, perhaps, even better that he should have some understanding of why what he manages to get can decently be considered an approximation of Justice. But above all it is a good, above and beyond Justice, for the citizen to meet his law and call it friend —or to see why he wants it different, if he does.

The present inaccessibility of knowledge of the rules, and worse, of even the main lines that organize the rules, plays twice into the other barrier, that of uncertainty and expense. Inaccessibility of knowledge increases both the labor cost and the uncertainty of advice. It does the same, one may add, for decision. By consequence, for the law-consumer, it puts a premium on peculiarly skilled or experienced advice or advocacy in the particular field. To pick the certainly right lawyer is to pay for that same and rare kind of lawyer. To pick the wrong one is to lose. To just pick is to gamble on a roulette-number—but with the possibility of winning reduced to one to one. It is a queer drift that has come upon us here. Let me say only this, with Teufelsdröckh: "If Access to Rights must be over a Bridge of Lawyers, and if Lawyers must also live, then there is Thinking to be done about how to keep little Rights, or the Rights of little Men, from being squeezed out of all Chance of Realization by the Charges at the Tollgate."

The small claims court is a noble institution—a beginning, reaching toward a good which, this time, is one phase of Justice. Let me say also that the type of legislative Justice which one most hopes for here is merely that type of enabling legislation which would empower a bar, as an organized unit, to take up the problem of truly bringing home—of making known and making accessible to every man—that "Equal Justice under the Law, Within," which from the beginning of our government has been the proclaimed counterpart of "Defense, Without." Indeed the drift has been queer which, as to Defense, Without, can give us a Defense Administration, taxes, bond issues, and conscription, as a substitute for Minute Men; but which, as to Equal Justice under the Law, Within, can leave the thing to bank account, or charity, or accident. I have profound admiration for the work of Legal Aid societies. And still, I seem to see here a problem for the Good.

The third point of technical need I want to mention touches again upon that Good which is law's contact with law's people. Savigny may not have phrased a bull's-eye with his idea of the necessary conditioning of all law by the people's *right-way-of-life*, yet right law which touches people must live *in* them. If law does not so live, it goes first technical; it goes then formal and remote. Remote law is not law to love, but law to dodge, or else to use. Remote law is law quite all right to evade, or to defraud; it is law which puts pressure on men to reach or fix officials; it is law which is a burden or a bludgeon; it is law which is the cynical tool of pressure-groups. One can almost say: it should be. Remote law is not your law and not my law, it is *their* law, that *they* put over on us, and it is up to us to put a counter over if we can. Remote law gets the treatment it deserves. I have but little quarrel with what it gets. My quarrel is instead with law's getting, with law's remaining, thus remote. My quarrel is therefore with technicians' ways which let it get remote.

Once, lawsuits were fought out over the winter about three feet of ground or some petty fifteen-dollar sum. They may have engendered as much bitterness among neighbors as they allayed, but they made law a living institution *in* the people. Once, despite its due measure of technicality, the scheme of the legal system was close enough to every day experience to let every man have some first understanding of what it was all about. One learned to follow lawyers' work, when court sat, as the modern American has learned to follow the tactics of baseball. American judicial opinions, moreover, had as a major original function to account not to a bar only, but to a people. Once, too, almost every lawyer lived a rounded life in a rounded community with a rounded practice, and he was known as wise, not as a black magician; was known as learned, not as merely shrewd; was known as a leader and a friend, first, as a technician, only second.

These things are largely lost, by drift and circumstance. By vision and rethinking, one fair part of them can be recaptured. But it does not recapture them merely to set up an administrative agency to do the veteran's or the laborer's legal work *for* him, or what have you more. When I watch the care, the skill, the patience, with which the Tennessee Valley Authority is knitting the active co-operation of the beneficiary into every least job undertaken for his benefit, I see a lesson in democratic government which carries over into all the work of law.[m] A man's rights must be accessible, but to be right rights, they must call also for some share on his part in initiating or in working out their procurement, their fulfillment. Else law remains remote, the government becomes an enemy or a dairy-cow, and the morale of official, citizen, and group alike bogs in morass, and pressure-groups become a by-word.

Do not mistake me. I have no quarrel with pressure-groups as such. They can voice need for all-of-us, as well as wish and selfish interest of their own. But the balance to pressure-groups is not and never will be *merely* other pressure-groups. The further needed balance lies in a citizenry alive, aware, and not habituated to "let George do it all."

Again, do not mistake me. For I have little use for empty cries for change of heart. My argument is that manageable changes in the legal techniques of the legal craftsmen, in phrasing their rules of law and in working with them, in managing their mediation of rights to the law-consumer, in rightly setting up the organs of justiciation or of administration—my argument is that such *manageable changes in legal techniques can bring law home again to law's people.* As means, or as end, I know no greater single good for law.

For when it comes to ultimate substance of the Good, I repeat that I can find no clarity, nor any conviction of reason or of deduction as to specific matters, from the broad ultimates others have found clear. I put my faith rather, as to substance, in a

[m] One has a tragedy in American government when Eisenhower feels necessity, at the same time, to express to Gordon Clapp his feeling that Clapp has been one of our major public servants—*and* to replace him as Chairman of the T.V.A.

means: in that on-going process of effort to come closer to the Good, that on-going process of check-up and correction, and further check-up and correction, which is the method and the very life of case-law. "Reason acting on experience"—better: "Reason at work upon experience, to find and state *explicit guidance for the future;* Reason, responsibly and explicitly accounting for *why* a rule or principle seems reasonable; Reason, re-examining in the light of reasonableness, on further experience, any and every prior ruling or prior reason given, and then reshaping, reformulating, redirecting, each time need may appear in further reason." That is the common law at its high best: the Grand Style. Perhaps because I know nothing better, perhaps because Judicial Justice has been so much discussed, let me leave it at that. But do not let me leave it at that without insisting that when law ceases to be remote, when law comes home, then a process works out among the citizenry of a democracy which is the exact analogue of the common law judicial sequence of self-correction, of judicial review of prior judicial decision—which is, indeed, its twin and needed brother.

If now, you ask me what guarantee I can offer that my own faith about the Good in this institution of our law is better than another's—what does Reason show me to warrant this particular faith of mine against mistake—I have no answer. Under the common law tradition, be a man judge, citizen, or scholar, They That Come After have as their office to correct him. When the machinery of work is healthy, and formalism does not hide on-going reason, They That Come After do their office of correction.

Meantime, a clear faith is a fighting faith. And as for guaranty, I can but rest on an ancient and magnificent summing up: *credo ut intelligam.* Which I prefer to render: *as a result* of my faith, I grasp it with my mind.

For such faith in the essential method of the common-law tradition as that tradition has stood in this country in its best years, and as it has come to stand again—that faith opens a new grasp of our political philosophy. When individual citizens or officers in office, from whatever sequence of divergent absolutes, come to cope as responsible citizens or officers with working out concrete "applications" of their absolutes to the problems of their fellows and themselves, answers are not to be had by deduction, nor out of authority. As in the common law, the new light of the fresh case recolors each problem of "application." One does his best. But the knowledge that review impends from his successors, in the new light of a new fresh problem, must come to any officer or citizen who thinks—new light, too, from a swing of administration, built on other ultimates, or on other immediate views of wisdom. The pragmatic way is no way to reach an ultimate or absolute, but it is the only sound way to *apply* an ultimate, however reached. The finest common law tradition sums up the manner in which the parties, the generations, the clashing groups of a democracy must work their way to wisdom.

SEMI-BALLADE ON THE GLORIOUS QUEST

Among our folk, as among the nations,
    Justice is never a thing, but a quest.
    The measure is always a little messed.
But a man must manage without vacations
and, if he must, on shortened rations,
    when questions press and press and are pressed.
    For Justice is never a thing, but a quest,
among our folk, as among the nations.

One suffers with fools, and with mistranslations,
    one labors with evil, or cynical jest—
Among our folk, as among the nations
    a pest is a pest and remains a pest.
    Yet God is kind though we foul the nest
and pour by the score our futile oblations
    to idiotics that reach no rest:
    Justice is never a thing, but a quest,
among our folk, as among the nations.

Shifting and subtle and torn the relations
    Which challenge and trouble and tangle and test;
Building is slow, though on sure foundations:
    here Law calls for the law-man's best.
    Queer the way it stirs the breast,
queer our rejection of imitations;
yet with our folk, as among the nations,
    Justice is never a thing, but a quest.

Envoi:
Lord, as we serve in our several stations,
    grant that we labor to Thy behest—
for with our folk, as among the nations,
    Justice is never a thing, but a quest.

{ 9 }

ON THE CURRENT RECAPTURE

OF THE GRAND TRADITION [a] *

There are many people—there are altogether too many people
—Gentlemen the Chief Justices of the various Supreme Courts in
these United States—to whom the basic question about you seems
to be whether you and your brethren are in the nature of Delphic
oracles, mere voices with a mission only of accurate transmission,
or whether, in sharpest contrast, you and your brethren are in the
nature of better-class politicians deciding cases the way you see
fit while you just manipulate the authorities to keep it all looking decent.

You resent that kind of misposing of the issue. I join you in
resenting it. Nevertheless, that kind of issue-posing is there, and
it is uncomfortable. When the bar does it, or the public does it,
the result has to be an undermining of confidence in the appellate
bench. Because a Pythian priestess type of job, a purely inspired
opinion into which the answer just flows, happens (in my guess)
not much oftener than one time in one thousand.

Today, however, I am concerned much less with the emotional
effects of the misposing on bar and public than with the effects,
emotional and other, on the appellate bench itself. If you are
addressed—and this outrageous sort of issue-posing is not gentle
in so addressing you—if you are addressed with the question:
Didn't you go hunting around for authorities after you already
knew how you wanted to decide? Don't you, now, know in your

[a] From 9 U. Chi. L. S. Record 6 (1960).
* An Address delivered to the Annual Meeting of the Conference of Chief
Justices, 1959.

215

soul that you then shaped those authorities up like a lawyer so as
to make the opinion look good? Do you mean to say, then, that
it was the Rules of Law *and not You* that tipped the scales?—
Against these questions for half, or even two-thirds, of the run
of cases, there can be only one answer.

What I now suggest is that this kind of queer but persistent
misposing of the issue by bar and public, coupled (as it is coupled)
with the facts of life about how appellate deciding is, *and has to
be,* done, has been producing among the appellate bench themselves an unease which hampers their own work inside themselves.
What I shall proceed to suggest is that a touch of history and of
analysis can turn this very unease into a welling fountain of new
strength; and also, incidentally, into a wherewithal for restoring
a faith and confidence of the bar that has long been in dangerous
decay.

My position is going to be that the course of history has led
not only bar and public, but you yourselves and your brethren,
into holding as a general picture of what your job is and of how
it should be done, a picture which is a snide false picture. It is a
picture which, thank God, is at odds, and in tension, with what
you have for decades been actually doing and with how you are
actually doing your vital work today. This tension, I argue, both
accounts for the unease and offers a machinery for stepping up the
work.

Let me get down to detail; but as I do, let me remind you that
American legal history is (the Supreme Court excepted) one of
the more neglected and is at the same time, for any lawyer, one of
the most accessible avenues to not only pleasure but illumination.
All a lawyer has to do is to read his earlier reports and statutes
not for their doctrine *alone,* but also or indeed primarily as a series
of documents from the times: Why the result? Why this road to
the result? And what is being simply taken for granted here, and
again specially, why?

To work: Since our reports first begin to accumulate—say 1810
—there have been two well-nigh complete revolutions in the way
and theory that deal with how you supreme appellate judges have
been going and ought to go about your job. You can test this
cleanly by looking, say, at 1859, 1909, and 1959. This is a matter of
plain fact. I shall proceed to urge that it is a most important fact.
But first I want to test in advance another proposition of fact on
which I expect to rely.

How many of you are familiar with the two revolutions of your craft-ways? No, that would be dice-loading. Let me rephrase: When I say: "There have been two complete revolutions, since 1820, in the general way in which American appellate judges have gone about their work, contrasting, in general, such times as 1859, 1909, and 1959," to how many of you does this assertion make any real sense? [Not one person suggested that it made any sense.]

Thank you.

In 1859, one era and manner of your work was perhaps beginning to wane, though it was still definitely dominant—say, like a moon one or two days after full. Roscoe Pound has called this general period our "formative period" when his eye was on the rather lovely building of doctrine in that time. In a happier phrase, he has also called it our "classic period." Then he was thinking of the method.

I call it our Grand Style, or the Manner of Reason. The essence is, I think, that every current decision is to be tested against life-wisdom, and that the phrasing of the authorities which build our guiding structure of rules is to be tested and is at need to be vigorously recast in the new light of what each new case may suggest either about life-wisdom, or about a cleaner and more usable structure of doctrine. In any event, and as overt marks of the Grand Style: "precedent" is carefully regarded, but if it does not make sense it is ordinarily re-explored; "policy" is explicitly inquired into; alleged "principle" must make for wisdom as well as for order if it is to qualify as such, but when so qualified it acquires peculiar status. On the side both of case-law and of statutes, where the reason stops there stops the rule; and in working with statutes it is the normal business of the court not only to read the statute but also to implement that statute in accordance with purpose and reason.

And also, if I may return to my opening: the writing judge has neither any illusion that he is or ought to be a Pythian priest, nor has he any illusion of freedom to move as he wills. He does recognize, indeed, the duty to make a solid case on the authorities. But my reading has turned up only one judge who (according to my sniffer) was completely ready to *distort* them in the interest of *his* will.[b] Reasonable, lawyer-like arrangement of authorities in a good cause, even if slightly skewed,—that I am not denying. What I am saying, and this is important, is that for most judges on most occasions—should I guesstimate over 90 per cent?—this was in no way under cover, and that policy—which means the *reason* of

[b] This was an exaggeration. I have found two.

the situation—was a normal, overt and sometimes lengthy subject of discussion. Thus, as of 1859.

By 1909 such practice had become exceptional, the ideal of it, *even the idea* of it was all but dead, and most lawyers, indeed most sitting judges, either knew, or thought, or felt, any such way of appellate deciding to be simply wrong, and, praise be, absent. Statutes, moreover, tended to be read unfavorably, and even when seen favorably, they tended to be limited to the letter.

I give you a flat fifty-year figure. Have you ever thought about the meaning and power of fifty years in our queer American legal tradition? With us fifty years can re-create the whole nature of the legal universe. We do not work with an unchanging canonized text like the Koran or the Mishnah or the Code Civil. We do not even have a carefully gathered and carefully taught doctrinal tradition such as might have grown up out of Coke, Blackstone, Kent, Story, Cooley, Pomeroy, Wigmore. Success of the case-book completely killed off that line of tradition-building. In result, the organ of tradition is the instructor. And a generation, there, amounts to hardly fifteen years. When you enter law school at twenty-one, a professor of thirty-five has the experience and authority of a father; one of fifty speaks like grandpa, from an ancient past behind which nothing ever has been different.

Hence, by the time any of you entered law school the way of work of 1859, the image of on-going constant *and overt* re-examination, redirection, rephrasing and general refreshment of the rules, in the light of sense not for the case alone but for the type of situation—that way of work and that image lay buried under formal thinking and formal ideals and a formal manner of reasoning and of writing—lay buried, for you, as if they had never been. Even after your experience in practice and on the bench, our test of a moment ago shows that the high tradition of the earlier nineteenth century is not vigorous in your minds as being a thing which once was *the* thing, which has just gotten temporarily displaced by one unhappy intellectual revolution.

But when you are now reminded of the fact that that way and ideal of work dominated the American appellate bench—great judges and mediocre judges alike—for more than half a century, then you should see and feel at once that the open and conscious quest for the reasonable rule *for the type-situation* which characterizes the work of the American State Supreme Court today, so far from being ground for unease, should be a basis for rich pride. What it means is that your branch of the profession has performed a truly amazing feat. Within fifty years, without conscious planning, in the teeth of the conscious image of duty and of correct craftsmanship misinculcated in your legal youth and insisted upon loudly and bitterly by the whole vocal bar, you have yet managed to work your way back to a daily way of judging which has almost recaptured the full Grand Tradition of the Common Law.

I speak of the American Supreme Bench in general; but I feel safe. I have studied New York at all periods, with closely examined mine-run samplings from 1939, 1940, 1951, and 1958. I have studied Ohio in 1844, 1939–40, 1953, and 1958. In Massachusetts, North Carolina, Pennsylvania, and Washington there have been sustained studies from fifteen or twenty years ago and then from full current samplings as well—all mine-run stuff, the reported cases taken in sequence as they appear. Nine other states, West, South, and Middle West, were studied in full current samplings. In each instance the material tested runs regardless of subject matter, accounts to "unfavorable" as well as "favorable" material, and reaches at least a majority of the judges on the court. There have also been a number of intensive borings, especially into Illinois material, to test the possibility of getting further light by approaches from other angles. Results: the historical comparisons show that the march toward recapture of the Grand Style is unmistakable, strong, steady, and increasing. The fifteen current samplings seem to me conclusive that almost no state can have escaped its influence. It is, I repeat, an amazing achievement, and it is more than time that it should become a source not only of conscious pride but of that even more effective craftsmanship which can be generated when men add to a sound feeling for the job a conscious study directed to improving the know-how of the craft.

Before moving on to a few suggestions which the best work, older or current, holds out for any work of every day, let me take a precaution against possible misunderstanding. When I speak of overt resort to and discussion of sense as an opinion-daily phenomenon of current judging among American Supreme Courts, I do *not* mean merely such discussion in regard to the *application* of the rule. Neither do I mean such discussion merely in regard to a *choice* between two so-called competing rules or principles. I refer to open, reasoned, extension, restriction or reshaping of the relevant rules, done in terms not of the equities or sense of the particular case or of the particular parties, but instead (illuminated indeed by those earthy particulars) done in terms of the sense and reason of some significantly seen *type* of life-*situation*. A short speech is no place to develop what has cost me a 500-page book.[1] I give a single illustration. Oregon had a precedent, based on soapy window-washing water on a sloping sidewalk, that was cast in terms of "not creating a hazard or adding to the danger of pedestrians who might use the sidewalk, by placing thereon, or, if so placed, in not removing therefrom, any matter that would cause a slippery or dangerous condition." Some snow fell in Portland, was cleared from steps onto an embankment, melted and ran, and, overnight, left a small patch of ice on the sloping sidewalk. The plaintiff slipped and was injured. What the court did was not to "apply." What it did, in the light of "negligence" "principle" plus some aversion to "strict liability," and in the light of three well considered Eastern cases, was to diagnose a new significant *situation:* "snow-clearance by the abutter," and to adopt a *new rule* to further general public convenience by freeing such clearing from risks of liability merely for refreezing.

The case simultaneously brings out another of the more striking phenomena of modern advance sheets. The courts search for, and then quote in some fullness, among out-of-state opinions as well as among home opinions, cases which give not only a rule but also *a persuasive presentation of good life-reason in the light of the type life situation.* Now I shall be slow to be persuaded that it is, as yet (though God grant it may soon be), the *general* habit of the bar to dig out and brief-quote this type of opinion in particular; and rarely is the presence of any such given reason even suggested by either digest or encyclopedia. The labor of this increasingly general quest thus indicates to me one of two things: either a hunger of the writing judge for situation-reason, before he can himself be satisfied, and then, in true Common Law Grand Tradition, his hunger also for merging that situation-reason with authority; or else it shows that, as a skilled man who wishes to keep or capture votes among his brethren, he knows this kind of material to be what they will go for. This is the sweetest dilemma any disciple and preacher of the Grand Tradition can ask to be impaled on. Either horn is honey. Neither will I be put off by any judge's conviction and assertion that he never writes to capture votes, that he writes merely his best version of the facts, the law, and the sound and right decision—let votes or heavens fall where they may. No judge of such conviction can

---

[1] THE COMMON LAW TRADITION: DECIDING APPEALS (1960).

deprive me of my comfort. For he could not be a judge unless he was a lawyer. And a lawyer either is no lawyer at all, or else as he shapes up a matter he puts its best foot forward. And a lawyer —including an appellate judge writing for his own conscience (but also to get his duty done, of a right resolution of the litigation in hand)—may indeed not think consciously about the particular tribunal he has in front of him. But his lawyer's instinct does a lot of that kind of work without his having to do conscious thinking.

With this as a background, let me turn to a few suggestions about both manner of actual judging and manner of opinion-writing which hang like bunches of good grapes, ready to be picked, on the vines of the better practice of your tradition.

The first of these is obvious: (1) The drive should be for *consistent* and *sustained* application and development of the best modern manner. Today, at unpredictable moments, there still pops up into consciousness and control the unhappy and obsolete 1909 image of your office as being purely formal, non-creative, powerless, indeed in a deep sense irresponsible: "It is the rule *and not* the court . . . etc." Whenever that image does so pop up, it interferes with the job. It interferes in the case in hand, which is bad; but, what is much worse, it slows and checks the smooth development of your general recurrence to the Grand Tradition. The doctrine I am preaching is, of course, not that a clear rule which leads to a right result needs anything more than mere clear statement in a single paragraph. The doctrine is instead that under the Grand and Only True Manner of deciding: (a) any rule which is not leading to a right result calls for re-thinking and perhaps re-doing; and, also and equally, (b) any result which is not comfortably fitted into a rule good for the whole significant situation-type calls certainly for cross-check and probably for more worry and more work.

(2) The second of the points is one which, between the 1939–1941 samplings I have studied and the current ones, seems to be on the perceptible increase. That is the practice, whenever time permits, of what I think of as a tidying-up of the whole particular little corner of doctrine, so as to afford the court a canvass of *all* the local experience to date, and so as to afford the bar a fresh and clean foothold. Note how comfortably this fits with any persuasive life-reason for a significantly seen type of situation which a court may locate in experience from across the border. Note also, where no such ready-made rationale is at hand, how the tidy-up provides

an authority-underpinning for any rationale the court may reach on its own. Note finally the dividends such a job pays not only to the bar in guidance, but to the court itself in speed of disposing of further cases in the same area. I have been proud of my Common Law Tradition, as I worked through my current samplings (in all, 350–400 cases) and met instance upon instance in which, even after such a recent tidying-up, the court was willing to review the field *once* more. I have been disturbed when, after two such jobs, a court has not felt that it was time to take a little skin off the back of slovenly counsel who despite the recent clean-up had been wasting court's time and clients' hopes and money.

(3) Save for the course of the prior discussion, the third point might well have been put first. It is a formula for avoiding both "Hard cases make bad law" and any splintering of "the law" into narrow jackstraw-decisions which offer to neither bar nor tomorrow's court any helpful pattern for guidance. In my judgment this formula is always helpful, in three cases out of five it resolves the chief difficulties almost automatically and in the rest it presses things toward sound solution. The formula is simple to state, and not hard to apply. It is this: As you size up the facts, try to look first for a significant life-problem-situation into which they comfortably fit, and only then let the particular equities begin to register; so that when the particular equities do begin to bite, their bite is already tempered by the quest for and feel for an appropriate rule that flows from and fits into the significant situation-type.

This kind of language means little by ear, or in the abstract. Let me try both to illustrate and to save time by taking a case most of you met (and were mistaught) while you were still students: *McPherson v. Buick*. That was a case in which the defendant not only had done every normal thing that in the then state of the art there was to do, but also had an astounding record of experience to show both its care and the soundness of its judgment. If you take the party-equities as a base-line and if you take "fault" of any kind as a principle, that pretty well cleans up the plaintiff. And Willard Bartlett's reminder that at the time of the accident the car was moving only at a stage-coach speed of eight miles an hour also becomes crushing argument. What Cardozo did, in contrast, was to take a significant *life-situation*, first, and to take these individual equities only against that background. I am not going to argue whether or not he was right or wise as to the doctrine in the particular situation. For my concern is with method; and not even the grand methods of the Grand Style give any assurance of sound outcome in any individual case. What they do is to double or treble the probability that the outcome will be sound. But the case does show sound method going to one value which would be live and real even if the particular case-result were most unhappy in its substance; to wit, the gain at least in predictability which can be achieved by a combination of looking first for a significant type of situation, and then doing a careful tidy-up. Thus before *McPherson v. Buick* the law of New York had for some demonstrable forty years been swinging around on this matter like a weather-vane. I urge that even Willard Bartlett's beautiful argument (which Law School never introduced you to—Have you ever read it? Who has?) was just another of the same: another *individual equity job*. The Torts boys praise Cardozo in this one because of his beautiful *new doctrine*. I agree, but that is not my point here. *I* praise him here because of his beautiful *old method*, and—as I hope my book makes unmistakable—I would praise that, even though I objected violently to his particular result.

See what he did. It is so simple. It is so grand. Instead of individual parties doing their best, or queer articles: "dangerous instruments," he set up a significant type-situation: consumer-purchase in a community which has to rely on increasingly ununderstandable basic technology. That typical situation, seen that way, stepped up the aspect of reliance and stepped down the aspect of fault. And the typical situation, as of course, included the need for marketing the product through middlemen. You will find no such overall picture sharply expressed in the opinion. What the opinion does is to *feel* that picture. Indeed, it is not the job, even of a great judge, to get fully explicit, all at once, about great social change. His job is to *feel* what he can, and to *see* what he can, and to *say* what he can. But his *method* has to be to *reach, first*, for the significant type-*situation*. Then, to diagnose a problem, and to prescribe an answer accompanied by an explicit life-reason: this not only helps toward a good answer, but is also priceless in affording easy wherewithal for tomorrow's intelligent application, or else for tomorrow's explicit correction, whichever tomorrow's case may prove to need. Finally, the good judge's office, in the Grand Tradition, is to do a careful and honest tidy-up in his opinion.

Out of a dozen more further matters there are three which press peculiarly for mention, even though the mention must be cut to the bare bones. There is, to begin with, the syllabus by the court. The propositions are these: (1) Whether or not there is a present practice for the court to prepare its own syllabus, it ought to. (2) A syllabus court which prepares the syllabus not *before* the opinion is written, but only *after* the opinion has been written, sacrifices the main value offered by the syllabus to the opinion, to the court, and to the law. (3) My argument is independent of any theory or doctrine to the effect that "it is the syllabus which states the law."

On the third point first: My book demonstrates, from Ohio, and I will undertake to demonstrate from any jurisdiction, that regardless of local theory on the point, a syllabus-court is up against the same multiwayed problems of handling prior authorities as is a non-syllabus court. My guess is that the diverging correct doctrinal possibilities merely rise from 60 plus to 80 plus, as syllabus and opinion come to interact in their operation and application.

Now on the first two propositions together, and flat, and simple: Elementary theory of argument makes it clear that if the points to be made are thought out, arranged, and also phrased, *before* writing begins, the result *has* to improve in

(a) clarity, and
(b) force, and
(c) speed of production. And *almost always* improves also in
(d) shortness and bite.

Again let me avoid being mistaken. When I apply the theory of argument to an appellate judicial opinion, I do not mean that an opinion is *merely* an argument. What I *do* mean is that whatever else it is, it is also and necessarily an argument: A conclusion has been reached and has been tested and has been found both right and solid. The opinion-writer now has a lawyer's job: the facts, issues, and authorities are to be marshalled so that on any point the rule announced is shown to any reasonable reader to be properly controlling, and so that the application of that rule is shown to any reasonable reader to be not only justifiable but wise. Only thus can a satisfying opinion come into being. The laws of argument apply: The points to be made are best thought out, arranged, *and also phrased, before* the writing begins. Of course the writing may show rearrangement or rephrasing to be required. Sometimes a judge may be forced to reverse his initial conclusion. But that cuts down not one tittle on the value of preliminary *phrased* organization.

It is a queer thing that you gentlemen, who, in order to make things clearer for yourselves to see and easier for yourselves to handle, force upon the bar in their briefs an organization by way of phrased points which come *first*, should in your own work and in your own product disregard that method. This calls for some soul-searching on your part.[2]

The second remaining "must" for mention is a question of judicial statesmanship: the value of a two-stage operation whenever any important change of doctrine either portends or is undertaken. Warning is a tremendous value to a counselling lawyer. Warning is also old practice. Take the familiar cases where the court says: "Now look: here is what we are *not* deciding." Or, beside and against these, take the cases where the court says: "Of course, if the facts were this other way, it seems clear that the outcome would be the opposite." Both caveat and prophecy, *when carefully considered,* give good warning. Both caveat and prophecy, even when carefully considered, offer the court a second think. Note now a new factor on the scene: we have today, in the law reviews, to a degree and with a general spread never before met in the history of our country, a forum for dubious or dangerous, even though carefully considered, suggested ideas of the State Supreme Court to be explored with freedom and with fullness, *before they bite.* To open an idea to such a forum is to widen materially the likelihood and range of information the court can hope to tap. Not infrequently such additional material can shift what seems the balance of wisdom. Meantime, the counselling lawyer has marked his chart with a danger flag, and transactions are so channeled that—no matter which way it goes—disappointments are reduced. That is pure gain for everybody.

Why, in the light of these facts, is not the principle of warning and the practice of two-stage operation made general? Thus, for example, when there is some novel ruling, it is almost always technically easy to add at the end an alternative which on the facts leaves the main, and meant, ruling still open, if real reason should unexpectedly appear, to be distinguished for cause.

A study of your current practices of distinguishing shows that purely technical distinguishing is today almost as extinct as the dear dodo. Today a distinction without a reason expressly given

[2] Up to this point, except for two additions to clear up what discussions in the Chief Justices' "workshops" showed to be expressions which had led to misunderstanding, the text is almost exactly as delivered. The following portions of the speech (save for minor later clarifications) were distributed, but had to be cut from delivery for lack of time.

is rare; and almost always the reason given goes to reason of fact, which is reason of life, as seen by the court. I therefore feel no hesitance at all in suggesting a standard technical procedure to avoid silly questions of face (*"Can We Overrule So Recent a Decision?"*) while a court still keeps its eye on the ball in a *two-stage* operation.

Finally, on this matter, and again in the interest of "general principle" (not coined for this argument, but built out of a careful examination of a century of our case-law experience)—finally: why should you not *generally,* instead of at odd moments, bring this principle of warning and this practice of two-stage to bear on the problem of overruling, as well as of any other change or warning? There is no time to develop this. I ask you only to think about three questions:

(1) If the argument and study in a case persuade you that a rule in the immediate area is ready to fall in the next wind, I am suggesting that warning of that is by any discoverable standard of decency as much needed as can possibly be the carving out of a little Swiss cheese hole in any pending decision.

(2) If the case in hand just slips in under an exception (so to speak, "on other grounds") to a rule which the argument has persuaded you no longer fits our people: why is this not the perfect opportunity to give, in regard to a rule, the warning notice which every man of you is willing to give with regard to an exception?

You will observe that what I am here urging, to wit, the considered expression that "When we get a clean chance, we will extirpate," does not even touch the problem of the *Sunburst Oil* case.

And yet, as far as my limited reading goes, this easier and more useful method has found more resistance among you gentlemen and your brethren than has even the bold move of deciding the pending case by the old rule, while announcing a new rule (or a new approach to a statute) for the future. I think that this difference is because you have been (rightly) trained to think protection against retroactive "law" to be not only decency, but *your* office; while you have also been mistrained to think that your office has no part in prophecy. But surely *any* good case-law judgment is in its best part a combination of prophecy and of clean guidance toward fulfillment thereof. In any event:

(3) Why do not the principle of warning, and the practice and policy of two-stage operation become a standard approach to possible overruling, prospective overruling, and to the case which

has, in itself, to be expected from the overruling—easing all of these, while it effectively warns the bar, and also opens up whatever may be elicited to inform the court before the final leap?

The last matter which refuses to be left without mention is that of the statutes. Here the image of 1909—"We must accept what is written, we have only to read the [so frequently non-existent] 'intent of the legislature,' we have no *power* to add," etc.—modified only by the 1959 willingness to abdicate self-will and to try to make sense—here, I say, the image of 1909 stalks not only active (though most intermittently) but vicious.

The simple basic principle which expresses both the Grand Manner and today's need is this: It is contrary to a Supreme Court's duty, and therefore to its power, to allow any statute to remain as an undigested and indigestible lump in the middle of Our Law.

Even the most formal judges of the Formal Period recognized this principle. Their response was sound in terms of office-instinct: The Law does call for wholeness. Their response was not good, in terms of measure. They refused to participate in the intrusion. They excreted what they could, via unconstitutionality. They walled off the rest by literalistic construction.

That is past, in regard to the particular. But it is still with us at odd moments, and vigorously whenever a court settles down to a sermon on its lack of power over the written word.

But in my current samplings

(a) I have found no single court which, even if it mouths the statute-image of 1909 today, cannot also be found *operating* in conflict with that image, and in an approach to the Grand Approach to statutes, on the same opinion-day or on the next.

(b) Nor have I found any court which, *judged on a sequence of cases,* is not moving with regard to statutes about as freely in the average as it is in the case-law field. This holds also for the 1939–1940 and 1944 work examined from six courts. What you get in the statutory field is a jerkier, less predictable movement: here more of a hitch, there a sudden jump, so to speak, under cover; with no adequate guidance, as to when which will occur.

That is not healthy judging.

According to the Grand Style, it is the office of the Supreme Courts in these United States to do, with statutes, too, what you have for now a demonstrable two legal generations been doing for the rules of our case-law. You must accept them, to start with: you are no independent agents. You must shape yourselves to what, in essence, they give you to receive; you are no officers to move as *you* see fit. You must also accept policy and basic measure, if, as and when the legislature gives them to you. Indeed— and here begins the tough duty—your job is *also* the perplexing one of remaining true to such policy and measure and at the same time to the nature and spirit of the inherited rule-machinery— of somehow handling the individual case according to all of these at once, as you labor in the vineyard of the heritage. You accept today from the Legislature, as your forebears of 1889–1909 would not, the Legislature's essential declarations of policy, and its outlines of measures. But as you do it, and very queerly, you still proceed to pick up, proclaim, and sometimes even trip yourselves on, the very noises that the foot-draggers of 1909 used to use in order to keep legislative policy from receiving any real recognition. For "We have no power," when that slogan was first popularized in the Formal Period, meant "Thank God, we can whittle it down to frustration."

Briefly, then: (1) A piece of legislation, like any other rule of law, is, of course, meaningless without reason and purpose.

(2) Few are the legislatures, even when equipped with tops legislative reference bureaus, who also have had time to give this particular bill the visiting Queen Elizabeth treatment, or who, in passing any bill, pass it with any real "intention," as to the question which is now before the court.

(3) Even when legislators do have demonstrable intentions— as with an open grab-bill—there can be times when a court has a duty of restrictive construction. (On this Breitel's forthcoming article advances—yet with sweet restraint—far beyond any earlier writing.)

In the net, then: as in the Grand Tradition, so in current practice, and even more in current need, the recapture of the Grand Tradition is almost there, but irritatingly is not yet there, quite. It needs to be fulfilled.

In regard to the How, my guess is that most of you who may disagree with me may be worried more about statutes than about anything else. In regard to statutes, and with my own mind on the way statutes have been viewed in our tradition in the first Elizabeth's time, and in Coke's, and in Marshall's or Shaw's, and in Hughes', as his viewing changed through his long legal life, and as I work over instance after instance of your current work— in regard to statutes, the essence comes to this: that except for occasional almost unwelcome reappearances you are almost back to getting at them in terms of "where the reason stops, there stops even the enacted rule." You are still, however, far short of the other duty, addressed to the undigested lump—the hard, the troubling stone in the law's stomach. That other, complementary duty is: Whither the reason leads, thither goeth the rule, as well. That is the principle of implementation by purpose. It is also part of a Supreme Court's duty, the duty to keep Our Law Whole, and a *working* Whole.

There is so much in this, my plea for conscious recreation of the responsible forward-guiding of our Common Law, which may offend all or some of you. To these I can only say in the words of old Oliver Cromwell: "I beseech you, in the bowels of Christ, bethink you that ye *may* be mistaken."

INSTITUTION, RULE,
AND CRAFT

ON THE NATURE OF AN INSTITUTION [a]

An institution is in first instance a set of ways of living and doing.[b] It is not, *in first instance,* a matter of words or rules.[1] The existence of an institution lies first of all and last of all in the fact that people do behave in certain patterns *a, b* and *c,* and do not behave in other conceivable patterns *d* to *w.* And the probability that an institution will continue coincides with whatever probability there is that people will continue so to behave. Every living constitution is an institution; it *lives* only so far as that is true. And the difference between a "written" and an "unwritten" constitution lies chiefly in the fact that the shape of action in the former case is *somewhat* influenced by the presence of a particular document, and of particular attitudes toward it, and particular ways of dealing with its language.

A national constitution is a somewhat peculiar institution in that it involves in one phase or another the ways of a huge number of people—well-nigh the whole population. If, like ours, it is a firmly established constitution, it involves ways of behavior deeply set and settled in the make-up of these people—and it

[a] This is excerpted from *The Constitution as an Institution,* 34 COLUM. L. REV. 1, 17–26 (1934).

[b] I should today focus first upon the *jobs* to be done, around whose doing ways both get organized and take on meaning.

[1] Some institutions—for instance, our present Constitution—have found words and rules serving them as midwife or even as ancestor; but in the main it is action which comes first, to be followed by delayed perception of that action, then by rationalization of the action delayed still longer, and finally by conscious normatization of what has been perceived or rationalized. Before these latter processes have been worked out, the lines of the action commonly have shifted. Veblen's eyes were keen: "A man's ethics are modelled on the conditions of his grandfather's time."

involves not patterns of doing (or of inhibition) merely, but also accompanying patterns of thinking and of emotion—attitudes, *e.g.*, potent and largely predictable, toward the verbal symbol "Constitution" and toward any person supposed to be attacking "It."

As an institution of major size, then, our working Constitution embraces the interlocking ways and attitudes of different groups and classes in the community—*different* ways and attitudes of *different* groups and classes, but all cogging together into a fairly well organized whole.

Perhaps it is as well to stop for an illustration. Any family is an institution. Any family is made up of persons. But not every aggregation of persons is a family. The persons in a family have one or another trait in common: either they live together, or they are related by blood, or both. We shall take for further development a case in which these two common factors concur. Yet what appears at once is the *divergence* of the ways of action of the persons concerned, despite the common factors. Mr. Hubb goes out to work and provides for payment of the bills. When he rises, his breakfast has been attended to; and the bathroom has been left free for his shaving. He, and no other, reads the newspaper while he eats. Before he leaves for his train, he fixes the furnace; and he receives certain instructions as to things to be brought back on his return. There is no need to go on. It is obvious that Mr. Hubb's patterns of behavior are not those of Mrs. Hubb, nor those of the maid, nor those of little Lorna. But it is equally obvious that the patterns of all four intercog like the wheels of a clock, and make a *whole* go round which we choose to call "a family," and which is more than and different from the constituent parts. It is obvious, moreover, that Mr. Hubb's behavior lies in good part in patterns, expected and reckoned with by the others. And normatized. If he should fail to come home to dinner, or should forget the ordered purchases, or should gamble away his paycheck at a poker-game, Mrs. Hubb would not only be upset in her co-operation, but would *feel* aggrieved. Meanwhile, each other member of the family contributes her own quite diverse patterns to the interlocking whole that goes on *as* a whole.

Now what holds of the gearing together of the ways of single persons into a small group holds of the gearing together of the ways of whole groups into a still larger whole. A factory combines management personnel, foremen, operating labor, repair staff, shipping clerks. A national corporation combines different factories (now taken as units) with the commercial divisions of the head office, the selling staff, the directors, the varied security-holders. A national government—but, again, why go on? The essential fact is that the larger the number of persons concerned, and the more intense their participation, (a) the more intricate the detail of the patterned clock-work, (b) the greater the range of room for slipping gears, (c) the larger and more internally complex the units which must commonly be taken as units if discussion is to remain intelligible.

THE CONSTITUTION: SPECIALISTS, INTERESTED GROUPS, PUBLIC

To sum up: no institution consists of *like* ways among all the persons concerned. It is the unlikeness plus the complementary crossplay of the organized ways which is the most convenient criterion for marking off an "institution" from a mere "way" or simple culture-trait.

As to our own working Constitution, even in so rough a sketch as this, it will pay to distinguish three categories of persons whose ways are concerned. The first are the *specialists in governing*. The second are what we may term the *interested groups:* aggregations of people more or less organized around some interest, who direct pressure upon the specialists or upon the general public in furtherance of their own particular desires. The third are those who, as to any given issue, are left over—call them the *general public*. They are important, as will appear; but important rather as is the audience in a theatre, as distinguished from actors and stage-hands, or from author and producer. Plays succeed or flop. So do constitutions. So does constitutional change. The audience, however, *initiates* neither play nor change.

By specialists in government I mean those people whose business is governing in general, or, perhaps more accurately, people *so far as* they enter into the *general* business of governing. This includes most official office-holders, be they legislators, executives, administrators or judges. But when, say, a legislator conceives his job to include getting the silver or aluminum or power people what they want merely because they want it, he will for my present purpose be dividing his time between specialization in government and activity as a member of an interested group. The classification by persons, or by offices, in other words, serves merely as an approximation to a classification of activity and attitude.—Somewhat obviously to be included among these specialists would be such party officials as devote a good share of their time to the problems of *de facto* government: Mr. Croker, Mr. Penrose, Mr. Curry. Beyond this, as suggested, the group shades off in terms of more or less time, more or less intensity, more or less success or influence, of persons partly specializing on such other matters as, say, road construction, saloon-keeping, labor union management, corporation law practice, gangsterism, or investment banking. The general position here to be maintained is that these specialists occupy, with reference to what the working Constitution is and how it changes, the key position, with various of the interested groups serving now to induce, now to inhibit, one or another change. One small group of specialists, the judges, hold a peculiar veto-power, called on fairly often, exercised only occasionally. The general public hold a further veto power, but one exercised rarely indeed. Referendum and recall of judicial decisions were devices aimed at furthering the exercise. Elections are an indirect and rather ineffective device for the purpose. Riot and revolution—when successful—are its final expression. In all but odd cases this power of the general public operates not as a veto of action taken, but as a deterrent from taking action or a stimulus to take action—for fear of what *might* happen.[2]

___

[2] *Excursus: On the nature of these concepts.*—It will be obvious that the categories thus laid down flow one into another, and even overlap. A man may be today an independent office-holder, tomorrow a lawyer with important political influence, the day after a bought-and-paid-for official working for an interested group. He may be president of the Civic Club and be simultaneously fighting a rate case for some utility. Neither he nor any other may, in the rate case, be able to tell whether his conception of good government, his conception of his clients' interest, his personal prestige and satisfaction in victory, his love of the game as such, or his prospective fee, is his fundamental drive. In so far the three "descriptive" categories fail of accurate description. And as of these, so of the other categories here suggested. "Way," for example, is the roughest inaccurate generalization of individual acts of individual people, all of a given line of acts being treated for convenience *as if* they were interchangeably alike. Of course, under the microscope, they are not so alike. Yet often, *for the purpose in hand*, the differences can safely be sunk in the similarities. The turning back or stopping of the clock at one session of a legislature can be treated as "the same" as at another. The fact that three new opposition members may protest, or even that some session may go by without clock-manipulation becoming necessary, does not obscure the presence of a governmental "way" general and predictable enough to warrant conceiving and applying the category. But in the main, the presence of a way is not a question of yes-or-no, but of more-or-less: *so far as* there exists significant regularity and significant uniformity of action in given circumstance among certain people, *to that extent* there exists "a way" among those people. Attendance at roll-calls of important legislative sessions (or, alternatively, pairing) may be regarded as a way rather well established. Similarly, *so far as* certain individuals are active regularly and in co-

THE RÔLE OF THE SPECIALISTS

It has been urged thus far that a working constitution is an institution, that it is an institution highly complex in nature, that it can be viewed with some adequacy as the interaction of the quite different ways and attitudes of three diverse categories of people, and that of these *the specialists in government stand at the focus.* I propose now to concentrate for a time upon the ways of these last. For not only is it they who are the prime movers in preserving so much of the Constitution as is preserved; it is also they who in all save most peculiar instances—on eleven occa-

---

operation, they can be said to be "a group." For instance—despite absences for fence-building or junketing—a legislative house. Again, *so far as* ways interlock in complement, they build into "an institution." The orderly progress of parliamentary debate is, *e.g.*, distinctly more an institution in this country than in some others. It is not, to be sure, when examined in detail, a way, but a complex. Only the speaker presides. Only one member holds the floor at a time; the others sit. "The rules of order" hold for all, but the predictable action of individuals which they call for is *different* action by *different* individuals, all organized into a going whole. The difference between "way" and "institution" is thus commonly merely one of emphasis and level of discourse. Where thought of as a unit in a larger whole, a complex may be treated as "a way," though the same complex, when treated as a subject for nicer analysis, would be thought of as an integration of interlocking parts.

The *outer boundaries* of a group or of an institution are almost never sharply marked. Each shades off into its neighbors. Some ways or men are closely, others not so closely, tied into the perceptible core. Are lobbyists, or pages, or inactive Senators, as much "The Senate" as floor leaders? The United States Steel Corporation—meaning thereby the persons *with* their significant ways and attitudes—might in one connection be considered to be the managing personnel, in another that personnel plus major stockholders, in still another that personnel plus all stockholders, and so on through bondholders, interested bankers, white collar staff, laborers, customers—or even customers of customers. A "basic" outfit is of necessity an outfit with outward boundary undefined.

The farther out one goes, to be sure, the slighter the nexus, the greater the outward range and angle-spread of radiation, the more disturbing the dynamic context of other groups and institutions built around other types of center. Yet the *core* is always clear—as clear as the boundary, in any given discussion, must be arbitrary. There is, certainly in a complex society, no escape from this fact: that the marking off of "*an interest*," "*a group*," "*an institution*" is an artificial abstraction from a complexly concrete mass of phenomena; nor any escape from the correlative fact: that the boundaries drawn will always be indefensible save as they become useful and significant *for the purpose in hand.* Hence all that is intended by the use of such terms, unqualified, is, throughout this paper, twofold: first (and descriptively) that in significantly high measure the attributes of the concept are present in fact in the life around us; second (and theoretically) that any increasing quantum of their presence or of their range or intensity where present would strengthen the truth-value of the proposition announced concerning them.

(Throughout the above my lasting indebtedness to Max Weber will be obvious. And Sumner must be added, and Ehrlich, and W. I. Thomas, and Underhill Moore, and that relentless teacher that *facts* must be regarded: A. L. Corbin. The last will not agree with my paper. But he will recognize his contribution to it.)

sions in our history, to be exact—arrange all amending of that Constitution.

Surely there are few superstitions with less substance than the belief that the sole, or even the chief process of amending our Constitution consists of the machinery of Amendment. Party system and campaign fund, protective tariff and secret ballot, patronage and Senatorial filibuster, judicial review and national banking: these sit as firmly, and most of them weigh as heavily, in our governmental structure as did ever indirect election of Senators or the power of the federal courts to entertain a suit against one State brought by a citizen of another. They were put into our working Constitution by the specialists. Two of them (filibuster and review) could each be taken out by the action of a single body of specialists. Their disappearance is less likely in fact than was, *e.g.,* the coming of the income tax, and hardly more so than a territorial reorganization of States into Regions, or an alteration of the two-Senator allotment. This feature of highly probable permanence is, as will appear, one essential criterion of what is Constitution, and what is not. Here it suffices to note that the amendment of the living Constitution to include these phases has been the work either mainly or exclusively of the specialists in government, and that the process of formal Amendment has not been found requisite in that work.

Whether it be to continue or to repeat, let me attempt further to make a seemingly unorthodox position unambiguous: *the working Constitution is amended whenever the basic ways of government are changed.* The reform of Cannon's committee rules was a striking instance; they had been fundamental. The entrance of the federal government into control of the air was a second. The N. R. A. may be hoped to be a third. Indeed, *amendment occurs typically by action of the relevant specialists alone,* and without alteration of the language of the Document. Of their own motion they can, and of their own motion or under pressure from interested groups they do, change the manner of government in vital aspects, widen it startlingly, ring out old pieces of the Constitution as bells ring out an Old Year. It is they who have remade the pattern of government as we have passed from a dominantly agricultural into a dominantly industrial and on into a dominantly financial economy. It is they who have tinkered, twisted, invented, on the governmental side, either to further shifts in economic institutions or to catch up with such shifts; to attempt some adjustment of the emergent new to the persistent old. By legislation. By executive or administrative practice. By building the wherewithal to elect or control executives or legislators. Under their hands much of the Document has been blotted out like the original text upon a double palimpsest.

"By action of the relevant specialists alone." Often a single person (a President), or a single group; more often several groups in active or passive concert. Occasionally, as mentioned, one peculiar group intrudes a veto: the judges. Their power so to do, if called upon, is the most vital reason for invoking the cumbersome machinery of Amendment. It is not the only reason. Neither, thanks to the awkwardness of the machinery, is their veto often an occasion for its invocation. In the main, when the judges interpose their Nay, men shrug and suffer. Yet this much is patent: unless the judges have vetoed, or unless it is confidently believed that if called upon they will veto, Amendment is in the main unnecessary, and is rarely resorted to. Where their veto occurs or is anticipated, the *working* Constitution (which includes judicial review) prescribes Amendment as the sole available process of amending.[3] This not because the Document so says, nor is it because the proposed amendment varies from the Document, or from its judicial "interpretation." *It is because one body of the relevant specialists happen to be unwilling to let the proposed amendment pass.* Why else are we concerned about the personnel of the Court?

Yet of certain Amendments, such as those on woman's suffrage or direct election of Senators, or, say, one admitting some hitler-like foreign-born to the Presidency, the use of the formal machinery would be reasonably predictable (unless perhaps in a time of overwhelming emergency) even though the Court's veto might *not* be expected. For the working Constitution consists not merely in powers of the specialists, nor merely in their existing ways of action; it includes no less their *attitudes* toward the Document and its language. It embraces deep-seated inhibitions among many of the most influential guildsmen (not judges alone) against departing openly from its express language, or even, at times, from what is thought to be the "intent" of less express wording. [Con-

---

[3] As an alternative, there is the remodelling of the Court—say, by way of increase of numbers; or even by way of introducing a retiring age sweetened, let us say, by duly attractive pension. But these are still in the realm of expediency and experiment. [This was written in 1933.]

sider, for instance, the power of the concept of "separation of Church and State," which one does not find mentioned in the Document.] In this the specialists resemble the members of the undifferentiated general public—save that some of the specialists have some knowledge of what the express language of the Document happens to be. The specialists are, then, self-limited in their powers of amending; or more accurately, they are limited in their discovery of their own *de facto* powers, or in the use of those discovered, by traditions regarding the Document which have shaped their imaginations and their consciences in the very process of becoming specialists.

The Rôle of the General Public

Less potent, I suspect, and if not that, then less frequently operative, are inhibitions based on the attitudes of the general public (from which distinguish at this point interested groups). Two factors characterize the general public's rôle. There is an unreasoned, unreasoning, tradition-founded loyalty to a symbol of national unity and permanence. Along with this there is a pervasive ignorance and indifference as to almost all detail. The loyalty, so far as I can observe, is in first instance to a phrase, without more: "The Constitution." It runs in infinitely decreased measure to the Document of 1789—which is currently enough supposed to begin: "When in the course of human events" or: "We hold these truths to be self-evident." Rather is the second line of loyalty to a slightly idealized picture of the Nation-As-It-Stands—including elections (pruned in dream of fraud, or blackjack, or of the triumph of the wicked enemy), including the present incumbents of highest office (somehow made National by panoply), including Prosperity (around the corner), including the People (always with silent elimination from that concept of particular objectionable elements, the negative selection varying to taste), including finally American Prestige as painted by pulp paper fiction, grade school history books and Fourth of July orations. All of which is somehow identified with the War of Independence and with a Document, and conceived loosely as having existed, with minor aberrations, from the glorious beginning.

This popular loyalty, though real, is blind. It is almost empty of *specific* content. Therefore (a) it leaves the specialists free to shape and reshape the working Constitution in *almost* any way they please, and *almost* to any extent on which they get together—whether they get together by concerted action or by drift. But (b) the combination of intense loyalty to a symbol with almost total emptiness of concrete content means an ever-present latent possibility that the symbol may become attached in the popular mind to almost *any* concrete content at all. And persons opposed to any projected change may work the hook-up. And simple and clear language in the Document may mightily facilitate such an arrangement, even though it should fail to stir the inhibitions of the specialists at large, or of the judiciary in particular.

Here, then, lie both the scope and the limits of the leeway which the general public affords the specialists. And be it noted that the scope is more real than the limitations. For the most potent limitation lies inside the skulls of the specialists. Whereas the public not only know nothing of the real operation of the Constitution—they also care nothing about it. What difference whether income taxation rests on "interpretation" or Amendment? What matter—to most—whether the 18th Amendment be on the books, and if on the books, whether it or a Volstead Act do the forbidding; whether New York has thirty-nine representatives, or fifty-two, or eighty-seven; whether Congress or the States regulate longshoremen's accident compensation; whether impeachment of judges calls for majority, two-thirds, three-fourths, or unanimous vote; whether "to receive ambassadors" does or does not imply the power of refusing recognition to a foreign government? What farmer cares whether a mortgage-moratorium or scaling-down clashes with the impairment of contracts clause? One can indeed in normal times conceive an uproar if the electoral college should proceed to perform its original Documentary function, or if the President should seek to dissolve Congress by action of the military arm. Bounds there are. But they are ample—as against the *general* public. The interested groups remain.

The Rôle of the Interested Groups

Wherefore one other type of limit should be mentioned. When action by the specialists on a point of constitutional change pinches the personal toes of Albert Jones too sharply, Albert is likely to react as he does to less fundamental change of similar effect. If part of a group, he fights effectively to block or undo the change. If only one of an unorganized class or ruck, he groans and gets nowhere, unless the pressure is painful and sustained enough to lock his fellows and himself together into an interested group.[4]

For the effective block upon constitutional change which ranges too far or in a direction undesired—alongside the self-limitation of the specialists, and the looming spectre of the Court—is the pressure of these interested groups. They are plentiful; and many or most of them are single-minded, and motivated in a fashion which reminds one of the Economic Man. To the extent that they are groups at all, they are organized; to the extent that they have found intelligent leadership, they are effectively organized, and their organization is effectively applied where it will do *them* the most good. They "see" bosses; they persuade administrators; they lobby bills into the legislature and out of committee, or out of the legislature and permanently into committee; they draw the teeth of legislation during passage, or in the process of its "application"; or, if the bill serves them, they get teeth into it, and give "due" unofficial aid in its enforcement; they discover barriers in the language of the Venerable Document, or in the cases "under" it, and press those barriers upon the courts. Nor is this all. They also "educate" the public; they offer generous aid in framing and forcing the issues of political campaigns. And I take the presence of such groups, and their activities in squeezing upon the specialists either directly or by way of first stirring the theretofore disinterested public, to be *essential* portions of the working Constitution of these United States. It is hard, without them, to see how our government would govern. The mind of a mere professor staggers in void when he attempts to conceive Manufacturers' Association, Beet Sugar Interests, Public Utilities, Federation of Labor, Magazine Publishers, Oil, or United Realtors abstracted from the national scene. Certain it is that, without such groups, governing would become for persons of this day and age unrecognizable. Yet I do not find them mentioned in the Document, save under an obsolescent clause about "the right of the people peaceably to assemble and petition the Government for redress of grievances." And even this clause touches only that relatively ineffective fraction of the Interested Groups which has to "assemble" in order to bring its grievances, or wants, to bear.

[4] Such as, *e.g.*, appears to be again emerging among farmers. Or must one subdivide into cotton, corn, tobacco farmers, and the like?

{ 11 }

THE BAR'S TROUBLES, AND POULTICES—

AND CURES? [a] [*]

The problem of unauthorized practice of the law is a problem of using the processes of the law to define and protect a monopoly. It immediately raises a series of obvious questions: What are the

[a] From 5 LAW AND CONTEMPORARY PROBLEMS 104 (1938); a part of a symposium on *The "Unauthorized Practice of Law" Controversy.*

[*] The American Bar Association has a Committee on Legal Aid Work, one on the Economic Condition of the Bar, one on Professional Ethics and Grievances, one on Unauthorized Practice, one on Legal Clinics, a section devoted to Legal Education and Admissions, a section devoted to Bar Organization and a Committee thereof on Coordination, and another on Public Relations. It is almost sure, shortly, to have one on Surveys of the Bar and of Legal Business. This paper attempts to make explicit some of what the Committees at work are discovering to vitally condition their work: to wit, that all such phases of the Problem of the Bar have a common line of cause, a common focus, a common line of cure. No less a part of the same picture is post-graduate education, on which see articles by Shafroth in 23 A. B. A. J. 777 (1937); 24 *id.* 11 (1938); and on which there is also a Committee.

An attempted sketch of the Whole must leave innumerable parts untouched, or suggested in a single sentence. It must risk unproved and locally inapplicable generalization. It must leave unnoted most of the documentation which exists. Its aim is perspective. It can hope to stimulate investigation—investigation seriously and carefully undertaken, with no light-hearted notion that finding facts is an off-hour job—investigation to determine whether the seeming general conclusions hold for any particular Bar, or any recognizable part of any particular Bar. If either gain in perspective or furtherance of real investigation is achieved, this paper has done all that it hopes to do.

The ideas involved are becoming common ground among the more careful thinkers in the field. My indebtedness to many of them I repeat: R. H. Smith, J. S. Bradway, R. Moley, Gisnet, A. A. Berle, P. J. Wickser, E. Cheatham, J. Michael (See my *The Bar Specializes,* 167 ANNALS 177 (1933)). Add I. Lazarus, C. E. Clark, L. K. Garrison, W. Rutledge, D. F. Cavers, F. Shea—and Emma Corstvet's singularly dispassionate and uncomfortable probing into which of the "known facts" are either

precise subject-matters of the proposed monopoly? Or, where statutes have already been passed recapturing invaded areas or pushing the monopoly into non-traditional salients, what are the precise subject-matters of the actual legally protected monopoly?

Then: Why does our society need to entrust *any* of these subject matters, examined one by one, to a monopoly? What is gained thereby for anyone but the monopolist? Is he for example so much better equipped to do this particular work than anyone else that it pays to keep all others out? Or is this job so important to the public that minimum qualifications for embarking on it need public testing and certification? Or is it, as an administra-

---

fact, or if fact, are known; and into what the known facts *really* show, or do *not* suffice to show.

Some of the most recent available and at least moderately significant fact material and analyses of the underlying conditions may be better cited: Lazarus, *The Economic Crisis in The Legal Profession*, 1 NATIONAL LAWYERS GUILD QUARTERLY 17 (December 1937) (reviewing the N. Y. City survey of lawyers); Committee for Cooperation between the Law Schools and the State Bar of California, *The Economic and Professional Status of California Lawyers during the First Five Years of Practice*, 12 STATE BAR J. (Calif.) 259 (1937); Garrison, *A Survey of the Wisconsin Bar*, 10 WIS. L. REV. 131 (1935); Stephens, *The Experienced Lawyers' Service*, 23 ILL. BAR J. 5 (1934); also *id.* at 216; Brenner, *Survey of Employment Conditions among Young Attorneys in California*, 12 STATE BAR J. (Calif.) 314 (1932); Am. Ass'n of Law Schools, *Report of Committee on Cooperation with the Bench and Bar* (Rutledge, Ch.) Program (1937) 42. Chicago Chapter, National Lawyers' Guild, *Report of Committee on Legal Service Bureaus* (1937). *Forthcoming*, with contents which I have in part either seen or heard discussed: American Bar Association, *Report of Committee on Economic Condition of the Bar*, 1938 (and see their Report for 1937, AM. BAR ASS'N, ADVANCE PROGRAM (1937) 247); *Report of Committee on Legal Clinics*, 1938; C. E. Clark and E. Corstvet, *Techniques for Exploring The Bar's Relation to The Community's Legal Needs: the Connecticut Study*. (Title subject to change); Am. Ass'n of Law Schools, Committee on Cooperation with Bench and Bar: *Manual for Objective Determination of The Bar's Economic Condition and the Bar's Relation to the Community's Needs for Legal Service*. (Title subject to change); Symposium in *Illinois Law Review* for February, 1938.

One hears, meanwhile, of projected studies in New Jersey and New York. Others must be in process. The hard thing is to keep the set-up of any study from either pre-determining questions, or from leaving questions ambiguous or even multiguous, or from relying on answers which cannot be wholly trusted to represent fact. *Figures* mean nothing *unless the stuff which makes up the figures* can be relied on. *E. g.:* Who knows how many lawyers are in practice, as lawyers, anywhere? No figures I have seen, with the possible exception of Garrison's Wisconsin study, give me any light on that, at all.

Does the Bar have to become a statistician? I fear even worse than that. I fear that the Bar may have to find folk among its members who can deal with *silly* statisticians as they have long done with silly "expert" witnesses generally, and who then look into the real meaning of the evidence. I have argued on p. 256 that the Bar is here the Bar's own client. A lawyer, in such a situation, masters the relevant extra-lawyer techniques, in the interests of his immediate client. He masters the techniques in two different ways: first, to understand and build his own case; second, to understand the weaknesses in his opponent's. What he does *not* do, is to shun study, or to lose understanding in anticipatory advocacy.

tive matter, perhaps necessary to add this or some other revenue-producing job (say notarization) to the monopoly subject-matters simply in order to support monopolists whose revenue from jobs for which we definitely need them will not alone eke out their existence?

Thirdly, why should these particular monopolists be given by law the monopoly-privilege?—again canvassing the subject-matters one by one. Is their service-record satisfactory? Are their charges reasonable? Do they serve all comers well and equally, and reliably, irrespective of person or pocketbook or position?

Fourthly: Who is worrying about unauthorized practice, and why? Is it the public, complaining of quacks? Is it the profession, concerned about the public welfare? Or who, and why? And do the proposed remedies fit the complaints made?

Such are the questions which underlie any discussion of un-authorized practice of the law, and any position taken on un-authorized practice of the law by anybody will either tacitly assume or openly posit as its base-lines some answers to such questions. *Any* position taken *must* do so.

The lines of my own approach to these underlying matters had therefore better be set out before I proceed.

An Author's Approach Stated

First, in a time of worry and crisis about anything the tradi-tional ways of doing and thinking about that thing are on trial, even when tradition is unambiguous. But today, this area of what is claimed to be unauthorized practice is one in which tradition speaks either with a forked tongue or not at all. Either the par-ticular job in question has, by pure social growth, come to be per-formed *both* by lawyers *and* by others, (say notary's work or collections) or the job in question is a new job with very little tradition, open to occupancy by either lawyers or others (say income-tax counselling or representation before a labor board). Tradition therefore either of what has been or of what has not been regarded as the lawyer's exclusive prerogative (or as the lawyer's proper outside limits of action) affords no decisive answer to any demarcation of the field.

Second, mediation between the powerful Law and Legal Insti-tutions which speak in the name of All-of-Us-at-Once and any lesser group of us, corporate, unincorporate or family—or even the occasional surviving lone individual—this I regard as an expert job, a necessary job, a permanent job. This equally whether the mediation take the form of advocacy or of counselling or of negotiation. It will always take skill to put a case well; specialization in that is a good thing to have, and it is well for the mouthpiece to be certified as competent. It will always take skill to steer away from dismissal of the complaint, to skirt the shoals of summary judgment, or to get the lines of sound appeal fitted to the procedure of the moment—or even to locate the effective office door among mazy administrative corridors. It will always take skill to tell a man in advance what action he may or can take, and show him how to take it, so as to have Law and Legal Institutions either neutral or active in his behalf. All these and others are matters in which a client's interests are invested in legal counsel. Other matters a-plenty occur in which a counseleés interests are invested in his counselor: investment counsel, insurance counsel, the friend who advises for or against that girl, or on whether to take that job, or on what surgeon or lawyer to consult. On such other matters skill is needed, too, and the need is permanent, too, and specialized and disinterested advice is most desirable. Perhaps the trouble there is that specialization has not developed far enough to enable us to organize a system of testing and certification.

Yet even with regard to the skills and tasks which have traditionally been entrusted to the lawyer one cannot wisely take as a base-line that as of course his monopoly must *or can* continue. The putting of a case, the negotiation of a settlement, the conduct of a trial of fact, representation before a tribunal or an administrator, to say nothing of debt collection or the handling of a trust fund—such "lawyer's" jobs I have found again and again done in workmanlike fashion by laymen, wholly unlearned in the law, who simply had specialized in the particular job in question. Again and again I have seen each of them poorly done by lawyers. And many "lawyer's jobs," such as the conduct of a case before a labor mediator or arbitrator, I have seen counsel almost regularly handle less skilfully than his principal, on either side. Such facts of course settle nothing. They do give to think: If laymen can do certain jobs as well as lawyers, or better, can they be kept out at all, or permanently, by legislation? Lawyers are not too popular as things stand, though they do have so heavy a representation in the legislatures. It is well to remember that man has seen not only legislation for lawyers' monopoly, but also legislation *throwing lawyers out* even of handling litigation before various specialized tribunals.[1] If laymen can do some jobs better or more cheaply and rapidly than lawyers, and they are specialized jobs, with articulate interests behind them, can a lawyer's monopoly—by law—stand up? Again, if there are some jobs, some central jobs, for which lawyers can with some safety be regarded as better equipped than any but exceptional laymen, and there are others where law-skills and lay-skills overlap, is a monopoly of more than the central jobs a wise one, a useful one, or one possible to be maintained? Yet again, if there be specialized jobs which require testing and certification for public protection, but in which law-skill is not the essential, is the public better served by lawyer's monopoly, or by allowing C.P.A.'s along with lawyers to counsel on tax matters, or approved technical experts, along with lawyers, to deal with patent matters? There are two base-lines in such matters: the public *will* be served; though the lawyer must be, as well. Two base-lines, not one.[2]

That is, if we can get the lawyer's central jobs performed, under any such conditions. Which brings me to my third main base-line,

[1] Juvenile courts; many small claims courts; under the German Republic all labor courts, even on highest appeal; and in each case with results dismayingly satisfactory to the parties. In the small claims courts the theory is that the cases are simple, and that the recovery is too small to pay a fee. In the other two cases the goal was adjustment, which the advocate's over-partisan training hindered. In mediation and arbitration the cases of parties inarticulate or so bitter that they need to talk through an outsider seem to about equal those in which the lawyer bothers the case by his over-technicality, claim-puffing, and one-sided approach. *This last is not inherent in the lawyer.* There was a time when A and B, having agreed, agreed also to go down to Lawyer Jones to have the thing drawn up. Lawyer Jones then counselled *both*—a function as useful as, today, it seems queer.

[2] Moreover, if the drive of the times is what I believe it to be, these base-lines are coming into critical conjunction. First, to a degree which distresses, in the main, rather more than elsewhere, in the larger city the pressure for fees is tending to disrupt any clear coordination of interest between the lawyer and most of his clients. Frequent results run all the way from practical hijacking through mere overcharge into distortion of the lawyer's own judgment in advising and into the occasional ruination of a case by fuss-budgeting activity to justify a fee. In such circumstances monopoly carries with it portent of abuse. *Such abuse need not be general,* in order to garrote the Bar. Indeed, as clients get together in groups, they acquire less of a black-art approach, more of a show-me-results approach to matters legal; and acquire also enough repetitive experience in particular lines of matter to form their own judgments about what good law work is. The mark of this in business is the formation of a legal department which proceeds to handle one business unit's legal work on business principles. The mark of it in the accident field is the Automobile Owners' Ass'n. These are a beginning, only.

Lawyers are going, then to *have* to SERVE, or lose monopoly. And that is a prospect which every right lawyer will be glad to see moving out of the field of preaching into the field of professional necessity. He does not—*if* his Bar locks shields, in a fashion equally Roman and Icelandic—have any fear of net results.

which is that no discussion of unauthorized practice can lead to really intelligent action until unauthorized practice is thought of not alone, but in conjunction with the economic condition of the Bar; in conjunction with Bar organization and activities; in conjunction with the well-done, ill-done, and undone legal business of the community; and in conjunction with admission requirements and quotas. Unauthorized practice problems, in terms of what to *do* about them in general, are inextricably interwoven with these other questions, to form a single pattern. The threads, one by one, are not only almost meaningless but are misleading unless examined in relation to the whole. This paper attempts a preliminary canvass of that whole and of the relation of its various parts. Details will of necessity be faulty. The generalizations will of course be inapplicable to many areas of the land or of the practice. The major emphasis here is on metropolitan conditions; the thesis is that these show in extreme and risingly crucial form maladjustments which have been making themselves felt in lesser but increasing degree most of the country over; and which, unless something is done about it *skilfully,* and along co-ordinated and sustained lines, will grow worse instead of better.

Lastly, let me make certain things as clear as words can make them, as to the presuppositions and objectives of this inquiry. I am a lawyer, and a teacher of law. I am proud of the profession. I am jealous for its standing and its growth. I believe in it. Nothing that I have to say *is* in fact, or is *intended* as, or can *fairly be read* as, an attack or an accusation or an Utterance of Grievance. The attempt here is single: to *describe a situation:* its What, its Why, its Whither. Since, like my brethren, I fail to enjoy the facts we see, I have proceeded to wonder about What to Do, and How.

But I am *not* here advocating any type or line of reform. This paper advocates not any solution, but an *approach* to a problem. The approach is the medical approach. There is an ache, within a body. What is it? Why is it? What can be done about it? What will this proposed course of treatment produce? What will this other? A Bar is in this like a body. There are toothache packets at the drugstore which are useful until dentists' offices open in the morning. There are other "palliatives" and "cures" which are definitively vicious in themselves, and doubly so in blind application. There are procedures which tend toward cure, although they hurt. But all really curative procedures, for baby or for Bar, are alike in this: they must look to causes, and wrestle with what has to follow on what has gone before. In this light I express occasional opinion on occasional possibilities of action. But I am *not* saying that in the present condition of Bar organization and Bar opinion any particular curative measure mentioned will be or even can be put into effect. I am *not* saying that, if successfully begun, such a measure will be or can be continued without deflection from its purpose by politics or jealousy or greed or blindness or inertia. Knowing the difficulties, I here advocate nothing. This paper looks to one thing only: to set out a little horse sense about a situation which when viewed little piece by little piece has not thus far made too much sense for horse or man. Horse sense about matters where emotions stir, where both vanity and interest and worry and a profession are involved—horse sense about such matters commonly makes unpleasant reading. The reason is simple: when we human beings are worried, we do and say silly things; when we are both worried about being crowded out and vain of our own work, we are in a jam, and act accordingly. When we look back on it, we mostly wish we hadn't. That is why it may be worth using hindsight ahead of time, this time. Unpleasant though this fellow Mr. Horse-sense Hindsight may be.

The scene to be surveyed is the Bar and the work the Bar seeks to do—always with an eye on the unauthorized practice of the law.

The first observation is that something must be seriously out of joint about the working relation between the Bar and that work which the Bar seeks to do. The evidence will not be denied. It piles up daily.

The Bar's Bother

Let us put on one side laymen's complaints about greed and high fees, for such complaints have been the lot of any priesthood of a mystery since man was man. Such complaints prove nothing because they are heard equally when the job of the profession is done well and when it is ill done. Let us put on one side also laymen's yowling about technicality, trickery, red-tape, delay, for even if business should be done with the utmost directness and despatch, it would still be complex enough to elicit such complaints a-plenty—especially a business in which every case means a minimum of one client foredoomed to disappointment. Let us turn rather to the Bar's own aches and groans. There we find unambiguous evidence that the Bar's work is out of comfortable cogging.

The Bar complains of "overcrowding." This means, in horse-sense terms, "not enough income to go around comfortably." For though the practice of law be a profession, the practitioner must eat. A profession is an activity in which service rates ahead of gain; but even in a profession, existence is a precondition to service. "Overcrowding" means that some practicing lawyers are having trouble staying alive. *They also serve who only stand and wait* is one of the noblest lines written in our tongue; but it presupposes, most unpoetically, rations for those who stand.

To these observations the cynic Caviller suggests doubt along a number of lines. Let us listen to him for a moment; let us, however, be as skeptical of his ideas as he may be of ours. "Is it gross income to the Bar that you are talking of," says he, "because on that I have seen no figures. If the Bar's gross income were not reduced by the mahogany front and the oriental rug, and the unnecessary but impressive extra square feet of office space and window; and moreover, if the Bar's *then* net income were equably divided among the Bar's members; and, further, if the Bar did not indulge a standard of living which is really the prerogative of *business* executives and financiers[3] and is essentially *unprofessional,* provided 'profession' means 'service-before-gain.' . . ."

It is time to withdraw the floor from this Caviller. He is distracting attention. Let us hear further from the Bar.

It complains of illicit solicitation of "business" by some of its members, and urges investigation and, on proper showing after hearing, disbarment.[4] The wiser speakers for the Bar link such illicit solicitation with overcrowding, they see economic pressure as a thing which breaks down legal ethics in some and strains legal ethics in more. As one listens to them, one becomes aware of two undercurrents of emotion. The member who has "arrived," and is safe, feels real disgust at business-chasing. The member who has struggled with temptation and won the wrestle at the cost of his body, is bitter at having others chisel and prosper.

[3] The Caviller may have been reading the Wisconsin survey, cited *supra* note to title. It there appears that by almost all the "tests" which an ingenious mind could devise, *available legal business* has in Wisconsin increased since 1880 almost outrageously beyond the increase of lawyers. Of course, incursions on the doing of such business are not covered, but many of the "tests" tried had to do with strictly lawyers' business; others sought to measure the community's *needs* for legal business. Either maladjustment in reaching those needs or maladjustment of income-distribution within the Bar, or and more probably the combination of the two, could reconcile the Wisconsin results with those from New York City. Perhaps a rising standard of living, and of professional outlay, needs its attention, too.

[4] "Disbarment" is a word highly interesting in its implications. It presupposes a Bar as a living, working *organism* from which an excision is to be made.

But the Bar, when it takes the floor, rarely draws the issue cleanly on this point. The Bar mainly attacks illicit solicitation by way of lumping it with outrageous action. The testimony is directed not in clear terms to "illicit solicitation of business," but to a wide and ill-defined offense dubbed "ambulance-chasing." Illicit solicitation gets somehow, rather implicitly, smuggled into that offense.[5] The cases cited do not run so heavily to the sin of getting business by use of runners, they run to fraudulent claims, to perjured testimony, to abuse of clients' trust and funds. For this there are two reasons. The first is that unethical practice has its own touch of the rot in an apple: once the rot sets in, it tends to spread. The second is that the Bar is the Bar, and has learned to argue cases, and prefers to characterize an undesired whole by some unchallengeably undesirable particular instance.

However, we are in the hypothetical chair, and we propose to force clarification of the issue. We rule that fraud, perjury, extortion and embezzlement be discussed first. We know that psychologically and sociologically they do not happen first, in any but a psychopathic lawyer. They are things which some few normal lawyers slide or slip into, over months and years; not evil ways initially planned, nor deliberately embraced from the outset. We know that. But we conceive that we can view the lesser slips more clearly when they are seen unconfused with major criminal acts.

The Bar proceeds, then, making reference to its own disbarment proceedings for its facts. It has occasionally found clients' funds withheld, mishandled, embezzled. Suggestions have even been made in bar associations of a small guild-tax to be laid on every complaint and every answer, to build a fund out of which the Bar's general reputation in such matters may be made good

---

[5] Illicit solicitation *per se* is even more important as a symptom than as an evil. If adequate and reasonably priced service were really and readily available to the bulk of the Bar's public, and that public knew where to find same, illicit solicitation would not too greatly bother. It would lose most of its gouging aspect, at once; and for the rest, would acquire a flavor which at present writing is moderately respectable: that licit semisolicitation which all of us can document *ad lib*. When a president of the A. B. A. [Earle Evans], some years back, explained to the students of a famous law school [Harvard] how a practice can still be built, he was to my mind performing a double public service. He was instructing the young in facts they very badly need to know; and he was bringing out for observation and discussion going techniques so familiar in lawyers' living that the speaker wisely thought instruction in them proper. Instead of being reprinted and circulated, the speech was allowed to drop out of sight. "And many a childing mother then And newborn baby died." Of course, folk who don't like to face fact didn't like it. But accurate presentation of facts is the first condition to cure of conditions. That lost speech would be worth much that has been printed.

against the terrific adverse publicity to the whole Bar of one silly outrage by one single member. Apart from embezzlement, the Bar has occasionally, too, uncovered perjury-mills which grind out false accident-claims, or uncovered corrupt and lasting conspiracies of lawyers, doctors, and witnesses which swell claims for workmen's compensation. Such mills, though sometimes large, are few. Exposure of them, as fast as discovered, has been a vindication of the honor of the Bar.—"And who provided the impetus to exposure, and the evidence?" cries the Caviller. The Bar, now just a trifle shame-faced, acknowledges that perhaps the insurance companies, who are not lawyers, but whose specialized business was involved, may have had at least some little share in that.

But fraud-in-essence goes far beyond perjured claims or mishandling of funds. It hooks up intimately with solicitation. Solicitation indeed engenders fraud in the claim, as when real injuries, though little, are made huge in court. And solicitation is frequently itself a semifraud, as when routine payments already in process from some government office are made to appear needful of expert advice—on contracts for half of the payment as a fee.

At this point—where not claims in court, but claims outside of court, come into focus—the Bar tends to attack less its own delinquent members than outside folk who have not been admitted to the practice of the law: unauthorized practice.[6] The chair does not quite understand this. The chair's accidental experience runs to finding lawyers and non-lawyers in about equal degree chiselling in between governmental payment of a routine claim and the prospective recipient. But the chair has no business interfering in debate. And what difference does it make? The abuse, whoever may be the abuser, is patent. Something is out of joint, whoever skims off the third or the half for no real service.

The Bar, however, has now swung into a favorite melody, well and skilfully played, and frequently: Outsiders never admitted to the practice of the law are cutting everywhere into the lawyer's traditional fields of work. Title companies are monopolizing title-search; trust companies are monopolizing the handling of estates and trusts, are even poaching on the drawing of wills; collection agencies are collecting; automobile owners' associations break in upon the Bar's duty and prerogative of representing automobile owners; C.P.A.'s are absorbing as much of modern tax business as does the Bar; little "bars" of non-lawyer specialists move into each

[6] See almost any unreported discussion of unauthorized practice; and see the shrewd and skilful paper by Clarence Case, 23 A. B. A. J. 941 (1937).

government department before which it pays to practice; interpreters and notaries and consuls and social workers move in to absorb what should be the legal business of foreign language groups; political fixers fix—and all of this is but the beginning. It is crawling with abuses. These people are not skilled lawyers. (How many lawyers are skilled lawyers, in the particular matter they are handling?) These people advertise, while lawyers are not permitted to—a terrifically unfair advantage; also, they serve as runners for unethical lawyers—even a trust company will retain a lawyer at a hundred a month to draft a thousand dollars' worth of wills, or more. These people solicit business in vile ways, and overcharge, and some are dishonest, and more make legal blobs. —At which point one hears little of the troubles which afflict grievance committees, and little of the need for raising standards of admission to the Bar. These are not really forgotten; they merely slip out of attention when Unauthorized Practice is the theme.

Again, as one reads and listens, one grows conscious of two quite different notes in the complaints: danger to the Bar's needed service being rendered; then, danger to the Bar's needed living being earned. This time, therefore, one feels that the notes come from a deeper level, a level much deeper. Not mere personal disgust with indelicate or unlovely ways of competition, nor mere personal bitterness at the success of such. The level here goes to the more nearly fundamental: a whole profession, a needed profession, is fighting in some alarm for its very continued life.

For it takes no Cynical Caviller to make us see that some of these encroachments on the practitioner's ancient fields are like the encroachments of the white man on the Indian: neither right nor law, neither tradition nor stubborn fighting by the gathered tribe, will over long hold up the dispossession. A title company simply can more effectively gather records than the ordinary lawyer can; and over the years it *can* therefore organize to do a job more quickly, more effectively, and more cheaply; it can issue insurance which the ordinary lawyer cannot, against its own error or negligence. It offers a better social machinery for the job. In such a case, over the long haul, there is only one answer: acceptance of the better machinery, and revamping and regulating it to get rid of its peculiar abuses and defects. Or else moving not to throw out the title company, *but to meet its competition.* It seems in Boston to have been possible for *specializing* lawyers, organized indeed into a conveyancers' association, to meet that competition.[7] That helps "the Bar" at large in Boston only indirectly; yet every lawyer well placed in a specialty is a lawyer both earning a living and removed from competition with the general.

As one looks through the list of "encroachments," certain conclusions become hard to escape. (1) Old lines of business are certainly drifting or being sucked into non-Bar hands, but with real probability that this is because they are being done more adequately or more cheaply or both by outside agencies, first; and second, because those outside agencies are making their serviceability *known,* such as it is. This holds importantly in the trust field, in the collection business, in the tax field, in the realm of political representation, to mention but a few. Abuses there are, on the side of lay "practitioners." But the steady drift of business is too steady, it recurs in too many fields, to permit the conclusion that the lay agencies, over the long haul, are not giving satisfaction.

(2) At the same time, and repeatedly overlapping, is a different phenomenon: much business which has never reached lawyers at all, such as petty claims in the metropolis, or estates and trusts based on life insurance and the trust company, much business which has only in the last decades come into existence at all, such as representation before government commissions of modern creation, has been *discovered* and has been *elicited* from "the public" by these other agencies. Lawyers operating by themselves along the old lines would certainly have been slow to know of its existence, and might never have discovered it at all. It is not business taken away by outsiders, but business whose presence and especially whose extent the Bar had never fully appreciated. It is business which the outsiders built. It is also business which suggests very strongly indeed that there is much legal work *still*

---

[7] R. R. B. Powell, now in process of studying the title insurance and Torrens situation, generously permits me here to use certain of his results on the facts. *But he is not responsible for my interpretations, which are my own, and which he has not been asked even to consider.* The insurance feature of title insurance appears (thus far) to engage in fact considerably less than 2% of title company income.—But even a 1% need for insurance hurts him whom it hits, and does not (on an insurance plan) turn on negligence. A competing *branch* of the profession, on the other hand, means singularly specialized and expert service. The Boston conveyancers seem to satisfy the Boston real estate trade.—Will this hold equally in a line in which the layman does not habitually consult a lawyer on every deal? That needs exploration. Meantime title companies (as by the discount to lawyers of which my former students tell me) and trust companies (as by carefully avoiding the drafting of instruments) show willingness to conciliate the Bar, and to work toward a *modus vivendi.* In which lie hints in regard to other fields as well.

lying around undone, untapped, waiting for some one. A need unfilled; a market ready.[8]—Yet the very lay organizations which have thus uncovered so much "legal" business are equipped to outcompete most of the Bar for some of the older legal business which the Bar *has* been attending to.

(3) The third conclusion is that the lay organizations thus far heavily noted in their "encroachment" show important common characteristics. They are *specialists;* each has worked out machinery for handling with maximum use of pattern, forms, routine, and concentration of expensive executive decision, a *semi-mass production of legal transactions or legal services* in a very limited field. Given the mass of roughly similar units of business, production can have its price cut in legal matters, as in others. It can be cheapened down into the region of petty business which most individual lawyers would shun as non-rent-paying. It will be strange if the Bar, once awake to the situation, cannot do legal service as well as can any lay organization.

(4) The fourth conclusion which emerges is that the Bar, through all of this development, has been very human. It is of the nature of any profession, when economically squeezed, to turn attention rather to income than to service; and any outsider or observer who feels disposed to make sport of that or to complain will do well to starve a little while he prepares his complaint, and to read some history while he starves. It is of the nature of any privileged class or group on whom a monopoly has been conferred by government to see the prerogatives of the monopoly quite as clearly as they see the duties whose performance is the reason for the monopoly's existence. The Bar is no exception. It is of the nature of man, when in trouble, to seek out a devil, and legislate against him, or incant, or burn. The teamsters did not examine the new pipe-line in terms of economics; they rioted against it. The dairy farmers did not examine the nutritive or economic virtues of filled condensed milk; they used their votes to get the stuff prohibited.

The lawyers, likewise, have not at first inquired deeply into how these ills have come about, and what they mean. They have turned to the simplest ineffective human devices man has known, in the proper, primitive fashion of *homo sapiens* in pain: Whip the

---

[8] On this the very careful Connecticut investigation, canvassing a sample of residences and of businesses in residence districts, gave results whose possibilities amaze. See Clark and Corstvet, *supra* note to title. If those possibilities prove out, to even a third, whether in Connecticut, or elsewhere, action is long overdue.

devils out of our midst by disbarment; legislate the competing devils out of the road by unlawful practice acts drawn so broadly that a legal aid society can feel forced to close down, lest it be transgressing; and, for the rest: shut down the output of lawyers (Did someone say "Philosophy of Scarcity?") and keep the young competitor under by longer training and by an apprenticeship during which he can be worked for his carfare.

It is all so very human, and understandable, and almost inevitable, that it would be tragic and pitiful and desperate if *homo sapiens* had not devised a better way. But he has. And the Bar—an intelligent body of men *when they are working for a client*—are recently beginning to discover that their own plight calls for the same resourceful and long-range sizing up of the situation which might be required of them in the interest of some *other* trade association whose motto was: *Service.* And whose continuance was conditioned on the motto's proving true. Today the Bar is counsel for a trade association in distress. Its full and most dispassionate skill is needed. *For its client is The Bar.*

How Did It Happen?

What, then, are some of the ideas which are beginning to come out of the Bar, and calling to be put together, that action may move in the direction of true cure, not of mere poulticing? They can be summed up in one single picture: with an automobile industry pouring cars and traffic accidents into the streets of the metropolis, with conveyor-belts at one end, one-way streets, traffic lights, and express highways at the other, with national labor organizations, national markets, nationally organized finance, with "private" businesses and industries numbering their respective citizenry in figures that look like the population-figures of cities, the Bar, in modern dress but in a buggy, attempts to cross the Loop. *Its* organization just about that of 1838—the most individually and individualistically organized activity in these United States. The very peanut vendor on the street will, for example, be found leasing his cart from Peanuts, Inc., returning it nightly to a central garage, or even working as a sales employee in a limited territory, his only independence being his commission. The farmer, the stronghold of individualism, joins a co-op, comes in under a federal government plan, crops for a landlord or a mortgagee. Only the lawyer—most of him—still ruggedly demonstrates the maxim: Divided We Fall.

For consider the conquest of America, well begun a short century ago, sweeping and swirling through the latter nineteenth-century decades: transportation, industry, capital and man power gathering, gathering, gathering together. Gathered into units, into corporate "persons," created by the lawyer's ingenuity. Consider the basic techniques employed: production techniques; specialize, subdivide and combine; standardize, standardize; cheapen by specialization, by standardization, by *mass*-production; use eyes and ingenuity to spot and eliminate traditional waste. Marketing techniques; standardize transactions as well as goods (or services), cheapen by standardization, reach the market of the whole nation, build for repeat orders; and advertise, and advertise some more; use eyes and ingenuity to spot and overcome traditional inertia. Form-contracts, Taylorism even in the office. Financial techniques, subdivision again and standardization, with each new wrinkle of any security thoughtfully provided by a lawyer—to bring capital together into newer, huger units. This, with all its exploitation and its draining of men, with all its incidental politics and bone-crushing, is the picture through which the Bar drives over a century, changing its dress and its manners—but not its buggy.

Organization, co-operation, co-ordinated group-work, specialized work, mass production, cheapened production, advertising and *selling*—finding the customer who does not yet know he wants it, and *making* him want it: these are the characteristics of the age. Not, yet, of the Bar.

These characteristics—modified only to write *need* for the first *want*—are compatible with the highest and noblest professional service. They can be made to conduce to finer, fairer, and more widespread service than the Bar now gives. But even more important (because eating does precede service) is that until the Bar *as a Bar,* not as an agglomeration of individuals, discards its buggy, the Bar will suffer much—and most of its individual metropolitan members will suffer more.

The canons of ethics on business-getting are still built in terms of a town of twenty-five thousand (or, much more dubiously, even fifty thousand)—a town with a single high school, where reputation speaks itself from mouth to mouth, even on the other side of the railroad track; and reputation not only of the oldster, but of the youngster. The youngster is watched when he hangs out his shingle; watched if he be a home-town boy, watched doubly if he be not. Word of law's work passes the time of day, along with side-taking as between the Mathematics teacher and the High

School Principal. All the lawyers are known, and people who have legal work to do are moderately aware of the fact; and they have little difficulty in finding a lawyer of whose character, abilities, experience, yes, and fees, they can get some fair inkling ahead of time. And—no little item—where reputation works and counts, the overhead becomes materially less. "Front" that socially and personally is waste is peculiarly a privilege and an expense of the metropolitan lawyer.

Turn these same canons loose on a great city, and the results are devastating in proportion to its size. If a small client does not know to whom to go, he does his pondering with all the folklore about lawyers stalking blackly through his brain—they overreach, they overcharge, they are not even to be trusted. This means, in result, undone legal business. A-plenty. Or it means turning to some non-lawyer who undertakes to help out. Or it means chancing it. If the client chances it, he very truly chances it: the conditions of metropolitan legal business make it no simple thing to reach into the grab-bag and pull out a lawyer who is able, experienced in the case at hand, not too taken up with other matters, and also reasonable in fee. Here, therefore, one needs stress on one line of points too often overlooked:

(1) Whether the client is fairly charged or not, if he *thinks* he is overcharged, he is for twenty years a walking, talking, publicity agent against the Bar entire.

(2) Whether he is well represented or not, if he *thinks* he got inadequate service (and neither the Law nor the Jury nor the Judge affects too much his own view of his Rights—which Somebody must have Done Him Out of—for he, too, is a devil-chaser) he is again a walking, talking, stalking publicity agent against the Bar entire. Gratuitous. He needs only a chance to tell his story.

(3) But if he goes to a non-lawyer, and gets poor service, he will still hold that against The Law.

(4) And if he goes nowhere, and gets nothing or worse, he will still hold *that* against both Law and Lawyers.

It is a true picture, this, of prospective small clients who need service and help in great cities. It is meat for the political fixer. It is meat for the ward-boss. It is meat for the siren-singing of the ambulance-chaser's runner. It is meat for the jailor who is tipster for the bondsman and the criminal court hanger-on.

For there *are* jobs to do, and jobs to get; jobs whose doing is badly needed, jobs which lawyers badly need to get to do. There are also cures available. But let us push the diagnosis further, first.

I do not mean to suggest that there are not within the metropolitan bar groups of lawyers who have effectively made the adjustment to business-getting which they need. There are indeed such groups. Outstanding is the adjustment of the so-called law factory, with its typical specialization on the higher brackets of corporation law. Within the relatively small world served by such a legal plant, its product and reputation have the same chance of becoming known by mere performance, reputation of a senior partner, or personal contact, which holds in a smaller town for the general lawyer in relation to the general community. No less to the point, in regard to the law factory, is another feature to which I shall recur: the careful development of specialization within the plant, and the accumulation, by forms, files, and specialized experience, of something approaching a mass production technique. The smallness of the fee, for example, for putting out an important bond issue, when taken in relation to the skill, authority, responsibility, labor, and speed of the personnel involved on the legal side is almost startling when compared with the general run of less specialized legal business.[8a]

Another type of adjustment lies in specialization on the business of business-getting. Here it is enough to mention the politically connected lawyer, with his road into patronage;[9] the solicitor of negligence suits, with his runners; the criminal lawyer who has built up his regular clientele. Indeed, in a broader sense, and with no suggestion of impropriety or even indelicacy in their building of a practice, there are, in every metropolis, the whole range of what we may think of as the middle and successful Bar. But one

[8a] Fees arising out of reorganizations based on the same bond issues are, of course, another story.

[9] Attempts either to control abuse or to allocate return in this connection have rarely moved with realistic hard-headedness. Perhaps too much is in the way. But when a Bar Association (as at least one has) taps off ten percent of every fee from patronage, to be administered for the relief of distressed lawyers, it moves toward combining sound engineering with group spirit. Substitute a graduated percentage scale for a flat one, and the road opens into a scholarship fund, as well (with a new problem, then, of a new kind of plum, best dealt with by letting law schools pick the scholarship men; they have both some expertness and a direct interest in students' quality). No less: no Association Committee could receive funds, over long, without acquiring some partial responsibility for holding down abuses in the patronage from which the funds flow. This means nothing at all, initially; but over the long haul it would mean a focus, both of criticism and of (possibly unwise) action. But a *focus* is a thing folk can deal with, if they only get it.

point for us here is that such lawyers draw their clientele either from organizations (business, labor, philanthropic) or from persons of moderate means; and the further point that their almost necessary office appointments provide for any accidental visitor who has to watch his dollars a psychic handicap to consultation which is too often forgotten as the lawyer considers the need for impressing his prosperous clients as being himself among the prosperous. And, perhaps, a still further point. When clients who are steady clients have to be guarded; when lawyer's service includes going up to the client's office; when fee-justifying seems to require putting on a show; when non-permanent juniors have to be kept from meeting the sources of business; when, in a word, *good* lawyers' thinking gets distracted from the lawyer's job— then, for some part even of the successful Bar, there is a most unwanted maladjustment—working itself out, as things human do, if left untended, by competitive disruption of the whole. In a word, while the upper reaches of political, of corporation, and of criminal practice find contact between client and counsel moderately simple, and while the person or group of moderate means has reasonable outlook of finding a lawyer to his liking and suited to his pocket, we are left with two thirds of the Bar and eighty per cent of the public who lack both the contact and the means of making it.

The Hurdle of Expense in Legal Service

The next matter which calls for attention is the cause of the exceedingly high price of legal services in this country. On the whole, the Bar is unaware of the existence of the phenomenon— and perhaps for that reason uninterested in its causes. The Bar has grown up with the causes as part of its natural environment, has adjusted to them as one adjusts to the pressure of the atmosphere, and would read with amazement that legal services could be performed at a level of charge materially lower than that with which they are familiar.

And, indeed, in these United States, certain of the causes may be regarded as permanent. These are the organization of our law itself, first, by fifty separate jurisdictions, alongside which run ten semi-independent federal circuits; and second, the fact that our basic legal technique is that of case-law, on which is superimposed spasmodic, unsystematic, and inadequately indexed statutory amendment, with the statutes themselves operating only state by state. This is the legal system that we have, and this is the legal system that we shall be living with. But to understand its effects upon the economic condition of the Bar and upon the Bar's service in a metropolitan community, we shall have to examine into why it is an incredibly *expensive* system. It is expensive because law is only local; because law, even for the locality, is hard to find, and slow to find, and calls for a book-equipment whose price would turn gray a Continental lawyer's hair. It is expensive because the foregoing facts produce a Bar whose members can become specialists in only very limited fields, at best, and most of whom are specialists in none. In any matter in which a lawyer lacks experience, the organization of our law itself heaps on him time-burdens in equipping himself to do a right job. One road out is to charge the client for the lawyer's self-education; that may be necessary, but it does not make for economy of service. Worse, the education may be wasted for the future: too often such a case never turns up again. No one who has never seen a puzzled Continental lawyer turn to his little library and then turn out at least a workable understanding of his problem within half or a quarter of an hour will really grasp what the availability of the working leads packed into a systematic Code can do to cheapen the rendering of respectably adequate legal service.—Let me not be mistaken. I talk not of supremely expert advice. Few, in any nation, can afford that. I speak of the work of the rough-hewn electrician who at least can be trusted *on quick call* not to blow out fuses or give advice which short-circuits, and sets the house ablaze. And again, let me not be mistaken. Few honor the virtues of case-law more than I do. But cheapness is not among those virtues. Neither for the society nor for the particular client. Whereas costly services are luxury services. Luxury services do not support a trade which verges on two hundred thousand strong. Unless, like current auto-models, they are *in demand*. Or unless, like used cars, they have come to be thought necessary, to get to work.

It is against this background of necessary relative expense that the Bar's organization, peculiarly in the metropolis, but even in the smaller centers, turns up in less-than-1838 adequacy in getting the price range down *as far as it will go*. With no desire to idealize those good old times which are perhaps "only good, because they are old," one can yet observe that a lawyer on circuit had a deal of opportunity to learn from or consult with his brethren, and that all reports indicate club-feeling to have been strong. One can observe that the youngster was almost forced into all-round learning, into learning from the whole group of his elders, at every circuit, and into learning about the very matters of most interest to him in his budding practice. One can observe that the tower of lawbooks to be mastered, and even of those to be used, bulked more like a woodshed than like the Empire State, and even that the law itself was then more fluid and more ready to yield to sense and "principle." One can observe that court and legislature put out about all the law there was to wrestle with, that administrative commissions did not dot the landscape, that the ranging intricate specialization of economic and even of social life had not yet set in—while today a rich man's problems, say of income tax, have become an unsounded mystery to a lawyer who may have practiced in the next street for a generation. In a word: the whole game was simpler, the beginner understood more of it, and Bar and practice were organized in such fashion as to teach him faster than today, and to make it easier for him to find and get advice he needed. Less time needed means less need to charge, and a greater portion of the public's business reached and done.

In the modern great city, this getting of advice by lawyers is not simple. We all understand and use the luncheon with the friend who knows—if we have and know a friend who knows: a practical, obvious, and wise device. It does not wholly solve the problem, but it tremendously reduces both the risk of error and the time required for the job in hand. We leave to chance, however, the knowing of the needed friend. And those who need him most are least likely to know him. So out of the idea of *group-movement* have we grown, indeed, that the "specialized lawyer consultation service" instituted by the Illinois State Bar Association—an excellent lead—is reported as hardly beginning to find the use it can. When one remembers what one blob by *any* lawyer, for lack of sizing up his problem, can do against the practice and reputation of the Bar entire, it becomes probable that the bulk of the Bar may be swapping the buggy for Shank's mare.[10] In times of economic stress for the profession, this may be short-range individual wisdom for many, but it is not long-range wisdom for the whole.

More generally than by such innovations as the experienced

[10] The smaller centers face the problem, too, in their own way. Though the legal problems arising are likely to be less complex, yet country and the small town are feeling the impact of the law, as well as the market, of the industrial, national economy. And where court-jurisdiction is divided by counties, and Bar-courtesy dictates turning local business over to the local man, the experience-swapping of the old-time circuit wanes.

lawyer's service, the Bar has moved against one feature of expense by the co-operative law library. Still more generally, it has once more—as with the trust and the collection and the landlords' protective association, the civil liberties union and the anti-boycott league—left laymen to show the road to organized and effective *legal* action along some specialized line. I have in mind the publication of law books, and especially of all the devices for speeding up the finding of the law: advance sheets, texts, encyclopedias, annotated leading cases, digests, citators—and last, swiftest, those aids in the current welter, the "services"—which are expensive. The Bar's own unwieldy effort, the Restatements, is no substitute for these. What remains in the way of aids is largely government work: semicodification, the federal index to state statutes, the work of legislative reference bureaus or of a council of state governments, and the like.

Yet all of this only slows, it does not stem the tide. The pooling of practical experience is the only available immediate road to importantly reducing the costs of finding law and of learning how to use it. There are some books which help. Most form-books are still unannotated hodgeporridge, but they show the way to better things. Many practice manuals are chockfull of good sense. I have even seen one moderately instructive book on how to prepare and try a case. And in a very few fields of law there are texts which do what *in a medical book is taken to be the author's duty as of course:* to wit, they present along with the rules of law a description and critique of the best known procedures in doing something effective about it.[b] A corporation trust company, on the other hand, makes profit out of specializing and routinizing the actual doing of something effective about it. So do all the various agencies, the useful ones, now so vigorously under attack for unlawful practice. So do the legal departments of banks and business outfits to whom enough transactions of a single kind come, to make experience cumulate, and to enable the building of routine. So do those government departments whose servicing is drawing off so many members of the Bar and negotiation with whom is affording so much new practice as well as so much new trouble in law-finding. Is, then, the individualistic Bar, familiar both with the value of the casual luncheon and with the efficiency of non-Bar legal work on every side of it, never to put two and four *together*

[b] In the quarter-century since this was written the how-to-do-it textbook has made some headway, but not enough to outweigh the increasing bulk and complexity of law-material.

and see that while $2 - 4$ is an unfortunate result, 2×4 can be one of real interest?

No one move is panacea, even if well and wisely made; nor will any cure come quickly. The metropolitan Bar suffers, for instance, also from unwieldy and unfortunate overhead—due in good part, as has been mentioned, to the double need for "front" when the mouth-to-mouth machinery of reputation-spreading is unavailable. Due partly, also, to a *need* for charging more than the traffic ought to bear, even when the service has been in fact routine and quick. A need, I say. Uncertainty and irregularity of income force high charge. The law-factory must be equipped to handle sudden peak loads; but the staff is always there to be paid. The small office moves on the same principle which its members rightly reprobate in bricklayer, plasterer, and electrician: it insists on high wage per hour or per day, to cover the uncertainty about how many working hours there will be in the oncoming year. Both deal with the uncertainty as if it had to be. Whereas a retainer which can be counted on means not only a lower price for legal service (more regular flow of business; more business of one kind) but an easing of worry-tension, and a lengthening of the lawyer's active life.

Now how much serious attention has the Bar as a Bar yet given to the subject of retainers? To educating the small businessman or small corporation in their value, and in the value of *consulting* service? To the possibility of developing, and on a moderately wide scale, *group*-retainers from persons whose legal needs are individually non-recurrent or infrequent, but who, taken in bloc, have like needs which *do* recur? Group insurance, even group medical service, are today as familiar almost as the grouping of men in mine or factory to handle the recurrent tasks, and so to raise income while production rises. But the Bar considers the problem still no further than from the angle of unethical *individual* solicitation of practice—or the angle of jealousy, or of fear of politics and patronage.

Indeed, as one observes the use of front and overhead largely unnecessary to the work, one is forced to grieve that too many of the metropolitan Bar have drifted into learning from Business chiefly the less fortunate excrescences which Business has to teach: useless magnificence of furniture, cream-skimming of return by the senior with skim milk to the junior, measurement of a man's worth in terms of business-getting power, methods of competition which verge too often on piracy, charge measured by what the *immediate* client can be made to bear. Whereas those things which give Business its excuse for existence are not yet learned: discovering markets for things people really need, but do not know they do; getting the consumer and the purveyor together, *distributing* what is wanted into the far corners; discovery of methods to unify service and to reduce unit-cost and price, and to purvey better, to more, for less.

The Bar has been largely a monopoly. It is busily engaged by legislation in seeking to become a monopoly again. Now of monopoly, and from the pure enterpriser's angle, we learn from most orthodox economists that "A monopoly which controls an article of very elastic purchase—a luxury or a costly convenience —must be careful not to put its price too high, lest its sales fall off and its gains decline or vanish. Wise selfishness may in such cases dictate a fairly reasonable price, not much above the cost of production." [11] Of course, wise selfishness always dictates also lowering the cost of production. Of course, the professional aspect of law dictates an attempt to spread law's service as far as effort can.—The three ideas, put together, speak for themselves. It would seem time for this particular monopoly to gather itself for concerted planning.[12] Only group planning, and group action, can help or cure.

Possible Curative Procedures

The first and obvious move is for the Bar, as a Bar, to apply business methods to the task of making contact with its customers. For long-range work along this line there will be need for careful and skilful sampling studies to develop what kinds of matter may come up frequently in the community on which legal assistance or counsel would be of value, and among what income groups, and what percentage of them get referred to anyone for

[11] 1 FAIRCHILD, FURNISS, AND BUCK, ELEMENTARY ECONOMICS (1926). In the third edition (1936) ch. XIII, the precise language quoted is somewhat modified, but the point is made more at length and more cogently. "The ever-present possibility that 'something just as good' may appear puts a very real check upon the greed of many a monopolist" (286). Or: ". . . the price which brings in the greatest immediate return . . . may stifle future demands" (287). "The last thing desired by any monopoly which has thus far escaped it is unfavorable public attention and legal investigation and control" (289).

[12] The bearing, at this time, of certain phases of procedural reform, is patent. The prepared case which is ready but not reached, with personal presence required at calendar call, and the common absence of any preliminary procedure to straighten out what issues are really in dispute, are magnificent instances of matters which not only raise costs but deter any client from ever doing it again, or letting anyone else do it at all, if it can be avoided.

such assistance, and among these, what percentage reach lawyers, and how the lawyers were found or why they were not found or not sought. Which would look like a large order, and a silly one, if a study in Connecticut had not already demonstrated that it can be done, and how to do it. But it does take some money, and it does take some skill, both in setting the study up—on which material is now available—and in execution.[13]

There is, however, no need to wait upon such a study of the market—one such as sales managers and advertising counsel have been making for decades. There is another thing already for the doing: call it publicity, or public education, or advertising the Bar's service, as you will. It consists in the Bar, as a Bar, using the newspaper, the magazines, and the radio to make members of the public who have never seen before come to see what a lawyer can do for them, and why they need his service. A legal ache is not like a toothache. The man who has it does not need to know he has it until matters have progressed too far for remedy. A contract with lopsided but enforceable catch-clauses needs to be caught before it is signed. Forfeiture conditions (which may be reasonable) still need to be known about in advance, warned about; at need some means must be devised for a client to tickle his memory by marks on the kitchen calendar—else the forfeiture is known only after it occurs. Such things few laymen realize, and most would be interested in knowing; and *sustained* publicity can not only inform them, but can slowly stir them out of inertia into action.

Provided, however, that there is a place to go which is convenient and which is made known. "Consult your neighborhood lawyer" will not work. Either he does not exist, or else too often he is hardly the man to consult. Perhaps, with such a campaign well under way, one could induce some good young men to open up in the neighborhoods, to save on rent and front, and to acquire a practice. But to date, they haven't.[14] Hence, a publicity campaign, to be effective, entails some further steps.[15]

[13] See Clark and Corstvet, and *Manual,* both *supra* note to title.

[14] The down-town address appears to have peculiar prestige-power. Which sets a man wondering how far four youngsters in partnership could average down expense and yet build up a sound practice by having three of them running three "local offices" of "Perkins, Petrosky, Picarello and Patrick, 120 Broadway."

[15] The kind of phonograph material one would have in mind would be such as this: "If you have a problem like this, or like the problems we have talked about, then see your lawyer. Tell him why you came. Tell us you went to him. [If you haven't a lawyer, see your neighborhood lawyer and tell us that]. If you don't know where to go, consult Bar Service, address.................... They charge a dollar

Beforehand, it is necessary to avoid a few misconceptions which lie close. There is no thought, of course, of any *individual* lawyer or firm advertising or being advertised in this fashion. It is "The Lawyer's Services," publicized by the organized Bar. But there are other misconceptions. Speeches, for instance, about law-and-not-men or about how the lawyer is the priest of justice, made by men of great name whose very reputation insures that they will never get down to brass tacks—such stuff in turn insures a flop. What is required is concrete, dramatic episode, worth waiting around to tune in on, or looking through the newspaper to find. If printed, the kind of occurrence which is news. With an arrangement with the editor whereby before the story is written up or published, the reporter contacts the Bar publicity man to make sure of the proper Bar angle coming out in the story; or, better, to give time for writing and more room for pointing the moral, and to achieve some independence of day by day occurrences, the institution of a specialty column on the subject. Conditions will vary from city to city. What will not vary is that a writer who knows his writing and his public will be needed; and that news-papers can be interested in the matter gratis, as human interest stuff which also serves their readers. What also will not vary is that a story for the laborer is not a story for the businessman, nor, often, a story for the petty retailer one for the clerk and his family. Not shotgun material, but successive rifle-shots (with dumdums for the mark and noise for the spectators) is what will function. The same type of thinking holds for radio work. Free time can be procured, but skit-writing and skit-acting are not jobs for well-meaning amateurs. Finally, it may be hoped that the cheapest type of enlightenment on what legal troubles and worries are lying around unattended to, will be found in fan mail from either a column or a weekly radio skit.

Fan mail needs answering, and aroused interest gets nowhere unless there is machinery for bringing the prospective client to

---

to look over your problem, and to advise you how to go about it. Law isn't much easier than living, and they may not be able to help you. But they will try, hard. They make no percentage or profit out of their advice. They are there to help you. If you have a problem like this or like the other problems we have talked about, then see a lawyer. If you don't know where to go, consult Bar Service, ad-dress....................."

David Diamond, reporting excellent radio work in Buffalo, 23 A. B. A. J. 940 (1937), adds at 941: "We cannot and do not ever say 'go see your lawyer.'" If the procedure rests purely in publicity, such caution is not only wise, but necessary. And the Buffalo publicity techniques deserve study. But why do they have to be thus crippled?

the man he seeks. Aroused interest which finds no attention goes sour. Any Bar which undertakes such a program must be prepared to furnish a consulting and sifting bureau. A charge of a dollar to get in will keep out cases which belong to the legal aid, and discourage a fair percentage of the cranks and psychopaths, and go some distance to meet the actual outlay of such a bureau. If advice is givable and given on the spot, a fee of a few more dollars will help further to meet expenses, and reinforce the notion that service costs something, and build up experience with *reactions to the charge*. Expectation of some charge must be prepared in the publicity. But reactions to the charge itself, in such a bureau, can put together what no single practitioner has ever dared to mention publicly—save over the confidential lunch or glass of beer—to wit: how to estimate what *this client* will bear. Such experience can then further put together what few single practitioners, in their most confidential moments, even think of, save in regard to some particular client, to wit, what will *its continuing* traffic bear? Whereas we need more. We need to know, in general, what *The Traffic* will bear, in terms of easing work in, rather than damming (*or damning*) work out. This is the problem of income to monopoly. I have no fear, as I state it thus, because the only conditions under which its income-features can be produced are conditions which *widen, strengthen, and lower the price of service of Bar to People.*

Personnel for such a bureau can be secured, under a salaried permanent head, either (and preferably) by donation of the services of the junior by each of a number of those leading firms to whom the cases will in no event be referred,[16] or by hiring able young men already hired by one of the leading firms, on one or two-year contracts (to avoid any suspicion that they may build up their own contacts, and jump the job).

The major difficulty, even though these should all be solved, remains: the reference list and its use. As to a list, there is no escape from the dangers of politics and wangling; but one can feel that, throughout the initial stages, insistence should be laid on

---

[16] This is not speculation. An office built to carry peak loads has, repeatedly, men that can be spared. This provides the edge in. What is then necessary is to secure the firm's engagement that the man loaned is loaned for a long enough period to make his breaking in worthwhile, and is not subject to irresponsible recall. This, too, is doable, though definitely less welcome. But the general public spirit of leading lawyers can be made by moderately intelligent salesmanship to yield as much for the Bar as for a hospital campaign. They are slow to see, but when they do see, they see with a lawyer's acumen. They can even be got to underwrite overhead for a two year try-out.

the fees in reference cases being materially lower than has been considered generally reasonable, and on the work going to competent men who have been having difficulty getting clients. Will this undercut the income of the other members of the Bar? I do not think so. I feel personal confidence that such a campaign, within a year, will not only leave unscathed or improve the income of the Upper Bar, but will be felt materially and gratefully throughout the lower income brackets. But some risk along this line must be taken. It must be taken because if the word ever gets around that this is just another gouge, the cause is lost—both free assistance in publicity and growing interest among the theretofore uninterested client-prospects. Complaints there must be; and open invitation to come in both concentrates and intensifies complaints. Yet in the first place, good work stands up; and in the second, a lawyer who has no eye on fat fees, and whose client's case comes to him already *prima facie* worth looking into, and with the client already responsibly assured that the lawyer is both competent and fair, comes under considerably less pressure than usual to hold out more than he will be able to deliver.

Two types of case are lumped together in the foregoing happy and lighthearted sketch. They will not stay together in any comfort. They are the case with some real money in it—the negligence claim, or the retainer, even small—and the case without. It is the former which will give color of peril to the project; not inside the list, where it would be easy to see to it that no man got two such lucky breaks in a single year or six months, but outside the list, for fear law services would follow Gresham's law, and the cheaper drive the dearer off the market. I pose the problem. To me, it seems a *political* problem, a problem of dealing with the votes of brethren who will fear ghosts that are not there; but brethren who have votes. The actual engineering is not hard. My space runs short, but I offer one of the easiest and least desirable of the various workable ways out: any case with as much as three or two hundred dollars actual, or three (or two) times that amount of contingent money in it, can be referred by the sifting bureau to the now existing Bar Association list. Not a noble solution. But surely one which would lay silly ghosts.

But not only are two types of case thus lumped, but two types of institution. A sifting and reference bureau is a necessary corollary of any intelligent publicity campaign. No less a corollary is a bureau which will pick up the legal burden of the little man to whom three to ten dollars for preventive advice means trouble with his butcher bill—or rather, since he pays cash, means two (or two more) meatless days for a number of ensuing weeks. He can pay something, and so does not belong in legal aid. He can mortgage the future, and pay more—but only pressing emergency makes any legal service seem to him worth that—as when his Jim has been arrested. Yet he too will be listening in on the radio, or reading; or will have heard from friends. To turn him away as overflow because he cannot pay all his way, is neither pretty nor wise: on him, too, depends the goodwill which keeps a campaign going. One of him, you may be certain, will be an Inquiring Reporter with a tale to write. A legal service bureau, akin to legal aid, but with a charge, is needed to take care of this; so is the type of inquiry one can learn from legal aid and from the hospital clinics, to keep fakers and grafters from drifting in. But whether to merge the legal service with the sifting and reference is a problem of overhead and of administration. To me the idea appeals somewhat—it might save time, rent, and effort.

And how does all this bear upon the problem of unauthorized practice of the law? Directly and immediately, in two ways. It will relieve a substantial portion of the existent suffering among the Bar. A substantial portion only—for only *competent* lawyers can an association or the allied associations dare put and keep upon the reference list. By so much, however, it decreases the major bother of unauthorized practice, and decreases it not for the moment only, but into the future, more and more. The road to the lawyer once found, and found good, remains open to a family and their friends, or to a business man for his future needs. For the latter the found road plus persistent publicity opens the ultimate possibility of the retainer; indeed, should the Bar ever get around to countenancing such a thing, the way opens for petty businessmen and even families to be moved *in groups* into the retainer field. Utopian, at the moment; but along such lines of developing business—and service—*where there is no possible competition,* lies one defense against *any* unauthorized practice.

The second direct effect rests in the balancing of one heavy competitive advantage of the unauthorized laymen: Our Advertising set against Theirs. The layman retains the advantage of direct solicitation. But who of those who do not run a racket,[16a] have been thus far using this method in great measure? On the advertising side, I prefer again to speak bluntly. It is open to a Bar which is actually rendering service, even where service does not pay in

[16a] If they do, they ought for that reason alone to be suppressed.

the particular case, and which can utilize in its publicity that fact plus the whole finer tradition of a profession, to capitalize such frauds and grafts as occur in unlawful practice to a degree and with an effect which no lay outfit could dare to, whose advertisement must be paid for, and which is seeking to draw business to itself. Does this mean merely *balancing* the layman's prior advantage?

Important as such direct effects might seem to be, I am inclined to rate more highly an indirect effect which (as being only an hypothetical upon an hypothetical) it might seem idle to discuss. That indirect effect is the development of techniques for semi-standardizing, and so cheapening, and so making available to a vastly larger clientele, a hugish number of normal legal services. On which follows the institution of a Bar clearinghouse for such techniques, and Bar facilities for consultation of another lawyer on matters which as of any given moment may have proved incapable of semistandardization. This, if it should happen, would mean a Bar which had moved in terms of American industry as well as of American business, of mass production as well as of selling technique; and also in terms of adjusting its operations to the conditions both of our queer law and of the Bar's own highly individualistic outfit-organization.

The curious thing is that this is really no hypothetical upon an hypothetical. It is instead an almost inevitable upon an hypothetical. *What is dubious of occurrence is a sane publicity campaign with its logically immediate corollaries.* Given these, however, the indirect effects referred to follow almost as of course. For how can a legal service bureau do its work, without that work leading to standardization precisely in the fields where that is most needed, and to widening service and market by lower service charge? Not only are there recurrent types of matter, but there are, over relatively short periods, recurrent new men to be broken in, and without expectation that they may stay on indefinitely. The former task provides the wherewithal and need to work out usable guidance materials; the latter, *unless the bureau be understaffed to the point of destruction,* forces that wherewithal into use. *Once prepared, it should be made available to any member of the Bar.* It will have major gaps, for any lawyer working on his own. It can, for instance, by very definition provide no light on the routine things to do and the dangers to watch in such a moneyed procedure as, say, title-closing or mortgage-taking. What it *can* do is to show up for the whole Bar's meditation and use that many matters which occur also among clients who can pay their way are vastly more capable of *communicable* schooling and even routinizing, in print, than any but one out of ten single lawyers have even taken time off to *realize*.[17] While the sifting service, unless it is so horribly understaffed in turn that it can neither keep records nor work up their meaning, will show what types of business are emerging in sufficient quantity to require putting a man to work to do the same job of gathering, digesting, and communicating experience with procedures and with difficulties to red-flag. Again, for the whole Bar's use. No divinity has decreed a buggy for the Bar.

With such things in prospect, but in prospect only, there is one matter on which the sifting service research crew can turn loose at once, and without waiting for any advertising campaign to bring any results: it can turn loose on any type of specialized matter which existing experience with unlawful practice has already shown to be a place where mass-production methods work and where the Bar needs better equipment for cheap and speedy service. No doubt about that need, nor doubt about where it lies, nor doubt about the feasibility of attack on it.

It is possible, however, in a number of such fields, that it may prove to be not economy of legal technique, but rather economy in *administration* due to the concentration of like cases, and to delegation of most of the work to routine employees, which gives the lay organization the competitive edge. And no individual-istically organized Bar can wholly meet that difficulty. Hence, where, after reducing the Bar's necessary costs so far as may be, such proves to be the case, I have wondered at times whether (in partial interest of a Bar's living) a compromise type of statute might not in the long run serve both Bar and public better than flat prohibition of the competing lay practitioner. I mean a statute which would allow the latter's service, but with a top limit on the value of the case or transaction concerned, a top limit measured high enough to pay him for continuing in his game to take the smaller cases. Whether or not there may be anything in such a

[17] At this point bows to Harold Seligson of New York—and to his collaborators. The courses he has organized in what one might sum up as Problems of the Younger Lawyer both do their own job and tend grandly toward doing the one I speak of. It is described 8 Am. L. S. Rev. 926 (1937). The accompanying papers give a good picture of the present state of the matter. [The American Law Institute has proceeded to develop similar How-to-Do-It materials and education, as have particular bars. But save perhaps in California there has been a tendency, it seems to me, for the take-home and reference material to be less developed than the oral presentation. Long-range, it is the former which is the more vital.]

vague idea, as to either commercial or co-operative lay lines of competition with the Bar, one thing stands clear: to use the criminal law to hog business *for* the Bar without making provision for reasonable attention *by* the Bar, at reasonable charge, to *all* that business, is to play not with fire, but with TNT. These lay competing agencies are not politically inert, nor have they served clients of that character. The agencies' life is at stake, and their customers have discovered how adequate and reasonable certain phases of legal service can be. Of course, certain statutes have passed, with no such preliminary precautions taken, and no explosion has occurred. Not yet. But I dislike to think, in an industrial state, of what is likely to happen to the Bar if such a statute is abused, when, e. g., (as is already in the definite offing) organized labor once wakes up to the possibilities of legal service not only for the union, but for its members, and businessmen discover one point at least on which business and labor have a common interest. I dislike to meditate on what a good publicity man could do with lawyers, in an anti-Bar-monopoly campaign, if he set out to use the material from the records of the Bar itself, and the methods of exploiting it which the Bar, in its pro-monopoly campaign, is teaching him.[18] Despite the record of the statutes passed without prior precaution and without apparent later row, the applicable word remains: Be ve-ry gentle with it!

There is another aspect of unauthorized practice which needs mention. Plainly, we need to distinguish, among our lay brethren, decent businessmen and co-operative outfits from lice and scroogers. Plainly we need suppression of these last. But, apart from economy, is there not a virtue in the former which is little mentioned, but which calls for the Bar's attention? I refer to *reckonability* of the *results* they get. In addition to standardizing the techniques for performance, they afford moderate assurance in advance that those techniques, so provided, will be *used* with average competence and good faith. Can we meet the competition there? We, supervised and knit together as leaves are in October?

Chanciness about result is tricky in its operation. When a lawyer feels his income chancy, he gambles on the worst, and zooms his fee for the case in hand. When a client feels his prospective service to be chancy, he does more than that: He stays away. Yet on the other end, when a college boy reads once in four years of some single headline-making fee—which he must know is chancier than any lottery—he gambles on the best, and pays, too—and

[18] As, by Case, *supra* note 5.

draws five cards, to join the Bar. In a jack pot. He does it, by the thousand.

But the chanciness of our service remains a vital factor in the unauthorized practice picture. Trust companies make clear that they, as corporations, survive the chance of your lawyer's death. Title companies, in their turn, make much of the insurance they offer. Whether or not the factual value of that insurance be very material, the client's *feeling* of assurance is. Now I strongly suspect some such feeling that the customer really knows where he is at to have a strong part in each other field of encroachment which has succeeded without indecent means in becoming a thing for lawyers to bother over. Can we offer to *our* public a similar feeling of safety about moderately competent *use* of the available techniques? Let me put the question this way: which of us would care to entrust his own interest to any first lawyer whom he happened to pull out of the grab-bag? Which of us would feel it to be *equal* nonsense to entrust his own interest to the first trust company, title company, collection agency, automobile owners' association, legal aid society, civil liberties protective association, landlords' guild, whom he happened to pull out of the bag? There is no positive assurance to be got out of mere size; there are men still alive who can recall real estate "finance" from which title companies were not wholly disassociated, and who can recall interesting relations between widows' trust funds and the duds left on the counter of a bank's securities affiliate. Size alone guarantees nothing—except easier possibility of supervision and more concentrated attack, more effective reform, in the event of abuse. But in any matter in which the customer's check-up comes quickly, if size is found together with continuance in business there is enough to show a *prima facie* record of moderately adequate performance. The law factory can and does claim that advantage over individual lawyers, and mints the public's understanding of a presumption which, though occasionally tricky, is nonetheless [even though the "name-partners" all be very dead] for any man a sounder base for action than a grab-bag. Few lawyers or law firms work today in groups big enough to meet this aspect of their better lay competition. For in the area of unauthorized practice— the wild 20's apart, and they were the whole country's and no peculiar possession of the Bar's competitors—in that area the exposures of dirty dealing or of gross incompetence relate peculiarly to the individual or the small fly-by-night outfit rather than to the bigger groupings with an address and a reputation, still less to co-operative lay legal ventures.

In which, for the Bar, there either is a lesson, or there is not. Monopoly legislation, at best, drives business merely Bar-wards, to be picked up—when it is not thereby dammed off—by any lawyer who happens to get it. The adverse advertising value of one client abused is not here to be labored, but it is to be recalled. And let the fact be looked at openly for once. Why, with the whole profession at stake, must it be pussyfooted? The fact is that a third or more of the lawyers now in practice in metropolitan areas are incompetent. *Law school faculties cheerfully give degrees to men to whom the faculty members would under no conditions entrust their personal business.* Bar examiners find no way to keep such men out of the Bar. Practicing lawyers, individualistically organized by tradition, feel no responsibility for training the green, raw rookies from the schools, even the good ones—though, I repeat, any error by any one of them blots and blurs not only the reputation but the very livelihood of all but the best established of the Bar.

Now either monopoly legislation or any Bar publicity campaign must face the fact that some of the resulting business—and a little is enough, for the harm to be done—must go to these incompetents. A publicity campaign must face the fact that wangling and favor, even with safeguards, will lead to the presence of some incompetents even upon the reference list; though this is not so troublesome; referred work can be watched. More bothering is the case of the clients who go not to headquarters, but to "some" lawyer—who proves to be the wrong one—and then get active in their counter-publicity. "Just one more gouge: the experience of Acidophilous G. Robins."

I see just one road out of this which would be workable in terms of human motivation. I shall describe it. As an intellectual exercise; for I cannot believe that a buggy-riding Bar could ever bring itself to act on an idea whose only virtue would be, by group-action and a bit of forethought, to drive the Bar's competitors to the wall. The fantasy has to do with an institution of pre-Soviet Russia, modified to fit American conditions. In the Russia of the Tsar, certain skilled crafts were organized into *artels*, of which the characteristic here in point was that the whole artel was responsible for defects in the work of any of its members. To apply such an idea to the American metropolitan Bar would be to invite the ruination of every worthwhile member. Yet almost the only people who really know the worth of a lawyer are his brethren. And the only way to make sure that their recommendations to non-friends are deeply sincere is by enlisting their own welfare in the recommendation. And the politics which lead to handing out patronage and even that share in the profits which goes with firm-membership are resisted even within the firm by quiet sabotage when it comes to entrusting the firm's business and reputation in a responsible matter to a known or suspected dud-like senior partner's son-in-law. And groups can build up the type of reputation in a metropolis which factories already have and which individualistic lawyers have been unable to. And whereas disbarment of the incompetent is unthinkable, the negative selection made familiar by Charles Darwin, applied by their own fellows, would force those same incompetents out of the practice, if they had group-reputations to compete against. It is a pretty fantasy: voluntarily formed artels, the members practicing on their own as now, taking new members only whom they trusted. A line of additional letters on the glass: "of the Marshall Artel." [19] A security afforded to the client, and known in advance, which no corporation could match. The policing done not by an overworked grievance committee, or a character committee which has to move on inadequate evidence, at best on evidence of what a man looks like before his work begins; the policing done instead by a man's mates, on the basis of his performance in the game itself. No monopoly, within the trade, because new artels would be free to form; perhaps, to keep risk within reason, a limited group-liability could be set on any one claim. . . . But why dream on. It is too sensible ever to happen. It simply would fit the Bar, with due attention to the essentially individual nature of law-work (which the factory, for all its virtues, has tended to forget and to blur) into the industrial structure of today, and provide, to *any* client, as against lay competitors, that *assurance* of service which today is available in the metropolis only at the price of unflawed diamonds. It would settle any questions of reference lists. It would semi-automatically drive shysters out of practice. It would have the quality of any sound social organization, the enlisting of solid self-interest, clearly seen and clearly

[19] *Artel,* or *Inn,* or *Guild,* or *Brotherhood* or what have you, so only the term can be, and be in fact, protected from piracy or use in misrepresentation—as a word like *Savings* is today. Even copyright might do it—though that would call for thinking through a most amusing set of problems.

directed to the simultaneous welfare of Bar and public. Well . . . good-bye, Dream. . . .[20]

QUOTAS AND NUMBERS

The dream goes, the buggy remains, and with it the problem. The problem is to get new business flowing, and to keep it flowing. I have indicated my doubts as to how far blanket monopoly legislation against unauthorized practice can accomplish this. But another proposal comes to the fore which has its values: one can both reduce the percentage of incompetents (insofar as incompetence is correlated with inexperience)—thereby furthering somewhat the whole flow—and one can also somewhat reduce the financial pressures on Bar members, by choking off the influx of new members. Moreover, it is a fair guess that admission quotas and *average* training and better talent (with the due percentage of exceptions) will over the country, go hand in hand. I believe both to be somewhat inevitably on their way. And I believe their result will be, slowly and a little, to increase the Bar's competitive position as against the unauthorized. Yet I crave permission to round out the picture by briefly canvassing some of the features of this quota picture which are receiving less attention than they deserve.

The quota idea has two roots which tap quite different soils. The one, the bread-and-butter root, calls for no further discussion.

[20] Consider, as the Dream departs, the Bonded Law List which finds so little favor with the Bar. After studying reports and canons, and listening, may one not say this? The Bar has not considered the question primarily from the angle of whether some type of Bonded List or its equivalent might provide greater security to a prospective customer, nor of whether providing such greater security might not open a greater flow of business to the Bar. In dealing with the Bonded List, the Bar's eye is less on the Bar's outcompeting the collection agency than on one lawyer's getting a headstart on another.

Yet the security afforded by a bonded list has value to the Bar at large. And one might start considering its use rather than its discouragement. The Canons and Resolutions I read do not seem to think of such things as an income pool from a bonded list—say, the first hundred dollars to any listed man, free to his own use, in absence of complaint; the second hundred fifty-fifty to the pool and him; thereafter thirds to the man, the pool, and the Bar, with the pool taking responsibility for what a lawyer shouldn't do. With listing accompanied by a contract to stay in the pool for a measured and fixed period. An outsider might find in this kind of thing a line of thinking which good thinkers get somewhere with. Present thinking seems concerned with whether a complaining customer will not be too easily satisfied, or a listed lawyer have too much chance to be engaged—in a word: it is lawyer-thinking, not Bar-thinking. How, then, can a Dream remain around?

The other does. It is the ideal of the lawyer as an American scholar and gentleman. It looks not only toward reducing the number of entrants, but toward eliminating a particularly high proportion of the candidates considered socially undesirable: Jews, radicals, uncouth prospective Lincolns; peculiarly and of necessity, boys who come from disadvantaged background. Any quota-administration, unaccompanied by the most careful checks, will work out that way. Now there are not many who believe as firmly as I do in the need for a lawyer being a gentleman of culture. But culture is an end-product, achieved as finely from bare feet and contact with good earth as from family background. Committees administering quotas *can* keep prejudice from working out misguided short-cuts; but not many Committees *will;* their enlisted self-interest runs the wrong way.

Again, if there were nothing to law practice and the position of the lawyer but trying cases, a good deal might be said for frank caste organization: gentlemen only, with gentlemen's restraint and responsibility, as advocates. English experience shows that. But, quite apart from all the other aspects of law practice there is an extra and more vital factor: the way of our Bar is to make the Bar the main road into politics, and the way of our politics is to elect only from the district of the residence, and people are best represented by men who know from youth up the conditions of those people's lives. To represent folk politically one should be able to think not only for them, but with them. To limit the entrance of boys of disadvantaged background is therefore a political calamity. For this reason alone no quota-talk should be even listened to which is not coupled, as a check, with a wide program for Bar scholarships for the able disadvantaged.

But more important to our immediate subject is the relation of the quota to unauthorized practice. I take it as inescapable fact that over the long haul the only way to deal with unauthorized practice is to modernize lawyer's practice until lawyers can compete on moderately even terms. That calls for imagination, for energy, and above all for a burning sense of need to use brains and imagination. The job, moreover, of developing new fields of activity for the Bar is not one which can be done and dropped. It is on-going. But when social invention is in demand, it is not among the comfortable and well adjusted that one looks first for the supply. The men who are going to work out new lines of action for the Bar and to explore new areas for its service are the men with no connections, and, it may be, with few manners; men with their whole own way to make, but with brains. In these men, in the disadvantaged, in persons who seem in advance to be without 'background', but who have brains . . . seems to be at the present juncture and for decades to come the real hope for the future of the Bar entire. It is amusing.—But again, there are signs that the ablest of the Bar are opening their eyes, and *seeing*.

A last word before I close. No war on unauthorized practice, however well conducted, is going to accomplish soon, if at all, what most of the fighters in the trenches hope from it, nor yet what the generals may be hoping. That is no reason at all for not moving into battle; existence is at stake. But it is the lesser middle and the poverty-stricken classes in the Bar who utterly need business to do. In the metropolis, these are not the groups who will most profit from the mere elimination of unauthorized practice. Indeed, there would be considerable thinning or lifting of fog about the problem if talk about The Bar in this matter could be broken down, and we talked instead about *which* of the heterogeneous conglomeration of persons who happen to be lawyers the talker happens to be thinking of. Some of the worried lawyers who are moving against unauthorized practice have in mind the rent, or a job in law which might open, or a job affording pay enough to live on. Whereas some have in mind owning a Lincoln, though they have a Ford; such members couple vigilance against unethical practice within the Bar with their interest in monopolies for "The Bar"— and yet go on, many or most of them, *unaware* of the plain fact that these two lines of action plus nothing more mean only more income flowing where enough flows already, the decrease of service, and the contribution of nothing to the Bar's true need. Still others of the Bar—including most of its kings—have no defined attitude of either sort, except that the Bar is in trouble, and they are willing to take time off to do something about it. From none of these groupings, *if they think no further,* will come action other than the mustard-plaster and the Sure-Kure, while the patient's stomach ulcer grows apace. Certainly all hope for the lesser middle and the near-paupers of the Bar lies in such measures as are suggested in this paper, in new business opened, and in new procedures for bringing together the lawyer and his possible client, in widening a market for what you may scoff at as Woolworth wares—which last, in law, too, can be very good indeed, and can be much sought after.

The other difficulty is this: let the economic condition of the Bar, at its low-income end, begin to improve materially and noticeably, and the tide of emigration will reverse itself. For decades now members of the Bar have been moving out—into business as sub-executives, into business as clerks, yes, more recently, into anything from driving taxis to elevator-running. Into government, all the way from dignified professional positions in the department of the Solicitor-General down into totally non-legal routine clerking. Into the police force, where physique has sufficed—and with good prospects, too. In result the Bar resembles the bituminous coal industry, the working outfits hedged in on every side by little submarginal mines ready, each one, to open again at once the minute prices rise sufficiently. By all means, if we can, let us get the machinery set for feeding lawyers oftener and most of them a little better. But when word gets out that there is food at last, we shall find more members crowding to the table than we have cooked for. That is one reason for trying to so work the thing out that service results as well as food. Another reason is that we still are a profession.

The Caviller Again

"So," says the Cynic Caviller, "you want to reduce the Bar to a dishwashing kind of service, or a moving belt?"

This Caviller makes me feel sympathy with whomsoever I may have insulted by twisting words in his teeth. Where did I say, where did I suggest "reduce" the Bar to anything? I want to see it uplift itself. I want to see what *can* be routinized, and get that much actually routinized, so that good energy and good imagination are left over for the jobs that call for both. Did I say other?

"You duck me," says the Caviller, "but this one you won't duck: Debasing Our Profession Into Business! Pure Business. You said so!" Did I, now? Or did I say Business-*getting*, dealt with in modern-age intelligence; Production-costs lowered, where possible, as an Engineer would lower them; but Service given as it is possible *only for a Bar* to render service?

"You duck again," exclaims our Caviller. "You Professor! You Reformer!"

No, I am not reforming. I only have my binoculars, from the cloister walls, upon our team. Superb players, so many of them. They only lack teamplay, coach, quarterback and signals. They have no interference, they never heard of passing. And all our boys have bet their shirts upon the game. That's all.

* * * * *

Antiquated in organization, in methods of doing business, in methods of getting business, in nose for where its services are needed, the Bar finds its buggy crowded to the wall. Specialized business outfits show how to specialize, standardize, and lower price on many services; they offer assurance of moderate adequacy in their work; they are easy to find; they make themselves and their service known. In the great city the Bar's overhead is uselessly high, much of its field of work lies fallow, it has no machinery for coming together with its customers. Its own thinking about its own troubles is still primitively individualistic. The condition grows worse.

The Job does not grow worse, or dwindle. Steady, and beautiful, stands the Lawyers' Work, to do. Eternal. But, as things stand, too many crowd in to the doing, even while much of it goes undone. Unique among professions for the huge spread in income between its top and bottom ranks, the Bar finds its glittering peaks to lure the young; it is, moreover, the only profession in which enormous fees when they occur cannot be kept out of the news.

Quotas may help, but cannot cure; and they need careful watching. Monopoly legislation may poultice somewhat, but unless accompanied by roughly equivalent service rendered by the Bar, contains uncomfortable likelihood of boomeranging. Real progress toward cure lies in *group action* to reorganize the getting of business and the doing of it in keeping with the age: in standardizing, spreading, and lowering the price of service. *Once Service is sure,* the Bar can outpublicize any lay competitor—wherever its Service can itself compete; but let Service fail, and the flank attack that opens can cripple and kill.

No move along this line in any manner impairs the lawyer's ancient and lovely task of individualized counselling. It merely reduces to routine what can be so reduced. But it does call for group action. Group action calls for many men to think things through. Whereas the Bar is human. Human beings in pain do not want to think things through; they prefer to chase devils. They prefer an opiate or a poultice to a cure, while the cause continues causing. Doubtless such will be the preference of the Bar.

{ 12 }

AMERICAN COMMON LAW TRADITION,
AND AMERICAN DEMOCRACY [a]

INTRODUCTION: The unspoken background which informs this paper is local, contemporary, and largely bourgeois "intellectual." There have of course been efforts over the years to broaden the base and correct the bias in observation by work over other regions of the country, other groupings of the population, nineteenth-century American history, and such phases of other cultures as I have been able to reach. But, as usual, the biases remain. I have also over the years formed views about human nature and about certain inherent aspects of institutions and their ways which condition both observation and interpretation. Of these the most important here is the conviction that what one may call the "higher" motives cannot be counted on for sustained large-scale operation unless provided with an implementing structure of patterns, ideology, and ideals which is largely learnable, and which takes off the run of individuals the major burden of heavily inventive or creative "application"; also that such a structure cannot hold stable unless it simultaneously feeds and enlists a large portion of the "lower" motives. A small-scale illustration is the institution of the common law *signed* opinion, with its personal pressures of ambition, vanity, and fear of public exposure of the writer as a fool, coupled with the implicit and often explicit restraining by brethren whose concurrence is sought, and the further effect of the authorities (guiding and restraining) and of the need for a sound rule for the future (guiding and pressing). The net effect,

[a] From 1 J. LEGAL AND POLITICAL SOCIOLOGY 14 (1942).

under the finer craft-style, is to develop out of most appellate judges a materially higher average of performance *on new jobs* than, left to themselves, they have had it in them to give.—Such slants as these need to be warned of.

On the side of "democracy," the substance of what is here offered is sown through the literature and through any man's corrective observation, though the arrangement has afforded me some additional clarity on certain of the problems. In particular, I have not elsewhere met the comfort on an approach at once to "civil liberties" and to "fascist" propaganda which derives from the separate analysis of a "refreshment of policy régime" plus the application of Holmes' thinking in the *Abrams* dissent. The relation of sociological and political philosophy to legal techniques in regard to the control at once of crime and of government officers, I have worked at elsewhere in Proc. Natl. Conf. Soc. Work, 1928, 127, below, p. 399; *Introduction* to HALL, THEFT, LAW and SOCIETY (1935) below, p. 412; and a study of the Sacco-Vanzetti Case partly published in MICHAEL and WECHSLER, CASES ON CRIMINAL LAW AND ITS ADMINISTRATION (1940) below, p. 431. One phase is developed with peculiar beauty in Dession, *Psychiatry and the Conditioning of Criminal Justice,* 47 YALE L. J. 319 (1938).

A powerful and incisive critique of the MS provided by Jerome Michael reached me after the material had already gone to press. Such use of his many suggestions as galley-correction permitted, I have made; and I wholly accept his basic position that the first part needs ripening. I do not, however, in the context of this journal, accept the criticism that the parts are out of balance. For I hold any general analysis or theory to be wisely accompanied *at the moment of publication* by some particular testing or application. This latter can never be complete, or completely persuasive. But it warns the reader (as the "issue" does, in a case-law opinion) what the framer of the generalizations has had particularly in mind; which aids criticism. And it forces the writer to follow his generalizations into the more concrete situation.

The concepts of craft, and of craft-style, represent an effort to find manageable ways to state, sharpen, and grasp for use the something in law-government which is more than individual character and personality, but is quite different from our rules of law, and is much more complex than can be communicated merely by such a loose term as "tradition." The line of thought is more fully developed in *On the Good, the True, the Beautiful, in Law,* 9 U. CHI. L. REV. 224, 227 ff. (1942), above, p. 167. The buttressing in regard to the contemporary manner of our common law appellate courts, and the application especially to administrative problems and to the manner of judicial opinions will appear in my forthcoming THE COMMON LAW TRADITION. The wherewithal to see the grand manner of the earlier period at work in its economic context is provided in *Quality of Goods in a Credit Economy*, rep. from 36 COLUM. L. REV. 699, 723 ff; 37 *id.* 341 (1936–7); the difficulties appear in *Horse Trade and Merchants' Market in Sales*, rep. from 52 HARV. L. REV. 725; 873 (1939). The theory of the non-opposition of law and justice, under an effective institutional set-up which includes the presence of sound juristic method, is developed in LLEWELLYN and HOEBEL, *The Cheyenne Way* (1941) chs. X-XII. The part played by the law and by the divergent aspects of the common law tradition in our history, and the role of the citizen-law-consumer—these are sketched in my forthcoming LAW AND LEADERSHIP [never finished.]

The convergence of my thinking with that of C. J. FRIEDRICH, CONSTITUTIONAL GOVERNMENT AND DEMOCRACY (1942; 1st edition 1937 *sub. nom.* Constitutional Government and Politics) will be obvious; I owe him also an acknowledgment for having led me, decades back, to Max Weber. The paper rests also on less tangible but no less vital stimulus from the thinking of Dewey, Commons, Roger Baldwin, John Childs, Ambrose Doskow, Felix Cohen, and David Riesman. And, of course, and particularly, of Emma Corstvet.

PHILOSOPHY is not sociology, and it has in consequence been with some misgiving that I have seen "democracy" made the focus of this first number of a journal dedicated to *sociology* in the legal field. For democracy seems to me an idea which at present writing falls more in the area of political philosophy than in that of a would-be science. A prospective science seeks to carry objective study as far as circumstances permit, and seeks to recognize as a limit that borderland where the objectively knowable becomes so mingled with speculation, desire, or the "truly right" as to lose claim to status as more than "philosophy" in that older sense of a man's best, carefully considered, somewhat-more-than-horse-sense judgments.[1]

My doubts have grown as I have set about preparing a contribution. What I have found to say lies so far this side of semi-science

[1] On "science," in this connection, compare my *Theory of Legal Science*, 20 N.C.L. REV. (1941).

as to be embarrassing to print in a journal which aims at progressive solid widening of what is objectively probable or even provable about things and relations in the legal field. Yet I suppose that an essay in analysis has some color of preliminary value; and there are times when speculative suggestion about relations can contribute to the advancement of objective knowledge. The difficulty is that to accomplish that, the speculations must lie in what will some day prove to have been the right direction. And although I think gambling in this matter a highly desirable intellectual enterprise, I also think such gambling to lie well beyond the border of legitimate sociology unless it either comes accompanied by particulars which in part test the speculation, or is itself a precipitate of long study of testable and tested fact-material. On the side of the American common law tradition, what appears below can in this view claim some respectability as being sociology. On the side of democracy, however, it cannot, and it does not. Yet in the matter of the relations between the two, it is possible that some validity derives from a careful watching of our common law tradition as it opens out in its relation to the society of which it is a part.

In any event, I see no escape from spending space on some analysis of the variant ideas which come packed loosely under the two assigned terms of the title. Each term, as commonly used, covers a number of ideas in shifting combination, and each covers at times (whether at once or in unpredictable alternation) ideas which are at war one with another. More particularly, in current usage, each term is shifted back and forth between ideals, which run free of various less pleasant aspects of our actual scheme of things, and allegedly descriptive concepts, which commonly enough focus on the more unpleasant actual aspects to the exclusion of the others. Believers talk the ideals; doubters talk the factual caricatures. Thus when you read Pound in praise of "the common law tradition" you get little inkling of the hitches and blindnesses which are, also, one past and present part of that tradition. Or again, Kent and his intellectual progeny do not refer, by "democracy," to the same phenomena of life to which Dewey is referring by the same label. Both sets of phenomena are in fact present, but neither is present to the degree or with the full effects suggested by the respective writers.

I shall attempt to gain clarity at the risk of complexity not by setting up any single ideal-type under either label, but by differentiating certain significant *phases* (perhaps, even elements) found under each. Each of such phases I shall set up as an ideal-concept of function and functioning. I shall set up each such ideal-concept as accompanied by a more or less accurately fitted *prevalent* ideal, actually held to a significant degree by some of our people. I shall set it up as accompanied further by something of institutional machinery of semi-effectuation of the held ideal. But no less vital to the picture is the conception, in each case, of prevalent counter- or cross-ideals with *their* more or less perfected institutional machinery, and with resulting tensions and wobbles of event. The upshot of the argument will be that our "democracy" has long depended upon a régime of tension and semi-balance. That that régime has presupposed more necessity than there exists, for cross-ideals, for cross-machineries, for cross-purposings. That to leave the matter, uncontrolled, to tension and to what *may* result in the way of semi-balance, is to overlook the fact that as voltage and grouped power increase, then slip in net balance packs a *new* kind of threat *to the régime*. The argument will be further that the better phases of our common law tradition show, on a small scale, a different and more effective way or organization, in which, for instance, Law (Certainty)[b] and Justice are set up not merely to *reflect* an upshot of tensions and drives, but instead to give *merged, moving*, reasoned *guidance*. That Law (Certainty)[b] and Justice need not be two, but can be one, and that machinery not only can be but has been devised on a largish scale to make that a normal rather than a strange phenomenon—to make that plain is, in my belief, a road to furthering similar and needed reanalysis of such problems as that of the leader and the led, the expert and the consumer of expertness, or the baffling phenomena of *non*-separability of powers. For fighting cross-ideals left in unresolved tension and conflict, with no effective machinery for guidance—these produce a very different way of work and result from that of a *single* machinery geared to take account of each of two differing lines of need.

The suggestion includes not merely the old but sound idea that there has been and must be, over and above disputant or otherwise rivaling persons, outfits or factions (above, that is, the "net" upshot of vocal and effective "interests") somebody or some body weighing the rivals and their claims in the light of their meaning for the whole and for tomorrow. The suggestion includes also the old idea that such weighing calls for general over-all thinking of

[b] I should today say: Reasonable Regularity; see COMMON LAW TRADITION, esp. 215 ff.

what as against any technical specialist is of a "lay" type. It includes the old idea that machinery for stiffening character, for maintaining sensitivity and *responsive* responsibility, for building mere men up to this over-all job, can in important part be provided by a clear and transmissible *craft*-tradition. It includes finally the old idea that sound ways of governing, sound in manner as well as in substance, *develop* the governed as no mere effective command can develop them. The argument is that the finer Common Law Tradition illustrates all these things; and the suggestion is that however obvious each is, their combination has slipped so far into neglect as to deserve stress.

DEMOCRACY
OFFICER-RESTRAINT AND THE LIBERTIES: REFRESHMENT

"Democracy" suggests (along with one neglected absolute) a political régime whose pervading accepted or dominant values are carefully left open to modification or displacement, and so are left open to utterance and agitation which may not only challenge those values but may also aim at their displacement by other means than violent revolution. This I shall call the *refreshment* phase of the democracy-idea. It is worth isolating as a separate semi-independent concept. It is worth note that from the angle of legal structuring this phase consists in a channeling for leeways and free play afforded by the whole régime, the *official* positive structuring being devoted far more to the safeguarding of such leeways (e.g. the Bill of Rights *re* the liberties) than to the implementation of movement within those leeways (e.g. the election-régime, the secret ballot). It needs note that "refreshment" occurs in fact differentially with regard to persons, groups, classes. One thinks of the negro messman who needed Pearl Harbor to get his chance to serve a machine-gun and a public; or of interned loyal Japanese citizens; and one thinks then of the peace-time analogues.

With refreshment of accepted values and policies taken as an objective, it is obvious that to that objective such matters as toleration, tolerance, liberty of conscience, speech, assembly, suffrage, organization and the like, stand as means and measures. Some of us do indeed feel these same measures and so much as can be managed of appropriate companioning attitudes to be means to other things as well—say, to a broadening and quickening of the individual spirit, to an enlivening variety of life, people, and interest, which have value in themselves apart from their implications for the political régime. And it may be admitted that the refreshment phase is bound up with this life-enrichment phase by strong tendency, by such contributing factors as the régime of technological movement and modern technology of communication, and by the relative improbability that any thoroughly bigoted simple two-party setup could ever condition itself to a régime of non-suppression. Despite that, the refreshment phase is intellectually severable, and it is severable in life. A live elite can do much refreshment, without much "popular" participation or quickening of the people's "spirit".

Again, a constitutional régime of refreshment implies per se little tolerance, no sympathy, and neither progress nor widening of horizon. It implies as a bare minimum only so much of "antagonistic co-operation" as is needed to make the blind and bigoted Big Endians who win this time leave open the chance for the equally blind and bigoted Little Endians to win next time, despite the patronage advantages enjoyed by this time's winners.

This having been noted, there remain two questions to which I do not have an answer. The first question is, whether such an active constitutional [2] refreshment régime can maintain itself in the absence of a considerable degree of supporting tolerance and cross-sympathies, running through a very considerable portion of the relevant population, i.e., in absence of sufficient "we-ness" feeling among some leaders, followers, or both, to induce restraint in victors and patience in losers. This presents a major problem of post-war: not only internationally, but within the nation. For we know that pressure, bafflement, and organization for conflict all sharply increase group-antagonisms; and the effect of our mass armed service on the welding of national team-attitudes is as yet wholly obscure. And we do not know at all what constitutes the minimum effective quantum and distribution of tolerance and patience needed to continue so much of refreshment as our own tradition affords. Still less do we know the quantum and distribution necessary to create such a tradition in any international political organization which may undertake tasks of real governing. Finally, our effective machinery for large-scale or mass-wise building of tolerance or even toleration lags so far behind our ma-

[2] I use "constitutional" here to mean the active basic setup. The secret ballot is a part of the "constitution" in this sense; and a party-system is a part wherever it is. I shall refer to the official Constitution by capitalizing. [I am amazed, in 1961, to find these words still apt.]

chinery for building their contraries as to make such machinery a curiously needed field of study.

The second question, also of post-war moment, but probably more on the international side and inside other nations than in ours, goes to the question of whether such a refreshment régime can maintain itself amid a large modern population unless the number of dominant parties remains manageably small. On both heads, the suggestion to be derived from the situation in American organized labor is almost as great as that to be derived from European "political" experience.

The final point to be made about the refreshment régime is that it is itself an absolute, and that it therefore is incompatible with any other absolute, and, again, that it is therefore forced on its own basic premises to maintain itself at need by forcible restraint of a rival movement. This I take to be sociological fact, although in discussing it I shall take the liberty to move for a moment into areas of philosophy. Any movement which in fact threatens future toleration after victory is a "rival" movement; and no other movement is. *At need,* therefore, a polity committed to any given quantum of refreshment is driven to restrain any such *rival* movement by force.

This is the point at which it becomes of basic importance to distinguish between a refreshment régime as a continuing end, and liberty of speech, agitation, and organization as a *means* to that end. The liberties call for restraint when and insofar as they cease to serve the end. Similarly, the rival movement calls not for suppression, but for restraint to the point at which it ceases to immediately endanger the régime of refreshment. It is of no moment to a refreshment régime per se that the rival movement may attack or even actively endanger any particular values which may be dominant for the moment—or which may have been dominant for the preceding century. That is why suppression of Communistic activity in this country would at this time[e] and into the foreseeable future be at odds with our Constitutional régime of refreshment. Some Communistic activity[e] in this country has indeed been an outrage, and much of it has been a noisome irritant; but none of it has come within howling distance of being

[e] It is plain that I am talking here of open agitation, not of undercover espionage. In regard to open agitation, I see no reason to change my fundamental views. But I am worrying, these days, about how to build up *at once* a fighting fervor and a wherewithal to leave, after either victory or defeat, a human race.

an active danger to our *refreshment* régime, nor does it threaten to, in terms of capture of political control. Communist activity in this country has its danger in a wholly different field. Given the prejudice against Communism which derives from its anti-capital and anti-clerical drives, Communist participation can go far to discredit and hamstring any liberal or "democratic" movement. That is a danger, and it is a live one. But it is not a danger which calls for *government* suppression.[3] It is, in terms of the refreshment régime, a risk of life to be faced and handled by liberal or "democratic" movements from within themselves.

For the same reasons, however, there are phases of activity of "fascist" character which do need careful watching, and which may come to need smashing restraint: this is because they move (as Communism does not) in terms which under war and post-war conditions have open to them terrific latent reverberations in *our* people (as Know-Nothingism, the Klan, and Red-hunts may suggest). Apart from the fact that a "fascist" movement can be made without straining to put on the garb of our overwhelmingly dominant American ideology and American emotion—a point which I prefer not to demonstrate—there is the other fact that from the beginning the American Constitutional (or Sunday) régime of refreshment has bulged and tottered in its struggle against the American factual (or workday) attitude of knock-em-out or run-em-out.

But again it is to be noted that restraint, not suppression, is the problem. Quite apart from the fact that it is seldom administratively feasible to preserve a refreshment régime while suppressing for not-yet-actively-perilous tendency, there is the other fact that any type of suppression is contagious; and there is the further fact that extremely useful ideas come frequently rolled up together with violent and/or absolutistic or totalitarian preachment. Until the latter becomes a real threat to maintenance of refreshment, it would be sad to use the force of government to keep us from being reminded by Communists that an economic system *can* labor at

[3] There is a separate issue in regard to schools run by the government. The refreshment ideal is a difficult ideal; it calls for training and inculcation; it does not grow in the growing young as a result of early direct life-experience.

It is the job of a refreshment régime to raise up the young in that aspect of the faith, and it is in my view altogether proper that active faith therein should be a condition to the appointment of a teacher in a government-run institution. By the same token, to require adherence to any particular prevailing *variety* e.g. of economic structure or régime flies in the face of the refreshment ideal. While to discharge or to discontinue any person on suspicion is at odds with the "reasonable regularity" aspect of our institutions.

making distribution of product turn less than ours does on sometimes the accident, sometimes the earned reward, of ownership;
or from being reminded by Fascists that a modern technology
calls for a fairish bit of centralized thinking for the whole, and
that pride of craft, in any craft, can have peculiar value as a
moving and sustaining force.

What this gives us, thus far, is a régime with a single absolutism,
but with that absolutism severely self-limited, and open-ended
with regard to any and all subsidiary or companioning content.
This régime is an ideal-concept, not remotely approached in fact.
The actually prevailing ideal is loose and foggy, but is widely held.
It is no mere dream-ideal, either; it is actively reached for and
partly achieved in fact. It is, moreover, an ideal in part institutionalized. There is an appropriate body of concepts backed by
an articulate philosophy. There are also popular slogans, well
understood and on call with some power of popular appeal: "A
man's got a right to his opinion!" "Wait a minute—let him
talk!"—"Wait till next election!" Unreckonably yet persistently,
there are "ways" at work, in individual and in group-work, which
fit with the ideal. There is an official symbol, the Bill of Rights
and the election régime, implemented with often practicable
measures. In many pinches the courts provide something of a
policing and enforcement machinery. This ideal with its imperfect
but effective institutionalization strains of course in severe and
often overwhelmed tension against counter-ideals and counter-
ways, which, though less formally structured, rest in emotion-
rooted practice, attitude, counter-slogan and even in known patterns of action available on call (the steam-roller; lynching, etc.) .

To the above formulation we must recur, for comparison, when
we come to what I shall call the "grand" phase of our Common
Law Tradition.

OFFICER-RESTRAINT AND THE LIBERTIES: REASONABLE REGULARITY

A Bill of Rights serves, as a means, more than the refreshment
aspect of democracy. With regard to refreshment, its objectives
are positive, creative, though they be unpredictable in content and
tendency; the restraints upon officials exist there for the sake of
ideas men hope may emerge from this or that portion of the
citizenry, as a result (in part) of restraining the officials. But a Bill
of Rights serves also, along with such similar measures as the con-

tracts clause, the due process clause, and the equal protection clause, a further and quite distinct function. To be sure, if the refreshment liberties be set up to be viewed merely as protections of the citizen as a person, then insistence on *nullum crimen, nulla poena, sine lege* and on reasonableness of classification for any purpose of benefit or burden, can appear simply as other and further protections of a significantly similar sort. But if the refreshment liberties be seen as *means* to deeper political ends, then restraints on officials take on quite another aspect when what is required by the restraint is non-individuated action, action by way of fixed protective procedures, action by way of open and known classification, and then by known rule and criterion general to the whole class.

This is the juice of Dicey's "rule of law" and of the German *Rechtsstaat*. Our thinking tends to whip it, along with refreshment, into a single syllabub of "civil liberties." And it is indeed related to refreshment in that *one* of its roots as well as *one* of its effects is to help keep governmental Ins from turning the general machinery of the peace against any bothersome leaders or members of the Outs. But it has also two wholly different lines of both genesis and purpose. The one has to do with man's feeling for Justice, quite apart from any matter of mere democracy. That feeling for Justice appears to dictate that it is *right* for what are felt as "like" cases to be treated alike. I have never seen the psychological or sociological genesis of this explored; but its existence I take as unquestionable. As a matter of governmental technique, the evidence is moderately persuasive that a *régime* operating on this basis enlists attitudes of support and patterns of behavior which serve it somewhat as a flywheel. The second and related line runs inside that staff of governmental officers which Friedrich calls the burocracy. The regularity régime serves there both to train and to police such officers; and (unless overstressed) it becomes perhaps the major factor in a viable long-range structure: again, a flywheel, but this time *inside* the organization.

In any of these aspects this *regularity* phase can serve "democracy." In none of them is it to be confused with "democracy": for certainly the two last-named aspects are compatible with a totalitarian or other absolutism; and a good case can be made along the same lines even for a rigorous criminal procedure on the general Bill of Rights pattern.[d] "Tyranny under the forms of

---

[d] What this tries to say is that I see no intellectual or sociological clash between absolute authoritarian government and a high-powered "rule of law" type of rule of

law" is over the long haul tyranny doubly hard to dislodge. Nor should it have needed Hitler to make clear to any thoughtful dabbler in history that classification and generality of rule (even plus fair procedure) are no full safeguard against what men call arbitrary despotism, if there be no restraints upon the content and manner of the classifications made and upon the consequences attached.

When, however, the classifications and consequences are required to be not only general, *but also "reasonable,"* and when minimum fairness and regularity of procedure is required as well, then there results a phase of *"reasonable" regularity* which Americans have come to associate with "democracy" as an inherent part thereof. And the concept of the "reasonable," with its combined, fused connotations of the accustomed and of the "right," infuses into the regular *and as a part thereof* a substance and content of "Justice." Again the ideal, though familiar and powerful and moderately well institutionalized, sits in strained tension with cross-ideals, cross-practices.[4] Note also, when the matter recurs in comparison with our common law tradition, that the conception of the "reasonable" which is a working part of the whole conception, is one which leaves full leeway for policy-shaping movement and semi "departure" in the large, and for individuated adjustment in the particular, each *as a part of* the "regular and regularized." It is partly for this reason that the phrase "constitutional

---

law plus a high-powered Bill of Rights type of protection of the person plus a high-powered adversary type of criminal procedure. I think there are holes in Acton's aphorism, despite its value. And I think it often pays to consider possibilities of which one happens to be able to offer no examples.

[4] One set of these cross-ideals clusters around the mere idea of the regular-in-terms-of-past-practice-and-thought, leaving out of account the need for individuation and for reasonable movement. Its formal expression is in the older blinder Constitutional decisions. An opposing set clusters around the idea of government by favor or by fiat—whether in business or in labor or in the "political" sphere; leaving out the element of the reckonably and impersonally regularized.

It is worth note that these unregularized and so to speak semi- or pre-legal *parts* of the legal régime are complementary and implementary proper working *parts* thereof (even when non-regular, and frequently unwise) whenever (1) their action moves in terms of the general objectives of purpose and manner to which the legal system is geared; *and* (2) it moves in terms of the leeways recognized generally by and within the structure for the play of judgment, to allow of cumulative experiment in good faith; *and* (3) when individuated or novel "discretionary" operation moves in terms of a *quest* for a *pattern* to guide treatment of what may at the moment seem a unique case. Put from the other side, the unregularized becomes *anti*-legal when it occurs in bad faith; or without quest for a pattern emerging or to emerge; or when it persistently jumps the recognized limits or even persistently pushes daily ordinary action out into limits which exist only to serve the case of pressing need. These criteria I do not recall seeing properly lined up in print.

democracy" is here avoided. Not only does it call up memory of
two many dubious decisions on constitutionality and of too many
passionate disputes. It also fuses and confuses the refreshment
phase with the reasonable regularity phase. Companions and
partners they are; but also better seen as only such. Finally, "constitutional democracy" insidiously calls up a picture of the regular
as somehow opposed to and as shackling both policy-shaping and
individuation of action, whereas it is vital, as J. R. Commons has
insisted, to perceive that with "reasonable" in the picture what
results is not a shackling, but a steadying[5]; not an opposition, but
a merger of the already ordered (often, even formulated) and of
readjustment.

If the foregoing can be grouped as the phases of "democracy"
which center on machinery for somewhat trammeling officers of
government, the phases to follow have as their focus the general
idea which since the 18th Century has been sloganized—most inadequately—by "equality."

"EQUALITY": LEADERSHIP AND SUFFRAGE

I suppose that, sociologically, it is agreed that in modern large-
scale society leadership "by the people" is a political slogan which
finds no counterpart in living fact. Real "government by the people" centers around the ideas of choosing and shaping policies and
measures, but rarely real choosing, never real shaping by the "the
people". The "democracy" idea concerned is rather that "the
people" shall have a voice (quantum indeterminate) (a) in originally selecting the men who do the choosing and shaping; (b) in
continuing or ousting such men; (c) in originally dictating, or,
after some accounting, in ratifying what such men have done. This
gets too complex for discussion here, and one meets such further
queer ideas as that "the people" means "all the people," and that
"voice" means an active and effective voice, as contrasted with
the facts about our political organization and about the com-
plexities of policy and measure. Perhaps one can set up a concept
of a working minimum in these terms: the "suffrage" phase—
which sits locked with "leadership"—looks to a moderately open
accounting by the organized governing officers for their major
policies and measures, coupled with the wherewithal for ouster at
reasonable intervals—ouster not for malfeasance alone, but for

[5] This is also why the attribute "general" in the concept of "law" misleads, as
against the attribute "regular."

general dissatisfaction; and those persons who can make themselves felt toward ouster must include some fair portion of the disadvantaged. The idealistic ideal steps up far beyond anything actual the fairness and fullness of any accounting, the range and effective organization of any suffrage-holders, and both their intelligence and their active political interest. The actual institutionalization is in terms of a theoretical official framework which has proved unworkable save in its broadest outline, and which has come to be "deplemented" largely by such things as a non-removable civil service, by committee organization of legislatures, by "expert" specialized commissions, and by a party organization built in large part to keep "the people" from having any say in any matter which can be kept away from them. Yet the ideal has shown itself to have a deep actual rooting, with rank-and-file movements recurrently breaking through into effectiveness, and, over a century and a half, with a slowly broadening base of effective suffrage, and at least since the Civil War with a slowly rising level both of accounting for policies and of intelligence in grasp of issues among the holders of the suffrage. Or so I read the record.

This appears to have gone hand-in-hand (and not alone in regard to our federal government) with a widening of professional, semi-"expert" governmental staff; and the recognized need for a staff of that general character, even among the policy-shaping officers, seems to me a marked characteristic of current administration in contrast, say, to those of Jackson, Lincoln, and even Wilson's later years. So that I am led to query whether there is not a rather close connection between what one might call our older primitive large-scale "democracy" with its ideology of general omnicompetence, plus its direct relation to the single leader, and a different, "staff" type of government companioning the wane of felt omnicompetence and simultaneously depersonalizing the leader-led relation. This despite the technology and technique of Franklin Roosevelt's "fireside talk." I grope here for ideas as well as for words; but if there is anything solid in the suggestion, it would follow that the major danger facing the "primitive" "democracy" would be demagoguery perhaps followed in the traditional manner by autocratic usurpation, whereas the danger facing the "expert-"staff type would be equally or more that of non-participation and of first allowing, then demanding that things be done for one, without individual and folk participation. The office-holder appears as the major blood sucker on the one set-up; the bounty-extracting pressure-group as that on the other. And the continuance or recapture of the personal relation with the individual leader I would suggest to be essential to soundness in the scheme of things, until an intellectual appreciation of the meaning of government for the whole as a Whole can be introduced mass-wide into the population; for lacking such an appreciation, only a personal relationship well handled—or a compulsion—serves to stir the ordinary citizen into really active participation.

DEMOCRACY
OTHER "EQUALITY" PHASES

There are four other aspects which travel under the "democracy" label, on the "equality" side, which need mention. One, that of general omnicompetence, I take to have ceased today to have standing anywhere as a creed, or even as an ideal. But our habits of thought and action still reflect some portion of a once widely prevalent attitude. The range of offices for which party or pressure-group service is conceived as an adequate qualification is still wide. We are slow to trust an "expert," we are quick to suspect him. Without analysis, moreover, we tend to take achievement in anything (certainly in business) as a sufficient indicator of ability to handle other things. And even while we flood high schools and colleges, we neglect man-placement. I read this to mean that as a people we have simply drifted into the use of "expert" staff in government, without, as a people, yet understanding such use.

The second remaining "equality" aspect is that of "distribution" out and "down" of society's product—a quickening attention to needs earlier dealt with on the one side by combined neighborliness and callousness to human wastage, on the other by unexploited land. One notes merely the old wisdom that this side of "democracy" can be in head-on conflict with that of responsible participation, unless "distribution down" is handled with a skill that we are far from having fully developed. To make the point, it is enough to conceive our traditional practices with veterans applied after this war by and to a group eight to ten millions strong, and to contrast them with the homesteading program which tied the opportunity provided to appropriate sustained self-help.[e]

Side by side, in idealistic theory, with "distribution downward"

---

[e] The further development, since this was written, of handout and of demand for handout is surely as disquieting as inflation, and rivals the worrisomeness of the international scene.

and with the "suffrage" side of the "leadership-suffrage" phase stands what one may call the phase of "opportunity downward"—personnel refreshment as distinct from policy refreshment. The two have a loose relation, but no necessary connection. The long series of those who were radicals-for-lack-of-recognition and have then become conservative leaders points the nature of the relation: most, but not all, of such have found the road to power partly by way of diagnosing in their radical years some policies which were called for by the times, but which were blind to the conservatives of their own younger years. But the connection is loose. In Hitler's régime for the recruiting of leaders one has, for instance, a machinery admirably designed to refresh an élite, but aimed at holding not only the action but the imagination of the recruits within a fixed ideological framework dictated from above; and the medieval Church in its best days offered a comparable machinery, except that a steadying tradition there provided more of the framework than did any living authorities. On the "democratic" side, I suppose that "opportunity" "downward" as we conceive it extends also to adult opportunity, and so, in causal relation, to opportunity for breaking into leadership along paths other than the ones already or authoritatively charted. Certainly it includes in our own past prevailing practice and present strongly held ideal plus still strong practice a material degree of "downward distribution" of leadership opportunity in the extra-political sphere; and I suppose that this is the area in which American political "democracy" most effectively mingles its waters with those of American life at large; our unexploited natural resources, markets, and ingenuity serving as a sort of constant vacuum to raise new men and new interests into position to be heard and felt. I take it also that "opportunity downward" on the more clearly political side has become of rising importance as greater groupings (or unorganized rucks) have come into being whom economic suction fails to reach, and that this is a major reason why politics and government have for forty years been rising in relative importance. And I take it as important to recall that "opportunity downward" in the political field need *not* mean "for the fit or for the wise," and need *not* hook up with more than a sham of "distribution downward," even under a régime of wide suffrage, as also that it often cross-purposes with "expert" leadership, and that it often works out in highly autocratic control of the rising or risen leader's immediate supporters.

For, finally, there is that phase of "democracy," inside of any subgroup, which has to do with the manner of reaching decisions:

some range of consultation, some fairness and openness of discussion. Call it the "procedure" phase. Even the ideal, here, is both uncertain and diffuse. And what there is of it wars with a much better implemented ideal of management and efficiency; a fact which holds true as well inside the machinery of official government as outside. Of all phases of "democracy," this aspect seems to me to have least hold on our people, save sometimes within small face-to-face groups. Yet its value, at least within such groups, is patent. Meantime, the institutional substitute (for it is no true implementation), so far as there is one, is found in the machinery of election and blanket-ratification—or disapproval—of decisions arrived at by other means; or, within smaller groups, in consultation with skilled or "representative" men, trial balloons, spies, polls, or other means of testing the leeways which exist for action, while goals and measures are determined by procedures other than "democratic." The labor field again presents the problem in its vortex, when a corporation's labor policy is subjected to enlarged "democratization of procedure" by collective bargaining between a dictatorial corporate management and a union also dictatorially controlled.

In sum, we find gathered under the one label "democracy" (as applied to American conditions) a "refreshment" aspect in regard to policy which by no means coincides with that as to controlling personnel; a "reasonable regularity" aspect which locks horns as often with "democratic procedure" as with "tyranny" or "efficiency"; a "downward distribution" drive in regard to product, suffrage, and opportunity both political and extra-political, countered by caste-building pressures; an omnicompetence attitude still at odds with needed specialized skills in government— each partly but imperfectly implemented by the full range of all that goes into political and extra-political-institutionalization, but each in tension with counter- or cross-institutionalizations sometimes stronger, sometimes not so strong.

The key-problem which emerges from the canvass would seem to be: to keep the "downward-distribution" aspects live, but to keep them live in terms of *active* participation of the beneficiaries. Out of this, if and where accomplished, all else seems to me to flow: leadership, balance, accounting, and the necessary expertise. Save that men, however intelligent or well-intentioned, are not to be trusted to maintain either a refreshment régime or one of reasonable regularity in the absence of restrictions upon officers which reach across the generations. The constitutional restraints symbolized by the Bill of Rights (though some of its provisions need amendment) perform a first part of this office. The other, and needed, implementing factor is a solid and articulate set of sound traditions of office; sound craft-traditions of action and of attitude.

OUR COMMON LAW TRADITION

The foregoing deals with a scene too vast to handle. "The" "key-problem" just presented is for instance a verbal gathering of a thousand diverse problems, a phrasing which only serves to hide the detailed variant jobs of finding ways and means, from time to time, and of moving the relevant welter of men into sustained effort to use such ways and means, if found. The ensuing portion of the paper is therefore directed to the tangible, and cuts into a field of infinitely lesser scope. But measures hereinafter suggested are urged not only as solid for use, but as already on a notable scale in actual process of coming into use in a key-area. Their relation to the vague vastness of American "democracy" lies in three points: The measures to be discussed pick up and somewhat advance the finer aspects discussed under "democracy," and pick them up at one of the more crucial positions. They sketch a *pattern* capable of use and adaptation in other areas of the problems of "democracy"; a pattern, moreover, capable of piece-by-piece introduction, each piece achieved being useful so far as it goes—with no need to wait upon wholesale movement. They shed particular light on the problems of an articulate sound tradition of office, and also on the manner in which "reasonableness" can become an integral part of "regularity": that is, they go to the nature and the building of the basic framework within which the other problems of "democracy" require to be worked out.

Certain facets of our common law tradition are familiar. Under it, law and the work of law are conceived as in an important sense judge-centered, or more accurately as centered in the highest available courts of appeal. In our system there are fifty-one of these, the Supreme Court's control over the highest State Courts being severely restricted. The decisions and opinions of a highest court not only provide the authoritative basis for determining much law never dealt with by the legislature, but under the American system those decisions also can lay down Constitutional limits on the legislature's action, and, finally, the ways in which such a court "reads" legislation become an authoritative gloss upon the meaning of the statutes. Jurists and scholars, even though they be judges writing off the bench, are only beginning to win a recognition remotely rivalling that of the highest available courts of appeal. The court's decisions, moreover, are persuasive and often controlling outside the State in which they are rendered; whereas a statute has its territorial limits of effect.

Equally important to the tradition is the importance in it and to it of the particular concrete case which comes before the court for decision. Rulings of wider import are made by the courts always under the impact of the concrete controversy; and if they require re-examination they are reviewed in the light of the further particular controversies in which they have come up for application. They can be and they are "distinguished" or "limited" as having had unnecessary and unwise breadth or direction of phrasing. This serves at once to test and to refresh rules of law by recurrent earthy contact with new experience—if the point recurs in litigation—while, on the other hand, it serves to hold vision and thought down to small areas and to condition thought by the partly accidental impact of what happens to be litigated. And though both judicial craftsmanship and scholars' work trend toward integration of the rules of law on a larger scale and around wider concepts, the particularistic mass of common law remains notably resistant to large-scale systematization or to clean logical structure within any attempted systematization. In detail and in large principle, common law is thus groping law, but it gropes out of the earthly rooted for better, but still earthy rooting. And this groping character holds trebly in our country, in which the whole vast area of law entrusted to the States lacks the ordering power of any single highest authoritative tribunal, while the stock of moderately common, vaguish concepts branches out into an intricate but patternless tracery of variant detail.

A further part of the common law tradition is the practice of publishing opinions which state the case, give the decision, and proceed to justify the latter; and our practice is also for any judge or judges who dissent to be free to publish their variant opinion, with its reasons, and for the ordinary prevailing opinion to be signed by the judge primarily responsible for its drafting.

Still a further part is the persisting omnicompetence of the highest appellate court. Its business is not divided among specialized tribunals, manned by specialists in particular fields. It sits on anything, determines anything, which is brought before it, quite irrespective of its technical ignorance. It is the business of counsel on the two sides to draw up, and provide the court with, any necessary technical information. The court voices, so to speak, as an official organ, not only The Law, but, in its sizing up of the situation and the controversy, the court voices also the residual *non-expert* horse sense of the community in the whirl of this technologically baffling world.

Finally, and as an aspect of what has been said above, the common law court of last resort faces inescapably an office of determining the law for the future. Its decision in the case in hand will become an officially recognized "precedent" for tomorrow and thereafter. Each such decision must. Willy-nilly, the common law court makes law with some speed as it proceeds from decision to decision.

Now it has been the practice to describe our common law tradition largely as if what lay at its heart were some phase or aspect of "law" or were some particular kind of "law"—howsoever you may choose to define that word. It concerns me here, however, to insist that each matter just referred to takes on a vital and exciting light if it be viewed, instead, as in first instance an aspect of a *craft-tradition,* as an aspect of a particular type of *tradition of the craft of judging in a court of last resort.* For it is in the craft-tradition of appellate judging that the major lessons of the common law tradition for "democracy" will be found.

Let it be noted first that one part of that tradition, one which is not found in any articulate rule of law, is that the court owes high duty not only to The Law, but also to Justice. Its duty is not to the one and is not to the other, its duty is to both at once, if it can find the skill and wisdom to serve both at once. All men know this, including the judges: it is only litigants or lawyers or partisans of either who forget it, and they only for the time being. Hence, in the craft-tradition, it is a standing discomfort and dissatisfaction whenever the court finds difficulty in working out a harmony of these two duties. This is that phase of American "democracy" termed above "*reasonable* regularity," at work in the daily labors of the appellate bench. It needs stress because the common law court deals not only with the particular decision, but with the rule which is to become a precedent and guide the future. It needs stress because if both continuity and reason in readjustment enter the picture in the highest court, a fortiori should they enter in other offices in which "policy" is a matter of *articulate* delegated duty.

Again, in the craft-tradition of the appellate courts, we find a number of attributes of work-in-the-office which are seldom phrased. I can try to describe some of them: effort at "impartiality"; effort to keep the mind open till both sides have been heard; effort to dissociate the "true essence" of the controversy from accidents of person, personality and the like; avoidance of a case in which a judge is or may be thought personally "interested." We might be tempted to sum this up as avoidance of conduct unbecoming a judge and a gentleman, if the matter were not patently positive rather than merely negative. A better phrasing would be: the handling of the matter, in action and in thought, according to the right tradition of judging. Some portion of this is institutionalized. "Independence of the judiciary" (qualified by short terms) and non-reduceability of salaries, seek both to make such "judicial" conduct possible and to further it. Rules of law against bribery, practices set against "influence," loose but useful practices of self-disqualification, even looser but still recognizable practices about judicial manners, the disciplinary pressure of phrasing an explanation of a decision in a published opinion, the policing power of possible open dissent by any member of the court who may see or feel outrage—these form a gap-filled hedge to mark and to half-police the tradition. But its juice lies in the realm of the *felt*. And it is most important that that juice should not be sought merely in personal uprightness or in "the judicial conscience," or in the judicial "intuition." For the perceptible lines of the *tradition* are what inform conscience and uprightness; they are what provide a main part of the material to intuit *with*. What else, for instance, determines *how far* innovation in decision is properly to go? Some distance is always proper; too much distance becomes very ticklish. Rules on the matter there are as yet none; nor are there rules for whither or how any movement is to be directed.[6]

It deserves attention that a fair number of aspects of "proper judicial conduct under the tradition" have been worked into the substance of the law, whether by Constitutional provision or by the courts on their own. Here the appellate judicial tradition crosses over into the political sphere, and links up with those aspects of "democracy" which relate to restraints upon officials.

---

[6] When such rules come into being, they will run along the general lines stated at the end of note 4, above, p. 293. The additional factor which marks the great judge from the "too political" or poor judge goes to substance, not to manner or motive. The innovations or variations of the great judge (a) prove to have been wise, to have been in fact keyed to what was needed; and (b) they are so phrased as to illumine later lesser judges. Craft-tradition cannot produce these results, if the man-material is defective; but it can *develop* such results, surprisingly, out of the general run of man-material.

One should mention such conceptions as the need for giving a chance to be heard, for notice of what the complaint is, for access to legal counsel, for sufficient evidence to support a finding of fact, for fair application of accepted rules of law (*with,* however, the implicit leeways the system offers, in such application), for confining a criminal prosecution to the question of whether a particular offense has been committed. In such matters the rights of Englishmen, as Pound has noted, have in our thought taken on the character of natural rights of man which courts feel it proper to protect in any appropriate circumstance.

Our Common Law Tradition: Two Contrasting Phases

The matters mentioned pervade all varieties of our common law tradition. But seriously affecting their operation and effect are two mutually incompatible further lines of factor. The one line, dominant roughly from 1885 to 1910, and still powerful in the ideology and practice especially of the bar, accounts for much of lay criticism (*and* misunderstanding) of courts and of our common law tradition. The other line, dominant in the 1830's and 1840's, and rising again into dominance in the 1920's, '30's and '40's, needs disentanglement from the former, if there is to be clear seeing either of the tradition itself or of what its grander manner or style means to our society.

What I shall call the formal style can be cast into ideal-type somewhat as follows, in terms of sociological description and of the appropriate legal doctrine: Separation of powers and the nature of judicial office combine to deny creation to the court. The existing legal materials contain all the answers; the dominant duty lies in their application. Justice is relevant, doubtless, in case of seeming doubt; but clarity and certainty of rule are the true goal for a court—the remedy lying with the legislature. In addition, the results of the courts' prior work are too well established and too well integrated to be lightly disturbed, and not only is any disturbing legislation to be "read" as severely limited in operation, but if it threatens too large a displacement of existing legal values, it becomes patently unreasonable and discriminatory, and so Unconstitutional. The existing legal scheme has as its office not to follow society, but to discipline society and to control it; criteria for handling cases are to be found therefore exclusively within the legal system, not outside it; and what a court deduces from the existing materials is what it is that court's duty to proclaim, come hell or high water, and that is what both judicial conscience and judicial independence are for. Within that frame of the received legal system, but only within that frame, one does his best to work out a satisfying disposition of the particular controversy. Opinions give the *legal* reasons, for the legal results, to the legally trained public, and a general public cannot be expected to understand. Neither sticky sentimentality nor an ear to the ground is any attribute of a sound court.

The waning [largely waned] way of work so stated in ideal type can at its peak be sweetly craftsmanlike, and often has been. It will be noted, however, to run counter to a number of what we have been treating as lines gathered under the label "democracy." It denies refreshment via court work (though of course even conscious effort to stand firm upon the old ways has never been able wholly to escape refreshment in fact.) It cold-shoulders refreshment of legal premise and general policy via the legislature. It denies accountability for *premises,* and affords accounting for action only in black-art terms and only to the initiate of the black art. It is ill-at-ease with refreshment of personnel; short-term elected judges are an anomaly in such a scheme of things; indeed, one of the most amazing marks of the power of the appellate craft-tradition has been the degree to which this ideology on and of the appellate bench has made conquest, over decades, even of short-term elected judges. The "regularity" phase of our American "democracy" this formal style of tradition furthered; but the furtherance was in recurring denial of the companion juice of "reasonableness," wherever "reasonable," even in a world of whirling change, meant readjustment. As part of the foregoing, but as a factor worth independent stress, the formal style was smug; self-satisfied and scornful, in-turned, blind to all premises but its own. And smugness has in things of law a power which it lacks elsewhere, save in a state-religion: for smugness in law means not only that I am exclusively correct, but that I have been appointed and given power and duty to impose my exclusive correctness upon all other folk. As is familiar, this became dire in the conflict of courts with legislatures and with the needs voiced by legislatures. It became no less dire as courts undertook to hold down or strike down action by the steadily budding new specialized agencies for government. At which point one must add another feature of the common law tradition, whose allocation may be in dispute. I should today allocate it to the formal style. Historically, it belongs to the tradition entire, and in its genesis it belongs to the grand manner. I refer to the treatment of governmental officers as having no standing whatsoever, as such, no presumption that their acts are "acts of state," and the like. This attitude in the craft-tradition was once a mighty bulwark of the free man against a king who was forced to act through officers. Today the matter has been partly rethought; it needs rethinking further to save the good heart of the idea, while yet recognizing the needs of modern government and of men who have to shape their affairs under modern government.

I mention these matters to get them out of the way. For the craft-"style" of appellate judging which has just been presented in peak ideal-type still colors most men's thought, today, about our common law tradition. Even lawyers, when the better of them awake as they have had to, to perceive that this style no longer pictures what is going on today, even such lawyers are by turn pleased—secretly—and shocked—openly—to observe the increasing use by the appellate courts of frank good sense, as one adjunct of decision. The lay public, including the bulk of men in the social disciplines, despite their belief in Justice, their sure knowledge that Law should serve Justice, and their constant consequent interest in improvement of our Laws, nonetheless view deflection by legalism as inherent in the picture unless particular men of peculiar power, insight, *and point of view* be somehow placed upon the bench. Which placing is a political feat for whose accomplishment procedures are not readily forthcoming.

I wholly concur on the importance of particular men; no institutional machine can get on without them. I recognize that transcendent single figures such as Mansfield once, and Cardozo during the crucial '20's, can go far to shape a legal epoch. But I am talking here not about single men, but about a craft-tradition that shapes men, and makes men—*most* men, almost all men—and brings out of ordinary men either better or worse than they would manage, just as men, to give. The formal style of the common law tradition crippled all but its few best men. The grand style of that tradition, on the other hand, stirs many merely average near up into the beginnings of greatness. In casting its characteristics into ideal type, I shall from time to time interpose a word of rationale; it is to be understood that the rationale suggested is unless the contrary is stated implicit, not explicit and conscious, just as the rationale suggested above for the contrasting style and manner is, at least in its totality, implicit rather than conscious and coherent. It is further to be understood that I do not conceive either manner, *pure,* to have prevailed, much less to have been universal, at any period. It is not difficult to find particular judges whose work has run with surpassing consistency along one line or the other; thus, for the formal style Parke, C. B., of the Exchequer, the Andrews of the 1880's in the New York Court of Appeals, the elder Sanborn of the federal bench; for the grand style, Mansfield, Cowen of New York, or more currently, say Lehman and Loughran in New York, Hart in Ohio. But "prevailingness" in the general daily work of the country has been of the pepper and salt or mixed tweed pattern, moving from bright to deep dark, then again to bright, in net effect. "Dominance" refers to the normal, the average, the to-be-expected, way of work; not to an unfailing or universal way. And in regard to the *growing* dominance of the "grand" style through the last [four] decades, I must lodge one word of caution: the courts have been groping, not consciously driving, into it. It therefore shows in their lines of deciding more clearly, as yet, than in their lines of writing opinions. What demonstrates the trend and points the future is the welcome given by citation and use to those opinions which are built in the "grand" manner, and the rising percentage of such opinions.[f]

The ideal-type is familiar to most in the work of Marshall; but let it be remembered that what Marshall was doing with the Constitution, the State-court judges of his day were doing with the precedents and statutes. There was (and is, again) a craft-"style." Thus: The first essential job of a case-law court of last resort is the shaping, out of the received authoritative materials, of a sound rule for guidance of the future: sound diagnosis of the trouble-area, and sound location and phrasing of a criterion for decision within that area. Criterion and phrasing must guide immediately and effectively, in dealing with problem-facts. To this end, the reason is as essential as the rule; the reason indeed informs the rule, and it is the applicability of the reason which tests the applicability of the rule. The reason must make life-sense, else it shows on its face that it has ceased to be an adequate reason. Law is thus daily tested for its sense in life, and the huge leeway of doctrine which the accepted seven-wayed techniques for handling or "reading" accepted authorities afford is to be used, (in the main cautiously, but always to be used) to make law for today and tomorrow accomplish sense in life. The individual equities of the individual controversy are to be sized up against the sound

---

[f] By 1960 I estimate the percentage, nationally, at close to 50.

rule for the type of controversy, as thus worked out; when so sized up, particular "justice" takes on perspective against the background of Justice in the type of situation—even as the particular controversy brings the background into touch with earth.[7]

"Judicial review" takes on in this approach a wholly different light. For there is no smugness in the grand style; its daily criterion of sound work is sought outside the legal system proper. What the legal system does is to provide materials which have behind them cumulated experience easy otherwise to overlook, and which also assure adequate steadiness in movement; and the *well-built* portions of the received legal system give guidance in the lines and manner of sound movement. But, again, the test remains living reason, explicit; and whether a reason is living must be determined from current life and from without. "Reasonableness" thus comes into its own *as a part* of "regularity," with judges' minds open to other persons' views on what may be the "reasonable." There is room, plenty room, still, for a decision of Unconstitutionality, but the review of statutes which becomes typical is a review not to strike down, but to discover an intelligent, intelligible purpose, to accept that purpose as a fresh line of policy, to modify not it to fit past law, but past law to take advantage of it—and then to implement it. Cardozo speaks somewhere of "informing a statute with a principle"; this is what he means. Meanwhile, as is the essence of sound case-law, the grand manner proceeds consciously and daily with its judicial review of *past judicial decision:* the on-going *better* shaping of rule and principle, in the light of each further experience.

One aspect of the intellectual process is peculiar. The steady search for "principle" is a search for simplification, for unities on a widening scale. The growing recognition, however, that princi-

[7] What makes steady innovation on the old rules, at a rather rapid rate, fit today with the *recognized* leeways afforded by the system, is that those leeways grow much greater as need grows greater. The classic example is Mansfield's adjustment of a dominantly feudal body of law to commercial conditions which had been pressing for a century before he mounted the bench. Similarly, today, we have a basic stock of rules and concepts which reflect our pre-industrial economy and which from 1880 to 1910 lagged in rate of remodelling far behind the industrial remodelling of our society, and lagged again (though less) even through the '20's and the '30's. Material readjustment has thus become a *daily* problem, as it had for Mansfield in commercial cases. This is doubly true because the present needed lines of readjustment run not to *substitution* of new rules, so much as to *specialization*. A classic example, already pretty well worked out, is the differentiation out of new rules on suretyship to deal with the professional surety, without too much disturbing the protection rules once built to save the Antonio who was helping out his friend.

ples are guiding lines, not premises for fixed deduction, that they must operate always not as flat "givens," but in terms of the persuasive power of their underlying reasons; this keeps the material live and flexible even while heaped-up particularism is yielding to some manageable compassability.

From all of this—which *describes,* let me repeat, the preponderant and increasing actual ways of our fifty-one highest appellate courts today—there emerge as it seems to me a number of exciting conclusions.

First, that serious opposition of Law and felt Justice is not only unfortunate, but is in good part unnecessary, in our legal system, granted the prevalence of a sound case-law *style.*

Second, (as one studies the breaking in of new judges) that at least on an appellate bench, the style of the court is transmissible and is largely transmitted; and that a sound prevailing style amazingly lifts the average level of output.[8]

Third, that a judicial opinion has a solid function of satisfying and persuading not only the bar, but the general public; and that it is for the health of courts, of law, and of public that it should do so. That well-built law, even in these days, does not require to be too far remote from the law-consumer to be felt as warm, and friendly, as Right. If the yearning for this were not powerful, and if a confidence that somehow it would happen did not lie deep, it is ununderstandable that our courts and judges could have maintained their standing despite forty years of the life-remote "formal" style. The American quarrel with life-remote decision has never been with the court as such, nor with the job of the court as such. It has always been turned upon particular jobs thought to be ill-done, or upon particular officers thought to be doing the job improperly. Only particular non-typical queer persons or groups have fulminated against the job, or against courts as such.

A fourth conclusion is that with the quest for life-sense once explicitly taken as the guide to use of the authorities, taken as a touchstone amid the divergent doctrinal potentialities of the authorities, advocates' technicalities come under control, and advo-

---

[8] Transmissibility of *any* style is best tested by studying the degree to which the work of any particular appellate bench maintains its character as new judges come on. They "are broken in." The influence of individuals shows clearly when a transcendent judge comes on and stays on: thus Cardozo on the New York Court of Appeals. Yet the degree to which the Cardozo *manner of* judging and opinion-shaping still marks that same court's daily work again evidences transmissibility—especially of a manner which can be felt to fit current need.

cates on each side are brought back to their function as "officers of the court," aiding the court to find and phrase the rules needed by all of us. On two sides, surely, and in divergent directions; but with the authorities marshalled on each side in support of one persuasive view of sense in life, as well as one view technically tenable in law.

Lastly, that if appellate courts can make sense and talk sense for people, serving as the residual general horse-sense organs of the people in any and in every type of matter, then such courts are a most appropriate body of review to determine whether other governmental agencies, (torn between politics, favoritism, enthusiasm, specialized expertness, woodenness, lopsidedness, ambition and vision) can give persuasive reasons that what they do is both reasonable in aim and reasonably regular in method. On the aims, an appellate court operating under the grand style of the common law tradition can speak as well as any other person and a deal better than most, subject always to the due voice of the electorate at the polls. On the methods, I submit that such an appellate court is *the* appropriate organ. For if there is one place where both citizenry and officials operating in a "democracy" need policing by their better moments for their more excited moments, it is on the aspects of refreshment and of reasonable regularity in method, discussed above.

I want to insist on this last point. People who distrust courts' views of the reasonable, as brought to bear on "expert" specialists' judgment, are caught in the image of the formal-minded judgments of formal-minded courts in days largely past and rapidly disappearing. But the judge who, in the grand style, has learned to *use* other officials' judgments about what is reasonable becomes a vitally needed policing officer to force the welter of lopsided expert judgments into a *net* life-sense for the whole of us.

Let me note further that alteration of the going practice of the courts is only in minor part to be expected by way of the advent of new personnel "with a different outlook" on matters social. The tradition too much shapes the man. Even such giant wills as those of Butler and Brandeis would have been shaken and reshaped by that tradition, had not each rooted firm in his own version of the tradition itself. What makes the advent of men "of different outlook" important today is that their advent can speed the *exclusive* dominance of the grander aspect of the tradition, so as to cut from under a future Butler the wherewithal to arm his point of view with his craft-conscience.

THE GRAND TRADITION, AND "DEMOCRACY"

On the side of refreshment of policy, the grand tradition of the common law offers its emphasis on continuity and articulateness, but coupled with its ongoing judicial review of prior judicial decision, and with its acceptance and development of statutory or administrative policies declared by other organs. Note the implications on the side of leadership-suffrage: The on-going review, the on-going acceptance and implementation of policies declared by others, lie both in the hands of specialists: on the side of method and reasonable regularity, these are *the* experts; on the side of content and substance, they are experts in that necessary but difficult task of forming judgment without single-phase expertness, but in terms of a Whole, *seen whole.* Yet under that method of opinion-writing which was Shaw's ideal felt as duty when he assumed office in 1831, they are experts who account to the public, to the general law-consumer, first, openly; second, fully; third, week by week and in detail; fourth, always after the event; fifth, not for wisdom merely, but also for reasonable consistency with the *order* of which they are a part: so that the essential bases of their action are both reasonably foreknowable and reasonably forefeelable. As human events go, modern appellate judicial decision is already among the more predictable, for anyone who has eyes to see the manner of the work; and this despite the fact that it will take another few generations of work in the grand manner before the technical legal material and the technical legal processes can be brought into that approach to simplicity of which both they and their problems are capable.

Now, in lump, these features are both impossible and improper to introduce unmodified into other phases of government; yet each has a lesson for such other phases. But the first lesson lies in the effective recapture of the grand manner itself. That recapture was not planned; against it stood the whole spinning weight of the ingrained formal style. Yet the full recapture is far along, the striking symptom being the capitulation of the Supreme Court of the United States, since 1937 or so, to the manner of decision which had been flooding up in the State supreme courts for two decades before. Hence I reason that craft-tradition of other office can grow, and can even be completely recast in effective manner, without the incidence of organized conscious effort. I reason further that if studied as such, if made the subject of skilled and conscious inculcation, such traditions can be grown and can be recast with considerable speed. In various of the governmental agencies we have had observable traditions, traditions properly designated as institutionalized craft-traditions, although of radically divergent character. Compare State; the Army (officer corps); the technical services (e.g. forestry); Post Office (contrast the carriers with the minor postmasterships).[g] What State and the Army require to learn from the grander common law tradition is that reasons need giving, not too infrequently, and that they need to be life-reasons, and that they need to be made understandable to a law- (and service-) consuming public. That the leadership phase of "democracy" is coupled with the suffrage phase, and that it is not enough to be expert, or even to be expert and correct. *"Responsibility" covers not only honor, but on-going accounting for audit.* What some phases of Post Office or of Veterans need to learn is a tradition of craftsmanship in performance. I see there and in other agencies defective craft-tradition as a problem primarily of individual men. It is individual leaders, and only such, who can pick up the job of organizing the speedy building of right craft-tradition where it is as yet absent. Yet individual leaders, or small groups, can do just that. Long history is not a pre-condition to a craft-tradition within an organization. Within less than a decade, for instance, the T.V.A. has worked out a set of perceptible craft-attitudes, and craft-ways clear enough and sharp enough to be used for the testing of personnel, communicable enough to be used to shape new men fast. In vastly less time, along quite different lines, Arnold's office did much the same. An extra touch or two of conscious study and conscious articulation can turn such a line of craft-building into the type of fly-wheel which, as in State and Army, can become materially resistant to shifts in top-place authority.

Note first, however, that it is not enough to simply have good men on the job, high or low. For individual men who merely organize a job without consciously institutionalizing the ways and ideals of the job as a craft with pride and standards, such men when they die or leave find writ in water their mark upon the further doing of the job—unless they happen in such lasting succession that a craft-tradition "grows." So far, government can learn from the organization of lasting business enterprise, as also from

---

[g] So far as my observation goes, Post Office has since this writing lost rather than gained in morale and craft-tradition; and so forestry under Eisenhower. Which is not to the point of either need or possibility, but to that of the need for patience. The general shift from Lincoln's time to the present is unmistakable.

the effect of single individuals on the style of particular appellate courts: say Cardozo on the New York Court of Appeals.

The second matter to note deals not with swift building of a craft-tradition, but with the manner of the tradition to be built. In contrast to the British-government manner or style of State— secret, self-sufficient in judgment and standard, accounting neither to the individual for particular decision nor to the public for general policy—Arnold's pattern worked in the finer common law terms: open policy declared and known in advance,[9] not only controlling subordinates, not only giving persons affected the wherewithal to argue their positions, but also affording open internal and external general check-up against improper secret grounds of movement and against partiality or discrimination. In contrast to the blinder Army style,[10] the T.V.A. for decades drove consciously and persistently in terms of enlisting, presupposing, even requiring, initiative, co-operation, responsibility from and among the "governed"—be they employees or consumers of service. What is needed here, and what is on the way although incipient only, is inter-communication and cross-study among the agencies and services which have thus begun sound, clear craft-building. For, patently, "governing" is the basic craft; and, patently, the finer common law manner, which is the finer "democratic" manner, is a basic pattern from which variants are buildable. Both T.V.A. and Arnold sought deliberately the "whole" view, as does the common law. But Arnold could have learnt from T.V.A., and T.V.A. could have learnt from Arnold; the two roads in are independent and converge, but never joined. I suggest that awareness of *the* problem, plus awareness of the existence of one highly suggestive model, may impend in the immediate offing as a factor speeding, deepening, and widening the range of the process, anywhere.

But the third thing to note is that such conscious craft-building and reference in so doing to the grand manner of the common law —that these are capable of study, adaptation, introduction, establishment single agency by single agency, single leader or group by single leader or group, no one dependent on another's effort. *One* man with tact, vision, and vigor can pick up such a job and get it done. This means procedure which is practicable in smaller

---

[9] And subject to change *with* notice, as new experience may require.

[10] That Army knows a better pattern, however submerged it may be, see a paper in *Harper's* about November, 1941, on discipline and morale, which I have not had opportunity to relocate.

units, where inertia is conquerable. And as one turns to observation of the law-work (which is key-work) in agency after agency through the last decade, one becomes persuaded that enough of men with the requisite energy and vision can be—have been [once, and have been again]—mustered, to make a material dent upon our general tradition of government, if only they will turn loose the possibilities of their positions. To me, the signs are also that awareness is looking up, if only by virtue of the attacks upon administrative agencies at large. Indeed, as Michael points out, where the judicial tradition of opinion-writing has been available as an easy bridge, one already finds the grand style rather well developed among administrative agencies. But how far the whole progress may be bogged by the flux of the war effort, or of war preparation, so largely in the hands of men lacking either common law or "democratic" training or ideals for doing—that is a problem.

Yet I suggest that such doing, and a craft-tradition of such doing by government officers, cut to the heart. To me, Lincoln's fear seems no longer to hold, that the great test of our institutions is to lie in the clamor for office, office being viewed as a way of living without work. To me, an *enough* of viewing office as a job to *do* appears abroad in the land to give some hope that such a way of viewing office can slowly be made dominant. It is, however, such an unorganized, an uninstitutionalized "enough," it leans still so heavily on individual ideals, it still so lacks the toughness, the man-shaping and man-sustaining power of the conscious craft-tradition as to leave open whether it can survive the current vortex. And craft-tradition, where present, is still frequently heavily of the wooden style, lacking on-going test against life-reason, or of the secret style, lacking accounting and accountability. Still, there is hope, there is almost promise.

Let me avoid one angle of easy misunderstanding. When I speak of "accounting" I do not refer to accounting to every citizen. This is a world of specialization; no citizen has time or knowledge to follow the work of every governmental agency, any more than he has to follow the daily work of the courts. But the *interested* citizen —of whom they are always many—*he* should be able to find out both the what and a why which he can understand; a why which, if it be an insufficient why, he can then make others understand. That, despite all accompanying distortions, is thus far our best machinery of getting issues out before the citizenry at large—and indeed for making issues unnecessary to get out. I fully understand that no common law grand *manner* can do away with issues of substance. The N.L.R.B. has been under attack far less because of its manner than because of the what of its doing, and of its mandate; and manner has been a peg to hang the attack on. Yet the point remains. Sound manner not only corrects substance, within, and lessens unnecessary grievance and misunderstanding; it also clarifies issues of substance, and makes them both easier to understand and harder to red-herring. And accessibility to the citizen of some general understanding is both a bulwark and a focal machinery of "democratic" law and government.

Indeed the matter goes further. Though the clamor for office as a way to living without work is no longer the pressing danger, it has been displaced by clamor for another way of living without work, a greater peril: the clamor to have the government simply do it for you. I believe it sociologically impossible under any régime at all comparable to ours to build into the present and the next generation by education, by direct publicity, or by the mere processes of growing-up a working counter-attitude to this; it could indeed be largely done by adequate handling of a citizen-army, but I see no signs that it will. But I submit that a craft-minded, craft-proud corps of administrative personnel, announcing policies in advance, and both acting and feeling need to give reasons— life-reasons—in the grander manner of the common law, offer a leverage both upon service-consumers and upon legislators which holds workable possibility of meeting and countering the danger. Such a pattern of personnel serves as a model of responsibility not only within but without. It stirs confidence, and pride, and a different attitude toward "the" government at large, in any citizen who meets with it, anywhere. A citizen's *general* attitude toward "government" builds importantly in terms of the contacts he has firsthand or has on close hearsay with particular government officers. Let these be reasonable, and give intelligible reasons, be firm, and insist on the citizen's reasonable participation where he has the wherewithal to participate, and the citizen's responsible "democratic" attitude is built. Government-as-an-enemy and government-as-a-hand-out do not comport with the rising level of police personnel, or of trial examiner—or of any official. And it is here, of course, that the "style" of the new army becomes critical for post-war. "Every man trained and eager to take over at need" spells healthy post-war "democracy." "The old army game" does not.

Contrariwise, "distribution downward," without rise in responsibility to meet it, is the bread and circus picture; and the downward pressure even of open taxation need yield nothing but the gutting of necessary services. "Distribution of opportunity downward," in turn, needs the training and steadying power of craft-tradition to raise and equip the new men in their work. "Expertness" in secret action denies accounting; yet leadership is given by no mass. From one end to the other of the problems of democracy, I thus submit that the grander manner of the common law tradition offers a pattern and a method for effective work, plus a demonstration that even under adverse conditions such patterns and methods can be made to spread on an effective mass or "democratic" scale, and to take hold, on an effective mass or "democratic" scale, of the relevant citizen consumer and participant.

{ 13 }

THE CRAFTS OF LAW RE-VALUED [a] [*]

Our order establishes itself at your school of law at a time and in an atmosphere which offer to men of the law more of challenge than of comfort. With the fate of the nation in the balance there is call for business men and call for medical men and call for men of the physical sciences. There is a call for architects and engineers and for the clergy. There is little call for lawyers. I find no pervading appreciation that law-skills can be mobilized to serve. I find no competitive demand in the armed services for law-trained men. I find no fear among civilians that if the law men go or are drafted the community must settle down to suffer for the lack of them.

I should suppose this to be a matter peculiarly apt for meditation at a gathering of men chosen from the head of the successive classes and whom one hopes to see rise to the head of the profession. For the head is the place in which men learn to look for vision and wisdom, co-ordination and balance, above all for rational and well-advised direction of affairs. And I should suppose that to any man who had taken thought about law and the men of law and their place in our society it must have come shattering to find his profession substantially ignored when other men gather themselves to settle down to deeper business and higher business than merely living. I should suppose that in our quiet moments we had prided ourselves on embodying as does no other craft of modern life the ancient American tradition of versatility, of ability

[a] From 15 ROCKY MT. L. REV. 1 (1942).

[*] Address delivered at the Installation Banquet of the University of Colorado Chapter of the Order of the Coif, held at the University Club in Denver, Colorado, on July 10, 1942.

at short notice to turn to any job and do it well. I should suppose that in our soberer moments we had taken pride and felt a surge of responsibility as we remembered that our work, alone among all lines of work, represented man's full effort at ordered, balanced co-ordination of People, State, and Nation, serving not parts or interests only, but the whole—not merely regulating or repressing, but gathering, guiding, directing the whole work of the whole national team. I should suppose that as we had watched men of law who were skilled men of law at work with men of any other line or craft, we had found our memories crowding with the instances in which grasp of the problem, wide-ranging grasp, and grasp of the men, sure-fingered grasp, and shrewd, practical invention of ways out or through or under had proved to be the work of the law-man in the group. You see it wherever a business outfit has good general counsel: one other man—be it the president, or the best vice-president, or the general manager—one other man out of the whole gang, *and* the general counsel, these are the leaders. You see it when a lawyer takes over the presidency of a University—that job which stretches even a good lawyer's versatility to the snapping point. You see it in Washington, where the general counsel of an administrative organization, if he is worth his salt *as a lawyer,* becomes a hub or the hub of policy and administration, where the better lawyers have been managing to combine so much order with forward-looking movement that you neither hear of their work nor have a chance to object to it as you struggle with the performances of men who are not themselves lawyers, and whose counsel do not happen to be good lawyers. If you, like me, have seen these things and known these things and had your quiet pride in them, it must have come shattering to you to find that we seem to be the only ones to whom an inkling of these things has trickled—to find that in the eyes of laymen high and low, military and civilian, our skills appear as badly worn spare tires, neither appealing nor reliable, and suited in the national need chiefly for the scrap-pile, to be remade into a makeshift something else. Nor do I find deep-throated crying for our vision.

Shock or no shock, the matter calls for thought from the head men of law-classes and of the rising bar.

I suggest to you that we can settle on at least two reasons why men of the law are invited into cold storage or the scrap heap when their country needs them most. I suggest to you first that we have confused ourselves, and so have confused the laymen, about the essence of our craftsmanship. We have fooled ourselves, we

have fooled our law professors, we have fooled the whole bewildered public, into the idea that the essence of our craft lies in
our knowledge of the law. And knowledge of the law we do have,
and we do need, but such knowledge is but the precondition of
our work. Yet the idea that the essence lies in this peculiar knowledge of the law, that idea gives us a sort of standing, the standing
of monopolists in a secret lore; and it may be we have discovered
that the priests of any black art can make the uninitiate pay well
for mystic service.

But the idea comes at a price. It comes at a price, for instance,
of turning out of law school prospective lawyers who know nothing
but the law, and have no simplest smattering of how to *lawyer*.
It comes indeed at a price of blinding our own eyes to our own
daily job, so that in the very process of counselling or of briefing
a case we study chiefly *what* courts have decided, and forget *how*
they go about deciding cases, and *how* they use the authorities
with which they work, and how and why those authorities themselves came into existence. The horrible mark of this among the
best of us was the desolate wail of the bar from coast to coast when
the Supreme Court finally got around to making some sense out
of the tax decisions. That caught the nation's leading lawyers
short, like lambs, in Wall Street. Yet the inevitability of it had been
written on the face of our economy for ten prior years: the question
was only just when, just how, the change would come. Had lawyers
consciously been viewing their work as a *craft of doing and getting
things done with* the law, instead of as a mere monopoly of knowledge of the law, those lawyers would simultaneously have been
viewing appellate judging as another, and a different, as being the
key-craft of law; they would have been studying that key-craft and
its methods, as well as its particular results; they would have been
ready. Let me say it again: the essence of our craftsmanship lies in
skills, and in wisdoms; in practical, effective, persuasive, inventive
skills for getting things done, any kind of thing in any field; in
wisdom and judgment in selecting the things to get done; in skills
for moving men into desired action, any kind of man, in any field;
and then in skills for *regularizing* the results, for building into
controlled large-scale action such doing of things and such moving
of men. Our game is essentially the game of planning and organizing management (not of running it), except that we concentrate on the areas of conflict, tension, friction, trouble, doubt—and
in those areas we have the skills for working out results. We are
the trouble-shooters. We find the way out and set up the method

of the way, and get men persuaded to accept it, and persuaded to pick up the operation. That is the essence of our craft.

But we do not say this, even to ourselves. Why not? Does it seem too plain, too ordinary, too much like what needs no license via bar examination? I do not know. What I do know is that *because* we do not say it to ourselves we do not study our own essence as we need to, we do not train every lawyer in it, we do not have and cannot yet phrase or apply standards of minimum competence in it, we do not require entrants to qualify in it, we learn it, each one of us, only by slow unreckonable accident, happenstance, or inborn artistry. What I do know further is that because we do not say it to ourselves we do not say it to others, and others even when they meet it in one of us, think it not a lawyer's peculiar craft, learned by lawyering, but think it an accidental human attribute of some particular lawyer. Does the Colorado Campus know, does the State know, that President Stearns may have been born with vision, or may have sucked it in from wherever, but that save for the skills in men and measures which he gathered as a lawyer and by lawyering, his policies would have collapsed, instead of building. *He* knows it. But it is not as a lawyer, it is as a university president, that he has been called into the war effort to help work things out. *He* knows that. It is infinitely less as a president than as a lawyer that he is proceeding to effect his contribution. And *he* knows that, too. *They* don't. They never will know it, nor will nor can they draw the consequence, until such men as you first know it, then become articulate about it, then act on it. Dean King and your faculty are ahead of you, on that, although it is your own finer craft-skills which they must turn to studying, to *implement* their goal of making law school work not alone at knowledge of the law, but also at the craftsmanship that is a lawyer's pride.

That is one reason why our fellow-Americans see us as useless, save as rear rank privates: they do not even know what our craft is, they do not dream of the value of the skilled law trouble-shooter in the welter of a national reorganization. There is another reason. It is a tender one. It rests upon a thing too often forgotten even by men foremost in remembering the first. For during the bouncing years of the exploitation of a Continent there seemed resources enough to take care of everybody, a boundless range of jobs to do, money to coin, and time so fleeting—and lawyers drifted like the rest along the current of swift opportunity. The then slant of thought which is now a tradition of thought is a client-wise, interest-wise, specialized, and special slant of thought. Most of us still hold pretty firm to the old idea that law should serve right and justice, and that right and justice demand to be viewed against the picture of a whole going Nation. But most of us, specialized and special, in continuing contact with particular clients or with clients of a particular class or range of interest, acquire views of right and justice, and so of the interest of the Whole, which can hardly be said to rest on rounded observation, or on rounded thinking.

Let me remind you that this is something of a modern phenomenon. A century ago the bar, even its leaders, enjoyed relatively little specialization. Sectional its thinking was, as were also its views of policy; but community by community, lawyers drew business from every economic level, every line of business, every type of background, every type of person. Right and justice, as they saw it, had a rounded basis, it had a rooting in the felt interest of a Whole. The easy place to see the mark of that is in the opinions of the time—Gibson, Shaw, Ruffin, Doe, Cowen, and on down the list. Technically clean work, admirably clean: but always with a conscious eye to need, to the need of the *whole* community, to *reason,* tested by the horsesense of current fact and life, to justice as measured by that kind of reason. Now this sense that law-work is not right work unless it makes sense for the whole as a wise man would see the whole—this sense that law is not good law if it does not make sense—this sense I do not find strong today among the practicing profession. Its absence is unhealthy in any law; its absence is vicious in a democracy; its absence is perilous in a democracy at war. For that great inarticulate welter pulling this way and that way which we call "the people," the folk of that welter have a deep and sure feeling about what law is for. It is for right, and it is for justice, and it is for the whole and not for any single part or party. When law is not so, something is wrong. When the work of law is not so, something is wrong. And whereas laws, many laws, may be very wrong indeed, The Law is right (and there again "The people" have a deep truth by the tail). This means, in people's eyes, that The Law must have been corrupted or abused or intricately tangled into folly by the lawyers. No wonder our skills are not perceived; they are thought bad. No wonder our skills, even where perceived, are in no great demand to win the war; men do not trust our *vision,* in their use. Technique without ideals is a menace: and that, all men know, and laymen fear. The other half of the same truth which we could teach them, reads:

Ideals without technique are a mess. But to show what is not a mess, but a salvation, one needs to put technique to work upon ideals, and with vision.

I have no belief in empty preaching. I have a very live appreciation of the problems known as rent and baby's shoes. I have no faith whatever in the accomplishment for national welfare of a lawyer who practices death by starvation, instead of practicing law. I know that clients must be got, and must be served. But the cold fact is that success in practice by way of what I may sum up as bigoted legalism has been on its way out for close to twenty years. It is seventeen years since the present Chief Justice made the same point, as a point already clear. I do not mean that a good man, with luck, cannot still achieve a handsome competence along that old road, nor do I mean that such a possibility will shortly disappear —for some. I mean that it is taking better and better men, and taking more and more luck, even for those, to work that out. I mean that one major portion of "the economic plight of the bar" of which so much is heard lies in the fact that *most* of the bar are still trying to practice law along the lines of a bigoted legalism whose banners were wavering by 1920, and, since, have been in full retreat.

Look at the facts—the cold ones. Before a jury you must make the jury believe your client *right*. Try facts before a court, and three times out of four or three and a half, you need the same. *Good* lawyers before an appellate court today spend over presentation of the facts, to persuade indirectly of the justice of their cause, an effort which exceeds the effort spent upon the marshalling of authorities. Mere legalistic correctness, when *unaccompanied* by good sense, travels today a road as tough as that travelled by mere appeal for justice, when unaccompanied by shrewd marshalling of authorities. Or take counselling. Good counsellors counsel today no longer for the maximum blood squeezage. They have discovered that that kind of counsel or of document bites back. It offends any customer who may read it. It offends a court. And a court can find ways through or under any language you can write. *Lasting relations* are built on a view of the client and the other party as in some sort a working team, though of course one seeks for his client a somewhat extra handsome slicing of the cake. Nowhere is this clearer than in the utter change that has in ten years come over the *style* of counselling in the labor field; the bitter-ender lawyer loses case and client. The interesting thing is that the lesson there is as old as the lawyers' proverb from the rounded days: the slogan went then that one ought to know his adversary's case well enough to win it. Applied today, to counselling, that means well enough to gather in the bulk of what your client really needs, on the basis of the other party's major premises, and with a result that is a working result, a reasonable mutual satisfaction.

Indeed, as one turns to any phase of that vast opening modern line of practice, of service and of earning a living, which has to do with governmental agencies, a lawyer meets not only professional opportunity, but the very lines of work the whole profession has been needing in order to recapture its vision of the Whole. Each agency, well-devised or poorly devised, well-manned or ill-manned, stands for an effort to deal with *some* aspect of a National need, a need of the whole which in the rush of things has gotten overlooked or shoved aside. To deal with any of the agencies, a lawyer must understand that adversary's case. See that case, in terms of what it has of reason and of sense, and then use a lawyer's ingenuity in invention and persuasion, and you find few good administrators who cannot follow any decent way of working out your client's basic need. And that takes you to the heart of the matter: for it is when an unreasonable administrator will not listen to *that* kind of argument that you can win your case in court, upon review.

Vision and sense for the Whole, and skills in finding ways, smoothing friction, handling men in *any* situation, with speed, with sureness: these mark our best. These things the country needs, and does not know good lawyers have. Indeed, even as we look upon our best, and know them, we do not ourselves see that they have merely found the way back to what all along has been the true heart of our craft. Our appellate courts have for two decades been piling up work and a tradition of work along these lines. Yet most of us, instead of welcoming that as boon and glory, have still shaken our heads, ploughed on along the dying lines of legalism, lost cases that we ought to have been winning. I say again, if *we* do not awake fully to what our craft is, if we do not make it both vocal and a living, reckonable thing, how may we expect our lay fellow-Americans in troubled crisis to know these services which they need, which we can give?

{ 14 }

THE MODERN APPROACH TO COUNSELLING
AND ADVOCACY—
ESPECIALLY IN COMMERCIAL TRANSACTIONS [a] [*]

"The law" of commercial transactions divides for the practicing lawyer into three rough groupings of material which he must view and use in sharply distinct ways and which require to be discussed separately. I propose to discuss certain most significant recent developments in these three groupings of material. In order to obtain a straight-running text I have thrown various qualifications

[a] From 46 COLUM. L. REV. 167 (1946).

[*] This paper is in substance that prepared for Dean Ribble's volume, "SIGNIFICANT DEVELOPMENTS IN THE LAW DURING THE WAR YEARS," planned for the returning lawyer. It is a continuation and complement of a paper I wrote shortly after we entered the war, for stay-at-home lawyers. *The Crafts of Law Re-Valued*, 15 ROCKY MT. L. REV. 1 (1942); also in A. B. A. J., Dec. 1942.

The argument of that paper was that if lawyers would see their professional crafts for what they are: in essence, hugely resilient and versatile skills for sizing up situations wisely, and then of getting things done, skills of trouble-shooting, trouble-evasion, and forward planning—then lawyers would not be moaning about their disutility in national crisis. That, furthermore, if those were the skills they made known to laymen as being their characteristic skills, laymen would develop more appreciation for the bar—and one may add, would bring them more good work to do. In the Services and at home, the War has done what a hundred papers or books could never hope to do: the War has jolted the best of the bar into work and thought along these lines. That is a development in our professional field which overwhelms in importance any other except the need for finding ways of world government; and it provides the key-lines of thinking with which to approach the greater problem. The present paper is therefore devoted to a wider theme than "The Commercial Transaction" which was assigned me by Dean Ribble, though I have tried to keep touch with the assigned topic by way of illustration and background; commercial law is my field, and theory does well to keep its feet on the earth.

and illustrations into footnotes; I urge any reader to disregard the footnotes on a first reading, though I believe they hold value for anyone who may desire to really work with the paper.

There is first the body of rules of law which one may call counsellor's rules or rules seen from the angle of the counsellor. These have to do with the shaping of a transaction while it is still capable of being shaped, and they run in terms of the degree of safety with which one can rely on the courts to act in particular predictable fashion if this particular transaction in hand should come to be presented to them.

For the counsellor has found that there are some solid, settled, clear rules on which he can build; they are safe, they are bedrock. But there are not as many of them as one might wish. Thus if a promise is to be supported (in the absence of a special statute such as the Pennsylvania Written Obligations Act[1] or the various recent New York statutes[2] which render consideration unnecessary in certain cases) the form of an explicit written bargain is the one really safe form of consideration, and the agreed return for the promise should be substantial; nothing less is *safe*. No "rule" that "the adequacy of consideration will not be inquired into by the courts" is solid counsellor's law, nor is a rule about "*any* bargained-for detriment" etc.[3]; nor, for the promisee's counsellor, is any "rule" of promissory estoppel a thing to be relied on (however strong the "trend" toward recognizing promissory estoppel may be) because until the reliance is clearly *sufficient* the outcome must remain uncertain, and a client has no business to be advised to change his position heavily to his prejudice before his legal rights

---

[1] PA. STAT. ANN. (Purdon, 1930) tit. 33, § 6.

[2] See N. Y. DEBTOR AND CREDITOR LAW § 243; N. Y. PERS. PROP. LAW § 33(2); N. Y. REAL PROP. LAW § 279; Hays, *Formal Contracts and Consideration: A Legislative Program*, 41 COLUM. L. REV. 849 (1941).

[3] The careful counsellor has noted long ago that the cases where merely nominal or technical consideration is held to support a promise lump in the non-business field and in situations where the real reason and drive for making the promise enforceable lies in the reasonableness of supporting Aunt Molly's promised benefaction to poor Susan, or to the Pottsville Hospital. Among the business cases, guaranties make out comfortably with as small a consideration as a binding extension of time, if that is clearly the bargained-for price of the intended guaranty; real estate brokerage agreements (especially when put in the form of binding options to the realtor) show signs (which I do not trust as permanencies) of winning irrevocability on the basis of almost nominal consideration; and pension plans relied on by employees over the years can yield contractual rights in the teeth of efforts to phrase them as utterly revocable gratuities. But in neither the brokerage nor the pension situation have the rules yet approached bedrock status; they represent still only real hazards to the promisor, rather than any basis for sound reliance by the promisee.

have been made safe.[4] On the other hand, from the angle of the promisor's counsellor, rules like those on promissory estoppel or "the law's" lack of interest in adequacy of consideration represent a hazard, a risk to be watched and avoided, because a court *may* bring them into application. Rules of law from a counsellor's angle therefore set themselves up according to the degree of solidity and reliability which they offer as foundation and tools for building, or else according to the nature and degree of the danger which they offer of producing an upset or other undesired result.

The second grouping of material is the body of rules of law seen from the angle not of a counsellor to whom the transaction has come early enough for him to shape the facts, but from the angle of an advocate to whom the transaction is brought only after the trouble has occurred. Bedrock law, so far as any of it is applicable, of course becomes important to such an advocate as setting the legal framework and pattern on and with the help of which he arranges the facts; in so far, the advocate views it much as does the counsellor. But that vast range of law which is not so clear or not so settled, of rules whose application is uneven, of "trends" in decision, of rules which courts commonly recite only to find a way around them if their direct application appears unfortunate[5]—that vast range is to the advocate not merely an area

---

[4] Few simple general statements of this breadth can hope to be wholly accurate. This one in the text is limited to the situation where the circumstances permit the terms to be clearly enforceable and reduced to signed writing. Sometimes circumstances do not so permit. Uncle Ezra "gives" George the fishing camp, but makes no move towards a deed; if Uncle Ezra is crotchety and the promise is unambiguously evidenced, a counsellor can properly meditate on the making of material improvements as greatly strengthening George's position, though he must explain to George that the improvements buy not a certainty but merely a good risk and then only if they cost enough labor or money to amount to something. And he will endeavor, by a tactful letter which informs of the plans, to fix the points of reliance and of Uncle's knowledge that George is about to rely. So, frequently enough, in the informal phases of business transactions. But the main point of the text remains: this is second best or third best in counselling, to be resorted to only in default of better, and only with the client's eyes open to the risks.

[5] *E.g.,* "Modification is a new contract and requires a new consideration," but "Waiver is the intentional relinquishment of a known right, and the right, once relinquished, cannot be reasserted." The second rule is a backdoor which may prove open when the first rule seems to bar the front way in. Or if an intermediary is being paid by one side and is also expecting pay from the other and makes full disclosure of these facts to both, the rules of "agency" will still leave him in trouble if he sues for his second commission, because an agent's duty is to get as much for his principal as he can, and for as little, and double agency simply *feels* self-inconsistent; the rules of "brokerage" give the intermediary a much stronger position because a broker's duty runs merely to bringing the parties together in a deal. My colleague Patterson soundly treats half of the law on

of risk, as it is to the counsellor; it is also to the advocate an area of opportunity: he may be able to win his case with the help of one or more of these available though far from wholly reliable rules. The advocate sees such rules not merely as threatening "chanciness," but also as offering chances; not chances in general and in the abstract, but chances in terms of what *he* can manage to do with them in this particular case in the particular available courts and, perhaps, against a particular known adversary. The advocate has his own single and utterly concrete case in hand; the counsellor has a concrete situation, but it is one which he must commonly view as affected by the hazard of bad advocacy in future litigation on a similar point which may result in a rule of law that can upset his transaction retroactively.

The third grouping of material for the lawyer who meets commercial transactions would appear to many not to involve "law" at all. It consists of the bodies of practical problems which present themselves for solution in counselling, and of the lines of practical technique which are being worked out for solution of those problems: it consists of the background, purposes, nature, legal techniques, of the commercial transactions themselves.

It seems to me that in the field of commercial transactions recent developments, including the effect of the war and the war years, show much less in the development of new rules of law than, first, in the spread of a new series of problems in this third area, and, second, in the spread among the more skilful lawyers of what one may think of as a professional as contrasted with a theoretical approach to the question of what the law "is," as applied to professional problems. Some of the new problems are good for the returning lawyer, or indeed for any lawyer, to meet in print, if only because working such things over is a good way to get old skills and habits of thought geared up again and oiled and working smoothly—all without risk to any client or to one's own reputation; and to that the latter portion of this paper will be devoted. But before that, there should be some discussion of this spreading, more "professional," and soundly realistic approach to what "the law is"—to what it "is" *for the practicing lawyer.* My view is clear that this approach hooks directly into and builds on any lawyer's experience during his war-work. Discussion of it should go far to make a returning lawyer realize with some com-

---

mistake, reformation, and annulment as in substance a set of backdoors into results which would be barred if one ran head-on into the more "standard" and regularly recited rules of law.

fort that the years spent in the Forces, so far from retarding him in his professional skill, have given him the possibility of bringing his professional attitudes and skills abreast of those which all but the best of lawyers who have remained simply in practice have required or will require three or four times the equivalent period to develop by what I may call "unassisted" practice. All that is needed is to bring to bear on legal work that style of analysis of the situation, that style of operational thinking, which are of the essence of work in the Services. Here is what we are up against, in terms of situation and facts and people and of how these people are organized and think and feel and act. Here, next, is what we want to get done. So, now, how do we *do* it? The same discussion should go far to make lawyers who have not been in the Services realize the degree to which sound work in law can and must build on and borrow the direct operational approach so well tested in the Services, or in engineering.

I. On Modern Counselling

Let me try to make clear what I mean by beginning in the area of counselling, and by beginning with what may look like absurdly elementary material: the parol evidence rule.

Disregarding for the moment the conflict of authority as to whether a signed writing which appears complete on its face can have oral terms added if they are such terms as might reasonably have been left out, one could make a moderately accurate "theoretical" statement of the rule in some such form as this: terms of an agreement reduced to writing and signed by both parties are not subject to variation or contradiction by evidence of any oral agreement previous to or contemporaneous with the signing. We can phrase it in terms of "oral evidence will not be admitted to vary or contradict," etc. We can open with a qualification about fraud, mistake, etc., and then go on to the rule requiring "clear and convincing evidence" of such matters. But however fully we state the qualifications, this type of statement of the rule is still no sound statement for professional guidance. For one thing, professional guidance needs to take account of *and to avoid* the conflict of view mentioned above as to whether terms can be added by oral evidence, or whether any seemingly complete document automatically takes in as a part of itself all implications or supplementations "of law" but nothing more, thus barring addition of any further terms, even though such further terms have been agreed upon. For a second and much more material thing, professional guidance is not satisfied by knowledge that the terms of the writing are exclusive without having also an indication of whether and when those terms will be "read" ("construed") by the court to mean what they are intended to mean. For a third thing, professional guidance remains inadequate until the possible out by way of alleged fraud, compulsion, or mistake has been looked over and either eliminated or minimized. Finally, an alleged subsequent modifying agreement can be as troublesome as one alleged to have been made previous to or at the same time with the writing, and the parol evidence rule does not even touch that aspect of the situation.

"Professionally," then, the "theoretical" parol evidence rule is only one piece of a broader rule about "fixing transactions by writing." For professional rules begin with a problem situation. They are about operations in that situation, they are functional, they must take account of all needed practical points of getting the job done. But the rules current in our lawbooks are not of this type, nor are they grouped in this way. So that the good counselling lawyer (faced, as men in the Services were faced, with a problem-situation to work through) sizes up his situation and his "theoretical" rules in their working aspects, and comes out with something like this:

(1) By reducing the transaction to writing, we get rid of any initial problem under the Statute of Frauds, unless "*the* consideration" is required to be expressed, in which case the form of its expression needs careful attention.[6]

(2) It will do us little good to get the terms of our agreement into a signed writing unless the terms thus written are clear. Only the unambiguous document gets the protection of the parol evidence rule. The benefits of the rule therefore depend on the same

[6] Mention of "the consideration" reminds us that in any deal which is at all complex we have the problem of lumping or allocating the consideration, and the problem of the effect of minor breaches; that these questions and those which arise under the heads of "dependent versus independent covenants" or of "severable versus essential breaches" are intimately connected with the question of "contractual regulation of the remedy"; that careful (not light or overgreedy) use of the language of conditions is commonly a more effective way of tightening up one's own rights in the event of the other party's default than is the language of promises, but that use of the language of conditions calls for special attention to the problem of waiver; and, finally, that overgreedy drafting which results in a patently lopsided document invites most courts to "construe" their way back into fairness—a point to which we shall be recurring. But a counsellor, making note of such matters as they occur to him, can come back to them after he has thought his way through this matter of getting the terms fixed in writing.

thing which is also so powerful in avoiding litigation based on cross-understandings: sound, clear drafting.

(3) Only a "complete document" gets the full protection of the parol evidence rule. So, since the authorities divide on whether a *seemingly* complete document can be added to by oral terms, and since some alleged oral terms can pretty vitally modify the net transaction without modifying any of the language of the document (as by adding a crucial warranty), we must consider a "merger clause" which states expressly that there are no other terms, express or implied, and that the transaction is limited to the terms of the document.

Before adding such a merger clause, however, we shall do well to look over the matter of trade usage. Few of us care to make deals in a commercial field without relying to some extent on trade usage. But how clear and uniform is the usage? Our technical terms (such as the description of the merchandise sold) will be read as meaning what those terms mean in the trade unless we define them differently in the document. Yet a merger clause *may* knock out some features of usage which we want in. The easiest way to handle this is to incorporate explicitly the rules or definitions of any relevant trade association, if there are any, and if we like them. If we don't do that, we face the job of choosing and phrasing our own terms on the major matters in question—a job which ought commonly to bear fruit in a standard form of contract for our client's use in transactions of the type. And in regard to that we must remember that the longer and more complex a form is which the other party just signs up, the less reliance can we place, these days, on any part of it standing up in court if it is challenged. Nothing is more striking, these days, than the courts' increasing unwillingness to enforce form-contract language as meaning what it says, on the crucial point of the case, *if the net effect of the form appears unfair in result*. It will not do to be misled by the fact that the courts go on talking as if their only office were to enforce whatever the parties have agreed, while they are in fact managing to get around the clauses on which unfair "protection" depends in the particular case.

(4) Again, only a final document, deliberately and unambiguously made the repository of the terms of the deal, gets full protection against parol evidence which would vary it by adding to it. And such a final document can wash out *prior* written agreements reached in the course of the negotiation, certainly by use of a merger clause. But it cannot wash out contemporaneous

writings, because they will be treated as all parts of a single transaction, to be read together.

(5) How then, can we make our document stand up as "final"? Its own say-so is not enough. We can get a *prima facie* position from the mere signing, but we can still be met by a claim of fraud, compulsion or mistake, a claim for instance that the other party's signature was procured by misrepresentation. The law of agency is probably our most useful resource here, plus perhaps a piece of the law of offer and acceptance. We can insert in conspicuous type, just over the place for the other party's signature, a provision that this contract (or order) includes and is subject to the provisions of this form (or the provisions on the back hereof) and a statement that the signer has read and understands those provisions, and a notice that no person (or no person other than an officer of the form-maker, or no person other than certain designated officers) has authority to alter the form or to contract or accept an order in any other manner than on and subject to the provisions of this our standard contract—or the like; or has authority to make any representations not stated hereon. We can, too, make an order form explicitly subject to acceptance at the home office, the ensuing risk of intervening revocation of the order (offer) being vastly less significant than the risk of having an over-enthusiastic representative close an unsupervised deal on terms unknown and uncontrolled. Finally (a matter curiously neglected) we can in the case of any person with whom we deal regularly send or leave a copy of our standard form for him to look over. If our form is fair, no business harm ensues; while the procedure rips to pieces most later claims of mistake or surprise.

If on the other hand the deal is single and the document hand-tailored to the deal, we need the document to be really read by the other party or by his counsel, we want an explicit statement of such reading and of his satisfaction before the signing, we want a witness or two to the reading and to that statement, and we want, when we get home, a memo of these things made by the witnesses while memory is fresh. It can all be done in casual conversation.

(6) We have now accomplished about all that can be accomplished in the elimination of "jury-risk." We have very fair hope of keeping before the court any question which may come up; and even the sending of a "mixed question of law and fact" to a jury —as, on the meaning of some term in the light of disputed trade usage—is pretty well out of the picture if we have done a decent coverage of the points in the deal which need coverage. We there-

fore recall that the way both to reduce the chances of evidence about fraud, mistake or the like being believed, and also to get a fair and reasonable construction of our document, is to make the document not only stay within the bounds of the fair and reasonable in fact, but to make it show on its face that it has so stayed within these bounds. For example, if we wish on behalf of the seller to provide that in the event of rejection or cancellation of any shipment we shall be at liberty to resell in any reasonable manner and then bill him for any net loss (regardless of whether "title has passed" at the time of rejection or cancellation), it costs only about ten extra words to give the buyer equivalent protection in the event that we, as seller, should fail to make an agreed delivery. The use of such extra words has value; it makes any court feel that this is a *decent* form, one to be construed liberally in furtherance of its plain purposes; and that effect is likely to carry over to other clauses of the form which we may be needing, such as, say, a power to suspend deliveries if the buyer is late in making payment or a power, after ten days' notice without the due payment by the buyer, to cancel unperformed portions of the contract (thus settling, our way, and without either jury-risk or risk of unfairness, the otherwise troubling problem of § 45(2) of the Uniform Sales Act).[7]

(7) Finally, we remember that the parol evidence rule protects only with reference to oral agreements alleged to be prior to or contemporaneous with the writing, whereas trumped-up claims or defenses can rest on alleged modifications made at any later time, and, certainly in the field of sales of goods, the delivery and acceptance of *any* installment is enough under the Statute of Frauds

---

[7] A clause enabling cancellation on any default in payment has been sustained, even where payment on the day was patently not material. But no counsellor has any business to expect such a clause to be sustained; it is also desperately vulnerable to "waiver" by inaction on one or two delayed payments, and it flavors the whole set of clauses with the arbitrary. A suspension clause plus a ten days' notice clause meets every legitimate need, and meets it free of either danger. The "grab-it-all" or "hog" school of drafting which is so rapidly losing caste and following was in reality a lazy school as well as a blind one: such counselling fails to build in either counsellor or client an appreciation of the long-run relations and purposes which involve mutual interests; it also leaves undone the counsellor's most useful and most satisfying job, to wit, the invention of a technique which will serve his client's need without offending or unduly disadvantaging either the other party or the wider public. Clients are indeed in business to make money, but the lawyer has as his job, also, the representation of the larger team of which any business is only a part.

When the problem is one of security there is both more reason and less danger in "grab-it" drafting, so far as it seeks mere security as contrasted with profit by forfeiture.

to let such trumped-up evidence in not only as to that installment but also the whole balance of the contract if deliverable within a year. Here is a wherewithal for completely unfixing everything we have been trying to fix, and only by occasional special statute, as now in New York,[8] can one by the agreement itself make a signed writing necessary to the modification. In some states we can partly meet this need by sealing the document, taking advantage of the old and waning rule that a sealed writing can be modified only by another writing under seal; but that is tricky business, and may turn and bite our own client in an unguarded moment when he forgets to seal a modification which he himself wants and needs. The better practice is again to have recourse to the law of agency: a clause can be inserted showing that no person other than an officer, over the officer's signature, has authority to agree to any modification. If the transaction is a hand-tailored one there is also real gain to be had from the queerly neglected, probably "unenforceable," but factually most persuasive clause which states that it is the deliberate intention of both parties, in the interest of clarity, avoidance of misunderstanding, and effective supervision of employees, to keep their relations under this agreement and also under any modification of it in written form and that each therefore agrees to confirm any modification by writing, promptly, and not to rely on or plead any modification until such a writing has been duly signed on both sides or confirmations have been duly exchanged. That leaves open of course the question of consideration for any modification which is in essence a concession on one side only; but that is not our problem here, except to remind that (as in New York) one may expect statutes (as the courts have also done half-heartedly) to be slowly opening the possibility of effective one-sided concessions, when asked and made in good faith and for sound business reason.[b]

Let me repeat that the most significant recent development on the "legal" side of commercial transactions has been the growth, the articulate growth among the better lawyers, of this type of problem-situation thinking and of operational approach to what "the law of the situation is." The particular problem chosen for illustration has, moreover, a significance that reaches beyond illustration. No single phenomenon in the commercial field is

[8] See N. Y. PERS. PROP. LAW § 33(2) [or, of course, the UNIFORM COMMERCIAL CODE, at least as to contracts for sale of goods, §§ 2-209(2), (4).]

[b] Here, too, the Code has value.

more striking than the drive to standardize transactions, to standardize them "our" way by forms which cheapen their handling,
which reduce both errors in performance and the costs of policing
performance, which, finally, cut down legal risks for "our" client.
Strong and widespread as this movement was before the war, the
war period has given it double impetus and has thereby opened
with respect to smaller businesses what long has been with respect
to larger ones a field for useful counselling and indeed for those
retainers which pay rent. I suspect one cause of this to lie in the
widespread procurement contracts: dealing as they did with complete production change-over, they forced study and meditation
with fresh eyes unblinded by routine. Involving as they did re-
negotiation, alteration and cancellation terms of drastic nature *and
all on one side,* they awakened businessmen to the possibilities of
drafting as World War I awakened the small investor to the meaning of bonds.[9] Meanwhile, in all aspects of the commercial field

[9] The fact of spread of this practice is brought home by the increasing collision
between buyer's forms and seller's forms. For twenty years that collision has been
interesting me as a theoretical possibility needing study because sure to become
an actual major problem. During these last years it has been turning up in practice
on all sides: each of the two parties to a dicker has built its own forms, and a
simple deal closed say on the phone proceeds then to be "confirmed" by the respective parties on two utterly variant forms. As counsel negotiate back and forth
to reach agreement on the final detailed terms, while the time for performance
approaches, counsel for the seller has a seeming *prima facie* advantage. He can, at
last, have the goods shipped with a covering invoice built his way. Under the
standard doctrine of offer and counteroffer this might seem to amount to a final
"counteroffer" which any acceptance of the goods must accept, regardless of any
contrary mere language used by the buyer. But this is not safe to rely on. At any
moment the courts may begin to use sense in the situation, treating the deal as
long closed, and closed finally, by the effective phone deal, in the terms then
agreed plus the general law and usage, and seeing all later efforts at imposition of
further terms by either party's confirmation or invoice as being mere efforts to
get modifications accepted. Delivery and acceptance then satisfy the Statute of
Frauds as to the original oral deal, and the courts have long been ready to disregard, at the buyer's option, an attempted imposition of conditions on a shipment
which has patently been made pursuant to a prior contract. [Under the UNIFORM
COMMERCIAL CODE the working law and practice of this situation becomes much less
tricky.]
    It will be noted that until some advance payment or some delivery and accept-
ance a deal so closed orally runs into trouble with the memorandum requirement
of the Statute of Frauds, especially where the sad, though waning, rule still prevails which requires the memo to state every term of the deal with accuracy. In
sense, any one of the successive proposed memoranda should be enough to admit
the contract to proof, as against the party who has signed it; but that is no position
for any counsellor to rely on, it is at best [, except under UNIFORM COMMERCIAL
CODE, §§2–201; and cf. 2–207,] a hope of what a court can be got to see. Here,
therefore, the seller is typically at a disadvantage, for he must commit himself

which touch security for financing, the documents have always and as of course been in the forefront, and always and as of course the situation has required to be examined as a whole. But even where it is not a question of documents, "the law" to the commercial counsellor must still be taken to be what it will do, or what he can get it to do for him: foundation, tool, or hazard.[10]

Is this inconsistent with an understanding that the essential office of the law is to govern, control, direct All-of-Us to the end of the Common Weal? Is it a denial that for the judge or for the legislator the law is not a matter of what is, but of what should be, of what officials are appointed or elected to follow and enforce, of what is to control and direct and limit officials in their action? It is not. Hand in hand with the developing appreciation on the part of the better commercial bar of what a realistic approach to "the law" can do for their work, there has been growing an appreciation of the realities of court work (see below): the courts are emerging as they should as conscious and powerful guardians of fairness, in the interests of All-of-Us; in the commercial field it has therefore ceased to be either safe or wise to do counselling or to draft papers of the old-fashioned lopsided type and then to rely

---

to action and expenditure while the buyer remains in too many jurisdictions without any obligation which the seller can rely on as enforceable. Again, though in a wholly different aspect, the value appears of preparing clauses for "our" side which are reasonable and fair. Such clauses, and such only, afford a basis for quick get-together.

[10] "If I were a court," my old chief W. W. Lancaster used to say gently but very firmly, when I had worked out what I thought a neat but novel road through a difficulty—"If I were a court, Mr. Llewellyn, you would persuade me. But I am not a court; I am counsel for a bank. Surely you can find a way which will not raise these—doubtless untenable—doubts." That did not mean that Lancaster was unaware of the need and beauty of creative counselling, of finding a good way through—though one which one might have to back by creative advocacy. What it meant was that in the particular matter in hand he felt the risk too great for the return until the possibilities of a safer road had been explored. That was judgment. It meant further that he had in mind the huge difference between uncertain law of a general character, which random chance may later put into the hands of botching counsel, without your knowledge, to upset your transaction, in a case of which you get no notice, and uncertain law when you are reasonably certain to be able to handle any litigation yourself, and so to build both record and argument as they should be built. Given the sure opportunity to back your invention, you can take extra risk to the extent of your own soundness as an advocate. But counselling out beyond bedrock remains risky, in the commercial field. It is rarely necessary. And lawyers can fool themselves as to their skill as advocates. Good advice is: before risking such a move, set up the lines of your brief, and then set up the lines of the best possible brief in opposition. If you have trouble building a good brief in opposition, consult some other good man. If you can't understand his argument, go back to invention of something better—because the court may understand it.

on literal interpretation under a principle of "Let him stand to what he signed." For the courts are not only resorting to "good faith" construction to give the agreement its intended business efficacy by freely inferring an unexpressed counter-obligation. They are going further. They are bringing the same idea of good faith and business fairness to bear to knock out arbitrary exercise of the most carefully expressed powers of cancellation, modification, and the like; or to find waiver of unreasonable clauses; or to make unreasonable exemptions themselves conditional upon reasonable efforts in good faith to perform the substance of the deal, conditional often enough upon actual and effective performance of that substance. These trends in "construction" are today clearly dominant; they are so sound that we must expect and welcome their further dominance; and the counsellor who does not take account of them in his drafting is misadvising his client and is endangering not only his reputation but his own competence. Not arbitrary exemption, but reasonable exemption (as in a "circumstances beyond our control" clause); not "protective" heaping up of powers in pure "discretion," but intelligent invention of a safe but fair way through possible difficulties, a way resting on commercial reason—these are what good counselling calls for today. And when such a way is found, the courts help. They are as helpful in interpreting and implementing *fair* clauses in *fair* contracts as they are skilful and stubborn in finding ways out of arbitrary ones.[e]

In similar fashion, both bar and bench have been developing an appreciation that until the rules of law themselves are effectively and realistically adjusted to what commerce needs immediately, and to what All-of-Us need indirectly, we are doomed to an unfortunate measure of waste in legal work, of unsatisfactory uncertainty and too frequent nonsense in result.

What has been said above shows that the whole contract-institu-

---

[e] Some bargain—"dominant" parties—issuers of travelers' checks, residence landlords, quality insurance companies, major auto manufacturers—argue the need for effective hog-drafting to protect themselves against jury-risk in cases of bad faith, fake claims, etc., insist that their own ingrained policy of customer-protection in any claims at all decent is an adequate safeguard to "the public interest," and that reservation of full discretion is necessary to their own safety. They also argue that hog-clauses tend to scare off most prospective or possible litigation. ("Did I sign *that?*") My own view is clear that (1) the business soundness of these arguments is limited to relatively few lines of relatively large and few clients; (2) that the legal tenability of hog-drafting is on the rapid wane—strikingly since 1950; and (3) that the effectiveness of the "scare-off" technique is also in material decline.

tion is in rapid process of remaking. Simpler, clearer, and better
adjusted rules, built to make sense and to protect good faith, make
for more foreseeable and more satisfactory results both in court
and out. It is therefore no accident that the developments in the
Bar's realistic understanding of their job have been paralleled by
the now pending work on a Uniform Commercial Code, in preparation by the Conference on Uniform State Laws jointly with the
American Law Institute—an overhauling, modernization, and
simplification of the older Uniform Commercial Acts, ironing out
discrepancies, filling gaps, meeting new needs, and supplied with
an official set of comments on purpose and application which will
draw the material together for immediate usability. The commercial lawyer should keep his eye on this Code [even if he is
practicing in a State which has not yet adopted it.]

II. On Modern Appellate Advocacy

The approach to advocacy which has been gaining ground so
rapidly these past years among the more skilful bar reaches of
course far beyond commercial transactions. It applies to any advocacy in court. But it has peculiar application to this commercial
field of law in which the rules and concepts and their application
are being forced by change of conditions (and by change in the
courts' perception of their office and function) into results that
depart from the older patterns. The advocates have worked out
their approach by trial, error, case by case insight into the needs
of their causes and into the general art of effective persuasion. It
has been a practical learning. It has been a learning appropriate
for discussion at this time because its spread is in a real sense a
war product. When a war is one which challenges the very bases
of your legal system, you cannot in comfort or in intellectual
honesty just go on doing what you have been doing; you have to
give yourself a fresh look at what it is all about and what it is
all for; and you do. And in any line of work, technical or professional, a hard fresh look at what it is all about and for is likely
to lead to sudden insight into more effective methods of operation.

Yet the change in the methods of the better advocates is not as
clear and conscious as that among the better counsellors. This is
because, as has been noted, the advocates have in the main done
their learning by trial and error, by "feel" rather than by con-

sidered theory.[11] They have not in the main become conscious of what it is which their methods of advocacy have been adjusting to: to wit, to a sharp change in the work and thought of our appellate courts which has been marked increasingly over now three decades.

Thus in presenting the better advocates' realistic, operational approach, one does better (as in any operational approach) by describing first the situation which the advocate is up against. His task is to persuade the court to his view of the law and of the facts of his case. What he is up against is therefore the court and *its* way of doing *its* work, *its* way of seeing the law and the facts of *any* case. The new development in this picture is not so much that the courts' ways have changed greatly in these war years as that the best advocates are beginning to realize more accurately (though often still dimly) what the courts' ways are. It is not, again, that the best advocates' best ways of work have changed greatly, but that those best ways are now becoming conscious techniques, and so available for more consistent use, available also to any man within the range of his own powers, no longer limited to the odd gifted few who are "born" artists in the craft and who then come to have "sufficient experience."

The realistic or operational approach to advocacy rests on facts like these (and they are carefully tested facts):[12]

[11] The reason is in good part that once the advocate sinks himself in his cause, he has tended to lose sight of the whole picture, to see it from his own side only. The counsellor, in figuring chances and safety-factors, has to reckon in more dispassionate terms: what can happen if, on the test case, the job of presentation is botched?

[12] Since I am here reporting conclusions from my own investigations, and since those investigations have purported to move along such scientific lines as method and material have afforded, I want to state three caveats or buttressings:

(a) As to conclusions, I find them to hold equally when I as a person violently disagree with the decision reached. The ground of difference proves to be rather regularly that the court's view of sense, decency and justice differs from mine, or else that the court has not seen doctrinal possibilities which I think I see. Mostly, when I can get hold of the briefs, I discover a failure of counsel on the side which I prefer to have done a sound advocate's job, as against a much better job on the other side.

(b) The development of the ideas presented began in studies which held the "situation" relatively constant, the courts varying.

(c) It proceeded into studies of the day-to-day work of particular courts, by page-to-page reading of reports, the "situation" varying, with the court held relatively constant. This procedure has thus far been extended to studies of daily work in six [later extended to fifteen] State supreme courts, which all show the general features here described despite striking and in each court characteristic peculiar lines of method and tradition.

(1) While the courts have and know a duty to the Law, their office forces on them also, and they have and know and labor to live up to, a duty to Justice, to decency and fairness of result.

(2) Despite this felt duty to Justice, it is also their office to stay within the Law as they seek for Justice; and they do so stay within the Law. But the range of *leeway* which our case-law system offers not only in *application* of the Law but also in its *readjustment* is much greater than most lawyers let themselves realize. And the fact that a case-law court's duty to its case-law system is (and always has been) a duty to take advantage of that leeway to further Justice and to improve the Law—that is a thing that the schooling of our lawyers has been slow to make adequately clear.

(3) Justice is a thing easier to feel than to think about. The conscious thought of courts runs rather in terms of "What is fair in this type of situation," or "What is good sense and decent in this type of situation"; and of course judgments on fairness or good sense or decency can and to some extent must differ, so that one needs to study the personnel of the court, and *their* ways of seeing sense.

(4) No court can feel happy with a decision unless the decision fits comfortably, under our accepted techniques of handling authorities, with the accepted body of the law. But the techniques which are accepted and in standard use are mutually contradictory and alternative techniques. This holds equally in regard to prior cases, to statutes, and to administrative regulations.

I give typical instances of each, just to remind of how the accepted and correct techniques run in opposing pairs or groups throughout each field.

(a) *Case-law:* (i) The prior decided case stands only for a point actually necessary to the judgment. Anything else in the opinion is dictum. Even if the rule carefully laid down would lead to the decision in the case and was unmistakably meant to, the case is still "distinguishable" if you can distinguish it on either the facts or the issue. You can, you even should, disregard any case which is thus "distinguishable." (Thus the court can and does avoid the misguesses or misphrasing or misjudgments of prior cases which they now see have gone off-line on the job of sense and justice.) *Per contra,* (ii) anything said by a prior court (whether dictum or not) can be picked up as: "The true rule was laid down" or "We said" or "We expressly held" in *Zilch v. Gahoozis.* . . . And any "distinguishable" case can be recognized as distinguishable, and yet be followed: "But we think the reason (or: the principle) of that decision equally applicable here." The court can even rest on "the tendency of our decisions" and cite cases none of which is in point, even in its language. (Thus they can and do capitalize the good judgments or phrasings of the past, where in their quest for sense and justice they find such phrasings or decisions helpful.)

(b) *Statutes:* (i) Statutes in derogation of the common law are to be strictly construed. Preambles and captions are no part of the statute. Nor can a statute go beyond its text. *Per contra* (ii) Remedial statutes (which are of course by necessity in derogation of the common law) call for liberal construction; preambles and captions show purpose; purpose is a necessary part of any text. More: a statute must at need be implemented to effect its purpose by going far beyond its text.

(c) *Administrative regulation:* (i) When interpretative regulations have been issued and the legislature later amends the statute without negating such regulations, it thereby incorporates the regulations as being the meaning of all unaltered language. *Per contra* (ii) Administrative usurpation is of course not sanctioned by an amending statute, which is directed only to correction of the legislative text.

These instances are, as noted, only illustrative. Our whole body of authoritatively accepted ways of dealing with authorities, ways in actual use in the daily work of the courts, is a body which *allows* the court to select among anywhere from two to ten "correct" alternatives in something like eight or nine appealed cases out of ten. That is, *technically* our system could find any of these alternatives to be correct. *Judicially,* our system does not allow most of them. That is not because the authorities and our accepted techniques for handling the authorities do not allow huge leeway. It is because judges have a duty to use the available leeways to make for sense and to accomplish decency, and because upright judges, these days, also want to and try to do just that. Whether consciously (as sometimes) or less consciously (as more often), they therefore use their two-faced or multi-faced accepted techniques to make the authorities take on some one of the (doctrinally) possible aspects which does seem to make for sense and to accomplish decency—always with the upright judge's ultimate and underlying drive to see the thing as best he can in terms of Justice-for-All-of-Us.

From these facts about the courts' methods and objectives a

number of practical rules or principles or guides for the advocate emerge at once.

First, and negatively: it is plainly not enough to bring in a technically perfect case on "the law" under the authorities and *some* of the accepted correct techniques for their use and interpretation or "development." If the case is really worth litigating on appeal (and perhaps half of today's appealed cases are), then there is an equally perfect technical case to be made on the other side, and if your opponent is any good he will make it. The struggle will then be for *acceptance* by the tribunal of the one technically perfect view of the law as against the other. Acceptance will turn on something beyond "legal correctness." It ought to.

Second, a "technically" perfect case is equally unreliable in regard to the interpretation or classification of the facts. For rarely indeed do the raw facts of even a commercial transaction fit cleanly into any legal pattern; still less so do the "trial facts" as they emerge from conflicting testimony. No matter what the state of the law may be, if the essential pattern of the facts is not seen by the court as fitting cleanly under the rule you contend for, your case is still in jeopardy. This is of course the reason for the commercial counsellor's concern with "fixing" the transaction by a well-drawn document which does fit cleanly into known and certain legal rules. But even documents can have their difficulties (especially in commercial finance). Thus despite any and every document and the parol evidence rule, the "form" of outright sale will regularly be disregarded if oral testimony and circumstances persuade the tribunal that the "true transaction" was one for security only. Despite any document and the parol evidence rule, the "form" of legitimacy may even become an adverse factor if the tribunal from oral testimony and circumstance is led to see in that form a "mask" for usury.[13]

Per contra, and third: *Without a technically perfect case on the law,* under the combination of the relevant authorities and some one or more of the thoroughly correct procedures of their use and interpretation, you have no business to expect to win your case. Occasionally a court may under the utter need for getting a decent result go into deliberate creative effort on its own; but few courts

---

[13] This notwithstanding what was accomplished by skilful counsel and a skilful judge in Jenkins v. Moyse, cited *infra* note 14. Even in that case both the trial court and the Appellate Division had "pierced the mask," notwithstanding New York's terrific penalty of both repayment promise and security being utterly void, if it was "usury." The lender had changed his counsel before the argument in the Court of Appeals.

like to. Such effort interferes with the court's sense of duty to the law; such effort requires also skill and labor from a hard-pressed bench. Sound advocacy therefore calls for providing in the brief a job all done to hand; it calls as of course for not stirring up any conflict between the court's two major duties. If there is any difficulty with or about the authorities, the solving rule that takes care both of those authorities and of the sound solution calls thus for careful, clear, adequate phrasing in the brief: "The true rule is . . ." (with any needed qualifications taken care of). A court can *recognize* the good solution which gives satisfaction in regard to a tough problem rightly worked out.

All of this serves only to lead up to the crux:

Fourth: the real and vital central job is to satisfy the court that sense and decency and justice require (a) the rule which you contend for in this *type* of situation; and (b) the result that you contend for, as between these parties. Your whole case, on law and facts, must make *sense,* must appeal as being *obvious* sense, inescapable sense, sense in simple terms of life and justice. If that is done, a technically sound case on the law then gets rid of all further difficulty: it shows the court that its duty to the Law not only does not conflict with its duty to Justice but urges along the exact same line.

The great change during these last few years in the approach of the best advocates lies here. As little as twenty or even ten years ago [i.e., before 1945], leading appellate advocates were still apologizing in private for that necessity of their profession that they termed "atmosphere." They meant the introduction, as a technical need, of matter and manner not really "legal" and in some undescribed way felt to be somehow illegitimate, which would make a tribunal *want* to decide their way. Today, as the courts' own sense of their felt duty to decency and justice becomes unmistakable in the decisions and increasingly articulate in the opinions, leading advocates have ceased apology and simply set to work. It is no longer a question of "introducing atmosphere." It is now a question of making the facts talk. For of course it is the facts, not the advocate's expressed opinions, which must do the talking. The court is interested not in listening to a lawyer rant, but in seeing, or discovering, from and in the facts, where sense and justice lie.

This leads to interesting corollaries. It is trite that it is in the statement of the facts that the advocate has his first, best, and most precious access to the court's attention. The court does not know the facts, and it wants to. It is trite, among good advocates, that the statement of the facts can, and should, in the very process of statement, frame the legal issue, and can, and should, simultaneously produce the conviction that there is only one sound result.[14] It is as yet less generally perceived as a conscious matter that the *pattern* of the facts as stated must be a *simple* pattern, with its lines of simplicity never lost under detail; else attention wanders, or (which is as bad) the effect is submerged in the court's effort to follow the presentation or to organize the material for itself.

Neither is it yet adequately perceived that the lines of argument just discussed lead of necessity to maximum simplicity on the legal side of a brief. Those who, complaining that "You never can tell on what peg an appellate court will hang its hat," throw in point after point after unrelated point, they scatter their fire, their impact, their unity of drive; they do it because they have not become clear that the vital matter is to satisfy the court that decision their way is imperative as a matter of sense and justice; they are still arguing as if "the law"—*before* the decision—were single and clear and in itself enough. Whereas in fact one, two or three good points in law (*i.e.*, technically sound and correct points) are enough, once the court is satisfied which way the case *ought* to, *must* come out. Indeed three points, or two, are commonly enough troublesome, as being scatterers of attention, unless a way can be found to make them sub-points under a single simple line which receives reinforcement and cumulative power from each subpoint as the latter is developed.

Again the gain to law-work from experience with the Services is

---

[14] For accessible examples of superb work, see: (1) Cardozo's statement of the facts in Wood v. Lucy, Lady Duff-Gordon, 222 N. Y. 88, 118 N. E. 214 (1917). That statement produces a picture of "long-term business agreement for profit" coupled delicately with "Is not the defendant acting in bad faith?" which in less than two paragraphs sets the issue: "Is this intended, valid, legal contract to be defeated by a trivial omission of expression?" (2) Davis' points as reported in Pennsylvania v. Mahon, 260 U. S. 293 (1922). There a statute intended to prevent subsidence of the surface of a city through removal of supporting pillars of coal quietly takes on the guise of a legislative gift to "Mr. and Mrs. Mahon," at the uncompensated expense of another, or a valuable right the Mahons had carefully contracted not to buy. Holmes was persuaded. (3) Lehman's combination of statement of facts, statement of legislative situation and argument in Jenkins v. Moyse, 254 N. Y. 319, 172 N. E. 319 (1930) is a fine example of "showing" purpose and reason for a result. There what seems to me a patent evasion of the usury statute in a more than moderately outrageous transaction becomes a proper use of a machinery intentionally left open by the legislature to keep persons in the borrower's troubled financial condition from being shut off from all access to the loan market, thus producing that essential sense in the statute which sustains the technically valid interpretation in favor of the lender.

clear. Once sense and justice are seen as the central problem, the technical job becomes one of concentrating one's effectives; of organizing them for mutual supplement and reinforcement at the single point of concentration which has been chosen for attack. Of course, there must be no slip-up, anywhere. The "law"-side must be done in correct doctrinal form, and must be adequate to sustain its part of the case. The solving rule must be clearly stated; its consistency with the authorities and its application to the facts must be made unmistakable. Of course. But again, experience in the Services offers a wherewithal for bringing the returning lawyer more than abreast of the developments in his art while he has been away. It brings him back with a contribution to the art.

III. Emerging Commercial Situations

The situations which are demanding the commercial lawyer's attention still concentrate on various aspects of security for short-term financing.

This is not at all as it should be. There are many non-financial aspects of commerce which reward for client and for lawyer the same kind of sustained counsellor's attention. Buying and selling, control of agents, marketing methods, afford a rich area for needed counselling, they offer that steady retainer work which can be useful to the smaller business and equally useful to the lawyer who needs a reliable backlog. As indicated above, work of this kind is likely to head up in the preparation of "our standard clauses" for sale and of another set for purchase; and some of the considerations involved have been discussed. One may add the need of going over carefully with the client, step by step, just how the order-getting, supervisory and execution portions of his business are being handled, so as to check up on what practicable, inexpensive operating machinery or shifts in machinery there may be to tighten control, reduce error, increase safety in the event of dispute—dispute with either customer, or employee; or, indeed, with supplier. To take the simplest instance, if there are four men in the shipping room it is not only a matter of business administration for the routine to include a record of which man is responsible for accuracy of content in any individual package; it is also, on the legal side, a matter of substituting effective personal proof by past recollection recorded for loose proof by way of the mere course of a regime; it is a matter, should there be a bothersome slip-up, of having a clear case against a single man which will stand up before a grievance committee or an arbitrator. On matters of this kind the counsellor who adds a sense of business feasibility to his legal knowledge can be of service from one end of a business through to the other; especially so in the formative and often loose-jointed operations attendant on reconversion or attendant, when a new enterprise gets well under way, on expansion.

Lastly, no forms and no advice to central officers can move toward real safety until operation-methods and simple, intelligible operation-routines and operation-instructions for the non-coms and enlisted personnel have been worked out.[15] That is simple sense. The responsible counsellor needs to be in on the working of them out, or at worst in on a final check-up of their adequacy. That is also simple sense. And the war has stepped up immeasurably counsel's perception of the need for a visit to the office and the plant to observe at first hand the step-by-step operating procedure, so as to spot where hitch or slip up can occur; it has stepped up his perception of the need for "execution" follow-through in business counselling; perhaps most, because good labor relations counselling has forced counsel into the plant, and an intelligent lawyer, when thus confronted with new stimulus, begins to think.

There is no hope of being able to cover here the new lines of clause which pop up for consideration in a thousand different lines of trade, but two of fairly general application may be mentioned. For one: a good deal of attention is being paid today to the problem of responsibility for patent or trade-mark infringement by goods sold. In the decided cases the courts have mentioned warranties of title and of merchantability, and there is even a case to be made for warranty of fitness for purpose when the seller knows of the buyer's purpose, say of further manufacture. An excellent set of principles of fairness in the situation, as between the buyer and the seller, is available in the 1945 A. B. A. Committee Report on Patent Clauses of Purchase Orders, to the Section of Patent, Trade-Mark & Copyright Law. The main line there taken is: anything that is a regular offering of the seller should be warranted by him against infringement; but what is

[15] Central officers can also do with instructions. It can be a tough thing when a well-drawn clause limiting a manufacturer's warranties to those expressed in the specifications on the confirmation is knocked out by an enthusiastic officer who incloses the confirmation in a pep-letter adding utter assurance of complete fitness for the buyer's otherwise unmentioned purpose—the inclosing letter not even going into the files which will be governing actual production.

specified by the buyer should be warranted by the buyer, so far as concerns his technical specifications. The sense is plain; but when the case-law is dubious the clauses need adaptation to the product and to the specific situation.

The second point has to do with transportation in ways unforeseen by the law of bills of lading, foreseen indeed much less in those simple statements of the law on delivery, payment, inspection which are phrased in terms of face to face operations. Direct night delivery by truck leaves no room for "protection" of the seller by way of order bill of lading, draft for the price, and use of the collection machinery of a bank; the goods beat the documents in by days. All right: we pay in advance or else we sell on credit; yet in either case the term needs to be explicit. And the inspection problem is not easy: tired drivers do not want to wait, and few trucking companies have facilities for handling rejected goods. A seller therefore needs a clause requiring his buyer to unload and receive; a buyer needs one giving full proper time for subsequent inspection and, if he is short of storage space, giving him appropriate power to reship "collect" to the seller, or else to resell for seller's account if instructions for disposition are not received within a named reasonable time after notice of rejection.[15a]

Now that labor relations work and tax work are bringing the lawyer into so much wider and so much more frequent and sustained contacts with businesses of smaller size, the day has come for real spread and development of "straight" commercial counselling of this nature. It is needed, both for commerce and for the bar. It has been slow to come partly because lawyers have been backward in adding to their technical equipment business sense and responsibility for business judgment, partly because businessmen when thinking "straight" business hate to think of trouble.

But in the field of security one party at least, the lender, already has his mind on trouble, and on its avoidance; so that the lawyer has long been regularly consulted.

What happened during the War was that with the need for financing war production and under government stimulus, commercial bankers discovered that mere contracts could be bankable, could even offer good banking security by way of assignment of the sums to be earned under them. (This had long been familiar, *e.g.*, in the construction business.) Whether and how far this type of

[15a] Note the value not only of substituting a specific for the legal "reasonable" time-limit, but also of keeping the specific time-limit reasonable in fact.

banking will continue is uncertain,[d] but against the contingency that it may, one point needs noting: any manufacturer who arranges for parts or materials by way of a subcontract or supply contract which he has reason to expect may be financed by assignment requires for his own safety the insertion of a "modification" clause. The law of assignments, after notice given, is either obscure or adverse as to the power of the notified "debtor" to make any adjustment at all of the assigned contract with the assignor, unless the financing assignee consents. The procurement of such assent is always a bother, and it is extremely likely to be overlooked. If a modification without the assignee's assent is made and operated on, and the assignor then becomes insolvent, there can be serious trouble. The "prime" party can cover this in any sub- or supply contract by a clause limiting the rights of any assignee: "Notwithstanding any assignment for security of this contract or any rights under it, the parties are free without the consent of any assignee to make any reasonable business adjustments of this contract in regard to quantity, materials, price, delivery dates or the like, the security rights of the assignee to attach after any such adjustment to the contract as modified"—or the like. Assignment other than for security should commonly be forbidden without the buyer's consent unless the product in question is routine-stuff. And it is sometimes wise to provide (as where problems of payroll may press) that, notwithstanding any assignment, sums due may be paid as earned to the supplier so long as the buyer (the "prime" party) remains without notice of the supplier's insolvency—though such a clause may bar effective financing, it is often reasonable in the circumstances.

The reconversion needs of quick and heavy financing have recently brought into greater prominence various devices addressed to inventory and other quick assets (accounts receivable) as bases of security.

The general problem is threefold, though the legal devices available do not as yet distinguish among the three business aspects. First, there is the business which is not yet so established that it can meet its general current needs by simple unsecured bank loan. Not too dissimilar is the line of business which once was of this character, and which therefore (like the auto retailer) resorted to a finance company rather than a bank for financing by way of trust

[d] It has continued. And "receivables" financing has moved out of the disreputable into the recognition it should long have had, of capitalizing for security the best and most liquid asset a business has.

receipt on the purchased cars as they came in, and resorted again for financing by way of assignment of conditional sales contracts as the cars went out to buyers on the installment plan. In such a case the practice of the whole line of trade may have become one of inventory and "receivables" financing. The second situation is that of the business in distress, with financing of inventory or of receivables an emergency measure which may tide the enterprise over the shoals, but which, if it does not, will milk the borrower's whole set of other creditors in favor of this last, secured, "new money in." The third situation is that of the successful but expanding business which needs temporary capital to go ahead abreast of opportunity.

The most troubling aspect of these developments is their persistent drive toward essential secrecy of the preferential lien which they seek; for which reason, even where a simple chattel mortgage on the stock in trade or manufacturer's inventory of raw materials is otherwise legally available, such a mortgage may be unwelcome to both borrower and lender. This desire for secrecy is in first instance a problem for legislative regulation; but it represents a source of danger in court which the wise counsellor will bear in mind as any set-up begins to approach the borderline of what might, apart from the courts' aversion to secret liens, seem, on doctrine, to be safe. Security is intended to *be* safe, safe in the pinch, safe even as against a court that loves not secret liens.

Perhaps the most ingenious of the devices now finding favor is the "field storage pledge." A portion of a borrower's premises is fenced off with a locked gate, or, if within a building, locked off, and is leased to a licensed warehouseman, and an appropriate warehouseman's sign is conspicuously posted at the entrance. It is essential that control be in the warehouseman's representative, not in an employee of the borrower; that everything brought in or taken out be checked and duly recorded by the warehouseman's representative; that he have sole control over the keys. He is then in a position to sign effective "warehouse receipts," negotiable ones, which the borrower can effectively pledge to a banker. Smooth operation requires sufficient advance planning to allow any necessary warehouse receipts to be withdrawn from the banker (typically against either trust receipt or substitution of further warehouse receipts) in time for any needed inventory to be withdrawn from the "warehouse" on the day it is needed. Only such smooth operation is secure. The warehouseman's charges are of course borne by the borrower, and are high, if viewed as service charges, unless the service bought be seen as that of making inventory available to secure loans.

I have not been able, myself, to see why this same device, minus the warehouseman, is not equally available to a seller who is willing to deliver at destination and wait for his money, but who wishes to retain "possession" so as to protect his seller's lien. Not warehousing, but public notice and actual retention of control as against the debtor, appear to be the essential ideas involved.

Trust receipt financing is also showing some signs of expansion. I do not counsel its extension into any unfamiliar area. Lenders not already skilled in operating with trust receipts are extremely hard to persuade or train to do the policing which is necessary to really safeguard themselves against loose practice (whether or not dishonest) on the part of the borrower. It is, for example, essential to real security that any proceeds of sales of trust receipted goods be turned over into special account or into the lender's hands within ten days after their receipt by the borrower.[16] The validity of the trust receipt lien[17] is also under a possible shadow because of the Supreme Court decision about to be discussed. And even in automobile finance, where the trust receipt has become an institution, the rise of direct delivery over the highway, with its normal elimination of any document of title covering the transportation, sets up a tricky situation in which the most careful co-operation of the manufacturer (as by making his bill of sale and invoice run direct to the financier) is needed in order to bring the transaction comfortably and clearly within the language of the Uniform Trust Receipts Act.

But the greatest turmoil in the commercial field has been unloosed in the area of financing by way of assignment of accounts receivable. Such accounts—book accounts for merchandise sold and delivered, or perhaps for services rendered, on credit—have until recently been viewed as "unbankable"; they happened not to fit into the picture of negotiable notes or acceptances capable at need of rediscount free of defenses, so that their general prime

---

[16] I have actually run across a recent situation—in a well-run bank, too—in which one side of the bank was financing an importer on trust receipt and another side of the same bank was making fresh advances by discount of trade acceptances arising out of the resale of the same trust receipted merchandise. This typifies the carelessness of too many lenders' reliance, and the need for constant follow-up.

[17] Though it is probably defensible in most cases as a non-secret lien, as a lien retained rather than one created, and as in any event defeasible by *bona fide* purchasers only when they purchase in ordinary course of trade.

liquidity (a full step, or two, ahead of merchandise in warehouse) was neglected. But many sound and expanding smaller businesses found working capital so valuable that it paid them to lay out the 9% to 17% or up (according to policing expense and "quality" of the accounts) which it then cost to get advances "on" the receivables.

There were three difficulties. In many states an assignment was good when made, whether against a subsequent assignee or against creditors in bankruptcy. In many other States this did not hold —certainly not as against a subsequent *bona fide* assignee—until notice of the assignment had been brought home to the particular debtor. The second difficulty was that enough receivables financing has been of emergency, last-ditch, eve-of-insolvency character to develop for receivables financing at large an evil reputation; secrecy of wholly legitimate receivables financing thus became a means of protection against calumny. The third difficulty was and still is that nobody knows what law governs the assignment of accounts receivable when the debtor is located in a state other than that in which the creditor is located or the assignment is made.

Into this mixed situation came first the V-loan program, familiarizing bankers with the workability of financing *contracts,* contracts still wholly unperformed, contracts merely for manufacture and sale; whereas with a receivable the goods have already been made, a customer has already been found, the delivery has been made as well, only payment waits (subject, of course, to possible defenses). With this V-loan development, bankers' eyes were opened, and they have recently been going into the receivables field, competing with the finance companies; the necessary consequence is a rapidly growing normality and respectability of this once scorned receivables financing: for what is "bankable" always duly becomes in point of reputation "good" and "proper" collateral.

The second thing that came into the situation was the Supreme Court's decision in *Corn Exchange Bank v. Klauder.*[18] It was there held that the 1938 Chandler Act amendment of the Bankruptcy Act, § 60 (a), was deliberate in its efforts to cut down secret liens, and that an assignment of an account receivable was therefore voidable in bankruptcy, in the absence of notice to the debtor, in any case in which the law of the relevant state made such notice necessary to perfect the assignment as against a subsequent *bona*

[18] 318 U. S. 434 (1942).

fide purchaser. Since then the legislative hoppers have been humming with bills designed to find a simpler means of safeguarding the lender than the common law's cumbersome and rather useless notification to each individual debtor.[19]

The two main types of statute deserve attention; it makes a difference to any commercial lawyer which type is chosen.[20] The one type, the so-called "simple validation" or "secret lien" statute, is built simply to ease receivables financing, without too much attention to any other phase of the general credit situation. It seeks to protect at once the borrower's old-time interest in secrecy and the lender's eternal interest in steady relations unattended by competitors' solicitation of customers or by competition from general creditors in case of the borrower's insolvency. It therefore simply validates the assignment when made. The other type of statute sees the "bad name" of receivables financing as already largely a thing of the past, finds the receivables business itself to prosper under the "open" type of statute, and finds the secret removal of a borrower's most liquid asset to be a hardship on merchandise and other general creditors which threatens the solidity of the general credit market. This is the "public notice" type of statute; not a filing statute requiring detailed filing as with conditional sales, but one requiring merely a general notice to be filed that X is financing his receivables with Y. That lets any prospective creditor know that he has no business to count on any receivables shown in a credit statement.

Whichever type of statute a state may pass, its effect on receivables where the debtor is in another state is, as has been noted, uncertain. And whether operating under the one type or the other or under the common law, the counsel of steady policing must be drummed into any lending client's ear. Each receivable should be separately listed in a paper whose heading can incorporate the general contract under which the financing occurs. (Better, in my

---

[19] In textile factorage—*i.e.*, outright purchase of accounts and collection direct by the financing "factor"—notification is not cumbersome, because by practice the factor controls in advance the credits to be given to the buyer. He is thus in the picture from the outset. This grows historically out of the older practice in which the textile factor was a selling agent, guaranteeing accounts *del credere*. But there is no convenient way of transplanting such practices to another line of business different in tradition.

[20] Regardless of type, there are important problems of detail. The Committee on Accounts Receivable of the Conference on Uniform State Laws (Chairman, L. Barrett Jones, Lamar Bldg., Jackson, Miss.) has prepared very workable drafts along each line which are in my view preferable to most of the existing statutes and which should be consulted.

opinion, is a general financing contract which looks forward to and controls any subsequent listing, each listing carrying an appropriate reference.) Remittances should be made and checked frequently, accompanied preferably by a specific statement (*e.g.*, on a carbon of the list) of which particular accounts have been paid when due, and which have not. Interim receipts by the borrower need to go into an ear-marked account, one preferably not subject to the borrower's drawings except for remittance to the lender. Unless some such precautions are taken, the rule of *Benedict v. Ratner*[21] may rise to knock out the whole set of assignments as being still subject to the borrower's disposition.

IV. THE CRAFTS OF LAW AND THEIR IDEALS

In closing, it seems right to stress that our bar and law alike require a large transfusion from the returning lawyers of fresh vision and of recaptured sense of what law is about, what the men of law are for. Here again, and even though we threaten somewhat to bog down in the lethargy after strain, the War has driven powerfully toward change. It has done more than make clear to us that our law has purposes which are precious and needs that call for lawyers' effort, that practice is not rightly a matter of client-nursing alone nor of merely winning cases. The War has also tremendously furthered the drive of conditions into long-term, lasting relations between private concerns, as between management and union; a drive which means that intelligent counselling and intelligent litigation strategy call increasingly for a point of view and for an invention of measures which take account of the other side as well as of your own; and which go beyond both to wrestle with problems not only of public approval but of the public interest. In a word, the drive of conditions has once again brought together the road to success at the bar and the road to fulfilling one's whole duty to the law.

May I quote a passage in which I once tried to get this clear? It is dated, in its allusions to a war in process; it is not dated, otherwise:

[The paper closed with quotation of the final passages from *The Crafts of Law Re-Valued, above,* pp. 320–2.]

[21] 268 U. S. 353 (1925).

{ 15 }

LAW AND THE SOCIAL SCIENCES—
ESPECIALLY SOCIOLOGY [a] [*]

FOREWORD

Our men of the Law have not been wise to let slip a standing
which, in this country, they used to have.

They used to be, as of course (along with preachers, prophets,
and successful generals), the people on whom other people called
to tell them what any trouble was all about. They used, also, and
again as of course (along with political leaders), to be the people
to whom other people turned when they wanted to know how to
get things done. A century or so ago, names like John Adams,
Alexander Hamilton, Andrew Jackson, Daniel Webster, Abraham
Lincoln, carried a sure flavor of knowing whither and of telling
how, for *All*-of-us. Such knowing of whither and such discovering
of how, for *All*-of-us, is still of the essence. It is, in essence, what
the institution of law and the men of law are for. Both we and
those whom we exist to serve should get that clear.

But it does seem that things have gotten in the way. This paper
represents one effort to remove an obstacle or two.

I

Law is still by common practice removed from any brotherly
contact with the social disciplines. This is in part the fault of the

[a] From 62 HARV. L. REV. 1286 (1949).

[*] This paper appears, by agreement, jointly in this *Review* and the *American
Sociological Review*. Each Review, however, carries its own FOREWORD, addressed
to its own public.

lawyers. "Questions of law," to lawyers, are questions about the doctrinally correct interpretation of rules of law, and jurisprudes of reputation (and, what is worse, of ability) have solemnly built "systems" which no less solemnly take "law" to consist exclusively of "norms" or of "imperatives," and the study "of law" has been seen even by university law teachers as being primarily the study of rules of law, and so on down the line until an outsider might fairly think that there is nothing to law except these authoritative rules, statutory or other, which explain how officials are supposed to behave in 2,461,879 various and subtly differentiated contingencies. And since it is plain, almost by definition, that nobody but a trained lawyer (and a very good one, too) can move with comfort and accuracy among these rules of law and their doctrinally correct quarter-shades of meaning, it is little wonder that the gentlemen from the other social disciplines stay out. Indeed if all the lawyer has to contribute is information about what the doctrinally correct rule is, then he is a proud member of the kind of discipline of which the sad German once remarked that "The Legislature may repeal my whole *Wissenschaft* tomorrow"—an attribute which somehow does not recommend the findings of a discipline to neighbors who think of their own work as "science."

Neither, over the years, do I find too much effective effort at neighborliness, let alone brotherliness, from the side of the social disciplines, or of sociology in particular. When I was younger I used to hear smuggish assertions among my sociological friends, such as: "I take the sociological, *not* the legal, approach to crime"; and I suspect an inquiring reporter could still hear much of the same (perhaps with "psychiatric" often substituted for "sociological")—though it is surely somewhat obvious that when you take "the legal" out, you also take out "crime." [1] When I was somewhat older I began to find law discussed as the most highly developed of "the codes" and the one backed by the state; but with little effort, for example, to explore the interesting differences

[1] Unless in one way or another either All-of-Us or somebody-claiming-to-act-for-All-of-Us gets busy dealing with undesired behavior, what room is there for a "crime" idea? The "sociological" or "psychological" lines of approach have their legitimacy, but that legitimacy must be based on and begin with some idea of what is "criminal." The questions to which such other approaches are addressed are: What behavior (past or prospective) is a general bother? Who is to do something about it? How? And of course old-line Law may be a bit backward in such matters. But, as Dession so shrewdly reminded us before Hitler did, the question of How is at least twofold. It involves not merely how to handle your man when you have him, but the problem of how to sort him out of the general public, to "have."

between a "code" made and staffed by professional specialists and one not so handled. And all along I have been meeting discussions of "law" in a context of "social control" of unspecified somebodies by other unspecified somebodies to unspecified ends by means which are indeed sometimes somewhat loosely indicated. It seems to me today that except for a little work in the field of crime and some in labor relations the quantitative side of sociology has tended to slight the legal, and that even the fine qualitative analysis which has marked the leading sociological thought of the last decade or so has left relatively undeveloped the pioneering work in regard to the "law" field of, say, Bentley, and the extraordinarily penetrating thought of Max Weber.

The contention here is that a different approach to law renders two-way contact and traffic between law and the *other* social disciplines easy, direct, and very fruitful on each end. For the shrewder observers have long seen that there is vastly more to law than any rules. Pound, for instance—one of the shrewdest—has for some three decades been insisting on a number of things on which most men of sociology and government still turn a stubborn back.[2] Rules he sees as an important part of law, and he sees them as rules *for* conduct ("precepts") not as that queer confusion which persists in the literature (both legal and non-legal) as "rules *of* conduct." Pound adds, as part of law, concepts, standards, principles, and ideals: a whole range of tradition-carried tools and shapers of men and of their work which more frequently than not run largely free of any verbal frame. Thus the drive for justice in legal work has power even though no man may be able to say what justice is; the ideal of uprightness for judge and for other officials has life and meaning even though no man may be able to reduce its content to words. Pound then goes on to include in law "a technique," a "taught" technique, for developing and applying these authoritative materials for control, guidance, decision, and he adds "the" judicial and "the" administrative "processes." All of these phrasings simplify more than is wise. "The" technique is really a rather elaborate and Janus-faced set of tech-

---

[2] No less striking is the degree to which Pound's work in its most original and fruitful phases still goes unused and above all undeveloped; as also, in its exaggerations and errors, uncorrected. Our institution of law lacks as yet one aspect necessary to its health: an on-going, on-growing critical constructive and constantly retested body of theory and of application of theory. But one would have thought that the universal recognition of Pound's standing would have led to an exception in his case.

niques; very considerable portions of them are not taught, resting largely in the inarticulate, though they are *learned* by most men of the law (for example, how do you tell when to hold a precedent or statute down, when on the other hand to let loose its growth-power?); and by the same token there are many and different kinds of process within the judicial field (consider the huge differences between trial and appeal, between trial to the court and trial to a jury, between a new J.P. and a skilled and experienced circuit judge) and of course even more so within the administrative. But such refinements are unnecessary to the main point, which is that with techniques and processes Pound has moved "law" out of the world of the purely normative, the world of words and meanings, and into the world of action, of human behavior, of patterns and ways of actually getting things done; and, what is more, of the people who get things done. You can have no techniques without technicians, no processes without people. Pound then goes on to add "the legal order," which he leaves not only undefined but almost unindicated; yet anybody can see that it includes a considerable quantity of "observance" and "support" and organization, and anybody can suspect that "the legal order" is meant to include also such going enterprises as courts, legislatures, law publishers, and police. All you have to do is to borrow a concept from sociology: *Institution,* and to make explicit that you include therein the relevant going practices and the relevant specialists and the relevant physical equipment and the manner of organization of the whole; and Pound's picture of law—the *institution* of law—becomes forthwith a something which any social scientist can look at, understand, make friends with, learn from, and comfortably contribute to.

The central aspect of an *institution* is organized activity, activity organized around the cleaning up of some job. In the case of the major institutions (of which the institution of law is one) the jobs concerned are vital to the continued existence of the society or group. Plainly, an important portion of any institution lies in the world of ideas: organization implies patterns for action, it implies lines of back-and-forth felt as correct and right, it implies problems of morale, of felt goal, and the like. Yet I want to insist peculiarly on the need for including and for stressing the *conduct*-phases of the institution—both patterned and unpatterned—and such things as physical equipment, and above all people, both the relevant specialists and the consuming and supporting public.[3] I should wish to gather in also not only active conduct but the relevant attitudes and relevant lines of *in*action, and the *inter*actions of any portion of the institution with any other institution; and the machinery for recruiting and for breaking in the institution's specialized personnel; and a dozen or so other obvious elements in any living major complex of the "institution" sort. Indeed the first direct contribution of the "law" discipline to sociology lies just here. For there has been a recurrent tendency in sociology, as careful thinkers have come to perceive more and more keenly the huge part played in life by ideas, by norms, by standards and ideals sharp or vague—there has been a recurrent tendency to move off the action-phase of what is there, and off the person-phase of what is there, and to take the set of norms or standards which are also there as *being, without more,* the institution, or the culture.[4] Now in the tongue of the court crier: Oyez! Oyez! Oyez! Which is to say: Hear and Attend! That way lies waste and positive error. The men of law have labored now for centuries over the most developed, explicit, and integrated bodies of norms and standards man has ever devised; the men of law have taken these bodies as being effective somethings in themselves, and their ingenuity in finding diverse and useful ways of laboring on that premise has been worthy of a Philadelphia lawyer. But the labors have either been barren,[5] or they have been actively misleading (the conception of a government "of law *and not* of men"), or else they have achieved a semblance of sense in result only through smuggling bits of horse sense into action and discussion by techniques akin to that of the wizard's hat, though largely unconscious in their operation.[6] From such error law has finally been driven, for help and light, into *supplementing* the "norm-and-standard" aspect by the whole rich range of *other* aspects of an institution. The lesson

[3] The best discussion of "institution" I have ever seen in print is the article of that name by Walton Hamilton in 8 ENCYC. SOC. SCI. 84 (1932). I think it interesting that those of us who tend to see "institution" as the central and most important concept in social science (I should reckon in Max Weber, J. R. Commons, Hamilton, Malinowski) have been heavily influenced in our thinking by work on the legal side.

[4] I have spotted this, for example, in otherwise admirable work of Murdock, T. Parsons, and Kluckhohn.

[5] I see Kelsen's work as utterly sterile, save in by-products that derive from his taking his shrewd eyes, for a moment, off what he thinks of as "pure law."

[6] Nowhere better illustrated than in Stammler's exposition of "right" law. The same procedure pervades PATTERSON, LECTURES ON JURISPRUDENCE (1st ed. 1940). It is indeed an almost superhuman task for a man of inherent sense to work sustainedly with the idea of law as being "merely" norm.

is plain in regard to any "institution" and in regard to "culture" at large.

The *rule* part of the law-institution is thus one *tool*-part of the institution; one hugely developed part; one part vital to communication over space and time and variant personnel; but one vital tool-part and no more than that, and a tool-part nowhere nearly so effective as it purports to be. And the variability and impermanence of the rules of law become not only understandable but interesting when the rules are seen as being not the very substance of the discipline, but instead as being *some* of the measures by which the men of the discipline go about the jobs of the institution.

II

What then, are the jobs of this particular institution? There is one interesting thing about it: Even a layman who may have fallen into thinking law and lawyers to be pure instruments of trickery or of oppression still thinks when he sees something "wrong" that "there ought to be a law about it." Even social scientists who shudder away from law as a child shudders away from a dark cellar or who curse it without bothering to understand, as a losing gambler curses "the luck"—even such folk find in themselves an uneasy, unreasoned but unyielding conviction that law is one of the major and central of our institutions. The social scientist has even marked off a discipline—Government, or Political Science—to express that conviction; though he has carefully left out of that discipline its black-dark cellar and foundation. The mere layman has a surer intuition: he lumps together in his feeling Law *and* Government (as also Law *and* Order). And when one looks to see, it is plain enough what the great and basic job is, on which the institution of law-and-government is focused. It is the job, for any group, for any community, for any political entity, for any society, of becoming and remaining and operating as *enough* of a unity, with *enough* team-work, to be and remain recognizable *as* a group or *as* a political entity or *as* a society. The fundamental Law-and-Government job is, then, the job that is fundamental to the existence of any society and of any social discipline at all: it is the job of producing and maintaining the groupness of a group.[7] Groupness does not just happen without machin-

[7] The case is one for lyrics as well as for study, and Miss Stein has set a persuasive pattern: A group is a group is a group is a group indeed.

ery and without work. It does not just continue, without machinery
and without work. Neither does it just operate, without work or
without machinery. The divergent drives, the frictions, the disrup-
tions inherent among human beings—these must be fought down
and conquered, and some net guidance must be achieved, else the
group or society blows up or dribbles apart or starves or perishes
in civil conflict.

Of course the institution of Law-and-Government operates according to the laws of institutions generally. Among these latter
there is one which deserves our particular immediate notice: to
wit, that institutions overlap in their functions as they do in their
operation, and that the more they are derived from growth as contrasted with conscious planned creation, the more striking is this
overlapping. So that there is no institution whose main job (or
jobs) is got done by that institution alone. Thus national defense
is not accomplished by the armed services alone; education is
achieved only in minor part by the machinery organized and specialized to that end; the market controls distribution neither
within the armed services nor within the family nor within such
areas as park, school, highway, or social security. And the organization of the team-work of our society is a product, in first instance, in large part of education in the family (turning new balls
of wild, semi-random energy into recognizable American five-year-
olds) and in the play-group and in the job; and in further large
part such organization is a product of the inherited, though changing, market. Let that be granted.

Nevertheless, the job of groupness is soundly viewed as essentially the job of this particular institution of Law-and-Government. First, because that is the only large-scale institution which
specializes constantly on that job, and the only one for which that
job is *the* major specialty. Second, because it is to Law-and-Government that we turn, in regard to the job of effective groupness,
whenever our other machineries fail to get that job done; Law-
and-Government is our machinery for conscious rekiltering, for
deliberate correction, for planned cure. And third (perhaps as a
phase of the other two), because Law-and-Government is the one
institution which is recognized in this matter as proper to speak
for the Whole of Us. So much so, indeed, that when in any group
or society there may be doubt on the point, you will recognize
an organ of Law-and-Government (for that society or for that
group) by the very fact that the organ does purport to speak for
the whole and does find that speaking recognized.

The whole vast job of team-work or groupness is too broad for easy study all-at-once. I have found the actual operations to cluster conveniently around certain subproblems or -jobs which it may pay here to run through in passing. Take a first four: There is the cleaning up of trouble-cases, which in various groups has been dealt with by tommy-gun or teargas, by legally binding compromise, by decree of a king or father or judge, by election or electrocution, revolution, oracle, or some combination or variation. There is as another subjob the channeling of conduct, habit, and expectation in such fashion as to prevent or reduce the emergence of such trouble-cases; and especially in a mobile society such as ours there is the peculiarly important job of *re*-channeling conduct, of creating new habit and expectation appropriate to the changing conditions of personal or group life, still without touching off too unmanageably much in the way of trouble-cases. There is, again, the allotment of the authoritative "say" and the regulation of the manner of its saying, in cases of emergency, or of doubt, or of innovation.

You will observe how many familiar lesser legal-governmental institutions gather comfortably under these heads, along with buttressing institutions which are not *primarily* (but only partly) legal-governmental. Around the trouble-case cluster judicial machinery, the vote (in elections, in legislatures, in the Supreme Court), the whole machinery of persuasion and negotiation, of contract-making in law, of "deal" in business, labor, or politics. Around the initial channeling job clusters that body of regulative law which has ceased to be challenged by litigation "on points of law" and which is therefore met in court only in case of doubt on the facts or in case of the perverse recalcitrance of some offender; here we meet the traffic-light, the filing of the income tax return, the general recognition of rightful possession and of the status of marriage, of governmental office, of citizenship; while such buttressing not-primarily-legal machineries as family and market have already been mentioned above. Re-channeling, in turn, opens up the whole law and practice of transactions (contract, will, deed, formation of new association or marriage, new issue of securities, patent, copyright), and of new legislation or regulation, or of change of leadership, in any group or society; in the less directly "legal" aspect, we have the whole range of innovation, collision, adjustment, and new emerging practice *inside* the areas of the legal freedoms and mobilities. Meantime, the regulation of the "say" cuts into the basic constitution of any group reallocation of powers, and also into all such prescribed forms as are included under Bills of Rights and due process or *ex cathedra* procedures, or under the committee procedure and "three-readings" procedure and parliamentary procedure of a legislature; and such real regulation of the say takes account no less of plain non-*official*-legal facts as personal prestige and unofficial organization of power and force of personality—in a word, of all the less official-"Legal" phases which enter nonetheless into the de facto Government of group, nation, or world—whichever be taken as the entirety which is the unit of observation at the moment.

III

The contribution to the legal discipline, even on the doctrinal side, of this approach by way of the institution-and-its-jobs is obvious. The approach opens up a whole new dimension; it removes thought, observation, and action out of Euclid's theorems into perspective, out of the flat into the round; it provides eyes and vocabulary for handling what otherwise would remain blind and puzzling, indeed hardly graspable situations. Thus, for instance, in the world of correct legal doctrine a question can answer only to Yes or No. Either, say, the right of filibuster (more accurately, not a right, but an Hohfeldian power-and-liberty, as against the Rest-of-the-Senate-and-as-against-the-Whole-Nation) is constitutionally guaranteed, or it is not; and it either is "law" or it is not. One can often hedge the Yes-or-No approach a little: (1) This is indeed the official law on the point, but it *should* be changed; or: it is indeed not the official law, but it *should (and may)* be made so. That is, one can step outside the world of correct doctrine to make a policy judgment *about* doctrine: about whether what is the flatly correct within the prevailing doctrinal system is also wise and good. Or (2) what the official law is on the point is doubtful; but the authoritative personnel will *probably* decide it to be thus-and-so. That is, one can step outside the world of doctrinal *materials* as they stand, and recognize that the authoritative judgment and action of authoritative *personnel* must *also* (and determinatively) be reckoned with. This second aspect is, from the standpoint of the world of "correct doctrine," bold, almost heretical, irreverent, and perhaps dangerous; it represents a partial advance-intrusion (shall I say "an infiltration"?) of "institution" thinking.

But even such inclusion of the possible reactions of crucial official personnel—judicial, executive, administrative—even this gives
no verbal wherewithal to pick up the doctrinal status of such an
odd-lot situation as the filibuster. On the other hand, from the
standpoint of the institution-and-its-jobs we can with reasonable
speed reach a reasonably accurate description even of the filibuster:
here is a minor institution of constitutional nature and importance
(individual power of important delay in crisis; small-minority
power of effective veto) but which has official standing neither as
Constitution nor as official "Law," being officially subject to
change by a single house (though it would seem to be Constitution
for that house, being safeguarded against change by simple vote);
yet it is an institution so firmly grounded in practice and in dear-
held senatorial tradition that its essence appears rather more firmly
seated in the national government than are many pieces of official
Constitution. The British would certainly call it constitutional,
as an important and solidly established phase of the allocation of
national power. And we should see things more clearly if we
adopted their way of seeing and describing such matters, so long
as we remember that *some* parts of *our* Constitution carry also an
extra attribute: that of judicial review of conflicting legislation.

I say therefore that on the legal side one gains power, via this
institution-and-its-jobs approach, to pick up, describe, and study
comfortably various queer situations such as practice-without-
recognized-explicit-rule, or the dead-letter statute, the influence
of tacit decencies, the position ("legal" position) of major-domos
or kings' favorites who have not yet become recognized prime
ministers. Much more important, however, is the new dimension
of insight afforded into the current everyday problems of the law.
Take an old one: Do the judges find the law *or* do they make it?
If you pose this question in the world of correct—or incorrect—
doctrine, you enter on a never-ending battle. If you pose it, on
the other hand, in terms of institution-and-its-jobs, you see at once
that the question is meaningless: because the judges in fact do
both at once. They make the law by voicing what had not been
voiced before, and how they voice it—both in spotting the issue,
and in phrasing it, as well as in the sharp or loose phrasing of the
solving rule, and in the limitation or extension and the direction
of issue and of phrasing—that "how" is creation by the judges. But
they create with given materials which come to them not only with
content but with organization, which not only limit but guide,

which strain and "feel" in one direction rather than another and with one intensity rather than another and with one color and tone rather than another, so that what judges have available to be *recognized* by them as right and just within the going system is largely given by those materials and by the situation around and before them, and their decision is in consequence quite literally *found* and *recognized*, as well as *made*. Which is as true here and today as it was in the ancient primitive interaction of themis and of folkway.

Again, the view of Law-and-Government as in essence a *single* institution opens up at one stroke an answer to two problems which have for centuries been eluding effective answer-in-words: that of the relation of rule and discretion, and of the relation of rules and the official. In the first place, no person who is thinking "Government" along with Law can ever fall into the misconception that things get done by rules of law alone *"and not* men"; instead, the picture becomes at once and of course that of an inter-action—of men acting under and within rules, and under and within a tradition both of goodwill and of know-how each of which is *part* of what we know as "under law." One then perceives, again as of course, that the "Law" pole of the institution is that in which it is regularity of action, reckonable advance guidance in detail, which is under particular and unrealistically exaggerated em-phasis; whereas the "Government" pole is that in which purely individual judgment in the particular situation moves with similar unrealistic exaggeration into the forefront. But something of *each* aspect is present in fact in every official action; and a very consider-able quantum of each aspect is present in every proper official action, in order that rules may be informed always with function, and that personal judgment may be informed always with a *drive* for rightness and for regularity. Indeed I think it a fair statement that official action within an area of discretion completely uncon-trolled as yet by explicit rule becomes rightly motivated according to how far that action is informed by a conscious or unconscious *quest* for such action as would be right and wise to repeat in like circumstances; and that such action becomes right in fact according to how far such a quest is successful. It is thus that one can test for *lawful* exercise of discretion, be the exercise wise or unwise. That formulation comes close to solving the true relation between discretion and rule in relation to the personnel of Law-and-Gov-ernment; and I suggest that that formulation is a direct and fairly obvious outgrowth of the institution-and-its-jobs approach.

IV

There are two further lines of sub-job which I find it useful to mark off. The one is introduced well enough by the problem of eliciting effective leadership and effective administration, just suggested by our discussion of the personnel and discretion factors in Law-and-Government. It is the *positive* job of the institution: the organizing and directing of the team in such fashion as to elicit positive drive, as to produce an unfolding of possibility, of vision, of health. This is a something importantly different from any mere machinery of allotting the "say," or from any merely negative machinery for keeping or getting people out of one another's hair. It is a *positive* net which needs positive achieving; its nature is suggested by paeans on free enterprise, by worries over taxation as crippling incentive, by a program of lessened working hours and bettered labor conditions directed to increasing output, and accompanied by effort to enrich resulting leisure—and the like. It is an aspect of the institution of Law-and-Government which must rightly be perceived as a part not only of the Government side but also as a part of the "pure-Law" side (for legal-helpful devices like contract and corporation and co-operative invite their own use; and the liberties within a legal system, and the lines of strain toward use of the liberties in one way rather than another, are quite as vital parts of the system as are any penalties or prohibitions)—it is an aspect therefore which is *in* and *part* of the Law-side, right enough, but which our thinkers since Swift's time have been curiously slow to stress.[8] But it is an aspect which the "plus-Government" phase of the groupness-institution almost forces to attention—again, as obvious.

The last line of sub-job which I like to mark off may not seem to you a sub-job at all. It pervades all the others, it is a problem of the *how* of working at and working out each and all of the others. It is the peculiar job of developing, maintaining, and bettering the craft know-how among the specialists engaged on any of the other jobs. For the basic jobs of an institution, its life-functions, can be handled either on a barebones level of just enough to keep the group or society from going under, or they can be handled on a high and successful level of questing for beauty, health, glory. And to achieve any portion of this latter,

---

[8] See VOYAGE TO LILLIPUT. Robert Lowie, moving in from ethnology, magnificently stresses this phase. Yet Lowie has completely missed, re law-ways, the know-how craft phases next to be discussed.

the know-how, the method, the reckonable tradition of the crafts-men, must be and stay itself on a high and successful level. (For permanence of effect I suspect that one needs, further, a solid tradi-tion of character and heart; but that is another story). Once this is perceived, it becomes clear that the stuff of official legal rules, offi-cial legal concepts, etc., presents itself under completely different aspects according to the particular craft-job which is concerned. Thus the judge, the counsellor, the advocate, the legislator, the policy-shaping administrator, the administrative subaltern or pri-vate, all see and use the official rule-stuff differently, and the more detailed study of the different crafts, of their craft-skills, -traditions, -ideals, -organization, -morale, -recruiting, presses, and presses hard, for attention.

Like everything that I have had to say and like everything that I shall have to say, neither this observation nor its consequences presents anything new. Instead, and again, it is obvious. The social disciplines have known for decades or centuries that communicable know-how is of the essence of technology. Such a thing as the trade or guild secret has been dealt with in the context of monopoly and competition, in the context of diffusion and invention, in the context of magic, priest-craft, specialist's technology, and general technology, and so in the context of specialization, education, and government. Again, the very idea of culture connotes culture-carriers, and the very idea of specialization implies not only spe-cialists but "lines" of sub-craft within the specialty, with separate skills and sometimes with separate recruiting. Max Weber, for example, has done lovely things with a concept of bureaucracy that reaches over into the Law-and-Government of enterprises quite other than the State. But I do submit that all of this (and much more) gains lovely and simple lines of unity and light when the concept of craft-and-craftsmen is introduced *consistently* as a major working tool.

A craft is, in essence, a recognizable *line* of work, practiced by recognizable craftsmen. Law-work, obviously, is not a single craft, though a particular man of law may practice more than a single one of the law-crafts—he may double in brass and treble in some-thing else: an advocate, a counsellor, *and* a legislator, for instance. Plainly, the degree to which crafts become specialized is a matter of practice: "advocacy" can be advocacy, or can become trial v. appellate, jury v. any other tribunal, plaintiff's side v. defendant's side, negligence v. any other jury work. But of importance is to note that if you have the concept of a craft in your head to think with and to see with, you have a tool of power. Thus, for example, you recognize that a craft means skills, that skills should mean moderately reckonable results, that licensing should turn on assuring the presence of the skills which lead to minimum decent results to the patron of the craft, and that both training and testing should be re-examined with such ideas in mind. You recognize that every craft ought to contain, if organized as such, its teachable rough carpentry, its still teachable but more delicate and advanced cabinet making; reckonable, testable. While of course on beyond will be the less communicable designing power, ability to originate, and the as yet often intangible skills we call know-how. But seeing the situation thus surely focuses in needed fashion such problems as the now so badly handled ones of training for and testing for the bar, and of policing performance at the bar. So it focuses the problems of any other craft in which performance is not to be left to chance. Hence I submit that this attack on the personnel and working of any and every institution is a curiously instructive, vital, unifying—and currently rather neglected—line of study.

And surely no institution urges as clearly toward such an attack as does Law-and-Government, where the rule-stuff is so highly developed, so carefully articulated, yet so hopelessly inadequate, in itself alone, to account for what actually goes on. And where, craft-job by craft-job within the specialized structure, the rule-stuff turns up such utterly different meanings. Observe, for instance: To the judge of a highest court of review "the law," say, of murder, is a moderately complex body of Ought-rules addressed in first instance to conscience under the felt obligation of the judge's office, rules which tell the judge that certain lines of action by the court which sat at trial are unquestionably correct and should be sustained; that certain others are unquestionably incorrect and should on proper appeal lead to reversal; and that still others raise a problem to be solved by an extremely intricate process of interplay of certain fixed official wording of rules on a statute book with certain past judgments of courts in dealing with such statutory wording and with some vaguish ideas of policy which are partly adumbrated in either the statutes or in the courts' past action, or in both, and, finally, with the flavor of felt justice in the situation in general and in the particular case. There exist no reliable rules or guides governing the proper course of this intricate interplay, other than "feeling" for the responsibilities and methods of the office, which is one main reason for divergence of views among appellate judges. There is only an indirect and distant touch of the truly imperative in the law of murder (or of anything else) as addressed to the supreme appellate judge: some highly unusual types of disregard of his conscience-duty can lead to disgrace and even impeachment or prison; and even honest but stubborn disregard of the traditional materials or of the traditional manner of their use could probably cumulate into perceptible repercussions. In contrast, for the judge at trial (who practices a very different craft from that of the appellate judge), the imperative aspect of "the official law" is materially greater. For he may, as the phrase goes, be "spanked" by the appellate court for doing some piece of his job incorrectly. The rebuke is only to pride and prestige, but it is a rebuke with teeth. This extra imperative aspect is diminished in fact and in effect as such, in the measure in which the trial judge can figure that the particular case will not be appealed; but such prospect does not alter the normative and semiimperative relation of "the official law" to the trial judge's office and conscience.

Now with either of these judges contrast the advocate, with a case to win. To him *in his craft work* the law of murder is first of all a framework within which he must move—a set of limitations. But secondly, it is a set of tools of persuasion. It affords him a wherewithal for arrangement of evidence; can he build up an obviously "reasonable doubt"? Can he persuade of self-defense, or of criminal insanity, or of the absence of such "intent" as is necessary to "first degree"? Is the language of the statute or the state of the decisions such as can be persuasively shown to take this defendant, on this state of evidence, outside the limited penalty provided by the statute (if the advocate is for the defense) or inside that penalty (if the advocate is for the State)? "The law" here offers not in first instance a guide to conscience, but in first instance, I repeat, a set of conditions limiting operations, and then, within those conditions, a set of tools usable to accomplish a given desired result. The advocate, in a word, faces "the law" as any person faces any institution, with only this difference: that the conduct-controlling purpose of other institutions and of the institution of law in particular is partly absent with respect to the advocate, because, in our system at least, his appointed task includes procurement of a fair trial even for a person who has wholly kicked over all the other purposes of "the law."

Contrast, again, now, the meaning of "the law" for the responsible maker or remaker of "the law." For him it is in first instance a tool, a device, for the shaping of other persons' conduct. The particular tool is verbal, and by ingrained tradition it is backhanded: It is regarded as unlawyerlike to address the persons sought to be controlled in the simple second person of the Ten Commandments or otherwise to say, directly, what is wanted. Instead, the approved method is to set up commands to officials from which a patient man can spell out threats or promises to other people, from which in turn a person of insight can often guess at what the lawmaker would like to see done.[9] But what is clear is that the responsible maker of law must see this law-stuff, actual or prospective, as an engineering device, as a wherewithal to get results, as a problem in cause and effect within the general working context of the whole institution of Law-Government. Given that institution as it is and as it goes, what pattern of law-words will so galvanize and organize the relevant official law-personnel as to make threats and promises come true; what pattern of law-words can hope indeed so to galvanize and channel the laymen to be moved that threats become unnecessary and promises stay within a workable budget? Speedy results, accurate, certain, cheap, and no unwanted by-product: an engineering, a technological goal and study. The other part of the study is the whither—but that is a study not of law-stuff as such, but rather of what ends law-stuff, along with all else of society, should be set to serve.

There is no value here in going on through other law-crafts. The point is that the craft-concept, by subdividing different jobs for seeing, taps and then organizes a range of light on "the official law" which legal thinkers, at least, have been a few centuries in getting into anything better than spasmodic use. The next point would be a suggestion that any other institution in society—say education—offers promise of similar illumination by a similar approach. What the crafts in any institution are, will differ; but always there are differing and complementary crafts. And always, as with the legal crafts today, to lose sight of the aspect of skills-and-knowledge—and standards, and goals—is to threaten the craft with technical and moral decay.

The craft-concept, moreover, offers a most peculiar value to sociology. For to study a craft is to study men at concrete activity, to watch the little coral beasties at work on their individual living and on their individual contributions of by-product. No discipline is healthy in which the practical-arts side is not in steady interplay

[9] This description is of the worst, taken as if typical. Yet there is enough pervading truth in it to let the cartoon have point.

with the theoretical: providing problems, providing experience and insight, testing and retesting theory. In sociology that interplay with the practical-arts side has been under-developed—at least until the emergence of such modern areas as "industrial sociology." Sociological concepts have tended to be too vast, too vague for convenient daily use. I think it interesting that social workers, who should be sociologists, tend rather into psychiatry for help, and that the relocation centers, which should have been calling for sociologists (or lawyers), recruited instead from anthropology. Turn your eyes and work loose on a sustained use of the craft-and-craftsmen concept, and you find of necessity that one foot remains planted in theory, the other in the practical work of craftsman Smithers, Tuesday next at 10:30 A.M. Your bridge goes up between practice and theory, and it carries steady traffic, two-way.

One can illustrate from the legal field both the process and its tendency into cross-bearings of unsuspected value. The trouble-case—grievance, dispute, offense—is one of the most important growing-points of legal doctrine and, no less, of the lesser legal institutions. The trouble-case and its disposition are of course part of the daily grist of legal craft-work. Mention has already been made of the interplay of past regularity and the unique upshot of the particular conflict: folkway and themis. That is general. But among the trouble-cases are mingled some which are big with portent: crucial cases. A challenge is made to some ancient landmark of practice and norm. The challenge either succeeds or it fails: a vital new impulse is thus either incorporated into the going system for keeps, or it is stamped out. What concerns me is not merely the shaping power of the single determination, but especially the way in which, around the somewhat accidental particular issue and particular proponents, drives of all kinds in the culture which theretofore have been inarticulate, unnoticed, misconceived, grow vocal, *organize* themselves—so that the determination brings not only new direction (or rejection thereof) but new consolidation of the working structure. You see what I am trying to indicate: an illumination of *major dynamics* and also of major structure, by way of the initially modest study of the run of the mine work of the crafts. I may add that I shall be very much surprised if deep and close study along this line should fail to reveal valuable parallels between the trouble-and-crisis-case process of culture-growth and an equivalent trouble-and-crisis-case process in the growth of the individual personality.

V

One other matter I should like to touch on before closing. The engineering approach to law-stuff which I have ascribed to the responsible lawmaker is of course appropriate not only to the maker of the official Rules of Law of the State, but to the person handling the control-machinery of any group, from the family on up. The Law-and-Government jobs, it will be remembered, are the jobs, for *any* group, of *any* size, of producing, maintaining, and directing that group's groupness. All regulatory machinery of any kind makes up a single field of study; indeed, it is fascinating, as one watches a new family struggle with children who are just coming to talking age, to watch legally untrained parents—*and* two- or three-year-olds—revert to or reinvent such lawyer's techniques as the distinction, the extension of a rule by analogy, literalistic construction of an announced rule, or construction according to the spirit which giveth life; or to see them redevelop almost *ab initio* the theory of notice and a hearing, or the theory against ex post facto law. And such observation of the law phases of every other institution or activity known to us has its potent value. But what I am immediately concerned about is the consequent amusing emergence of a new tiny branch of sociology: the sociology of dogmatics, which deals with what happens when people try to get their rules for guidance into words that have authority. The sociology of dogmatics hooks up interestingly with the phenomenon of changing period-style in the law-crafts, and by that route brings to the institution of law and to the citizen's desires and needs with respect to that institution a light and a hope which have been badly missing in this country for some four generations. I refer to the ideal of a government "of laws and not of men" and to the ideal of a tribunal in which cases are decided "by the law," irrespective of the person of the judge. Both of these ideals are justified ideals, and the theory that government and law do in fact work largely irrespective of the person of the official is a theory which *ought* to be substantially true. Neither—as will promptly appear—is what is now being said at all in conflict with what I said above about the inherent factor of the man in any work of law at all.

What is inherent is that the man must always enter into the result: it is he who must read the words of the rule of law, it is he who must size up the facts as to whether a rule of law applies. No rule of law ever applied itself. But what the sociology of dogmatics teaches is that in the measure that a craft-tradition runs clean, clear, reliable, you may expect much the same *kind* of reading, much the same *manner* of application, much the same classification of the situation, from *any* trained craftsman. Divergencies thus shrink in number and in degree in the measure of the clarity of the craft-tradition. To that extent the "man" element can and does shrink within the meaning of the phrase and of the ideal. If, moreover, the current period-style (as was the case in the great days of our early 19th century, and as is becoming increasingly the case again today) stresses the spirit and purpose, not the mere letter of the rules of law, then the constant struggle between old, frozen form and new, emergent need and situation tends into a steady, rather than into an unreckonable and happenstance attention to the latter. That is indeed not enough to insure regularity of result. For if the prevailing rules of law are drawn not to purpose, but according to external criteria, if the definitions are not functional but are fixed by marks independent of function, then the conflict remains unpredictable between the drive of form and the drive of need. Let, however, a period-style in the crafts which stresses purpose and function take over also the shaping and phrasing of the rules themselves, and you come into possession of rules of law which come close indeed to deciding cases independently of men: for they are rules which talk well nigh alike to every craftsman, of whatever background or temperament, who has been trained in and is responsive to that period-style. In such a regime, indeed, the creative activity of the man-in-office looms particularly large; but it is for all that a relatively predictable activity, fitting with the spirit of the rule—it therefore fits also with the slogan of "law and not men" and with the ideal which informs that slogan.

I find it not queer, but natural, that the sociology of dogmatics (which is one little branch of the sociology of institutions) should find itself concerned with period-style, which is a branch of esthetics. I find it not queer, but natural, that the combination should proceed to resolve jurisprudential controversy, to clear up the working meaning of a noble ideal of government, and to point the way for effective reform of our rules of law by showing what they must be like in order to do the work they are for. I find it not queer, but natural, that the resulting light on the institution of

Law, by simultaneously illuminating the whole problem of the crafts and of the teamwork phase of all institutions, should give fresh perspective on all of social science. As between disciplines, as between persons, as between nations: it pays to be neighborly.

{ 16 }

THE CONTENT OF A JURISPRUDENCE COURSE [a]

. . . I stand thus for a compulsory third year special course in Jurisprudence, in every school that trains lawyers for their great profession. It is feasible to give. It is a joy to teach. And, after the first floundering, the students take it with enthusiasm as well as profit.

But when it comes to what is to go into such a course, let me speak in warning. You have two-semester hours, maybe three. To have three semester-hours for Jurisprudence is like having three semester-hours for the LL.B. course in Law. Make no mistake about that. Jurisprudence is as big as Law, and bigger. And as a teaching matter, it is twice as big, because a student *gets* not what you tell him, but what he *goes and gets* out of the telling, and makes his own. He has to think it through, test it out, make it his own; and to get him to do that is slow going. In three semester-hours you can scratch a bit in one corner or two corners. Jurisprudence as a whole subject, you will never even get to looking at.

That makes very little difference. It makes very little difference, because the job does not call for "covering" Jurisprudence. The job calls for putting together what a student knows of law, and for getting *some* meaning out of the putting; and there is not one corner of Jurisprudence in which two or three semester-hours of work will not give you a very satisfying result on that main job.

But I am much concerned to make clear that it is utterly impossible to "cover" the whole of Jurisprudence, because that makes clear in turn two other things. The first is that seven courses in

[a] Excerpt, at 591-2, from *A Required Course in Jurisprudence*, 9 AM. L. S. REV. 590 (1940).

Jurisprudence, in different schools, which have no single common topic, can yet be each and all superb courses for the job and for the student. The second is that anybody planning a course can afford to spend no time in lamentation on omissions. He can begin by knowing that he will have to omit seventy-four semester-hours of valuable work in Jurisprudence. The important thing is to get whatever he does choose into such shape as to make his men *think* about it, and put what they know of law together around it.

Indeed it is almost startling to run over even a few of the angles of approach and areas of inquiry which open in Jurisprudence— any one of them capable of filling six semester-hours as full of good meat as any egg; any one of them capable also of profitable, though less extended treatment, if only the treatment of whatever is chosen for treatment be intensive, and go deep, and get into concrete material from all over the prior or contemporaneous courses in law. Here, for instance, is the philosophical foundation of law —which you might think of as the beginning of Jurisprudence— and which can be handled either from a comparative angle or from that of a particular chosen philosophy. Do that beginning right, and you will never get much beyond the beginning, in any two or three unit course; at Columbia, we have wanted to get into other matters, and so have just been forced to begin "without the beginning." But that beginning is a rousing and worthwhile field of study.

Another is the nature of law, and its definition, and the values to be had from one or another definition; or the nature of justice, either ideal justice or what men feel to be justice, and the bearing of the quest for justice on the content of law and the ways of judges and lawyers with law. I suppose those would be questions in the philosophy of law as distinct from the philosophical and metaphysical foundations of law.

Then there is the discipline which Wigmore calls legal method, and which Kantorowicz called dogmatics, and which I should call casuistry: study of how one goes about getting a right answer to problems, out of the authoritative given materials, and within the framework of the accepted techniques. It is a very different thing to just get the hang of doing this in a dozen courses, from what it is to look the process and the art over as a special job, and to figure out how the job is best done. And if there be one thing which can wake a law-class up to the depth and color there is in cases, it is for them to start reading cases for a while not to get the rule laid down, but to get hold of how the writing judge went to work to find, test, phrase, and apply the rule laid down.

All of such things, or any of them, occur to anyone as possible subject matter for a course in Jurisprudence. But there is a wholly different slant available. There is a theory of legal institutions to be inquired into, quite as illuminating as any theory of law: What is a court? Why is a court? How much of what we know as "court" is accidental, historically conditioned—how much is essential to the job? The problem of administrative tribunals can also become very interesting, in that light. The "lawyer" is another legal institution, and so is "contract," and so is "trust." And "res judicata" and "day in court" have a good deal more to them than the doctrines on the subject.

Again, I should suppose that study of the relation between law and what law accomplishes is Jurisprudence, quite as solidly as is the inquiry into how law comes into being, or comes to undergo change. I should suppose that the relation between our discipline and the social sciences is Jurisprudence, and a kind that rewards study, too. I should think an amazingly fine course in Jurisprudence could be built around the life-work of a Holmes, watching his ideas ripen, watching influences at work on him, watching the interaction of the doctrine of the time, the time itself, and the man. Or again, history read for its meaning is Jurisprudence: say, over a hundred years, the relative roles played by the courts, the legislatures, the writers, political leaders, and the movement of the times, in the shaping and working of our law.

No, by the time one comes thus to the end of a first page of possible angles into Jurisprudence, one finds the wherewithal to fill one solid year and more of course-work. Choice must be made, ruthless choice. Only two things seem to me vital, as to subject matter: there ought to be *some* study of some part of our legal techniques, viewed just as such, because such study cross-illumines all the cases any boy has read. And there ought to be *some* study of the quest for justice, for that is one of the more hidden things in law, and yet the finest of them all. . . .

{ 17 }

THE STUDY OF LAW AS A LIBERAL ART [a]

You ought to find an unusual number of striking resemblances between what I am about to say and the notable speech delivered last fall at the Michigan Centennial by a certain Dean whose monument we are in process of dedicating. You ought to; I certainly did, when I went back to his paper after finishing this one. I am certain that these resemblances are not coincidental. I find them most gratifying. For I believe firmly that when two intelligent and curious people, both working in the same context and looking to the same purpose, open their eyes and really seek to see what is about them, they ought to see many things alike, so much alike that their very seeing draws them together into a team. This belief in no way quarrels with Miss Mentschikoff's observations of this morning regarding the way in which a person's experience must condition and screen his seeing and his judgments about it. You will note that, for instance, when we come to the difference in emphasis between Levi and me in regard to the use of independent reading as a tool in legal education.

But to work:

Surely there have not been many things which so obscure the pursuit of wisdom as does the misposed issue. In American legal education the first and worst of such misposings has been and is: How far "must" the University Law School sacrifice its University Mission to the sad practical fact that its graduates must earn a practical living in the practical practice of practical law? Joseph Story saw the matter thus a century and a quarter ago. I heard it

[a] Address at the Dedicatory Celebrations, University of Chicago Law School, April 30, 1960.

375

thus misposed as recently as the last meeting of the American Association of Law Schools by a Harvard Law professor of distinction who was on his way to Yale.[b] Story surrendered unconditionally, and American legal education is suffering still from his abdication of a University's responsibility. As we shall see, his surrender was abject.

What needs emphasis first, however, is that the surrender rested on false thinking. The truth, the truth which cries out, is that the good work, the most effective work, of the lawyer in practice roots in and depends on vision, range, depth, balance, and rich humanity—those things which it is the function, and frequently the fortune, of the liberal arts to introduce and indeed to induce. The truth is therefore that the best *practical* training a University can give to any lawyer who is not by choice or by unendowment doomed to be hack or shyster—the best *practical* training, along with the best human training, is the study of law, within the professional school itself, as a liberal art.

Story's writings make plain that this was not an idea strange to him. But he wanted students, he wanted them quick, he deemed the current market for a decent product to be slender. He posed the false issue. He bid for students by limiting the curriculum to a single year, and by cutting out every aspect of breadth, depth, or vision on which his own best work had theretofore depended and continued to depend. So, in utter disregard of the older tradition that the study of law must reach as wide as a world and as high and deep as man's best wisdom about government—the tradition subscribed to equally by Benjamin Franklin, our universal genius, by Thomas Jefferson, our classic liberal, by James Kent, the most rounded and solid legal conservative of that day, and by Story himself in eloquent terms, in 1817—so, as the barest training for a legal cobbler, Story successfully launched the Harvard Law School. By Holmes' time it had degenerated into what was hardly even a decent trade school. Small wonder.

Note now the sequence of events, note the way in which past error, especially a crucial past misposing of an issue, can baffle even genius. Attention (that is, here, to the posed or misposed issue) conditions seeing as much as do the context and the background with and out of which we see.

Langdell, who rebuilt the school into what was long the lead-

[b] And the misposing pervades and distorts half of the report of the British-Canadian-American Conference on Legal Education, Sept. 5-8, 1960: 14 J. LEG. ED. 13-173 (1961).

ing institution of the country, saw three deep truths. The first was, that a University training in law, indeed a liberal arts study of *anything*, for the *doer* in the art, if it is to be right, must be technically solid, technically reliable, in a word, craftsmanlike. You must learn to draw, before you can be free to distort, or merely to feel and express. You must learn to draft, before any legal vision you may have or learn can take shape in a workable, working measure. The second thing that Langdell saw was that history, carefully studied, is one good road to understanding. Depth is of the essence, and the time-dimension is one main road to depth. Langdell's third insight needs no less attention, in these decades when so much noise is devoted to "What Fields of Law and How Much of Each Shall We Include in the Curriculum?" That third deep insight went to a method of instruction, and also to a sub-ject-matter of instruction, each of which ran independent of any such particular "Fields of Law" as Contracts, Trusts, Equity Juris-diction, or any other of those "Subjects" which still typify and stultify a Law School Catalog. Langdell's new method of instruc-tion was by way of detailed discussion of an historical sequence of selected appellate cases, presented in the concrete, presented in full, studied before the class-hour by the whole class, and available, during the hour, for microscopic re-examination. Langdell's new subject-matter which transcended any particular doctrinal sub-ject-matter was legal analysis, legal reasoning, legal argument, and legal synthesis. A genius. Put together with a quest for develop-ing out of the disordered case-law of that day some underlying principles of substantive doctrine, one had here a combination that, in contrast to any cheap trade-school teaching, could well appear worthy of the efforts of a University, and it is no wonder that (especially in Ames' watered-down popularization) the idea began to sweep the discipline.

But the curse of Story was still on it. The resulting technical skills, though sharp and well instilled, were narrow, and they re-mained so. The wherewithal for vision was not given. The circuit was both small, and closed. It called for a man of the personal power of a Hand or of a C. C. Burlingham, Sr. to break out of such training into the study and understanding of the liberal art.

We have three rather striking monuments to that. Thus when Keener was called to Columbia in 1890 to put that law school on a footing worthy of a great University, he brought with him two policies: (1) "The" case-system (for the embattled crusaders did not bother to distinguish, for instance, Langdell's lawyer-oriented

learn-how-to-do-it-yourself "case-system" from Ames' scholar-ori-
ented learn-my-lovely-doctrine "case-system") —"The" case-system
must control *all* courses, with lectures driven into bootleg, and
with books, other than case-books and law reports, all but anath-
ema as tools of learning. (2) All that noise which is not "law"
must go out; a "law" curriculum must cast out Ishmael. Columbia
University, in the interest of acquiring a University-type Law
School, had therefore to amputate from any official "law"-con-
nection what became the Department of Political Science. Thus
the Roman Law perspective of a Munroe Smith, the scholarship
and vision of a Goodnow, the power and range of our greatest international lawyer, John Bassett Moore, flourished not within the
law curriculum, nor for it, but across the barbarian border,—
though law students were permitted to take some of their courses.
Indeed, even as Columbia was beginning to move into correction
of this early error, Thomas Reed Powell himself had to wait for
a call from Harvard Law School (which, tardily, but over the last
decades with a gratifying, though intermittent, persistence, has
also been trying to out the "damned spot" stained in by Story)—
Powell had to wait for a call from Harvard to find his recognition
as a full-fledged *law* professor.

The second monument dates from a full quarter-century later,
but was again a lasting one. In 1906 Roscoe Pound had issued
what more than 50 years later is still a classic call for general
regeneration of the American approach to matters of law, of law-
administration, of law-appreciation, of the courts' work in relation
to society and human need: it came close to being a call for law
to be viewed and treated as a liberal art at work.[e] That call was in
intent and major substance national; but tone and method and
material reached out into a whole world, even as they reached also
down into the daily work of every lawyer. It was a document of
greatness, and one of promise. But by 1914 we find Pound writing
that the clarion is no longer needed. In 1915, when, already our
foremost jurisprude, he became Dean at Harvard Law School, he
deliberately took his own Jurisprudence course *out of the undergraduate curriculum*. He kept it out, lest his bulk of graduates be
distracted—or contaminated. "Heavy, heavy, over thine head"
hangeth the curse of Joseph Story.

The third of the monuments lies, in time, half-way between the

[e] *The Causes of Popular Dissatisfaction with the Administration of Justice.* The
reprint in 20 J. AM. JUDIC. SOC. 178 (1937) is accompanied by Wigmore's description of the circumstances and immediate effects.

other two. This Law School [Chicago] was founded in 1903. Like a prospective Greek colony, we looked for a Mother-City, we turned to the then Athens of the American legal world, to Harvard Law School. They loaned us a man for an organizing Dean, they offered also their prestige and backing. After all, had not Massachusetts colonized Northern Ohio? There was, however, in the Chicago project a disturbing factor, a man named Ernst Freund, an innovator who was dedicated to the study of law as a liberal art. His background had been in the tradition of those German "law"-faculties which were not limited in theory to what Langdell and Keener saw as "law." The difference appears even in the name: *"Rechts-*UND *Staatswissenschaftliche Fakultät:"* the faculty of Law-Government. Freund, now, was proposing to enlarge the vision, the labor, the educational prospect and plan of our new "Law" school by founding in these United States the discipline now known as Legislation. He was proposing, even, to recognize as a proper part of a "Law" school's training the then unheard-of art-and-problem we know today as Administration, which is still, after another half-century, obscured and hamstrung in our Law Schools as mere "Administrative Law." Freund was a Whole-seer, and a Seer *for* the Whole—not only a student but a teacher of law, I repeat, as a liberal art in the rich sense of that term. Such thinking was, for Story-and-Langdell-bounded vision, either terrifying or disgusting. We have a letter from Dean Ames, of the then Harvard, in which he regretfully threatens to withdraw the light of his countenance from a program thus corrupted. I have no record of how Ames was tamed, or of how Freund was turned away from too open blasphemy, or both; but somehow (and I assume it was the blarney-tongue of Harper) the new venture was held together.

In consequence, via Ernst Freund of the University of Chicago, the professional study of law as a liberal art was launched again in these United States.

That way of study of law has since then gone forward steadily. The progress, one does note with regret, has been as slow as it has been steady. It has also, all along, been cursed with the original sin, which, as we have seen, cut down the range even of the genius of Langdell. Indeed, in Chicago herself, there have been periods during which it was a little hard to be sure that all three of the necessary things were twined into that "three-fold cord" of legal education which in Bible language "is not quickly broken." Those three necessary things, for any study of Law (or of any other activity) as a Liberal Art are these: (1) neat, clean, effective technical proficiency, which we may think of as the mechanical or physical underpinning of the practice of any liberal art. (2) The second necessary thing, which I like to think of as the intellectual aspect, is making clear the meaning of the art for neighbor, for nation, for the practitioner, the artist, as a man, and finally for mankind at large. (3) The third thing, which I see as spiritual, is the drive and quest of the art, and within the art, for beauty or for service or, best, for both together.

Each of these three strands deserves more detailed talk.

Consider the indispensability of pure technique. Surely each —any—member of the practicing art must be able to *do* what is needed, must be *able* to do it with at least a journeyman's accuracy and dispatch, for *any* consumer of the art's service, and at *any* time. (Let me say here, fast, that this minimum competence of *each* mint-marked law graduate does not appear, as yet, in these United States.)

Let there be no mistake. I am not here tangling with any single law school or any group of law schools. Neither am I making exception of any law school at all, not even of this one. I have, in the course of a long and often misspent life, tried to get this same point across in three particular law schools other than Chicago; by name and in chronological succession: Yale, Columbia, and Harvard. The point made no headway at all, in my time, at any of those schools. None of them was really interested in any question of *minimum* reliability of their *minimum* product. They basked in the sunshine of their A-Men and their B-Men. Neither can I honestly state that even your present Chicago faculty has proved wholly immune to this virulent bacillus.

Yet any whole-view must set itself into the perspective to which a whole-view belongs. And the whole-view begins with a simple fact. A liberal art can be as liberal as you please, and it should be—*any* liberal art should be, including law. But one thing, I repeat, sits firm: any man who proposes to *practice* a liberal art must be *technically competent.* I choose a single example which does not even involve the lawyer's responsibility of every lawyer to his client. In the entrance hall of Al Barnes' amazing collection and arrangement of paintings one meets head-on a huge reclining nude done by Renoir with infinitely sharp and accurate drawing and perspective (with, incidentally, a cold green tone that reminds of David.) It hangs there side by side with the same subject, in the same pose, in the same size, done by the same

Renoir with the luscious reds and soft, almost fluid, contouring of his later work. The pair of pictures make clear to anybody, once he has a chance to think, the fact: technical cleanliness is the only reliable foundation. The matchless second picture could never have been painted by a man who lacked competence to paint the first. Technical skill is not *a* foundation only. It is *the necessary* foundation. Appreciation of a liberal art *can*, sometimes in high degree, be got without it; though even in regard to appreciation an amateur performer can commonly get lengths or laps ahead of the appreciator who can do nothing but appreciate. But for the practicing artist technique is the foundation.

I pause for a moment to deal with an objection. It can be argued that in this era of specialization technical proficiency can be entrusted by the artist to a subordinate as some entrust their spelling to a capable stenographer. We hear of laboratory scientists— outstanding in research as a liberal art—who, the phrase goes, would be "lost" without their artisan but effective technicians. And there may have been great captains—for surely the military art has not infrequently been practiced also as a liberal art—there may have been great captains who were not too good at handling close-order drill (though, few, I suggest, who were deficient in thinking about the techniques of supply). Despite such possibilities I argue firmly that in the particular matter of law, American law, as we approach the 7th decade of the 20th Century, no such delegation can be envisaged, and each individual prospective craftsman requires to go out individually and adequately supplied with his personal basic kit of effective techniques and with some personal basic competence in their use. The American law school, even that of the University of Chicago, is not devoted to the training of Justinians, or of any Justinian's successor—of any man who, on mere emergence from his training, can command the *technical assistance* which, without any technical adequacy of his own, can produce the fighting power of a Belisarius, plus Hagia Sophia in six short years, plus a Corpus Juris Justinianum in seven. The American law school has as its task to turn out a graduating *class* of craftsmen *each* of whom can stand on his own legal feet.

It goes without saying that the second strand of the cord must be built as firm and vibrant as must the first. In part this second comes of itself in the achievement of the first. You cannot, for instance, really learn the two arts of reading: fast reading and utterly exact reading, without some insight into the meaning of what has been read. You cannot learn a law-craftsman's architecture and detail in writing, his power of arrangement along with flavor, his master-accuracy of phrase, without study of what the writing is for nor yet without some understanding of the nature and circumstances of those to whom the writing is addressed. Yet what the institution of law-government does for—and indeed does to—the participant or consumer individual, or group, or community, or state, nation, and *in posse* world—this calls for further and explicit study on its own and in the large. This is not all. Each major one of the individual crafts of the institution needs likewise its own study as a whole. There is a theory of advocacy, or spokesmanship, or rhetoric (which aspect lends the name is immaterial)—a theory which has formed the basis of a liberal art since classic times; a theory, moreover, which is empty and vain save as it builds on and with deep understanding of the psychological and ethical nature of cause or of client, of tribunal or other addressee, of society and of the law-governmental phase thereof. There is, too, a philosophy of advocacy, one which can set itself, without shame, beside any branch I have met of philosophy or of political theory; and in which the modern can advance well beyond the classic. There is, moreover, an esthetics of advocacy (I do *not* mean merely rhetoric as a branch of literature), as there is of each single other of the law-governmental crafts, which represents as significant and valuable a general branch of esthetics as has thus far remained substantially unstudied.

And what I have said for advocacy, or spokesmanship, can be said of course in essence for protective counselling, or for the various aspects of legislation, or for the craft of the trial judge, or that of the court of appeal, or of the administrative wheel-horse, or of the administrator with the reins. Let me reach forward for a moment with this observation: for those (and they are the majority) who come to us either without much interest in beauty or else without much interest in service, it is the combination of the theory and philosophy of the crafts with some advancing and tested *skill in the crafts* which stirs interest and excitement and growth. In forty-five years of rather diversified observation I have met with little else that has been enough in itself to stir any of these students except for a moment or for a few. But education in a school must be directed to *all,* and must be directed not to moments but to years, to a life-time.

One tradition of exposition includes the occasional arrival of an adversary who gets beaten off. It can be a useful tradition; but it is abused when the adversary is set up merely to be knocked down. Hence my adversary today will be very real, and very troubling. "Three years," he says, "is what we have, and only three. Today, moreover," he says, "our graduates do not go out on their own: they hire into an apprenticeship with skilled employers; they get a further training which we can count on to be added unto ours. And where," he says, "in this interesting continuation of a B.A. course which you suggest, is there anything about the *laws* of which we are about—I use your own phrase—to 'mint-mark' these graduates as being Bachelors. Finally," he says, "—or was I mistaken?—I thought I heard you say that your ideas had found little interest at any of the leading law schools in these United States. Was it during forty years and more? And aren't those schools still leading?"

In spite of my skillful—and not too unfair—adversary, I shall now urge that I am not the only man in step in this parade.

The question of knowledge of the "laws" or rules of law, as a subject of instruction, nay, as *the* main subject of instruction, that is the heart-question. Nor is there doubt that the tradition of thinking of "the law" as consisting at least centrally of "the rules" (and principles) is ancient, nor doubt that that tradition has body. Neither can it be gainsaid that organizing such rules into semi-coherent "fields" of law has value, nor yet that a law graduate should have some working understanding of how to deal with the particular peculiar lines of organization our culture has hit upon—which, I admit, are as fundamentally baffling as is our spelling. But what I urge in defense is four-fold:

(1) Langdell and his "case-system" soundly discovered, I repeat, a subject-matter of instruction which ran beyond the bounds or lines of any "Fields" of law, and which was more important than such "Fields." It was not teaching of the rules of law, or of the fields of law, but the teaching of that wide new subject-matter, and the fact that back in the simpler Harvard of 1875–1900 that teaching used to lead to pretty sound technical training of *any* Harvard graduate at all, which gave to anything labelled "the" case-system a *general* prestige-value which more recent facts have for forty years and more belied.

(2) Case-system teaching is tremendously time-consuming; and although as one enters on it some concentration of doctrinal material is vital, the information about rules of law which can be acquired by way of such time-waste is horribly limited. On the other hand, the intensive work of case-teaching—accompanied by

the intricacies of our general case-*law* system—leads to unique specialization among our law-instructors; and a specialist, especially one who is a teacher, loves his baby, thinks his darling more important than any other darling, works out his gospel, and argues, fights, even sometimes intrigues for more hours per semester to spread the Perfect Word. Case-teaching in the upper years is thus a vicious instrument for producing unplanned concentration of good teachers' minds on propagating, at all costs, tiny, mostly unimportant, intricacies of narrow positive doctrine in case-class and by the case-method—because that is the only method that remotely excuses such procedure for any teaching at all except the training of prospective specialists in some narrow field of law. This, again, perpetuates the teacher-scholar's thinking that a man must use *as his central teaching focus*, "the law" or the rules and principles of the particular "field" in which he is one of the few experts and architects. It is so pleasant to work over and try to inculcate in class the whole of one's results in such a field.—Still, it is *not* good doctrine that "What is Fun for the Law Professor is good for the country."

(3) While the second point just made is not as yet familiar, nevertheless, all over the country, the last quarter-century has seen a tremendous and gratifying ebb in the old-style central emphasis upon the rules of law as a central subject-matter even of a case-course organized around a "field of law." I say "gratifying" not because a law student should not meet, learn, and practice the art, on a large scale, of synthesizing cases into first a small-scale and then a large-scale structure of doctrine. The student should indeed be up against this—once, twice, three times, perhaps, for a slower student, four, five. But five times is enough, even for a slow student, and *all five times together have no need to occupy as much as a single year of curricular space.* Meantime the new material which has everywhere been forcing its way in to rival the rules of law, that is material which itself contributes to the second, the "meaning" strand, of our threefold cord; it is "policy" discussion on the wisdom of the rules—discussion which seeks to bring out how they work, how far they do things worth doing, how far they may need change and improvement. And this is good to do. It drives toward the whole, it drives toward meaning. It moves also, somewhat, in terms of the concrete.

But difficulty has resulted, unless not only the individual instructor, but the faculty as a group, pause, look, and take thought. The difficulty is simple. It is this: the number of class hours available in three years does not increase. If to the old task of developing the rules of law, you simply pile on a further equivalent-sized task of exploring their effect and importance and value, then you leave no elbow room: the *less gifted* student becomes the sardine in the box. Moreover, as life has become more complex, the original subject-matter of the rules themselves has also swollen. The sardine gets not only packed, but squeezed.

The answer is of course quite clear; like most plain truths, it has gone largely unnoted. To achieve the values of policy discussion in a modern context, the student needs enough information about the particular rule under inquiry so that he can think instead of merely palaver or emote. Off-the-cuff, bald of information, is not policy-discussion, it is vaporing. "We should," said Levi, "pursue our efforts to bring the problems and methods used in law teaching closer to the actual." That means actual problems. But it means, just as vitally, enough *information per problem* to make it actual to the *less* informed and *less* gifted student. It means also enough *class-time per problem* for the class-work to get actually down into it, in its specific itness. This inescapably results in cutting, relentless cutting, of the doctrinal material covered. It means highly intensified treatment of a vastly smaller body of rules. Cut down thus on scope of the material, and your class-hours do indeed suffice to do the job of technical training, they suffice also to enrich it with exploration of meaning, they suffice to go on into the arts of policy-evaluation, of imagining curative measures, and of documentary and legislative drafting: all merging in the pursuit of a true liberal art. But leave the matter, as most case-book makers, most faculties, and most individual law teachers have been doing, to mere drift, and you find that the new, flooding, loose material shows little bite in itself, but yet manages by flow, dilution, and distraction both to wash out the base of any technical training and—as examinations show yearly—to make uncertain, for many or most, even a knowledge of the rules.

No, a liberal art is not well taught by mere yearning, nor yet by drift. There must be machinery not only of inspiration but of communication, and of practice; it must be machinery which has teeth that mesh. To spread out without discrimination, to heap up material and objectives without rethinking and appropriate refinement of method—that is to invite the kiss of death. Re-design of our production-apparatus is in order. We need a Kaiser, to get us riveting our boathulls from the top.

Let me take just a moment to suggest one (it is of course *only
one*) among the possible fruitful ways of gathering materials for
more intensive discussion. A man could begin by following Langdell in selecting a whole sequence of decisions on one single topic
from one single jurisdiction. This meets, one may note, one part
of Levi's sound demand for historical understanding. And every
teacher in a federal law field knows the gain in comfort, solidity,
and understanding which comes from being able to focus on a
single tribunal; the trouble is that while the Supreme Court roots
in the common law tradition and does resemble our other courts,
neither it nor its issues typify them. Every good teacher in a
federal field knows, too, how useful it can be in study and discussion for the student to be familiar at first hand with much or most
of the background of cases and doctrine which the court had at
hand as it approached the case in hand.

One would certainly, also, instead of editing out of the opinions
either any facts at all or any supposedly collateral issues, leave
these in (at least in careful digest), so that the case would have at
least some of the full-bodied flavor with which the case presented
itself in life to the appellate tribunal. Now a detailed series
of comparable fact-situations, not skimped, but generous, and
spotted around a single rule or issue, can do an interesting job
of providing some real basis for intelligent judgment about the
working and wisdom of a rule; no less, about what factors influence courts in their work, and why; and often, even, how. I
find myself hungering for three further types of material on any
topic: some reasonably full indication of what can be gleaned
from available social science material or current lay literature
about the problem and the bearing thereon of the times; some
knowledge about the sitting judges and the general contemporary
history of the particular court; some indication of and quotation
from counsel's argument, and, where one can get at it (one very
often can) such material from the record as proves illuminating
in regard to the argument, or the decision, or policy. The point
to be made is that material presented in any such fashion, and
appropriately developed in class, would cut the number of rules
or topics "covered" in an upper-year case-class to a tenth or a
twentieth, *leaving the rest for independent reading*. It need not
therefore be unguided reading. There is nothing I know which
would prevent an instructor who loves his material from building
a syllabus to guide and to communicate or even preach his more
prized ideas. But it would be *undiscussed* reading, leaving class-

time free for real and deep discussion. I have never heard that Socrates was seriously worried over "coverage in class," as dictated by some conception of a "field," rather than of the full implications of a "narrow" question.

Such a selection and arrangement of material would make problems of wisdom or "policy" both clean and "actual," and this both in the large and with respect to the particular parties. It would make the manner and motivation of the court's work a matter not of speculation or off-hand guess, but of serious study. It would really whet study and understanding of such craft-skills as counselling, litigation, issue-shaping, arrangement of issue and of argument, legislative invention, and drafting. Indeed, such sharp, *detailed* focusing of the dramatic interplay of situation, rules, institutions and persons offers a branch of humanistic study that can stand up with literature and with the best of history.

(4) The last point on which I find myself far indeed from isolation is in regard to the need for supplementing any of our many types of case-class instruction by one, two, or seven other methods, especially in the upper years. For more than forty years, and all over the country, we have been witnessing experiments, many successful—some fantastically so—but still so tied to the skills and person of particular instructors that little has as yet emerged which is available as a discipline, like "case-teaching," for easy general access. I shall at this time call attention merely to one negative aspect of this ferment. There is one thing of which I have seen and heard nothing—unless perhaps in some of the work here in Hutchins' time—to wit, the large-scale employment of *reading*, and reading *not in course*, as a normal device for acquisition of acquaintance with the stock of inherited knowledge, with the body of inherited thought, and with the meaning, operation, and problems of the law-governmental institution in the contemporary world. Said Levi: "We pay insufficient attention to the classics of legal writing other than those which happen to be opinions or law review articles." He could not be righter. But neither is he right enough. His mind was, and wisely, on a liberal artist's need for understanding his tradition both of institutions and of thought; and a man raised on the great Books thinks then first of "classics." I am more pedestrian. That same liberal artist has need also for a reasonable supply of simple information about the current state and past achievements of his art. I would therefore greatly broaden Levi's statement: "Almost irresponsibly, the general practice of American legal education is to encourage the

silly American superstition that to know anything about anything you must take a *course* in it. Practically no attention is paid to the values of any reading which is not directly course-connected, which means, for the most part, class-connected. The nose of any but the gifted is held down to the assigned case or the specific collateral reference, and even the latter is likely to be addressed less to vision than to further detailed discussion of doctrine already raised in class. The planned use of reading, classic or homespun, in *substitution for* courses, so as to make room for more intensified class-work—this is almost non-existent. And so is deliberate writing, for such purposes."

There is here in American legal education—as a direct inheritance from Langdell—an insularity difficult to understand and impossible to defend. A prospective Ph.D. in government or economics or history or international relations takes courses, and he profits by them; but the bulk of his acquaintance with the achievements, tools, and thinking in his discipline *he goes and gets*. He reads, and he reads on his own. If he comes out less sharply knowledgeable about much of it than if he had taken an intensive course in each part of it, he yet comes out with a range and depth of contact which the relatively intensive character of worthwhile courses bars, over the needed *great* areas, from the work of any but one teacher in a hundred. Now American law instructors are the most specialized in the world. By the same token, their knowledge outside of their own specialties is typically vague or almost absent; yet each one of them is aware of a need for *some* acquaintance with the nature of the general body of our doctrine. It comes like the blow of a bludgeon to find a man with such queer equipment insisting with conviction and emotion, and by attitude and behavior, that for the general run of *unspecialized* students *no* knowledge of that particular scholar's particular field is really much worth having unless such knowledge has the meticulous accuracy and the ground edge which that particular scholar, with his diamond-cutting mind, has managed to put on it, and which—in the teeth of the annual lessons to him from his own examinations—he still proposes to inculcate next year by his same accustomed manner of case-teaching, which each succeeding examination demonstrates to have been inadequate. Forgetting all his F's and all his D's and all his scraping C's—*his own failures*—he argues not for less material and higher concentration, and, to fill in background, for a syllabus and an adequate supply of books for the reading room. He argues instead for increasingly extensive non-coverage in class by *his* course in the same old way.

In contrast, let me urge with passion that if one-tenth of the energy and skill which in the past ten years has gone into the production of case-books had gone instead into the production of reading lists and critical syllabi to guide, we should already have available a machinery for moving legal education, all over the country, into its rightful status as the study of a liberal art: truly *in*tensive work *in* class, *ex*tensive work outside. What we need is not more time for professional law study, but better employment of the time we have; not more courses, but fewer, with much more time open for outside reading and writing; not wider class-coverage but class-coverage narrower and deeper, varying from three or four times narrower and deeper in the first year up into five to twenty times narrower and deeper in the upper years. In a word, what American industry faced with the advent of World War II: re-thinking, re-designing, re-tooling. À la Kaiser, I repeat.

I must not leave unregarded the last, the spiritual strand in this our threefold cord. Its first aspect, the quest and study of beauty in and within the institution of law-government, has been curiously overlooked by students of esthetics. There is some discussion of rhetoric, seen as literature, and Mencken noted that some of the best American writing was buried in briefs no one of which has ever been read by half a hundred pairs of eyes. But who follows up the esthetics of the trial in court, where the advocate writes his drama as he goes, and produces it, and himself acts the main part— all with a counter-author and a counter-cast writing and acting unreckonably against him?—a branch of esthetics never yet even discovered by most estheticians. Who looks into the architecture of draftsmanship? Some have, a little, in regard to the finer type of legal treatise; and every author of a *good* treatise, or of a *good* case-book, or indeed of a good law review article, knows and rejoices in the thrill of an architecture honest and powerful. But once again, is it proper for the Law Professor to monopolize for his personal benefit or enjoyment? How often—for teaching, or even for theory alone—have the esthetics of statutory or documentary draftsmanship come in for study, appreciation, and expression to the student?: the architecture of a German Civil Code, the chaste compression of phrase in a Code Napoléon, the shift from the gruesome prolix obscurity of an American statute book of 1910 to the relatively clean organization and clarity of the better phases of a

Uniform Commercial Code. Who in the literature or in the class-room has followed up the implications of Jerome Frank's insight that a court "reads" a statute as a performing violinist "reads" his music or an actor "reads" his part? And the esthetics of the law-government arts of action—say negotiation, chairing, client-han-dling, or appellate judging—(I do *not* mean merely the writing of the opinion)—these, except for the work on the last of that con-summate artist and appreciator, Walton Hamilton, are substan-tially as unmentioned in print as they are unattended to in thought. Literary men have indeed from time to time noted the esthetic qualities in surgery, and Benêt has celebrated a small-town doctor's handling of practice and patient with the same fervor with which he depicted Dan'l Webster mastering the Devil. But in the main, law-governmental esthetics, the quest for beauty in the work, that well of daily intangible reward to the craftsman, also and at the same time that unfailing fountain of craftsmanship which is effective craftsmanship—that, to the loss of the profession and to the damage of the public lettered or illiterate, blushes not only unstudied, and untaught, but unimagined.

This is not because the esthetics of law-government are esoteric. On the contrary, they are rather earthy, and they afford, along with pleasure, immediate practical return. For an instance, I think I have demonstrated [d] that the concept of period-style, brought to bear upon the manner of American appellate judging, deepens understanding of process and of meaning, and that it also yields the wherewithal for prompt improvement (for wheel-horse, and for lead-horse, and for driver—for anybody but the genius who needs no teaching) of both appellate advocacy and appellate judg-ing. More, it goes far, in the service of Law-Government and of our polity, to allay the crisis in confidence which has for four decades been festering in the bar about the work and reckonability of our appellate bench. Yet, in application to law and government, that concept of "period-style," nay, any concept of "style" at all, has remained almost unknown.

One can indeed note this one minor hopeful sign: in the past fifty years the general literary level of legal composition (I dare not say the same for composition on the governmental side) has risen beyond ready belief or understanding. Legal books and articles not so very long ago had the dull indigestibility of a pro-

---

[d] THE COMMON LAW TRADITION—DECIDING APPEALS (1960). And compare the illumination derived from divergent modes of judging: Wetter, THE STYLES OF JUDICIAL OPINIONS (1960).

verbial new bride's biscuit; today you can read them, many you read with pleasure, not a few are written with distinction. The level of opinion-composition has risen less strikingly; for this is the daily product of a great group who publish not when nor what they choose to, but constantly and without selection and because they must. For all that, the rise in average level is amazing. The double phenomenon means that one aspect of a liberal art, the steady and somewhat successful quest for satisfying form, is live at least on the law-side of law-government; and it means to me that in practice and the times there is a market for legal esthetics, one which waits only upon a production-apparatus. It means, finally, with the rise in literary level among the scholars, that *if they wish* to give attention to the wider job, and to *teach* it, instead of merely having personal fun, they have the capacity. They can. The matter goes to will. It has become a situation like that which faces any ordinary State's Attorney. He has *power* to move here, he has *power* to move there, he has *power* also to direct his choosing to serve his own pleasure or his own advancement. But his time and facilities admit of doing only ten per cent of what he has the *power* to do. The easiest way is of course not to rethink the job, but to roll down the groove the predecessor officers have carved.

In regard to the quest for beauty in law-government I urge that such old easy following is out of date. Our legal scholars, our law-teachers, have begun to discover the esthetic values in the law-crafts for themselves; the shift both in opinion-writing and in the manner of judging makes palpable also that a market sits a-waiting. An opportunity, nay, an obligation, has thus opened. For right work, the old groove will no longer do.

As to the other main phase of the spiritual, the drive for service, the case is better, but still far from good.[e] We do have at least general recognition among men of good will that law-government has service to perform. It would be hard to find anyone in legal education who would on this thing of service parallel Patterson's: "It is hard to see how esthetic theory has much to do with law." Most, if pressed and if outside of enough highballs to break down reticence, would admit that law-government is a service institution: in service lies its soul—service for client or cause or class, or for some dream which embraces all classes and even a world.

[e] On this Frank Newman was admirable, at the Conference referred to above, p. 376, note b.

It makes no difference how you feel in regard to message or mission in the other liberal arts; this one must by its nature put service beside beauty, or ahead. One aspect of that is to look into what is good for the Whole, the Entirety, and to puzzle among conflicting or competing claims, and necessary though it is to cut the teeth and to practice the jaws on matters of this sort in detail and in the small, attention is called for also in the large and in the over-all, else the Whole Art goes empty.

On this last, today, we meet trouble.

The trouble starts with the current American idea that—church schools apart—it is not for a school to inculcate beliefs, unless perhaps in George Washington, the flag, and the United States. Any other approval, moreover, if practiced by individual teachers, is thought to imperil not only student independence, but faculty unity: let the cobbler stick to his last! Few, and to my mind unfortunate, are the faculties which have worked their recruitment to produce a substantially uniform political complexion.

The teacher, moreover, especially the teacher in his middle years, is typically up against two further and personal blocks. On the one hand, his very competence in one, two, or three relatively narrow "fields" has tended to dampen any inner conviction of competence in regard to over-all judgments. On the other hand, if his whole-drive for the ideal is religious, he feels hesitant to thrust it upon a whole class, many of whom do not share his religion; if it is not religion-linked, the man is typically revolted at the idea of "imitating" the kind of "empty mouthings" of his elders against which he has found it necessary to rebel.

Finally, there is the tradition of the ordinary modern American intellectual: he feels shy about open expression of the things which most deeply move him, those by which he lives; and he commonly distrusts the value of mere preachment, anyhow, to change the heart or stir the soul.

Take the last first: the intellectual is out of step on this. Work can be done by words. Neither the Rotary speaker nor his audience has any doubt of the effective value of what has its known label: a speaker's "message." Nor has Billy Graham. Concede that words are neither all, nor enough. They can still pack a wallop. And as for shyness, that is no quality for a teacher to indulge, especially no quality for a law teacher, who must from one to three quarters be a ham.

No, the question goes flatly to the merits. There is something here worth teaching. It is of the essence of the profession in any aspect, it is trebly of the essence of the profession as a liberal art. It represents that line and variety of obligation without which all the rest becomes a menace. And much of the job depends so largely on knowledge and on vision. Yet neither the needed insight nor the needed informed responsibility comes, to any but the more gifted, by mere exposure and osmosis.

Yet, once again, there is the problem of responsibility for the Mint-mark—as to *any* person stamped. The questions therefore are two: First, can this informed obligation of service be *taught* at all, to all, or to almost all? Second, if so, can it be taught with decency, and with safeguard of a teacher's self-respect? To both questions the answer is: Yes.

Can it be taught at all? It is almost amusing to see the eagerness with which the same law teachers who shun all mention of high ideals roll up their sleeves to inculcate those low ideals (which still are true ideals) known as the better doctrine or the wiser rule or the true principle in some particular aspect of some particular "field." And often with success. It is fascinating to observe how any course which reaches for wide vision and perspective evokes from the class embattled discussion that both roots and flowers in the deeper and higher purposes of law-government. Above all, any teaching which goes to skill in any of the crafts, if accompanied by inquiry into what that craft is for, and by occasional posers on what to do in a situation fraught with ethical difficulty, brings out of a class a fighting discussion which induces not only a sense of craft-responsibility, but a sense informed.

Finally, as a method, there is the occasional pure soul-searching or revivalistic sermon. Most good law professors can preach rather well. And many a sermon—if sermons come only rarely, and if they come with power—many a sermon kindles many a man. Kindling is not enough; but kindling starts the fire. There is no reason to be reticent about what you know they need to know, and think and feel they ought to think and feel. Respect can come by observation and osmosis; knowledge cannot. Neither do the tenderer virtues come by themselves except with age; and the problems of today's world cannot wait for the inexperienced to *live* their way through into experience and suffering enough to not only see whole, but to judge wisely about both vision and duty. The law student needs in these matters to have the wells of wisdom open not only in the little, but in the large. We, I say therefore, are free to offer what we have, within the finest traditions of our universities and of our polity, provided only that we in no way demand agreement or penalize dissent. The teaching of law as a liberal art requires that we put forth our best. The student is entitled to it. But such teaching requires also that we leave the student free. That is what leaves *us* free.

The times are ripe. This last year I have addressed group after group of law students from all over the country, explaining how what has seemed to many a departure by our appellate bench from steady duty into personal vagary has been instead and in fact a recapture of our highest common law tradition of judicial duty and steadiness. I have never been so received. Each time, the boys have gone quietly crazy with belief, and with relief. There is a hunger in the land which the responsible law teacher can neither ignore nor neglect—a hunger for responsibility in our profession.

In another connection, I urged long ago that the nature of law-government as a service-institution and of legal esthetics as functional esthetics means that right work in this liberal art finds the Beautiful twined by nature with the Good.[f] I urge now that since law-government is also a discipline of sharp-drawn effective measures for the control of human action, and since such measures can be built only by sound technique based on sound knowledge of humanity, based also on accurate observation, right work in law-government twines in the True as well. Technique, the intellectual side, the spiritual—the true, the beautiful, the good—a liberal art indeed. Truly, if each strand be spun strong and solid in itself, that threefold cord cannot be broken quickly, or at all.

[f] Above, p. 193.

THE CHICAGO LAWYER'S PLEDGE [1]

In accepting the honor and the responsibility of life in the profession of the law, I engage, as best I can,

> to work always with care and with a whole heart and with good faith;
>
> to weigh my conflicting loyalties and guide my work with an eye to the good less of myself than of justice and of the people; and
>
> to be at all times, even at personal sacrifice, a champion of fairness and due process, in court or out, and for all, whether the powerful or envied or my neighbors or the helpless or the hated or the oppressed.

[1] This pledge is offered at the graduation luncheon to the outgoing class of the University of Chicago Law School, for those who choose to take it. Over the last ten years no one has chosen not to take it.

CONTROLLING BEHAVIOR:
HOW AND WHY?

LAW OBSERVANCE VERSUS LAW ENFORCEMENT [a]

Law, like social work, begins when someone takes to doing something someone else doesn't like. One way of attacking this problem of human conduct is by centering on the individual whose conduct is making trouble. That gives us case work, and, with luck, individual cures. That method of attack takes the social system for granted. The job is to get the individual adjusted to the system. Different in matter, method, and aim is the attack by way of study of the system to see what it is and how it works. This is, to be sure, of service later in undertaking individual cures; but it is, with luck, of service even more in opening up a chance of modifying the system and of reducing the need for cures. This paper moves along the second line: that of study of the system, of mass and not of individual effects.

I propose to ring changes, perhaps *ad nauseam*, on three simple facts: first, that law observance is a question not of legal rules, but of the formation of folkways that can be and will be learned chiefly without direct reference to particular rules; second, that law and folkways alike are not general and common to our society, but are different and specific according to groups, occupational and other; and third, that for mass, as contrasted with individual, attempts at control, the problem of lawmaking and of law enforcement centers on informed, sustained effort to find the particular persons whose conduct is concerned, and to devise means for affecting the conduct patterns of those particular persons.

I should like to begin with the proposition that law, as we know it in modern society, is not a good, but an evil; it is a thing to

[a] From PROCEEDINGS OF THE CONFERENCE ON SOCIAL WORK (1928) 127.

regret; it is an expression of our somewhat startling incapacity to arrange our affairs in any decent fashion. At the same time, that incapacity being present and obvious, law as we know it becomes necessary as a makeshift to fill the gap; it is necessary as a make-shift; it is a clumsy, rickety thing, but it is our own and some of us still love it. Let me illustrate. If what we think of as law ob-servance should ever be or become universal, it is clear that law enforcement would have no reason or room for existence. And the concept of law would be in grave danger of vanishing with it. What would be left would be the ways of the society, the patterns of action which people learn and live. Those ways are not law. Technical law, as we know it today, is the set of rules specifying what government officials shall or may do when other people do or fail to do specified things. Law, as we know it today, presup-poses a government. And it presupposes also that there will be people who do not walk in the ways desired; indeed, those are the only people with whom our rules of law normally concern them-selves. Those who, as the phrase goes, observe the law, the law pays little attention to. It will thus be clear that I am using "law" to mean official pronouncements or official action aimed at keeping the action of other officials or other people within desired lines or limits. This is of course not the whole of law; but it is the whole of such law as is contemplated by the terms "law observance" and "law enforcement." It will be clear, too, that I am using "folk-ways" to mean any established practices, any pattern of action actually observable among some group of persons—especially prac-tices which not only exist but are accepted by the group con-cerned. The term thus used is loose and broad; it requires as care-ful specific analysis as does "law," but limitations of space require the use of shorthand terms.

What is meant, now, by this phrase, "observance of the law"? It is a phrase which rests upon confusion. It is a phrase which assumes that in some manner the law contains precepts, that the law tells us what to do. Such is not normally the case. The words of the law are not: "Keep hands off the goods of others," but "Any person duly convicted of larceny shall be sentenced" to so many years in prison. Undoubtedly there is behind this rule a purpose or policy of inducing people to keep hands off the goods of others. But the rule and the policy the rule is supposed to further may or may not be on speaking terms. If you happen to believe that im-prisonment breeds crime, you may have your doubts even about the simple case I have instanced. When it comes to whether the policy of farm relief will be accomplished by the McNary-Haugen Bill, the possible divergence fairly aches its way to attention. I start, then, with distinguishing the legal rule from the policy which it is supposed to effect. To this I shall return. As to the rule itself, I urge that in strictness its only application is to people who do things we wish they wouldn't; in strictness, it can be observed only by judges and sheriffs and jailers.

But there is another and more important reason why we cannot "observe" the law: we do not know what the law is. How can we? We commonly train a man for three years before we let him begin to claim that he can find out what it is. We pension a whole profession to tell us what it is, when any of us by accident needs to know. Even as to things of daily life we do not know. What is larceny? Is it larceny to embezzle? Is it larceny—is it an offense at all—to run an electric connection around my power meter, or to tap a telephone wire and steal valuable information? You do not know, and neither do I; and what would be the difference if we did? We live adequately without knowing. What we in fact set about "observing" is not the law, but those taboos on meddling with other people's goods which we grew up with. Prescribed patterns of conduct, prescribed inhibitions, resulting attitudes which vouchsafe rough predictability of what we should do even in a novel situation: these are what we really "observe." And, in the main, we observe them not at all because they conform to the law, but irrespective of whether they do or not. The law has nothing to say on making subject and predicate agree, nor on the manner of beginning a letter, nor on whether you will accept a given job, nor on your power to dispose of your street car seat by gift to a lady. There is law with an apparent policy of discouraging indulgence in alcohol. And the bulk of us abstain or do not abstain from alcohol and theft for the same reason that we abstain or do not abstain from double negatives: the ways of our environment indicate that course of conduct. Rarely, very rarely, we check conduct, or embark on conduct, or modify conduct, with a conscious eye to the law. When we do, it commonly has to do with fresh-baked law, new law—and it must be that most freakish of new law: new law that for some curious reason we happen to know about.

All of this brings me to the following propositions: First, law observance, so called, to be generally effective requires that folkways in conformity with the purposes of the law concerned shall have been first developed. It is the folkways, not the law, which are known; it is the folkways, not the law, which our present scheme of things offers some guaranty of people learning and following. Second, hence, when there is new law made, it presents itself as a problem of inducing change of folkways. And this involves working out patterns of action which conform, and finding the people whose conformity is desired, and putting those patterns of conduct across with those people. This is so obvious that I should feel ashamed of taking your time to say it if it were not so regularly overlooked. New law on the books, without more, is an exhortation. In the case of a delinquent we recognize that exhortation, not buttressed by a sound technique of habit change, is commonly almost worthless. In the case of new law the very exhortation often does not reach our ears—until the rod falls.

I come now to the fact which the criminologists tell us accounts for much of our delinquency: folkways in our complex and changing society are neither uniform nor stable. They vary by groups. Children exposed to the conflicting ways of various groups run risk of failure to firmly ground themselves in ways that will keep them clear of the law. Then arises that particular phase of law enforcement. Having trained the dog to snap, we beat him; he is a vicious brute. That is infinitely easier than training him over again; it also hangs responsibility on a less awkward peg.

But my concern is with another aspect of this fact that folkways are not uniform, that they vary by groups. And it is this: while folkways vary thus, each group being concerned with its own, much law purports to lap over the whole of society. Such law therefore finds observance group-wise, according to the varying folkways. It finds opposition and evasion group-wise, too. There are peculiarly Italian crimes, says Sutherland: personal violence in personal disputes. There are peculiarly Finnish crimes: public drunkenness and disorder. One may go on: there are offenses of the central markets, from bucket shopping to the grand manner of financial jobbery; and offenses of the petty markets, such as short weights or city milk graft. Observance, then, and opposition, group-wise. What is equally to the point, the folkways of our society at large do not extend to very vigorous support of law as such. There is indeed common to most of us a passive benevolence toward law enforcement; so in all cases where we lack knowledge of the facts, or where the outcome does not seem to touch matters near to us: benevolence, but passive. For, equally common, is that carryover of our youth which makes us know it is a scurvy thing to peach on anybody. Equally common also is that attitude of an age of specialization: let the cop do the dirty work; what else are we paying him for? Equally common, finally, is a total absorption in one's own affairs, which call for time and energy; and a natural diffidence about rushing into this law game when we do not know the ropes—or the wires! So that benevolence to law enforcement remains largely passive, with an exception. There are the interested groups. There is the Antisaloon League, Mr. Comstock's organization, the S. P. C. A., the Ku Klux Klan, the League for Industrial Rights, the American Legion, the American Bankers' Association. Here again, however, the interest is not in law as law, but in the mores dear to the group concerned. At times enforcement of those mores proceeds by flogging, or by terrorization; at times it proceeds against the doing of acts legally indifferent or even laudable in law. In such case the group fights for its mores not by enforcing, but by displacing, law. But more typically we find the militant group urging, backing, vigorously supporting some phase of law enforcement which happens to coincide roughly with the group desires, using the law to force other people into line. And this, I take it, must be set against its opposite: interested groups operating in criticism, pressure, passive and active opposition to some policy of law which runs counter to their mores, or to their desires.

I draw the conclusion that most law, today, is indifferent to most people; that group ways and group interests, where at all strongly developed, are likely to lead the group concerned into flat disregard of whatever law becomes too inconvenient; that active support of phases of law enforcement depends on there being groups whose particular interests, or dear-held mores, the phase in question seems to further. Am I arguing that law as law has lost all meaning to our community? Not quite. There is this passive good will toward law in general—a fossil deposit of the days when law was held right in itself, and sacred. (Perhaps, even, a newer point of view is gaining ground: that the rules of the game are worth abiding by: a sense of civic sportsmanship. But query: most of us still show some tendency, when the umpire isn't looking, to play to win.) There is, too, in the average citizen a disposition to conform personally to the law when it happens to touch him—if it does not make too much trouble; that is the one case. Or if the chance of discomfort from non-conformity looms large, that is the other case. And here it is worth note that a deal of confused thinking has been done on the deterrent effects of severe punishments. They may be futile in dealing with the professional criminal. They may be footless in preventing crimes of passion.

But when the question is one of urging the great well-meaning public into conduct which happens to be slightly inconvenient, severe punishments in the offing—known to be in the offing—are capable of effect. The effect may come at too high a price; but that is another matter.

So that I am arguing not that law as law has no effect, but that in the main it has in itself too little effect to be of moment in producing conduct which conforms to the policies concerned. And it seems to me that little is gained by decrying this fact. Whereas much might be gained by recognizing it, by ceasing to think of the passing of a law as having some inherent magic potency. At the same time it would be useful to deposit on the dump heap that paleozoic holdover, the idea that law is the same for all.

You will have noticed, cropping up through all the foregoing, references to laws which affect different groups in different ways. This is true of the simplest and most generally applicable of our laws. Pass by the obvious inequality of effect of laws about theft, trespass, vagrancy, and so forth as they apply to the haves and the have-nots. Come to the simple property taboos mentioned before. For you and for me it is about enough to have a simple rule of hands off, in regard to goods of other people. But suppose you are the assistant trust officer of a bank. You have a fund with loose proceeds to invest. That fund you hold for Mrs. Smithers, who will get the income for life; after her death young Harold takes the principal. Mrs. Smithers needs a security with quick immediate return. Harold needs a principal, safe at all costs to income, and preferably in a corporation which ploughs a goodly share of earnings into plant. Your superior has an investment banker friend with some sluggish securities on hand unsold; or perhaps it is the investment company associated with your bank which wishes to unload slow movers. Or, if the securities offered are peculiarly desirable, should you load up for Mrs. Smithers and Harold, as against Mrs. Roberts and Richard, whose fund you also hold? Here no plain rule of mine and thine will do. You need elaborate and detailed rules of action, elaborate and detailed far beyond the needs of persons who are not specialists. And if any of those rules of action are to be provided by law, the law will likewise move into detail which to the non-specialist is meaningless, and from whose knowledge he is mercifully spared.

Now regulative law is used for two main purposes. Within any group, and as to that group's own affairs, regulative law is used —to some extent—to buttress the group's own folkways at significant points; the state lends aid to help the group line up its own; so, for the community at large, with the law on sex offenses, or on homicide; so within that most prevalent of smaller groups, the family. There the law works indirectly by privileging moderate "correction" of the children; it works directly by helping a parent to secure the return of a runaway. But even more, regulative law attempts control of relations not so much within a group as between groups, marking out the limits or the obligatory methods of one group's impingement on another. Workers may strike, but not to secure the discharge of a fellow worker; they may not "picket," but they may employ one "peaceful emissary." [b] The father may "moderately correct" his child, but may not abuse him. In case of abuse the law suddenly recognizes the family, not as a unit, but as conflicting individuals, and proceeds to police their relations. Again, in this regulation of contact between groups, the law may simply stake off the ring, lay down a few rules prohibiting the use of brass knuckles and gouging, and leave the parties to battle or bargain to an issue. This it does in much of that wide field of adjustment we speak of as "the" open market. Or the law may attempt to prescribe certain specific conduct for one group, as when the rates of a public utility are laid down, or its obligation to serve all comers; or when specific safety devices are prescribed for an industrial process. Whether such attempts at group control are directed to the internal or to the external phases of group activity, one thing is clear: to be either intelligent or effective, the control must move in terms of the particular group activity; it must be drawn to fit each particular group; it must be special law and not general. And in the main it turns out to be special law, and not general, even when it lacks intelligence or effectiveness or both. This means that the vast bulk of regulative law has reference to the conduct of relatively few persons: few, that is, for each rule or set of rules; different persons for different sets of rules. So that law observance becomes for most law the prerogative of the few who happen to be concerned. And law enforcement becomes a question of properly influencing the conduct of those few.

It becomes convenient here to distinguish those persons who specialize in what we may call a legitimate activity which is subject to regulation from those whose line is regarded as wholly unlawful. They are significantly different in the problems they raise;

[b] I see no reason for trying to bring these statements into complex accuracy after thirty-two years of rapid change in the relevant body of rules.

yet, as I hope to show, they are also significantly similar. First, then, as to regulation of the legitimate activity: proper fire safeguards in places of public meeting; avoidance of combination prices in supposedly competitive selling; compulsory disclosure of the ingredients of packaged food, etc. The line of activity in such a case is either highly organized or it is not, and the problem differs accordingly. If not highly organized, the problem is one of ignorance, of inertia, of possible severe economic pressure against any change involving expense to the single enterprise, and of difficulty both in getting uniform action and in policing. All of which may be accentuated if the line is such as to lend itself to the mushroom, fly-by-night form of doing business. Licensing is one hopeful road into regulation; it gives ready notice of location; it raises some funds for inspection. Well nigh essential to success, however, is the working out of ways of compliance, ways such that they can be introduced without killing off the business; and, along with that, reasonably uniform pressure on all competitors. Beyond this, the problem of education to conformity does not greatly differ from that of educating a loosely organized trade up to intelligent bookkeeping or cost accounting. And from the trade associations the government can learn. One of the lessons will be patience, when regulation is desired to jump too far ahead of trade practice.

If, on the other hand, the line is highly organized, two things become possible. One is to direct both education and pressure to a relatively small group of executives, who, if they will, can shape the conduct of their whole organizations. The other is to police more cheaply. It is easier, too, to procure a rough equality of pressure; it is easier to procure from competitors or customers some assistance in detecting violations; it is easier to procure rather expert advice on what can and what cannot be done without injuriously affecting the legitimate phases of the activity. All this in the ideal case. There are flaws in the ideal. The more highly organized the activity, the less chance there is, politically, of getting what seems to be, or even to portend, adverse legislation by the legislature; the more danger there is that, once passed, the legislation will fail of enforcement. There is still a certain odor of oil around the capital. Nor have I heard of great present interest in the Department of Justice as to the bearing of the antitrust laws on aluminum. Finally, the more highly organized the activity, the more the policy behind a specific measure is likely to fail of reflection in the measure. This first, politically. The teeth of the law may be extracted in committee. Section 20 of the Clayton Act was touted, you remember, as a charter of liberties for labor. But toothless it came into the world, and toothless it will go out. Second, attempts at regulation of highly organized business are rarely drafted by men as skilled as those whom they attempt to regulate. And—this is important—they are commonly drawn in terms of what the supposed offenders have been doing; whereas equally necessary is study of what else the supposed offenders may proceed to do. For a highly organized activity, thanks to skilled legal counsel and a high executive I. Q., can undergo very rapid changes of conduct pattern, under pressure; but such changes can be either in conformity with both a measure and its policy, or equally well they can be around the measure and in the teeth of its policy. Once again the question becomes one of education, of inducing so called observance. It can be done. We have the trade practice submittals of the Federal Trade Commission as cogent evidence. We have the Department of Labor of New York issuing, in 1927, 166,000 orders with reference to the labor and factory laws, with which substantial compliance was had without resort to the courts or police. And may it not be urged that both the technical problems of dealing with a technical activity and the delicacy of the task of persuasion to conformity go some distance to explain the huge development in these latter days of specialized administrative departments of government? [1]

All this brings me to a question: whether some similar type of specialization is not a condition to more adequate control of those equally specialized activities which we regard as wholly illegitimate. The criminologists have made a promising beginning at breaking up this catch-all concept "crime" into sub-groupings with a trace of living meaning. They argue cogently that traffic offenses, public drunkenness, and burglary show no significant a priori likenesses. They point out that homicide among Italians is largely confined to other Italians as the victims; and, more significant still, that it is by way of disappearing in the second generation. There is, then, homicide and homicide. But even more strikingly there is divergence among the lines of professional crime, crime for a living. I mentioned before that such lines differed from legitimate lines in various ways. Chief among these are

---

[1] Peculiarly difficult to reach by regulation are those cases where executives, directors, etc., exercise discretion in their own interests, in opposition to the interests of the group they supposedly represent. This is the problem of government; and we seem to be quite as far from solving it in the business and social field as we are in the more purely political.

that professional crime commonly presupposes secrecy in the business, so that one major problem becomes that of detection. It normally presupposes also secrecy of the channels of trade and that the professional criminal cannot be induced to conform to law without abandoning his occupation. There remain the points of similarity: that professional crime depends upon profit, and profit upon a market, and a market upon the nature of the goods concerned; and, finally, that an unprofitable market is a discouraging field of enterprise. It seems obvious that this is a matter of informed, specialized inquiry. Let me take a simple example. The books of the New York Public Library persisted in disappearing. This was a field peculiarly of juvenile delinquency; the opportunity was open to all, but the rewards of theft so petty as to make juveniles the likely prospects. A statute was passed making exhibition for sale of a book bearing a library stamp an offense. The library officials saw to it that every second-hand book dealer in the city received notice of this statute. Promptly the thefts decreased almost into nothingness. The market had become unprofitable. There has never been a prosecution under the law. There is no need.

This suggests important differences between such goods as raw silk and woven silk and furs. Woven silk could be made readily to carry identifying marks on every yard. Forthwith the risks and costs of marketing stolen piece goods would rise; they might be made to soar to the point of no return. The problem of furs and of raw silk would remain. And it seems to me highly suggestive that the agencies of private interested groups have moved much further into this type of specialized study of particular lines of crime than have our police.[c] One thinks of the Bankers' Association, the jewelry men, the insurance men who deal with wilful destruction of insured goods or realty, the present move against fraudulent claims, the investment bankers' attack on fraudulent promotions, the credit men's approach to fraudulent bankruptcies. Such groups have not solved their problems. But they have begun the saner type of study. They seem to me particularly interesting because they set specialized skill against specialized skill; and because they move mass-wise against narrowing specific lines of opportunity for criminal aggression, and the particular market for the proceeds of aggression of some particular kind. On the side of

[c] I suspect this statement to be largely dated, and in process of rapid further dating.

the individual delinquent they seem interesting in that they promise to reduce the urge and opportunity to become professional.

But there remain certain phases of crime-for-a-livelihood of which a word should be said: commercial prostitution, gambling, and the illicit liquor traffic. These are peculiar in that they require a reasonably wide market and in that they further require an ultimate consumer who fully knows the illegality of the trade. And I take it such are precisely the reasons why these lines find operation difficult without corrupting the police into protection. The only point I wish to make is this: it has been our practice to approach the prohibition of these activities by way of pressure on the purveyor, leaving the consumer largely to himself. This is to leave the demand vibrant and profitable, while seeking to choke off the supply. It is a curious piece of legal engineering. It is a charmingly unbusinesslike approach for a community dedicated to the business man. Not only is the purveyor, by hypothesis, peculiarly ingenious in obtaining corrupt protection; not only, even when that fails, is he equipped with the most competent talent for legal defense, and largely impervious at least to fine if he should lose. The very publicity of legal proceedings against him becomes a business asset to him, whereas the consumer shrinks even from the publicity of an arrest. And while the purveyor gambles cheerfully, and in money terms, his present profits against his possible losses, and writes off a contingent reserve against his fines, the consumer must put his reputation on the table as an additional stake. Altogether one thing seems fairly clear: the present approach is as foredoomed to ineffectiveness as social activity well can be. Effective prohibition calls for coping with the market. If the wide public does not sufficiently desire prohibition to swallow what this costs in burdens to consumers who happen to be caught (and there need not be so many), then it might be well to stop pretending that we want law which we do not want. I would not be understood to deny the utility, at times, of laws concededly unenforceable and unenforced, as a first step toward public education along particular lines. But I would argue that the price of such education advances very rapidly as non-observance becomes not only widespread, but conscious and purposeful.

Well, you will say, Llewellyn's argument comes to this: first he denies the existence or the possibility of law observance; and then he treats law enforcement as a technical problem of producing or inducing this same law observance which he says is quite impossible. Then he divides society into a lot of so called groups, and talks as if the groups were really solid, and as if the people he treats as group members took over the supposed folkways of their groups in block; whereas our main problem is trying to reeducate youngsters and adults who have failed to get, from anywhere, conduct patterns solid enough to see them through life. Finally, you will say, he talks as if the closing of illicit avenues to gain would prevent youngsters from going wild. He is content to leave society organized in terms of money measurement, money incentive, high pressure salesmanship to make people want what they don't need, and buy what they can't afford, so as to break down all their resistances to easy, illegitimate gain; he is content to leave youth shut in from legitimate adventure, open to the pulls of life and groups in flux, given over to commercialized external recreation, with a mobility both from hour to hour and from year to year which defies all the ancient devices of control and education. And he asks us to believe that study of specialized groups, licit and illicit, with an eye to the particular problems of prohibitive control each raises, will cure all that.

And if you should thus accuse, I think I should admit the accusations, with these three exceptions: first, that any merely repressive ways of tightening up the present control machinery I should regard as temporary expedients, good, so far as our present order of things is good, but bound to raise trouble by their very effectiveness so far as our present order denies normal human outlet to a sigificant number; second, that this same process of microscopic study of the living ways of specific subgroups in our society seems to me as essential to any technique of single case adjustment and re-education as it does to the effective adjustment and control of mass relations between these shifting but real clumps of humanity I have chosen to call groups; third, that I have not been asked to talk on whether our civilization was worth having, but on how to keep people moving inside the paths that civilization has marked out, for good or ill. Certainly, I shall insist again, in closing, that law observance is a question of folkways rather than of rules; that rules and folkways are not uniform but diversified in our society; and that any problem of law enforcement is a technical job of altering the conduct patterns of specific individuals. And I shall insist again that all law, as we know it, is at least this far an evil, as its very necessity evidences that our society has outgrown the only really adequate means of government which man has thus far invented.[d]

[d] Today "the only really adequate means of government" is a dated concept. Modern means of communication and of force-application have made possible terrifically effective government which, over a couple of generations, can prove efficient to almost wholly remodel folkways and even mores, on a mass scale. Indeed before Hitler and Soviet Russia, and without modern technology, sociologists should not have overlooked the work of the Zulu Chaka and, to a somewhat comparable extent, of the Mongol Genghis.

{ 19 }

THEFT AS A BEHAVIOR PROBLEM [a] [1]

It has for some time been time we had this book of Professor
Hall's. When any phase of crime-control is talked about, the
tendency has too often and too strongly been to emote instead
of thinking. Some criminologists have indeed talked gratifying
sense; and from them Dr. Hall has learned. Some practical men
have acted sense—they are the most numerous group who have.
Some—fewer—practical men have even talked sense. Professor
Hall has learned from them as well. But about *the Criminal Law*
neither the one group nor the other (to say nothing of the
lawyers) has done much talking of sense;[b] still less, about the law
of theft, which is the heart of the really *criminal* Criminal Law.
Yet not only can we not get along in this matter without law;
we also need vigorous changes in our law—changes which can be
diagnosed and understood only by studying the society the law
purports to govern.

Hall gathers together the sense talked thus far—about the
problems of theft, and the ways of theft, and the control of theft.
And about the part law plays, has played, can play, in that control. Dr. Hall adds, in all of this, a deal more sense of his own,
which we have needed. Hence Criminology has needed this book.

[a] From JEROME HALL, THEFT, LAW AND SOCIETY (1st ed.), Introduction.
[1] This Introduction builds on my paper in Proc. Conf. Social Work, 1928, 127;
on a manuscript submitted to Jerome Michael for use in his survey of the values
of an Institute; and of course on the book in hand. Emma Corstvet, Sheldon Glueck,
Robert Lynd, Thorsten Sellin, and Herbert Wechsler read the manuscript, and
gave freely to its improvement.
[b] This must be taken as of its date. But even today talk which assays high in
sense is talk which it takes care and patience to locate.

But Criminal Law has needed it desperately. To the law of Theft in particular it is the most important contribution I have met.

Being a lawyer, perhaps I shall be pardoned for turning first to the legal aspect of the book. Technical it may seem, to a non-lawyer. I can only promise him that, given a bit of patience, he will find that technicality both illuminated and illuminating.

To a lawyer concerned with control of crime, Dr. Hall's message is the motto of Imperial Rome: Divide and Conquer. Let me pick one phase of the thesis for illustration.

Hall demonstrates that the traditional category of Larceny is all but meaningless for purposes of control. It embraces eighteen or eighty divergent varieties of conduct. Each one of the varieties embraced calls, whether in prevention or in treatment, for its own peculiar line of handling. "Theft-for-sale versus theft-for-personal-consumption" yields a first line of cleavage. For within theft-for-personal-consumption professional activity is, on the whole, rare; whereas within theft-for-sale it is occasional or casual activity which is relatively rare, and which when found is more commonly than not both juvenile and a prospective first step toward ultimate professional criminality. Within the field of theft-for-sale, again, Jewels, Silks, Furs, present each one its distinct problem of prevention and detection. Yet these three have aspects significantly similar, aspects which shed light on the whole problem of illicit gain. In all three the key to partial prevention has lain in concerted action by such organized business units as are particularly open to attack; in the joint employment of a specialized force of lay police; in the devising of protective measures, specialized to the ways and needs of the particular business and to the particular patterns and the particular personnel of predatory actions; and finally in intensive education of the interested business units toward moving along the lines thus found to be the safest. Hence forgery of checks (a different "crime") more significantly resembles these three phases of theft than any of the three resembles, say, larceny from a dwelling, pocket-picking, or theft of motor cars. While motor theft in turn proves to split into at least three utterly different types of offending: first, "borrowing" for a joy-ride, the car being abandoned, normally, in good condition; second, theft for a gain limited by the value of the car (resale; stripping and resale of accessories; plus "theft" by owner, to defraud the insurance company or the mortgagee); and, third and most serious, the "borrowing" of the car to use not for pleasure, but in a bank hold-up or worse. In this last case as in the first, the car will be found, in due course, abandoned and normally in good condition; but to define "the" offense in terms of "taking for a temporary purpose," evidenced "by return or abandonment in good condition" is to confuse the chauffeur's joy-ride, the city juvenile's delinquency, and the professional gangster's favorite trick for baffling pursuit.[2]

So, then, for purposes of control, the motto for our too-inclusive traditional legal categories is Roman: Divide and Rule. Divide in terms which have some real relation (a) to the lines of behavior in question, and (b) to the persons whose behavior comes in question.

This is *not* to deny the values of integration, or of semi-systematic synthesis. It *is* to deny the values of such synthesis until meaningful units have been discovered which become worth synthesizing. The present outmoded categories of criminal law need to be broken down into such meaningful units; rules need to be reformulated (as administration already has in part been organized) on the basis of units of activity and study which have meaning in the life of today and tomorrow, rather than of day before yesterday alone. *That once accomplished,* one can attack the problems of reintegration.

If this thesis be not sound, all sense is nonsense. Though sound, it is neither law nor familiar to lawyers. To law and lawyers, then, our author offers help.

But his work gives sociologists and criminologists no less to chew on. That careless slogan: "I hold with the sociological, *not the legal* definition of crime," rings with disappointing frequence in the ear.[c] Hall makes it clear indeed that legal definition must, to be effective, follow the lines of the social problem. But he makes it no less clear that *without* legal definition, attempts to cope with

---

[2] Wechsler properly points out that merely penalizing this last, say in the case of bank-bandits, would have little practical *in terrorem* value (as well hang for a sheep as a lamb!) nor would it help detection after the robbery. Yet to see the problem as it is has double value. It leads, first to not drawing a statute aimed at either thieves or bandits so as to include mere joy-riders. It leads, second, to considering whether carrying sawed-off shotguns or tommy-guns in motor cars, and, especially in *stolen* motor cars, is not properly placed on a par with bank robbery: occasionally the wolf-pack is picked up on its way to the hunt [or, in case of mowing down, on the way back from the attempt or kill.]

[c] I doubt if this is any longer true. But an impatience across the border, in pyschiatry or sociology or the like, with "the law" as being off-base and somehow in the way—that is an unthought-through flavor which has not left us; and I think the analysis which follows still has current value, even though our best crime-fighters have moved far ahead.

crime will in modern society be a hopeless undertaking. Even such admirably organized private agencies as the Silk Protective Association would be in trouble if the law and the lawmen were not available to stiffen the social framework, to provide that general policing within which they do their special policing, and to deal with offenders and recover stolen goods when tracked down. Gang warfare—or that of private police—(rudimentary law-stuff though it be) is, alone, inadequate to serve the policing needs of any but a parasitic subgroup whose life is drawn from a larger community rooted—in part—in Law.

Hall makes it clear, too, that *predatory* crime cannot be understood either in the abstract, or as a matter of acts, *mens rea* and the like. Much less can it be understood as being merely "Crime." Only its analysis into a series of *particular lines of activity* gives it tangible, observable body. A thing many criminologists, more sociologists, and most lawyers, need still to learn.

I have no desire to suggest that there are no lawyers who understand the need of subdivision, intensive subdivision, of the cross-chopping welter which the existing categories of criminal law have naïvely been supposed to "cover." The work of an intelligent prosecutor is enough to blow any such suggestion to the Fijis.[d] Neither do I wish to suggest that there are no criminologists who have gotten under the skin of their material: compare the marking off of delinquency and the juvenile court movement[e] and the study of boy-gangs, delinquency areas, and legitimate play facilities; or the recognition of such special categories as "police offenses," "political offenses," "crimes of passion"; or the attempts to introduce control groups into etiological studies; or the canniness with which the finer criminologists in these latter days approach the interpretation of our nobly loose statistics.

What I do claim is that I have seen no monograph or book which has so consistently or successfully endeavored

(1) to carry subdivision through *consistently, and to the limits of its utility,* in terms of what we now know about *significantly different lines* of criminal activity; and

(2) to *keep* the significant differences clear *throughout,* instead of forgetting them as one chapter passes into the next; and

[d] And we have now for years had Wechsler and his team at work (often enough misguidedly, but in blinding advance over mere traditional law) on the Model Criminal Code.

[e] Which has matured even to the place—in spots and on occasion—of considering possible needed correctives by way of civil rights for juveniles.

(3) to marshal social and economic history, legal history, modern criminological research, modern practical experience, modern legislative experiment, *and common sense,* into a meaningful whole; and, finally,

(4) to recognize, in every phase of the suggested program, the practical difficulties present, the available means for meeting them, and the lines of trouble-making exception which need to be watched.

In a word, Hall's merit lies not merely in the use of an open mind, of a wide range of knowledge, of practical experience and judgment, and in their application to a major legal problem; it consists no less in *thinking through* implications of what various others know, but have rested too largely content with just knowing.—Or with knowing too exclusively.

For attempts to cope with crime have found their bane in *uneven development of different aspects of knowledge among the various groups concerned.* This uneven development has in each group coupled ignorance or underestimate of what others had to offer with overestimate of the group's own full competence. It has been furthered by the all-too-frequent lumping of all "Crime," or all "Criminals," or all "Accused" into a single indiscriminate pile. What the softboiled who wish to reform the underprivileged victim of circumstance have to contribute has, for instance, little meaning for the hard-boiled whose attention is on the dyed-in-the-wool professionals [or hard-case juveniles] who are their thorn. Or take the "efficiency tables" of the old-fashioned Crime Survey (which reflect thinking too prevalent still), though they lose all significance unless every man arrested be first assumed guilty; and contrast such tables with that considerable number of constitutional guarantees (and rules of evidence) which take as their baseline that *every* accused must be assumed [not only] innocent [of the offense in hand, but also lily-white throughout his whole past life.] As against any aspect of such brute lumping observe Hall's care anent petty theft: he sees relatively few psychiatric, relatively many socially-conditioned cases—but 'ware the occasional kleptomaniac. And 'ware the pickpocket, typically a professional; and 'ware the stripping of motor-cars for accessories, another professional racket. Or observe the care with which, though the line of his major interest here is the professional, he yet takes account of the casual receiver for consumption, and discriminates as to automobile joy-riding, and marks off that petty theft which (as we have just seen) he then skeptically proceeds to treat as in turn needing further subdivision.

"Uneven development," I said, "of different aspects of knowledge among the various groups concerned." The police, and the Jewelry men, and the New York Grand Jurors' Association, have discovered that jewelry-thieving has aspects of its own. How many lawyers have discovered that? How many criminologists? The psychiatrists have discovered many things about mental constitution, or about compulsions. How far are police and Jewelry Protective Agencies aware of these? How far are the psychiatrists aware of what the social ecologists have dug up about the effect of neighborhood on the recruiting of professional depredators? The criminal lawyer and (less so) the political scientist, know much about the interaction of organized criminals and organized political machines. How many sociological studies have we about "the social process" there involved? Business men and bar associations see Crime Waves, and go to work promptly as if the law had only professionals to deal with. Social workers see boys going wrong, and go to work as if man were utterly, and all men equally, malleable.[1] Ministers get sentimental, and petition the judge for mercy; the judge acquiesces once, and gets fooled; twice, and gets fooled; thrice, and gets fooled—and turns into a Jeffries. While most of the great artists, in this game as in others, know not what they do. They record experience, which is useful; but they give advice that others have no wherewithal to follow. Legislators, meanwhile, are swept by this influence or that, this theory or that; they draw statutes which enclose six lines of case in one "offense," or in one line of treatment. Juries see individual cases and begin to dodge the consequences of the statute. Judges "construe." The statute fails of its purpose. Administrators, thirsting for results from which law blocks them, have no choice but to invent bald fictions; they distill the illicit but potent liquor of Discretion. We of the public, embarrassed by the inadequacy of literal law and clattering machinery, wink at the bootlegging; we praise the bootlegger; we enjoy the product—only to discover that, here as elsewhere, out of the bootlegger's company rises the racketeer.

---

[1] Thirty years of metropolitan and suburban developments have handsomely dated this statement. Yet can we not still urge that what the most skilful field people have discovered about "hard" youth is known to few lawyers, law-makers, or voters?

The need is for integration of the soundest knowledge among *all* the groups. The need is for significant subdivision of subject-matter, from the angle of how control is feasible; but it is no less for integration of all available knowledge, all available techniques of attack, within each such subdivision. The need, then, is for discrimination as we either subdivide or integrate. Professor Hall has provided all of these.

*   *   *

To so provide them, he has limited his field. A monograph is no encyclopedia. Whereas the office of an introduction is to set a monograph against a general background. Hence—to work.

The office of criminal law is threefold. It is, first, wherever there is not already present an overwhelming agreement about the un-desirability of certain conduct, to single out and stamp certain types of conduct as sufficiently undesirable to require govern-mental opposition. I have little concern in this Introduction with this first office. Theft—at least most theft—is sufficiently disap-proved in our society to make discussion unnecessary; sufficiently, also, to make the general nature of Hall's subject-matter clear without extended attempts at definition. Much needs to be said about borderlines of what should be treated as theft, but little about the core. The core is here our concern.

The second office of the criminal law is to serve as an effective tool in checking the conduct desired to be checked. So-called sub-stantive law, the set-up of administrative agencies, and the regula-tion of procedure, all join in this. I have indicated often enough that I find them hard to sever; that I think any tendency to sever them obstructive to the thinking immediately required by our present day; and that where such a clean-cut purpose as the check-ing of much predatory theft is observably a datum in our society, I feel the most presently useful line of attack to lie in treating so-called substantive law, administrative set-up, and procedural regu-lation as a single interlocking whole. A material part of that whole, though one deserving of separate classification, consists of those *de facto* official actions—often enough rising to the dignity of established practices, sometimes to the sanctity of established prac-tices viewed by the practitioners as both necessary and right—which are variant from or even flatly contrary to the official legal norms. Most police, *e.g.,* seem to me to view the third degree as both necessary and right. Such practices may be potent furtherers of valid purposes which underlie an ill-drawn substantive rule and a sputtering administrative scheme.

When, as so often, one of the aspects is at variance with another —as when procedural technicality seems to defeat the substantive rule, or administrators insist on operating as the rules say they should not operate—we have words to describe the happening. We have words to describe also such results as the occasional ousting of such officials, or the effect of a local clean-up in an exodus of theretofore protected gentlemen of the gun. Still, the most fruitful baseline of study remains the net operation of the whole official set-up, taken as a whole. It is that net operation—it is the substantive rule only as it trickles through the multiple screen of *action* —which counts in life.

The third office of the criminal law is to hold the discretion of officials within certain bounds dictated by political considerations which often war with the checking of criminal activity. The unjustly accused is to be given his chance. Malicious accusation is to be kept from being an assassin's tool. Official arbitrariness or persecution is to be constrained within bounds.

One vulnerable aspect of Professor Hall's book is his failure to take any proper account of this third phase of criminal law. I have of course no quarrel with specialization inside a discipline. I recognize that the second office of criminal law is quite wide enough to consume any man's attention, especially in a single monograph. Nonetheless, an Introduction has its own function; and on this point an express corrective to Hall's emphasis is needed. *The problem of checking crime must at times be complicated by the problem of checking officials.*

I shall, however, follow Hall in centering upon the second matter listed: the shaping of tools to check certain types of activity concededly undesirable, which we group as "theft."

To check theft is to control human behavior. The only approach to controlling human behavior is to take it as a problem in behavior. The control of human behavior is a problem of human drives and human conditioning:

(a) (i) of persons to be controlled;
    (ii) of persons to do the controlling; and
(b) of existing patterns, largely built by and learned in groups, patterns both of response and of stimulus; and
(c) of guessing into the as yet unknown, either

(i) as to what to do with an individual, where an individual is in question, rather than a mass, or

(ii) as to a mass, where no mass reaction has as yet been discovered.

The problem, I say, is one in human behavior, neat and clear. For the purpose in hand, the objective needs no philosophical inquiry; it is given. The tools, as tools, are to be judged by their results.[3] The problem is not only complex as any problem of influencing vast numbers of people is complex. It is made doubly intricate by two contributing factors: (1) We are by no means clear as to who it is whose behavior we desire to check or re-orient. Some we know. Others—most—we do not. As to these last, until we know them, *mass* operations are our only means. The former (those that we do know) can be dealt with case by case—*if* they can be dealt with at all. (2) We can bring to bear directly only one minor part of our political establishment—police, courts, D.A.s, wardens. Economic and social factors we can hardly touch. Most even of the political establishment is (and properly) devoted to other ends. Even so much of it as can in this connection be called upon is in good part otherwise engaged; "offenses" are not limited to theft. Even where not otherwise engaged, our available fraction may, *e.g.,* believe in socking 'em where we think leniency promising, or believe that a particular gangster is less useful in jail than as an ally at the polls.

The control of behavior, in a word, is hard enough (as educators know) when you know whom to focus on, and have complete command of what you hope to be your controls. And it always involves the previous patterning of your would-be controllee. This "controllee," to the educator's distress, reacts not like a chemical solution from which the desired precipitate can be had with some sweet certainty. He—or she—reacts as an individual compounded of genes and social conditioning. What to do, the educator guesses —often wrong. Even when he guesses right, he finds countervailing factors present and active, to plough up his sowing. When the Great Thief lands in the Cabinet (official or unofficial), or be-

---

[3] Not by any single instances. There is the fact and factor of variable personnel. Yet there are tendencies in institutions as in people, though with institutions an adequate statistical base is rarely available, and the student must have recourse to art.

There is, of course, a needed philosophical inquiry into the relation of reform, incapacitation, and deterrence, where they conflict—as they so often do.

comes Head of State, then what can be effectively argued to be wrong with thieving?

All this is multiplied, as to criminal behavior. Rarely does the acting official have the curious but often potent status of the educator, as regards his subject, or patient, or victim. Rarely does he have as much contact with the patient's patterning and background. Stirred—as he must be—with the imminence of danger, rarely does he have that patience, that sympathy, which distinguishes an educator from a mere presence on an "educational" payroll. And more often, most often, the identity of "the patient" is wrapped in nebulosity. There is the uncaught offender. There is the possible offender of the future. How deal with a patient whom you cannot locate? How reform one who scorns reform?

And always, there is the organ-base, throbbing below all else: *Have* these officials sense? *Will* they use even the sense they have? If so, to what end will they use it?

*   *   *

All of this drives to three points as the centers of attention:

(1) The political problem: to get officials who have some sense, and who can be trusted. I must disregard that here, and for the moment—as Professor Hall has disregarded it.[g]

(2) The persons to be controlled: we need sharp distinction between rifle-shots at those we know, and shot-gun stuff into what we hope to be the general direction of them we know not. And Glueck well insists that, for treatment or for prevention or detection, the persons concerned, according to their psychological make-up and their conditioning, can be usefully grouped around conceptual types.

(3) *The patterns of action,* so far as discernible or predictable. *E.g.*—even as to known prospective offenders—*to cut off the market* is to bother prospective (even professional) thieving-for-resale *in that market.* Or, as to possible future delinquents, in districts so crowded as to bar decent outlet for play, the provision or development of legitimate play-facilities may materially reduce criminal recruiting. This is a matter less of existing pattern than of pattern-shaping. The urge for action, the urge for prestige, are there, in the kids, by nature. An outlet they will find, for most. Legitimate outlet lessens pressure toward illegitimate.—As for *existing* patterns, compare Hall's discussion of checking thefts in silk.

[g] But consider its vitality. Take the impact of Wilson in Chicago, 1960 f., and the counter-stir.

Patterns—present or prospective—exist among possible victims (business practice) or among existing pirates (hijacking and re-marketing methods plus gang-ways), or among prospective recruits —or, finally, among law-enforcement personnel. All are important. Indeed, until we develop better means for spotting individuals, patterns of action will remain our most effective focus of study toward checking predatory theft.

Of patterns four things may safely be said: (1) In the main, they are best understood in their more specialized forms, not in their more generalized. While "boy-gang" has won its place as a fruitful concept, "theft-gang" loses meaning except in terms of the com-modities and lines of attack and marketing employed. For whereas boy-life is relatively unspecialized, theft-life, especially when or-ganized, is not.

(2) Patterns are subject, in some degree, to being changed by shifting conditions. Any type of theft-for-sale must be affected by the market. So far as the market is bottle-necked, it becomes *the* vulnerable point. Hall's chapters on receiving stolen goods are elo-quent of this.

(3) Patterns of any group affect those of any other group with which the first group interacts. Police who deal constantly with the professional criminal—whether antagonistically or co-operatively —cannot escape the influence of professional criminal patterns. Though they remain wholly honest, they are likely to develop techniques for dealing with offenders which give lamentable re-sults when applied, let us say, to political demonstrators or to pickets who are really peaceful.

(4) Patterns of action either are or are not reinforced by a sense of their rightness; and that sense of rightness may pervade a whole society, or may be limited to the acting group; and at times the norms of the group may be at odds with the norms prevalent in the rest of society. Theft-for-sale, as a trade, seems normally to the person engaged in it right enough. In this lies one main difference, as to prognosis for reform, between the established criminal and the general run of one-time serious offenders whom one may think of as in part victims of circumstance or passion.

These are not all the differences between the two. Lack of prac-tice and lack of gang-support are likely to make the isolated of-fender-by-circumstance easier to detect and catch; his conscience may lead him to confession; his access to skilled counsel is less likely; his ability to hamstring prosecution by intimidation of witnesses or political influence is rarely on a par with that of the tradesman in organized crime.

All of which seems to me to call for clean-cut severance of the two, *as regards the applicable legal rules*. Present criminal procedure is well enough adapted to dealing with the non-tradesman. We do need, for court purposes, and *in non-political* cases, to get rid of the privilege against the accused being made a witness against himself. That is a fossil.[h] But in the main, the procedure serves.

Not so, with the tradesman in crime. Here the social problem is no longer an offense, but a line of livelihood. Constitutional and criminal lawyers should surely be able to devise a scheme whereby, say, a special status of "Criminal Association" could be created, subject to proof and judicial determination; the operative facts to be such things as frequenting of criminal hang-outs for six months out of a given year, or association with some minimum number (four, five, six) of persons already convicted of any of a given list of serious offenses, *non-political* in character, for a similar period. Prior conviction of offenses against property *for gain,* or for carrying concealed weapons, and the like, might well be receivable in evidence as bearing on the charge. Time spent in jail, for the proper kind of offense, and within the year preceding or succeeding three months of such association, might well be made the equivalent of further association. The operative effect of pinning the status on a man would be *not any immediate penalty,* but, rather, a loss of privilege: first, a more summary procedure in the event of later indictment or information on a charge of a serious *non-political* offense; and second, limitation of bail, enlargement of any penalty on conviction, in the court's discretion, and some limitation on the parole provisions otherwise applicable.

I put forward such a suggestion with diffidence, but with con-

---

[h] Within the *essential policy* of our prohibition against double jeopardy we also need, of course, to get rid of any prosecution for perjury against a defendant who has successfully testified in his own behalf. The Fifth Amendment rooted in a régime of no right to counsel, nor to confrontation, nor to cross-examine witnesses against one, nor to subpoena witnesses in one's favor, with touches of torture in the offing and indefinite imprisonment without habeas corpus. Its policy is dead, even in regard to individuals. But of course any man should be permitted (sworn or unsworn) to lie on the stand in his own behalf without danger of a second prosecution if the jury believes him on the first.

Note that such a revision of our law (not unlike the current German one) would have no need, if carefully drawn, to touch the question of wire-tapping and the like one way or the other.

viction. The diffidence rests somewhat on such a consideration as the injustice of cutting off possibilities of reform. It rests more on suspicion of the ease with which police could find pegs on which to hang unsolved crimes, or to satisfy personal grudges. It rests most of all on distrust of legislators; we have considerable evidence that our legislators can be stampeded into using such a status-idea to brand political radicals rather than tradesmen in crime.[4]

The first doubt could be largely met by permitting a counter-proceeding, after due lapse of time, to remove the status. The second continues to trouble. I find, of course, no serious difficulty in listing the necessary exemptions: police, clergy, social workers, lawyers, and the like; nor in building a similar procedure to determine what are criminal resorts.—Conviction as to the value of such a move rests on a certainty that the only sound road out of the slough of criminal procedure lies in devising a sieve that will throw different jobs into different channels adapted each one to its peculiar job. The separation out of the juvenile court opens the road into the future.

It is typical of the blindness and perversity with which we handle criminal law that the nearest approaches we now have to such an idea—all as well-intentioned as the road to Hell—remain both sorry idiocies. The use of vagrancy or criminal syndicalism—each in essence as a status concept—to strike down political radicals, is simple outrage; it is the ancient and typical perversion of criminal law to keep the Ins in, which Bill of Rights, throughout three centuries, have sought, as yet in vain, to wholly stem. Will we never recognize what even Tsarist Russia knew: that political offenders are a class apart? On the other hand, a Fourth Offender law cleaves still to the ancient theory that all criminal procedure must look alike, and leaves the essential fact—the line of livelihood—officially irrelevant to the issue in trial. While the New York move against association with criminals has as its penalty not what is wanted: a better break on getting conviction for a real offense—but only an immediate minor penalty.

Such considerations will make it clear why Hall's proposals about the law of criminal receiving rouse my enthusiasm. His at-

[4] Miss Corstvet wholly repudiates this line of suggestion. To her the chance of its being misapplied against *political* offenders too far outweighs the chance of its sane use. I agree in the prognosis. But I accept, to date, the scientists' position that it is no business of his what use any inherently worthwhile theory or suggestion may be put to. Veblen, in his *Place of Science in Civilization,* states the dilemma as no man before or since has stated it.

tention goes to the line of business as the essence, and to the problem of proof as the essential point of technique. And, in the broader aspects, to this particular line of business as a focal point of attack on the whole.

* * *

Discussion of background tempts on and on—nowhere more siren-like than in regard to crime. Under existing criminal law, for instance, theft for sale hugely outbulks any other category of serious offense. With the categories of stock-jobbing, swindling, and corporation and financing fraud in process of extension, Criminal Depredation for Gain will shortly bulk still larger. Yet in relation to "Crimes" at large, thievings bulk small.

One is forced to subanalysis of Crime. In terms of motivation: gain, passion, politics. In terms of livelihood: the secret livelihood, where we have little more than *in terrorem* measures and policing available, unless highly organized units such as banks are the points of attack; as against the open livelihood, where checking up of accounts, bonding companies' checkup on whether the individual is gambling, and the like, can be used; or special private police; or tear-gas installations; or such preventive measures as a provision that any profits made by an officer or director of a company in its stock within three months prior to a directors' meeting shall inure to the company. Whether either point or personnel of peril is *known,* defense is aided.

Or again, we must subanalyze in terms of available reinforcing patterns and norms: theft is sufficiently tabu, for most, so that only extraordinary temptation will bring transgression. Even for many on the margin, fear of the cop will adequately raise the threshold. Whereas violation of motor-regulations is still, for most, a question of expediency. Speed, fun, opportunity and pride have consistently outrun the building of self-acting patterns (or of the later-developing norms) of conformity to motor-regulation. Developing these last is a question of education. We know that where governmental force can be concentrated consistently and intelligently, it can be done: though in New York City pedestrians still jay-walk when they choose, in Memphis and Albuquerque they have waited for the lights, for years. New Haven in 1934 lay between, with the balance in favor of the light. This is a matter of conditioning the public from outside.

What seems clear, as a conclusion, is that in all these matters of petty police administration, from safety devices and building codes through child labor regulation and spitting on the sidewalk, we have two fields of activity differing not unremotely as, in regard to heinous offenses, the field of the caught differs from that of the uncaught and potential offender. If the outfit to be controlled—a factory, a bank, a stock exchange—is organized, stable in location, and known, force can readily be brought to bear. So also can persuasion. And fines [,or preferably non-reimbursement confinement,] should regularly run against responsible officers *as well as* (if fines) against the outfit. For responsible officers *can change the ways of the outfit.* If we have outfits scattered, small, and mobile, on the other hand, inspecting costs are high. Licensing is then normally the only sane way to lift the cost. If we have, finally, a wholly unorganized class to deal with—such as the operators of pleasure cars—we need highly intelligent conditioning at all points of concentration. But we need more. Outside such points we must enlist a host of non-governmental agencies (the insurance companies being, *e.g.,* more effective than the newspapers—and herein lies one value of compulsory liability insurance) and we need the most careful canvass of what preventive measures can be brought to bear at the bottle-neck (tests for drivers, renewed at intervals; tests of cars before license. Could one add licensing of garagemen and mechanics, based on competence, and requirement that unsafe cars be reported?)

Throughout, the single question remains the center: *human behavior* is to be controlled *by human behavior.* Hence: *who* are the human beings in question *on any given issue?* how are they organized? to what stimuli will *they* (as they now exist) respond in the desired manner?

Why all this should need to be said, I cannot understand. A glance at law, practice, or the literature of criminology makes it clear, however, that it does need to be said. Professor Hall's book stands out in that it does not need to be said to him.

*   *   *

Professor Hall has approached his subject from the basic assumption that rules of law reflect the felt needs of the society. Perhaps this is too well known to require proof. Sound scholars, for all that, prefer to test assumptions. Dr. Hall tries the assumption out, in the Appendix, on Carrier's Case, a turning point in the law of larceny. The results are novel in legal literature. They substantiate the hypothesis. In careful detail. In this instance.

Chapter One builds on this Appendix: a single intensive study has been done; more sweeping interpretations can then be risked. The response of rules on theft (judge-made or legislative) to the march of events is followed through the highly creative 18th Century.

Yet Chapter One suggests repeatedly not only a response, but a lag. How great, then, is the lag? Does it lead to distortion? What forces break it down? Chapter Two looks into some of the shackles which early legal views or theories place upon the adaptation of old rules to new conditions. The conclusions must be that unpleasant facts of distortion exist; that the early theories have yielded chiefly, and piecemeal, to the direct pressure, over very small areas, —*only* over small areas—of highly interested and influential groups who think not of the whole, but of what they want (Carrier's Case, too, represented indirect financial interest—that of the King); that the results, over any longer period, tend to become chaotic, whether judicial or legislative shifts are in the forefront; and that a wherewithal for predicting which way the rat will jump in any individual instance is not yet at hand. Note how long "choses in action," which the rising banking and commercial interest would seem to require to see made a subject of larceny, held out against emerging common sense. (Does this mean that pick-pockets and highwaymen long thought such "choses-in-action" as they acquired too dangerous to dispose of—while drawers or acceptors were prepared to furnish duplicates? Bank of England notes—the first to be covered—ran to Bearer. How commonly was other bearer, or blank indorsed paper, made—or transferred after it had been stolen?)

I trust that one other conclusion becomes hard to escape: the major concepts of any legal century are likely to need revision in the next legal century. Roman Law of the late Empire managed to serve Europe fairly well until the arrival of the machine. But why? Surely because it had already adapted itself to a high commercial and urban civilization—and had in addition been worked over by Azo, Bartolus, the humanists, the Pandectists, till it had ceased to be *Roman* Law, save where *Roman* Law fitted later conditions. Ehrlich, on this, is persuasive.

But medieval English law has no such background. It contained sense, in spots, from which moderns could profit. I have tried above, in regard to "Criminal Association," to suggest the possible value of a modification of that use of "known" reputed fact which was the basis of William's Inquest and the early jury. For all that, both machinery and concepts need constant overhauling, as conditions change. Conscious effort *can* reduce lag.

Hall is not satisfied with showing lag, however, nor yet (later) with advocating cure. He wants to see the *effects* of lag. He wants also to add to the study of the rules an indication of the behavior which went on under those rules. This is so unusual, in the study of criminal law, as to merit high praise. The results, in Chapter Three, are so striking as to force the praise higher. Yet I wish Chapter Three had either been put first, or integrated, as a running comment, into Chapters One and Two. I advise the reader to take Chapter Three first, and to keep his right thumb in it, for reference, as he then reads the story of "substantive law" that runs before it. Or else—*after* reading Chapter Three, to reread those others. Three enriches the colors of the others as sunset enriches the colors of an October hillside.

For in Chapter Three it appears that that Benefit of Clergy which Kipling did not understand, exempting some from the inexorable death penalty, spread on the one hand outward till it seemed to include the entire population—while on the other hand the percentage of offenses which it touched at all was steadily narrowed under pressure from the particular lobbyists of the moment. It appears, too, that transportation of convicted felons once played almost the same rôle which parole and suspended sentence seek to play today. And that the history of transportation demonstrates the vital part which economic pressure and lack of economic opportunity play in theft for gain. It appears, finally, that when rules head one way, and felt needs head in another, administrators will twist and wriggle to meet needs despite the rules—building up *practices* which shock as being "illegal," but which are as inevitable as they are needed; which also leave a somewhat terrific room for abuse. Thus what we see as the glory of English administration in the 18th and early 19th Centuries, in somehow almost regularly softening the law and keeping at least the decent convict from the gallows, presages the District Leader's notations on the Court Clerk's docket, as to whom the former gentleman is "interested" in. The lesson is clear: either official rules must be remade to fit conditions—for some years to come—or else corrupt discretion creeps in beside legitimate.

Thus Hall achieves his own background, showing over a period the interaction of official rules and social need, and the effect of each on administration—and some reasonable suggestion of the effect of administration on each. The net lesson is that social need is a result of social and economic conditions; that social need is the true crux of the problem; that the problem is a problem in human behavior; that rules mean little—save distortion of control—except as they are sifted through administration; and that rules *plus* administration are a unit as being governmental devices to control behavior.

* * *

Doctor Hall turns then to application of his buttressed insight to contemporary problems. As indicated above, the lines of attack are four: (1) Receiving stolen goods as a bottle-neck problem in theft-for-sale, the *trade* being the essence, and the difficulties of a theory outmoded for footing on "a specific offense" being criticized in terms of the problem of proof. (2) Specialized depredation (silk, jewels, furs); the extra-legal measures of reduction which have worked, plus the dangers inherent in purely private lines of protection. Of those there is one which Hall does *not* mention: private police have values, as against theft, which are not paralleled in their work against strikers. As with courts, and criminal law, the riders gallop, with unequal beauty, in several directions at once. (3) Auto theft, and the closer analysis of the meaning of this new category of criminal statistics.—A lovely job. (4) Petty larceny as a field in which "modern" lines of reformation treatment can *often* be tried out without encountering the emotional and political opposition felt in "babying convicts." Here, too, belongs auto-joy-ride "theft," [1] save perhaps in the case of psychopathic personalities.

On these, enough has been already said to introduce them. What deserves repetition is that Professor Hall's approach to them rests on hypotheses as to human behavior and institutional development which he takes not out of the air, but takes from sociological literature. *Which he not only takes, but tests for their applicability* to the legal and social phenomena of theft before he attempts their application.

The book is in consequence cautious, thorough, and illuminat-

[1] I cannot recall a time when I had more difficulty in making contact with my fellow-man or figuring the how-and-why of his gizzard than when, as a committeeman for the Commissioners on Uniform State Laws preparing a statute against auto-theft, theft-for-use was proposed as a flat felony, and I explained the juvenile "car-for-a-party" theft, and found a number (of non-Commissioners) at the table who "knew all about that, and meant exactly that." It is of course this granitic-stupid type of mind which threatens us with an atom-war.

ing. It is, even, lit with common sense and practical experience. To lawyers, sociologists, criminologists, and practical men concerned with theft it is to be recommended—with the certainty that any one of them will learn from it things he needs to know. It may even be commended to interested members of the general public. They have sense—if they are interested. The book talks sense—for anybody interested.[j]

[j] It is pleasant to report that the book—and the man—achieved real success.

WHO ARE THESE ACCUSED? [a]

Who are the two men whose names recur, whose lives and honor are the immediate stake in all this story? [1]

Nicola Sacco, an Italian, resident in Massachusetts from his eighteenth year. A solid workman, who learned his trade outside of hours, a shoe-worker, a "good cobbler" and "edger." A simple-hearted devoted husband and father. A lover of nature—who in prison found difficulty writing to his friends unless blue sky heartened and cheered him through the bars. An idealist, bent on improving the lot of working-men, so strong, so unafraid in his convictions that on trial for his life, before a jury whom he knew to be prejudiced against such views, he preached his beliefs, prepared to be a martyr to his faith.

Nicola Sacco, (the same Nicola Sacco?), a foreigner discontented with our institutions, yet content to abide among them. One who forsook all decent views for Socialism, even for Anarchism. Living and earning here, yet fleeing to Mexico in fear of being drafted to defend the country. The user of a false name. A man who would lie lightly to his employer to cover up a morning on leave which he had spent in talk and not on business. A gun-toter. An agitator.

[a] This was originally prepared as part of an unpublished study of the Sacco-Vanzetti case. The present portion has been published in MICHAEL AND WECHSLER, CRIMINAL LAW AND ITS ADMINISTRATION 1085 (1940), and in JOUGHIN AND MORGAN, THE LEGACY OF SACCO AND VANZETTI 178 (1948).—I have retained, marked "M-W," the Michael and Wechsler notes.

[1] (M-W) See Commonwealth v. Sacco, 255 Mass. 369, 151 N.E. 839 (1926), 259 Mass. 128, 156 N.E. 57 (1927), 261 Mass. 12, 158 N.E. 167 (1927). The full record of all the proceedings has been published as THE SACCO-VANZETTI CASE (1929). For discussions of the case, see FRANKFURTER, THE CASE OF SACCO AND VANZETTI (1927); FRAENKEL, THE SACCO-VANZETTI CASE (1931).

A man too indifferent to American ways to seek during twelve years of freedom to learn English decently, too stupid to learn English decently during seven years in jail. An associate of that Vanzetti whom we know to have been convicted of an attempted holdup in Bridgewater.

Bartolomeo Vanzetti, a man who had forsaken his home in Italy and a good living with a farmer-family whom he loved, because his conscience would not let him be a party to exploiting men. A man who, though without wife and children, astonished his neighbors by his steadiness and effort at his work. A man who, ready to throw himself into the place of danger in defense of his fellows, was chosen to go up to New York to discuss the further defense of Salsedo, a radical held incommunicado by the Federal authorities in their wild deportation drive of 1920; that Salsedo whose "questioning" is suspected of having driven him to seek relief in suicide. Vanzetti, a man whom person after person, of judgment, insight, and sensibility, learned to know after the time of his imprisonment; and whom each of those who learned to know him came to honor, respect, admire, even love. A man framed up before the present trial (on a charge made against Sacco, too, until for Sacco an unshakable alibi was proved) in order to make easy the conviction in the case in hand.

Bartolomeo Vanzetti (the same Bartolomeo Vanzetti?), a radical leader, a speechmaker, an anarchistic agitator; closely concerned with that Salsedo who was dangerous enough to induce the Federal authorities to hold him incommunicado till, seemingly, he confessed his guilt by suicide. A gun-toter, Vanzetti, as well. A man convicted previously of another desperate crime of violence. A man the more dangerous because of his brains and gift of leadership. A draft-dodger. A liar, who lied copiously and confessedly on his arrest. A believer in violence. An associate, a sympathizer, a "comrade" of those radicals who threatened and even exercised outrageous violence in efforts to terrify the authorities into giving him up without punishment.

Opinions differ, you may observe, about these two. Two things are certain: they were Italians and radicals; they were accused of murder.

From one angle, it makes no difference which of these two views of these two Italians you accept. Angel or devil, a man has a claim to a fair trial of his guilt. Angel or devil, he has a claim to a fair trial, not of his general social desirability, but of his guilt of *the specific offense* charged against him. Such is the letter of our law.

Such also is our law's spirit. For letter and for spirit there is a reason. Law is administered by men. We do not trust men to be wholly wise, or wholly fair. Above all, we do not trust men to be wise or fair to those with whose opinions, with whose interests, with whose dear-held beliefs their own interests, their own dear-held opinions, clash. "General social desirability" of others, through most of history, has meant to men in power such attitudes and actions and opinions as do not threaten their own continuance in power. Our forefathers learned this from John, learned it again when York and Lancaster were warring, learned it yet again from the early Stuarts and the later. Their learning left its mark upon our law. It is *not* for the official to judge whether an accused is socially undesirable. Only the legislature passes on that point, and the legislature must pass upon it not for single men, nor after the event, but for whole classes, and for whole classes chosen in advance.[2] The only job and the only privilege of the official—district attorney, court, or jailer—is to deal with those who by some specific action have brought themselves within the classes thus laid down. By some *specific* action. Again we wish a safe-guard. There must be some *objective* certainty, that men can fix upon and see and prove, before we trust officialdom to act. It is too easy to find "general" indications against one's enemies—be they Bolsheviks, or Democrats, or rivals for the Tenth Ward leadership. So the job of police and prosecutor is to bring suspects to book. The job of court and jury is to see *whether* the suspect has committed *the particular offense*—not even in this determination of the fact will we trust the executive official, the official *who is in power*.

This, I say, is the spirit of our law as it is the letter. And you will observe that it is for the protection of each of us that this is

[2] (M-W) *Cf.* U. S. Attorney-General Jackson in a letter to Senator Russell, Chairman of the Senate Committee on Immigration, with respect to a bill which passed the House on June 13, directing the Attorney-General to deport Harry Bridges "notwithstanding any other provision of law" as a person "whose presence in this country the Congress deems hurtful" (N. Y. Times, June 20, 1940, p. 12, col. 3): ". . . It would be the first time that Congress, without changing the general law, simply suspended all laws which protect a named individual and directed the Attorney General to disregard them and forthwith to deport 'notwithstanding any other provision of law.' . . .

"What becomes of equality before the law, of the impersonal and impartial character of our government, if it is to select unpopular persons to suffer disadvantage or punishment? . . .

"As an American I would not, for the sake of my own liberty, deny the protection of uniform and indiscriminatory laws and of fair hearings to even the humblest or meanest of men. As an official of the United States I cannot in good conscience do other than recommend strongly against this bill."

so. Each one of us may be tomorrow objectionable to some one of the authorities. This far our law seeks to protect us from him. No man can tell when his own opinions will become intolerable to the new officials. Think of the numbers of theretofore respected citizens whose views became "socially dangerous" almost overnight when Bolshevism broke into power in Russia, or Fascism in Italy. But there is a deeper wisdom in these rules. They are not chiefly for the direct protection of unpopular minorities. More deeply, more far-sightedly, they are *for the indirect protection of majorities against themselves.* No majority can remain healthy long without an opposition. No man can tell in advance which piece or fraction of the thousand oppositions contains the fertile seed of new advance. There is but one hope: let them *all* fight for their place in the sun—all, short of such turbulence and riot as makes life with them intolerable. This not for them, but for ourselves. *We* who are in the saddle need the stimulus, the new ideas, the challenge, the stirring, that their wild rantings offer. I see, then, no cause for laughter, no cause for bitter sneer, no cause for indignation, when radicals caught and accused of this or that grapple themselves for protection to these very institutions which in their freedom they rant upon and curse. Such action may be no credit to the radical. On that I should not care to pass, excepting case by case, in full possession of each set of circumstances. But it makes no difference to anyone else whether that action is creditable *to the radical* or not. It is *we,* it is *our* institutions, it is *our* law, which are in question. *It is for ourselves* that we must guarantee to this recalcitrant fair trial—fair trial of whether he has committed a specific, clear offense. *We* need to let him run, lest *we* grow stagnant. *We* need to keep faith with *ourselves,* that the law we have made for ourselves and all who live among us shall be applied alike to all who live among us and to ourselves.

Yet this deep wisdom (which most of us in our more sober moments see and know, which most of us in any moment of excitement will forget)—this deep wisdom is a wisdom only partial. The other part is this: that men are not single acts, but living beings. That men are wholes. That a man's history is an index to his acts. That a man's value depends in good part on who that man is.

From one angle, I said above, it makes no difference which of two views of these Italians you accept. And that is true; likewise, that is one part of wisdom. But from another angle, from another part of wisdom, it will make all the difference in the world. For if a man is bad, if a man is a menace, any excuse to get him out of the way may be better than none. If a man is bad, if a man is a menace, why should we worry too much over whether he may or may not have done this one act charged? He will have done a plenty of other things as bad or worse. "He ought to be hanged, anyway." And even if you should reject these two positions, no sane man can avoid agreeing on a third: if a man is bad, if he is a menace, it will take *much less evidence* to convince you that he has committed the particular offense than if he were an honored citizen. "That's just the kind *he* is!" will get short shrift—with the trier of fact, with *any* trier of fact—beside "I can't believe such a thing of *him!*" If you believe, therefore, that these two Italians were dangerous men, ungrateful beneficiaries of a long-suffering America, men of violence, undesirable in every sense: then (1) you will think they got what they deserved, and guilt or innocence of the Braintree murder will seem to you of relatively little consequence, and you will be disposed to say: why all this stir, even if the machine did maybe slip a cog, about two scoundrels?; and (2) you will find very slight evidence quite ample to convince you that the Braintree murder in particular must be laid at their door. This, even if the jury had not spoken; even if the Lowell Committee had not reported.[3]

If these should be your beliefs, bear with me none the less for a moment while I question whether you are wise. It is not likely that I shall be able to persuade you. Persuasion in these matters is not easy. They cut to the closest, to the most intense of loyalties. They fire emotions which make argument seem ridiculous, insulting. In these matters a man's position stands unchallenged because it rests on the unchallengeable. There is but one right way, there is but one right opinion, there can be but one right feeling. And any "argument" which moves from some different premise is an affront. Indeed, an argument which assumes that a different

[3] (M-W) The Committee's report appears in THE SACCO-VANZETTI CASE (1929), v, 5378i. The Committee, consisting of A. Lawrence Lowell, Robert Grant and S. W. Stratton was appointed by Governor Fuller to advise him, in connection with an appeal for executive clemency presented on behalf of the condemned. The Committee concluded that the trial was fair, the motions for a new trial properly denied and the defendants proved guilty beyond a reasonable doubt. With respect to the fairness of the trial, the report concluded (*id.* 5378n.): "To summarize, therefore, what has been said: The Committee have seen no evidence sufficient to make them believe that the trial was unfair. On the contrary, they are of opinion that the Judge endeavored, and endeavored successfully, to secure for the defendants a fair trial; that the District Attorney was not in any way guilty of unprofessional behavior, that he conducted the prosecution vigorously but not improperly; and that the jury, a capable, impartial and unprejudiced body, did, as they were instructed, 'well and truly try and true deliverance make.' "

premise may be tenable is an affront.—All this I know, as who does not who has lived with his fellowmen for a few years, and used his eyes? Yet I would ask you: bear with me for a moment while I question whether you are wise.

For I think we have slid, in some remarks I made above, quite typically but quite unfortunately, quite as men do but hardly as men should, into an evil fallacy. "If a man is bad, if he is a menace, it will take no such great evidence to convince you that he has committed this particular offense." But what do we mean by "bad" or by a "menace"? Is a known gunman under suspicion of another hold-up? A known penman under suspicion of another forgery? A known drunkard under suspicion of driving while intoxicated? That is one thing. Or is a man whose opinions on the property *system* or our *system* of government we do not like— whose *opinions* we hate, fear, loathe—under suspicion of murdering a stranger to him in cold blood? Is that the same thing? Mark you, the crime charged is not assassination of some high official, who might be thought by the accused to be or represent the hated System. Nor is it, say, a bombing in the process of a strike, where fierce conviction of necessity to use violence if one is to win through to the "rights of man" might come in question. It is a cold payroll hold-up matter, done for gain; for all that one can see, for private gain. The bad men, the menacing men, who are charged thus with doing murder upon strangers, for gain, are men whose opinions, whatever one thinks of their wisdom, or of their rightness—or of their dangerousness to our institutions in the large— are based fundamentally upon the fellowship of man, upon the need for human decency and human kindness of each man toward his fellows. And the men in question, the accused, have both shown unmistakable courage in pursuing these opinions, have both gone with some cheerfulness through the sacrifices these opinions have seemed to make necessary. "Bad," and "a menace;" may be. But *this* kind of "bad," *this* kind of "menace"—is that so safe a conclusion? Is it so fair a conclusion? Is it so reasonable? Is it reasonable at all?

As a matter of common sense—common sense, that is, in sober quiet thinking, when a common sense man has really settled down to think—I say we have slipped when we think that because *these* men are "bad" they may be taken without too meticulous inquiry as guilty of *this* crime. But there is more. As a matter of law, of that law which is an integral part, in letter and in spirit, of the institutions we hold dear, the trier of fact must not even be allowed *to take the risk* of being unable to bring this type of common sense to bear. As a matter of law the prosecutor will not be permitted, of his own motion,[4] to show the jury in a trial for "ordinary" murder what the social or political views of the defendants were. Indeed, the law goes much further. The prosecutor will not be permitted, of his own motion,[5] to show that the defendant has been previously convicted of a crime. He will not even be permitted to show that the defendant has previously been convicted of a crime *of like nature, in like circumstances.*[6] Here, in its vigor to save an accused from prejudice, to save him from even the *chance* of prejudice, the law keeps from the jury the most relevant and persuasive of facts. In this extreme case of the rule's application it seems to me to outrage common sense. But that the rule holds, *even* in the extreme case (I should say, even in the absurd case), evidences more than the inertia of the law. It evidences the vitality of the *policy* of keeping the jury, the trier of fact, from being influenced by *irrelevant* "badness," *irrelevant* "undesirability" of the accused, in passing on his guilt or innocence of a *particular* offense. Not only against the prejudices, the policy-views, of the official in power, but against the prejudices, the policy-views, of the triers of fact does American law, in keeping with the best spirit of American institutions, set up its barriers—in favor of *any* man who is accused.

If, then, we are faithful to the form of government we have inherited, and to the spirit which breathes through that form of government, we cannot allow a radical, however we may despise his views, and though those views attack our government itself, to be more quickly believed guilty of *any specific offense* than would a man whose views on government we would ourselves go to the stake for. If *we* are faithful to our form of government we must set out, with gritted teeth, to judge the evidence for its own

[4] We shall see later, and in our present case, that this does not hold where the accused himself first opens up the question. But our present inquiry goes not to the manner of the trial, but to the question whether it makes any difference to a good American what manner of trial a foreign radical has had.—It would not hold, either, in an accusation of political assassination, where views could be used to show motive.

[5] If the accused should take the stand in his own behalf, prior convictions could be shown against him, as against any other witness, to make him seem unfit to be believed. But the accused would *himself* have to take the initiative. And the theory of the law is that the convictions are to be weighed *only* for the purpose of wiping out the accused's own testimony.

[6] There is an exception, not here in question, when a series of crimes are charged to be part of a single, continued plan.

value, although the defendant be the rankest revolutionary. *That we owe not to him but to ourselves.*

But what of the other aspect of the "whole man" in the case? "If a man is bad, if a man is a menace, any excuse to get him out of the way may be better than none." What he has not yet done, he may yet do. Proof fails (by pure misfortune) as to all the ill he must have done already. A stroke of luck, if we can put him out of harm's way now. Why any pother, then, when he *is* put out of harm's way?

As to this, I can but recur to what is said above. It is a repetition; but it repeats only what is too often forgotten as soon as heard. *We* have dedicated ourselves to institutions which put sole judgment as to when the state may move against a man—against *any* man—into the legislature and the Constitution. Perhaps that is an unwise way of ordering matters. But if it is, then the very fabric of our government is woven of unwisdom. *We cannot have the fabric and reject it, both at once.* To have it, to accept it, is to accept its spirit with its letter. "We need to keep faith with *ourselves* that the law we have made for ourselves and all who live among us shall be applied alike to all who live among us and to ourselves." Let that fail, though it fail upon the veriest wretch, and *we* shall have failed. The country that we cherish will have failed. You may take or reject our American institutions. But you cannot take them, you cannot honor them, without taking on yourself the burden of indignation, of wrath, of reform, if you should find that a man has been put away *for what he has not done.* A man. *Any* man. Foreigner, radical, or revolutionary; draft-dodger or desperado. *It is not that man, it is your institutions which are at stake.*

{ 21 }

THE ANTHROPOLOGY OF CRIMINAL GUILT [a]

Criminal guilt is not a single idea. Under the single label are a number of strikingly different ideas, which in common thinking are met in various quite different combinations. We are going to be thinking and talking at cross-purposes unless we get at least the major divergencies out in the open to be looked at.

Begin with "guilt." The core of the "guilt" idea is action that runs counter to a group standard for action, an accepted group standard which is taken for the case in hand to be important. Little things can be made big things by the culture—thus the obligation to wear a collar while delivering an inaugural address —or by the person, as when one English barrister retired from practice because one of his pleadings would not stand up—or by a combination, as when a little girl "dies of shame" at spotting her dress at her first party. But you dilute the "guilt" idea into near meaninglessness if the infraction in question doesn't much matter.

Mattering, however, turns up from either end. Sometimes the infraction matters to the offender, as in our little girl's case even if nobody else noticed. Sometimes the infraction matters to the group, as when a Cheyenne Indian killed another Cheyenne and the resulting blood-stench threatened to drive away the buffalo; or as in the troubling modern case of the political offender whose heart is not only pure but high. The psychiatrist is peculiarly concerned about guilt felt by the individual when the group sees no need for the feeling; the criminologist is peculiarly concerned

[a] From the N. Y. U. Series on Social Meaning of Legal Concepts: CRIMINAL GUILT 100 (1950).

439

about guilt felt by the great-group, *but not* by the guilty individual: the "hard case," the "criminal for a living." The job
of effective raising and training of the young is in very real part
the elimination to a reasonable degree of each of these two situations, and the development, to a reasonable degree, of coincidence
of individual and of group-feeling about guilt. I will not say: "as
ethnology teaches." I will say instead: "as horse sense indicates
and ethnology illustrates."

Meantime, and from the standpoint of the group, "guilt" proceeds to turn up as a question of fact, and a troubling one. Among
people after people, for instance, we see *secret* offenses treated
as peculiarly punishable—secret killing; or secret sorcery (banned
utterly by the Chagga king). And let me greatly protest against
the smug and to me naive misinterpretation of this phenomenon
on the part of those students of procedure who, taking modern
legal procedure as just plain "rational" (God save the mark!), have
attributed the early heavy penalties for secrecy of offense to inadequacy of primitive procedure to try the facts. I do not find
as much evidence of current *social* dissatisfaction among primitives with primitive prevailing procedures to try facts as I do of
current dissatisfaction among moderns with modern prevailing
procedures. And the man who wants to understand why secret
offenses are feared and hated and stamped on in a primitive culture would do well to meditate upon modern reactions when a
"bandit gang" or a "sex fiend," etc., is supposed to be at large
and at work in some neighborhood, or spies at work in the country. Secrecy of the offense can step up unbelievably Bentham's
"secondary" uneasiness effects of serious crime. This is doubtless
especially so insofar as a primitive community's legal system
loads a major share of post-crime procedure onto the aggrieved
person or group, for secrecy hamstrings all "self-help" machinery;
but you will not understand our recurrent "red"—or Know-
Nothing, etc.—scares, from Haymarket through to today, unless
you take any real danger concerned as the smallest of three ingredients, of which the other two are (a) a sort of cross in the
politico-economic area between heresy and blasphemy and (b) a
fierce terror at secret and *therefore* infinitely widespread and
disastrous operations.

Finally, the idea of "fault" gets mingled in among the intellectual inhabitants of the "guilt" concept. This approach moves
in terms of "guilt" being impossible unless the offender has had
the wherewithal to avoid offending; sometimes it is even sug-

gested that he must have an intent to offend, or even to commit the particular type of offense, in order to be "guilty." What ethnology does for us here is to point up the fact that a system of law is ever and again faced with problems of felt public menace which drive in many situations to make fault in the offender partly or even wholly immaterial to "guilt" as laid down by group authority. The most familiar instance is the breach of a religious tabu so powerful that breach puts tribal welfare in jeopardy, so that execution in expiation is seen as a social necessity: as Oedipus of the legend faced necessary supernatural punishment for his guilt of an utterly unwitting offense, so various peoples have felt themselves forced to deal with unwitting tabu-breach either through the priesthood or through the secular arm. It used to be the practice to contrast this with modern law, with some complacency, until ex post facto laws and the offense of being born with particular types of parentage came into recent prominence. Perhaps now we shall do well to rethink how far our own law provides exceptions to the notion that fault is a necessary part of "guilt": martial law or the stranger who is nonetheless held "to know the law"; with which one contrasts the privileged killing, say by sniping, of persons in a different kind of uniform or the psychologically irresponsible and peculiarly dangerous killer who fails to meet the "legal" test for criminal "insanity."

The first of these, martial law, is the one which can closely parallel the primitive approach to unwitting infraction of a tribe-endangering tabu. It is of particular importance to us because it shows criminal law moving wholly without thought of punishment, but instead purely in terms of engineering considerations addressed to the public safety. This challenges us to meditate on whether our own basic general approach in terms of punishment or penalty for serious crime may not be a false road in. I think it is. It is, moreover, if a false road in, one which misleads not only the lay public and the bulk of bar and bench, but even supposedly enlightened advocates of reform. It would, for instance, not surprise me, before this program is over, to hear someone referring to the barbarity of an outmoded "legal" test for criminal responsibility which leads to "punishing" some offenders who are really sick, etc., with the implication that punishment is all right, for the well. But if the suggestion I derive from the ethnological data is sound, any such thinking is hopelessly skewed; the only piece of our prevailing legal system which ought to be taken for granted in such a discussion is civil liberties protection against arbitrarily seizing an individual for treatment; beyond that the first and basic question ought in all cases to be one of what treatment *public safety* requires, or permits.

To sum up thus far, the single label "guilt" covers in various combinations at least these different major ideas with regard to an offense: (1) individual sense of guilt; (2) group-imposed standard of guilt; (3) fact that some person committed the offense; (4) fault in the offender.

And when we turn to the *criminal* phase of "criminal guilt" we find an equivalent complexity. The one core idea is that some*body* is supposed to do something about the offense in question, as representative of the whole relevant community. It must be some*body*, not merely conscience or the supernatural—though it may be a religious somebody. And the something to be *done* must have teeth, though a verbal rebuke can in some circumstances bite harder than a flogging.

Let us, moreover, not be misled when, as in cases of blood-vengeance by kin, aggrieved persons step forward to savor their own vengeance while they also lift the brunt of the community's work; they move, until blood-vengeance is put under legal control, as community representatives and indeed more often than not under community pressure. This is what the early Old Testament makes clear, this is still seething beneath the "law" of the Njal-Saga; this, also, is what that primitive people recently captained by Churchill have found to be an exceedingly useful device for enforcement of the criminal law: the privately-run prosecution. From which a further challenge arises to our thinking: Are we quite sure that channeling the utter whole of criminal prosecution into the District Attorney's office may not be an overdoing of a basically good idea? Are we quite sure that it does not thrust upon the District Attorney a bulk and burden of uncontrolled and non-responsible discretion which is at fundamental odds with our whole theory of officials responsible and acting under law, and which drives almost inherently in the direction of abuse? I suggest, moreover, that our almost complete absorption of enforcement machinery by the State has an unhappy by-product which, these days, we can ill afford: it drives another wedge between the law-supporter, the law-consumer, and his law. It still further substitutes George for a citizen's own shoulder at the wheel. It grazes away still more of those grassroots which Lilienthal has rightly seen and preached as vital to the right working of our style of government.

Thus far, the "criminal" side of "criminal guilt," however interesting, would seem to present a clear picture; but that is only because we have as yet not dug into the other ideas which are packaged under the label "criminal." The second aspect of the core-idea branches out to include, as "criminal," any action of any kind against which society moves, officially, by way of law and law enforcement officers. This aspect turns at once to war with so much of the content of the "guilt" idea as involves personal sense of guilt (the conscience-sin-repentance phase of "guilt") and even with so much of the "guilt" idea as suggests importance of the offense. For petty police offenses are happily included; so are all those offenses which are officially declared but which, for whatever reason, lack resonance among the law-consumers and law-supporters. One thinks of significant types: the conqueror's measures before the conquest has become accepted; the policing measure (safety, revenue, conservation, traffic, or other) which is felt as imposition or nuisance or outrage—in a word any unwelcome restraint whose purpose is not felt and re-sponded to. Thus the only two aspects of the "guilt" idea which at the same time spread over this whole ground of the "criminal" are the phase of officially imposed standard of guilt and that of fact-of-guilt: Is the deed in question officially a *criminal* deed? Is it *this person* who did (or is otherwise responsible for) the deed? Here the questions divide: the question "of law" and the question "of fact." But in a very real and deep sense the two questions merge into a unity as against all other *types* of question. They merge on the *legal* level, they merge into a *legal* question: Is this a man who is going to be handled no longer as a citizen, but now as a criminal wrong-doer?

It is no accident and no product of word-juggling that our question of "criminal guilt" comes thus to a first focus on an area to which the modern religious phase of guilt, the conscience phase of guilt, the moral phase of guilt, the psychiatrist's phase of guilt are not irrelevant if, as and when any of them happens to be present, but to which each of these phases is for all that *un-essential*. It is no accident because in our polity the heart of the whole scheme of law against serious crime lies in this *purely legal* question: Is this the man who has forfeited the rights a man is born with?

Do not mistake me. I am not suggesting that the criminal code is not important. To take an historic instance, the old indiscriminate extension of the death penalty over almost everything at large was hugely important, to individual offenders, to inefficiency of operation ("As well be hanged for a sheep as a lamb," etc.), to colonial policy. So, today, it is important that the legal rules about receiving stolen goods are bafflingly inept and that our law on sex offenses is out of line with the facts of life. But when you get into the deeper meaning of the most important of these matters, they start moving over into the other problem. Thus the matter of criminal receivers is at bottom only a single aspect of the need for carefully and separately engineered rules and handling of the whole problem of *serious-crime-for-a-living*. But the mere setting up of such a category to be thought about cuts into the very essence of our approach to the basic question: Is this the man?

Again, do not mistake me. I am not urging or advocating a "legalistic" as contrasted with a sociological or human or psychiatric approach to serious crime. What I am doing is to point out a fact about certain choices of policy which underlie and inform the whole implicit working philosophy of the going institution which we call "government and law." That fact is that the "legalism," so-called, of our legal system's approach to serious crime represents indeed considerable real legalism and blindness on the part of the legal profession; but it represents even more, much more, overwhelmingly more, a set of policy-choices inherited and unthinkingly cherished in our lay tradition, policy-choices of which legal rules and procedures and lawyers' attitudes are in first instance reflections—though sometimes distorted reflections.

The basic policy-choice is that of distrust of officials. It is expressed in requirements of criminal procedure which shackle all efforts to cope with serious crime. It is expressed in similar requirements about the rules of criminal law ("equal" and general, and before the event). It is expressed in an adversary system of trial which has been developed to the point of sometimes absurd and function-defeating excrescence—as well see most easily by contrast with that other branching off the single trunk, the English. The net can perhaps be sloganized as an "arm's length" system of criminal law. The main features are familiar. An offender is viewed in first instance not as a person, not as a member of a going team whose attitude or action is bothering the team's smooth working and who therefore needs straightening out. Instead, he is viewed as a person quite outside, whom the officials are to take hold of only if they can pin upon him some specific act. The act must have been described as an offense in advance, in words, by official law; and it must then be charged in the particular case, also in words. It is something of a game or contest of verbal jackstraws to see whether the accused or his act can be pulled by his counsel out from under the government's arrangement of words without moving any of the latter. The actual trial of fact must be before a tribunal artificially sterilized of knowledge of the facts, under a procedure which rigidly eliminates a great deal of relevant evidence and in which one major object of prosecution and defense is to catch each other by surprise, and another major object is to obscure the jury's judgment by appeal to its emotions. The defendant (and any witness) is still happily surrounded by a protection against self-incrimination which had real value when an accused had no right to counsel, or to notice of charges, or to confront and examine witnesses against him, or to subpoena witnesses on his own behalf, and when self-incrimination meant in first instance talking under torture.

The foregoing sketch of our modern American adversary proceeding in serious criminal cases is deliberate caricature. It is intended to remind, and to remind hard, that what remains a rather majestic and altogether vital set of ideals has come with time to be encrusted and hampered in operation by machinery, attitudes, practices, which are of dubious value. That machinery needs overhauling, and from the bottom up, if the ideals are to become and remain either real in fact *or regularly renewed and revitalized in the consciousness* of the observing or participating law-consumer and law-supporter. The ideals themselves are solid, they are eternal: fair and full notice of charges, time to prepare, right to hear and right to answer, right to a *fair* and open-minded tribunal (both "ignorant" and "impartial" are only measures aimed at *fairness*), right to call witnesses, right to a helper and spokesman who knows the ropes. It is a solid ideal, no less, that there should be fair warning in advance of acting, that the action may be an offense. But surely all of such matters are humanly capable of being worked out by measures which are reasonable rather than piddling, purpose-guided rather than form-ridden, moderately and reasonably flexible rather than petrified. But, again, it is all but impossible to work out *and work with* this sounder type of measure if the fundamental tone of the institution is the arm's-length tone: you there, I here, in a pure adversary contest: one in which almost any conflict between truth-interest and adversary-interest is resolved in favor of the latter. Again I invite attention to the British procedure in trial for serious crimes. I suggest further that our own penalty-and-punishment, as contrasted with a prevention-and-cure, approach to criminal law is intimately bound up with the general arm's length system. An adversary-type of trial is indeed conceivable which moves then after conviction into a pure cure-and-prevention line of treatment (I include, of course, execution in prevention); but it is psychologically a difficult combination, a sort of institutional semi-schizophrenia.

Meantime the attitudes of law-supporter and law-consumer essentially buttress the American arm's-length approach of the official institution. We do not view our officials in first instance as part of Us. Most of the time, for most of us, our officials are He and They, unless we have some "in" of which we know that we should rightly be ashamed. Even the touch of Us-ness that goes with Uncle Sam is lacking in regard to state or city government. Partly by consequence, partly for other reasons, there is a continuous rallying power in the civil liberties ideals, as applied to the criminal law and its enforcement. The law-supporter also goes whole-hog for the "punishment-penalty-vengeance" attack on the treatment phase of serious crime; he feels no Us-ness with the offender, save in peculiar circumstances. (I wish I had time here to explore the why of that; there is a good deal to be said which is commonly left unmentioned by the psychiatrists.[b]) Where the law-supporter does bog down in understanding and enthusiasm of support of today's official approach is on the details of the adversary style of trial. Even this is not because it does not fit the law-supporter's book; a hundred years ago men regularly rode or drove in to the county seat for the trials, and followed them with the enthusiasm of today's baseball fans, and they would still if other amusements had not crowded the trial off the boards. But to those who lack a fan's appreciation of the fine points of the game, the adversary trial seems from outside like

[b] In particular, it pays to stir into the pot (a) the simple social pattern learned in childhood: offense-punishment; (b) the hangover of magic-thinking, in which one exorcizes evil by appropriate action; (c) the quest for a simple answer, when a complex problem eludes diagnosis. Give me a few solid ingredients like these, and I am quite willing to accept in addition some of the more reasonable suggestions of the psychoanalysts.

backhandedness or trickery which approaches a travesty on justice; a dragging, awkward, unreliable machinery at best; at worst, one which is manipulated. In consequence, there is today one thing of which you can be sure: for the ideals of fair play which underlie the adversary system of trial you can stir up real enthusiasm among the law-supporters. But there is not one sole excrescence of trial machinery that will find one sole jot of support from any person in the country except a lawyer. This combination states an asset for reform, if the asset can be put to work.

When, with this picture of our own official system in mind, one turns for light and stimulus to ethnology, the one thing which turns up as a pretty general datum is the buttressing, among the less developed cultures, of the work and ideals of criminal law by the work and ideals of education, religion, current morality, and in consequence, of individual conscience. Rather regularly, in primitive cultures, criminal guilt is felt guilt, and official action against crime has live support. To observe that, and to observe that in general it simplifies the problems of controlling crime, is again simply to confirm horse sense; and it is also, and somewhat horribly,—with the help of Hitler's regime and Stalin's—to remind us that at a sufficient price in regimentation of all mind-and-habit-shaping institutions, even a highly complex industrial society can achieve such buttressing, and that if we do not (as I do not) wish to pay that price, then we have a job to do, to find a substitute.

Beyond that, one has to pick and choose, in order to find really vital suggestion from ethnology. I get, for instance, almost no illumination of modern problems out of the sprawling criminal law of the Barama River Carib, or of the Eskimo. I get little out of the developed legalism of the Chagga or Ashanti: we can outmatch their best. But when one begins to observe the highly geared drive for rehabilitation of the offender which pervades Cheyenne criminal law, one begins to prick up his ears. When one turns to the New Mexican Pueblos, and finds an established system to deal with both petty and grave offenses on that same basis, with punishment not only in fact but as a matter of conscious philosophy relegated to the role of an educational tool, then one does more than prick up his ears. One settles down to learn.

Here is a completely different approach to problems of criminal law. Offenses are foreknown as such, so far as experience is at hand, but hitherto unprecedented offenses can be fore*felt* as such when they run clearly counter to the tone and purpose of going institutions. A "trial" lies half in an inquiry by officials, an inquiry reaching "real evidence" (tracks, etc.), and all available testimony, including that of the suspect or accused; what he has to say in argument or extenuation is part of this phase. The officials will go drum up evidence for him on their own or at his instance. *They want to find him innocent:* he is part of their team. What is known as the "trial," the second half of the procedure, is formal on the point of fact, except in an exceptional case. Its purpose is instead to bring the erring brother, now known to be such, to repentance, to open confession, and to reintegration with the community of which he *was and still is regarded as an integral part.* As contrasted with arm's-length attitudes, the law, the procedure, the treatment, the attitudes, the emotions are *parental.* There is infinite patience in the tribunal, infinite long-suffering. Typically, also, there is infinite ultimate inflexibility: it is the offender who will have to do all the ultimate yielding. The results, 95% of the time, make our results look weak, uncertain, costly. But when the parental system ever goes wrong, the results do raise the hair. Let officials turn the machinery to work out a personal grudge; or to enrich themselves corruptly; or to put down political dissent—and one begins to understand why our forefathers, through the centuries, found it worth blood to win through to measures which could partly control officials.

As usual, when one comes home from an ethnological exploration, and looks around, one sees that it has all been there at home in front of him, all the time, just waiting to be noticed. The parental system is that by which we make and administer the criminal law of and within the household, the school, the system under which we each grow up. It is the system of the business unit in our adult lives, indeed of and within practically any working unit in our society which has not been reorganized, say by collective bargaining. It is plainly, when it works well, superior to any conceivable adversary system of trial, to any arm's-length system of regulating offenses against the group concerned, so far superior that we should scorn, even fear, the introduction of lawyer-style adversary procedure into any group for whose welfare we were ourselves concerned. But it will be observed that the keynote and grandeur of the parental system lies in the feeling of groupness, of We-ness, between the culprit and both the group-government and the group-public—a We-ness which makes "criminal guilt," in this context, regularly take on the aspect of *sense* of guilt in the culprit, either live from the beginning or latent and waiting to be roused into vigor by the tribunal. But the sense of guilt in question is not merely a recognition of having done wrong, not merely a contrition; it is at the same time, and no less vigorously, an active drive to come back in and to proceed then to do right—and it is companioned by sure knowledge that welcome waits, and help. This last is what our prison chaplain can promise only for God, not for the rest of us in our society. Let this feeling of We-ness, of love, acceptability, acceptance, and welcome—let this wane or die or be lacking, and a parental type of system becomes a chancy, too often an evil, thing.

Against this background I submit that a considerable number of our problems take on light. One is forced to ponder the need for finding some way, as between the arm's-length and the parental approaches, for combining the best features of both. One observes with fresh interest how modern reform-and-rehabilitation "treatment" procedure wars with the trial procedure and the rules of criminal law onto or over which the "treatment" procedure is grafted. One observes with fresh interest the need for introducing into youth and juvenile courts a touch of that protection of the citizen from being "taken over" which informs the Bill of Rights for adults.[1] One watches with excitement the growth, for instance, in discharge cases in some portions of the labor field, of a grievance procedure which carries in embryo real possibilities of that sound *human* system of criminal law which may some day displace both the overly arm's-length and the overly parental. One observes the thrusting into military law, by way of reform, of considerable quantities of the less satisfactory and over-lawyered parts of the arm's-length approach; and one observes it with worry, until the fact dawns that here indeed is a combination of the best features of both: the C.O. who is worth his salt will move, and move effectively, completely outside "the book," and by his own parental system, using and building his own sense of criminal guilt among his men—and cutting in shrewdly on the fact-of-guilt phase; but "the book" will be there to hold down

---

[1] Some of my students make a very solid point here: that the desirable relative *degree* of "parental" admixture in a sound system may well turn in part on the personal importance of the result. Death or indefinite forced labor is not the same stake as a fine or a year or five days or bed without supper. The "informal" fact-determining and "Can-we-grab-him-and-treat-him" approach becomes less seaworthy as the risk of an administrator's error increases in its quantitative impact.

the C.O. who never should have been made C.O., and who cannot be trusted at all on parental terms.

And so it goes. My time is up, my job hardly scratched. Yet I submit that there is virtue in the visit to the "primitive"—the so *primitive*—cultures.

{ 22 }

GROUP PREJUDICE AND SOCIAL EDUCATION [a]

One puffs up the importance of whatever problem he happens to be concerned with. The deeper you get into any problem of this complex world, the wider grows the range in which you discover your problem to be vital, and then tend to see it as exclusively vital. And the more you pack your mind with such implications, the less chance is left for sound perspective. Thus, for example, the whole world comes easily enough to shape up almost purely in terms of possible exhaustion of natural resources, or in terms of improvement or debasement of the human stock; or in terms of decay or recapture of spiritual values, or of the lag between man's powers to exploit natural forces and man's ability to control the uses to which the exploitation is put. Indeed, I think I could make a pretty powerful case for the limited span of human attention as being the focal problem of our world, to which one could with some persuasiveness reduce such matters as ignorance, waste, political apathy, threat to all long-range spiritual values, the lopsidedness of our thinkers, and even group prejudice.

In any event it is clear that both you and I must be on our guard against getting the present camera so close to the objective that one tremendous foot will obscure both the man and the landscape. Despite that, I shall urge that the problem of group prejudice comes as close to being a key problem of the modern world as any problem you can find; that it is for the foreseeable future a permanent problem; and what I may loosely call education is for that foreseeable future the only available line of palliative or

[a] From CIVILIZATION AND GROUP RELATIONSHIPS 11 (ed. Maciver. 1944).

451

solution. But by "education" I mean not merely formal education in schools nor the general initial rearing of the child; I mean the whole learning process that goes on as long as man is alive to learn. I mean, in a word, that there are ways of diminishing or conquering group prejudice, and that those ways can be put to work on adults as on children. They are hard and they are slow, but they are workable and they are good. And the way to begin is to begin.

The heart of what I have to say sums up thus: the country first, and then the world, face problems of effective and intelligent organization and reorganization on an ever-widening scale. Organization forced and controlled either merely from the top or by any single group among us will in your view and mine pollute the very springs of significant human living.[1] But grass-roots organization raises problems of producing enough mutual understanding to keep faction feeling from dwarfing all sense of the whole, enough mutual understanding to get the urges of our leadership as of our citizenry into something of an automatic balance, and to keep those urges so balanced. I shall try to show that group prejudice is the most fundamental handicap or obstacle or trap along that road. I shall try to show also that we misconceive group prejudice when we think of it as primarily a prejudice *against* some one or more particular groups: as anti-Semitism, anti-Catholicism, anti-Anything-in-particular. It is instead at bottom a

[1] This is not nearly as clear in fact as you and I tend to think it is. Very real values came eventually out of a unification of France which rested on ruthless suppression by the cruder North, first of an Albigensian and then of a Huguenot civilization curiously similar to ours, and, in between, of a Burgundy which I at least greatly admire. The Normans in England moved in a manner and with an organizing power and "racial" vigor that reads amazingly like a modern Nazi invasion, save only that they found the conquered land, to their surprise, becoming their "heartland." The Romans, on the other hand, whose long-range efforts we seem today to approve, drained their conquered territories in the "best" modern Nazi style and employed a thoroughness in subjugation penalties which the Nazis have not yet dared to match (December, 1943).

These matters deserve more thought than most of us give them. But I do not think that they have any business to affect our attitudes, our emotions, or our fighting convictions. There is only one sound reason even to begin to submit to a hypothetical future "verdict of history" about the nonworkability of a way of life one holds precious. That reason appears only if, after throwing all you have into the fight, you have been crushed flat. "Verdicts of history," even when they happen to prove "favorable," take a few hundreds of bitter years to get themselves rendered.

What we can do, however, is to observe that when organization is called for, it *is* called for, and to observe that *grass-roots* organization does not just happen; it calls both for grass roots and for machinery and for long, persistent upkeep effort on the machinery. For a fine example see LILIENTHAL, TVA—DEMOCRACY ON THE MARCH (1944).

prejudice *in favor* of "My Own Group" as against *all* others, "pro-us" prejudice eternal, live, and waiting, ready to be focused and intensified against *Any* Other Group. And this makes things look very different, once you see it. For I shall try to show that our very ways of growing up produce this basis and drive for overwhelming group prejudices in all directions, and that our ways of living on as adults reinforce those prejudices at every turn. I shall therefore argue that corrective machinery must, if it is to be *effective*, operate on a mass scale, a truly people-wide scale, as contrasted with the de-prejudicing of any few and favored individuals. I shall argue that such meetings as this are drop-in-the-bucket stuff, if they just happen and pass, and that they are at their very best only drop-out-of-the-oilcan stuff—useful as a drop or three of oil can be useful or even indispensable in a squeaking joint, but doomed to be temporary and very minor palliatives unless and until we can get down to causes and to cures which both reach to the root and go to the mass. And because I find only short-range value either in merely viewing with alarm or in merely crying out for change of heart, I shall proceed (so far as I have been able to get) to speak of concrete measures of relief and cure. The measures will have four characteristics: First, they will be measures which promise, so far as employed, to work. Second, they will be measures which are capable of employment in our here and now, and with means and personnel which are at hand. Third, they will be measures which can be put to work in the little as well as in the large; which do not depend on any preliminary wide-scale political or social reform; which open for immediate work by individuals or by smaller groups as well as by a nation. Lastly, they will be measures already sufficiently under way to be making real dents on the problems; though only dents.

Let me clear up one point, however, before going further. This discussion is going to be one of conditions as we find them, whether or not we like what we find. It will therefore be an unpleasing discussion, because in this matter conditions are unpleasing in the extreme. It is going to be a discussion not of ideals and good things, but of hard-headed and hard-eyed means and measures to deal with continuing conditions which in spots are not only hard and tough but also nasty. I happen to be a realist in jurisprudence, in sociology, and in psychology, and the job of a realist is to begin by seeing exactly what he is up against and by striving to keep what he wants and hopes for and will fight for from ever getting in the way of spotting what he is up against. The second job of a realist

is to find ways and means that will *work,* in moving toward where
he wants to go: to implement ideals with hands and feet that stand
on and can take hold of the here and now. Now there is abroad
in the land a silly and false line of thinking—or better, of nonthinking—which proceeds on a queer assumption that such hard-
eyed study of ways and means, of hands and feet and machinery,
betokens or even proves a lack of interest in ideals and right goals.
It is a line of nonthinking which rests on an assumption that all
right answers are *single,* so that to answer "Yes" to anything is of
necessity to answer "No" to everything else. Thus it is the same
line of nonthinking which leads to such conclusions as that "we
must win, simply because we are right" or that it is enough,
generally, in this world of ours to behave rightly and feel rightly.
Whereas the whole course of human history indicates that while
faith and ideals can sometimes win battles, faith and ideals alone
cannot win wars; that while faith and ideals can move societies,
they cannot, alone, *build* societies nor yet build up new generations within societies; that while it is death to be without them,
yet they cannot, alone, continue life. They provide the breath and
the blood and the spirit of life and society, but they provide
neither the bony structure nor the muscle nor the nervous integration and balance nor yet the food and digestive machinery. And
since I am speaking to people whose faith and ideals I can presuppose as definitely as I can presuppose my own, I shall, deliberately,
insist throughout this lecture on the *What-Else-in-Addition* that
is essential to make those ideals take on working reality.

The first point I want to make is that the basic process of
"socializing" the newborn human animal is a process of "anti-
socializing" him at the same time. For a century ahead, at least, it
seems to me that this has to continue so.[2]

Look it over. The fundamental fact is that the human being is
a *group* product, and therefore develops into a group member,
absorbing many vital aspects of his environing group.[3] The next
fact is that this building of groups (like this building of the new-

---

[2] Although I get glimmers of procedures, here and now politically impossible,
which *could* produce an effective mere socializing on a mass scale.

[3] *E.g.,* at ten, at six, even at three, the boy line of any tradition produces (in the
mass) sharply different reactions and attitudes from the girl line; or the French or
the Dutch from the American. Subdivide any of the suggested categories, so as to
make more and more things "equal" and you will still get the suggested result: *e.g.,*
American upper-income single-child boy *vs.* girl; French-Breton white agricultural
vs. Wisconsin white agricultural, or either *vs.* Mississippi white share-cropper
agricultural.

born into effective group membership and so into being a person instead of a cross between an angry wildcat and a haphazard cyclone, appears, as it just proceeds to happen, to be almost in equal measure a consolidating business and at the same time and by the same means an *excluding* business. I happen not to have noticed this much in the literature (except for Sumner), although it is too obvious not to have been remarked on many times.

It is in any event vital for our problem. Sumner—as so often— cut to the heart of it; man lives in an In-group; and to any In-group any and every other group is an Out-group. An In-group or We-group is indeed hard to conceive except by contrast to the Others who are not In, but are Out, not We, but They.

This has four different aspects, all vital to our problem.

The first is the fact and the utter necessity of channeling each new small ball of random energy into *group* ways before it (he or she) can become either at all bearable or recognizable as a "person." If you have not thought about this before, think about it now. It is quick to prove. In the matter of bearability, imagine a baby born with the physique and muscular control of twenty-one years and meditate on a baby's horrible but now frustrated rage at weaning or being left alone or at colic or simple undiagnosed desire, plus the young child's pleasure in watching fire grow and in smashing anything that either resists or smashes with a noise. In the matter of recognizability as a person, consider speech (which language differences show to be one of our sets of group-ways) and ask yourself whether you are prepared really to recognize as a "person" any human being with normal organs of hearing and speech who at twenty-one still babbles.

The second aspect is equally quick to see, and the matter of language offers the quickest way to see it. Not *human* group-ways, but the group-ways of *My Particular Group,* are what each budding "I" is slowly shaped to fit into *and so to demand of others.* The American child does not grow up speaking or expecting French. He plays "Farmer in the Dell," not *"Sur la pont d'Avignon."* He knows of Washington, Lincoln, Roosevelt, not of Charlemagne, Jeanne d'Arc, Pétain. His heart rises to the Stars and Stripes and is bothered when he has trouble with certain high notes in *Our* national anthem. If you see this, you must go on to see further: if he is being raised Back Bay, "The Irish" are different, threatening, and bad. If he is "Boston Irish," he looks with scorn upon a waning effort of civilization typified by Back

Bay. Save in an utter crisis of the nation, "My" group is not, for most purposes, The People of these United States, it is for most and for deep purposes "The people I grew up among," and pretty narrow: *"Unsre Leit";* "White folks is white folks"; "Public School is so indiscriminate"; "the dirty Harps," "the lousy Orangemen."

The third aspect is this, and you will please take time enough to get it clear: Those ideal, ethical, social values which mean not only bearability of the person but forward drive, input of extra work, service, the quest for loveliness, that wonder by-product, nobility of soul—these are instilled and develop only out of In-group, out of We-group rearing and training. They are directed to, focused on, produced by "Us-ness." They are what Civilization most vitally needs. They represent its Soul. But for all except the inspired they grow out of, and so by the nature of that growth are most limited to, the In-group, the felt We-group. I speak of mass phenomena, of bulk occurrence, not of occasional transcendent individuals. I speak of voting power, within a political democracy, of the many who, if a leader gets too far ahead, make him a "leader" without followers.[4] The raising, then, of the growing ego to have and respond to these "In-group," these "We-group" ways, attitudes, ideals—this is not only our necessity for keeping our society alive, but it is our hope for all that is worthwhile.

But the fourth aspect is what shocked men as Sumner underscored it. Man lives in an In-group, a We-group. The recognized and cherished virtues in social contacts apply with full effect to all other members of that We-group: loyalty, honesty, self-re-

[4] My reading shows no leadership toward One-ness that compares in immediate effectiveness with that of Moslemism in its earlier conquest. Certainly, in part, because the choice was simple: Confess belief or die. Certainly, in part, because the mechanism of "confessing belief" was equally simple: one short formula. But beyond both of these lay a power, not as yet analyzed to my knowledge, of producing in the conquerors, despite differences in language and other vitally recognizable ways, a seemingly unparalleled feeling of "We-ness" with those who had confessed belief. My very insufficient reading on the point suggests a degree of acceptation of the conquered which as against any comparable case would be as "sociologically impossible" as is the modern student-run Law Review of these United States: a scientific periodical matching in quality the best professional journals of the law or of any other discipline, responsibly edited by men who are still ungraduated, unadmitted students, with decision-making staffs turning over every year, with no editorial personnel in office or training for more than a rough two years, and with entrance on such training preceded by a bare year's study in the discipline. I have managed finally to explain to myself this last "sociological impossibility"; the results persuade me that no line of inquiry is more fruitful than inquiry into such impossibilities.

straint, courtesy, support in need, self-sacrifice; as contrasted with concealment, deceit, overbearingness, contempt, disregard, robbery, killing—which are in savage societies the normal and proper ways of dealing with members of *any* They-group. Take the last first: in our own society the righteous and laudable killing of "Out-group" or "They-group" members is indeed limited to war and the general war area of thought (*e.g.* the spy about to get away with military secrets). But it needs only that you note our celebration of aviation aces or of enemy casualties in general to make clear that we—like all other men but prophets—still run our ways, our morals, our ideals, on two different levels which divide flatly according to We-ness and to They-ness. The things you need to see if you have not yet thought about them are these: (1) that you can sympathize to the heart with deceit and killing ("successful ambush") when directed against a They-group *and any of its impersonal individual members* (contrast: one lone hunted escaper from a prison camp, hungry, weary, just inside your door with the hounds approaching); (2) that deceit, robbery and killing apart, you have They-group attitudes toward a considerable number of "they's" within these United States. If you practice law, how long since you have been willing to hire a woman as a law-clerk? If you own a house, what do you think of having a colored family "buy in" next door? If you are a union man, what is your attitude toward "rugged individualists" on the neighboring machine? If you are a Republican, how do you feel about a New Dealer? If not robbery, bold fraud, killing (which we in our civilization reserve for They-groups at *war* with us), at least we indulge, within our own America, the other ancient attitudes toward our They-groups: distrust, disgust or ridicule, fear, hate, checked in minor part but only in minor part by religion, morals, manners, and the compulsion of the law. I challenge you who listen. Do you dare claim your souls are clean, in this? No snobberies, disgusts, fears, or hates where you feel yourselves (not personally, but as *group* members) at an advantage? No inverse snobberies, resentments, fears, or hates where you feel yourselves (not personally, but as *group* members) discarded?

These are the facts of life in this matter, as they result. But to see our problem, we must go on into *how* they result. And that goes back to an eternal phenomenon: the newborn infant.

An In-group, a We-group, is the only machinery known to us, I repeat, for producing out of each small groping squaller that something different which we can recognize as a *person*. The psychologists tell us of certain needs for "security" in the growing human being; and it appears to be "family," or persons who are family members known *and designated as such* ("father," "mother," "brother," "uncle," "nurse"), who first satisfy and reinforce and then symbolize that security. You must really see this, and feel it. You see it when any man stranger is hailed by a lisper as "Dad-dy" and approached accordingly. It is a queer man stranger who does not respond. You see it at a later age when a dinner guest is introduced as "Mr. Struthers" and therefore let alone unless he makes advances, whereas if he is introduced as "*Uncle* Jack" he is promptly climbed on and has his hair pulled (and knows he has to take it). He has been labeled, *pro hac vice* he has been made a We-group member. This carries over throughout life. If you want "the govamunt" (which too commonly spells milch cow or sloppy waste) or "the burocracy" (which spells blindness, tyranny, or red tape) to appear live, close, warm, strong, a right subject for affection, respect, and pride—then you speak of "Uncle Sam."

But at the same time you see that even so early and by this mechanism, the We-group circle demonstrates its closing; inward, and also outward. There are freedoms of behavior within, there is a tightening up of teamwork as against the outside, from "company manners" on through to "not washing dirty linen in public." There is the building up of loyalties, tolerances, ways of adjustment, the recognition of "Our" ways, "Our" standards, "Our" rightnesses, to which the budding "I" must shape himself, and does. What I want to suggest is only that the concept of "We" as it is thus in fact created in the child is at the same time and by the same almost-necessity a concept of "They" as being persons to whom the same duties, the same sympathies, are *not* owing, and *as against* whom the "We's" line up together—as of course. The child as he becomes a *person* acquires, by the very process of becoming one, these two ingrained and contradictory sets of attitudes, patterns of action, emotion, and thought. The "We" set is the set on the growth of which both the child and his civilization utterly depend. But to build that set he *has* to build also that "They" set which threatens to disrupt both him and his civilization, and which applies to anyone who is not part of his "Us."

Now I do believe it to be humanly possible to rear individual children with an almost indefinitely expansible set of "We" attitudes, and with no sharp crystallization of these socially disruptive

"They" attitudes. But there is no *large*-scale rearing of this type that now goes on. The current multitude of "names" of scorn and insult "upward" or "downward" or "crosswise" are enough both to witness and focus the contrary: "Sissy," "Lilyfinger," "Mick," "Kike," "Nigger," "Spic," "Hunyak," "Wop," "White Trash," "Damnyankee." Or consider the high tolerance and unity that find expression in "the effete East," "the sticks," "rube," "city slicker," "agitator," "goon," "white collar." Whether by section, by national or race origin, by occupation, by financial or social position, by residence with reference to the railroad tracks, the labels are there to gather, there to spread, there to intensify "They" attitudes. The labels have, also at times, a terrifying indiscriminate over-breadth: consider, today, with the Chinese as our allies, and the overwhelming Philippine majority on Bataan, "yellow bastard." And those labels are group labels, impersonal, to stick as labels on any person, and make him thus cease to seem wholly a person. To us, as to the savage, "man," "full man," "real person," means "one of Us."

All of this could in itself be relatively harmless; it could in itself conduce even to a fuller and more enjoyable life; but only on one condition. That condition is that the wider Unity shall be so powerfully felt, perceived, and acted on that the great *Team* with its team play and team membership definitely dominates all factions and all faction feelings. Within a felt dominant Unity you can call names, curse, and seem to scorn, because the felt unity talks more deeply than your words. Within a sufficiently felt unity, felt differences can produce more of affection than of irritation. Again the family shows the picture. If it is a family instead of a failure, it remains a team. That even the family becomes so often a failure instead of a family gives us a first indication of the power of the *divisive* drives which rise in our culture from the very shaping of the child into a person.

Now it is in my mind, with no particular desire to glorify any nonexistent rosy past, that this particular problem of group prejudices—this problem first of the outbalancing of "We" attitudes by "They" attitudes and, second, of their too great outbalancing—that this problem was not so severe before our nation was industrialized. I do find nastily divisive currents, say, in our earlier nineteenth century. The Sections were forming up, the States then showed an isolationism greater than today's; the social and political bitterness of the "safe" men against Jackson's "rabble" makes today's anti-Rooseveltism seem thin as dishwater;

the Know-Nothings do not present a pretty picture; nor are melted tar and knife-edged fence rails gentle instruments. Yet, looking all that fairly in the face, I cannot find it so distressing as the picture of today. And the reason is clear. The reason is that the mere growing up in a community of 1830 or 1840 gave you, whether you wanted it or not, *some* view and *some* understanding of a *Whole* of which you were a part and of that Whole as something to which you owed a real responsibility. Then factional battles were as bitter and often as dirty and cruel as a family blowup; but even when drowned in interest, hate, and physical or emotional drunkenness, they were yet carried on over a heavy undertone of the *felt team* that still consisted of the *Whole*. I have never been sure of this, and study of Civil War times, both North and South, has made me less sure; it *may* be only that the divisive forces were still, one by one, too little organized, too small in size and in gathered strength to tear things utterly apart, no matter how far each part had lost sense for the Whole. Nonetheless, I still think I describe accurately.

What bothers me today is that today I see no as yet adequate machinery at work in civil life and on the mass scale for leavening our "They-group" attitudes with this needed underlying feel and consciousness of Total Team, while the They-group attitudes apply to all who do not happen, by training, to be strictly "We," and today that means for each of us to an ever-widening major fraction of the population.

For observe first that merely growing up, today, has no need to produce any understanding at all—except in national crisis—along the line of the great team. In the country, certainly in a one-crop area, there is little but lopsidedness to be had: the whole industrial or financial phase of the world is "They." In a city big enough to have high-school districts, the situation is worse, because "They" are not only present but "They" are close at hand, for active, personalized enmities to develop, while the whole, even of the city itself, it is far too big for a youngster to fathom by mere growing up. The best long-tested American institution to meet this, and it is both peculiarly American and a social invention of amazing power, is the single high school of the smaller Mid-Western town or city. I am not touting such a high school as a wholly "democratic" institution, nor as perfection. I am fully aware, for instance, that the Negro (or the Mexican) gets little comfort from it. I know, even at its best, the overdominance of those better situated economically and the snobberies and heartburnings which result. But I trust I am enough of a sociologist to recognize in snobbery (which I abominate) probably the most potent single force for self-improvement in a mobile society. And I state categorically that the nearest working approach thus far offered on a wide scale in our civilian life to the fabled melting pot is found in just these high schools. The *bulk,* the overwhelming bulk, of the kids comes out of them with some real living feeling of a Total Whole, and with some real *approach* to living "We-group" attitudes that have bridged, for instance, the railroad tracks and a fair portion of the religious, economic, racial, and political gulfs within the community.

The sociological processes involved in furthering or breaking down group prejudice are relatively simple to see and to describe, and it is very queer that they have received so little attention. I am not referring to "processes" of the large, loose sort called "accommodation," "co-operation," etc. I am referring to the detailed daily mechanisms by which individual persons, in types of situation which occur and recur as recognizable types, proceed to react with some mass reckonability.

The first point is that the We-attitudes are almost always expansible to a material degree, and that when their scope is expanded to include new persons it tends strongly to be so expanded *en bloc*. The new person is *accepted*. If a child receives Mr. Struthers as "Uncle Jack," he takes the new uncle utterly. When you discover your outsider to be "just like one of us," you "take him in." Note the processes of thought and feeling. You adopt him *into* your We-group. Without greatly thinking about it, you thereby in your own feeling *divorce* him from his old group. You also feel that you have been very generous and that he owes both equivalent gratitude and an obligation to react wholly like "one of us." Here lies danger, as danger lies also in your sudden shift from trial acceptance or acceptance with reservations, conscious or unconscious, into real acceptance.[5] But the process is a widener of understanding and of the range of feeling. One perceives that *some* "real people" can grow elsewhere.

But the second point is that such expansion tends strongly to be limited to the particular person concerned. As a mass phenomenon it depends first of all on *recurrent* and *close* contacts

[5] This has its dangers of throwback, precisely because it obscures the need for detailed adjustment to and working out of the remaining powerful divergences. Complete acceptance sets up expectations of complete fitting in; and disappointed expectations kick back with peculiar violence. The phenomenon is most strikingly observable in cross-group boy-and-girl relations before and after marriage.

with that person, an "otherwise" acceptable individual. But to get beyond the phase of taking in just him (and of *pro tanto* seeking to take him out of his "own" group), to move into an attitude of wider openness to and understanding of They-groups in general, there must be in the picture also some *grouping* which can be seen and felt as a wider We-group of which both acceptor and acceptee become a part. That is just what the single local high school offers, and over a four-year period. In primitive life the newcomer is adopted into the family or the tribe—he is drawn wholly in, and wholly out of his old group. In our society both or more of those concerned can become members of a We-group different from their old We-groupings: they can marry and form a *new* family; they can enter the high school; they can become active both in "the party" and in the same party "club."

The third point has to do with certain vital attitudes toward evidence and occurrences and troubles. The We-attitude is one of sympathy and indulgence toward the individual concerned, and it is that of reading all evidence fast and firmly to the glory of Our group. The They-attitude is one of suspicion and condemnation of the individual in question, and it is that of reading all evidence fast and firmly to the discredit of His group. Bad taste, evil intent, dirty dealing, crime, are alleged of an individual, or some happening suggests them. If he is of your We-group you "cannot believe it of him," "there must be some mistake," " 'We' aren't like that"; at the worst, he is utterly nontypical of Us, thank God. But if he is of one of your They-groups you take the report at once, at face, and on its worst interpretation; "There, you see: that's just the way 'They' are"; the worst at once displays to you the essential character of Them All—"And we won't forget it, either!" It is the good which is exceptional, as to Them. The likable and fine is therefore read exactly in reverse. The best that *any* of Us does is *typical* of Us; each of Us swells with pride. The unmistakably fine on the part of one or three or forty of Them, seen from the outside, leads only to a grudging recognition that there *are* exceptions—*if* the report is true.

Now these destructive They-ways of interpretation—these ways of reading and using that new experience which is the adult's line of ongoing education—these ways intensify in the measure in which there exist well-integrated particular patterns of adverse, scornful, fearful, or hateful concept about the nature of any particular They-group concerned—"Capital" and "the Bosses" or "Labor" and the "Unions"; "Bourbons" or "Communists";

"Jews," "Catholics," "Babbitts," "Bible-Belters," "Long-Haired Professors," or Big Endians and Little Endians of any other label. And the devastating effect of such They-ways of reading each particular incident piles up in terms of the multitude of incidents which come to superficial notice, which come devoid of any healthy backlog of contact at first hand with an adequate number of persons of the particular They-category; which come devoid, as well, of any healthy backlog of *recurrent* discovery that the sloganized "They" pictures handed down within the We-group have proved with some regularity when tested in action and actual contact to be distorted calumnies. One recalls Lincoln Steffens' amazement and distress as the political bosses against whom he was crusading turned out so regularly to be people—people who in so many ways plainly earned his admiration. Thus the rapid modern increase of "news," even apart from any deliberate distortion, becomes less a reducer than an increaser of any group prejudices which have become organized into integrated and current sloganized *whole*-patterns. In some aspects the "conqueror of distance" in the physical sense tends rather to increase "social" gulfs. (In contrast, some of the continuing radio programs can develop contact enough with groups different from oneself to bridge gaps—if one will only listen regularly to such programs depicting one's They-groups; as do some of the comic strips, which I suspect get a much less selective audience.)

Put these three factors together: (1) whole-hog acceptance, if any acceptance at all—almost removing the accepted individual from any persuasiveness regarding his still wholly unaccepted group. (2) The dependence of acceptance on recurrent and favorable personal contact in the context of a felt group of which both the acceptee and the acceptor are working parts, and the relative rarity of those conditions. (3) The set adverse and differential "type" interpretation of any surface or secondhand experience, and today's multiplication of such experience.

These are the ongoing disruptive mechanisms or machineries, ever new because they are re-created in raising almost every child into the social virtues and with the social values which we need.

What can be set against them is this—slow, painful, but effective: (1) To run, in close and continued contacts, into not one or two, but into a series of persons from an Others- or They- or Out-group, and to begin to see them from inside a wider felt group-unity, this is materially to change one's They-attitude not only toward them as persons, but toward all further surface experience which concerns each of the particular Others-groups. (2) More-over, since the basis of group prejudice is the We-group attitude as against all other groups, that basis is severely shaken by solid countering experience with even a single They-group. Such experience is not enough, for most. It can be bulkheaded off, and tends to be, leaving other "hates" or "fears" quite open still. But the second job on another They-group is thrice and more as easy as the first. (3) For a person to do this with members of a series of marked and known Others-groups breaks down those same attitudes toward *all* Others-groups—within a given limit. The limit varies with the person; but it is always wider than the circle of the direct experience. Its radius is determined, so far as I can see, in the first instance, by the *felt* range of the greater Whole within which the Others-groups have, as they have been met, been seen as included. Almost always that seeing has a series of peripheries, reaching outward with differential intensity and with queer exclusive criteria. But the essential game is won with the first major and *general* breakdown of the Others-attitude.

What the high school mentioned above accomplishes is to get this done early in life, at least on the community scale, and commonly to get it done with regard to several different Others-groups at once; yet late enough in life so that it requires some conscious thought to digest the results—thought which goes then some distance to drive them home.

One must, however, in the single high school and elsewhere, note one qualifying and danger-producing factor: close contact of members of different groups can, under unfavorable circumstances and absent highly skilled management, result in increased bitterness. Where the background is one of established ideology, especially where one group is on the rise and resentful, the other on the defensive and afraid, individuals are prone to meet not as people but as representatives, with loyalties set and with closed fronts, and the contacts are likely to be those of war. That fact gives some color of reason—only, in my view, a color—to the attitude of the Army toward our colored citizens in this war.[b] The reason why I think the choice made to be a mistaken choice is that the overwhelming tendency of any decent army is to work out group loyalties in terms of the "outfit," which transcends any type

[b] My particular heart goes out to the colored messboy who needed Pearl Harbor to get a chance at a machine-gun, and to the American Indian who needed Iwo Jima to join the four-man team who planted the flag.

of group background of its members, so that mixing "unlikes" into "outfits" breaks down prejudice.

And that is why the Armed Services are providing today the most hopeful antiprejudice *mass-scale* operation we have ever seen. It has been skilfully done, the mixing of the population into the smaller units: continuous contact in a common setting of a new group-loyalty lived with, lived in, small enough to see and grasp and stir pride, yet an inescapable part also of a National Whole—with the members of different They-groups so many and so mixed that they cannot be felt and fought as mere "representatives." Here is a thing to give heart, and to set against the political dangers of a prospective pressure group of twelve millions of veterans. It is doubly hopeful because it occurs among the young, who will be raising the next generation. While, at the moment of saying this, the heart bleeds to see one body of our people larger than the body drawn into the services still substantially cut off from the most effective prejudice-dissolving processes.

One must not, however, count too heavily upon the effects of armed service. Veterans return to a life organized along civilian lines; and how far Joe and Stan will then prove to have been cases of merely "personal" acceptance remains a problem. I count here, somewhat, on the Legion posts to do a thing our ordinary political clubs have done less well. In the latter it has been found useful, repeatedly, to lump the club around a group unity of another kind, largely Polish or Irish or whatever. The Legion's unity ought to be of a cross-group kind, and can be more so, according to the way in which Posts come to be established.

I find hope, too, despite blindness and setbacks, in the labor field. I find a definite trend there in the direction of more understanding between managers and labor leaders, and in the direction of each group's undertaking some burden of "selling the other to its constituency." Leaders have leverage, and not only in lessening the enmity against "adversaries." You see what can be done when you see the skill with which the cafeteria workers in this city were brought to accept colored workers into the union and on the job: use of a time of labor shortage, use of Mrs. Roosevelt's entertainment of Marian Anderson ("You don't think you are better than Mrs. Roosevelt?"), careful selection of the first colored workers to be hired for "front" work, flat head-on meeting of the first few cases of "either she goes or I go"—and the *unreasoning* barrier went down. There remains friction; but it is dwindling friction, and contact within the wider unity has come and continues.

But as one moves into his own small effort, in neighborhood or any other groups, along such lines, and in regard to building chances for contact, and then effective contacts, between any groups, it pays to remember that bites too large are fraught with indigestion. Group prejudice roots deep because it roots in infancy. It roots deep because it roots in the very origins of our finest loyalties and loves. It is tricky because of these things, and also because "acceptance" leads so lightly to overexpectation, and seems always to imply a debt on the part of the person accepted. Lurking for the occasion of sudden crisis or sudden disappointment are all the nasty feelings and all the nasty labels: "So you're only a dirty ——, after all!" (Fill in to suit.)

An individual's own part begins slowly and continues long. You do some reading, detailed sympathetic studies made from inside some group that is strange and, preferably, a bit obnoxious to you. You do steady, heavy policing of your own reactions to incidents and especially to hearsay about particular happenings, trying out the very troublesome job of weighing *fairly* what you read and hear—or half see. You discover that it is hard to see a person as a person, rather than as a member of a group, without resenting and reacting in resentment. You take on membership and work in at least one group in which you have a chance to move—*very* carefully—toward steady and satisfactory contacts with members of different and partly antagonistic groups, and you build by work more than by talk on the wider value and purpose that joins all; which means you must be choosing for your work a group that has a purpose worth having. It is all prosaic and humdrum and time-consuming and terribly slow. It is baffling because other people will not understand and will insist on doing the wrong things, or on choosing the wrong times. It is uncomfortable because it really disturbs some of your own most comforting and well-laid prejudices; and nothing is so pleasant, so effort-saving, as such a prejudice. Yet I think this game, played over the years by each of us, is our necessary contribution to our citizenship.

And I know it is fun, and a source of richer living. Some of us even get into a position of leverage and bring down suddenly a whole section of some wall of prejudice the others have been undermining through the years. But without that prior undermining no leader could bring it down—except as, on occasion, some shrewd heads and hands are in a key position at some actual or possible mixing bowl and shape not the people but the conditions of their meeting and their work—in terms not of Great

Ideals alone (the Flag, the Nation, Brotherhood of Man) but of small daily jobs in face-to-face tangible outfits, too, so that the people reshape—educate—themselves into not only a new We-group, but a We-group built around a conscious job: that is, a Team.

{ 23 }

YES, IT TAKES MASS PRODUCTION [a]

The job is the education of an entire democracy for democracy. Knowing what a pretty good education for democracy would be like, if we had it, is a good deal like knowing how nice it would be to split the atom if we could split it.[b] We have a few hundred or a few thousand men and women who actually manage something of such education for five times or ten times their own number of youngsters. But that is a good deal like having a number of laboratories where a few atoms get split—at a cost which makes atom-splitting, or education for democracy, an experiment, a luxury product, a procedure only for skilled professionals seeking less to teach than to learn. Fine rarities are fine things. But a democracy is a mass thing. The character of a democracy is determined in part by its transcendent individuals; but it is determined vastly more by the nature of its masses. Can the needed education be put on a mass production basis? Can it handle and channel into growth and freedom children not by the score or the hundred or the thousand, but by the million?

That is the issue, and there is no use ducking either the issue or its implications. An authoritarian system can and does handle a moderately effective shaping of its children by the million. Whatever troubles Russia has today, the generation of young Russians have lost Tsarist Russia forever. Whatever troubles Germany has or will have, the young Germans are, as a people, being effectively made into a different people from that of pre-Hitler days.

[a] From 28 SURVEY-GRAPHIC 621 (1939).
[b] We have, since, achieved the atom-split. I wonder whether effective mass-education, even "for democracy," may, if achieved, produce equivalent new problems.

468

In each case the managers of the education-mill may fail of their precise objectives; but in each case the conditioning of the young is proceeding fast, in relatively homogeneous directions, by schooling, by regimented organizations for the young, by control of the printed and spoken word, by elimination of competing stimuli and inhibition of undesired lines of response.

That is the competition which democracy is up against. I understand this issue of *Survey Graphic* to rest on the assumption that democracy is not as yet adequately equipped to meet that competition; that it needs changes in the character of its mass and of its masses, if it is to survive such competition, let alone be more worthwhile to itself; that our democracy needs *new* lines of education on a scale which will produce effective change. I share such a conviction myself. Anyone who shares it will have to face the implications.

The first implication is the need for considerable rethinking about the machinery of the needed education. Conscious education—and that is what is here under discussion—is done by people. People operating on a large scale have, thus far in man's history, had to work in patterns. Whether there ever will be a large enough number of folk capable of intuitive and artistic guidance of youngsters along continuously reshaping experimental lines, I do not pretend to know; perhaps a proper education for democracy will some day uncover some unsuspected wealth of such ability. But at least for the next generation our teachers will, to 95 or 99 percent, be just others from among our people who have themselves gone through the type of education which many of us see as insufficient. Those teachers will therefore need patterns to learn from and to rely on for guidance; they will need fairly clear, fairly simple, fairly standardized patterns, which call for no high intelligence or art to use.

But can patterns of forward-looking education be devised, Butterick-patterns for mass use by the just plain folks of our educational machine? My answer is, yes. But that, in turn, calls for some rethinking of the objectives of an education for democracy.

There is, for example, a fairly widespread ideal among forward looking educators about training young people to get at the facts, and to make up their own minds about the meaning of the facts. That ideal has a touch of validity. The validity lies in the definite desirability of inculcating an interest in such facts as a person can get, and in the desirability of not accepting any particular authority in blind tribute to it or to authority as such. But this touch of validity is bound up in a single lump-ideal and slogan with a vast absurdity, and with a sad nearsightedness.

The absurdity lies in the conception that in matters social or technical—in any matters beyond the scope of personal finger-and-eye experience—any of us can get even an approximate firsthand acquaintance with "the facts." Our very "facts" are, regularly, taken on authority. They must be. Scientists' authority, newspapers' authority, textbooks' authority, teachers' authority, neighbors' authority. And our facts, too, are changeable and shift from day to day and year to year; atoms, and space, and maps, and the meaning of the Constitution, refuse to stay what we once *knew* they were. Our "facts" are therefore simply the more solid, and sometimes the more lasting, among the opinions we accept and rely on.

The nearsightedness in the "make up your own mind" ideal, on the other hand, lies in failing to connect up the true goal of education about "the facts" with the true goal of education as to judgment-making in political, or social, or economic matters. For both in getting "the facts" and in forming a judgment about what it is wise or good to do or to try to get done, or about how to get the wise or good thing done, the problem of the bulk-folk in a democracy, of those folk whose education is the education of the democracy for democracy—that problem is not one of a person's making up his own mind, but it is one of building up intelligent choice among the offered opinions and solutions. Any opinion or solution is indeed to be weighed somewhat in terms of its seeming substance, and of whether it seems to make sense. But, even more, it will be, and it should be, weighed in terms of who is offering it.

Effort to get the facts and to think for oneself is indeed a vital part of education, and the unleashing of such effort is a vital goal. That is sound. But it is unsound to overlook the plain truth that such effort gets us just up to the point of making our own choice among competing authorities about both what the facts are and what to think about them. One's own choice of authorities, made intelligently and honestly, makes good democracy. It is not only the best that can be had; it is also enough. It is, moreover, the kind of thinking which in the favored of the Lord brings out leadership and brings that leadership to maturity.

In regard to this problem, I submit that one very simple pattern is available, ready for use by any teacher with any normal pupil; a pattern the repetitive use of which well nigh compulsively inculcates over the years a workable degree of critique upon competing authorities, and well nigh forces some inquiry into why a given authority is to be trusted. The pattern is this, to be used from kindergarten through into adult education: every statement of "truth" holds as an essential term the introductory phrase: "X says that . . ."; and no "truth" is known, or is to be remembered, if that vital term is not part of its statement and memory. "My geography book says that Albany is the capital of New York." "Warren's History says that Columbus discovered America." "The Deodont ad says that Deodont whitens the teeth." "Mr. Smithers says that stealing is naughty." "The *Bugle* says Japan is a menace." "Candidate Loud says that Senator Louder is a liar."

That "facts" and "truths" of wisdom (or unwisdom) can be mastered so, and can be remembered in this very fashion, our own pre-literate culture bears potent witness. Our loss of the habit of tagging the saying with the sayer dates from an intervening period when more print could be trusted, moderately, than can be trusted now. The recapture of the simple pattern which once ran: "Uncle Eben always said . . ." is in these days of multiple and interest-serving voices the one technique capable of mass-inculcation which can move a whole people from blind credence and helpless groping into forced conscious choice.

For you have to choose, when two "truths" with differing tags of source oppose each other. You have to think critically, too, when two conflicting "truths" with a single source-tag meet in your memory. You may even be moved by source-tags to start asking why any particular source puts out the kind of "truths" it does. All of which is no panacea, nor any road to development of a utopia. It is only a line of action simple enough and unmistakable enough for use by very ordinary teaching personnel among very ordinary pupils to produce quite indirectly and even in the absence of artistic instruction, a level of selection among offered "truths" and leaders which at present is by no means ordinary; to produce *mass-wise* not the desirable level of critical thinking, but a materially higher level than we have. Preaching of democracy is good. It is needed. The ideal and its beauty need to be instilled and to be made vivid and to be kept alive. But preaching is not enough. We need techniques.

Let me set one more problem of technical education for modern democracy, a commonplace problem enough, but a neglected one; and one whose answer is also to be found, if at all, along similar

lines of simple, mass-usable techniques of indirect effect. A sur-
vival-danger to democracy is divisiveness. A survival-condition of
democracy is that the way of flat suppression of the rival or conflicting group be adopted only as an utter and last resort. Now, if
my observation does not mislead me, the carry-over of the ethics
and working attitudes learned in the childhood face-to-face group
into the affairs of the larger society works moderately well so
long as the individual comes to view any larger group among his
later contacts as a "We-group" of which he is a responsible part,
rather than as an "Others-group" of which he is no part. Wherever
lines of conflicting interest appear, the individual proceeds to find
himself a "We-group," big or little, and lines up with it against
the respective "Others." Through family, neighborhood, community, race, religion, section, party, work-group, "class," or what
have you, I repeat, the ethics and attitudes of the face-to-face group
carry over moderately well, for most, over most of the time, into
this whole range of a person's later "We-groups." The point about
this is that it just happens; it requires no particular extra-instruc-
tion or labor in adaptation; it is as close to a natural process as
any phenomenon of society. With it, however, goes what is no
less a natural phenomenon: there are other ethics and other attitudes learned and ready, for any "Others-group"; and every "We-
group" implies an "Others-group." They are outsiders; they are
the enemy; *they are not like us,* and we can and will believe anything of them.

This is a matter which only conscious instruction can abate,
which only conscious planning and working of an adjustment-
machinery can lessen. It is the root of deep divisive hates, and deep
divisive hates are luxuries democracies these days can ill afford.
The matter focuses up thus: no groups at odds have ever, taken
in the large, played wholly clean; and if one ever had, it still
would by its rival have been seen as using dirty play. Now when
a person of our group is found doing dirt, and we condemn him
(assuming that we do, instead of thinking that is as good as They
deserve, anyhow) we do it with a fine-flavored background of
knowledge of how untypical he is of Us. We regret, then we forget; it is he, not We, who is that way. But when any *one* of an
"Others-group" plays dirty, or is obnoxious, he promptly typifies
the whole, and They, all of Them, are remembered and stig-
matized by what that lone one did. Bad faith, underhandedness,
violence, corruption—it needs but rumor of a single case to make

these into lasting marks of Them and of all Their works. Such, with the fear and rage and self-righteousness that have to follow, is the seed of red riot and of what is almost worse, the festering internal hates that can cripple a people.

This is a more complex problem to find machinery for than is the simpler one of lifting the level of intellectual critique; its roots are deeper, and its vices are themselves imbedded in our very "We-group" machinery out of which we build up our finest team play and loyalties and loves.[e] I do not dream that I have found a pattern that will serve to cure. But I do know that at this point and for this purpose some workable mass production machinery must be found, if education of a democracy for democracy is to develop the grander scale of team play needed to sustain itself against the totalitarian threat, or indeed to develop its own potential richness of life. The brotherhood of man is too vast a concept for most to lay easy hold of, and too amorphous; the Christian ethic finds verbal acceptance too often in company with "Kill the These" or "Lynch the Those." National unity is easier; but again it does its work only with the adversary in the picture. And here our existing mechanisms do function pretty well against the time of national emergency; we effectively get the stage set for all Americans to throw themselves into a single national "We-group" as soon as the proper Others loom on the scene, a danger imminent. But not until then. Until then we see Americans who are unlike ourselves not as Americans but as the niggers or the wops or the bosses or Wall Street or the great unwashed. Whereas the problem here goes to the every day and to the other side of the railroad track [—or, for New Yorkers, of the Hudson.]

No one who has watched artists work in such a field as industrial relations can doubt that even rooted and snarling antagonisms can be much allayed. The human material allows of it; and techniques exist. As yet they are not techniques available to ordinary people in the mass, nor used by such. Yet it is moderately clear that they are not too complex for use in education: "The other gang have the same kind of troubles with their people that we are up against. They have a few liars, a few skunks, a few who are just in it for themselves and don't care what happens to anybody. Most of them just don't know all the facts—how can they understand? Look at what they're hearing about us from their liars. Maybe we don't know all the facts, either; their whole gang

[e] See above, p. 462.

can't really be like that—they're people, too. Take them one by one, they're an awful lot like us."

You will have observed the trouble with this line of attack. Here is an attitude which encounters not passive acceptance of a simple pattern of learning, like the one mentioned before, but which encounters resistance, loyalty, fighting argument. Thus it calls for some art in use. Not for too much art; the basic idea is easy enough, and the concrete application seldom hard. But there is another intellectual difficulty: this line of operation is on a more mature level of thinking than the other. School work occasions for it, moreover, turn up in such things as literature, civics, history, upper-bracket studies; social occasions appear also much oftener in the more highly developed group life of the upper grades. Nonetheless, the line of procedure suggested is much closer to practicable pattern form for general use, much more clearly capable of indirect effect by repetitive actual application to particular cases, than is any ideal, however beautiful, which has as a technique merely the call for a change of heart.

But the real difficulty with this line of approach is not intellectual, nor does it rest in the emotions of the pupil. It rests instead in the emotional resistance of the teaching personnel, and of the supervisory personnel. This type of understanding of "Out-groups" is not wanted. The urge against such understanding is direct and primitive, because "We-groups" are in their nature felt as right and fine and precious, and because they derive so much of their felt rightness and fineness from the presence of "Others-groups" to contrast them with. Further, loyalty-building procedures can be seen to be endangered by any approach which would eliminate the rousing appeal of "Boys, go out and get 'em!"

All this shows how much thinking is needed before the kind of techniques we require can be developed for mass use. The fact-learning pattern proposed above is capable of institution and acceptance in any educational machine, and can get much of its work done under pure routine operation among quite indifferent personnel. It is therefore a *first rate* procedure.

This one is only third rate, because of its limited range of application, its requirement of some minor skill for its effective use, and its much smaller percentual effectiveness: it will, for instance, bounce off the emotional resistances of many pupils. Above all, and on the matter of practical introducibility, it must meet with

fighting barriers to its acceptance among supervisory personnel—
barriers only in part removable.

For this very reason, the unsolved problem makes a fundamental point: the need to articulate goals for education of a
democracy for democracy which go to the heart, but which are,
for all that, obtainable by mass operation through a mass personnel overworked, overcrowded, undertrained and underpaid.
Further, these goals must be thought through until there emerge
techniques and patterns utilizable in routine fashion, patterns of
teaching whose indirect effects, when they are employed by the
poorer cobblers among our teachers on children underprivileged
as to food, surroundings, equipment and, it may be, heredity, will
still raise the level of thought and feeling, and set the pupils freer
for democracy. Here lies the crux of educational thinking for the
next decade.

{ 24 }

THE LAW, HUMAN DIGNITY, AND HUMAN
CIVILIZATION [a]

"Human dignity" and "Human Civilization" are not simply
to be coupled for consideration from the angle of law and legal
institutions. They require separate consideration. That fact flows
from the nature of law and the work of law in a modern society.

For from the standpoint of a developed legal system, legal work
proceeds almost wholly by way of classification and treatment of
categories. Only poorly built categories call for much individuated
exception, the presence of which or the need for which is therefore in all but odd cases a symptom of inadequate initial structuring. Sound legal structuring does indeed call for ongoing redirection of categories, so that the lines of the categories may be always
subject to their reason; and it calls for the edges of categories to
be flexible under the influence of reason and fresh experience; but
that goes to remodeling of the categories, rarely to individuation
inside them. What cannot be categorized to satisfaction is capable
only of *bad* legal treatment, or else of what one may call *semi-*
or *pre*-legal treatment, say of the untrammeled juvenile court type.
Such semi- or pre-legal operation is not anti-legal, but is complementary or implementary, and is (although not "formed" or
formulated) a right and true part of the legal structure itself,
whenever it moves in terms of the general objectives of purpose
and manner to which the legal system is geared; and when it
moves in terms of the leeways recognized by and within the structure for play to allow of judgment and cumulative experiment in

[a] From SCIENCE, PHILOSOPHY AND RELIGION, 3d SYMPOSIUM 297 (1943).

good faith; and, finally, when the individuated or "discretionary" operation moves in terms of *quest* for a *pattern* to guide treatment of what may at the moment seem a unique case. Put from the other side: the semi- or pre-legal uncharted movement is anti-legal when it occurs in bad faith, or occurs without quest for some possibly emerging pattern; or when it persistently jumps the recognized limits or even persistently pushes daily action out toward limits which exist only for the occasional case. But a failure of such complementary or implementary action, when it is needed, or a failure to reach for proper remodeling of categories—at need by interstitial individuated action—that spells legalism and woodenness, i.e., "law" which has lost touch with law's reason for being.

Against this picture Human Dignity appears in two major aspects. One is that that concept suggests lines and limits within which categories and consequences are wisely, and rightly, to be restrained. The abolition of chattel slavery and the "race or color" amendment language suggest the problem of such "reasonable" limits on classification; so does the concept of second-class citizen. Such limits are negative in flavor; they only set certain outside prohibitory marks. On the side of consequences, the problem is suggested by cat-of-nine-tails flogging as a punishment.

But Human Dignity also enters the picture on the positive side. Categories can be built in an effort to recognize, encourage, even produce human dignity. The problem is suggested, in successive degrees of positive drive, by minimum wage and work conditions; by freedom to organize and compulsory collective bargaining; or, say, by an effective combined unemployment relief, industrial reconditioning, placement and morale program.

Both as to the limits set and as to any positive measures, human dignity is an informing ideal and goal. At no time, however, is it a sole goal, for *any* legal system. The very idea of classifying denies some individualization, and denies recognition of a very fair portion of dignity which may be not self-righteous, but righteous. There is, for instance, no reason inherent in the nature of our polity for recognizing conscientious objection; such recognition is a luxury-product—a luxury-product of great long-range value, but one entirely dependent upon the existence of some immediate surplus of man-power and organization-power. The idea of classifying, moreover, serves another valid ideal which oftentimes competes with that of human dignity, and that is: that phase of Justice which lies in relative equality, at least within categories of "likeness." Again, or in some ways as a part of the same idea, The Law is a team-organizing and team-directing institution, not merely a repressive institution; and first, survival of the team, second, the dominant team-objectives, will and should crush out any human dignity that cannot be otherwise handled. Thoreau presents that problem, or in a lesser way Mormon polygamy. Conscription presents it hugely. Most strikingly, martial law presents it.

In result, the effective large-scale operation of ideals about human dignity within a legal system is a product of surplus. Not solely so; the "necessary" causative factors are not of themselves "sufficient" causative factors. The matter in question is also and equally a product of idealism, and of the supremacy of particular ideals. But it is vital to remember that surplus is the pre-condition to *large-scale* (which means *legal*) effect of the idealism.

And it is only with that established that one can come to the relation of The Law to Human Civilization. Human Civilization I take to be the total machinery which society has grown itself to carry on its work and traditions, and, in our own variety, to refresh itself and to leave some room for individuals to build themselves into different kinds of people. Civilization can only in thought or in particular details be separated from The Law. But plainly it can be seen as setting some limits on The Law. Those limits are not what men used to think they were, when The Law is in hands well enough equipped and organized, and ruthless enough; and thorough and sustained in its attack on the shaping of the young. This means that any The Law informed by the ideal of human dignity is a The Law limited much more than one which is not so informed. Civilization therefore enters the picture, second, as providing the wherewithal for the human dignity ideal to be in some degree maintained: as providing the requisite surplus. It enters the picture, third, as providing rearing machinery for the young, and living machinery for the adult, which either inculcate and encourage the prevalence of the human dignity ideal, or do not, or (as in our own Civilization) do both at once, and still at individually unreckonable cross-purposes. In this last situation, the particular role of The Law becomes clear: it is to offer institutional structure (Constitutional provisions, courts), symbols and slogans (Bill of Rights, Free Speech, Right to Strike), and rearing machinery (schools) to make the ideal of the soberer man or moment have teeth even against the impulse of the more passionate moment or man. It is also to build this institutional structure solid enough, and in a form remote enough from easy change, to make it have teeth across the generations—a job for which some kinds of legal institution are peculiarly fitted, especially when they are intrenched, tradition-hallowed, and interlocked with supporting ways of action and thought.

WHAT LAW CANNOT DO

FOR INTER-RACIAL PEACE [a] [*]

In the context of the topic assigned to me "Law" is a tricky term, and "Peace" not much less so. I have long been of the opinion that for the last century or so discussion and controversy about "Law" could have been much reduced if a few unhappy mistranslations had not crept into common and misleading usage. Thus what has been written in Latin on Natural Law, or on what kind of thing is rightly and truly to be honored in the legal field —such writing has been almost entirely about *ius,* and practically everything written in this connection removes itself largely from the field of reasonable controversy if you translate *ius* as you ought to, and read the word as meaning not "law," but "right-law." Again, those portions of Savigny and especially of Puchta which have been most subject to misunderstanding and attack are those in which *Recht* is used not to describe the lawyer's rules in a modern state but to refer to that right-way-of-life-and-heart which gives goal, support and body to the lawyer's technical rules.

I need to make these points because they come close home indeed to the question of "law's" relation to inter-racial peace. For surely the question of what "law" can or cannot do to build, as distinct from destroying, inter-racial peace, that question is addressed by necessary implication in first instance to *ius,* to right-law. It is, however, also sure that something more is envisaged than

[a] From 3 VILLANOVA L. REV. 30 (1957).

[*] A paper delivered at the School of Law, Villanova University, April 26, 1957 as part of a symposium on "Inter-Racial Peace" held on the occasion of the dedication of Garey Hall, the Law School building.

doctrine, however ideal, *in hominum vacuo*. Plainly the picture is one of right-doctrine which is also a going part of a going governmental system, equipped with machinery and personnel to do something about it.

But I should like to submit that one derives interesting and illuminating further suggestion from the Savigny-Puchta concept. I do not mean merely that there is no limit to what *Recht* can do for inter-racial peace if *Recht* is present on an adequate scale in the sense of the right-way-of-life-and-heart. That is true, and no goal could be truer; but it offers little by way of effective measures. No, what I mean is that in any matter of crisis or of change there is a strong case to be made to the effect that no piece or body of doctrine, however glorious in ideal or phrasing—that no piece or body of doctrine can be fully *right*-law unless it is so built as to have heavy impact upon its own people, and so upon the people of some one particular time, place and cultural tradition. Indeed, in regard to matters of change or crisis I am prepared to argue firmly that right timing therefore also becomes a vital aspect of the rightness, of the true *ius* character, of the relevant portions of *right*-law.

In any event, three things seem very clear. The first is that the machinery of law-government has no need to lag behind or to lag with or to uncreatively just fit into the existing ways of people in their race relations, whether inside a nation or between nations. On the contrary the machinery of law-government can be built (as has been done in part by our Constitution and by our Supreme Court and by our system of armed services and of elections) to set up ideals still far from full attainment, to set up tension, steady or sudden, in the direction of those ideals, and in some degree to block off or to beat down obstruction. But the second thing is no less clear: put tension on too suddenly, too sharply, too hard, and your wire can snap, can even snap back into that devastation called destruction and reaction. It is a fine trite truth that the art of statesmanship lies in finding workable measures, in introducing them with patient skill, in following them through with firmness, and with courage, *and also with tact*. Trite truths are commonly enough deep truths. Our problem is that this one gives little practical guidance to most of us. For the third thing which is also and sadly clear is that when we are middled in the actual workings of inter-racial conflict, readjustment, and laborings toward peace, then only the event itself gives clear indication of which measures have been workable, which not, what has been vision, what error, what has been wise, what brash.

Meantime it may be that some further light on the limits of what can be done by way of the machinery of good or right law-government, manned by plain people who are not demi-gods, it may be that some further light can derive from looking a moment at this idea of "peace." I take it that the discussions at these meetings, certainly those of today, reach far beyond any idea of a simple absence of active danger to or attack upon limb and life. Peace in that sense of "The Peace" can be had, and had inter-racially, by way of the machinery of law-government; and there is not even any need that that machinery have about it any element of rightness. Consider the brutal law and policing of Englishry under the First William, or of occupied Europe under Hitler and Himmler; or if that does not seem to you sufficiently inter-racial, try thirteenth century Mongol occupation of any Western country, or today's Kenya or South Africa. Indeed, in this bare-bones aspect of "peace," racial differences rather simplify than complicate the ruler's fiat "peace" problem.

But I take it that what is under contemplation here is a richer, more active, more fruitful kind of peace, one which reaches quietly on out into "goodwill toward men." And there one slogan has often been that you *cannot* "legislate" a change of heart or "legislate" friendship or even tolerance or any other thing of mind or spirit or of attitude.

One can accept the slogan so far as concerns any direct commands by way of the law-government of a many-wayed, many-grouped, society in rapid movement. "Kiss and make-up," even inside the family, is a command which presupposes a pre-existing, a going, a lasting regime that offers a basis for resumed relations, for revived and remembered affections and patterns of team-work. In such a situation even the compelled gesture of get-together can have its impact on the habit and the heart. Not so, if the gesture rests on no such basis, or when it even stirs disgust. But is such a limit "the limit of effective legal action," or is it but the limit of certain ways and measures—measures none too well conceived, measures ill-designed? There is, says boyhood's proverb, more than one way to skin a cat. The tool chest of law-government has long been rich in tools, and the crafts of law-government have for millenia been as rich in wisdom as in wisdom's misuse. Let us then not too lightly leap to "what *cannot* be done."

Take a piece or two of material once widely supposed to have been pretty silly, material with which we have, however, a decade or so of experience. Fair Employment Practices laws and commissions, for example. You will recall that everywhere the commissions have moved on velvet feet with velvet paws with velvet patience for evasion. But slowly outfit after outfit which had been lily-white has begun to turn up one or another theretofore unfamiliar type of personnel. This has results. The hard-bitten lawyer who finds a woman associate in his office (not that women are protected under Fair Employment) awakes against his will to the fact that a woman can be not only a lawyer but a good lawyer —he has watched one work, he has worked with one. Everywhere, the "No Social Relations" tabu tends to yield, in modern man, to an opening up of some contact and some understanding for any member of your team; and that does queer, slow things to the traditionally received mere "anti" labels of ignorance. It does queer, slow things also to that deliberate ignoring which is worse than ignorance.

All observations, however, with due caution, please! I have said that the process does queer things in eating away "anti"-feelings and in building some understanding, some liking. This our machinery of right law-government can go far toward getting started, toward spreading, toward freeing from any flavor of the strange. But I have said also, please, that the process of having "Other" kinds of folk, "Different" folk, "Outsiders," in the team of your working outfit is a *slow* process. It is very slow. And about that there is not much which even the best law-government machinery can do. Team is not magic, team can breed rivalry and irritation, too. I have actually heard, *e.g.*, of Democrats, Catholics, raised in the same parish, school and block, each Irish (or Polish or Italian) in background, who were yet in bitter war over control of a single political club. Neither will it do to overlook that the slowly spreading understanding and often friendship which has developed so often during the war and under the Fair Employment regime, first, is as yet far from typical of our population; and, second, has yet to be subjected to the corrosive effects of severe hard times and ensuing survival-competition within the team itself. On this last, law-government can of course help some, insofar as it can cushion any economic bother. But it is not my office today to go into questions of either means or price, on that.

Here, if you will allow me, is a place where I feel a need to lodge a personal caveat. My faith in jurisprudence as in legislation has always rested on the need for seeing the facts straight, as the beginning for the man of law-government. The facts of life and of man-in-society confront the craftsman with his problems, they utterly condition his powers, they offer him also, under God's guidance and help, the only tools he has. A hard-eyed view of what the law-governmental craftsman is up against is thus of the essence of his coping with the problems of his necessary, nay, his noble craft. This approach I have been preaching for more than a quarter of a century. I called it realistic. It is realistic. It is a matter not of goal, but of method. "Neo-realism," a—shall I say *another?*—"mistranslation" sounds like the name of a philosophy. It has never been a word or a philosophy of mine. And I do not want either any echo of an outdated controversy (not, by the way, inter-racial) or any possible present misconception to permit any one of you to get any idea that I like or approve or urge any of a number of things which I observe as being—to me—very troubling facts-of-life that have to be wrestled with.

May I feel free, then, to grapple with worries which in these days are no light burden?

For I come now to places where, so far as I can spot the facts, the values of our civilization move into a civil war which (among other things) interferes with inter-racial peace; where also, so far as I can spot the facts, the price of a gain can rise high; and where the problems of timing become very restless. Let me try out a sequence of oversimplified but suggestive situations, when it is the machinery of official law-government which seeks to remove racial discrimination.

Hospitals: (which I think could be made today into regulated public utilities, at least for purposes of anti-discrimination.) As to patients, admissions to private rooms raise problems no more serious than the "outrage" felt years back by people with "real cars" and "real" status when Ford began to pay "mere" workmen five dollars a day and to let us ordinary folk climb into Model-T's; while emergency work and wards entail an element of common suffering that goes some distance toward an even deeper common feeling than that of "team."

Much more troubling is the matter of professional staff, where the limited facilities and opportunities produce a bottle-neck not unlike that envisaged above in regard to industry in a depression.

But at least so far as concerns supervisory personnel, how far is this different from the other professions, or from industry at large. The number of colored foremen or chief engineers, of Nisei bank vice-presidents, of American Indian senior law partners, is not noticeably large; nor does the Fair Employment aspect of law-government seem to me to have done much to increase that number. Indeed I do not see how it can. In contrast, it has been suggested that what law-government might well have been unable to do in the professions to open up opportunity and welcome in high place in this country for Catholics and for Jews has over the generations been partly accomplished by the arrival of Chinese, Nisei, Negroes, and Women, all to be happily discriminated against, thereby pushing the Catholics and Jews into opportunity and acceptance.

Hotels: Here I seem to see privacy enough to make the social price of "forcibly" opening them rather negligible.

Restaurants: The social price in terms of tension rises. But tables can remain separate.

Bars: Typically, people are much closer together. And there is alcohol. Doubts rise, as to the *price* of "legal" compulsion. I wish I could see a smooth way in regard to bars. But in much of Chicago the matter is working out moderately well.

Beaches: There is little alcohol, but any crowded beach is a place of constant intrusion and of constant need for restraint. There is rarely such continuity of personnel as can lead to understanding. And crowds can mobilize too easily into trouble.

Yet this is not a thing which right law-government cannot handle. One piece of inter-racial relations has to do with any group's pleasure in feeling at home in recreation. If you use the machinery of right law-government to provide (by way of condemnation and taxation, at need) adequate and appropriate facilities within easier reach, for example, of any colored neighborhood, you will find folks grouping up largely for their own pleasure. This is to be sharply distinguished from any unthought-through, unimplemented official law-government *mere* insistence that anybody is entitled to admission to any beach. Of course this latter is called for. My point is that, *alone,* such a measure not only is not enough, but may move against its own purpose.

Against such a background of troubled meditation one approaches the explosive question of *Schools.*

In graduate schools it seems to me that both horse-sense and experience show the job-team pattern to be available in a very satisfactory form.

In primary schools my observation and my readings combine to make me believe that (parents apart) inter-racial peace is an as-of-course aspect simply of being and working together, certainly if the start is made say in the two lowest grades, letting the integration move forward from there.

High school and college open up problems on which I am not reticent. You simply have limited me to twenty minutes in which to deal with a two-hour subject. Let me say simply that where resistance is strong, I should think it wisest to take high school last, and only after experience with the college had become available to demonstrate the unfoundedness of many fears, and, along with the primary school picture, to let the unparalleled turn into the familiar. So many things terrify because they have never been met with, looked at, lived with, *and found to be no worse than most of life.*[b]

Two things remain to say. The first is that it is an honor to be able to acknowledge in public the impressive work of the Roman Catholic Church in this task of furthering a true peace among mankind. You know, but you will let me state, that this goes back to earliest origin. You know, but you will let me state, that it is a matter for deep, full pride to see such a great tradition currently live and flourish in a time of trouble.

The other thing which remains to say is this: the machinery of even the rightest of right *ius* is subject to the limitations of human inventiveness. Just as to build for speed is to sacrifice carrying-capacity, and vice-versa, so building in law-government has through the ages had to labor sometimes with handling conflicting functions. I was visited yesterday by two ancient gentlemen of an American Indian tribe. They had come a long way to Chicago. They had complaint to make. Though why to me is not easy to make out, yet the ground of the complaint is clear indeed. Twice in the last few years an Indian and a White had gotten into conflict. Each time the conflict arose out of the White's bringing illegal liquor onto the Indian reservation. Each time there resulted a quarrel and a killing and a trial. Regardless of what you or I might think to be the so-called merits of any case or cases, with curiously few exceptions the results in cases like this, since

[b] What seems to me most striking in the events since the above was written is threefold: (1) The slow wearing down, by law-governmental means, of the law-governmental defenses set up to maintain segregation; (2) the entirely foreseeable incursion of mobile forces to break up any quiet good-faith efforts at compliance with the law, and the slowness with which foresight was put to work to avoid such outside interference; (3) the seeming success of step-by-step moves locally, where intelligence and care were used both in internal arrangements and to keep roving hoodlums off.

long before Custer, have been that if the defendant White has killed an Indian he is "Not guilty," but if the defendant Indian has killed a White, "Guilty" he is. Note that this is not a question of White and Negro, nor yet a question of the Deep South. In every other bar you can find a picture of the brave Custer, who became a general by killing children, and killing them without provocation.

This matter of what I shall call racially differential verdicts is an inter-racial problem of no small import. It derives, moreover, directly from our general official American law-governmental system. It derives from the fact that we have deliberately built that system to serve values which conflict among themselves. "A jury of the vicinage" has been ordained with special intention to make it possible not only for the law-government set up by any distant central establishment to be set at naught, but also for the so-called "facts" to be "found" in the teeth of the truth—all in the interest of the prevailing emotions or prejudices of the vicinage. On the whole, I think this to have been wise, at least for criminal cases. I do not mean that I think juries should lightly disregard their oath of office, any more than I think that judges should in their search for justice disregard the letter of the rules of law. I do mean that it does not pay to overlook or forget any real and built-in reason of an institution. And the "of the vicinage" idea is as purposeful as is an appellate court's duty to justice. On the whole (with some changes in procedure) I think that if it were given to me to do over, I should redo this jury job, for criminal cases, close to the original design.

Thus, when you think about what "Law" cannot do in regard to inter-racial peace, take on yourselves the burden of facing up to what your own fundamental legal machinery for escaping from your own fundamental law makes it sometimes impossible for even your own fundamental law to get done.

Pressed by my own limitations of imagination and ingenuity, I should, I repeat, have to leave to a local jury the power to sometimes defeat rules even of Constitutional law in the interest of local emotion. [Yet I keep reaching for some way to hold such verdict-rendering within bounds, even more so than the Supreme Court has yet managed by its wise use of the "due process" concept.]

Meantime I shall do some unpleasant dreaming about the faces of those ancient Winnebago gentlemen.

MEN

{ 26 }

WESLEY NEWCOMB HOHFELD—TEACHER [a]

When a master-craftsman has laid down his tools for the last time, there falls upon those who have worked with him and under him a heavy loss—a loss too heavy to be realized at once. With increasing realization comes a need for expression, for some tribute, however inadequate, to the memory and to the work of the master who is gone. To that end this number of the JOURNAL has been given: to some presentation of Professor Hohfeld's contributions to the working science of the law, to some development of his analytical methods in their practical application, to some study of the evolution of that Law to which he devoted his life, to some indication of the problems which confront us to-day in carrying on the work which lay closest to his heart: accurate, adequate adaptation of our law to the changing needs of this society in which and for which it exists.

Something has been written in these pages of Professor Hohfeld as a scholar, and as a writer. But it does not seem fitting that a number such as this, edited by men who were his colleagues or his students, should be without some appreciation of his work as a teacher of the law.

He was no common teacher. *"A man for the upper third"*—quite so—sincerely, frankly so. Each man must do his work in that way in which he best can do that work. "Hoh" taught the upper third—and he *taught* them.

He had little of that grace in putting forth his thoughts—or meeting men—which makes for general popularity, for quick, unthinking so-called comprehension. His approach was neither

[a] From 28 YALE L.J. 795 (1919).

light nor facile. Perforce his appeal was largely limited to those who by temperament and training could and would see something of the full depth of his learning and the power of his mind.

And to them he did appeal. Under him one was led step by step, with sure solemnity, into the presence of the Law, in all the majesty of its great system; the Law—a growing, constantly adjusting whole—inconsistent, it may be, as mankind is inconsistent, yet ever glorious in freeing itself from inconsistencies. To have the vision lifted beyond the little point at hand, out of the single "field" staked off as "Bills and Notes" or "Equity"—carried up into the high places, to look out over the whole land, hills and valleys, ploughed land and fallow, spread out in its wonder—this was the inspiration to be had in Hohfeld's classes. It was to be had in all his classes, to be had increasingly from year to year, as one's own eyes were opened, one's perception schooled. But most of all did it await "Hoh's" students in the Conflict of Laws. There, amid the conflicting claims of varied jurisdictions, the nature of the Law grew clear—to him, to us—; there, out of chaos came perspective; there, and there only, it has seemed to me, could a man see Hohfeld's mind trace out again the path of his own deepest thinking. There, working over what was, for sound theory, practically uncharted ground, he fought his way out of the inconsistencies of current doctrine, seeking the explanation which explained; and found it—doubted, examined it—tested, tried, and fortified it, till it *stood,* foursquare, complete. There—still unwritten—was his greatest single individual contribution; still unwritten—but given to his students.[b] And it was amid the conflict of the laws that he worked out in their completeness the massive outlines of his jurisprudence. It was in that crucible of conflict that his fundamental concepts took their final shape; only when tested there do they dawn in all their import upon the mind. Hohfeld—teacher! There was the triumph of his teaching.

And so it was he led us up on to the height. Much—so dishearteningly much—was, even at the last, too vast, too far, too unfamiliar to be grasped in its detail; but the height, once gained, the vision, once seen, was not to be forgotten.

It was no easy climbing. "Hoh" was no believer in the royal

[b] Hohfeld's projected *The Logical and Legal Bases of the Conflict of Laws,* for which he had gathered extensive notes (all the needed passages from Story had, for instance, been located and typed on cards) consisted of the theories later written up by his colleague, Walter Wheeler Cook, under the same title. It was Hohfeld's cleanest thinking. A statement and application of the basic theory appears, interestingly, in the same issue as the present paper. See 28 YALE L.J. 813 ff. (1919).

road. He had scant sympathy for mental laziness or physical, for scattered energies or surface-thought, for what he used to call the small and common coin of legal learning. But for any who came seeking, keen-eyed and earnest, he was a willing guide. And as an opponent in discussion he was in some ways generous to a fault. Let a man object, let a man fight the conclusion, let a man bend his every energy to the attack—"Hoh" grudged him, in class-room or office, neither time nor labor nor occasion.

Such teaching bore its fruit. Some students, as we have come to know since Hohfeld's death, he filled with reverence such as few men dream even of inspiring. And ever increasing comes testimony from his students of the value of his rigorous training: value in practice—value in their thinking and their doing.[1]

His teaching bore its fruit. The "upper third" is not the whole. That there should be in his classes those who did not, could not— and some, indeed, good men, who would not—understand: this was to be expected. It was to be expected that these men should not love him. And with his sickness creeping on him, Professor Hohfeld grew at times impatient of ununderstanding, carried over at times into classroom intercourse the discipline to which in his own mental work he had so drilled himself. And that grace which makes such things pass off as nothings, the gift we call a *way* with men, he did not have.

He was a lonely man—perhaps for lack of that same *way* with people. Perhaps, too, we owe much to that loneliness, much of his depth, much of the huge breadth of the foundations of his thought. Night after night it took him back to the office, in which he had worked through all the day, to work again, read, think, amidst a tangle of books and papers, long past the hour of closing. It is

---

[1] Hohfeld's method, Hohfeld's faith, and much of Hohfeld's personality speak in the following lines from the close of his first paper on *Fundamental Legal Conceptions*: ". . . It might be difficult at first glance to discover any essential and fundamental similarity between conditional sales of personalty, escrow transactions, option agreements, agency relations, powers of appointment, etc. But if all these relations are reduced to their lowest generic terms, the conceptions of legal power and legal liability are seen to be dominantly, though not exclusively, applicable throughout the series. *By such a process it becomes possible not only to discover essential similarities and illuminating analogies in the midst of what appears superficially to be infinite and hopeless variety, but also to discern common principles of justice and policy underlying the various jural problems involved.* . . . An indirect, *but very practical,* consequence is that it frequently becomes feasible, by virtue of such analysis, to use as persuasive authorities judicial precedents that might otherwise seem altogether irrelevant. . . . *In short, the deeper the analysis, the greater becomes one's perception of fundamental unity and harmony in the law.*" 23 YALE L.J. 59 (1913). The italics are the present writer's.

hard to recall a night when, looking out as my day closed, I did not find his office window bright.

But welcome as a student was who came into his office, it is not in his office that one's memory pictures "Hoh"; but in his class-room, there behind the desk—in his class-room when some man had interposed a question. There he sits, crouched somewhat forward on the desk; his black-haired eagle-face seems set with anticipation of the clash of views, his heavy shoulders tense, for all their student's stoop,—there he sits, silent through several seconds. You too grow tense for the struggle; but as you watch his eyes, you thrill with a dawning wonder, almost awe—slowly, alone, you see him climbing up into the mountain, to see this little question set out against the background of the whole, to look again upon the body of the Law as one,—and signal down to you the way to join him.

{ 27 }

ROSCOE POUND [a]

(A review of his JURISPRUDENCE)

It has proved extremely difficult for me to work out a review of this book—chiefly, I think, because the book will mean such different things to different groups of men. Thus if you are the ordinary reasonably intelligent but very busy lawyer, a review ought probably to state that this holds rather little for you, and, so far as it does hold anything, is too expensive, at its enormous price, and that it is too sprawling in its organization to be accessible.

But if you are a lawyer with an interest in the wider aspects of his profession who is also taking some time off for serious reading, this may be a very good book for you indeed. One thing is sure: there is nothing gathered in English which reports the same general range of legal thinking as does this. In the main, moreover, the ideas, like their sources, are translated into language—and often into application—which we can all understand. And the whole is infused with the powerful and critical home-grown insight about us-folk, our legal problems, and our legal ways, which has been the foundation of Pound's greatness and which has been so strikingly absent in so many (I do *not* mean, e.g., Radin or the Cohens or Seagle or Cairns) who have quarried abroad not to enrich, but to substitute. If you are this inquiring lawyer, you will meet skillful presentation and critique of law-directed thinking especially from the German and the French, with Greek and Latin not neglected, informed by an encyclopedic acquaintance

[a] From 28 UNIV. CHI. L. REV. 174 (1960).

with Anglo-American judicial writing up to say 1930 which few
have ever matched. The result will lift your eyes, stir your mind,
and, it may be hoped, refresh your soul. It will also ornament
your shelf: bound in handsome brown with Roscoe Pound's signature in gold, and with the paper thick or thin as may be needed
to make all five volumes harmonious in bulk.

If you are another type of reader or public, you begin carpingly
by asking why the end-results of the most prolific writer on Jurisprudence in our language should come feather-bedded in wide
margins, half in extra-large type and fatted paper, with much
of the most pungent older stuff cut out, and with an index which
screeches its inadequacy. As one of the professionals in the field
who began with this reaction (one goes on, e.g., to find no substantial mention or understanding of Arnold, of either Cohen, or
Cahn, Fuller, Isaacs, Michael, Radin, or Seagle, all of whom were
writing while Pound was still in powerful spate)—as one such,
let me start here by reminding my brethren that if they read they
will find these volumes full of cliché ideas—somewhat in the
manner of Shakespeare. Pound is indeed no Shakespeare; nevertheless, to take an instance, the basic content of, say, *Law in Books
and Law in Action,*[1] *The Limits of Effective Legal Action,*[2]
Spurious Interpretation,[3] *Mechanical Jurisprudence,*[4] etc., is the
basis of our forward-looking thought of the '20's and '30's and has
provided half of the commonplace equipment on and with which
our work since has builded. It is not to the point that I have not
found these particular papers reproduced in text in the present
volume, much less rearranged and expanded as is *Justice According to Law;*[5] their flavor and ideas are nevertheless present. So is
the turning of eye and mind to other-than-English sources, where
Pound, even more than Wigmore and Kocourek, and Radin, laid
the foundation for the American lawyer to broaden and deepen
his vision—a foundation which even world tragedy and threatened
disaster have found it hard to persuade that same American lawyer
that he truly needs (including among such American lawyers most
of the "sophisticated" snooters at Pound).

Thus before I come to my own estimate of the value of the
present work I should like to repeat first that for the practicing
lawyer whom the author used to so impress with the sweep and

[1] 44 Am. L. Rev. 12 (1910).
[2] 3 A.B.A.J. 55 (1917).
[3] 7 Colum. L. Rev. 379 (1907).
[4] 8 Colum. L. Rev. 605 (1908).
[5] (Pts. 1–3) 13 Colum. L. Rev. 696 (1913), 14 *id.* 1, 103 (1914).

learning of his after-dinner speeches, these volumes are a store-house of what today is called continuing legal education.[6] Secondly, that the modern sophisticate finds here much of the fundament on which he rests, and that most of him will find also a rude, shrewd challenge to his provincial self-sufficiency, a challenge to move on into the work recorded in other tongues than ours (including the Scandinavian, and the Russian), and proof that such moving is needed and can pay.

These matters out of the way, what does this work, in the light of Roscoe Pound's work in general, mean to the contemporary jurisprude?

The author tells us that the job was planned and begun in 1911,[7] completed in 1952, and twice revised (1949–1952, 1956–1958).[8] It must be taken as the final full word of a titan who during forty or so of his 65 years of prolific legal writing threatened to make American jurisprudence a one-man show. Significantly, his first listed article, back in 1896, was *The Influence of Civil Law in America*.[9] Significantly again, in the ten preparatory years, even while only five out of eighteen items appeared in other than local Nebraska publications, yet well more than half were jurisprudential. The first great paper, that "mother of symphonies," came in 1906: *The Causes of Popular Dissatisfaction with the Administration of Justice*.[10] A paper—not merely a review—about Pound's work is listed as early as 1914.[11]

One gets the impression that the major lines of the present book

[6] Such a lawyer should add, especially, (1) STONE, THE PROVINCE AND FUNCTION OF LAW (1950), the best one-volume job on the whole field; its author was also responsible for much of the up-dating of the Pound footnotes. (2) REUSCHLEIN, JURISPRUDENCE—ITS AMERICAN PROPHETS (1951), which gives not only the best available whole-picture of Pound's work, but also deals rather surely with many American writers whom Pound neglects. (3) COHEN & COHEN, READINGS IN JURISPRUDENCE (1951), which is an admirable selection of first-hand material, and which, in supplement to Pound's material, builds up the institutional and operating side of law. (4) CAIRNS, LEGAL PHILOSOPHY FROM PLATO TO HEGEL (1949), tough going, but extremely useful in the way in which it brings the elders to bear on current problems and thinking.

[7] Vol. I, p. xi. SETARO, A BIBLIOGRAPHY OF THE WRITINGS OF ROSCOE POUND 4–5 (1942), notes, in addition to the well-known *Scope and Purpose of Sociological Jurisprudence* (pts. 1–3), 24 HARV. L. REV. 591, 25 *id.* 140 (1911), 489 (1912), an original OUTLINES OF LECTURES ON JURISPRUDENCE CHIEFLY FROM AN ANALYTICAL STANDPOINT (67 pp.) from 1903, and an original READINGS ON THE HISTORY AND SYSTEM OF THE COMMON LAW (404 pp.) from 1904.

[8] Vol. I, p. xii.

[9] SETARO, *op. cit. supra* note 7, at 3.

[10] 29 A.B.A. REP. 395, reprinted 40 AM. L. REV. 729 (1906), 14 AM. LAWYER 445 (1906), 20 J. AM. JUD. SOC'Y 178 (1937).

[11] SETARO, *op. cit. supra* note 7, at 139.

shaped up rather early, along with the major insights. Thus as against Pound's *Outlines of Jurisprudence*, 3d ed. 1920, and 5th ed. 1943 (the two editions with which I happen to be familiar), the present table of contents shows not too much elaboration of basic plan between 1920 and 1943, and very little since. It is worth noting, perhaps, that 1943's "Conditions of non-Restraint of natural *powers*" has turned into one of "natural *freedoms*" (where the plural is of course peculiarly useful to clear thinking); and that the "Law and ethics" of 1920 (an emphasis on writing and theory) and the "Law and morals" of 1943 (with necessary emphasis on practice and mores, along with theory) has moved, in plan, into a rethought, reanalyzed, combination: "Law and Morals— Jurisprudence and Ethics." The text does not realize this more mature plan, but even so, it represents a gratifying advance over one of Pound's less happy early ventures.[12]

The over-all scheme divides thus:

1. *Jurisprudence.*—History and "schools," some 350 pp.: mostly meat, sometimes deep insight, sometimes superficiality. Thus I, pp. 34–38 on Greek philosophy and Roman law seems to me mere words; and Savigny, in this part and elsewhere, is dealt with in conventional stereotype and as if Kantorowicz's blinding paper[13] had never been written, and indeed as if "the" historical "school" had not, with Goldschmidt, blossomed in codification. In contrast, Ihering receives thoughtful treatment.

2. *The End* [= Goal] *of Law*, 187 pp.—One asks chiefly: Why the singular? This type of over-simplifying of a complex set of issues recurs. For instance, notwithstanding some four decades of insistence by Sunderland, Green, and especially J. Frank, on the difference—peculiarly in a jury-culture—between appellate justiciation and justiciation at trial, Pound still writes of "*the* judicial process"; and again, notwithstanding the report in 1941—a time when Pound was a central figure in the discussions—of the U.S. Attorney General's Commission on Administrative Procedure, we

---

[12] LAW AND MORALS (1924). This little book, though heavily documented, gets almost nowhere, and Pound's wisdom shows in not using it as one of the prior works to be incorporated *verbatim*, or nearly so, into the final word. But that word (ch. XI) is itself not satisfactory in this area; its concern is too much with doctrine. Doctrine is indeed one lesser phase of the relation of law and morals; but the bridge and the tension lie in practice—here would have been, e.g., a place to discuss fiction in general, and such matters as modern American consent divorce, with "ethics" as they hit judge and practitioner, legislator and layman. Kant, Stammler, Kohler, etc., have stuff, but one wants to see ethics, for lawyers, get down from "books" and into "action": the court-room and the office.

[13] *Savigny and the Historical School of Law*, 53 L.Q. REV. 326 (1937).

find the relevant discussion here full of *"the"* administrative process, as if administrative processes did not come in Heinz varieties.[14]

3. *The Nature of Law,* 464 pp.—Theories of law; law and the state, and morals; justice according to law (this last as fine and full as anything in the book.)

4. *The Scope and Subject Matter of Law*: interests, 371 pp.— This is discussed below.

5. *Sources, Forms, Modes of Growth,* 362 pp.

6. *Application and Enforcement of Law,* 34 pp.—It escapes me why this is a separate "part," rather than being added to "justice according to law," or else really developed on its own by the author of *Limits of Effective Legal Action* and co-editor of the *Cleveland Crime Survey* of 1919.

7. *Analysis of General Juristic Conceptions,* 507 pp.—Rights, powers, non-restraints, duties, persons, acts, things.

8. *The System of Law,* 713 pp.—Classification, proprietary rights, obligations, reparation, enforcement, comparative civil procedure. (But why should "Law" be *"private" law?*)

Save for the problems of crime and governmental organization and operation (which are hardly brushed) international matters (which are scanted) and taxation,[15] the range is thus huge; it is worthy of Reuschlein's intitulation, "The Pre-emptive Pound." [16] The underlying data and literature have, as mentioned, a vastness unfamiliar in American scholarship; Wigmore had something of the same omnivorous quality, Radin had much of it and Seagle some, but in general it has been rare since Kent and Story. One of the main values of the present volumes lies in the results of these explorations, whenever Pound lets his results take shape with enough detail to carry meaning. Thus, for instance, the comparative treatment of Gény and Duguit [17] is, except for its

---

[14] This is strikingly so in one of the later-written (and useful) additions, in which Pound, contrary to his older practice, recognizes and responds to an attack. The passage—it is III, 469–72, based on *The Judicial Process in Action,* 1 N.Y.L.F. 11 (1955)—is sprightly and has power; but it misses the beauty of Dewey's exciting analysis (first put forward about coevally with Pound's own first major effort on the theory "of judicial decision": *Logical Method and Law,* 10 CORNELL L.Q. 17 (1924)); and the reason Pound misses here is, I think, almost wholly because for him "the" judicial and "the" administrative stand as obscuring over-simple entities between the eye and understanding.

[15] Among matters not mentioned in the Index are Taxation, Budget, Defense, Military Establishment, National Defense, and War.

[16] REUSCHLEIN, *op. cit. supra* note 6.

[17] Vol. I, pp. 181–89.

source,[18] the most illuminating job on the subject I have read; and Gény is among us the most neglected of the valuable Continental authors.

It is indeed in relation to this job on Gény, excellent in itself, that I can perhaps best indicate my own troubles with the book at large. The points are two, and they are applicable throughout: (1) In the very process of discovering and lauding Gény's *Science et Technique,* Pound pushes off the *Méthode* as having "no more than incidentally raised the questions as to values *and made some suggestions as to a measure.*" [19] (My italics.) But the guts of the *Méthode* lies in the most magnificent single job that has ever been done of *mediating,* by way of a single, simply formulated, way of work ("measure"), between *any* ideal, and *any* authoritative text, and what proves in each case in hand to need doing. Gény's formula is not all-sufficient, but he added to it literal volumes of specific application until, if you really read, you get by that very reading to where you can do it for yourself in your sleep, and do it not so badly. This is genius: it is also lawyering, it puts jurisprudence to work, for anybody. It is an instance of that *technique* which the later book stresses as a matter of theory— and, as Pound sees it, rightly. Holmes muffed this aspect completely.[20] Patterson muffed it.[21] Even Pound's versatile and sensitive sniffer really missed the *technique,* too; nevertheless, in a day when Duguit was the fashion, Pound smelled out Gény as the sounder man.

This is Pound's sniffer at work. It is an amazing sniffer. It reminds me most of the general genius of the American case-law judge: *most* of the time it is *amazingly on-target. And so rarely in the bull's eye.* For Pound is of course not in the bull's eye here. He recognizes Gény's quest for "starting points" for legal reasoning; but he just plain ducks discussion of what those starting points are or should be. He recognizes the importance of *technique,* in general. But he turns his back, then, on the *craft-*

---

[18] Pound's *Fifty Years of Jurisprudence* (pts. 1–2), 51 HARV. L. REV. 444, 777, at 464–72 (1938), is abbreviated in the current text, whereas it deserved to be much expanded.

[19] Vol. I, p. 182.

[20] Holmes' *Natural Law,* 32 HARV. L. REV. 40 (1918), started off as a review of Gény's *Méthode.* I cannot believe that Holmes ever got beyond Gény's second-rate philosophical introduction. The latter's philosophy matures in the later work, but it never achieves a stature comparable to the method of the *Méthode.*

[21] JURISPRUDENCE—MEN AND IDEAS OF THE LAW 353–54 (1953).

aspect, the daily working aspect for daily working lawyers, of this great *Méthode* of Gény's—even while, I repeat, he is sniffing out the greatness which has been missed by almost every other American writer except Cardozo.[22]

The second point illustrated is Pound's preference for the study of theory, verbalized theory, writer's theory, over study of results, or of how it gets done: over process and know-how either in the concrete or in theory. Gény's *Méthode* (if I may quote from Pound in a not dissimilar context about our appellate courts) seemed to him only to "ring changes on the familiar," so he went on to Gény's theoretical discussions.

Let me try to state it this way: Pound has contributed, for my guess, more than any other individual (unless perhaps John Dewey) to making legal thought in this country result-minded, cause-minded, and process-minded. Yet such lines of thinking leave little mark upon the whole, and almost no marks upon the structure, of these final volumes.

In illustration: by 1903, we have *Outlines, Chiefly from the Analytical Standpoint*. Those 67 pages get developed, with love and skill, into more than 1200 working pages of the final word. Contrast the relative non-use here of the famous and seminal basic articles published up to say 1910. The Theory of Interests itself, the Poundians' delight, which one might have hoped to see developed as the true center of a Sociological Jurisprudence, as the place where one really gets down to cases, comes in for only 371 pages. The *Interests* themselves are slighted. They are developed with no similar love. Take as an instance "Security of Transactions," an old, old friend: In connection with Ehrlich[23] there is indeed a suggestion about the importance of *what* is relied on by the people doing the transaction; for a moment Pound shows there even in regard to commercial matters the sensitivity which he brought so powerfully to his System. But by the time the guts are reached (the Interests) it is as if neither Ehrlich, nor Ely (unmentioned[24]) nor Cohen & Cohen (also unmentioned[25]), nor Hershey's work (though it, too, is cited previously)—nor, to push forward, the interesting effects of a compulsory labor bargain on the old law of offer-and-acceptance—

[22] NATURE OF THE JUDICIAL PROCESS (1921), *passim.*
[23] Vol. I, pp. 334–37.
[24] So far as discovered.
[25] So far as discovered.

had ever been around.[26] Neither is there any concrete discussion of one of the leading modern German figures, Heck, although there is a 1914 paper of his cited,[27] and although his influential *Interessenjurisprudenz* surely demanded the attention of any follower of Ihering, and had long been in full print, directly devoted to "interests" and even to transactions.[28] Fuller's paper on form in contracts[29] is another source of value which goes unregarded. In the case of my own *What Price Contract?* [30] one can be sure that the disregard was not due to oversight, because Pound and I, at the time, had been collaborating in the Encyclopedia of Social Sciences article on Contract of which the paper was an immediate offshoot; and one can be sure that the disregard is not due to Pound's regarding the author as valueless, because he treats me in the main with more than gentleness: he sometimes even uses me to build on. Such treatment, or neglect, of the workings of a major "interest" can, it seems to me, be explained only by lack of interest. In similar fashion, the elaborate development of "the" theory of the corporate "person" [31] proceeds without touching the exciting and troubling problems of the government corporation, and substantially as if there had never been the *commandite,* *G.m.b.H.,* or close corporation problem, and certainly without treatment of Berle and Means or of the SEC. So the theory of inheritance[32] is developed from "The Indo-European peoples," but says nothing, for example, of the seeming effects of English primogeniture on colonial expansion, or of the philosophy or effects of modern inheritance taxation. So, finally, in developing either Proprietary Rights[33] or Property as an Interest,[34] there is no wrestling with that shift of American "private" property law into the "public law" field which has characterized zoning, water, minerals, and urban redevelopment.

[26] This is the type of systematizing point frequently developed in Parts 7 and 8: in a business negotiation "for a contract" one has the familiar offer, counter-offer, etc., sequence. In a labor negotiation "for a contract," points get tied down one by one. The two theories "of formation of contract" have never been harmonized: Which is *the* right theory?

[27] I have mislaid the reference.

[28] *E.g., Grundriss des Schuldrechts* (1929); *Begriffsbildung und Interessenjurisprudenz* (1932); *Interessenjurisprudenz* (1933).

[29] Fuller, *Consideration and Form,* 41 COLUM. L. REV. 799 (1941).

[30] 40 YALE L.J. 704 (1931).

[31] Vol. IV, p. 191 and *very* nice at 260–61.

[32] See especially vol. III, 142 pages.

[33] Vol. V, pp. 77–195.

[34] *E.g.,* vol. III, pp. 105–55.

Now, let me repeat, no man in his senses who has either read Pound or seen Pound in action can believe that ideas of this kind are beyond his reach. *Nothing* has ever been beyond his reach. Such ideas are instead, I suggest again, outside his range of interest; the inoculation of Pound with Ehrlich simply did not take.

Try this hypothesis, to put all of this together.

Suppose that Pound's native bent has all along been really in those areas of "System" with which he began, and which he has managed to develop, these later years, in the teeth of all or any of those multitudinous demands on his time which have derived from administrative or from emergency pressures: Pound has always loved abstract theories. He has always loved them best when they came readily available, in other peoples' writing, for his own careful, penetrating, and *systematic* analysis. One can instance his sorting and dissection of the various single-line theories of "juristic person," already referred to. Each theory he tests with clean scalpel, as to whether it explains the whole. Each theory fails. At the end comes a brilliant synthesis;[35] but the origin-of-theory aspects of *Interpretations of Legal History* (where Pound, independently, matched one of Pareto's most significant contributions) has no part in either the presentation or the synthesis. It is quite characteristic that Dewey's theory[36] (which is the best) is not mentioned (much as Dewey's exploration of the appellate judge's operation is left to Cairns' interpretation). Dewey's lines of thought just do not fit the Pound mind. The Dewey emphasis, indeed the Dewey necessity, was always to reach for effects, for function, for "what it has been *doing*."

My net judgment comes to this:

If, contrary to the basic Pound nature (gathering, observing, portraying, arranging—with a reasonable feel for growth), the times called—as they did call,[37] for process-and-result-directed

---

[35] Vol. IV, pp. 260–61.

[36] Dewey, *The Historic Background of Corporate Legal Personality*, 35 YALE L.J. 655 (1926).

[37] There was at the turn of the century a ferment-period of process- and result-directed work in the social disciplines (sparked and symbolized, I have always thought, by the first Roosevelt). Consider, in general, Chicago and Wisconsin in Economics, Sociology, Government, Philosophy. Consider, more particularly, Dewey, Veblen, Ely, Ross, Mitchell, Commons, Merriam, Thomas. Consider, then, in law, and in relation to a proud Nebraskan, the following titles *in addition to those mentioned above: The Decadence of Equity*, 5 COLUM. L. REV. 20 (1905); *Do We Need a Philosophy of Law?* 5 COLUM. L. REV. 339 (1905); *Executive Justice*, 55 AM. L. REGISTER 136 (1907); *The Need of a Sociological Jurisprudence*, 19 GREEN BAG 607 (1907); *Common Law and Legislation*, 21 HARV. L. REV. 383 (1908) (Here Pound

work, then the most versatile legal scholar in our history could produce that, too. And he did, out of a cornucopia, until the 1914 papers; one can even add, though in much lesser measure, *The Theory of Judicial Decision* in 1923.[38]

If, moreover, there is in the Pound nature a deep, passionate love for the American judicial approach to the things of law, and so for judicial supremacy (*two* things)—then there ought to be—and there is—one functioning and functional piece really developed in the final book—"the judicial process"—and that may explain why *Justice According to Law* grows and shines in these final volumes.

But if the Pound nature did not take, by its nature, to problems of *how* things *work*, and especially not to the dirty detail and to the working out of theory about detailed *process*, then one can understand why pressures of time and circumstance could keep the Old Master from developing theories of process, while at the same time setting him free to develop theories of structure.

I cannot tell. What I can report to jurisprudes is this:

The number of holes you (or I) can pick in these volumes is, if you are a pick-ax fan, gratifying. They are not at all that gathering and ordering of Pound's insights and knowledge for which many of us have been hoping. You find here, for example, few traces of his thought about judicial organization, or about the bar, or about dealing with crime.

On the other hand, the number of holes in your (or my) equipment for sound thinking on our own problems, *of today*, which these volumes offer good cement to fill: that is dismaying.

Ave, Caesar!

"made" his first goal: the *Harvard Law Review*. That *Review* was only five or ten years late, in recognition); *Enforcement of Law*, 20 GREEN BAG 401 (1908); *Liberty of Contract*, 18 YALE L.J. 454 (1909). These go on: *Puritanism and the Common Law*, 45 AM. L. REV. 811 (1911) (rather deep); *The Scope and Purpose of Sociological Jurisprudence* (pts. 1–3), 24 HARV. L. REV. 591 (1911), 25 *id.* 140 (1911), 1489 (1912); *Democracy and the Common Law*, 18 CASE & COM. 447 (1912); *Social Problems and the Courts*, 18 AM. J. SOCIOLOGY 331 (1912); *Social Justice and Legal Justice*, 75 CENT. L.J. 455 (1912); *Courts and Legislation*, 7 AM. POL. SCI. REV. 361 (1913); *The Organization of Courts*, 70 LEGAL INTELLIGENCER 86 (1913); *The Administration of Justice in the Modern City*, 26 HARV. L. REV. 302 (1913); *Legislation as a Social Function*, 18 AM. J. SOCIOLOGY 755 (1913).

By 1924 the net tone of the titles has completely changed.

[38] (Pts. 1–3) 36 HARV. L. REV. 641, 802, 940 (1923).

HOLMES

Draw me not without cause; sheathe me not without honor.

Father-forged, tempered in war—purged in white blast
when greed cracked wide all steel that bore a flaw,
the fine blade ground to edge against the law,
drove through tough hide time forms upon the past.
Arrogant flame! And edge and point for lies!
Untarnished by all use, unmarred by mould,
he flashed forth truth too dazzle-bright to hold,
till slow years schooled and shielded duller eyes.
After such conquest? Fierce to the time-dim mark
where freedom *is* control: gay, bold, and keen,
self-patterning with priceless damascene—
Justice' own Sword. Instant to call of duty.
Blade prophet, priest and captain of our Ark:
Never without cause drawn. And sheathed in beauty.

MR. JUSTICE HOLMES [a]

Gather in one place the tributes to a man, and you will know if he has been indeed a hero. Unless he is the full man, the kindler of spirit, tribute will flatten into platitude, tribute repeated will dull, will stale. Here, to hand, are papers spread over fifteen years.[1] Do not pick them up lightly; they are perilous. You will not bring yourself to put them down unread; nor, having read them (or if they are old friends, having reread them thus in sequence) will you again be quite the same. For in the reading you live your way into contact with a ranging glory. A man, a soldier, a scholar of parts, a prophet. A gentleman of old Boston, a jurist, the judge among judges, a living power in the history of the country. A friend of youth. A thinker who has broken to triple team those battling horses Depth and Range and Fact. A worker in words as the great among pencil-draftsmen have worked in line: three strokes, and he has said all that he sees, said most that there will be to see for half a century; three strokes of black flat on white, and you have body, you have color, you have vibrant form.

Holmes. The volume is well called Holmes—and there is in Holmes due portion of its authorship. Into each one of the authors he has entered; they bear his mark—the mark of the leader whose

---

[a] A review of the book of that name edited by Frankfurter (1931). From 31 COLUM. L. REV. 902 (1931).

[1] The series continues, in the Columbia, Yale and Harvard Law Reviews for March: Cohen, Frankfurter and Laski again; Cardozo's introduction to the present volume. One regrets that for the papers by Redlich, Littel and Lippman it was not possible to substitute that of Hughes in the Harvard Review, or Hughes' radio speech for the 90th birthday, and Yntema's beautiful study in the Yale Law Journal. Not that the three papers included lack value if they stood alone, but that the other contributors, "touched with fire," set a cruel standard.

leadership involves "no effort to enslave his followers." [2] More, each of them has risen to his theme as to a challenge. Holmes, in each paper; yet the writer, too; and Holmes in the writer.[3] For as you thrill to the reading you will find that the subject has called out in each the best that lies in each; you will find each putting forth his heart to portray the Holmes *he* sees; you will find that Holmes to be the idealization of what he holds most precious among the things that he himself has striven for. Morris Cohen sees the lonely thinker, the philosopher, the fighting idealist; he glories in Holmes' rejection of one-absolute-for-all, in his constant awareness of law's normative side, in his steady grip—even while prophesying realism—on logic and the rational in law.[4] John Dewey writes of the Holmes who cuts behind the fallacious certainties of formal logic in decision, of the free mind, of the experimentalist, of the man of faith in the ultimate power of intelligence. Frankfurter's well-known review of the first twenty-five years on the Supreme Court (one frets at having to wait another generation for his review of the second twenty-five) reads, save for its nicer plan, save for the straightness of its telling, like an Icelandic saga of the Constitution, with Holmes as Sigmund, Sigurd, Odin, all in one; as the smoke swirls above the dying fire the teller's voice grows magic: Holmes' theory of the Constitution and Frankfurter's weave in and out and mingle in the flow. One vital point on which they mingle rightly must be quoted: "These limitations are not self-defining *and were intended to permit government.*" And Learned Hand—himself a doubter, a scholar, a judge whose very penetration causes him turmoil in decision from which springs richness and wisdom in opinion granted to few—Learned Hand pays homage to sure courage among doubts, to joyous workmanship which earns its leisure, its "agitation in the presence of fair women," to a man of hidden deeps whose passing insight is worth another's treatise. And sets forth in ocean-simple prose like Holmes' own the view of life they share. "The houses little children make upon the beach are crude and ill-fashioned, and the tide soon comes and sweeps them

---

[2] FRANK, LAW AND THE MODERN MIND 259 (1930)—a further tribute to Holmes.

[3] A lover of style will find fascination in the marks of Holmes' style upon the style of the papers. Cardozo, *e.g.*, commonly offers baroque at its best; Holmes has the vigor and simple loveliness of early Gothic—with touches of the sophistication of the primitives. Cardozo's paper here is cathedral-like in the mingling of the styles.

[4] These two last in a study contemporaneous with the book: *Mr. Justice Holmes and the Nature of Law,* 31 COLUM. LAW REV. 352 (1931).

away, as time will sweep away our bravest monuments. But neither time nor tide can spoil the play, nor take away one tittle of the joy that came with making them."

A catalog of catalogs, a tribute to tributes, becomes tedious. I must pass over Laski's study (reinforced in the March YALE LAW JOURNAL with striking parallels to Spinoza), pass over Wigmore's. But it needs note that not from any lawyer's hand, but from Elizabeth Shipley Sergeant's, comes the finest picture of Holmes the man, the man-in-judge-and-artist, and so the proof a law-trained hero-worshipper must cherish, that not only we of the craft, not only they of political science, or they of philosophy, but all who have eyes and have humanity can be set ablaze by "Justice Touched With Fire."

What wonder that Cardozo, opening the volume, raises again the query which comes at times to troubled, eager youth—as once it came to that eager youth whose picture at graduation from Harvard [5] we ponder over with Cardozo's words—"whether law in its study and profession can fill the need for what is highest in the yearnings of the human spirit. Thus challenged, I do not argue. I point the challenger to Holmes."

Here and there in the volume appears a note of gentle criticism. To me, a welcome note. Supreme greatness needs no apology. It scorns retouching.[6] Only through knowledge of what may be deemed defect can one pierce to understanding of the strength. Holmes, regrets Cohen, finds the existing régime of property and profit well enough conceived. His realism, says Dewey somewhat sadly, at times "seems almost to amount to a belief that whatever wins out in fair combat, in the struggle for existence, is therefore the fit, the good and the true." But skilfully and justly our authors use such matters to point the glory of that tolerance which is "eternally vigilant against attempts to check the expression of opinions that we loathe and believe to be fraught with death," the glory of a fighting faith rooted in realization that "time has upset many fighting faiths."

More use of the same tools would add yet more. It has seemed to me curious that no man has brought Holmes' architecture in

[5] Opposite p. 20. And compare the passage, p. 192: "It cost me some years of doubt and unhappiness before I could say to myself: 'The law is part of the universe—if the universe can be thought about, one part must reveal it as much as another to one who can see that part. It is only a question if you have the eyes.'"

[6] Portraitists "beautified" the pock-marks from the face of Washington. They thought thus to increase his stature; they deprived us of the image of that power which, marked with pox, commanded by its presence.

words into closer relation with his architecture of his life. As to
his daily life, his personal relations, this is done by Hand, by Laski,
by Sergeant. Cardozo and Wigmore insist upon the consistency
of crafsmanship in "small" cases as in great, in private utterance
as in Opinion of the Court. But surely this same consistency, this
same sense for form, lights up the three score years and ten of work
with law. One will go far to find more constant, more sustained
digging in detail than shows in the work of the young seeker
Holmes, be it in history, be it in analytical study, be it in background. *Until the whole, first shadowy, shifting, dim, took shape,
sharp outline, trembled to testing, and grew sure—and stood.*[7]
Patience to grub was conditioned for him on the will at length to
see law whole. Once seen—and the vision was taking clean, well-
nigh final outline in the eighties—patience to grub waned fast.
Each to his own true bent. It may have been ambition, urge to
power, urge for more public action, which took him from Harvard
Law School to the bench. But if it was, it was informed by a thrill-
ing intuition into self. It is possible, even perhaps likely, that, with
his intellectual goal thus achieved—in prophecy which still "commands the future, a valid but imperfectly realized ideal" [b]—
Holmes as a professor might have done little more than counsel
young men genially, and flatten out. To build that prophecy into
reality called, before building could begin, for the sweat of a
hundred backs with shovel, pick and crowbar. Such excavation,
for the architect, had lost its charm.[8] So—to the bench—where
the cases presented themselves, and of themselves, with facts and

[7] As one who for some years now has been occupied in turning up (after one
year or five) the places where prior thinkers have set forth each successive idea
which one has chanced upon, I can bear witness to a peculiar quantitative quality
of Holmes' prose. It takes meaning in exact measure as his eyes see. There is never
doubt. Though the idea be thrown out in a single passing phrase, you will know
how much of it, precisely how much of it, Holmes had seen at the time—sometimes more than you yet see, sometimes less, sometimes the same. If it is not
more, there will be no use in looking further into Holmes' writings *of the same
or earlier date.* Max Weber's work has the same rare quality, interestingly enough,
though in his case the style is elephantine involuted awkwardness. This matter is
one then not of beauty, but of finding words which *are the skin* of living thoughts.

[b] Yntema's phrasing.

[8] A different type of sweating he took on. Not only to work out his picture of
the whole, but then—while his shelves grew heavy with the work of social science
—to fight off temptation to elaborate, the demon that would encrust and curtain
vision with over-carving of the surface; instead to stay year in, year out, at
seeing it more simply still, again and again reviewing each part's relation with
each other part, finding words, leaving undying record of each phase of each relation—till the blind must take it in.

relevant authorities already gathered—where the unique insight and vision of the master could, on his own terms, illumine half a century more, into a present which will halt and stumble further decades in its struggle to keep pace with him. Greatness must be inborn; but greatness, too, grows out of balance, out of architecture, in the living-out.

There is one matter still to raise, a misconception among the profession akin to the lay misconception that Holmes in his personal views is liberal or even radical as to the social scheme. The misconception has to do with the modernity of Holmes' statesmanship. On one point and one only[e] do I find a trace of such modernity, and even there in such general terms as to strip it of the most modern flavor. That is, in the conception that room must be left to the new nation for its being, that to this end state powers and restrictive formulas must suffer where they must. In this reestablishment of the theory that "it is a Constitution" (as Frankfurter well argues) Holmes has seen modern needs and met them. But met them with philosophy, not with a detailed knowledge. The premises of individual decisions are often far from modern. For the rest, the striking expression remains: "My agreement or disagreement has nothing to do with the rights of a majority to embody their opinions in law," with only the qualification of vigilance against attempts to check *opinions* that we loathe. These views were in many aspects obsolete or obsolescent when the young Holmes took his commission in the Twentieth. The *modern* need which began then and has rolled up bewilderingly since was the need for the social technician, for him who in the whirring, clanging maze of modern economic life could find sense, see out-of-gearness, invent remedy. A Brandeis sustains a new industrial or business regulation because he sees and demonstrates its utility. A Holmes sustains it in mild wondering approval, patient tolerance, magnificent disinterest. Modern in any sense of a man of the industrial era, or of a man equipped to deal with its peculiar needs, Holmes is not.

And only by realizing this will one reach the meaning of his work. Beside the social technician who speaks the peculiar needs of our time must stand the man who reaffirms the humanity of

[e] Beryl Levy thinks the dissents in the Massachusetts labor-conflict cases to open an innovating approach to tort law in general.

I should give even money that I can turn the essential idea up in THE COMMON LAW, as part of Holmes' first unifying analysis.

all time. How strangely, how gloriously, they meet, they complement: side by side, each leaning on the other. Each is the other's need. For greatness is not single in its aspect.

All but a few who wrestle with technique go under; it is technique which masters them; left to themselves with problems of technique, they turn into robots. What is to aid? Men and lawyers, in this machine-made age, must struggle with technique or fail. Whence are they then to draw vision and fire to preserve humanity? "Thus challenged, I point the challenger to Holmes" —to that full grandeur great not because it is modern, but because it is eternal.

{ 29 }

HOLMES [a] *

Men reflect institutions. Men are made of the institutions they have grown into, absorbed in whole or in part, and recombined into an individual personality. But to some men it is given themselves to become an institution. Holmes molds America.

It is a strange thing, in a dollar-ridden world, to find an associate justice, one out of nine, and not the titular chief, saluted and mourned as this nation's most distinguished citizen. It is a strange thing to find a President calling as of course to pay a nation's respects to a justice who is no longer sitting. It is a strange thing to find the cloistered bench (ununderstood, misunderstood, or disregarded) turned into a pathway to the admiration, the

[a] From 35 COLUM. L. REV. 485 (1935). An Appendix by Lawrence R. Eno assembled a useful and I think unique bibliography *about* Holmes.

* For Holmes' effect on other men, for his range, for the superb art with which he wove his qualities into a life rich and powerful as an ancient Oriental rug, see Book Review, 31 COLUM. L. REV. 902 (1931), for his place in the history of American legal thought, and the rôle of accident in the picture, see *On Philosophy in American Law,* 82 U. OF PA. L. REV. 105 (1934). See also PUT IN HIS THUMB 108 (1931).

The best study of his constitutional law work is Frankfurter's, in MR. JUSTICE HOLMES (1931) 46; the finest string of the five-word jewels is Wigmore's, *ibid.* 212; the best appreciation of the personality is Elizabeth Shipley Sargent's, *ibid.* 183. No satisfactory biography exists. Neither is there in print any collection of the anecdotes, but Frankfurter has promised to gather them and submit the gatherings to the secretaries and other friends for authentication, addition, and amendment. There is already a myth-lore full-blown. It should be included. But it should not be confused with its historical base.

To write of Holmes a second time causes acute embarrassment: follow the series of papers by Frankfurter, or Laski, or Cohen. Or this. A man has in the first writing been stirred to give more than he had to give! Contrast, *e.g.,* HUGHES, THE SUPREME COURT OF THE UNITED STATES (1928), with Hughes, *Mr. Justice Holmes,* 44 HARV. L. REV. 677 (1931).

affection, of a people. A people not of lawyers, but of laymen.[1]
A pathway trodden with no will for show, without display.[2]

In part, one doubts not, this is accident. Age is of the essence
of a national institution. This man grew old.[3]

But how many who grow old touch age with fire? How many
keep live their interest in the "lambkins," how many kindle the
spirit of each individual lambkin into blaze? This is a time for
tribute. Tribute comes best out of experience that either sears or
glorifies.

One instance of each. Some young squirt achieves editorship of
a law review. He calls in a stenographer. He writes to ask Holmes
for a contribution. The letter is institutional; for decades we all
have sent it, as our first. The reply is no less institutional: Holmes
declines. Declines *in own-penned longhand*. An absurd tradition;
surely the typewriter has been invented. But a tradition whose
application lifted, even while it shamed; for Mr. Justice Holmes
had, each time, taken time in his declining to make the letter
somehow personal to this young squirt whom he had never seen.
One more lambkin he had awakened to the burden, and the
majesty, of an ancient culture. The man lived in the faith that
being a gentleman of Massachusetts required one, at whatever

---

[1] This is the astounding thing. Any craft honors a master craftsman. Read the roll,
from Coke to Cardozo. Yet non-craftsmen, too, are stirred by Holmes. Non-craftsmen
of course misunderstand him. They think the venerable conservative a radical,
because he had the detachment to refuse to substitute his judgment for that of
the legislature. Still . . . the Better Bar fell into the same error.

The Great Dissenter was known, as men always will be, by his *crucial* work. It
is beside the point that he did not like the designation. How could he like it?
When he dissented, it was not from desire, but from Puritan conviction—though
there was a touch of young perversity at work as well: dissenting opinions were
not subject to have his "plums" removed from their environment of "stinking
dough." *To concur a hundred times in routine matters is but to give body to the
Great Dissent that counts.* Cohen's last paper on Holmes is notable for its clarity
on this. *Justice Holmes* (March, 1935) 82 NEW REPUBLIC 206.

[2] Without that display known in these days as "publicity." Within a very narrow
circle, Holmes did show off—and loved it. His tongue and pen were graceful as a
cat, his soul as vain. I do not mean the vanity, vanity, of Ecclesiastes; Holmes'
vanity was robustious small-boy-pleasure in real workmanship; it was "Mother!
See what *I* did!"—and "What *I* did" was always so hugely worth the seeing.

Within a very narrow circle. For he was quite content to go unread, ununderstood, if only the work stood up, to him, as art. "Only one man in a thousand
will get your meaning," said the secretary. "Boy, that is the one man I am writing
for." This is not display. It *is* showing off. A bit perverse. And rather glorious.

[3] He was proud of his age, as proud as of his ancestry or of his record in the
war. It was an ill turn that deprived him by days of birthday number ninety-four.

sacrifice, to be a Massachusetts gentleman. Nor is the longhand [4] to be confused with that other feature at once of tradition and of personality which can never be outmoded: the patience, the skill, that has made every existing Holmes letter an individuality— whether accolade or inspiration.

The second matter: At the suggestion of Morris R. Cohen, both this review and Yale's joined Harvard in celebration of the Ninetieth Birthday. Never in teaching have I seen such radiance as that work, and the work of the man whom it was meant to please, shed on those boys. Teachers and undergraduate editors together conceived of the event as a national occasion, submitted to a major (commercial!) broadcasting station that wild idea, and sold it [b] . . . Holmes speaks to youth. Only as you harden against youth will you find growing strange to you the wisdom of that wise young man of mighty years.

It is this which moves one to faith that Oliver Wendell Holmes has only begun to be an institution. Those who hold [5] that he did not leave his mark—save perhaps on individuals[6]—need but

[4] In the last years, letters were more likely to come, *still in longhand,* from his secretaries. Sometimes, even then, with a Holmesian touch.

The Massachusetts gentleman was sometimes Massachusetts overmuch: "Once I risked buying a secondhand book. And when I opened it, what do you think I found? *A hair! !*" This the same bodily *continuum* that had delivered the Abrams dissent, while pressures intended to be passed on to him were thrust upon his wife: "My dear, there are some things in which even a man's beloved does not cross her husband's conscience."

[b] This broadcast was before the days when casters understood that such things had value. Young Herbert Wechsler, Columbia's editor-in-chief, was the idea-man and negotiator. "And who will pay for this?" asked the broadcast executive. "*You* will pay for it!"—Here is another great tradition, that of the American law review.

[5] So, almost, M. R. Cohen, *supra* note 1.

[6] There were the friends. There were the colleagues. ([Stone, after about five years on the Court:] "Most of what I know comes from a certain old gentleman.") There were the individual scholars who sent in books or papers, and were forthwith re-energized. There was the succession of secretaries. Over sixty when he mounted the ultimate bench, Holmes was yet willing to break in a cub a year to the work of the Supreme Court of the United States. One wonders whether this particular labor was not in part a guilt-compensation for that abrupt departure from the Harvard Law School for the bench. Not even a Holmes could run free of the impact of such a personality as Ames.

But the motivation is immaterial to the precedent. Brandeis and Stone carry it forward; they, too, are educators. Taft joined in. Hughes did not. Cardozo lent a new and endearing touch: secretaries not from *my* school, but in rotation from *all* the schools with which I have been closely associated.

[Consider how this tremendous contribution to our judging and our training has come to spread across the country: Gray's invention, which Holmes built out; Frankfurter's successful seeding.]

look forward. The mark is there. It is still in becoming. "A valid but imperfectly realized ideal," wrote Yntema four years ago.[7] An ideal *being* realized: "His work commands the future." For Holmes, Holmes almost alone, has cracked open the law of these United States. The time-deep calcine crust is burst forever.

It was in 1881 that lectures called *The Common Law* appeared —setting contract up in terms of risk assumption, risk allocation; washing "malice aforethought" down into terms of reasonable foreseeability; showing the mingled elements of history, morals, and administration in the field of tort. It was in 1896 that he pronounced for the analyst the rule of "cynical acid," and—in the same lecture—for the reformer or judge the need for social and economic background.[8] But ten years later Carter was still teaching at Harvard that law is but discovered by the judges.[9] In 1914 Corbin was all but impeached for *Law and the Judges,* which said only and quietly that law did move, and that the courts, slowly, moved it. Even in 1924 I heard a lawyer, for whose technical skill any lawyer must have profound respect, say words: "Mr. Justice Holmes is an able, learned, witty, charming—*and exceedingly dangerous* man!" [e] Carterians, and such Viewers-with-Alarm, we have with us still. Nonetheless the cracking open is in progress. As to old learning, it is no longer heresy to argue that judges have "molecular" law-making power. Men have learned that from Holmes.[10] It is, despite the efforts of the American Law Institute, despite its blackprint void of cases, no longer heresy to argue even that there is no brooding omnipresence in the skies, but that the true measure of law *to the unwilling man who is to be controlled* is: what, in particular, can or will anybody do about it, here and now? It is no longer heresy to see constitutional law as a field in which economic forces, prejudices and personalities play in an intricate, semi-concealed game, law, politics and statesmanship

---

[7] *Mr. Justice Holmes' View of Legal Science,* 40 YALE L. J. 696, 703 (1931).

[8] *Path of the Law,* COLLECTED LEGAL PAPERS 167 (1921).

[9] LAW, ITS ORIGIN, GROWTH AND FUNCTION (1907).

[e] John Hardin, of Newark.

[10] Or at second hand, *e.g.,* from Cardozo.

One of Holmes' triumphs (indirect but glowing) is Cardozo's succession. Two New Yorkers—and one magnificent—and one Jew were already on the bench. In that situation, a *Western Republican* Senator visited a *Western Republican* President, to strongarm, over the President's choice, the appointment of *the* single possible successor (though that successor happened to be Jew, Democrat, and from New York).

together, with Scottsboro new trial and Texas disenfranchisement emerging in "due" balance from a single sitting.[11]

Nor has any man save Hale so eloquently stated the social obligations imposed by the judicial function. "I have tried to see the law as an organic whole. I also have tried to see it as a reaction between tradition on the one side and the changing needs and desires of a community on the other. . . . I have considered the present tendencies and desires of society, *and have tried to realize that its different portions want different things. . . .*" He had tried to see these things "in a dry light."—With the conclusion, as to tradition and the present, "that the wisest are but poor guides." [12]

No. Holmes' work, though unfinished, is finished; though undone, is done. Unfinished, because an entire further generation must still be raised in his understanding before that understanding can control the law. Finished, because no more is needed for the raising; men enough with full desire to do that raising this one man Holmes has raised for us already.—Undone, because the personnel of any court (so long as mere nose-count determines Constitutionality as it might properly determine ordinary civil cases) can cripple insight, and has. Done, because Holmes has provided every man possessing eyes with vision. He has given American law, private or constitutional, the technical key to sanity and self-sanation: Look! See! Move! The need to see; the room to move, but always in consonance with tradition. A key. The fact as clear as the job is pressing.

But I do not wish this to be brutal eulogy. I believe a man seen best when he is seen also as a *man,* one of the *homo,* only so-called *sapiens,* tribe. It lends charm to the young Holmes' observation that the law of prescription rests essentially on the *fact* of

---

[11] Patronage can build a machine, in the Court or out. Consider the possible effects of assignment of opinions. In part, this is a question of safety: Roberts' phrasing, *e.g.,* will be duly cautious. But in part a man can be wooed and moved by opportunity for reputation. So Holmes, when his chance came, as Senior Justice, to preside, threw Stone, the then junior, a reputation-maker with the Maple Flooring Case. One does not think this an accident. Nor is it to be quarreled with. But Polonius' "Do not dull thy palm with entertainment" has dubious application to a new-fledged comrade whose vote in a divided court is needed.

Contrast the realism of such procedure (or indeed the half-realism of the Duplex Printing Case) with the Court's approach to political parties in Texas.

[12] Fragments noted when an unpublished Holmes speech was read aloud. The crumbs stir hunger. Sir Matthew Hale's injunctions to himself appear in 2 CAMPBELL, LIVES OF THE CHIEF JUSTICES 198 (3d ed. 1874).

person and thing together, when the old Holmes, on his retirement, is discovered "losing" half his library—borrowed from the Library of Congress, the borrowing forgotten as the books sat their way into an emotional ownership. It lends significance to those letters, each one of which was a gem, to discover that his oral humor rested thirty per cent on easy—even lazy—juxtaposition of high judicial office and profanity, or of great age and youth. It lends glory to the gallant fighter for human rights and social needs to discover that he was interested in neither; but could fight for them, *and fight!* This man to whom modern painting was "a bottle of guts"; to whom The Massachusetts Twentieth Cavalry was throughout life a symbol of the Best; who, to our knowledge, has neglected records while writing opinions;[13] who loved French novels and left undigested the very economic and sociological works he himself had acclaimed as needed guides; this man who at times would rather turn a phrase than think.[14] —Why does pulse race, why do eyes water dangerously, as we think of him no longer here?

Because he was human. Because that secretary who had been lured to a morning drink was made to feel not only that it was a transgression, but that Mr. Justice would have been glad to transgress with him. Because not only Holmes, but the world, appreciates a lovely woman. Because wit is salt.

The letters; the over-fastidiousness; high courage viewed at once as commonplace to a gentleman and as the base of living; the recognition of homage as simply due; the grace and finish of most personal contacts, the scorching superior irony of a few; the dispassion and lack of interest in the moving phases of a world; the payment on the nail of any price exacted by a held ideal—this Holmes was a noble of an *ancien régime*. But without the cruelty: to this noble, the weak had rights. Without the social irresponsibility: "I *like* to pay taxes! It's the price of civilization." His country was his residuary legatee.

But that is not enough. Nor is it the guts of the matter. We are dealing with no *bon vivant,* no mere good fellow or master of the language; nor yet with a mere, though great, aristocrat. Clear, devastating, magnificent, stands America's most distinguished

---

[13] But this was choice of work. Holmes has been known to save one day of record-reading, only to put in two or three on building an opinion which satisfied.—The particular reference is to a tale from Taft, reported in THE COMMON LAW TRADITION, at p. 21.

[14] But phrases turned *to a purpose,* and to thought already done.

citizen. A gentleman and soldier who even in the orgy of the '70's could develop a road to public weal and private integration no later Adams had the skill to find.[15] He who has led America's Law into the future. Be it by charm, or by persistence, be it by style or by wisdom—all these he used—Holmes opened wide the door. The door stands open.

Then Death plucked at his ear, and said: *LIVE!* I have come.

[15] Holmes should have been an Adams. In culture, if not in genes, that was his essential line. But how could he be an Adams? He had charm, and wit.

INDEX